COLORADO
BIRDS

A REFERENCE TO THEIR
DISTRIBUTION AND HABITAT

Robert Andrews & Robert Righter

PUBLISHED BY
Denver Museum of Natural History

Dedication by Robert Andrews

To my parents Robert and Dorothy Andrews for their unceasing love and support and
the special friends I have met through our common fascination with birds, most
especially Tim Gates, my first bird-watching friend, who died March 6, 1990

Dedication by Robert Righter

To all the past and present ornithologists, biologists, and bird-watchers whose efforts
greatly contributed to the formation of this book

Book design by Hugh Anderson and Michael Williams, Archetype, Inc.
Cover Photograph by Wendy Shattil/Bob Rozinski © 1992
Illustrations by Don Radovich

Published by the Denver Museum of Natural History,
2001 Colorado Boulevard, Denver, Colorado 80205

Manufactured in the United States of America

First Edition, 1992

Library of Congress Cataloging-in-Publication Data
Andrews, Robert, 1952–
    Colorado birds : a reference to their distribution and habitat /
Robert Andrews and Robert Righter.
        p.   cm.
    Includes bibliographical references and index.
    ISBN 0-916278-68-9 : $24.95
    1. Birds–Colorado. 2. Birds–Colorado–Geographical
distribution. 3. Birds–Colorado–Habitat.   I. Righter, Robert,
1939– . II. Title.
QL684.C6A53 1992
598.29788–dc20   92-5872
                                                    CIP

CONTENTS

It has now been 27 years since the Denver Museum of Natural History published *The Birds of Colorado* by Alfred M. Bailey and Robert J. Niedrach. Colorado has changed dramatically in the ensuing years, and so has our knowledge of its avifauna. There have been several changes in bird species occurrence, distribution, and nomenclature since 1965. In recent years, with the Colorado Bird Distribution Latilong Study and the Colorado Breeding Bird Atlas Project, knowledge of birds in our state has accumulated rapidly. There has been a growing need for an updated, definitive treatment of the distribution and status of Colorado birds, and this book fulfills that need.

Robert Andrews and Robert Righter have prepared a remarkably comprehensive and well-documented summary of the current state of knowledge about the distribution and status of Colorado birds. They logged countless hours in the field and consulted records from other field observers and organizations like the Colorado Field Ornithologists, Denver Field Ornithologists, and Colorado Bird Observatory. They also examined data and specimens from several museums, including the Denver Museum of Natural History, to piece together the historical jigsaw of bird distribution in the state. This volume will prove an invaluable addition to the bookshelf and fieldpack of any amateur or professional student of Colorado's natural history.

To the serious student of birds, this book can be used to identify the many gaps in our current knowledge, and thus stimulate further investigation of these captivating creatures. Studies investigating changes in the status and distribution of bird populations often provide unexpected dividends by revealing otherwise unperceived changes in environmental quality. I believe this book is an investment toward those dividends.

The mission of the Denver Museum of Natural History is to encourage and facilitate the understanding of our world and its inhabitants. We are proud to publish *Colorado Birds* enroute to fulfilling that mission.

CHARLES R. PRESTON, PH. D.
Chairman of Zoology
and Curator of Ornithology,
Denver Museum of Natural History

Since 1965, with the publication of the *Birds of Colorado* by Alfred M. Bailey and Robert J. Niedrach, as much and perhaps more new information has been gathered regarding the status and distribution of the birds in Colorado than in all the years prior to 1965. In our opinion, we felt a new publication was warranted.

The idea for developing an updated annotated checklist for Colorado birds was conceived by Bob Righter, Charlie Chase III, and Bob Andrews in the spring of 1987. Charlie dropped out due to a time conflict with his studies at Florida State University.

From the beginning we all felt strongly that this state bird book should have maps and graphs accompanying the text to maximize the presentation of the information. So as not to compromise this vision nor to restrict the scope of the book, we bullheadedly felt that the best course would be to self-publish.

For this book to be as accurate as it could possibly be, we knew it must be subjected to a rigorous peer review process. Therefore, almost 50 reviewers, whose perspectives range from the American Ornithologists Union, museums, educational institutions, regional experts, various government agencies, including Colorado Division of Wildlife, U.S. Forest Service, and U.S. Fish and Wildlife Service, have all given their input and the species accounts reflect their enormous contribution.

It was during one of these review processes that Betsy Webb, Curator of Zoology at the Denver Museum of Natural History, suggested we contact Betsy Armstrong, head of their publications department. This has led to a very significant association with the Museum whereby the project was then able to fully benefit from its vast storage of knowledge. The dimension, scope, format, and presentation could not have been achieved without the Museum's expertise.

ACKNOWLEDGMENTS

The below listed individuals, in alphabetical order, were reviewers for this book.

David Bolster	Formerly CU-Boulder; Upland Sandpiper
Clait Braun	Colorado Division of Wildlife (D.O.W.); grouse and pigeons
Toni Brevillier	Colorado Springs
Dan Bridges	Statewide, all species
Bill Brockner	Evergreen area
Mike Carter	Colorado Bird Observatory; Barr Lake region, Bear Creek Park, Bailey Bird Nesting Area
Charlie Chase	Statewide, all species
Walter Collins	Grand County
Gerald Craig	D.O.W.; raptors
Alexander Cruz	CU-Boulder; Blackbirds and cowbird
Coen Dexter	Grand Junction, all of Mesa Co., served as coordinator for information from that region
Warren Finch	Served as our initial editor
David Fleck	CU-Boulder; Scrub Jay
Peter Gent	Statewide, all species
Kenneth Giesen	D.O.W.; grouse
Van Graham	D.O.W.; cranes
Walter Graul	D.O.W.; Mountain Plover
Richard Hoffman	D.O.W.; grouse
Harold Holt	Statewide, all species
Bill Howe	U.S.F.W.S.; So. Platte drainage in northeastern Colorado; North Park
Mark Janos	S.E. Colorado, Delta, Grand Junction
David Jasper	Grand County
Hugh Kingery	Regional Editor American Birds, Birding Bird Atlas; all species
Fritz Knopf	U.S.F.W.S.; Mountain Plover; Orchard Oriole
Ron Lambeth	D.O.W.; Mesa Co.
Dave Leatherman	N.E. Colorado
Rich Levad	Mesa County
Brian Linkhart	Flammulated Owl
Thompson Marsh	Statewide, all species
David Martin	Statewide, all species
Jack Merchant	Eagle County
Duane Nelson	Records Committee Chairman, Colorado Bird Observatory; statewide, all species
Cate Ortega	Formerly CU-Boulder; Blackbirds, cowbird
Charles Preston	Curator of Ornithology, D.M.N.H.; statewide, all species, particularly raptors
Don Radovich	Gunnison area, contributed the exquisite drawings for this book
John Rawinski	U.S.F.W.S.; San Luis Valley
Jack Reddall	Statewide, all species, permitted us access to his vast collection of records for the Eastern Plains
Warner Reeser	Estes Park and Rocky Mountain National Park
J.V. Remsen Jr.	A.O.U. Committee on Classification and Nomenclature; provided information on Louisiana State University specimens; statewide, all species
Lonnie Renner	D.O.W.; cranes
Richard Reynolds	U.S.F.S.; Owls - Purple Martin
Jim Ringelman	D.O.W.; waterfowl
Ron Ryder	Dept. of Fishery and Wildlife, C.S.U.; Waterfowl
James Sedgwick	U.S.F.W.S.; *Empidonax* Flycatchers
Scott Seltman	Extreme Eastern Colorado and adjacent Kansas
Dave Silverman	Pueblo and Wet Mts.
Kip Stransky	Durango area
Michael Szymczak	D.O.W.; waterfowl
Van Truan	Pueblo area
Judy & Doug Ward	Moffat Co. & Leadville
Bruce Webb	Formerly CU-Boulder; Owls
Lois Webster	Mountain Plover
Brian Wheeler	Hawks

II. The individuals listed below provided important information on specific records:

Jerome Besser	Al Hay	Bill, John, Inez Prather
Mary Jane Black	Phil Hayes	Joe Rigli
Henry & Vi Bossman	Joe Himmel	Pam Rizor
Steve Bouricius	Mark Holmgren	Bill Rowe
Richard Bunn	Bob Jickling	Marilyn Rowe
Jerry Cairo	Barbara Jubrias	Larry Sanders
Kevin Cook	Frank Justice	Dick Schottler
Virginia Dionigi	Jan Justice-Waddington	Mildred Snyder
Patty Echelmeyer	Joey Kellner	Joe TenBrink
Norm Erthal	Mike Ketchen	Helen Traylor
Margaret Ewing	Clara King	Linda Vidal
Phyllis Fischer	Paul Lehman	Helen & Art Wainwright
Elva Fox	Cindy Lippincott	Jim & Rosie Watts
Dave & Carolyn Griffiths	Joe Mammoser	Elinor Willis
Glen & Jeane Hageman	Brian Millsap	Roberta Winn
Dave Hallock	Mark Nikas	Chris Wood
Laurens Halsey	Paul Opler	John Yaeger
John Hardister	David Pantle	Vic Zerbi

III. The data that were used in making decisions on the status and distribution of the birds in Colorado were in part derived from the records of the many dedicated and knowledgeable bird watchers of Colorado. In our opinion each one should be rightfully acknowledged. We were very sensitive to the problem of wanting to recognize these individuals in this book and at the same time very concerned about not wanting to leave a valued birdwatcher off such a list. Some of the problems confronting us were that many have moved out of state, some have passed on, and some do not belong to an organization; therefore, their name does not appear on a list that we could access. Colorado ornithology, however, should be very appreciative of these unnamed bird-watchers.

IV. The individuals and organizations listed below have been important in providing information, opening doors to information, and doing other important work for this book. Names are listed in alphabetical order.

Betsy Armstrong: who first had the foresight to recognize the potential of this book and secondly the skills to see it through to its final form

Dave Armstrong, CU-Boulder: Provided us with maps.

Colorado Bird Report: Norm Erthal, Dave Martin, Scott Menough, Dick Schottler, provided us quarterly bird reports.

Christmas Bird Count: Rocky Mountain Region - Helen Downing

Colorado State University: Zoological Collections - Myron Baker, Jean Boylan

Cornell Laboratory of Ornithology
Colonial Bird Register - Jim Lowe

Denver Museum of Natural History
Archives: Kris Hagland, Eloise Howerton
Publications : Betsy Armstrong
Zoological Collections: Betsy Webb allowed us access to the collection; Ric Peigler showed us where everything was.

Field Museum, Chicago, Illinois: Collection Division - David Willard

Museum of Northern Arizona: Collection Managers - Scott Cutler, Terry Merkel

National Wildlife Refuges
Arapahoe - Eugene Patten; Alamosa - Monte Vista - Rick Schnaderbeck; Browns Park - Jerre Gamble

Tammie Nakamura - scanned original map onto computer

Phyllis O'Connell: Advised on computer technology in early stages

Allan Phillips: Examined critical specimens

Sandy Righter: Intangibly and tangibly provided much support; Sandy spent countless hours on the gazetteer section.

Martin Twarogowski: Labored well over 350 hours to produce over 1,500 maps and graphs.

University of Colorado: University of Colorado Museum Collection - Shi-Kuei Wu, Cate Ortega

United States Fish and Wildlife Service, Patuxent, MD
Breeding Bird Survey - Sam Droege

Western State College
Collection Department - Seth Adams

Introduction to Colorado

Colorado surpasses most states of the United States in having both a diverse and fascinating avifauna and spectacular natural scenery.

Although Colorado lacks a coastline and an international border, and generally does not have the large-scale migrations of other parts of the continent, Colorado does have one of the largest state bird lists (444 species) of any state, especially for an interior state. Several of North America's most important avifaunal regions meet and mix in Colorado, a result of its central location, diverse topography, and great elevational range. Colorado's birds include those from alpine tundra, boreal forest, western coniferous forests, western shrublands, eastern deciduous forest, northern plains grasslands, and southern plains grasslands.

There are 444 species of birds that have been confirmed in Colorado. Of those, 396 are represented by extant specimens, 36 by photographs that have been published or are on file with the Colorado Field Ornithologists Records Committee (RC), and 12 are supported by excellent written details on file with the CFO. A total of 267 species are confirmed to have nested in the state, including four former breeding species (50 years ago or longer), plus five species that have recently been suspected of breeding but which have not yet been confirmed.

The Geography of Colorado

Colorado's dramatic geography is divided into three regions: the eastern plains, the mountains, and the western plateaus.

The plains, which occupy the eastern part of the state, form the Great Plains Province. The mountains run north and south through the center of Colorado and form the Southern Rocky Mountain Province. West of the mountains in the western third of Colorado are the plateaus, mesas, and canyons that form the Western or Colorado Plateau Province. Two other geomorphic provinces also occur in the far northwestern corner of Colorado: the Uinta Mountains are part of the Middle Rocky Mountain Province, and the Yampa Basin is part of the Wyoming Basin Province. Colorado has a total elevation range of 11,083 feet. The lowest point is 3,350 feet along the Arkansas River near Holly, Prowers County. Colorado's highest mountain is Mt. Elbert (14,433 feet) in the Sawatch Range in Lake County, which is the second highest mountain in the contiguous United States. The geography and geology of Colorado are described in greater detail by Gregg (1963), Armstrong (1972), Chronic and Chronic (1972), Chronic (1980), Mutel and Emerick (1984), Erickson and Smith (1985), and Rennicke (1986).

The Great Plains Province

Eastern Colorado lies within the western Great Plains. The plains at Colorado's eastern border are at about 4,200 feet on the uplands and 3,400 feet in the river valleys, and they rise westward to reach 5,000—6,000 feet where they meet the mountains, and 7,500 feet on the divide between the South Platte and Arkansas Rivers. These plains occupy about 40 percent of the state.

The eastern plains are generally flat to rolling. Locally, there are areas of greater relief formed by high, isolated buttes or mesas edged by bluffs and canyons. These higher areas occur predominately along Colorado's northeastern and southeastern borders. Along the border with Wyoming and Nebraska in Weld and Logan counties in northeastern Colorado are the Pawnee Buttes, Chalk Bluffs and the Peetz Tableland. Farther south is Fremont Butte, in Washington County and Twin Buttes in Cheyenne County. South of the Arkansas River are the Rattlesnake Buttes in Huerfano County and Two Buttes in Baca County. In Las Animas County along the border with New Mexico are Raton Mesa and Mesa de Maya. These features rise up to 4,000 feet above the surrounding plains. The Palmer Divide is between the South Platte and Arkansas rivers and forms a higher area between the lower valleys to the north and south. At its western end where it merges with the mountains, it reaches 7,500 feet. The Spanish Peaks, on the line between Huerfano and Las Animas counties, are volcanic mountains rising over 12,000 feet. They are considered by geologists to be part of the Great Plains but are biologically part of the mountains.

There are two major river valleys in Colorado's eastern plains. The South Platte River leaves the mountains southwest of Denver and flows northward and then northeastward, and exits the state into Nebraska at Julesburg at Colorado's northeast corner. It receives numerous tributaries that flow eastward out of the Front Range, such as the Cache la Poudre and Thompson rivers and St. Vrain, Boulder, and Clear creeks. Farther out onto the plains, its only tributaries are small streams that are dry most of the year. The South Platte Valley occupies much of the northern half of the eastern plains.

The Arkansas River leaves the mountains west of Pueblo, and flows eastward into Kansas, leaving Colorado near Holly. Once leaving the mountains, the Arkansas River receives only small tributaries that are usually dry. Its drainage comprises all of the southern half of the eastern plains. A portion of east-central Colorado between the South Platte and Arkansas drainages lies within the drainage of the Republican River, which flows eastward through Kansas and Nebraska to empty into the Missouri River.

The Southern Rocky Mountain Province

Colorado's mountains are comprised primarily of two north and south-running parallel ranges with several large enclosed basins called parks between the ranges. Collectively, all of the mountains are commonly called the Rocky Mountains, with individual names given to the numerous distinct ranges that form subunits within the Rocky Mountains. On their eastern side, where they meet the Great Plains, the mountains rise abruptly and are sharply delineated from the plains. Westward toward the western plateaus, the transition is more gradual and less cleanly defined. Colorado has 884 mountains higher than 11,000 feet, including 54 higher than 14,000 feet (Rennicke 1986).

The eastern parallel range starts at the Medicine Bow and Laramie mountains, which enter the state from Wyoming west and northwest of Fort Collins. Southward, they merge to form a chain that runs south to near Colorado Springs, and is called the Front Range north of the South Platte River and southward is called the Rampart Range. South of Colorado Springs no continuous range fronts the plains, only isolated mountains: the Pikes Peak Massif west of Colorado Springs and the Wet Mountains southwest of Pueblo. West of Pikes Peaks are the low Arkansas Hills, which occupy the area between the South Platte and Arkansas Rivers and through which the Arkansas River flows, via the Royal Gorge, to reach the plains. South of the Wet Mountains are the Spanish Peaks, already described as geologically part of the Great Plains, and the Culebra Range, which is part of the western chain.

The western range starts near Steamboat Springs as the Park Range, with the Rabbit Ears Mountains forming a low eastward extension. South of the Park Range is the Gore Range between Vail and Dillon. The Williams River Mountains, north of Dillon, and the TenMile Range, south of Breckenridge, form a connection to the Front Range. The Mosquito Range is east of Leadville and Buena Vista. West of the upper Arkansas River from Leadville south to Salida is the Sawatch Range. Southeast of the Sawatch Range, the western corridor angles eastward as the Sangre de Cristo and Culebra ranges.

Between the parallel chains of mountains are the parks. These basins are almost completely enclosed by the surrounding mountains. They are such a distinctive feature of the Southern Rocky Mountains that they were once known as the Park Mountains. There are four main parks and many minor parks. Just south of the Wyoming border, with the Park Range to the west, the Rabbit Ears Mountains to the south, and the Medicine Bow Range to the east, is North Park. It lies at about 8,000 feet. Just south, surrounded by the Medicine Bow, Front, and Gore ranges, is Middle Park, at about 7,300 to 8,000 feet.

Farther south, and located nearly in the center of the state, is South Park. It is bounded on the west by the Mosquito Range, on the north by the TenMile Range, on the east by the Tarryall and Kenosha hills, which are extensions of the Front Range, and southward by the Arkansas Hills. South Park is the highest of the parks, with an elevation of 8,800 to 9,800 feet. Lying between the Wet Mountains and the Sangre de Cristo Range is the small Wet Mountain Valley at about 7,900 feet.

In south-central Colorado is the largest of the parks, the San Luis Valley. It is 100 miles long and up to 50 miles wide, and is larger than Delaware. It is bounded to the east by the Sangre de Cristo and Culebra ranges, and to the west by the Cochetopa Hills, and the La Garita and San Juan mountains. The valley extends southward into New Mexico, with the low San Luis Hills forming a barrier just north of the state line. The San Luis Valley has an elevation of about 7,500 feet.

West of the two parallel north-south mountain corridors are other isolated ranges. The Elkhead Mountains are between Steamboat Springs and Craig. North of Glenwood Springs is the White River Plateau, a portion of which is known as the Flat-tops. The Elk Mountains are south of Aspen, and to their south are the West Elk Mountains. In southwestern Colorado are the San Juan Mountains, with their main mass between Ouray and Silverton and extending southeastward into New Mexico. This mountain range covers more than 10,000 square miles (larger than Vermont), and is the largest single range in the U.S. Rockies (Rennicke 1986). The San Juans are a volcanic range and are geologically unrelated to the rest of Colorado's mountains. Northeast of the San Juans are the low La Garita Mountains and Cochetopa Hills, which form a connection with the Gore Range and the Sangre de Cristo Range. West of the San Juans are several peripheral ranges: the San Miguel, Rico, Needle, and La Plata mountains.

The Continental Divide, separating the Pacific and Atlantic drainages, traverses the state from north to south, following the Park Range, Rabbit Ears Mountains, Front Range, Ten Mile Range, Sawatch Range, Cochetopa Hills, La Garita Mountains, and San Juan Mountains. The highest point on the Continental Divide in Colorado is Grays Peak (14,270 feet), in the Front Range in Summit County and the lowest is Muddy Pass (8,772 feet), in the Rabbit Ears Range, Grand/Jackson counties. The east side of the Divide is drained by the North Platte River in North Park, the South Platte River along the Front Range and South Park, the Arkansas River, and the Rio Grande River in the San Luis Valley. The northern part of the San Luis Valley has an internal drainage with no outlet. The South Platte and Arkansas valleys are often collectively known as the East Slope. The west side of the Continental Divide, called the West Slope, is drained by the Colorado River and its tributaries.

The Western Plateau Province

West of the Rocky Mountains is an area of moderately high plateaus and mesas deeply dissected with deep canyons and broad valleys. Major plateaus and mesas in this province include, from north to south, the Yampa Plateau, Roan Plateau, Battlement Mesa, Grand Mesa, Uncompahgre Plateau, Sleeping Ute Mountain, and Mesa Verde. Some of these, such as Grand Mesa, reach as high as 10,000 feet, while most others are somewhat lower. Between them are rolling or hilly uplands and numerous valleys. Some of the valleys are fairly broad with gradual borders, while others form deep and narrow canyons. The main river system in western Colorado is the Colorado River, which rises in Rocky Mountain National Park and flows west and southwest through Middle Park, Gore and Glenwood canyons, the Grand Valley, and exits the state through Ruby Canyon into Utah west of Grand Junction. Its main tributary is the Gunnison River, which joins the Colorado from the south at Grand Junction. The Uncompahgre River is a major tributary of the Gunnison River, joining it at Delta. Other rivers in this part of the state include the Green, Yampa, and White rivers in northwestern Colorado, and the Dolores, San Miguel, Mancos, Animas, Piedras, and San Juan rivers in southwestern Colorado.

The Avian Habitats of Colorado

Most of Colorado's native vegetation is grassland, coniferous forest, aspen forest or shrubland.

Most of eastern Colorado was originally grassland, but much of it has been replaced by agriculture. About 40 percent of Colorado is coniferous forest (Erickson and Smith 1985), which consists primarily of piñon-juniper, ponderosa pine, Douglas-fir, lodgepole pine, and spruce-fir. Much of western Colorado and the mountain parks is shrubland. Other habitats such as riparian forests and wetlands are of much more limited distribution, but are important to birds.

In the following discussion, only the most common plant species are mentioned, but many others also occur. The emphasis is on tree and shrub species; grasses are mentioned only where they are dominant, and other forbs are generally not listed as there are so many species. The following is a simplified system. Exact species composition, especially of the secondary species, varies widely from area to area. Most habitats form mosaics or mixtures with other adjoining habitats. Such areas, known as ecotones, are often more diverse in both plant and bird species than either adjoining habitat. More details on the vegetation of Colorado can be found in Marr (1961), Gregg (1963), Harrington (1964), Armstrong (1972), Peet (1981), Baker (1984), Mutel and Emerick (1984), and Weber (1987, 1990).

Grassland

Flora: Colorado's grasslands, also often called prairie, are dominated by a mixture of blue grama and buffalo-grass (see Appendix 2 for scientific names). In the grasslands adjacent to the foothills, buffalo-grass is often missing. During wet years or in locally moist spots, medium-grasses and tall-grasses also occur, such as needle-and-thread, sand dropseed, side-oats grama, western wheatgrass, and big and little bluestem. In sandy areas, grasslands are dominated by sand bluestem and sand sagebrush. Other shrubs, such as rabbitbrush, saltbush, and winterfat, also occur locally in grasslands. Prickly-pear cactus is often numerous where grasslands have been heavily grazed. On the southeastern plains candelabra cactus occurs, and yucca is found throughout the eastern plains.

Distribution: This is the dominant natural vegetation through most of Colorado's eastern plains. It occurs from 3,500 feet to about 5,500–6,000 feet at the lower edge of foothill shrublands and forests. Grasslands are also found in the mountain parks, most notably in South Park and the Wet Mountain Valley but locally in North Park and the San Luis Valley. Many smaller mountain parks contain grasslands. Much of the area covered by grassland is short-grass grassland. Mid-grass and tall-grass grasslands also occur locally, primarily in locally moister areas such as depressions and near the foothills. Sandsage grasslands occur mostly in northeastern Colorado, especially along the south side of the South Platte River and in Yuma County. Grasslands occur in dry areas, usually with less than 20 inches of precipitation, which comes mostly in spring and summer.

Large areas of this habitat have been converted to cropland. Most of the grassland that remains has been used for cattle grazing, which has altered the vegetation of the original grassland, favoring the short-grasses and weedy forbs. Therefore, the tall-grasses have become much rarer. In many areas overgrazing has occurred, reducing the density of grasses and often permitting extensive growth of prickly-pear cactus. In some areas, primarily near the foothills, much grassland has been converted to urban and suburban uses. The most extensive areas of grassland are in the Pawnee National Grassland in northeastern Colorado and the Comanche National Grassland in southeastern Colorado.

Avifauna: Relatively few species of birds occur in grasslands. The most common and widespread species is the Horned Lark. The Lark Bunting is also quite common in most eastern Colorado grasslands. In northern Larimer and Weld counties, McCown's Longspur is an abundant species and the Chestnut-collared Longspur is local. The Western Meadowlark is a grassland bird, but is now more common in many agricultural areas than in short-grass prairie. Species such as Cassin's Sparrow and Brewer's Sparrows occur in grasslands with numerous shrubs. Grasshopper Sparrows are most common in areas with taller grasses. Densities of most small grassland birds fluctuate widely in response to annual variations in precipitation. Some raptors, such as the Swainson's Hawk and Ferruginous Hawk, occur primarily in grasslands and breed locally where trees or bluffs provide nesting sites. Burrowing Owls are found mostly in prairie dog towns. Ferruginous Hawks, Bald Eagles (in winter), and Mountain Plovers are also associated with prairie dog towns. Some species, such as Vesper Sparrow and Brewer's Blackbird, are more numerous in mountain park grasslands than on the eastern plains.

The destruction or modification of native grasslands by human activities has caused a serious decline in some grassland species. The Mountain Plover and Long-billed Curlew are both much less numerous and more locally distributed than they were a century ago. The Greater and Lesser prairie-chickens occur locally in sandsage grasslands. The grassland-foothill shrub ecotone is the habitat for the rare and local plains subspecies of the Sharp-tailed Grouse.

The greatest diversity of bird species in grasslands is during summer. This habitat provides so little food and shelter in winter that it supports very few species, the most numerous being the Horned Lark. Some species that do not breed in this habitat may occur there in migation, often in large numbers, such as Rock Wren and Mountain Bluebird.

References: Giezentanner (1970), Stahlecker and Behlke (1974), Knopf (1988).

Lowland Riparian Forest

Flora: This habitat is dominated by the plains cottonwood. Other tree species may also occur locally, such as box-elder, green ash, Russian-olive, and American elm. The last three species are non-native species that are cultivated in towns, and have spread into the river-bottoms. Except in northeastern Colorado, tamarisk (salt cedar) is also a frequent species (Lindauer 1983). An understory of the peach-leaved willow is frequent, and lower shrubs such as snowberry are also common. Sandbar willows occur on river sandbars. Depressions often have plants of moist habitats such as cattails. Some riparian areas lack trees.

Distribution: Along rivercourses in the western valleys and on the eastern plains, where it is nearly continuous along the larger rivers and is localized along the smaller rivers, which are often dry for much of the year. This habitat ranges from 3,350 feet along the eastern border to about 5,500 feet at the edge of the foothills. The vegetation in most of the towns and cities of the lowlands is comparable, although a much wider diversity of trees are found. Areas occupied by this habitat are always moist due to the presence of surface and subsurface water.

Human activities have greatly altered the annual water regimes of the South Platte and Arkansas rivers on the eastern plains and hence the vegetation. Prior to white settlement those rivers had water primarily during the spring runoff in spring and early summer and were dry most of the rest of the year. Cottonwoods therefore occurred only in local groves. These rivers now have water all year due to dams and irrigation, enabling the cottonwood forests to become continuous along the rivers (Knopf 1986). Tamarisk is an introduced species that is rapidly expanding in riparian areas (Lindauer 1983). Many riparian areas have been converted to human uses such as residential, industrial, and highway construction, gravel mining, and recreation.

Avifauna: Although it occupies only 0.2 percent of the area of Colorado, it is the richest in diversity of birds (Bottorff 1974). Many of the species also occur in urban areas and foothill riparian forests. Important breeding species include Yellow-billed Cuckoo, Eastern and Western Screech-Owls, Great Horned Owl, Red-headed Woodpecker, Northern Flicker, Eastern Kingbird, House Wren, Brown Thrasher, Yellow Warbler, Orchard Oriole, and Northern Oriole. Many species of migrants, such as flycatchers, thrushes, warblers, and sparrows, occur in this habitat in spring and fall. Tamarisk is important for only a few species such as Bewick's Wren and Blue Grosbeak. Although species diversity is much less in winter, it is still more diverse than most other habitats. The lowland riparian forests of eastern Colorado were corridors through which many eastern species, such as the Blue Jay and Common Grackle, reached Colorado.

References: Stelter (1979), Knopf and Olson (1984), Knopf (1985), Knopf and Sedgwick (1987), Knopf et al. (1988), Sedgwick and Knopf (1986, 1987, 1990).

Foothill Riparian Forest

Flora: Although dominated by narrowleaf cottonwood, several other tree species and many shrub species are also numerous, such as box-elder, red-osier dogwood, willows, mountain maple, alder, and river birch. Especially in the mountains, conifers, mostly notably the Colorado blue spruce, form a mixture with the cottonwoods.

Distribution: Along rivercourses in the foothills, lower mountains, and mountain parks from 5,500 to 10,000 feet.

Avifauna: Similar to lowland riparian forests, although less diverse (Knopf 1985), especially in winter. Some species, such as Warbling Vireo and Lazuli Bunting, are present in the lowland and foothill riparian areas, but are more common in the foothills. A few species are lacking (as breeders) in the lowland riparian areas, such as Cordilleran Flycatcher, Veery, Swainson's Thrush, and MacGillivray's Warbler. This habitat is richer in species than adjacent uplands (Knopf 1985).

Semidesert Shrubland

Flora: The common shrub is greasewood, but shadscale, four-winged saltbush, rabbitbrush, and big sagebrush are common locally and in some areas may be the dominant species. Greasewood tends to be most common on the more alkaline soils, and four-winged saltbush often dominates on drier and less alkaline soils.

Distribution: Primarily in low drainages in western and southern Colorado, mostly from 4,000 to 6,5000 feet but also from 7,500 to 8,000 feet in the San Luis Valley. The most extensive areas are in western Moffat and Rio Blanco counties, along the Colorado, Gunnison, and Uncompahgre rivers in Mesa, Delta, and Montrose counties, southwestern Montezuma County, and in the San Luis Valley.

Avifauna: Few species occur in this habitat and most are also found in grasslands or sagebrush shrublands. Birds include Chukar, Gambel's Quail, Sage Thrasher, Loggerhead Shrike, and Black-throated Sparrow. The low species diversity is greatest in summer.

Sagebrush Shrubland

Flora: Big sagebrush is the dominant species in northwestern Colorado, North Park, and in the Gunnison Basin. Mountain sagebrush is the dominant species in most other areas. A variety of other shrubs and a few trees are also found, primarily where these shrublands adjoin other habitats, such as semidesert shrublands and piñon-juniper woodlands. Mountain sagebrush often adjoins or mixes with aspen forests.

Distribution: Primarily in western Colorado and the mountain parks, primarily from 5,000 to 8,000 feet, but also locally down to 4,000 feet and up to 9,500 feet. The most extensive stretches are in Moffat and Rio Blanco counties, in North and Middle parks, and in the Gunnison Basin. There are also numerous patches elsewhere, such as in southwestern Colorado, the periphery of the San Luis Valley, in Eagle County, in the valley of the upper Arkansas River in Lake and Chaffee counties, and in the valley of the Laramie River in northwestern Larimer County.

Avifauna: This habitat has a relatively small number of species, although it is more diverse than semi-desert shrublands. Many of the most common species are primarily restricted (as breeders) to this habitat, such as Sage Grouse, Sage Thrasher, Brewer's Sparrow, and Sage Sparrow. Green-tailed Towhee may also be common locally. Species diversity is greatest in summer.

References: Braun et al. (1976), Knopf et al. (1990).

Foothill Shrubland

Flora: The most common and conspicuous species is Gambel oak. Other shrub species that also occur are mountain mahogany, skunkbrush, serviceberry, bitterbrush, rose, currant, ninebark, buckbrush, rabbitbrush, and hawthorn. Some of these species may form pure stands or may dominate, such as mountain mahogany in the northeastern foothills north of central Jefferson County and serviceberry in Moffat and Rio Blanco counties (Costello 1964). Gambel oak may attain the size of a small tree, especially in western Colorado.

Distribution: These shrublands occur statewide, mostly from 5,500 to 8,500 feet. The most extensive areas are in northwestern and north-central Colorado. Gambel oak does not occur along the Front Range north of Jefferson County, but other species range north to Larimer County. In western Colorado, these shrublands are more extensive and occupy a wider elevational range than in eastern Colorado. They are bordered below by grasslands, semidesert, and sagebrush shrublands, and piñon-juniper woodlands; and above by ponderosa pine and Douglas-fir forests. This habitat is absent from the periphery of North, Middle, and South parks.

Avifauna: This habitat has a fairly diverse avifauna, especially in summer. Many of the species of this habitat are more common here than elsewhere, although no species is restricted to it. Species that tend to be more common here than in other habitats include Sharp-tailed Grouse, Band-tailed Pigeon, Common Poorwill, Dusky Flycatcher, Scrub Jay, Virginia's Warbler, Lazuli Bunting, and Rufous-sided Towhee. Green-tailed Towhees are most common in shrublands dominated by species such as serviceberry or mountain mahogany. Many other important species also occur commonly in adjoining habitats. In winter, diversity is generally low, but it may support large numbers of a few species, such as American Robin, where it contains fruit-bearing shrubs.

Piñon-juniper Woodland

Flora: Piñon pine is the dominant tree, usually mixed with Utah juniper, and in some parts of the state one-seed juniper. Junipers are more drought–tolerant than piñons and may form pure stands in some areas, especially at lower elevations. Various shrub species also are found, particularly where these woodlands intermix with other habitats.

Distribution: These woodlands occur widely in western Colorado, east to southwestern Grand County, in the periphery of the San Luis Valley, and in the southeastern foothills east to western Baca County and north to central Chaffee and southwestern El Paso counties. Isolated stands occur north to Larimer County. These woodlands occur mostly from 5,000 to 7,000 feet, but in some areas are as low as 4,000 feet or as high as 8,500 feet. The woodlands are usually bounded by grassland and sagebrush and semidesert shrublands below and foothill shrublands above.

Avifauna: This habitat has a number of species that either are restricted to it or are most abundant in it, including Gray Flycatcher, Pinyon Jay, Plain Titmouse, Bushtit, Gray Vireo, and Black-throated Gray Warbler. In fall and winter Steller's Jay, Scrub Jay, and especially Clark's Nutcrackers descend into these woodlands where piñon cone crops are ample. Where the berry-like cones of junipers are abundant, birds such as Townsend's Solitaire, Western Bluebird, Mountain Bluebird, American Robin, and Pine Grosbeaks are attracted to this habitat in fall and winter, often in large numbers.

References: Stelter and Nagy (1979), Lanner (1981), O'Meara et al. (1981), Sedgwick (1987).

Ponderosa Pine Forest

Flora: The dominant tree is the ponderosa pine. At upper elevations, the forests are fairly dense, but at lower elevations they are much more open. Where this habitat meets the foothill grasslands there is a pine savanna. In cool ravines and on north-facing slopes, Douglas-fir occurs commonly, or even dominates. Numerous shrub species and several other trees are found where these forests meet the piñon-juniper woodlands and foothill shrublands below, and lodgepole pine and aspen forests above.

These forests are used extensively by humans. Suppression of fire, a decrease in heavy grazing, lumbering, and a wetter climate early in the century have combined to create denser forests than would normally occur (Mutel and Emerick 1984).

Distribution: Foothills and low mountains in eastern and southern Colorado, primarily from 5,500 to 8,500 feet, but in some areas as high as 9,500 feet. These forests range north to Larimer County in eastern Colorado and Mesa County in western Colorado. They extend east to Elbert County on the Palmer Divide. In northwestern and central Colorado west of the Continental Divide ponderosa pine forests are absent, although individual trees occur in other coniferous forests.

Avifauna: This is generally the most diverse coniferous forest. Diversity is greatest in summer. Williamson's Sapsucker and Pygmy Nuthatch occur primarily in this habitat, which accounts for their scarcity in northwestern Colorado. Many other species are also numerous in these forests, such as Steller's Jay, Western Bluebird, Solitary Vireo, Grace's Warbler (southwestern Colorado only), Western Tanager, and Chipping Sparrow. Where ponderosa pine forests are mixed with Gambel oak shrublands, Wild Turkeys and Band-tailed Pigeons occur.

References: Cruz (1975), Winternitz (1976), Hudler et al. (1979), Aulenbach and O'Shea–Stone (1983).

Douglas-fir Forest

Flora: Dominated by Douglas-fir and usually mixed with ponderosa pine, lodgepole pine, or quaking aspen. Junipers may also occur, as do many foothill shrub species.

Distribution: Occurs throughout Colorado in the higher foothills and lower mountains, mostly from 5,500 to 9,000 feet, but as high as 10,500 feet in some areas. These forests are bordered by ponderosa pine forests or foothill shrublands below and lodgepole pine and quaking aspen forests above.

Avifauna: No species are restricted to this habitat; its avifauna is a mixture of species from adjoining forests.

Reference: Winternitz (1976).

Lodgepole Pine Forest

Flora: The lodgepole pine is the dominant species. Douglas-fir, quaking aspen, Engelmann spruce, and subalpine fir frequently form mixtures. Some shrubs are also present, but this habitat is often depauperate in plant species. These forests are often very dense and uniform.

Distribution: The middle and upper mountains, mostly in northern and central Colorado, and only in scattered locations in southern Colorado. It is found mostly from 7,500 to 10,500 feet, but also down to 6,500 feet and up to 11,500 feet. It is bounded below by Douglas-fir forests, and above by spruce-fir forests. It is most extensive in areas that have been disturbed by fire or logging.

Avifauna: This is the least diverse forest type in Colorado, especially where it grows in dense, uniform stands. Most of the species that occur are wide-ranging species occurring in most coniferous types, such as Mountain Chickadee, Yellow-rumped Warbler, and Dark-eyed Junco.

References: Roppe and Hein (1978), Nicholls and Egeland (1989), Hallock (1990).

Aspen Forest

Flora: Dominated by quaking aspen, usually with a rich understory of shrubs and forbs. Often mixed with conifers such as lodgepole pine, ponderosa pine, Engelmann spruce, and subalpine fir. In western Colorado, it often adjoins sagebrush shrublands.

Distribution: Statewide in the mountains, primarily from 7,500 to 10,000 feet, but a few small groves as low as 6,000 feet or as high as 11,000 feet. Generally occurs on relatively sunny sites disturbed by fire or logging.

Avifauna: These forests have richer diversity of birds than the adjoining coniferous forests. Some species are more numerous here than in other habitats, such as Red-naped Sapsucker, Tree Swallow, and Warbling Vireo, although no species are entirely restricted to this habitat. House Wrens are common in this habitat as well as in foothill and lowland riparian forests. Flammulated Owls often nest in aspens. In their limited Colorado range, Purple Martins occur primarily in aspen forests.

Reference: Flack (1976).

Montane and Subalpine Riparian Shrubland

Flora: Riparian areas in the montane and subalpine zones are quite diverse, and generally form a mosaic with adjoining habitats. They may be composed entirely of shrubs, form a mixture of trees or shrubs, or have isolated groves of trees. They also often merge with moist or wet meadows. Common shrubs and low trees include many species of willows, bog birch, river birch, alder, and red-osier dogwood. Several tree species are present, depending on the elevation, including narrowleaf cottonwood, Colorado blue spruce, and white fir. From 7,000 to 10,000 feet the most common combination is narrowleaf cottonwood and Colorado blue spruce (and white fir in southern Colorado) with numerous shrubs. Above 10,000 feet willows and bog birch dominate.

Distribution: Along drainages primarily from 7,000 to 11,000 feet, but also locally to 6,000 feet or 11,500 feet.

Avifauna: Because of its hetergeneous nature, this is a fairly diverse habitat compared with adjoining forests, especially below 10,000 feet. Important breeding species include Willow Flycatcher, Swainson's Thrush, MacGillivray's Warbler, Wilson's Warbler, Fox Sparrow, Lincoln's Sparrow, and White-crowned Sparrow. In winter, this habitat is used by White-tailed Ptarmigan.

References: Hadley (1969a), Eckhardt (1979), Hallock (1984), Knopf et al. (1988).

Limber Pine and Bristlecone Pine Forest

Flora: Limber pine and/or bristlecone pine dominate. Relatively few other plant species occur in this depauperate habitat. Individuals of those two species occur scattered in adjoining forests.

Distribution: Locally in higher mountains from 7,500 to 11,500 feet, generally on dry, windy, exposed sites. Limber pine also grows locally at lower elevations, even on the plains such as at Pawnee Buttes, Weld County. Bristlecone pine occurs primarily in the southern half of Colorado.

Avifauna: Relatively few species occur in this habitat, mostly common and wide-ranging species from adjoining habitats such as Clark's Nutcracker and Dark-eyed Junco.

Spruce-fir Forest

Flora: The dominant species are Engelmann spruce and subalpine fir. Those two species are generally mixed, but may occur in pure stands, especially at the lower elevation range of this habitat where only the spruce grows. The shrub understory is generally poorly developed; the primary shrubs include blueberry and whortleberry.

Distribution: Higher mountains statewide. It is best developed from 10,000 to 11,000 feet, but also occurs to 9,000 feet and 11,500 feet.

Avifauna: Because of the climate at high elevations, these forests have relatively small numbers of species. The species that do occur often are restricted to this habitat or are most common in it, at least while breeding. Important species include Boreal Owl, Three-toed Woodpecker, Hammond's Flycatcher, Gray Jay, Clark's Nutcracker, Brown Creeper, Golden-crowned Kinglet, Ruby-crowned Kinglet, and Pine Grosbeak. Some wide-ranging coniferous species, such as Mountain Chickadee, Yellow-rumped Warbler, and Dark-eyed Junco also occur. Diversity is greatest in summer; most species either migrate south or move to lower elevations for winter.

References: Gutiérrez (1970), Wagner (1984), Hallock (1988).

Krummholz

Flora: Reclining, wind-blown thickets of Engelmann spruce and subalpine fir, with some limber pine and bristlecone pine. Numerous thickets of bog birch and willows are interspersed among the conifers.

Distribution: In the higher mountains from 11,000 to 12,000 feet between spruce-fir forest below and alpine tundra above. The lower limit of krummholz is called treeline (the upper limit of upright trees) and upper limit is called timberline (the upper limit of trees of any size or shape).

Avifauna: This habitat has a very limited avifauna. Most birds are summer residents only. The most distinctive species is the White-crowned Sparrow. Other species of spruce-fir forest and subalpine shrublands also occur. White-tailed Ptarmigan use this habitat, especially in winter.

Alpine Tundra

Flora: Primarily forbs, including grasses and sedges. In depressions, low clumps of willows are also found. Many different communities are recognized, primarily related to snow cover. Technically, the term tundra should not be used in Colorado as the term is applied to areas with permafrost, which occurs very rarely in Colorado (Braun 1980). However, the term alpine tundra is so widely used and recognized in Colorado that we continue to use it.

Distribution: On the higher mountains above treeline from 11,500 feet upward. Most of the major mountain chains in Colorado are high enough to have alpine tundra, but it is limited in some chains, and is lacking on the lower chains. The most extensive stretches are found in the Front, Gore, Mosquito, and Sawatch ranges, and the Elk and San Juan mountains.

Avifauna: Only a few species occur in this habitat. The primary breeders are White-tailed Ptarmigan, Horned Lark, and American Pipit. Prairie Falcons, Common Ravens and Rosy Finches nest on cliffs and forage on adjacent tundra. Open country birds of lower elevations also occur, primarily in late summer and early fall. Such species include Northern Harrier and Mountain Bluebirds. Only the White-tailed Ptarmigan occurs regularly in winter.

Reference: Zwinger and Willard (1972).

Canyons and Cliffs

Distribution: At all elevations in the foothills and mountains, and locally on the eastern plains.

Avifauna: The species found nesting or roosting on canyon walls and cliffs depend primarily on elevation, with most species found in the foothills and lower mountains. The main species are Turkey Vulture, Golden Eagle, Prairie Falcon, Peregrine Falcon, White-throated Swift, Violet-green Swallow, Common Raven, Canyon Wren, and Rosy Finch. Spotted Owls are found in forest patches on canyon walls. Black Swifts nest on cliffs adjacent to or behind waterfalls.

Natural Streams and Lakes

Distribution: Statewide. Most natural lakes in Colorado are found in the mountains, but natural intermittent ponds are found on the eastern plains. At lower elevations, most smaller natural streams are intermittent, flowing primarily during spring and early summer.

Avifauna: A wide variety of species are found in natural wetlands, depending on the area of the state, elevation, and particular characteristics of each wetland. The richest natural wetlands are found in North Park and the San Luis Valley. North Park is Colorado's primary duck breeding area. Ring-necked Ducks and Buffleheads breed on beaver ponds and kettle ponds in the mountains. Common Mergansers, Spotted Sandpipers, and American Dippers occur along mountain streams and Harlequin Ducks formerly occurred. Wood Ducks breed along shaded watercourses at low elevations. Moist meadows fringing streams and lakes are used by many birds for nesting or foraging, such as White-faced Ibis, many ducks, Sandhill Crane, Common Snipe, and Savannah Sparrow.

Cattail Marshes

Flora: Dominated by cattails.

Distribution: Statewide at lower and middle elevations (mostly below 6,000 feet and from 7,500 to 9,000 feet), mostly in the western valleys, mountain parks, and on eastern plains.

Avifauna: A small number of species breed in this habitat. Most are found primarily in this habitat and some are restricted to it. The main breeding species are American Bittern, Virginia Rail, Sora, Marsh Wren, Red-winged Blackbird, and Yellow-headed Blackbird. Where cattail marshes fringe ponds or lakes, other species such as Pied-billed Grebe, Eared Grebe, Western Grebe, Clark's Grebe, Ruddy Duck, American Coot, and Black Tern use these marshes. Blackbirds and Short-eared Owls may roost in marshes in winter, and where the marshes are unfrozen a few Virginia Rails and Sora may also be found.

Reservoirs

Flora: Variable. Many reservoirs have an extensive growth of smartweed in their shallows, and a few with relatively little fluctuation of water levels may have cattails. Many reservoirs have fringes of lowland riparian forest. Reservoirs that are lowered substantially for irrigation have a distinctive group of plants that grow on the exposed muddy or alkaline flats.

Distribution: Statewide along rivers, but mostly in western valleys, mountain parks, and on eastern plains. The greatest concentrations are along the South Platte and Arkansas rivers in eastern Colorado. Most reservoirs are constructed either for flood control or for irrigation; both are also extensively used for recreation.

Avifauna: A large variety of species use reservoirs; only lowland riparian forests equal or surpass reservoirs in their species diversity. Some, especially new reservoirs and those in the mountains, have few or no birds, but most have large numbers of birds, primarily in migration and winter. Most species of loons, grebes, ducks, gulls, and terns are found on reservoirs. Most species of shorebirds are also found around them, primarily around irrigation reservoirs that have low water levels and exposed mud flats in late summer and fall.

Relatively few species of water birds use reservoirs for nesting. American White Pelicans and California Gulls nest on islands, and Double-crested Cormorants and Great Blue Herons nest in groves of tall trees standing in reservoirs. Western Grebes summer on most reservoirs, and nest on those with stable water levels and aquatic vegetation such as smartweed. Reservoirs in southeastern Colorado with exposed alkaline shorelines have small nesting populations of Snowy Plover, Piping Plover, and Least Tern. A few Ospreys nest around some mountain reservoirs.

Some reservoirs remain partially or entirely open in winter due to warm water associated with power plants, chinook winds, or continual flow of water from rivers or canals. Such reservoirs support large numbers of wintering birds, primarily waterfowl (especially Canada Geese and Mallards, but also other species such as Common Mergansers) and Bald Eagles.

Agricultural Areas

Flora: The main nonirrigated crop is winter wheat. Irrigated crops are corn, alfalfa, sugar beets, and vegetables. In the western valleys, apples and peaches are grown in orchards.

Distribution: Primarily in the western valleys, the San Luis Valley, and on the eastern plains. Locally in other mountain parks, and in the foothills and lower mountains.

Avifauna: Exclusively agricultural areas have relatively few bird species, but where fields are interspersed or edged with houses, shelterbelts and windbreaks, riparian forests, or wetlands, a much wider variety of birds is found. Among the most important species are the American Kestrel, Ring-necked Pheasant, Mourning Dove, Western Meadowlark, Red-winged Blackbird, and Common Grackle. Dickcissels are especially common in alfalfa. Stubble wheat fields are an important winter habitat for the Horned Lark. Corn fields interspersed with grassland are important for both the Greater and Lesser prairie-chickens in winter. Agricultural areas, especially cornfields with interspersed tall trees, often have Lewis' Woodpeckers. Migrant cranes often feed in fields. Recently plowed fields often attract Franklin's, California, and Ring-billed Gulls. European Starlings, Red-winged Blackbirds, and House Sparrows are abundant in winter where livestock is kept and fed.

Reference: Stahlecker and Behlke (1974).

Urban Areas

Flora: Extremely variable. Small towns and residential areas in cities at lower elevations usually have cottonwoods and elms as dominant trees, but many other tree species and many species of shrubs are also planted. Fruit-bearing trees and shrubs such as Russian-olive are often more numerous in residential areas than elsewhere. Conifers are also planted in urban areas, often far outside their natural range.

Distribution: Statewide, primarily in the western valleys, mountain parks, foothills, and eastern plains (especially at the base of the foothills).

Avifauna: A wide variety of birds occur where vegetation is abundant. Primary species include Mourning Dove, American Robin, European Starling, Yellow Warbler, Common Grackle, House Finch, and House Sparrow. Urban parks and golf courses often have large numbers of Canada Geese. In business or industrial areas where vegetation is scarce or lacking, primary species are Rock Dove, European Starling, and House Sparrow. The Chimney Swift occurs primarily in towns, nesting in buildings. The Mississippi Kite nests principally in town parks in southeastern Colorado.

Organization of the Species Accounts

Names: Each species account begins with the English and scientific name of the bird as given by the AOU Checklist and its supplements (American Ornithologists' Union 1983, 1985, 1987, 1989, 1991). Subspecies are not included except for field-identifiable subspecies.

Summary: The next section is a short summary statement that provides readers with a quick overview (the big picture). The summary does not mention all areas and seasons; for a complete discussion see the text.

Status: The status section begins with one or two codes. The first (given for all species) tells whether the species' occurrence in Colorado is based upon a specimen (indicated by SP), a photograph (PH), or only by sight records (SR). Breeding species (B) and former breeders (FB) are also indicated when appropriate.

The text of the status section deals with the abundance and distribution of the bird. It begins with the season(s) in which the species is most common, and proceeds to the season(s) in which it is least common. The name of each season is boldfaced where it is first used to facilitate locating specific information. The time-span covered by the book is from the start of Colorado ornithology (late 1800s) to the present. We have included records published through the end of 1991, although some unusual published records have not been included because they have not been yet fully evaluated by the CFO Records

Committee. We have discussed changes in abundance and distribution through historical times when appropriate. For species which have not always been present in Colorado, the first observation in the state is listed. For species which have been present since the first ornithologists arrived, the earliest known observations were listed by Marsh (1968).

Wherever we state that there are a specific number of records for a certain area and season (17 fall records, for example), we have a complete listing of all records that are available to readers who want more information. Because many old references were not precise, sometimes we have to hedge and say "about 17 records." The notation "17+ records" implies that we suspect our list of records is incomplete.

Many published observations have been excluded because they lacked details. In most cases, we do not mention such undocumented reports. However, in cases where an unusually large number of undocumented reports exist and where we feel it is important to emphasize that observations need to documented, we have mentioned this. Our intent is not to criticize for failing to document reports (indeed, the CFO Records Committee has not always requested documentation for species we feel need to be documented). All species or categories, such as winter records or west slope records, that we feel need to be documented are indicated with an asterisk. Of course, any observations in areas or seasons where there are no records should be carefully documented. Reports of the CFO Records Committee include information on all records evaluated by the committee (Reddall 1973a, b, c, 1974a, b, 1975, 1976a, b, Andrews 1978, 1979, Chase 1981a, b, 1982, 1983, Gent 1984a, 1985a, b, 1986, 1987, Bunn 1988, 1989a, b, Nelson 1991).

Many species accounts include high counts. We have included only especially notable counts and have made no effort to find high counts for every species. Only single-party counts are included, generally those made at a single site or limited area; no CBC high counts are included. It is true that these counts may have limited scientific validity due to wide variation and biases in how they were made, but they do provide interest to many readers.

Habitat: Following the status section is the habitat section. Whenever possible we have tried to indicate differences in habitat use in different parts of the state or at different seasons. We have used the term *forest* to indicate any more or less closed canopy tree-dominated habitat and *woodland* to any open-canopy tree-dominated habitat. Using that definition, only piñon-juniper seems to qualify as a woodland, and all others are forests, although most can have a woodland aspect in some areas.

Records: In many species there is a records section. This lists the most unusual records by date and location. For species with 10 or fewer state records, we have listed them all. For species that are accidental in one season or in one major region of the state, those records are also listed individually. All specimens known from Colorado are listed if there are very few. Where specimen records are listed, the collection in which the specimen is held is indicated by abbreviation, and the catalog number is included if available. References for sight records have not been included unless a publication provided additional useful information. Uncited records were generally obtained from Bailey and Niedrach (1965) or from the appropriate issue of *American Birds* (Mountain West Region), the *C.F.O. Journal*, or local newsletters such as the *Lark Bunting*. Many recent records have been sent to us by observers; those letters are on file.

We have usually not included specimens collected by Edwin Carter in Middle Park, Grand County and at Breckenridge, Summit County in the late 1800s, and now deposited in the Denver Museum of Natural History collection. There is significant doubt about the localities of these specimens because there were so many improbable records that have never been repeated; see the Orchard Oriole account for an example.

Notes: Some species have a notes section which includes miscellaneous information. For many species reference is made to the National Audubon Society Blue List (Tate 1986). This is a list of species that are declining or which should be monitored for other reasons, but which are not yet endangered or threatened.

References: Many species have a reference section. This includes only references that were not already cited in the status or habitat sections. Although most of the references we have cited deal directly with distribution, abundance, or habitat, we have included some references about breeding biology, etc. when those studies were conducted in Colorado. We avoid citing unpublished reports or theses. We have cited some information from people as personal communications or unpublished reports; these are kept on file and are available to readers.

The literature cited section contains numerous recent references on Colorado birds. We have not attempted to list all of the references from earlier years. Bailey and Niedrach (1965) provided an extensive and useful list of references. The most useful older references include Cooke (1897, 1898, 1900, 1909), Cary (1911), Sclater (1912), Bergtold (1928), and Niedrach and Rockwell (1939). Marsh (1968) and Holt (1970) provided important historical information. Important statewide references published since 1965 include Holt and Lane (1987), Kingery (1988), and Holt (1989). Inkley et al. (1981) examined statewide patterns of species diversity. Ryder (1986) reviewed Breeding Bird Survey results for Colorado. In addition, there are many useful local checklists for counties, national wildlife refuges, national parks, national forests, national grasslands, national monuments, and state parks.

Useful references on the birds of adjacent states include: **Wyoming:** Oakleaf et al. (1982), Fitton and Scott (1984), Dorn and Dorn (1990). **Utah:** Twomey (1942), Behle and Perry (1975), Cook (1984), Behle (1981, 1985), Walters (1983), Behle et al. (1985). **Arizona:** Phillips et al. (1964), Monson and Phillips (1981), Jacobs (1986), Rosenberg and Terrill (1986). **New Mexico:** Hubbard (1978). **Oklahoma:** Sutton (1967, 1974), Johnsgard (1979), Wood and Schnell (1984). **Kansas:** Rising (1974), Johnsgard (1979), Thompson and Ely (1989). **Nebraska:** Johnsgard (1979), Ducey (1988).

Maps: Most species have maps showing their distribution in Colorado. The patterns show areas where the species is known or would be expected to be widespread. Symbols indicate localities of one or several records or small localized populations. See the legend for a more detailed explanation of the patterns and symbols. Maps are not included where all records from Colorado are listed in the text. For most species these maps are the first detailed published maps. Therefore, many maps should be considered to be preliminary, and we urge observers to provide additional information by sending it to us or publishing observations in the *C.F.O. Journal* or another ornithological journal.

Seasonal occurrence graphs: These graphs show arrival and departure dates, peak periods of abundance, and relative abundance throughout the year. When this information varies significantly in different regions of Colorado the graph has separate levels. It would be useful to have more published information from different geographic and elevation areas. See the legend for an more detailed explanation of the patterns and symbols.

Elevation graphs: These graphs show relative abundance at different elevations from 3,500 to 14,000 feet. Where there are significant seasonal differences in elevational distribution separate columns are provided. See the legend for an explanation of the patterns and symbols.

Monthly records graphs: These graphs show the monthly distribution of all records of the rarest species. They show all records from Colorado or from a specified region of Colorado. Individual birds that were seen during several months are included only in the month during which they were first seen. The number of records listed in the text and shown on the graph sometimes don't match because records without specific dates are not included on the graph.

Other information: While researching this book, we consulted over 30 local bird checklists. Although most of them proved useful, we encountered great difficulty in utilizing that source. The available checklists varied so widely in what information was included and how it was presented, and especially in the abundance categories used, that the usefulness of this source was greatly reduced. We believe that if all local checklists adopted a standardized format, they would be far more useful to both birders and researchers. We have proposed such a format (Andrews et al. 1992), based upon the format and categories used in this book.

We have assembled a large quantity of material while researching this book. The information is maintained on a computerized database. Any reader desiring to examine the material upon which the species accounts were based can request access to this database by contacting the authors. An article will appear in the *C.F.O. Journal* further describing the database and its use. We strongly urge all readers to contribute any additional information they currently have or which they obtain in the future which would improve the accuracy or completeness of this book. Such information could be published in the *C.F.O. Journal* or another ornithological journal, or could be sent to the authors c/o Zoology Department, Denver Museum of Natural History, 2001 Colorado Blvd., Denver, Colorado 80205. Written or photographic documentation of unusual observations should be sent to the Colorado Field Ornithologists Records Committee at the same address.

Abundance Categories Used in Text

Abundant:	>100/day in appropriate season and habitat
Common:	25–100/day
Fairly common:	10–25/day
Uncommon:	1–10/day; usually seen daily
Rare:	1–5/day and 1–10/season; usually not seen daily
Very rare:	10–40 records (for the state as a whole, or within certain areas or seasons)
Casual:	4–9 records
Accidental:	1–3 records
Note:	Abundance categories indicate the average number of birds that would be seen by an observer over many trips in several years in the appropriate season, area, and habitat. It does not indicate the number that can be seen by a specialist studying or searching for a particular species. Exceptions are grouse and owls, in which the numbers as defined above would grossly underestimate the true abundance of the species.

Topographical Regions Used in Text

Eastern plains:	All of eastern Colorado from outer edge of foothills east.
Western Valleys:	Includes the valleys of the Yampa, Green, White, Colorado, Uncompahgre, Gunnison, Dolores, San Miguel, Mancos, and Animas rivers. The eastward extension (along the Colorado River, for example) varies with the species; maps should be consulted.
Foothills:	5,500 or 6,000 to 7,500 feet; includes mesas on western slope, Black Forest, and much of Las Animas County and southwestern Baca County.
Lower mountains:	7,500 to 10,000 feet.
Higher mountains:	10,000 to 11,500 feet.
Mountains:	Lower and higher mountains combined.
Mountain parks:	North Park, Middle Park, South Park, Wet Mountain Valley, and San Luis Valley; for some species, minor parks (such as Estes Park, Moraine Park, etc.) may also be included; maps should be consulted.
Above timberline:	>11,500 feet.

Codes and Abbreviations Used in Text

B:	Species is a confirmed breeder in Colorado
BBS:	Breeding Bird Survey
CBC:	Christmas Bird Count
CM:	Carnegie Museum, Pittsburgh
CSU:	Colorado State University
CU:	University of Colorado, Boulder
DMNH:	Denver Museum of Natural History
FB:	Species formerly bred in Colorado
FMNH:	Field Museum of Natural History, Chicago
LSU:	Louisiana State University
PERS. COMM.:	personal communication to authors
PH:	Species recorded from Colorado on the basis of photographic records
RC:	Records Committee (Colorado Field Ornithologists)
SDNHM:	San Diego Natural History Museum
SP:	Species recorded from Colorado on the basis of extant specimens
SR:	Species recorded from Colorado on the basis of documented sight records
WSC:	Western State College
*:	*species, or categories that require either photographic or written documentation*

Legend For Maps

Primary range: where the species is most common (usually fairly common, common, or abundant). On summer maps, the primary and secondary patterns show the known or probable breeding range, unless specified otherwise by the map label or in the text.

Secondary range: where the species is less common (usually rare or rare to uncommon).

Symbols indicate where the species is least common or show isolated populations.

▲ Spring

▼ Fall

◆ Spring and Fall

✳ Winter

⊞ Early Winter

■ Summer: confirmed breeding

☐ Summer: probably breeding

⊕ Summer: nonbreeding

▣ Summer: breeding (minor sites), used only to distinguish between major and minor breeding sites on the same map

╪ Summer: former breeding

● All year

⊗ Records in several seasons (as specified on map label)

▲̲ Underlined symbols indicate specimen records (given only for rarest species)

[▲] Symbols within brackets indicate records at unknown sites within the county

? Records at that site, but time of year unknown

Legend For Seasonal and Elevation Graphs

Common to abundant

Uncommon to fairly common

Rare

Very rare

● Casual or accidental records (one or several days)

 Casual or accidental records (more than several days)

[●] Record within that month, but specific date unknown

Abbreviations

N = North
S = South
W = West
E = East

Apx. = approximately
Mi. = miles (mileages given are approximate air miles)
Mt. = mountain or mount
Mts. = mountains

N.W.R. = National Wildlife Refuge
Res. = reservoir
R.M.N.P. = Rocky Mountain National Park
S.R.A. = State Recreation Area
S.W.A. = State Wildlife Area

Colorado Counties & Location

County	Location	County	Location
Adams	northeast	Kit Carson	east central
Alamosa	south central	Lake	central
Arapahoe	northeast	La Plata	southwest
Archuleta	southwest	Larimer	north central
Baca	southeast	Las Animas	southeast
Bent	southeast	Lincoln	east central
Boulder	north central	Logan	northeast
Chaffee	central	Mesa	west central
Cheyenne	east central	Mineral	southwest
Clear Creek	central	Moffat	northwest
Conejos	south central	Montezuma	southwest
Costilla	south central	Montrose	west central
Crowley	southeast	Morgan	northeast
Custer	south central	Otero	southeast
Delta	west central	Ouray	southwest
Denver	northeast	Park	central
Dolores	southwest	Phillips	northeast
Douglas	northeast	Pitkin	west central
Eagle	northwest	Prowers	southeast
Elbert	east central	Pueblo	southeast
El Paso	east central	Rio Blanco	northwest
Fremont	northeast	Rio Grande	south central
Garfield	northwest	Routt	northwest
Gilpin	central	Saguache	south central
Grand	north central	San Juan	southwest
Gunnison	west central	San Miguel	southwest
Hinsdale	southwest	Sedgwick	northeast
Huerfano	south central	Summit	central
Jackson	north central	Teller	central
Jefferson	central	Washington	northeast
Kiowa	southeast	Weld	northeast
		Yuma	northeast

Major Placenames

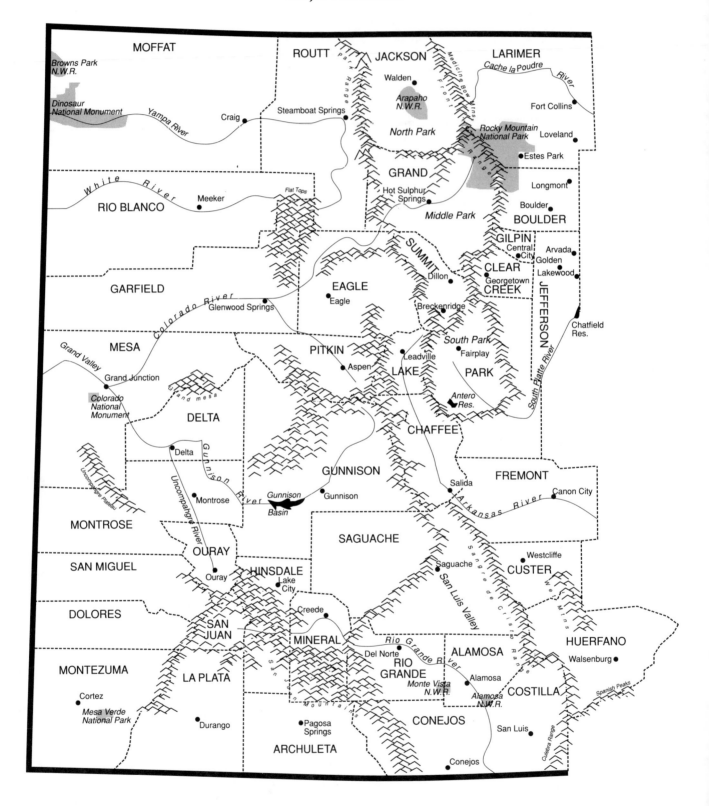

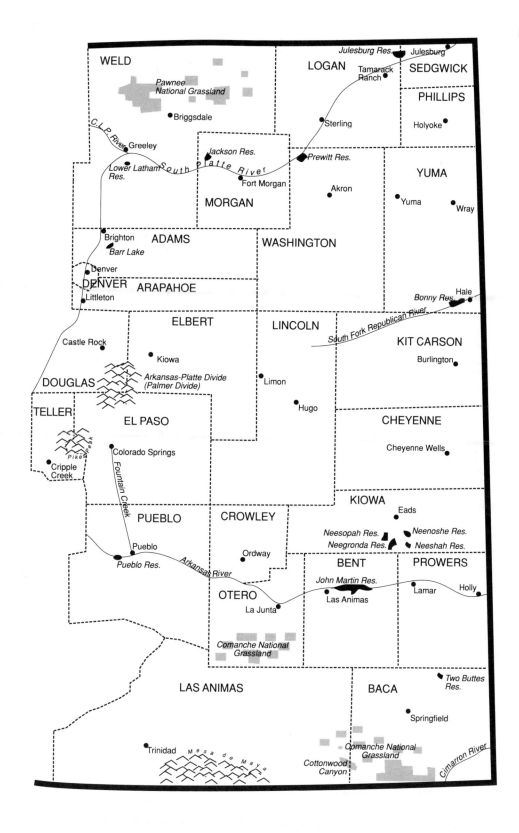

50 Miles

WELD

Pawnee
National Grassland

LOGAN

Julesburg Res. Julesburg

Tamarack
Ranch

SEDGWICK

PHILLIPS

Briggsdale

C.L.P. River

Greeley

Sterling

Holyoke

Jackson Res.

Prewitt Res.

Lower Latham
Res.

South Platte River

Fort Morgan

MORGAN

Akron

YUMA

Yuma

Wray

ADAMS

WASHINGTON

Brighton

Barr Lake

Denver

DENVER

Littleton

ARAPAHOE

Bonny Res. Hale

South Fork Republican River

ELBERT

LINCOLN

Castle Rock

Kiowa

Arkansas-Platte Divide
(Palmer Divide)

Limon

KIT CARSON

Burlington

DOUGLAS

TELLER

EL PASO

Hugo

Pikes

Creek

Colorado Springs

CHEYENNE

Cripple
Creek

Cheyenne Wells

Fountain Creek

KIOWA

Eads

PUEBLO

CROWLEY

Neesopah Res.

Neenoshe Res.

Neegronda Res.

Neeshah Res.

Pueblo

Ordway

BENT

PROWERS

Pueblo Res.

Arkansas River

John Martin Res.

Lamar

Holly

OTERO

Las Animas

La Junta

Comanche National
Grassland

Two Buttes
Res.

LAS ANIMAS

BACA

Springfield

Trinidad

Mesa de Maya

Comanche National
Grassland

Cottonwood
Canyon

Cimarron River

Regions of Colorado Used in Gazetteer

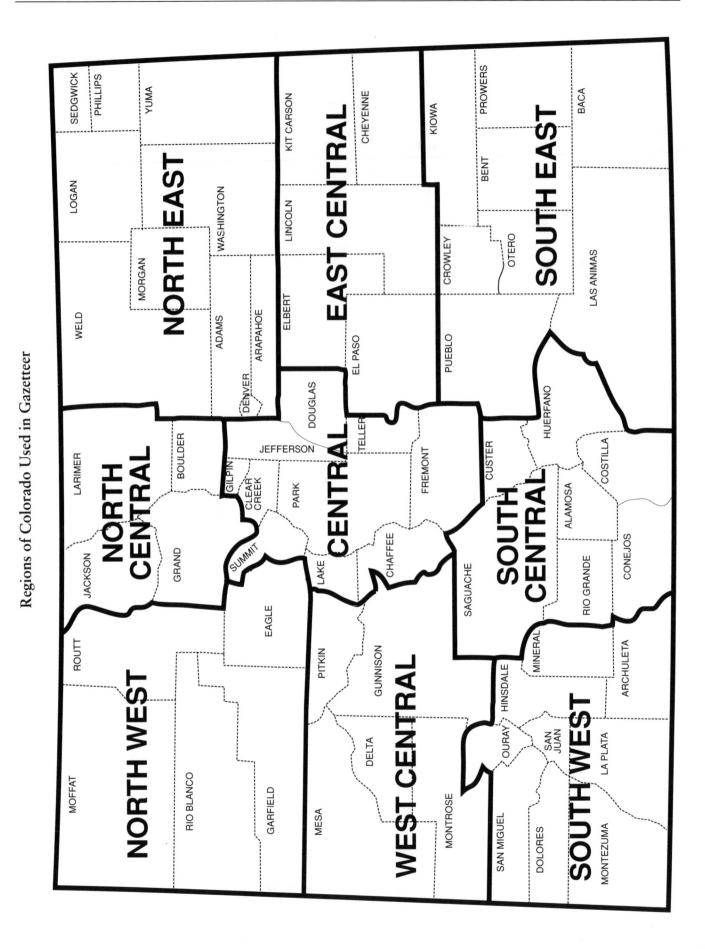

Placenames & Locations

Adobe Creek Res.	(Bent/Kiowa) 4,128', 12 mi. N of Las Animas, Bent County; same as Blue Lake
Alamosa	(Alamosa) 7,544', town, see map
Alamosa N.W.R.	(Alamosa) apx. 7,500', 5 mi. E of Alamosa, see map
Allenspark	(Boulder) apx. 8,400', town 12.5
Antero Res.	(Park) 8,940', SW corner of county, see map
Antonito	(Conejos) 7,888', town in SE corner of county
Apishapa Creek	(Las Animas) apx. 7,500', 18 mi. NW of Trinidad, in far W part of county
Arapaho N.W.R.	(Jackson) apx. 8,100', just S of Walden, see map
Arapahoe Peaks	(Boulder) apx. 13,400', W part of county on Continental Divide
Arkansas-Platte Divide	apx. 7,500', between Denver & Colorado Springs; same as Palmer Divide, see map
Arkansas River Valley	apx. 4,700' near Pueblo to apx. 3,400' near Holly, see map
Arvada	(Jefferson) 5,337', suburb NW of Denver, see map
Aspen	(Pitkin) 7,908', town, see map
Aurora	(Arapahoe/Adams) 5,342', suburb E of Denver
Austin Bluffs	(El Paso) apx. 6,050', a bluff in N part of Colorado Springs
Baculite Mesa	(Pueblo) 5,393', 5 mi. NE of city of Pueblo
Bailey	(Park) 7,750', town in NE part of county
Barr Lake	(Adams) apx. 5,000', 4 mi. SE of Brighton in NW part of county, see map
Baseline Res.	(Boulder) apx. 5,350', just SE of city of Boulder
Bayfield	(La Plata) 6,900', town 15 mi. E of Durango
Bear Creek Canyon	(El Paso) apx. 7,500', just SW of Colorado Springs
Beetland	(Washington) apx. 4,250', town in extreme NW part of county, near South Platte River
Bennett	(Adams) 5,483', town 25 mi. E of Denver
Bent's Old Fort	(Otero) apx. 4,100', national historic site apx. 8 mi. NE of La Junta
Bergen Park	(Jefferson) apx. 7,800', town 15 mi. W of Lakewood
Berthoud	(Larimer) 5,030', town 10 mi. N of Longmont
Berthoud Pass	(Clear Creek/Grand) 11,315', NW Clear Creek County & SE Grand County
Beulah	(Pueblo) 6,200', town in SW part of county
Big Thompson Canyon	(Larimer) 7,523' - 4,982', between Estes Park & Loveland
Billy Creek S.W.A.	(Ouray) apx. 6,900' to 7,500', 8 mi. N of Ridgway
Blackhawk	(Gilpin) 8,056', town in SW part of county
Blue Lake	(Kiowa) same as Adobe Creek Res.
Blue Mesa Res.	(Gunnison) 7,519', 12 mi. W of Gunnison
Bluebell Canyon	(Boulder) apx. 5,700', SW edge of city of Boulder
Bonny Res.	(Yuma) 3,600', SE part of county, see map
Book Cliffs	(Mesa) 6,000', 10 mi. N of Grand Junction
Boot Lake Res.	(Adams) apx. 5,000', 12 mi. E of Brighton
Bootleg Res.	(Adams) same as Boot Lake Res. in early references
Boulder	(Boulder) 5,363', city, see map
Bow Mar	(Jefferson) 5,500', suburb on SW edge of Denver & NW of Littleton
Boyd Lake S.R.A.	(Larimer) apx. 5,000', 2 mi. NE of Loveland
Breckenridge	(Summit) 9,603', town, see map
Briggsdale	(Weld) 4,840', town 25 mi. NE of Greeley; site of Crow Valley Park
Brighton	(Adams) 4,982', town, see map
Browns Park N.W.R.	(Moffat) apx 5,400', NW part of county, see map
Brush	(Morgan) 4,231', town 9 mi. E of Fort Morgan
Brush Hollow Res.	(Fremont) 5,492', 9 mi. E of Canon City & just NW of Penrose

Buena Vista	(Chaffee) 7,954', town 23 mi. N of Salida
Buford	(Rio Blanco) 7,100', town 25 mi. E of Meeker
Burlington	(Kit Carson) 4,163', town, see map
Burnt Mill Rd.	(Pueblo) apx. 4,700', from SW edge of city of Pueblo
Byers	(Arapahoe) 5,200', town 38 mi. E of Denver
C.F. & I. Lakes	(Pueblo) apx. 5,000', 7 mi. S of Pueblo; on some maps shown as St. Charles Res.
Cache la Poudre River	(Larimer/Weld) headwaters on N side of R.M.N.P.; flows E, joining South Platte River at Greeley (Weld), see map
Cameo	(Mesa) 4,820', town 7 mi. NE of Grand Junction
Cameron Pass	(Jackson/Larimer) 10,276' northwest of R.M.N.P.; between Medicine Bow Mts. & Never Summer Range
Campo	(Baca) 4,339', town 20 mi. S of Springfield
Canon City	(Fremont) 5,332', town in E part of county
Capulin	(Conejos) 7,810', town 18 mi. SW of Alamosa (Alamosa)
Castlewood Canyon State Park	(Douglas) apx. 5,900', 5 mi. E of Castle Rock
Center	(Saguache) 7,645', town 23 mi. S of town of Saguache
Chambers Lake	(Larimer) 9,153', W part of county, 7 mi. from N edge R.M.N.P.
Chatfield Res.	(Douglas/Jefferson) apx. 5,300', SW edge of Littleton (Arapahoe)
Cheraw	(Otero) 4,130', town 12 mi. N of La Junta
Cheraw Lake	(Otero) 4,130', adjacent to Cheraw
Cherry Creek Res.	(Arapahoe) apx. 5,350', within Aurora, a SE suburb of Denver
Cheyenne Wells	(Cheyenne) 4,296', town, see map
Cimarron River	(Baca) apx. 4,300', in SE part of county, see map
Clear Creek	(Jefferson) apx. 8,000'-5,300', flows from W of and through Golden
Clifton	(Mesa) 4,710', town just E of Grand Junction
Coal Canyon	(Mesa) apx. 6,000', 9 mi. NE of Grand Junction
Coal Creek	(Adams) apx. 5,100', in early references, same as the upper portion of Sand Creek in central part of county
Cochetopa Dome Res.	(Saguache) 11,132', 35 mi. NW of Saguache in NW part of county
Colorado National Monument	(Mesa) apx. 4,500' - 6,000', 9 mi. W of Grand Junction, see map
Colorado River	headwaters W of Continental Divide in NW corner of R.M.N.P.; flows W, exiting state W of Grand Junction, see map
Colorado Springs	(El Paso) 6,012', city, see map
Colorado Springs S.W.A.	(El Paso) apx. 5,500', 16 mi. SE of Colorado Springs; often referred to as Hanna Ranch
Comanche National Grassland	(Baca/Las Animas/Otero) apx. 4,400', S Baca, E Las Animas, & S Otero counties, see map
Conifer	(Jefferson) 8,270', town 12 mi. SW of Lakewood
Continental Divide	Enters state from the N above Steamboat Springs (Routt) then swings E, close to Boulder (Boulder), then proceeds SW, exiting in SE Archuleta County
Cortez	(Montezuma) 6,200', town, see map
Cottonwood Canyon	(Baca/Las Animas) 4,800', mostly in extreme SW part of Baca County, see map
Cottonwood Pass	(Gunnison/Chaffee) 12,126', E part of Gunnison county & W part of Chaffee County
Coventry	(Montrose) apx. 7,200', town, 35 mi. SW of town of Montrose
Craig	(Moffat) 6,185', town, see map
Crane Park	(Garfield) 10,385', in the Flat Tops, 11 mi. NE of Glenwood Springs
Creede	(Mineral) 8,852', town, see map
Crestone	(Saguache) 7,863', town in E part of county, 16 mi. N of Great Sand Dunes Monument
Crook	(Logan) 3,711', town in NE part of county, 27 mi. NE of Sterling
Culebra Range	(Costilla/Las Animas/Huerfano) apx. 13,500', SE Costilla, SW Las Animas, & S Huerfano Counties, see map

Curecanti National Recreation Area	(Gunnison) apx. 7,500', 25 mi. W of Gunnison; includes Blue Mesa Res.
De Weese Res.	(Custer) apx. 7,900', N central part of county, located just outside Westcliffe
Deadman Mt. Lookout	(Larimer) apx. 10,500', 40 mi. NW of Fort Collins, W of Red Feather Lakes region
Deadmans Canyon	(El Paso) apx. 7,200', N of Colorado Springs at U.S. Air Force Academy
Deckers	(Douglas) 6,400', town 20 mi. SW of Castle Rock in SW part of county
Deer Trail	(Arapahoe) apx. 5,183', town in W central part of county
Del Norte	(Rio Grande) 7,874', town, see map
Delta	(Delta) 4,961', town, see map
Denver	(Denver) 5,280', city, see map
Deora	(Baca) apx. 4,400', town 25 mi. NW of Springfield in NW part of county
Devils Head	(Douglas) 9,748', mt. 8 mi. E of Deckers in Rampart Range
Dillon Res.	(Summit) 9,156', central part of county
Dinosaur National Monument	(Moffat) apx. 5,900', SW part of county, see map
Dinosaur Ridge	(Jefferson) apx. 6,300' just S of I-70 & S of Golden; site of hawk watch
Dove Creek	(Dolores) 6,843', town in W part of county 35 mi. NW of Cortez (Montezuma)
Dry Willow Creek	(Yuma) apx. 3,500', near Wray
Durango	(La Plata) 6,512', town, see map
Dye Res.	(Otero) apx. 4,100', 3 mi. N of Rocky Ford
Eads	(Kiowa) 4,213', town, see map
Eagle	(Eagle) 6,600', town, see map
East Carrizo Creek	(Baca) apx. 4,800', 4 mi. E of Cottonwood Canyon in SW part of county
Eastlake	(Adams) 5,270', town in W part of county, 13 mi. N of Denver center
Eaton	(Weld) 4,839', town 7 mi. N of Greeley
Echo Canyon Res.	(Archuleta) apx. 7,100', 4 mi. S of Pagosa Springs
Echo Lake	(Clear Creek) 10,597', 7.5 mi. SW of Idaho Springs
Eckert	(Delta) apx. 5,700', town 8 mi. NE of Delta
Edwards	(Eagle) 7,220', town 13 mi. E of Eagle
Elba	(Washington) apx. 4,700', town 7 mi. S of Akron
Eldora	(Boulder) 8,700', area in SW part of county, 17 mi. SW of Boulder
Eleven Mile Res.	(Park) 8,561', 25 mi. E of Antero Res. in SE part of county
Elk River	(Routt) apx. 7,500', headwaters in Park Range, flowing S to where it joins the Yampa River apx. 7 mi. W of Steamboat Springs
Elkhead Mts.	(Moffat/Routt) apx. 10,000', range in NE Moffat County & NW Routt County
Elliot Ridge	(Grand) apx. 8,000', 12 mi. W of Hot Sulphur Springs
Encampment River	(Jackson) apx. 8,700', 30 mi. NW of Walden in extreme NW part of County
Endovalley	(Larimer) apx. 9,000', R.M.N.P.
Englewood	(Arapahoe) 5,306', suburb S of Denver
Escalante Canyon	(Delta) apx. 5,000', 11 mi. W of Delta in extreme SW part of county
Escalante S.W.A.	(Delta) apx. 5,000', 5 mi. W of Delta
Estes Park	(Larimer) 7,522', town just E of R.M.N.P.
Evans Ranch	(Clear Creek) apx. 8,000', 8 mi. W of Evergreen (Jefferson)
Evergreen	(Jefferson) 7,040', town 20 mi. SW from Denver center
Evergreen Lake	(Jefferson) 7,040', adjacent to Evergreen
Fairplay	(Park) 9,953', town, see map
Fall River Road	(Larimer) apx. 11,900' to 9,000', R.M.N.P.
Fern Lake Trail	(Larimer) R.M.N.P.
Fisher Peak	(Las Animas) 9,627', 6 mi. S of Trinidad
Flat Tops Wilderness Area	(Garfield/Rio Blanco) apx. 10,500', a high, isolated range within the White River Plateau, NE Garfield County & E Rio Blanco County

Florence	(Fremont) 5,187', town 8 mi. E of Canon City
Fort Collins	(Larimer) 4,984', city, see map
Fort Collins Nature Center	(Larimer) apx. 5,000', near Fort Collins
Fort Garland	(Costilla) 7,936', town 26 mi. E of Alamosa (Alamosa) in N part of county
Fort Lewis	(La Plata) 7610', town 5 mi. W of Durango
Fort Logan	(Denver) apx. 5,300', area within city of Denver, extreme SW corner
Fort Lyon	(Bent) 3,870', town just W of John Martin Res.
Fort Morgan	(Morgan) 4,330', town, see map
Foster Res.	(Weld) apx. 5,000', far W part of county, 7 mi. NE of Longmont (Boulder)
Fountain	(El Paso) 5,546', town 15 mi. S from Colorado Springs center
Fountain Creek	(El Paso) apx. 5,700', flows S out of Colorado Springs, see map
Four Corners	Apx. 4,800', refers to area where Colorado, Utah, Arizona, & New Mexico meet; SW corner of Montezuma County
Four Mile Canyon	(Boulder) apx. 6,300', runs W from Boulder
Fraser	(Grand) 8,550', town 20 mi. SE of Hot Sulphur Springs in SE part of county
Front Range	Refers to the mountains starting at the N end of the state with the Medicine Bow-Rawahs and proceeding S through Boulder County to Jefferson County. See map.
Fruita	(Mesa) 4,498', town 12 mi. NW of Grand Junction
Garber Canyon	(Douglas) apx. 6,900', 10 mi. W of Castle Rock
Genesee Mt.	(Jefferson) apx. 7,500', 5 mi. SW of Golden
Genesee Park	(Jefferson) 8,284', mt. in Genesee Park
Georgetown	(Clear Creek) 8,519', town, see map
Gill	(Weld) 4,670', town 9 mi. E of Greeley
Glade Park	(Mesa) 6,750', town a few miles SW of Colorado National Monument
Glenwood Springs	(Garfield) 5,746', town, see map
Golden	(Jefferson) 5,675', town, see map
Granada	(Prowers) 3,484', town 17 mi. E of Lamar
Granby	(Grand) 7,935', town 10 mi. SW of SW edge of R.M.N.P.
Granby Res.	(Grand) same as Lake Granby
Grand Junction	(Mesa) 4,586', city, see map
Grand Lake	(Grand) 8,369', lake & town on SW edge of R.M.N.P.
Grand Mesa	(Mesa/Delta) apx. 10,500', 30 mi. E of Grand Junction, see map
Grand Valley	(Mesa) apx. 4,600', broad valley in which Grand Junction, Fruita, & Clifton are situated, see map
Grant	(Park) 8,580', town in N part of county, 19 mi. S of Georgetown (Clear Creek)
Great Sand Dunes National Monument	(Saguache/Alamosa) apx. 8,500', 25 mi. NE of Alamosa
Greeley	(Weld) 4,663', city, see map
Green Mt. Res.	(Summit) 8,100', N part of county, 20 mi. SW of Hot Sulphur Springs (Grand)
Gregory Canyon	(Boulder) apx. 6,100', just W of city of Boulder
Grover	(Weld) 5,071', town 17 mi. NE of Briggsdale
Guanella Pass	(Clear Creek) 11,669', 8 mi. S of Georgetown
Gulnare	(Las Animas) 6,800', town 18 mi. NW of Trinidad
Gunnison	(Gunnison) 7,703', town, see map
Gunnison Basin	(Gunnison) apx. 7,200', SW part of county, see map
Gunnison River	Headwaters W of Continental Divide N of Gunnison (Gunnison); joins Colorado River at Grand Junction (Mesa), see map
Gypsum	(Eagle) 6,334', town 7 mi. W of Eagle
Hale	(Yuma) 3,600', town, see map
Hall Valley	(Park) NW of Kenosha Pass

Hamilton Res.	(Larimer) apx. 5,000', 10 mi. N of Fort Collins
Harts Basin	(Delta) 6,000', 12 mi. NE of Delta; also known as Fruitgrowers Res.
Hartsel	(Park) 8,860', town 8 mi. E of Antero Res. in SW part of county
Hasty	(Bent) 3,870', town 2 mi. N of John Martin Res.
Hayden	(Routt) 6,336', town 22 mi. W of Steamboat Springs
Henrys Lake	(Jefferson) apx. 5,400', in Lakewood
Hereford	(Weld) 5,260', town 24 mi. N of Briggsdale, very near Wyoming border
Highline Canal	(Mesa) apx. 4,700', leads into Highline Lake
Highline Lake	(Mesa) 4,697', 20 mi. NW of Grand Junction
Highline Res.	(Mesa) same as Highline Lake
Hoehne	(Las Animas) 5,700', town 10 mi. NE of Trinidad
Holbrook Res.	(Otero) 4,162', 8 mi. NW of La Junta
Holly	(Prowers) 3,397', town 27 mi. E of Lamar
Horse Creek Res.	(Otero/Bent) 5,068', 15 mi. NE of La Junta; also known as Timber Res.
Horse Creek Res.	(Adams/Weld) apx. 5,000', 13 mi. E of Brighton
Hotchkiss	(Delta) 5,351', town 20 mi. E of Delta
Hovenweep National Munument	(Montezuma) 5,883', 28 mi. W of Cortez along extreme W edge of county along Utah border
Howardsville	(San Juan) apx. 9,900', town 5 mi. NE of Silverton
Hoy Mt.	(Moffat) 8,831', 9 mi. SW of Brown Park N.W.R. in the NW part of county at the Utah border
Hudson	(Weld) 5,024', town 22 mi. NE of Brighton (Adams)
Huerfano River	(Pueblo/Huerfano) apx. 5,600', 18 mi. SE of city of Pueblo
Hygiene	(Boulder) 5,090', town 4 mi. NW of Longmont
Idaho Springs	(Clear Creek) 7,540', town 12 mi. E of Georgetown
Idalia	(Yuma) 3,960', town 7 mi. NW of Bonny Res.
Idledale	(Jefferson) 6,460', town 15 mi. SW from Denver center
Ignacio	(La Plata) 6,432', town 18 mi. SW of Durango
Jackson Res.	(Morgan) 4,438', 20 mi. NW of Fort Morgan, see map
Jefferson	(Park) 9,500', town 15 mi. NE of Fairplay
Jim Hamm Pond	(Boulder) apx. 5,000', just W of Union Res. (Weld) & 4 mi. E of Longmont
Jimmie Creek	(Baca) purportedly in W Baca County but probably a local appellation no longer in use
John Martin Res.	(Bent) 3,851', see map
Julesburg	(Sedgwick) 3,477', town, see map
Julesburg Res.	(Logan/Sedgwick) apx. 3,500', 40 mi. NE of Sterling; same as Jumbo Res. or Jumbo Lake, see map
Jumbo Lake	(Logan/Sedgwick) same as Julesburg Res.
Jumbo Res.	(Logan/Sedgwick) same as Julesburg Res.
Kenosha Pass	(Park) 10,001', 20 mi. NE of Fairplay; NW part of county
Kersey	(Weld) 4,617', town 8 mi. E of Greeley
Kim	(Las Animas) 5,690', town 65 mi. E of Trinidad
Kit Carson	(Cheyenne) 4,285', town 25 mi. W of Cheyenne Wells
Kossler Lake	(Boulder) apx. 7,500', 5 mi. SW of Boulder center
Kremmling	(Grand) 7,364', town 16 mi. W of Hot Sulphur Springs
La Garita	(Saguache) 7,840', town 35 mi. NW of Alamosa (Alamosa)
La Jara	(Conejos) 7,602', town 15 mi. S of Alamosa (Alamosa)
La Junta	(Otero) 4,066', town, see map
La Plata Mts.	(La Plata/Montezuma) apx. 12,000', 16 mi. NW of Durango
La Salle	(Weld) 4,676', town 5 mi. S from center of Greeley
La Veta	(Huerfano) 7,013', town in SW part of county

La Veta Pass	(Costilla/Huerfano) 9,382', E part of Costilla County, W part of Huerfano County
Lafayette	(Boulder) 5,237', town 10 mi. E of city of Boulder
Laird	(Yuma) 3,400', town 7 mi. E of Wray
Lake City	(Hinsdale) 8,671', town, see map
Lake De Weese	(Custer) same as De Weese Res.
Lake Estes	(Larimer) apx. 7,500', just E of Estes Park
Lake George	(Park) 7,968', SE part of county, 2 mi. W of Teller County
Lake Granby	(Grand) apx. 8,400', NE part of county at SW edge of R.M.N.P.
Lake Hasty	(Bent) apx. 3,800', just E of John Martin Res.
Lake Henry	(Crowley) apx. 4,300', 5 mi. NE of Ordway
Lake John	(Jackson) apx. 8,100', 10 mi. W of Walden
Lake Meredith	(Crowley) apx. 4,300', 3 mi. SE of Ordway
Lake Sangraco	(Adams) apx. 5,300', extreme SW corner of county
Lakewood	(Jefferson) 5,440', suburb to the W of Denver, see map
Lamar	(Prowers) 3,622', town, see map
Las Animas	(Bent) 3,901', town, see map
Lasauses	(Conejos) apx. 7,500', town in NE part of county 15 mi. SE of Alamosa (Alamosa)
Latham Res.	(Weld) same as Lower Latham Res.
Lay	(Moffat) 6,170', town 20 mi. W of Craig
Leadville	(Lake) 10,152', town, see map
Lily Lake	(Larimer) 9,057', R.M.N.P.
Limon	(Lincoln) 5,366', town, see map
Littleton	(Arapahoe) 5,632', see map
Livermore	(Larimer) 5,800', town 18 mi. NW of Fort Collins
Longmont	(Boulder) 4,979', city, see map
Lookout Mt.	(Jefferson) apx. 7,400', 15 mi. W of Denver center
Lory State Park	(Larimer) apx. 5,300', 6 mi. W of Fort Collins
Lost Park	(Park) apx. 10,000', area in NE part of county, 9 mi. S of Bailey
Loveland	(Larimer) 4,982', city, see map
Loveland Pass	(Summit/Clear Creek) 11,990', E edge of Summit County & W edge of Clear Creek County
Lower Latham Res.	(Weld) 4,664', 6 mi. SE of Greeley; same as Latham Res., see map
Lykins Gulch	(Boulder) apx. 5,700', 8 mi. N of Boulder
Lyons	(Boulder) 5,374', town 15 mi. N of Boulder
Mack	(Mesa) 4,520', town 20 mi. NW of Grand Junction
Mack-Mesa Res.	(Mesa) apx. 4,700', adjacent to Highline Lake, 20 mi. NW of Grand Junction
Manitou Lake	(Teller) apx. 7,800' within Manitou Park
Manitou Park	(Teller) apx. 7,800', 28 mi. N of Cripple Creek in NE corner of county
Manzanola	(Otero) 4,252', town 20 mi. NW of La Junta
Marshall Pass	(Saguache) 10,842', in extreme NE part of county
Masters	(Weld) 4,490', town 25 mi. SE of Greeley
Maybell	(Moffat) 5,920', town 38 mi. W of Craig
McCoy	(Eagle) 6,690', town extreme N edge of county near Routt County line
McLellan Res.	(Arapahoe/Douglas) apx. 5,300', S edge of Littleton
Medicine Bow Mts.	(Jackson/Larimer) apx. 10,500', the shared border of Jackson & Larimer counties, see map
Meeker	(Rio Blanco) 6,249', town, see map
Mesa	(Mesa) 5,650', town 25 mi. E of Grand Junction
Mesa de Maya	(Las Animas) apx. 6,000', SE part of county, see map
Mesa Verde National Park	(Montezuma) apx. 7,800', 10 mi. SE of Cortez, see map
Michigan Creek	(Jackson) apx. 9,000', 20 mi. SE of Walden

Michigan River	(Jackson) apx. 8,000', flowing NW from the Medicine Bow Mts. to the North Platte River
Middle Boulder Creek	(Boulder) apx. 9,000' to 5,400', flows from SW of and through Boulder
Middle Park	(Grand) apx. 7,600', the towns Kremmling, Hot Sulphur Springs, Granby, & Tabernash are situated within this area, see map
Mile High Duck Club	(Adams) apx. 5,000', 2.5 mi. NE of Barr Lake
Milner Pass	(Grand/Larimer) 10,758', R.M.N.P.
Milton Res.	(Weld) apx. 4,900', 20 mi. NE from Brighton (Adams)
Minturn	(Eagle) 7,817', town 25 mi. E of Eagle
Monte Vista	(Rio Grande) 7,663', town 12 mi. SE of Del Norte
Monta Vista N.W.R.	(Rio Grande), apx. 7,650', 10 mi. W of Alamosa (Alamosa), see map
Montrose	(Montrose) 5,794', town, see map
Monument	(El Paso) 6,960', town 15 mi. N of center of Colorado Springs
Moon Gulch	(Gilpin) apx. 9,000', N part of county, SW of Rollinsville
Moraine Park	(Larimer) apx. 8,200', R.M.N.P.
Morrison	(Jefferson) 5,800', town 12 mi. SW of Denver
Mosca	(Alamosa) 7,550', town 13 mi. N of Alamosa
Mt. Antero	(Chaffee) 14,269', 17 mi. NW of Salida in SW part of county
Mt. Bross	(Park) 14,172', NW edge of county near S Summit County
Mt. Elbert	(Lake) 14,433', 13 mi. SW of Leadville; highest point in Colorado
Mt. Evans	(Clear Creek) 14,264', 9 mi. SE of Georgetown in S part of county
Mt. Goliath	(Clear Creek) 12,216', 7.5 mi. SE of Georgetown in S part of county
Mt. Lincoln	(Park) 14,268', W edge of county near S Summit County
Mt. Shavano	(Chaffee) 14,229', 15 mi. NW of Salida in S part of county
Mt. Zirkel	(Routt/Jackson) 12,180', on Continental Divide 12 mi. S of Wyoming border
Muir Springs	(Morgan) apx. 4,300', area 8 mi. W of Fort Morgan
Navajo River	(Archuleta) apx. 7,300', 18 mi. SE of Pagosa Springs
Nederland	(Boulder) 8,236', town SW part of county
Neegronda Res.	(Kiowa) 3,876', S central part of county, see map
Neenoshe Res.	(Kiowa) 3,932', S central part of county, see map
Neesopah Res.	(Kiowa) 3,922', S central part of county, see map
New Castle	(Garfield) 5,550', town 12 mi. W of Glenwood Springs
Newell Lake	(Weld) 4,956', 2 mi. E of Berthoud (Larimer)
North Park	(Jackson) apx. 8,100', area bordered on the W by Park Range, on the E by the Medicine Bow Range, & on the S by Rabbit Ears Range, see map
Nunn	(Weld) 5,185', town 20 mi. N of Greeley
Olathe	(Montrose) 5,346', town 10 mi. NW of Montrose
Orchard	(Morgan) 4,400', town 20 mi. NW of Fort Morgan near W border of county
Orlando Res.	(Huerfano) 5,905', 10 mi. N of Walsenburg
Ouzel Falls Trail	(Boulder) 9,450', R.M.N.P.
Ovid	(Sedgwick) 3,521', town 7 mi. W of Julesberg
Palmer Divide	Same as Arkansas-Platte Divide
Paonia	(Delta) 5,674', 28 mi. NE of Delta
Parachute Creek	(Garfield) flows into Colorado River from the N 38 mi. NE of Grand Junction (Mesa)
Paradox Valley	(Montrose) apx. 5,300', W part of county
Park Range	(Routt/Jackson) apx. 11,000' on W side of North Park
Parker	(Douglas) 5,870', town 12 mi. NE of Castle Rock
Pawnee Buttes	(Weld) apx. 5,500', 30 mi. NE of Briggsdale
Pawnee National Grassland	(Weld) apx. 5,000' N part of county; in two sections—one section NW of Briggsdale and one section NE, see map

Peetz	(Logan) 4,432', town N central part of county, 25 mi. N of Sterling
Pennock Pass	(Larimer) apx. 9,000', 5 mi. NE of border of R.M.N.P.
Penrose	(Fremont) 5,330', town 12 mi. E of Canon City
Pikes Peak	(El Paso) 14,110', 15 mi. W of Colorado Springs, see map
Pingree Park	(Larimer) apx. 9,000', area 1 mi. N of R.M.N.P., along the South Fork of the Cache la Poudre River
Piñon Canyon	(Las Animas) apx. 6,600', NE corner of county
Plateau Creek Valley	(Mesa) apx. 5,500', starts 24 mi. E of Grand Junction and continues E for 9 mi.
Platteville	(Weld) 4,820', town 14 mi. SW of Greeley
Poudre Park	(Larimer) 5,676', town 14 mi. NW of Fort Collins
Poudre River	(Larimer) same as Cache la Poudre River
Prewitt Res.	(Washington/Logan) apx. 3,900', 24 mi. NE of Fort Morgan in NW corner of Washington County, see map
Prospect Res.	(Weld) 5,010', extreme S border, S central part of county
Pueblo	(Pueblo) 4,695', city, see map
Pueblo Res.	(Pueblo) apx. 5,000', 8 mi. W of Pueblo, see map
Rabbit Ears Pass	(Jackson/Grand) 9,426', near where Jackson, Grand, & Routt counties meet
Rabbit Ears Range	(Jackson/Grand) apx. 9,000', along S border of Jackson County & N border of Grand County
Radium	(Grand) 6,910', town 27 mi. SW of Hot Sulphur Springs
Rampart Range	apx. 9,000', a range running N-S between Denver and Colorado Springs
Rand	(Jackson) 8,620', town 20 mi. SE of Walden
Rangely	(Rio Blanco) 5,224', town 50 mi. W of Meeker
Raton Mesa	(Las Animas) apx. 9,300', 9 mi. SE of Trinidad
Red Feather Lakes	(Larimer) 8,342', in NW part of county 23 mi. N of north edge of R.M.N.P.
Red Lion S.W.A.	(Logan/Sedgwick) apx. 3,700', NE part of Logan county & NW part of Sedgwick county, adjacent to Julesburg Res.
Red Mt. Pass	(Ouray/San Juan) 11,008', S part of Ouray County & NW San Juan County
Red Rocks Park	(Jefferson) apx. 6,000', 15 mi. SW of Denver center
Redlands	(Mesa) 4,650', town 4 mi. W of Grand Junction
Ridgway	(Ouray) 6,985', town 10 mi. N of Ouray
Riverside Res.	(Weld) apx. 4,500', 25 mi. SE of Greeley
Roaring Fork Valley	(Garfield/Pitkin) from Aspen 7,908', to Glenwood Springs, 5,746'
Rocky Ford	(Otero) 4,178', town 12 mi. NW from La Junta
Rocky Ford S.W.A.	(Otero) 4,200', 3 mi. N of Rocky Ford
Rocky Mountain Arsenal	(Adams) 5,150' on NE edge of Denver county
Rocky Mountain Biological Lab	(Gunnison) apx. 10,500', 30 mi. N of Gunnison, near Gothic
Rocky Mt. National Park	(Larimer/Grand/Boulder) 14,256' to apx. 7,500', see map
Royal Gorge	(Fremont) apx. 6,000' at rim, 5 mi. W of Canon City
Russell Lakes	(Saguache) 7,796', 10 mi. S of Saguache
Rustic	(Larimer) 7,160', town along the Cache la Poudre River, 30 mi. W of Fort Collins
Rye	(Pueblo) 6,900', town 30 mi. SW of Pueblo
Saguache	(Saguache) 7,697', town, see map
St. Charles River	(Pueblo) flows from the SW part of county, joining the Arkansas River apx. 8 mi. E of Pueblo
St. Vrain Creek	headwaters W Boulder county & SW Larimer county; enters South Platte River SW of Greeley (Weld)
Salida	(Chaffee) 7,036', town, see map
San Juan Mts.	a high range in SW part of state, see map
Sandhills	mostly in Yuma County, N & NW of Wray
San Luis	(Costilla) 7,965', town, see map

San Luis Lakes	(Alamosa) apx. 7,550', 18 mi. NE of Alamosa
San Luis Valley	apx. 7,500', S central part of state, Monte Vista N.W.R., Alamosa N.W.R., & Great Sand Dunes National Monument
Sangre de Cristo Range	mt. range borders the E side of San Luis Valley, see map
Sawhill Ponds	(Boulder) apx. 5,350', gravel pits 4 mi. NE of Boulder
Security	(El Paso) 5,730', town 8 mi. SE from center of Colorado Springs
Sedalia	(Douglas) 5,860', town 7 mi. NW of Castle Rock
Sedgwick	(Sedgwick) 3,500', town 14 mi. SW of Julesburg
Shadow Mt.	(Grand) 10,154', 2 mi. E of Shadow Mt. Res.
Shadow Mt. Res.	(Grand) apx. 8,400', on SW edge of R.M.N.P.
Sheep Lake	(Larimer) 10,505', R.M.N.P.
Silver Lake	(Boulder) apx. 10,200', in SW part of county
Silver Plume	(Clear Creek) 9,118', town 2 mi. W of Georgetown
Silverthorne	(Summit) 8,790', town 3 mi. W of Dillon
Silverton	(San Juan) 9,318', town in center of county
Smith Lake	(Adams) apx. 5,000', 4 mi. SW of Brighton
South Cheyenne Canyon	(El Paso) base apx. 7,000', at the SW edge of Colorado Springs
South Platte River	Headwaters E of Continental Divide; flows from South Park to Eleven Mile Res., then flows NE, exiting state in NE Sedgwick county, see map
Spanish Peaks	(Huerfano/Las Animas) apx. 13,000', 20 mi. SW of Walsenburg, see map
Spicer	(Jackson) apx. 8,400', 20 mi. SE of Walden
Spring Creek Pass	(Hinsdale) 10,901', 12 mi. SE of Lake City
Springfield	(Baca) 4,365', town, see map
Squaw Mt.	(Clear Creek) 11,486', 4.5 mi. S from Idaho Springs
Stapleton Park	(Jefferson) apx. 7,500', a Denver Mountain Park 5 mi. SW of Golden
Steamboat Springs	(Routt) 6,695', town, see map
Sterling	(Logan) 3,935', town, see map
Sterling Res.	(Logan) apx. 4,000', 13 mi. NW of Sterling
Stonewall	(Las Animas) 7,800', town 30 mi. W of Trinidad
Strasburg	(Adams) 5,380', town in extreme S central part of county 35 mi. E of center of Denver
Sullivan	(Arapahoe) 5,477', locale along Cherry Creek in Aurora
Summit Lake	(Clear Creek) 12,830', on flank of Mt. Evans 13 mi. SW of Idaho Springs
Sunset	(Boulder) apx. 8,000', town, 10 mi. W of Boulder
Sweetwater Lake	(Garfield) 7,709', Flat Tops, E central part of county
Sweitzer Lake	(Delta) apx. 5,000', 2.5 mi. SE of Delta
Tamarack Ranch	(Logan) apx. 3,700', see map
Tarryall Creek	(Park) flows from NW part of county, 12,000', joining the South Platte River in SE part of county, apx. 7,500'
Taylor River	(Gunnison) headwaters in N of county, apx. 10,300', flowing S to join the Gunnison River N of Gunnison, apx. 8,000'
Timnath Res.	(Larimer) apx. 4,900', 8 mi. E of Fort Collins
Timpas	(Otero) apx. 4,100', 17 mi. SW of La Junta
Tomichi Creek	(Gunnison) apx. 10,200', in far SE part of county from town of Gunnison eastward
Totten Res.	(Montezuma) 6,157', 3 mi. NE of Cortez
Trail Ridge Road	(Grand/Larimer) high point 12,183', R.M.N.P.
Trinidad	(Las Animas) 6,025', town, see map
Trites Lake	(Saguache) 7,577', part of Russell Lakes; 10 mi. S of Saguache
Twin Lakes	(Lake) apx. 9,200', 13 mi. S of Leadville
Two Buttes Res.	(Baca) 4,230', N edge of county, see map

Unaweep Canyon	(Mesa) SW part of county, 8 mi. from Utah border
Uncompahgre Plateau	apx. 50 mi. long plateau; primarily from SW Mesa County through Montrose County
Uncompahgre River	headwaters in N San Juan Mts.; flows N entering Gunnison River at Delta (Delta), see map
Union Res.	(Weld) apx. 5,000', 4 mi. E of Longmont; same as Calkins Lake
U.S. Air Force Academy	(El Paso) apx. 7,300', 8 mi. N of Colorado Springs
Upper Sand Creek	(Saguache) apx. 9,000', NW edge of Great Sand Dunes National Monument
Vallecito Creek	(La Plata) apx. 7,800', NE part of county; flows into Vallecito Res. which is 20 mi. NE of Durango
Valmont Res.	(Boulder) apx. 5,360', 5 mi. E of Boulder
Villegreen	(Las Animas) 5,500', town 55 mi. E of Trinidad
Walden	(Jackson) 8,099', town, see map
Walden Pond	(Boulder) apx. 5,350', a pond adjacent to Sawhill Ponds
Walden Res.	(Jackson) apx. 8,100', 2 mi. W of Walden
Walsenburg	(Huerfano) 6,185', town, see map
Walsh	(Baca) 3,956', town 20 mi. E of Springfield
Ward	(Boulder) 9,253', town 13 mi. NW of Boulder
Waterton	(Douglas/Jefferson) apx. 5,500', town 17 mi. SW of Denver center
Watson Lake	(Larimer) apx. 5,200', 6 mi. NW of Fort Collins
Weldona	(Morgan) 4,340', town 12 mi. NW of Fort Morgan
Wellington	(Larimer) 5,201', 10 mi. NE of Fort Collins
Wellington Res.	(Larimer) apx. 5,200', within the Wellington S.W.A., 12 mi. NE of Fort Collins, 2 mi. E of Wellington
West Elk Mts.	(Gunnison) apx. 12,500', range 25 mi. NW of Gunnison
Westcliffe	(Custer) 7,888', town, see map
Westcreek	(Douglas) 7,520', SW part of county
Wet Mts.	(Fremont/Custer/Pueblo/Huerfano) apx. 9,500', the range E of the Wet Mt. Valley
Wet Mt. Valley	(Fremont/Custer) apx. 7,800', bordered on the E by the Wet Mts. & on the W by the Sangre de Cristos; Westcliffe and De Weese Res. are situated in this valley
Wetmore	(Custer) 5,990', town 30 mi. NE of Westcliffe in NE corner of county
Wheat Ridge	(Jefferson) 5,445', suburb on NW edge of Denver
Wheat Ridge Greenbelt	(Jefferson) a greenbelt that is situated in NW part of suburb of Wheat Ridge
White River Plateau	(Rio Blanco/Garfield/Eagle/Routt) high plateau with many parts over 10,000', covering area in E Rio Blanco & Garfield Counties, NW part of Eagle County, & SW part of Routt County. The Flat Tops are within this area.
Whitewater	(Mesa) 4,660', town 9 mi. SE of Grand Junction
Wiggins	(Morgan) 4,540', town 15 mi. W of Fort Morgan
Wild Basin	(Boulder) apx. 9,000', R.M.N.P.
Williams Fork River	(Grand) Middle Park, headwaters in Williams Fork Mts., apx. 12,400', flowing N into Colorado River E of Kremmling, apx. 7,300'
Willow Creek	(Dolores) apx. 7,500', central part of county
Windsor	(Weld) 4,800', town 12 mi. SE of Fort Collins (Larimer)
Windsor Res.	(Weld) apx. 4,800', 11 mi. SE of Fort Collins (Larimer)
Woods Lake	(Eagle) apx. 9,300', 18 mi. S of Eagle
Wray	(Yuma) 3,516', town, see map
Yampa River	flows from S Routt county N to Steamboat Springs, then west through Dinosaur National Monument (Moffat), see map
Yuma	(Yuma) 4,132', town, see map

SPECIES ACCOUNTS

Order Gaviiformes
Family Gaviidae

Red-throated Loon
Gavia stellata

Very rare in fall and early winter in eastern Colorado.

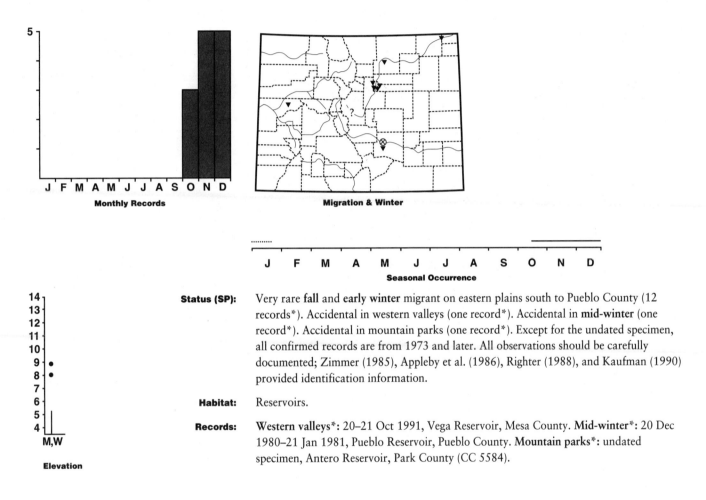

Monthly Records

Migration & Winter

Seasonal Occurrence

Elevation

Status (SP): Very rare **fall** and **early winter** migrant on eastern plains south to Pueblo County (12 records*). Accidental in western valleys (one record*). Accidental in **mid-winter** (one record*). Accidental in mountain parks (one record*). Except for the undated specimen, all confirmed records are from 1973 and later. All observations should be carefully documented; Zimmer (1985), Appleby et al. (1986), Righter (1988), and Kaufman (1990) provided identification information.

Habitat: Reservoirs.

Records: **Western valleys*:** 20–21 Oct 1991, Vega Reservoir, Mesa County. **Mid-winter*:** 20 Dec 1980–21 Jan 1981, Pueblo Reservoir, Pueblo County. **Mountain parks*:** undated specimen, Antero Reservoir, Park County (CC 5584).

Pacific Loon
Gavia pacifica

Occasional migrant in fall and early winter in eastern Colorado.

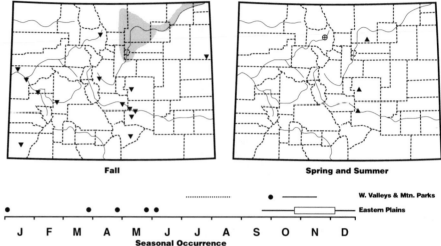

Fall   Spring and Summer

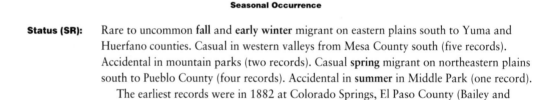

Seasonal Occurrence

Elevation

Status (SR): Rare to uncommon **fall** and **early winter** migrant on eastern plains south to Yuma and Huerfano counties. Casual in western valleys from Mesa County south (five records). Accidental in mountain parks (two records). Casual **spring** migrant on northeastern plains south to Pueblo County (four records). Accidental in **summer** in Middle Park (one record).

The earliest records were in 1882 at Colorado Springs, El Paso County (Bailey and Niedrach 1965), followed by others in 1887, 1898, and 1955; all other records have been from 1972 and later. During the 1980s, five to 10 were recorded in most falls, and in 1989 there were 23 records. The increase in the number of observations is probably due to increased observer awareness of this species and its identification.

Habitat: Reservoirs; occasionally on small lakes.

Records: Fall in mountain parks: 25 Oct 1976, Antero Reservoir, Park County; 27 Nov 1977, Shadow Mountain Reservoir, Grand County. **Summer in mountain parks:** 8 July 1984, Granby Reservoir, Grand County.

Notes: (1) This species formerly known as Arctic Loon. (2) There is a specimen (15 Nov 1887, Breckenridge, Summit County; DMNH 7003), but it is doubtful that it was collected at Breckenridge.

Common Loon
Gavia immer

Migrant, mostly at low elevations; occasional in summer and winter.

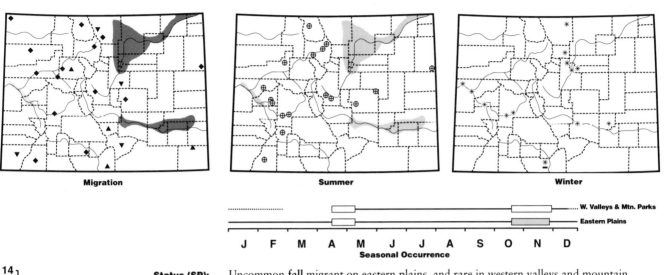

| Migration | Summer | Winter |

Seasonal Occurrence

W. Valleys & Mtn. Parks
Eastern Plains

J F M A M J J A S O N D

Elevation

Status (SP): Uncommon **fall** migrant on eastern plains, and rare in western valleys and mountain parks. Peak numbers occur from mid-Oct to late Nov. High counts: 13 on 2 Nov 1986, Sweitzer Lake, Delta County; 20 on 6 Nov 1990, Pueblo Reservoir, Pueblo County. Most mountain records are from the Grand County reservoirs and Antero Reservoir, Park County, but records also exist from North Park, the San Luis Valley, and smaller parks such as Estes Park, Larimer County. Accidental in mountains outside parks (one record). Rare **spring** migrant in western valleys, mountain parks, and on eastern plains. Most observations are in mid- and late Apr.

Very rare **summer** resident in western valleys (14 records), mountain parks (13 records), and on eastern plains (31 records). Casual in mountains outside parks (four records). Most records are of birds in nonbreeding plumage, but some birds in breeding plumage have been seen. Nesting in Colorado is not suspected; the nearest breeding site is in the mountains of northwestern Wyoming.

Very rare **winter** resident (30 records) on eastern plains, primarily near foothills. High count: up to five in winter 1986-87, Pueblo County. Casual in western valleys in Mesa, Delta, and Gunnison counties (five records). Accidental in mountain parks (one record).

Habitat: Large reservoirs and lakes.

Records: **Mountains outside parks:** July 1897, Sweetwater Lake, Garfield County (Cooke 1900); 12 July 1976, Lake City, Hinsdale County; 5 July 1980, Kossler Lake, Boulder County; summer 1981, Grand Mesa, Mesa County; 18 Oct 1988, Cameron Pass, Jackson/Larimer counties. **Winter in mountain parks:** 24 Feb 1953, La Jara, Conejos County (Daniel 1953).

Yellow-billed Loon
Gavia adamsii

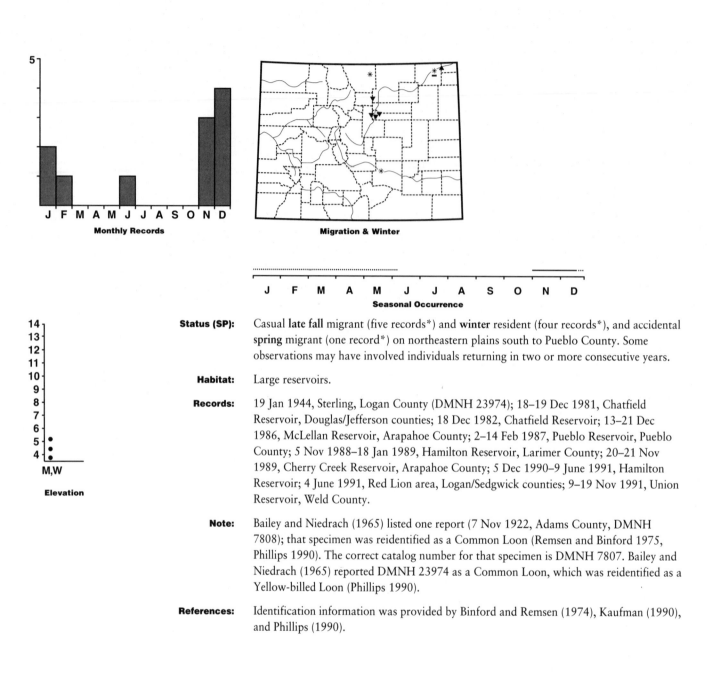

Monthly Records

Migration & Winter

Seasonal Occurrence

Elevation

Status (SP): Casual **late fall** migrant (five records*) and **winter** resident (four records*), and accidental **spring** migrant (one record*) on northeastern plains south to Pueblo County. Some observations may have involved individuals returning in two or more consecutive years.

Habitat: Large reservoirs.

Records: 19 Jan 1944, Sterling, Logan County (DMNH 23974); 18–19 Dec 1981, Chatfield Reservoir, Douglas/Jefferson counties; 18 Dec 1982, Chatfield Reservoir; 13–21 Dec 1986, McLellan Reservoir, Arapahoe County; 2–14 Feb 1987, Pueblo Reservoir, Pueblo County; 5 Nov 1988–18 Jan 1989, Hamilton Reservoir, Larimer County; 20–21 Nov 1989, Cherry Creek Reservoir, Arapahoe County; 5 Dec 1990–9 June 1991, Hamilton Reservoir; 4 June 1991, Red Lion area, Logan/Sedgwick counties; 9–19 Nov 1991, Union Reservoir, Weld County.

Note: Bailey and Niedrach (1965) listed one report (7 Nov 1922, Adams County, DMNH 7808); that specimen was reidentified as a Common Loon (Remsen and Binford 1975, Phillips 1990). The correct catalog number for that specimen is DMNH 7807. Bailey and Niedrach (1965) reported DMNH 23974 as a Common Loon, which was reidentified as a Yellow-billed Loon (Phillips 1990).

References: Identification information was provided by Binford and Remsen (1974), Kaufman (1990), and Phillips (1990).

Order Podicipediformes
Family Podicipedidae

Pied-billed Grebe
Podilymbus podiceps

Migrant and summer resident at lower elevations and in mountain parks; rare in winter.

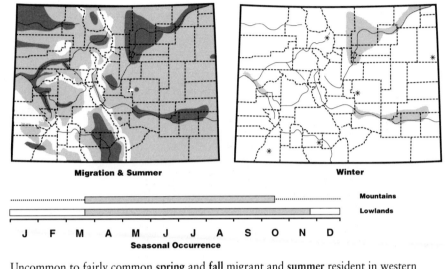

Migration & Summer   Winter

Mountains

Lowlands

J   F   M   A   M   J   J   A   S   O   N   D
Seasonal Occurrence

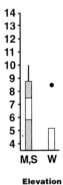

Elevation

Status (SP) (B): Uncommon to fairly common **spring** and **fall** migrant and **summer** resident in western valleys, mountain parks, and on eastern plains. High count: 49 on 30 Oct 1981, Chatfield Reservoir, Douglas/Jefferson counties. At large reservoirs that lack nesting habitat, it is primarily a migrant. Rare migrant in foothills and lower mountains outside major parks. Rare **winter** resident in western valleys and on eastern plains; accidental in mountain parks (two records).

Habitat: Breeds on small lakes bordered with dense vegetation, especially cattails. In migration and winter, also occurs on large reservoirs.

Records: **Winter in mountain parks:** has wintered at Monte Vista National Wildlife Refuge, Rio Grande County (Ryder 1965); winter 1978–79, Grand Lake, Grand County.

Horned Grebe
Podiceps auritus

Migrant at lower elevations, especially on eastern plains; rare in winter.

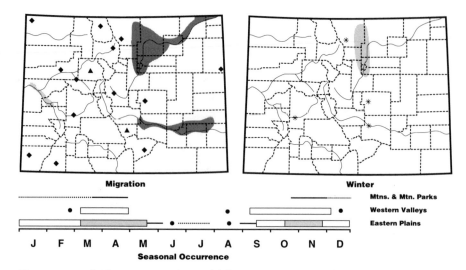

Migration   Winter

Mtns. & Mtn. Parks
Western Valleys
Eastern Plains

J   F   M   A   M   J   J   A   S   O   N   D
Seasonal Occurrence

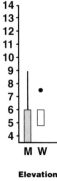

Elevation

Status (SP): Uncommon to fairly common **spring** and **fall** migrant on eastern plains. Rare in western valleys and mountain parks. Spring migrants begin appearing at low elevations in mid- and late Feb. High count: 200 on 9 Oct 1976, Union Reservoir, Weld County.

Rare **winter** resident on eastern plains. Most records are on reservoirs near foothills (especially power plant reservoirs), where open water is more likely in winter and which are more thoroughly studied by observers. High count: 10 on 6 Feb 1987, Hamilton Reservoir, Larimer County. Accidental in mountains (one record). Accidental in **summer** on eastern plains (one record); several June and August records probably pertain to late or early migrants.

This species has increased in Colorado since early in the century, probably due to the construction of numerous reservoirs. Sclater (1912) considered its occurrence in Colorado to be "doubtful" and Bergtold (1928) listed only four reports.

Habitat: Reservoirs.

Records: **Winter in mountains:** winter 1977–78, Lake Estes, Larimer County. **Summer:** 19 June–27 July 1977, Barr Lake, Adams County.

Red-necked Grebe
Podiceps grisegena

Occasional migrant in eastern Colorado.

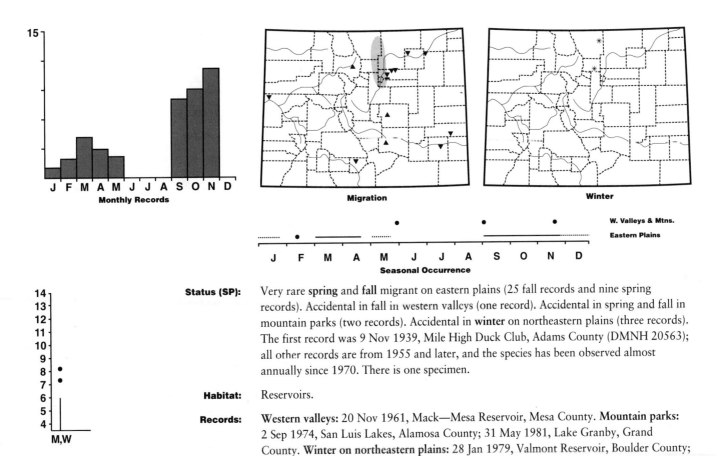

Status (SP): Very rare **spring** and **fall** migrant on eastern plains (25 fall records and nine spring records). Accidental in fall in western valleys (one record). Accidental in spring and fall in mountain parks (two records). Accidental in **winter** on northeastern plains (three records). The first record was 9 Nov 1939, Mile High Duck Club, Adams County (DMNH 20563); all other records are from 1955 and later, and the species has been observed almost annually since 1970. There is one specimen.

Habitat: Reservoirs.

Records: **Western valleys:** 20 Nov 1961, Mack—Mesa Reservoir, Mesa County. **Mountain parks:** 2 Sep 1974, San Luis Lakes, Alamosa County; 31 May 1981, Lake Granby, Grand County. **Winter on northeastern plains:** 28 Jan 1979, Valmont Reservoir, Boulder County; 9–12 Feb 1980, Valmont Reservoir; 28 Nov 1988–20 Jan 1989, Hamilton Reservoir, Larimer County.

Eared Grebe
Podiceps nigricollis

Migrant and summer resident in lowlands and mountain parks.

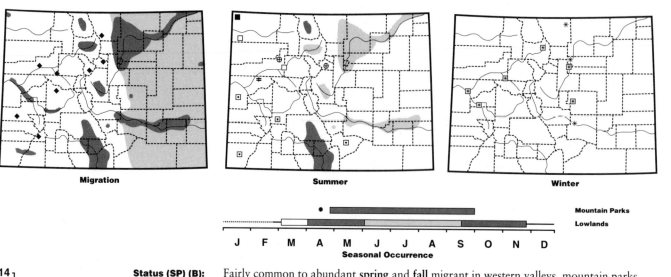

| Migration | Summer | Winter |

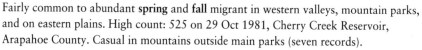

Seasonal Occurrence

J F M A M J J A S O N D

Mountain Parks
Lowlands

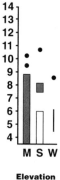

Elevation

Status (SP) (B): Fairly common to abundant **spring** and **fall** migrant in western valleys, mountain parks, and on eastern plains. High count: 525 on 29 Oct 1981, Cherry Creek Reservoir, Arapahoe County. Casual in mountains outside main parks (seven records).

Abundant **summer** resident in North Park and the San Luis Valley. In years when water levels are favorable up to 750 pairs nest at Walden Reservoir, Jackson County and 450 pairs nest at San Luis Lakes, Alamosa County (Nelson and Carter 1990a). Uncommon to fairly common locally in other mountain parks and on eastern plains, and at Browns Park National Wildlife Refuge, Moffat County. Rare in western valleys, with nesting records at Unaweep Canyon, Mesa County and in southwestern Gunnison County. Accidental in higher mountains (two records).

Very rare in **early winter** on eastern plains near foothills (20 records). Casual in western valleys in Pitkin, Mesa, and Delta counties (five records); accidental in early winter in the mountain parks (one record). Casual in **mid-winter** on eastern plains near foothills (four records).

Habitat: Breeds mostly on shallow ponds and lakes bordered with cattails, although it breeds at some lakes that lack cattails. In migration and winter, occurs on reservoirs, and occasionally on rivers.

Records: **Summer in high mountains:** 13 June 1925, Echo Lake, Clear Creek County; 13 Aug 1991, Crane Park on Flat Tops, Garfield County. **Early winter in mountain parks:** 7–13 Dec 1982, Grand Lake, Grand County.

Reference: Gorenzel (1977).

Western Grebe

Aechmophorus occidentalis

Common migrant and summer resident at low elevations and in mountain parks, and breeding very locally; rare in winter at low elevations.

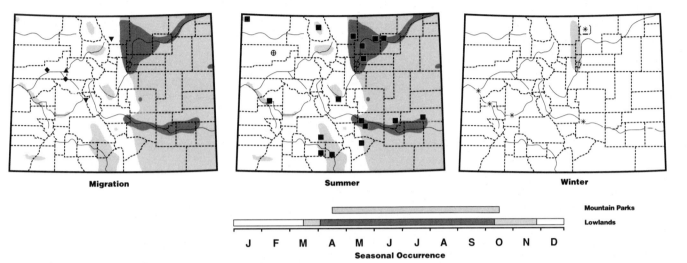

Migration   Summer   Winter

Mountain Parks

Lowlands

J F M A M J J A S O N D

Seasonal Occurrence

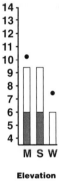

Elevation

Status (SP) (B): Spring and **fall** migrant, abundant on eastern plains and fairly common to abundant in western valleys and mountain parks. High count: 4,500 on 18 Oct 1980, Jackson Reservoir, Morgan County. Accidental in mountains outside of parks (one record).

Locally uncommon to abundant **summer** resident in western valleys, mountain parks, and on eastern plains. Breeds very locally only in those years when appropriate water levels are maintained throughout the breeding season, but in many years do not breed. Birds often start breeding, and fail because water levels either rise or fall dramatically before the eggs have hatched. Many reservoirs have populations of nonbreeding summer residents.

Rare to uncommon **winter** resident on eastern plains near foothills, and in western valleys in Mesa, Delta, and Gunnison counties. High count: 25 on 16 Jan 1983, Boulder, Boulder County. Most winter records, especially mid-winter records, are from the 1970s and later. There is one winter specimen.

Early in the century this bird was unusual in Colorado. Hersey and Rockwell (1909) did not record it in the Barr Lake area, Adams County (where it is now abundant), Sclater (1912) listed it as a rare fall migrant, and Bergtold (1928) said there were about six records. The first breeding record was in 1940 in Saguache County (Bailey and Brandenburg 1941). Bailey and Niedrach (1965) listed only four breeding sites; there are now at least 17 locations.

Habitat: Large reservoirs, and rarely on ponds. Breeds at lakes in shallow water with dense emergent or flooded vegetation such as cattails, smartweed, or willows.

Records: Mountains outside parks: 16 Aug 1985, Cottonwood Pass, Chaffee County. **Winter specimen:** 27 Dec 1921, Weld County (DMNH 9362).

Clark's Grebe

Aechmophorus clarkii

Migrant and summer resident at lower elevations and in mountain parks; most common in southern Colorado.

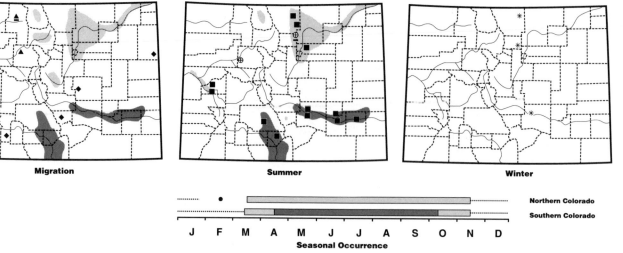

Migration   Summer   Winter

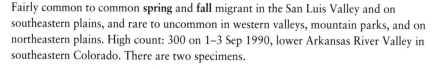

Northern Colorado
Southern Colorado

J F M A M J J A S O N D
Seasonal Occurrence

Elevation

Status (SP) (B): Fairly common to common **spring** and **fall** migrant in the San Luis Valley and on southeastern plains, and rare to uncommon in western valleys, mountain parks, and on northeastern plains. High count: 300 on 1–3 Sep 1990, lower Arkansas River Valley in southeastern Colorado. There are two specimens.

Locally fairly common to common **summer** resident in the San Luis Valley and on southeastern plains, and rare to uncommon in western valleys north to Mesa County and east to Eagle County, in North Park, and on northeastern plains. There are 12 known breeding sites. Many reservoirs have populations of nonbreeding summer residents; breeding occurs very locally only at sites and in years when water levels are appropriate. At some sites in southern Colorado, Clark's Grebes outnumber Western Grebes or are the only species of the pair present (Bunn 1986).

Casual **winter** resident (eight records) on eastern plains near foothills from Larimer County south to Pueblo County.

Virtually all Colorado records are in the last 10 years, after the splitting of this species from the Western Grebe and subsequent awareness of identification field marks.

Habitat: Large reservoirs, and rarely on ponds. Breeds at lakes in shallow water with dense emergent or flooded vegetation such as cattails, smartweed, or willows.

Records: Specimens: 25 Apr 1948, Steamboat Springs, Routt County (DMNH 25514); 6 June 1976, Union Reservoir, Weld County (DMNH 37740).

Order Pelecaniformes
Family Pelecanidae

American White Pelican
Pelecanus erythrorhynchos

Abundant summer resident and migrant on eastern plains and occasional elsewhere; nests at three locations.

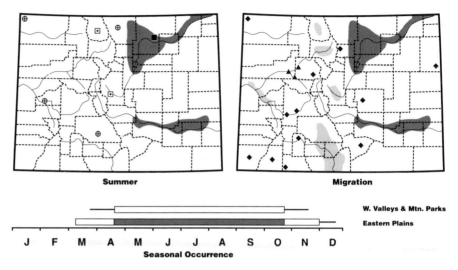

Summer   Migration

W. Valleys & Mtn. Parks

Eastern Plains

J F M A M J J A S O N D
Seasonal Occurrence

14
13
12
11
10
9
8
7
6
5
4

M,S

Elevation

Status (SP) (B): Abundant **summer** resident on eastern plains, and rare in western valleys and mountain parks. Many reservoirs have large populations of nonbreeders, especially on eastern plains. This species breeds at three locations. Pelicans started nesting on an island in Riverside Reservoir, Weld County in 1962, and 500–1,000 pairs nest there annually (Miller 1978). About 800–1,000 young fledged there in 1991 (R. Ryder, pers. comm.). Nested at Antero Reservoir, Park County in 1990 and 1991; 200–300 birds were present, and eight young fledged in 1990 and 61 in 1991 (C. Loeffler, pers. comm.). Ten birds attempted to nest in 1991 at McFarlane Reservoir, Jackson County, but fledged no young (J. Dennison and C. Loeffler, pers. comm.). Accidental in mountains outside parks (one record).

Abundant **spring** and **fall** migrant on eastern plains. Rare in western valleys and mountain parks. Rare in mountains outside parks, mostly flying overhead. There are several observations of individuals spending the **winter** at eastern plains reservoirs; all of these records pertain to injured birds unable to fly.

Habitat: Large reservoirs. Breeding sites are on islands. Individuals or flocks are often seen soaring over other habitats far from reservoirs.

Record: **Summer in mountains outside parks:** up to 35 in July 1991, Red Feather Lakes, Larimer County.

Note: Most birds that breed or summer in Colorado winter along the Gulf of Mexico (Ryder 1971a, 1981).

Brown Pelican
Pelecanus occidentalis

Status (SP): Casual in **spring** and **summer** (seven records*).

Records: One about 1 July 1908, Woods Lake, Eagle County (DMNH 16280) (erroneously given as Pitkin County in Bailey and Niedrach 1965); 9 May 1991, Limon, Lincoln County (photographed sitting on top of a McDonald's); 3–4 June 1991, Union Reservoir, Weld County; one to two 23–26 June 1991, Chatfield Reservoir, Douglas/ Jefferson counties; 24 June 1991, Barr Lake, Adams County; 1 and 9 July 1991, Antero Reservoir, Park County; 22 July–8 Aug 1991, Cherry Creek Reservoir, Arapahoe County.

Order Pelecaniformes
Family Phalacrocoracidae

Double-crested Cormorant
Phalacrocorax auritus

Migrant and summer resident, primarily in eastern Colorado; a few in winter.

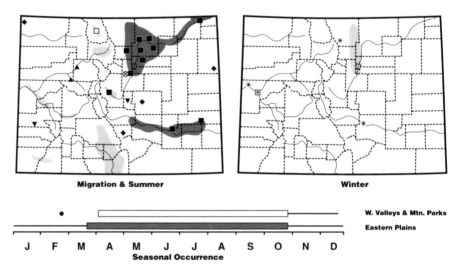

Migration & Summer   **Winter**

W. Valleys & Mtn. Parks

Eastern Plains

J F M A M J J A S O N D

Seasonal Occurrence

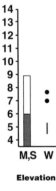

Elevation

Status (SP) (B): Locally abundant **summer** resident on eastern plains, and rare in western valleys and mountain parks. Some birds seen in summer are nonbreeders. Breeding was first recorded in Colorado in 1931 at Barr Lake, Adams County (Bailey and Niedrach 1937). There are now 11 nesting colonies, eight on the northeastern plains, two on the southeastern plains, and one in the mountain parks at Antero Reservoir, Park County (where nesting first occurred in 1979).

Common to abundant **spring** and **fall** migrant on eastern plains. High count: 1,400 on 17 Oct 1989, Rocky Ford, Otero County. Rare in mountain parks and western valleys. Rare in migration and summer at Evergreen Lake, Jefferson County, and probably at other lakes in the foothills and mountains.

Very rare **winter** resident on eastern plains near foothills (about 26 records). Casual in western valleys in Mesa County (five records). Accidental in mountains (one record).

This species has become much more common since the early part of the century. Sclater (1912) and Bergtold (1928) considered it to be a rare migrant with perhaps six records. Construction of reservoirs is probably the main reason for this increase in numbers and expansion in range.

Habitat: Reservoirs. Breeding colonies are usually in flooded groves of cottonwood trees.

Record: Winter in mountains: 1 Jan 1973, Lake Estes, Larimer County.

Neotropic Cormorant
Phalacrocorax brasilianus

Occasional in summer and fall at lower elevations.

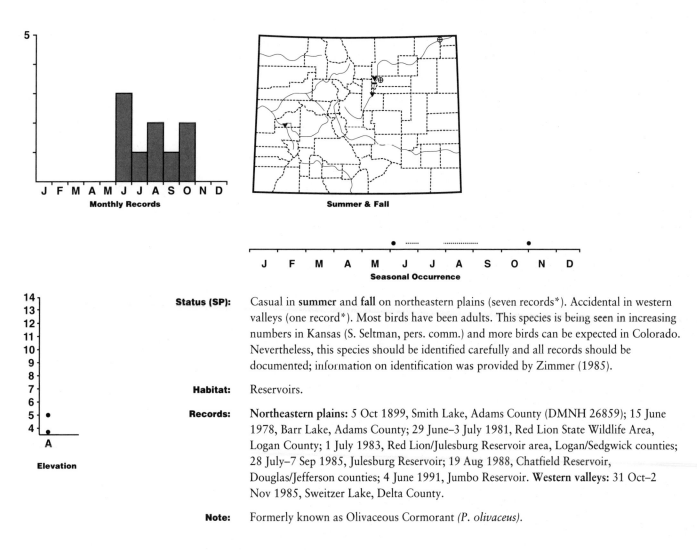

Monthly Records

Summer & Fall

Seasonal Occurrence

Elevation

Status (SP): Casual in **summer** and **fall** on northeastern plains (seven records*). Accidental in western valleys (one record*). Most birds have been adults. This species is being seen in increasing numbers in Kansas (S. Seltman, pers. comm.) and more birds can be expected in Colorado. Nevertheless, this species should be identified carefully and all records should be documented; information on identification was provided by Zimmer (1985).

Habitat: Reservoirs.

Records: **Northeastern plains:** 5 Oct 1899, Smith Lake, Adams County (DMNH 26859); 15 June 1978, Barr Lake, Adams County; 29 June–3 July 1981, Red Lion State Wildlife Area, Logan County; 1 July 1983, Red Lion/Julesburg Reservoir area, Logan/Sedgwick counties; 28 July–7 Sep 1985, Julesburg Reservoir; 19 Aug 1988, Chatfield Reservoir, Douglas/Jefferson counties; 4 June 1991, Jumbo Reservoir. **Western valleys:** 31 Oct–2 Nov 1985, Sweitzer Lake, Delta County.

Note: Formerly known as Olivaceous Cormorant *(P. olivaceus).*

Order Pelecaniformes
Family Anhingidae

Anhinga
Anhinga anhinga

Status (SP): Accidental in **fall** (one record*).

Record: 24 Sep 1931, Coal Creek, at Aurora, Adams County (DMNH 12247). A second specimen from the same site in Sep 1927 (DMNH 12296) was reidentified as the Australian species by A.R. Phillips and is assumed to have been an escape.

Order Pelecaniformes
Family Fregatidae

Magnificent Frigatebird
Fregata magnificens

Status (SP): Accidental in **fall** (one record*).

Record: 14–16 Sep 1985 (DMNH 39020). This bird was originally seen in flight near Chatfield Reservoir and Lakewood, Jefferson County and was killed at Green Mountain Reservoir, Summit County after attacking a wind-surfer; the bird was near starvation (Webb 1985a, Webb and Reddall 1989). Its occurrence in Colorado can probably be attributed to Hurricane Elena.

**Order Ciconiiformes
Family Ardeidae**

American Bittern
Botaurus lentiginosus

Migrant and summer resident at lower elevations and in mountain parks.

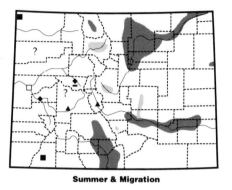

Summer & Migration

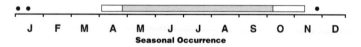

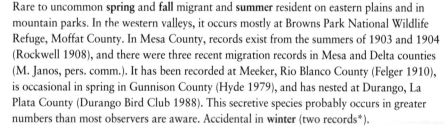

J F M A M J J A S O N D

Seasonal Occurrence

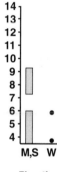

Elevation

Status (SP) (B): Rare to uncommon **spring** and **fall** migrant and **summer** resident on eastern plains and in mountain parks. In the western valleys, it occurs mostly at Browns Park National Wildlife Refuge, Moffat County. In Mesa County, records exist from the summers of 1903 and 1904 (Rockwell 1908), and there were three recent migration records in Mesa and Delta counties (M. Janos, pers. comm.). It has been recorded at Meeker, Rio Blanco County (Felger 1910), is occasional in spring in Gunnison County (Hyde 1979), and has nested at Durango, La Plata County (Durango Bird Club 1988). This secretive species probably occurs in greater numbers than most observers are aware. Accidental in **winter** (two records*).

Habitat: Cattail marshes and sometimes in adjacent wet meadows. Rarely seen outside of marshes around lakes and in riparian areas, primarily in spring and fall migration.

Records: Winter*: 11 Jan 1915, Crook, Logan County (DMNH 4265); 4 Jan 1976, Colorado Springs, El Paso County (DMNH 39417).

Note: This species is declining throughout North America, and is on the National Audubon Society Blue List (Tate 1986).

Least Bittern

Ixobrychus exilis

Rare migrant and summer resident in eastern Colorado.

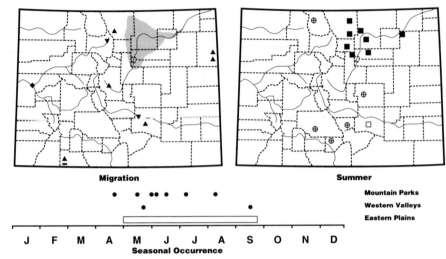

Migration   Summer

Mountain Parks
Western Valleys
Eastern Plains

Seasonal Occurrence

J   F   M   A   M   J   J   A   S   O   N   D

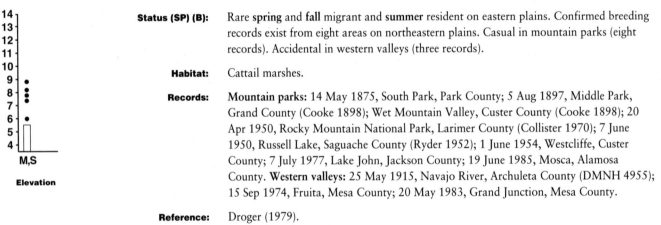

Elevation

Status (SP) (B): Rare **spring** and **fall** migrant and **summer** resident on eastern plains. Confirmed breeding records exist from eight areas on northeastern plains. Casual in mountain parks (eight records). Accidental in western valleys (three records).

Habitat: Cattail marshes.

Records: **Mountain parks:** 14 May 1875, South Park, Park County; 5 Aug 1897, Middle Park, Grand County (Cooke 1898); Wet Mountain Valley, Custer County (Cooke 1898); 20 Apr 1950, Rocky Mountain National Park, Larimer County (Collister 1970); 7 June 1950, Russell Lake, Saguache County (Ryder 1952); 1 June 1954, Westcliffe, Custer County; 7 July 1977, Lake John, Jackson County; 19 June 1985, Mosca, Alamosa County. **Western valleys:** 25 May 1915, Navajo River, Archuleta County (DMNH 4955); 15 Sep 1974, Fruita, Mesa County; 20 May 1983, Grand Junction, Mesa County.

Reference: Droger (1979).

Great Blue Heron
Ardea herodias

Summer resident at lower elevations and in mountain parks; rare in winter.

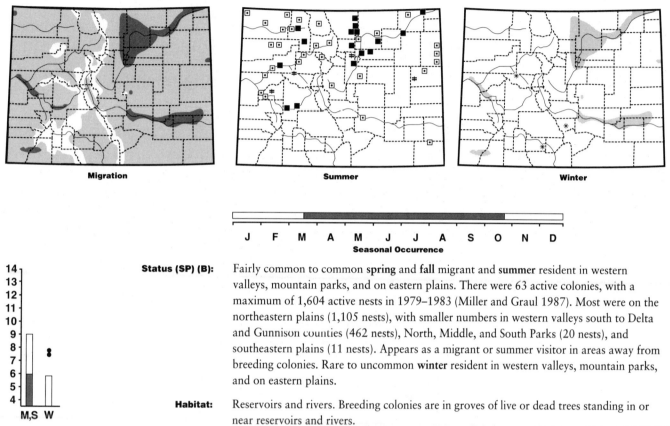

| Migration | Summer | Winter |

Seasonal Occurrence

J F M A M J J A S O N D

Elevation

14
13
12
11
10
9
8
7
6
5
4

M,S W

Status (SP) (B): Fairly common to common **spring** and **fall** migrant and **summer** resident in western valleys, mountain parks, and on eastern plains. There were 63 active colonies, with a maximum of 1,604 active nests in 1979–1983 (Miller and Graul 1987). Most were on the northeastern plains (1,105 nests), with smaller numbers in western valleys south to Delta and Gunnison counties (462 nests), North, Middle, and South Parks (20 nests), and southeastern plains (11 nests). Appears as a migrant or summer visitor in areas away from breeding colonies. Rare to uncommon **winter** resident in western valleys, mountain parks, and on eastern plains.

Habitat: Reservoirs and rivers. Breeding colonies are in groves of live or dead trees standing in or near reservoirs and rivers.

References: Ryder et al. (1979), Vos et al. (1985).

Great Egret
Casmerodius albus

Rare migrant in eastern Colorado and occasional elsewhere; breeds at two sites.

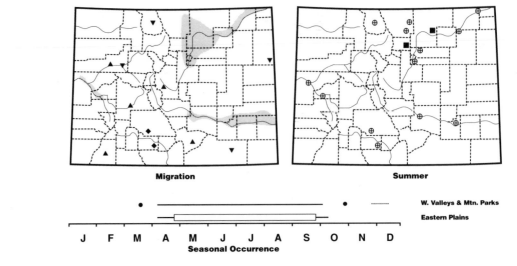

Migration   Summer

W. Valleys & Mtn. Parks

Eastern Plains

J F M A M J J A S O N D

Seasonal Occurrence

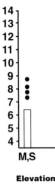

Elevation

Status (SP) (B): Rare **spring** and **fall** migrant on eastern plains; may be locally uncommon in late summer and early fall. Casual in western valleys (10 spring records and four fall records). Casual in mountain parks (four spring records). There is one specimen.

Rare nonbreeding **summer** resident on eastern plains. Casual in mountain parks (four records) and accidental in western valleys (three records). **Breeding** has been confirmed at two sites. One or two pairs starting nesting in 1972 in the Great Blue Heron colony in northeastern Boulder County (Morgan 1975) and several pairs have nested each year since. A pair nested in 1983 at Riverside Reservoir, Weld County, but not earlier (Miller 1978) or since (R. Ryder, pers. comm.). Accidental in **early winter** (one record).

Habitat: Reservoirs, ponds, and rivers.

Records: Specimen: 29 Apr 1933, Barr Lake, Adams County (DMNH 12368). **Summer in mountain parks:** 8 July 1950, near Monte Vista, Rio Grande County; July–8 Sep 1977, Walden, Jackson County; summer 1984 at Saguache, Saguache County and at Monte Vista. **Summer in western valleys:** 19 July 1977, Grand Junction, Mesa County; up to nine birds all summer in 1984, Grand Junction; 10 June 1989, Harts Basin, Delta County. **Early winter:** 22 Nov–18 Dec 1988, Grand Junction, Mesa County.

Snowy Egret
Egretta thula

Uncommon migrant and summer resident at lower elevations and in mountain parks.

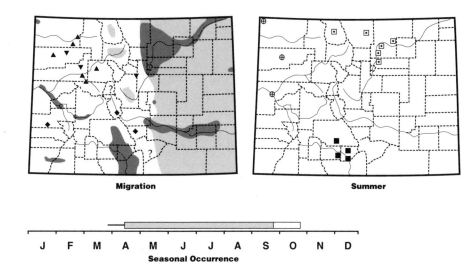

Migration | Summer

Seasonal Occurrence

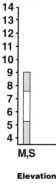

Elevation

Status (SP) (B): Rare to uncommon **spring** and **fall** migrant and **summer** resident in western valleys, mountain parks, and on eastern plains. May be fairly common locally in late summer and early fall on eastern plains. High count: 50 on 31 Aug 1985, Lower Latham Reservoir, Weld County. Breeding is known from 10 sites: four in the San Luis Valley, five on northeastern plains, and one in North Park. Nesting was first recorded in eastern Colorado in 1937 at Barr Lake, Adams County, and in the San Luis Valley in 1940 at Trites Lake, Saguache County (Bailey and Niedrach 1938, 1965). Occurs as a rare nonbreeding summer resident throughout the lowlands and mountain parks. Accidental in mountains outside parks (two records).

Habitat: Reservoirs, grassy marshes, wet meadows, and rivers. Nesting colonies are in trees or shrubs adjacent to reservoirs or marshes.

Records: **Mountains outside parks:** 1907, La Veta, Huerfano County (Cary 1909); 17 Aug 1976, Evergreen, Jefferson County.

Note: Snowy Egrets banded in Colorado have been recorded in winter from both coasts and the interior plateau of Mexico (Ryder 1971b).

Little Blue Heron
Egretta caerulea

Occasional migrant, mostly in eastern Colorado; nested once in San Luis Valley.

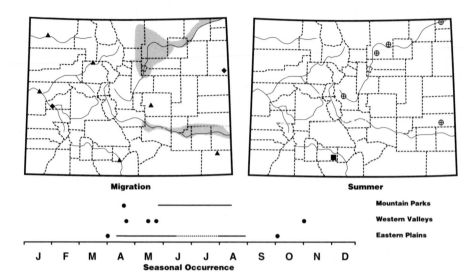

Migration   **Summer**

Mountain Parks

Western Valleys

Eastern Plains

Seasonal Occurrence

J F M A M J J A S O N D

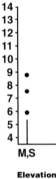

M,S

Elevation

Status (SP) (B):   Very rare **spring** and **fall** migrant on eastern plains (19 spring records and 10 fall records). Most records are from northeastern plains, probably due to the greater number of observers in that part of the state. It would be expected to occur more often in southeastern Colorado than elsewhere. Casual in western valleys (four spring records and one fall record*).

Very rare spring migrant and **summer** resident in the San Luis Valley at Monte Vista National Widlife Refuge, Rio Grande County and Alamosa National Wildlife Refuge, Alamosa County. It was first recorded in the San Luis Valley in 1974. One pair nested in 1988 at Monte Vista National Wildlife Refuge for the first confirmed **breeding** record (Ryder et al. 1989); three chicks were produced, all of which died. Two were collected 5 July 1988 (DMNH 39515, 39519) (Webb and Reddall 1989). The birds apparently have not nested since 1988, probably due to low water levels (R. Ryder, pers. comm.). Casual in early summer on eastern plains (five records) and accidental in South Park (one record*).

The earliest definite record was 20 Aug 1956 at Platteville, Weld County, and there have since been at least 86 reports of this species. Unfortunately, many reports have not specified the age of the bird, and many reports of immatures do not have details on file. Although reports of adults do not require documentation, all reports of immatures should be carefully documented. Wilds (1984) and Kaufman (1990, 1991) provided useful information on the identification of immatures.

Habitat: Reservoirs, edges of marshes, grassy meadows, and rivers.

Records: **Western valleys***: 23 May 1973, Maybell, Moffat County; 27 Apr 1974, Fruita, Mesa County; 15–16 May 1977, McCoy, Eagle County; 1 Nov 1984, Sweitzer Lake, Delta County; 26–30 Apr 1988, Harts Basin, Delta County. **South Park***: 2 July through Aug 1983, Antero Reservoir, Park County.

Tricolored Heron
Egretta tricolor

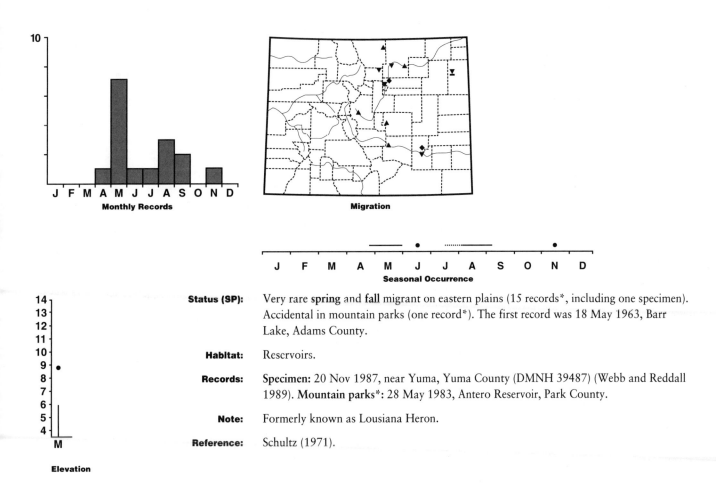

Monthly Records

Migration

Seasonal Occurrence

Elevation

Status (SP): Very rare **spring** and **fall** migrant on eastern plains (15 records*, including one specimen). Accidental in mountain parks (one record*). The first record was 18 May 1963, Barr Lake, Adams County.

Habitat: Reservoirs.

Records: **Specimen:** 20 Nov 1987, near Yuma, Yuma County (DMNH 39487) (Webb and Reddall 1989). **Mountain parks*:** 28 May 1983, Antero Reservoir, Park County.

Note: Formerly known as Lousiana Heron.

Reference: Schultz (1971).

Reddish Egret
Egretta rufescens

Status (SP): Accidental in **spring** and **fall** (two records*).

Records: Young dark morph bird Aug 1875, Colorado Springs, El Paso County (DMNH 26971); subadult dark morph bird 27–29 May 1991, Blue Lake, Bent County. A report in 1880 at Golden, Jefferson County (Cooke 1898) is best discounted because the specimen is not extant.

Cattle Egret
Bubulcus ibis

Migrant and summer resident at lower elevations and in San Luis Valley; breeds locally.

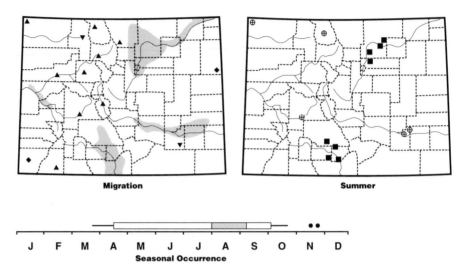

Migration   Summer

Seasonal Occurrence

J F M A M J J A S O N D

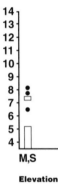

M,S

Elevation

Status (SP) (B): Rare to uncommon **fall** migrant and rare **spring** migrant on eastern plains. May be fairly common to common very locally during late summer and early fall, such as at Lower Latham Reservoir, Weld County. High count: 150 on 24 Aug 1986, Lower Latham Reservoir. Rare in western valleys and San Luis Valley. Casual in other mountain parks (five spring and early summer records). Accidental in mountains outside main parks (one spring record).

Uncommon **summer** resident locally in the San Luis Valley and on northeastern plains. Nesting was first recorded in 1977 at Riverside Reservoir, Weld County, and Russell Lake, Saguache County (Miller and Ryder 1979), and since then at Barr Lake, Adams County (1980), Milton Reservoir, Weld County (1981), and Monte Vista National Wildlife Refuge, Rio Grande County (1983). Rare nonbreeding summer resident in western valleys, mountain parks, and on eastern plains away from nesting sites.

The first state record was 12–13 Sep 1964, Cherry Creek Reservoir, Arapahoe County, and there have since been several hundred reports. There is one specimen.

Habitat: Nests around reservoirs and marshes. Foraging birds and migrants are seen in wet meadows (especially near livestock) and at reservoirs and ponds.

Records: **Mountains outside parks:** 15 May 1976, Estes Park, Larimer County. **Specimen:** 1978, Russell Lake, Saguache County (CSU).

Green-backed Heron
Butorides striatus

Rare migrant and nonbreeder in eastern Colorado and occasional elsewhere; two breeding records.

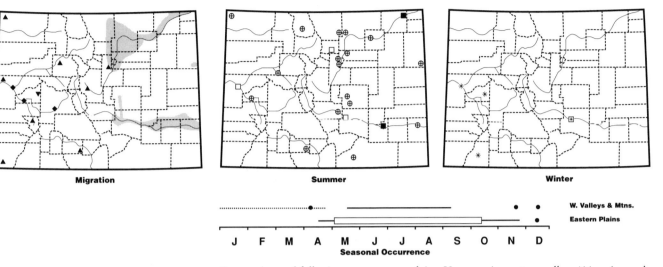

Migration	Summer	Winter

W. Valleys & Mtns.

Eastern Plains

J F M A M J J A S O N D

Seasonal Occurrence

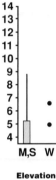

14
13
12
11
10
9
8
7
6
5
4

M,S W

Elevation

Status (PH) (B): Rare **spring** and **fall** migrant on eastern plains. Very rare in western valleys (11 spring and 11 fall records) and accidental in the mountain parks (three spring records). Accidental in mountains outside parks (one record). Rare **summer** resident (55 records) on eastern plains and accidental in mountain parks (four records), mountains (one record), and western valleys (two records). Most summer records probably pertain to nonbreeders. There are two confirmed **breeding** records. There are four possible breeding records involving birds carrying nest material or immatures seen in an area where adults summered. Accidental in **winter** (four records, including three mid-winter records*).

Habitat: Wooded rivers and edges of reservoirs and marshes.

Records: **Mountains outside parks:** 1 June 1980, Idledale, Jefferson County; 9 July 1983, near Conifer, Jefferson County. **Breeding*:** adult on nest 26 June 1973, Rocky Ford State Wildlife Area, Otero County (photo in Kingery 1973a); nest with two eggs, 18 May 1982, Tamarack Ranch, Logan County. **Possible breeding:** 1984 and 1985 at Sawhill Ponds, Boulder County; 1988 at Clifton, Mesa County; 1989 at Pueblo, Pueblo County. **Winter*:** 19 Jan–26 Apr 1976, Durango, La Plata County; 15 Dec 1984, Pueblo, Pueblo County; Jan–Feb 1981, Grand Junction, Mesa County; 24 Feb 1986, Hotchkiss, Delta County.

Note: Formerly known as Green Heron.

Black-crowned Night-Heron
Nycticorax nycticorax

Summer resident at low elevations and in some mountain parks; uncommon in winter.

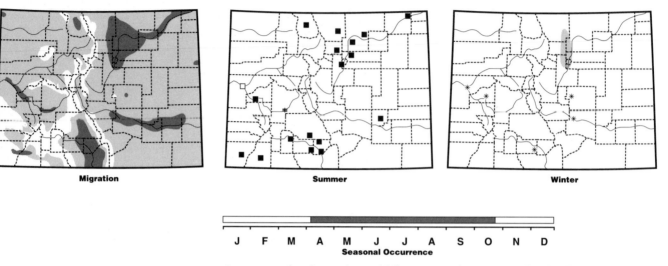

Migration   Summer   Winter

J F M A M J J A S O N D
Seasonal Occurrence

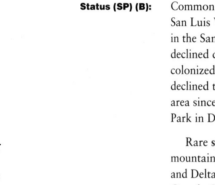

Elevation

Status (SP) (B): Common to abundant **spring** and **fall** migrant and **summer** resident locally in North Park, San Luis Valley, and on eastern plains. Rare in western valleys. Most breeding colonies are in the San Luis Valley and on northeastern plains. At some breeding sites numbers have declined dramatically, while at others numbers have held steady or new sites have been colonized. At Gunnison, Gunnison County a colony with 50 nests in the 1950s had declined to only six in 1978 (Hyde 1979), and the species has not nested in the Gunnison area since (D. Radovich, pers. comm.). During the 1970s, a colony was established in City Park in Denver County.

Rare **spring** and **fall** migrant in Middle and South Parks and in foothills and lower mountains outside parks. Uncommon **winter** resident locally in western valleys in Mesa and Delta counties, in the San Luis Valley at Monte Vista National Wildlife Refuge, Rio Grande County, and on eastern plains near foothills. High count: 31 on 16 Jan 1990, South Platte River, Denver County.

Habitat: Reservoirs, rivers, and marshes. Breeding colonies are usually in willows or other shrubs near ponds and marshes. Most winter birds are found along rivers.

Reference: Ryder (1971b).

Yellow-crowned Night-Heron
Nyctanassa violacea

Occasional in migration and summer in eastern Colorado.

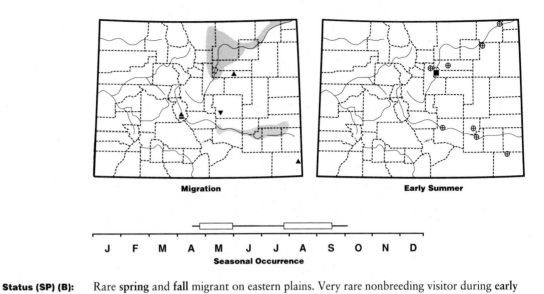

Migration   Early Summer

J   F   M   A   M   J   J   A   S   O   N   D

Seasonal Occurrence

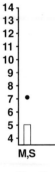

Elevation

Status (SP) (B): Rare **spring** and **fall** migrant on eastern plains. Very rare nonbreeding visitor during **early summer** (14 records); most birds seen in mid-July and later are probably migrants or post-breeding wanderers. Confirmed **breeding** in 1983-1985, Denver County (Gent 1987). There were only five records before the 1960s, all in spring; the first fall record was in 1968 and the first early summer record in 1969. There are two specimens.

Habitat: Reservoirs, rivers, and marshes.

Records: Specimens: 1 May 1908, Salida, Chaffee County (DMNH 26972); 3 May 1914, Byers, Arapahoe County (DMNH 6987).

**Order Ciconiiformes
Family Threskiornithidae**

White Ibis
Eudocimus albus

Status (SR):   Accidental in **fall** (one record*).

Record: One immature 20 July–8 Aug 1985, Neesopah Reservoir, Kiowa County (Bridges 1985). A specimen said to have been taken at Barr Lake, Adams County in 1890 (Bailey and Niedrach 1965) is best discounted because the specimen is not extant.

Habitat: Reservoir shoreline.

Glossy Ibis
Plegadis falcinellus

Status (PH):   Accidental **spring** migrant (three records*).

Records: 26 Mar 1986, Sweitzer Lake, Delta County; 7–9 May 1989, near Erie, Weld County (photos in RC files); 4 July 1990, Orlando Reservoir, Huerfano County. Because of the difficulty of separating this species from the White-faced Ibis, all reports should be rigorously documented. Pratt (1976) and Kaufman (1990) provided information on the identification of this species.

Habitat: Reservoir shorelines and wet, grassy meadows.

White-faced Ibis
Plegadis chihi

Migrant in lowlands and mountain parks, mostly in spring; breeds primarily in the San Luis Valley.

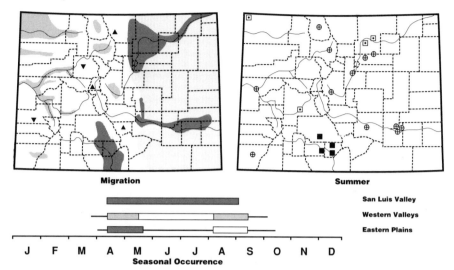

Migration   Summer

San Luis Valley

Western Valleys

Eastern Plains

J F M A M J J A S O N D
Seasonal Occurrence

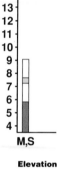

Elevation

Status (SP) (B): Fairly common to common **spring** migrant in the San Luis Valley and on eastern plains; rare to uncommon (locally fairly common) in western valleys and other mountain parks. Very rare in mountains outside parks (14 records). High count: 627 on 26 Apr 1987, Crowley/Otero counties. Rare **fall** migrant in western valleys, mountain parks, and on eastern plains.

Very rare nonbreeding **summer** visitor (about 14 records) in western valleys, mountain parks, and on eastern plains. The main **breeding** area is in the San Luis Valley, where colonies occur at Russell Lakes, Saguache County, Monte Vista National Wildlife Refuge, Rio Grande County, and Alamosa National Wildlife Refuge and San Luis Lakes, Alamosa County. About 115–150 pairs nest at the Monte Vista and Alamosa National Wildlife Refuge colonies. The species nested at Lower Latham Reservoir, Weld County in 1970 for the first breeding record outside the San Luis Valley (Stamper et al. 1972). Nesting has also occurred at Browns Park National Wildlife Refuge, Moffat County, Gunnison, Gunnison County, and Riverside Reservoir, Weld County.

Habitat: Wet meadows, marsh edges, and reservoir shorelines.

References: Ryder (1967a, 1971b).

Roseate Spoonbill
Ajaia ajaja

Status (SP): Accidental in **spring** and **fall** (two records).

Records: 1 Sep 1913, Riverside Reservoir, Weld County (DMNH 7388); flock of seven on 24 May 1938, near Hovenweep National Monument, Montezuma County.

There are two additional records that are doubtful. One was captured alive at Silverton, San Juan County about 15 June 1888 (Morrison 1888). Although the identification is probably valid, it is hard to believe that this species would occur in a closed mountain basin at 9,300 ft. It may be that the details of this record became garbled, and therefore we believe this record is suspect. A specimen was said to have been collected at Pueblo, Pueblo County (Smith 1896). Since there were no firm details about the date and location, and since the specimen is not extant, we believe it should be discounted.

Order Ciconiiformes
Family Ciconiidae

Wood Stork
Mycteria americana

Status (SP): Accidental in **fall** (two records*).

Records: 30 Aug 1902, Ft. Logan, Arapahoe County (DMNH 7417, 14711); 25 July 1934, Denver County (DMNH 12379). Other specimens mentioned by Morrison (1888), Cooke (1897), and Bailey and Niedrach (1965) are not extant, and should discounted.

**Order Anseriformes
Family Anatidae**

Tundra Swan
Cygnus columbianus

Rare migrant at low elevations and in mountain parks; a few in winter.

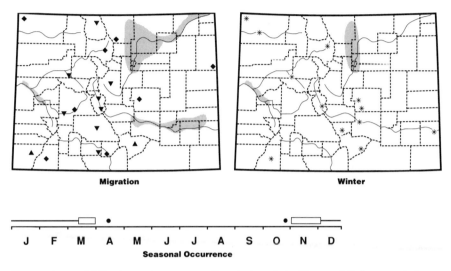

Migration   Winter

Seasonal Occurrence

J F M A M J J A S O N D

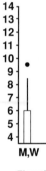

Elevation

Status (SP): Rare **spring** and **fall** migrant in western valleys (primarily in Mesa and Delta counties), mountain parks, and on eastern plains. It probably occurs somewhat more regularly in fall than in spring. High count: 28 on 19 Nov 1977, Chatfield Reservoir, Douglas/Jefferson counties.

Very rare **winter** resident on eastern plains near foothills (about 27 records) and casual in western valleys (about 13 records). Accidental in mid-winter on extreme eastern plains (one record) and in mountain parks and valleys (three records).

Habitat: Reservoirs.

Records: **Mid-winter on extreme eastern plains:** 13 Jan 1990, Holly, Prowers County. **Mid-winter in mountain parks:** Dec 1977–5 Jan 1978, De Weese Reservoir, Custer County; 7 Feb–1 Mar 1981, Shadow Mountain Reservoir, Grand County; late 1987–4 Apr 1988, Salida, Chaffee County.

Trumpeter Swan
Cygnus buccinator

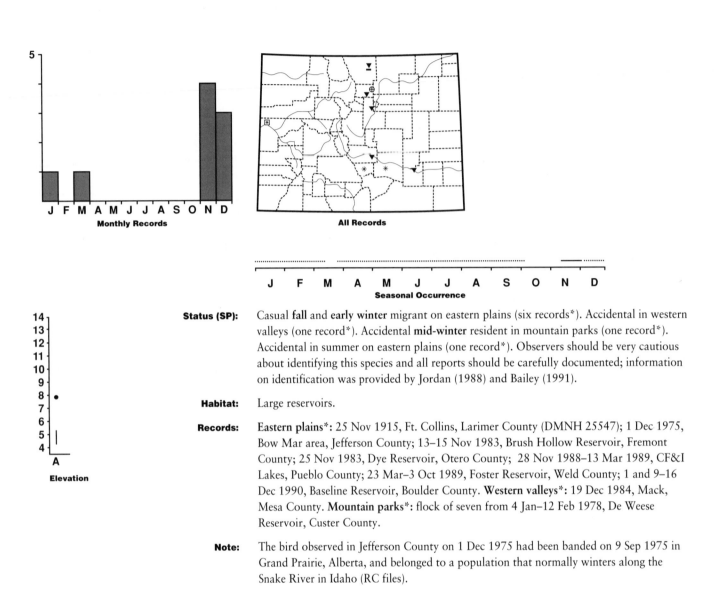

Monthly Records

All Records

Seasonal Occurrence

J F M A M J J A S O N D

Elevation

Status (SP): Casual **fall** and **early winter** migrant on eastern plains (six records*). Accidental in western valleys (one record*). Accidental **mid-winter** resident in mountain parks (one record*). Accidental in summer on eastern plains (one record*). Observers should be very cautious about identifying this species and all reports should be carefully documented; information on identification was provided by Jordan (1988) and Bailey (1991).

Habitat: Large reservoirs.

Records: **Eastern plains***: 25 Nov 1915, Ft. Collins, Larimer County (DMNH 25547); 1 Dec 1975, Bow Mar area, Jefferson County; 13–15 Nov 1983, Brush Hollow Reservoir, Fremont County; 25 Nov 1983, Dye Reservoir, Otero County; 28 Nov 1988–13 Mar 1989, CF&I Lakes, Pueblo County; 23 Mar–3 Oct 1989, Foster Reservoir, Weld County; 1 and 9–16 Dec 1990, Baseline Reservoir, Boulder County. **Western valleys***: 19 Dec 1984, Mack, Mesa County. **Mountain parks***: flock of seven from 4 Jan–12 Feb 1978, De Weese Reservoir, Custer County.

Note: The bird observed in Jefferson County on 1 Dec 1975 had been banded on 9 Sep 1975 in Grand Prairie, Alberta, and belonged to a population that normally winters along the Snake River in Idaho (RC files).

Greater White-fronted Goose

Anser albifrons

Rare migrant and winter resident in eastern Colorado; occasional elsewhere.

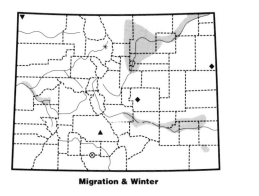

Migration & Winter

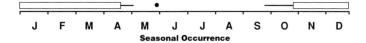

J F M A M J J A S O N D

Seasonal Occurrence

Elevation

Status (SP): Rare **spring** and **fall** migrant and **winter** resident on eastern plains. It may be locally uncommon in migration, especially at reservoirs in southeastern Colorado. Most winter records are from northeastern plains near foothills. Very rare migrant and winter resident in western valleys in Mesa and Delta counties (about 23 records) and one record at Browns Park National Wildlife Refuge, Moffat County. Casual in the San Luis Valley (about six records). Accidental in Middle Park, Grand County (two records).

Habitat: Reservoirs, marsh edges, wet meadows, and cropland (especially cornfields).

Records: **Grand County:** reported as occasionally numerous by Carter, in Cooke (1900); 2 Jan 1966, Shadow Mountain Reservoir.

Note: There were no records of this species overwintering, at least in the Denver area, prior to the winter of 1964–65.

Snow Goose
Chen caerulescens

The two field-identifiable color morphs are treated separately.

White morph

Abundant migrant in extreme eastern Colorado, and winter resident in southeastern Colorado; rare in other areas.

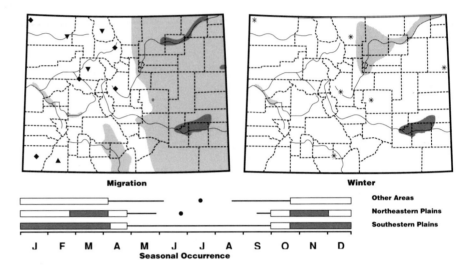

Migration **Winter**

	Other Areas
	Northeastern Plains
	Southestern Plains

J   F   M   A   M   J   J   A   S   O   N   D
Seasonal Occurrence

M,W

Elevation

Status (SP): Abundant **spring** and **fall** migrant and **winter** resident in the Arkansas River Valley from Crowley and Otero counties eastward. At the peak of migration there are about 10,000 on the eastern plains, and 5,000 winter on the southeastern plains (Colorado Division of Wildlife 1989). In the Bonny Reservoir area, Yuma County and in the South Platte River Valley from Morgan County northeastward it is an irregularly abundant migrant and rare winter resident. Rare to uncommon migrant and winter resident elsewhere on eastern plains west to foothills. The migration corridor of this species has shifted westward into eastern Colorado in the last decade (Colorado Division of Wildlife 1989).

Rare migrant and winter resident in western valleys, mostly Mesa and Delta counties. Rare migrant in mountain parks. Winters occasionally in the San Luis Valley (Ryder 1965, USFWS 1989). Accidental in South Park (one record).

Very rare nonbreeder in **summer** on eastern plains (about 13 records). Accidental in South Park (one record).

Habitat: Reservoirs, marsh edges, wet meadows, and cropland (especially cornfields).

Records: **Winter in South Park:** winter 1971–72, Antero Reservoir, Park County. **Summer in South Park:** 9 July 1991, Antero Reservoir.

Note: There is one specimen of a Snow X Canada Goose hybrid: 11 Dec 1965, Eads, Kiowa County (DMNH 35630) and several sight records.

Blue morph

Migrant in extreme eastern Colorado; occasional in other areas.

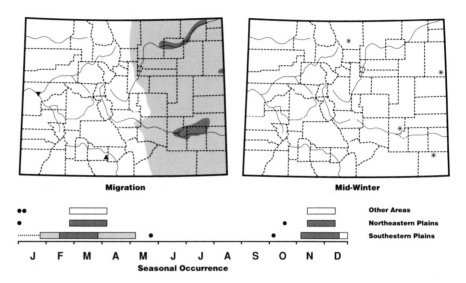

| | Migration | Mid-Winter |

Other Areas
Northeastern Plains
Southestern Plains

J F M A M J J A S O N D

Seasonal Occurrence

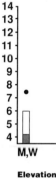

M,W

Elevation

Status (SR): Uncommon to fairly common, and irregularly common to abundant, **spring** and **fall** migrant in the Arkansas River Valley from Crowley and Otero counties eastward. Irregular migrant, rare to abundant, in the Bonny Reservoir area, Yuma County, and in the South Platte River Valley from Morgan County northeastward. Rare migrant elsewhere on eastern plains west to foothills. Accidental spring migrant in mountain parks (one record) and fall migrant in western valleys (one record). This species is usually seen scattered in flocks of white morph Snow Geese.

Very rare **winter** resident on eastern plains (about eight records). Winter status of this bird is difficult to assess; the numerous February observations in the Arkansas valley could be either winter residents or migrants.

The earliest record was Apr 1938, Deer Trail, Arapahoe County, and there were few records before the 1970s. Starting in the 1920s, this morph has become more frequent in areas on the western Great Plains that formerly were used only by the white morph (Cooke et al. 1988).

Habitat: Reservoirs, marsh edges, wet meadows, and cropland (especially cornfields).

Records: **Mountain parks:** 23–24 Mar 1974, Monte Vista National Wildlife Refuge, Rio Grande County. **Western valleys:** 18 Dec 1977, Grand Junction, Mesa County.

Note: Hybrids between Canada and domestic geese look very similar to blue morph Snow Geese and are often reported as such (R. Ryder, pers. comm.). Observers should be careful in identifying this morph away from extreme eastern Colorado.

Ross' Goose

Chen rossii

The two field-identifiable color morphs are treated separately.

White morph

Rare migrant and winter resident at low elevations and in the San Luis Valley.

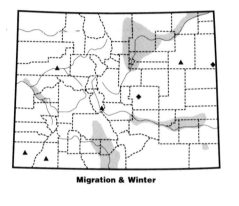

Migration & Winter

J F M A M J J A S O N D

Seasonal Occurrence

M,W

Elevation

Status (SP): Rare to uncommon **spring** and **fall** migrant and **winter** resident in western valleys (mostly Mesa and Delta counties), the San Luis Valley, and on eastern plains. Accidental in the upper Arkansas River valley (one spring record). Accidental in **mid-summer** on eastern plains (one record).

This species is increasing in Colorado. Since 1960, it has increased dramatically in frequency in central North America (Prevett and MacInnes 1972, Frederick and Johnson 1983). The earliest record from the state was 23 Dec 1906, Longmont, Boulder County (DMNH 416), but virtually all records have been from the 1970s and later. This species was not listed from western Colorado by Davis (1969) or from the San Luis Valley by Ryder (1965). The first record from the western valleys was in 1974, and most observations have been during the 1980s (Janos 1985a). The first San Luis Valley record was in December 1965. Most observations are of single birds or small flocks of up to 10 birds, but during the 1980s there were several observations of larger flocks (up to 200 birds).

Habitat: Reservoirs, marsh edges, wet meadows, and cropland (especially cornfields).

Records: **Upper Arkansas River:** 22–31 Mar 1986, Salida, Chaffee County. **Mid-summer on eastern plains:** 23 June 1990, Ft. Collins, Larimer County.

Blue morph

Status (SR): Accidental in **winter** and **spring** (two records).

Records: 21–23 Apr 1987, Neenoshe Reservoir, Kiowa County; 12 Feb 1990, Lower Latham Reservoir, Weld County.

Brant

Branta bernicla

The two field-identifiable subspecies are treated separately.

Brant

B. b. bernicla

Status (PH): Accidental in **fall** and **winter** (three records*).

Records: 16 Jan 1964, Two Buttes Reservoir, Baca County (photos taken but not published); 24–31 Oct 1981, Cherry Creek Reservoir, Arapahoe County; flock of four 10–11 Nov 1990, Barr Lake, Adams County. A specimen mentioned by Cooke (1897) is not extant.

Habitat: Reservoirs.

Black Brant

B. b. nigricans

Status (PH): Casual in **fall, winter,** and **spring** (five records*).

Records: A bird banded in Alaska was recovered in fall in the early 1950s at Loveland, Larimer County (Hansen and Nelson 1957); 30 Nov–7 Dec 1968, Ft. Collins, Larimer County (Pakulak et al. 1969; includes photograph); 17 May 1980, near Briggsdale, Weld County; 2–3 Nov 1984, Boulder, Boulder County (photos in RC files); 11–21 Feb 1988, Lower Latham Reservoir, Weld County.

Habitat: Reservoirs and ponds.

Canada Goose
Branta canadensis

Abundant migrant and winter resident and local summer resident at low elevations and in mountain parks.

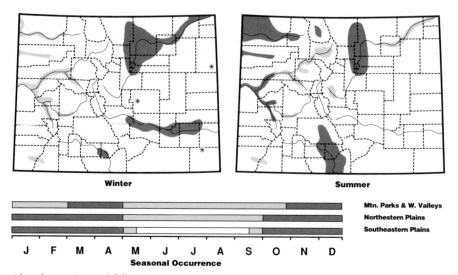

Migration   Winter   Summer

Mtn. Parks & W. Valleys
Northestern Plains
Southeastern Plains

J F M A M J J A S O N D

Seasonal Occurrence

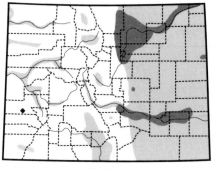

Elevation

Status (SP) (B): Abundant **spring** and **fall** migrant in western valleys, mountain parks, and on eastern plains. At the peak of migration there are about 150,000 on the eastern plains and much smaller numbers in the western valleys and mountain parks (Colorado Division of Wildlife 1989).

Abundant **winter** resident in western valleys, the San Luis Valley, and on eastern plains. The statewide winter population is about 120,000–130,000 (Colorado Division of Wildlife 1989). About 50,000–70,000 winter on the plains near northeastern foothills, 5,000–20,000 on extreme northeastern plains, and 20,000–30,000 in the Arkansas River valley in southeastern Colorado. Smaller numbers winter at Bonny Reservoir, Yuma County, and Two Buttes Reservoir, Baca County. Several thousand winter in the San Luis Valley and in the western valleys along the Green, Colorado, Gunnison, Uncompahgre, and Dolores rivers. The species first began wintering in north-central Colorado in the late 1950s (Szymczak 1975).

Locally uncommon to common **summer** resident. The statewide breeding population is about 5,000 (Colorado Division of Wildlife 1989). About 1,200 breed on plains near the northeastern foothills; this population is resident. About 550 resident birds breed on extreme northeastern plains in the South Platte River Valley. A total of about 1,400 breed in mountain parks: 500 in North Park, 46 in Middle Park, 200 in South Park, and 600 in the San Luis Valley. The birds in the San Luis Valley are resident, but those in the other parks are migratory. About 1,500 breed in western valleys, mostly along the Green, Yampa, and Little Snake rivers in the northwest and the Colorado, Gunnison, and Uncompahgre rivers in west-central Colorado. Small numbers also nest in the Cortez area, Montezuma County, and statewide in foothills and mountains.

By the late 1950s, there were only two significant populations of geese in the state, which were breeding in the northwestern valleys and wintering on the southeastern plains, and with migrants elsewhere. Since 1957, restoration efforts such as nesting boxes and releases have established populations in previously occupied areas and in new areas. Populations of this species have thus increased 30–fold (Colorado Division of Wildlife 1989). In many areas, the species has become so common it is now a nuisance.

Habitat: Reservoirs, ponds, gravel pits, rivers, marshes, wet meadows, croplands, city parks, and golf courses. Breeding habitat varies. On the plains near the northeastern foothills, birds nest mostly around reservoirs and gravel pits, while riverine areas are the main habitats in northwestern and northeastern Colorado (Colorado Division of Wildlife 1989). In winter and migration, they occur primarily at reservoirs and feed in grainfields.

Note: This species has many subspecies that vary greatly in size. Most subspecies can't be separated with certainty in the field. Very small geese (Cackling Goose, *B. c. hutchinsii* or *B. c. minima*) are observed very rarely in migration and winter primarily on eastern plains.

Wood Duck

Aix sponsa

Resident at low elevations, mostly in eastern Colorado, and occasional in the mountains.

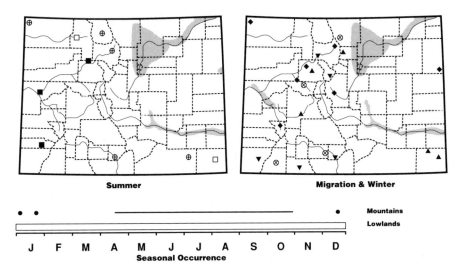

Summer   Migration & Winter

J F M A M J J A S O N D

Seasonal Occurrence

Mountains

Lowlands

Elevation

Status (SP) (B): Uncommon to fairly common **resident** in the Grand Valley, Mesa County and on eastern plains, breeding locally. In western Colorado outside the Grand Valley, breeding was recorded in 1950 at Willow Creek, Dolores County (Bailey and Niedrach 1967) and in 1984 at McCoy, Eagle County, and was suspected in 1987 at Hayden, Routt County. Very rare at all seasons in western valleys outside of the Grand Valley (about 24 records). Very rare in migration and summer in mountain parks (about 13 records). Very rare in migration and winter in mountains outside parks (eight records).

This species has increased dramatically in Colorado in recent years. Bergtold (1928) considered it almost extinct in the state. Bailey and Niedrach (1965) called it uncommon, and most of the records they listed were migration and winter records in northeastern Colorado. They listed the 1950 nesting in Dolores County as the only breeding record. From the 1970s on, this species began nesting on the eastern plains, with breeding now recorded from at least 11 sites. It was first recorded in the Grand Valley in 1968, and began breeding there in 1986.

Habitat: Reservoirs, lakes, and rivers shaded by tall overhead vegetation.

Green-winged Teal
Anas crecca

Common migrant in lowlands and in mountain parks and breeds in mountains; local in winter.

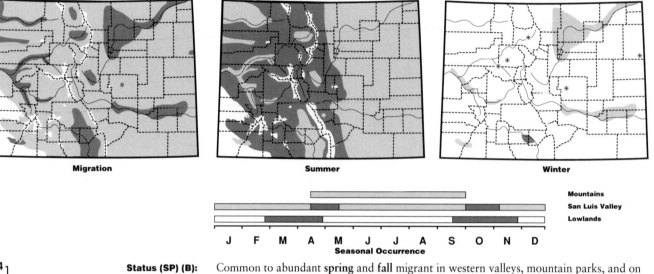

| | Migration | Summer | Winter |

Mountains
San Luis Valley
Lowlands

J F M A M J J A S O N D
Seasonal Occurrence

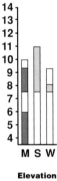

Elevation

Status (SP) (B): Common to abundant **spring** and **fall** migrant in western valleys, mountain parks, and on eastern plains. Uncommon to common **summer** resident in North Park, the San Luis Valley, and in mountains outside parks. Rare to uncommon in western valleys, other mountain parks, and on eastern plains (primarily northeastern). Common winter resident in the San Luis Valley in Rio Grande and Alamosa counties, and rare to uncommon in western valleys and on eastern plains.

Habitat: Breeds in beaver ponds, marshes, and wet meadows. Also occurs on reservoirs and ponds in migration and in winter.

American Black Duck

Anas rubripes

Occasional in migration and winter in eastern Colorado.

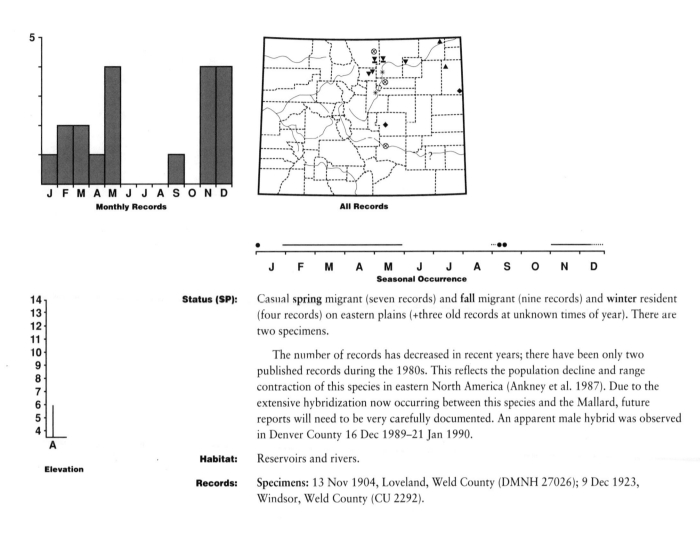

Status (SP): Casual **spring** migrant (seven records) and **fall** migrant (nine records) and **winter** resident (four records) on eastern plains (+three old records at unknown times of year). There are two specimens.

The number of records has decreased in recent years; there have been only two published records during the 1980s. This reflects the population decline and range contraction of this species in eastern North America (Ankney et al. 1987). Due to the extensive hybridization now occurring between this species and the Mallard, future reports will need to be very carefully documented. An apparent male hybrid was observed in Denver County 16 Dec 1989–21 Jan 1990.

Habitat: Reservoirs and rivers.

Records: Specimens: 13 Nov 1904, Loveland, Weld County (DMNH 27026); 9 Dec 1923, Windsor, Weld County (CU 2292).

Mallard
Anas platyrhynchos

Abundant resident at lower elevations and migrant and summer resident in mountain parks.

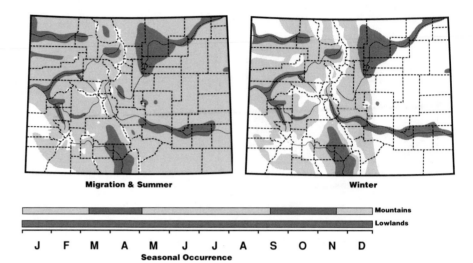

Migration & Summer   **Winter**

Mountains
Lowlands

J F M A M J J A S O N D
Seasonal Occurrence

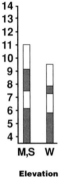

Elevation

Status (SP) (B): Abundant **spring** and **fall** migrant and **summer** resident in western valleys, mountain parks, and on eastern plains and fairly common in mountains outside of parks. Numbers are greatest in migration and winter, when reservoirs in eastern Colorado may have thousands. Peak migration periods come during Mar and Apr and Oct and Nov. Populations tend to be somewhat lower and more localized during the summer. About 60,000 Mallards breed in the state (Colorado Division of Wildlife 1989).

Common to abundant **winter** resident in western valleys, the San Luis Valley, and on eastern plains, and rare to uncommon in other mountain parks and mountains outside parks. Up to 20,000 birds winter on some eastern plains reservoirs.

Duck numbers in Colorado increased starting in the 1950s and reached a peak of over 450,000 birds in the early 1970s, but since have declined significantly (Colorado Division of Wildlife 1989). During the late 1980s, between 100,000 and 150,000 ducks wintered in Colorado; the vast majority were Mallards.

Habitat: Reservoirs, ponds, marshes, rivers, and city parks. Also occur in croplands or abandoned fields while feeding or nesting.

Northern Pintail

Anas acuta

Common migrant and winter resident at low elevations and in the mountain parks; local in summer.

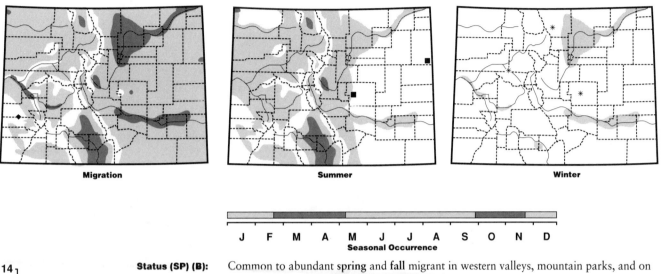

| Migration | Summer | Winter |

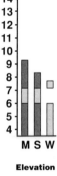

Elevation

Status (SP) (B): Common to abundant **spring** and **fall** migrant in western valleys, mountain parks, and on eastern plains. Rare to uncommon in mountains outside parks. Fairly common to common **summer** resident at Browns Park National Wildlife Refuge, Moffat County, in North Park, South Park, and the San Luis Valley; locally rare to fairly common in western valleys, mountains outside parks, and on eastern plains (mostly northeastern). Rare to uncommon **winter** resident (locally fairly common to common) in western valleys, the San Luis Valley in Rio Grande and Alamosa counties, and on eastern plains.

Habitat: Reservoirs, ponds, marshes, and rivers. Also occur in croplands or abandoned fields while feeding or nesting.

41

Garganey
Anas querquedula

Status (SR):   Accidental **spring** migrant (one record*).

Record: 21–28 Apr 1990, Jackson Reservoir, Morgan County. Spear et al. (1988) found that most interior North American records of this species were in Apr and May, and they believed these birds were wild rather than escapes.

Blue-winged Teal
Anas discors

Common migrant and summer resident at low elevations and in the mountain parks; occasional in winter.

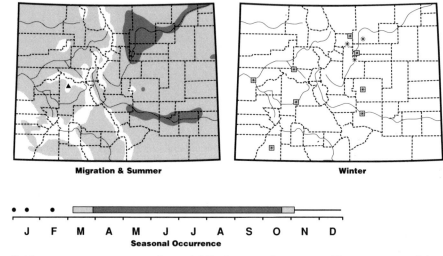

Migration & Summer   Winter

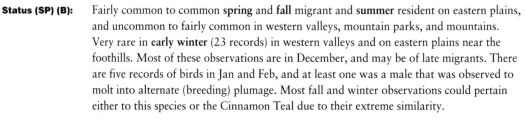

Seasonal Occurrence

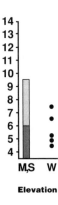

Elevation

Status (SP) (B):   Fairly common to common **spring** and **fall** migrant and **summer** resident on eastern plains, and uncommon to fairly common in western valleys, mountain parks, and mountains. Very rare in **early winter** (23 records) in western valleys and on eastern plains near the foothills. Most of these observations are in December, and may be of late migrants. There are five records of birds in Jan and Feb, and at least one was a male that was observed to molt into alternate (breeding) plumage. Most fall and winter observations could pertain either to this species or the Cinnamon Teal due to their extreme similarity.

Habitat: Reservoirs, ponds, marshes, and rivers. Nest in croplands, abandoned fields, grasslands, and wet meadows.

Cinnamon Teal

Anas cyanoptera

Common migrant and summer resident at low elevations and in the mountain parks.

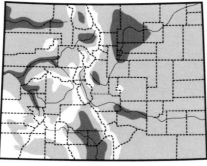

Migration & Summer

J F M A M J J A S O N D

Seasonal Occurrence

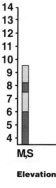

Elevation

Status (SP) (B): Fairly common to common **spring** and **fall** migrant and **summer** resident in western valleys, mountain parks, and on eastern plains near foothills, and uncommon to fairly common in mountains outside parks and on extreme eastern plains. This species appears to displacing the Blue-winged Teal (M. Szymczak, pers. comm.). This is one of the earliest returning migrant ducks, and the numerous observations in Feb are of migrants.

Habitat: Reservoirs, ponds, marshes, and rivers. Nest in croplands, abandoned fields, grass-lands, and wet meadows.

Northern Shoveler

Anas clypeata

Common migrant and summer resident at low elevations and in mountain parks; local in winter.

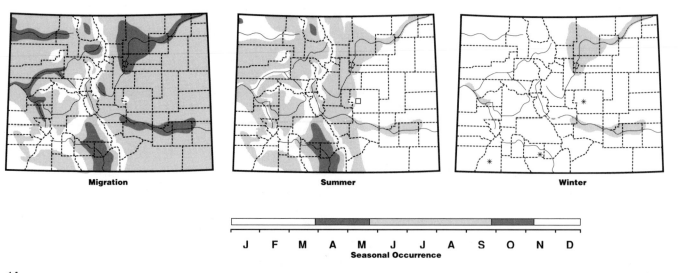

Migration	Summer	Winter

J F M A M J J A S O N D
Seasonal Occurrence

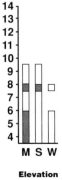

Elevation

Status (SP) (B): Common to abundant **spring** and **fall** migrant in western valleys, mountain parks, and on eastern plains. Uncommon in mountains outside parks. Fairly common to common **summer** resident at Browns Park National Wildlife Refuge, Moffat County, in North Park and in the San Luis Valley. Rare to uncommon in western valleys, mountains outside parks, and on eastern plains. Rare to uncommon **winter** resident in western valleys from Mesa County southward, the San Luis Valley in Rio Grande and Alamosa counties, and on eastern plains; at some sites it may be common to abundant. High count: 2,500 on 12 Jan 1980, lakes in Denver and Jefferson counties.

Habitat: Reservoirs, ponds, marshes, and rivers. Nest in croplands, abandoned fields, grasslands, and wet meadows.

Gadwall

Anas strepera

Migrant and summer resident at low elevations and in mountain parks; local in winter.

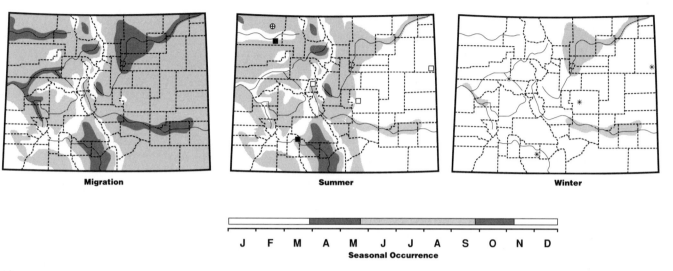

Migration   Summer   Winter

Seasonal Occurrence

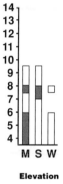

Elevation

Status (SP) (B): Fairly common to abundant **spring** and **fall** migrant in western valleys, mountain parks, and on eastern plains. Rare to uncommon in mountains outside parks. Uncommon to fairly common **summer** resident at Browns Park National Wildlife Refuge, Moffat County and in mountain parks; rare to uncommon in mountains outside parks and on eastern plains. Rare to uncommon **winter** resident in western valleys, mostly in Mesa and Delta counties, the San Luis Valley in Rio Grande County, and on eastern plains; may be locally fairly common.

Habitat: Reservoirs, ponds, marshes, and rivers. Nest in croplands, abandoned fields, grasslands, and wet meadows.

Eurasian Wigeon
Anas penelope

Migrant in eastern Colorado, mostly in spring, and occasionally elsewhere.

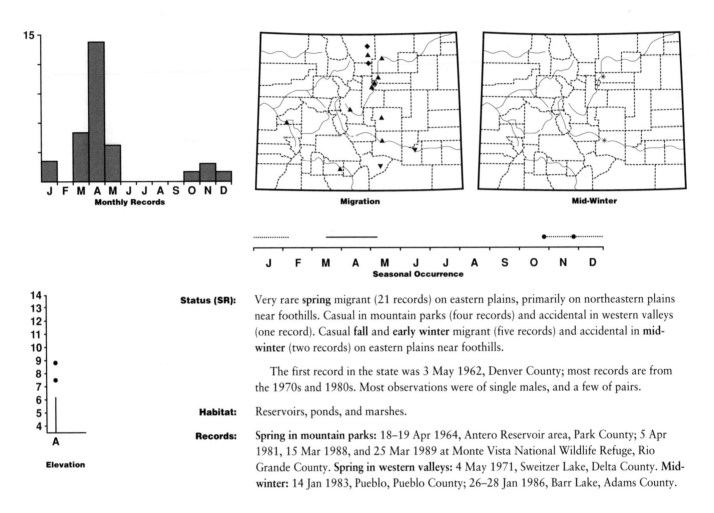

Migration **Mid-Winter**

Monthly Records

Seasonal Occurrence

Elevation

A

Status (SR): Very rare **spring** migrant (21 records) on eastern plains, primarily on northeastern plains near foothills. Casual in mountain parks (four records) and accidental in western valleys (one record). Casual **fall** and **early winter** migrant (five records) and accidental in **mid-winter** (two records) on eastern plains near foothills.

The first record in the state was 3 May 1962, Denver County; most records are from the 1970s and 1980s. Most observations were of single males, and a few of pairs.

Habitat: Reservoirs, ponds, and marshes.

Records: Spring in mountain parks: 18–19 Apr 1964, Antero Reservoir area, Park County; 5 Apr 1981, 15 Mar 1988, and 25 Mar 1989 at Monte Vista National Wildlife Refuge, Rio Grande County. **Spring in western valleys:** 4 May 1971, Sweitzer Lake, Delta County. **Mid-winter:** 14 Jan 1983, Pueblo, Pueblo County; 26–28 Jan 1986, Barr Lake, Adams County.

American Wigeon
Anas americana

Occurs throughout lower elevations and in the mountain parks; most numerous in migration.

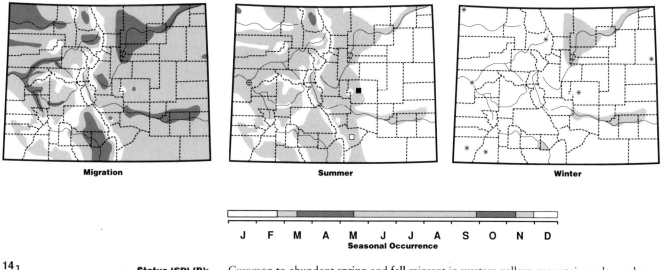

| Migration | Summer | Winter |

J F M A M J J A S O N D
Seasonal Occurrence

Elevation
M S W

Status (SP) (B): Common to abundant **spring** and **fall** migrant in western valleys, mountain parks, and on eastern plains. Rare to uncommon in mountains outside parks. Fairly common to common **summer** resident at Browns Park National Wildlife Refuge, Moffat County and in North Park; rare to uncommon in South Park and the San Luis Valley, in mountains outside parks, and on eastern plains. Rare to locally common **winter** resident in western valleys, in the San Luis Valley in Rio Grande and Alamosa counties, and on eastern plains.

Habitat: Reservoirs, ponds, marshes, rivers, and city parks. Nests in croplands or abandoned fields.

Canvasback

Aythya valisineria

Migrant at low elevations and in the mountain parks; very local in summer and winter.

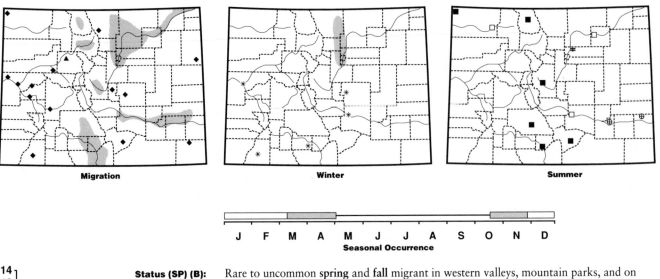

| Migration | Winter | Summer |

Seasonal Occurrence

J F M A M J J A S O N D

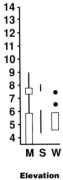

Elevation

M S W

Status (SP) (B): Rare to uncommon **spring** and **fall** migrant in western valleys, mountain parks, and on eastern plains. Rare to uncommon **winter** resident very locally in western valleys (mostly in Mesa County) and on eastern plains (mostly near foothills). Occasionally winters in San Luis Valley (Ryder 1965). Rare and very local **summer** resident in northwestern valleys (mostly at Browns Park National Wildlife Refuge, Moffat County), in North Park and the San Luis Valley, and on eastern plains. Some summer birds are nonbreeders.

Habitat: Reservoirs and ponds in migration and winter; in summer in marshes and on ponds.

Redhead

Aythya americana

Occurs throughout lower elevations and in the mountain parks; most numerous in migration and least numerous in winter.

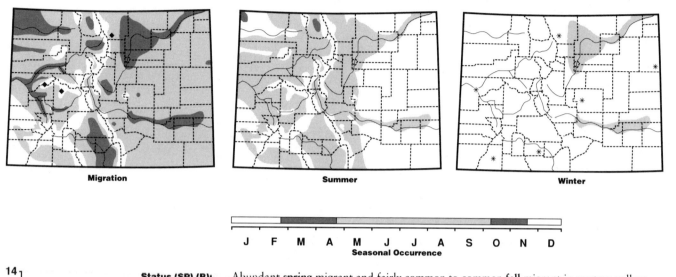

| Migration | Summer | Winter |

Seasonal Occurrence

J F M A M J J A S O N D

Status (SP) (B): Abundant **spring** migrant and fairly common to common **fall** migrant in western valleys, mountain parks, and on eastern plains. Although this species still occurs in Colorado in large numbers, it has been declining seriously since the early 1980s in central North America (Ryder 1991a). Fairly common to common **summer** resident at Browns Park National Wildlife Refuge, Moffat County, in North Park, and the San Luis Valley; rare elsewhere in mountains and on eastern plains. Many birds seen in summer may be nonbreeders. Rare **winter** resident (may be fairly common very locally) in western valleys and on eastern plains, primarily near the foothills.

Habitat: Reservoirs and ponds in migration and winter; in summer in marshes and on ponds.

Elevation

Ring-necked Duck

Aythya collaris

Migrant and winter resident at low elevations and in mountain parks and breeds in the mountains.

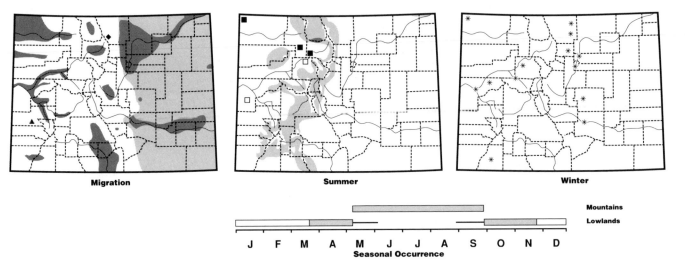

Migration	Summer	Winter

Mountains

Lowlands

J F M A M J J A S O N D

Seasonal Occurrence

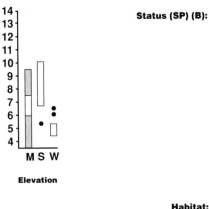

Elevation

Status (SP) (B): Uncommon to fairly common **spring** and **fall** migrant (common to abundant very locally) in western valleys, mountain parks, and on eastern plains. Rare to uncommon **winter** resident (common to abundant very locally) in western valleys and on eastern plains, primarily near foothills. High count: 1,000+, 2 Jan 1980, Boulder County and 29 Dec 1981, Valmont Reservoir, Boulder County.

Uncommon to fairly common **summer** resident locally in mountains and mountain parks, primarily along or west of the Continental Divide; most common in the Park and Rabbit Ears Ranges south and west of North Park. Also recorded breeding in northwestern valleys at Browns Park National Wildlife Refuge, Moffat County. This species has evidently increased in recent years as a breeding species in Colorado; Bailey and Niedrach (1965) noted only three nesting records (all 1949 and later).

Habitat: Reservoirs and ponds during migration and winter. Summer birds occur on mountain lakes, beaver ponds, and marshes near coniferous and aspen forests.

Greater Scaup
Aythya marila

Rare migrant and winter resident in eastern Colorado.

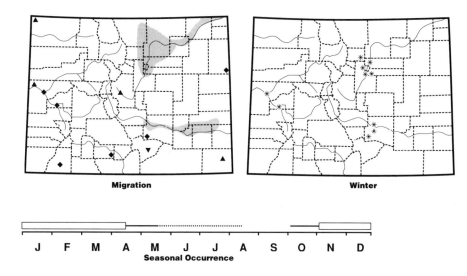

Migration	Winter

Seasonal Occurrence

J F M A M J J A S O N D

Elevation

M,W

Status (SP): Rare **spring** and **fall** migrant on eastern plains. Very rare in western valleys (13 records), primarily in Mesa and Delta counties. Accidental in mountains and mountain parks (two records). Rare local **winter** resident (uncommon very locally) in western valleys in Mesa and Delta counties and on eastern plains near foothills. Accidental in **summer** (one record).

Habitat: Reservoirs and ponds.

Records: **Mountains and mountain parks:** 9 on 11 May 1974, Park County; recorded at Monte Vista National Wildlife Refuge, Rio Grande County (Ryder 1965, USFWS 1989). **Summer:** one all summer 1991, Clifton, Mesa County.

Lesser Scaup
Aythya affinis

Migrant at low elevations and in mountain parks, and breeds in mountain parks; rare in winter.

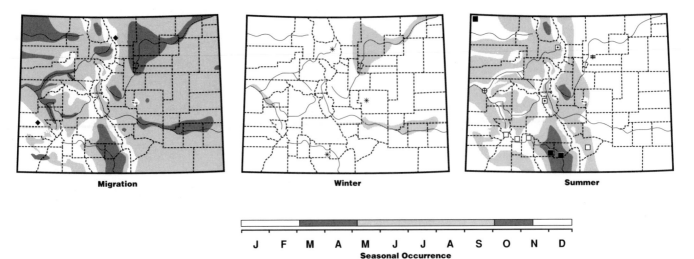

| Migration | Winter | Summer |

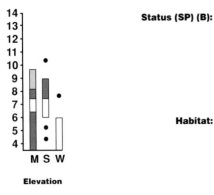

Elevation

Seasonal Occurrence

J F M A M J J A S O N D

Status (SP) (B): Common to abundant **spring** and **fall** migrant in western valleys, mountain parks, and on eastern plains. Rare to uncommon **winter** resident locally in western valleys and on eastern plains; also recorded in **winter** in Middle Park and the San Luis Valley. Fairly common to common **summer** resident in North Park and South Park. Also recorded breeding at Browns Park National Wildlife Refuge, Moffat County and very locally in mountains and on eastern plains. Some summer birds are nonbreeders.

Habitat: Reservoirs and ponds in migration and winter; in summer in marshes and on ponds.

Harlequin Duck
Histrionicus histrionicus

Former breeder in the mountains; one recent record on plains.

Status (SP) (FB): Former **summer** resident in mountains (three records). A male was said to have been collected 15 May 1875, Tarryall Creek, Park County, but the specimen was not located (Bailey and Niedrach 1965). A pair was collected 21 May 1876 (DMNH 387, 388), but the location is uncertain. The label on the male specimen says Michigan Creek, Jackson County and the label on the female specimen says South Park. It was "common" in San Juan County (Drew 1881). The only **breeding** record was of a downy juvenile collected 15 July 1883, Vallecito Creek, La Plata County (CM 21786) (Parkes and Nelson 1976). Apparently a small breeding population occurred in the mountains that became extinct after the 1880s.

Accidental in **fall** on eastern plains (one record*).

Habitat: The specimens were collected on mountain rivers. The recent sight record was at a reservoir.

Record: **Eastern plains*:** 24 Oct 1976, Barr Lake, Adams County.

Oldsquaw
Clangula hyemalis

Rare in fall in eastern Colorado; occasional elsewhere in the state and in winter and spring.

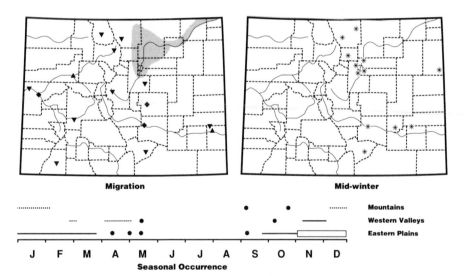

Status (SP): Rare **fall** migrant on eastern plains, and very rare **mid-winter** resident (17 records) and **spring** migrant (15 records). Very rare in western valleys, mostly in Mesa County but also in Garfield, Gunnison, and La Plata counties (eight fall records, four spring records, and one winter record). Casual in mountains and mountain parks in fall and winter (four records).

Habitat: Reservoirs.

Records: **Mountains and mountain parks:** 10 Dec 1959–8 Feb 1960, Estes Park, Larimer County; 11 Nov 1970, Lake Granby, Grand County; 7 Sep 1982, Walden Reservoir, Jackson County; 24 Oct 1982, Antero Reservoir, Park County.

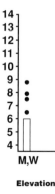

Elevation

Black Scoter

Melanitta nigra

Very rare in fall in northeastern Colorado.

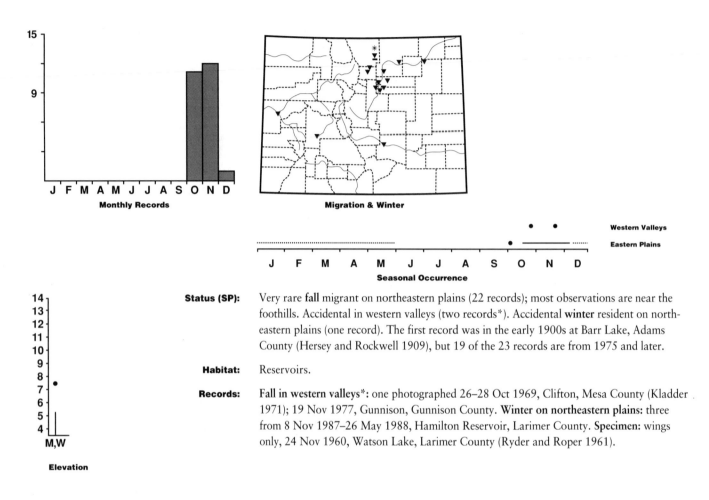

Monthly Records

Migration & Winter

Western Valleys

Eastern Plains

Seasonal Occurrence

Elevation

Status (SP):	Very rare **fall** migrant on northeastern plains (22 records); most observations are near the foothills. Accidental in western valleys (two records*). Accidental **winter** resident on northeastern plains (one record). The first record was in the early 1900s at Barr Lake, Adams County (Hersey and Rockwell 1909), but 19 of the 23 records are from 1975 and later.
Habitat:	Reservoirs.
Records:	**Fall in western valleys*:** one photographed 26–28 Oct 1969, Clifton, Mesa County (Kladder 1971); 19 Nov 1977, Gunnison, Gunnison County. **Winter on northeastern plains:** three from 8 Nov 1987–26 May 1988, Hamilton Reservoir, Larimer County. **Specimen:** wings only, 24 Nov 1960, Watson Lake, Larimer County (Ryder and Roper 1961).

Surf Scoter
Melanitta perspicillata

Rare in fall in eastern Colorado; occasional in other areas and seasons.

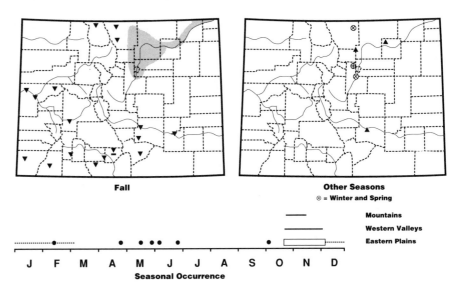

Fall **Other Seasons**

⊗ = Winter and Spring

——— Mountains

——— Western Valleys

▭ Eastern Plains

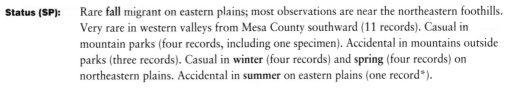

Seasonal Occurrence

J F M A M J J A S O N D

Status (SP): Rare **fall** migrant on eastern plains; most observations are near the northeastern foothills. Very rare in western valleys from Mesa County southward (11 records). Casual in mountain parks (four records, including one specimen). Accidental in mountains outside parks (three records). Casual in **winter** (four records) and **spring** (four records) on northeastern plains. Accidental in **summer** on eastern plains (one record*).

Habitat: Reservoirs.

Records: **Mountain park specimen:** 12 Nov 1988, San Luis Lake, Alamosa County (Jeske 1989). **Fall in mountains outside parks:** 25 Oct 1980, Red Feather Lakes, Larimer County; 20 Oct 1984, Lake Estes, Larimer County; 20–22 Oct 1985, Rocky Mountain National Park. **Summer***: pair in breeding plumage 26 June 1974, Henrys Lake, Jefferson County.

14
13
12
11
10
9
8
7
6
5
4

A

Elevation

White-winged Scoter
Melanitta fusca

Rare in fall in eastern Colorado; occasional in other areas and in winter and spring.

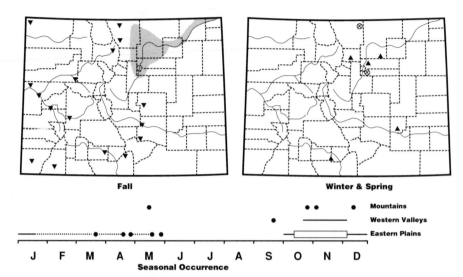

| | Fall | | Winter & Spring |

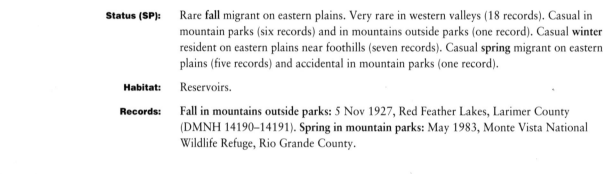

Seasonal Occurrence

J F M A M J J A S O N D

Status (SP):	Rare **fall** migrant on eastern plains. Very rare in western valleys (18 records). Casual in mountain parks (six records) and in mountains outside parks (one record). Casual **winter** resident on eastern plains near foothills (seven records). Casual **spring** migrant on eastern plains (five records) and accidental in mountain parks (one record).
Habitat:	Reservoirs.
Records:	**Fall in mountains outside parks:** 5 Nov 1927, Red Feather Lakes, Larimer County (DMNH 14190–14191). **Spring in mountain parks:** May 1983, Monte Vista National Wildlife Refuge, Rio Grande County.

Elevation

14
13
12
11
10
9
8
7
6
5
4

M,W

Common Goldeneye

Bucephala clangula

Fairly common winter resident throughout Colorado where open water is available.

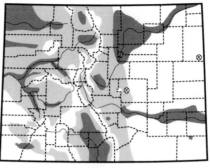

Migration & Winter

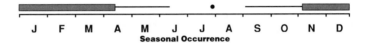

J F M A M J J A S O N D

Seasonal Occurrence

Status (SP): Fairly common to common **winter** resident in western valleys, foothills, lower mountains, mountain parks, and on eastern plains. At sites where all water remains frozen throughout the winter, it may appear only as a spring and fall migrant. Accidental in **mid-summer** in mountain parks and on eastern plains (two records). There are several undocumented summer reports in the mountains and western valleys; such reports need to be carefully documented because Barrow's Goldeneye would be more likely than Common.

Habitat: Reservoirs, ponds, and rivers.

Records: **Mid-summer on eastern plains:** 30 July 1977, Cheraw, Otero County; 1981, North Park, Jackson County.

14
13
12
11
10
9
8
7
6
5
4

M,W

Elevation

Barrow's Goldeneye
Bucephala islandica

Rare winter resident and migrant in lowlands and mountains; a few breed in the northern mountains.

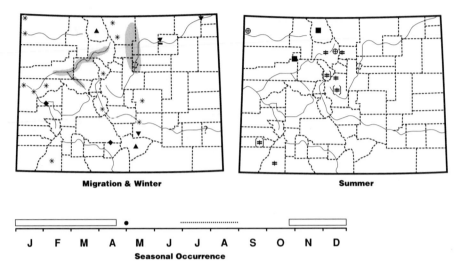

Migration & Winter   Summer

J   F   M   A   M   J   J   A   S   O   N   D

Seasonal Occurrence

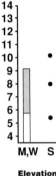

14
13
12
11
10
9
8
7
6
5
4

M,W S

Elevation

Status (SP) (B): Rare winter **resident** and **spring** and **fall** migrant in western valleys, mountain parks, and on eastern plains near foothills. In some years, it may be locally uncommon along the Colorado River and its tributaries and adjacent reservoirs from Grand County west to Garfield County. Accidental on extreme eastern plains (three records, including two specimens).

Casual **summer** resident in mountains and mountain parks. There were 10 breeding records from Grand, Summit, Boulder, Park, Dolores, and La Plata counties from 1876 to about 1900 (Brewer 1879, Morrison 1888, 1889, Cooke 1900, Henderson 1909, Bailey and Niedrach 1965). There were two confirmed breeding records in this century. A pair with five young was photographed 10 Aug 1982 at Walden, Jackson County. In the Flat Tops Wilderness, Garfield County, breeding was suspected in 1989 (Kingery and Kingery 1989) and confirmed with a brood 6 July 1990 (Anonymous 1990, Kingery 1990a). There have been seven other summer records since 1969 in Moffat, Garfield, Jackson, and Grand counties; additional breeding records in the northern mountains are likely.

Habitat: Winter birds occur on reservoirs and rivers. Summer birds have been seen on mountain reservoirs and ponds in forested areas.

Records: **Extreme eastern plains:** undated specimen, Lamar, Prowers County (CC 6983); 6 Nov 1938, Jackson Reservoir, Morgan County (DMNH 19640); 21 Nov 1990, Julesburg Reservoir, Logan/Sedgwick counties.

Bufflehead
Bucephala albeola

Migrant at low elevations and in the mountain parks, and occasional in winter; breeds near North Park.

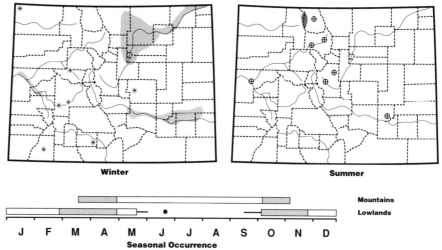

Migration   Winter   Summary

Mountains

Lowlands

J F M A M J J A S O N D
Seasonal Occurrence

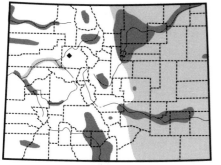

Elevation

Status (SP) (B): Uncommon to fairly common **spring** and **fall** migrant in western valleys, mountain parks, and on eastern plains. High count: 400 on 3 Nov 1991, Hamilton Reservoir, Larimer County. Rare **winter** resident (locally uncommon) in western valleys and on eastern plains. May be common to abundant at Hamilton Reservoir, Larimer County.

Uncommon **summer** resident on the east slope of the Park Range, Jackson County, where breeding was first recorded in 1987 (Anonymous 1988, Ringelman and Kehmeier 1990, Ringelman 1990). There are about 50–100 pairs breeding in that area (J. Ringelman, pers. comm.). It is unknown whether this breeding population has always been present or is a recent phenomenon. Casual nonbreeder in western valleys, other mountain parks, and eastern plains (eight records 1981 and later).

Habitat: Reservoirs and ponds. Breeding birds occur on glacial depressions called kettle ponds and beaver ponds adjacent to mature aspen forests; the birds nest in old flicker holes in dead or dying aspens (Ringelman 1990).

Hooded Merganser
Lophodytes cucullatus

Rare in migration and winter at low elevations and in mountain parks; one recent breeding record.

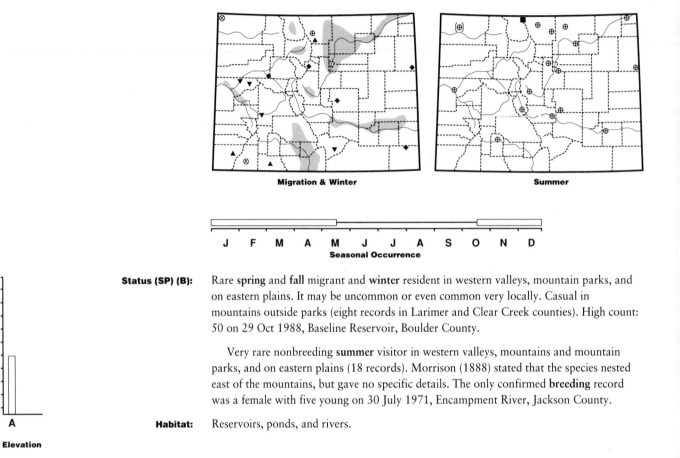

Migration & Winter

Summer

Seasonal Occurrence

J F M A M J J A S O N D

Elevation

Status (SP) (B): Rare **spring** and **fall** migrant and **winter** resident in western valleys, mountain parks, and on eastern plains. It may be uncommon or even common very locally. Casual in mountains outside parks (eight records in Larimer and Clear Creek counties). High count: 50 on 29 Oct 1988, Baseline Reservoir, Boulder County.

Very rare nonbreeding **summer** visitor in western valleys, mountains and mountain parks, and on eastern plains (18 records). Morrison (1888) stated that the species nested east of the mountains, but gave no specific details. The only confirmed **breeding** record was a female with five young on 30 July 1971, Encampment River, Jackson County.

Habitat: Reservoirs, ponds, and rivers.

Common Merganser

Mergus merganser

Common winter resident at low elevations and in mountain parks; breeds, primarily in western mountains.

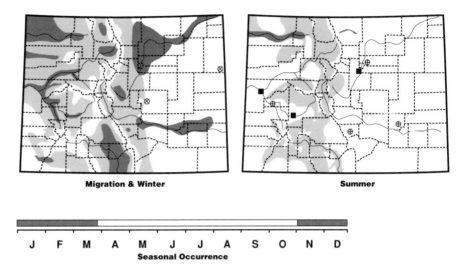

Migration & Winter   **Summer**

Seasonal Occurrence

J F M A M J J A S O N D

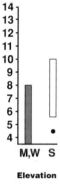

Elevation

Status (SP) (B): Fairly common to abundant **winter** resident in western valleys, mountain parks, and on eastern plains. In mountain parks, it may occur primarily or exclusively as a spring and fall migrant. High count: 4,500 on 3 Dec 1989, Cherry Creek Reservoir, Arapahoe County.

Rare to uncommon **summer** resident in central and western Colorado. It occurs in the mountains west of the Continental Divide, in North, Middle Parks, and South Parks, and in mountains east of the Divide along the Poudre River, Larimer County. In the San Luis Valley, it is found along the Conejos and Rio Grande rivers. Occurs in the western valleys primarily along the Yampa River and tributaries in Moffat and Routt counties and along the Colorado River downstream to Eagle County, and there is a breeding record along the Gunnison River at Grand Junction, Mesa County. Also breeds on northeastern plains: since 1971 along the South Platte River at or upstream from Chatfield Reservoir, Douglas/Jefferson counties, and since 1981 near Ft. Collins, Larimer County. Occasional nonbreeders may occur elsewhere in western valleys and on eastern plains.

Habitat: Reservoirs and rivers.

Red-breasted Merganser
Mergus serrator

Rare in migration and winter at low elevations.

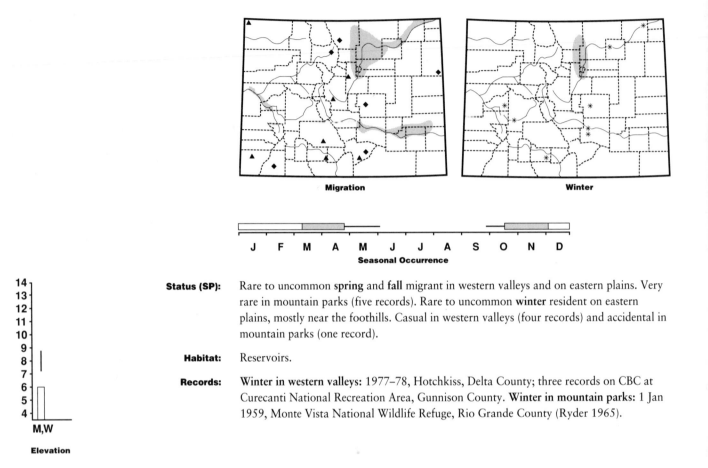

| J | F | M | A | M | J | J | A | S | O | N | D |

Seasonal Occurrence

Elevation

Status (SP): Rare to uncommon **spring** and **fall** migrant in western valleys and on eastern plains. Very rare in mountain parks (five records). Rare to uncommon **winter** resident on eastern plains, mostly near the foothills. Casual in western valleys (four records) and accidental in mountain parks (one record).

Habitat: Reservoirs.

Records: **Winter in western valleys:** 1977–78, Hotchkiss, Delta County; three records on CBC at Curecanti National Recreation Area, Gunnison County. **Winter in mountain parks:** 1 Jan 1959, Monte Vista National Wildlife Refuge, Rio Grande County (Ryder 1965).

Ruddy Duck

Oxyura jamaicensis

Occurs throughout lower elevations and in mountain parks; most numerous in migration and least numerous in winter.

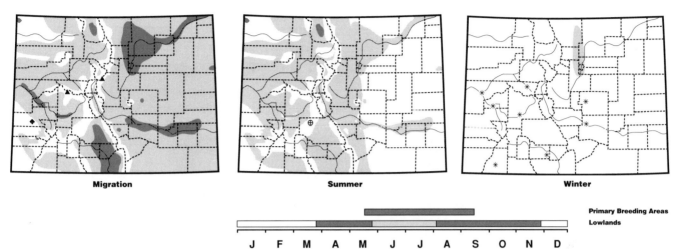

			Migration				Summer				Winter

Primary Breeding Areas

Lowlands

| J | F | M | A | M | J | J | A | S | O | N | D |

Seasonal Occurrence

Elevation

Status (SP) (B): Fairly common to abundant **spring** and **fall** migrant in western valleys, mountain parks, and on eastern plains. High count: 2,000 on 27 Apr 1938, Barr Lake, Adams County. Rare in mountains outside parks. Fairly common **summer** resident at Browns Park National Wildlife Refuge, Moffat County, in North Park and the San Luis Valley, and rare to uncommon in western valleys and on eastern plains. Rare **winter** resident in western valleys from Mesa and Pitkin counties southward, in the San Luis Valley at Monte Vista National Wildlife Refuge, Rio Grande County, and on eastern plains near foothills.

Habitat: Reservoirs and ponds. Breeding birds are found on ponds and in marshes.

Order Falconiformes
Family Cathartidae

Turkey Vulture
Cathartes aura

Fairly common migrant and summer resident in foothills and western valleys.

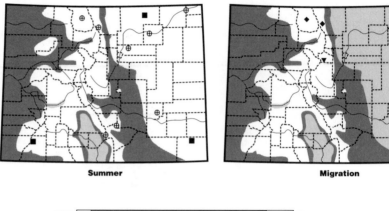

Summer   Migration

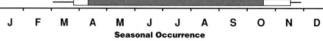

J F M A M J J A S O N D
Seasonal Occurrence

14
13
12   •
11   •
10
9
8
7
6
5   •
4   •
M,S W

Elevation

Status (SP) (B): Fairly common to common **spring** and **fall** migrant and **summer** resident in foothills statewide and in western valleys, east to Grand, Eagle, and Pitkin counties. High count: 233 on 30 Sep 1990, Boulder, Boulder County. At the Dinosaur Ridge hawk watch, Jefferson County, 407 were seen in spring 1990 (Nelson 1990). It is uncommon in migration and summer in the Gunnison Basin and the San Luis Valley, where it is observed primarily around the perimeter of the valley. It is rare in North Park, where it has not been recorded breeding. Rare to uncommon in lower mountains and accidental in high mountains (three records). Rare in migration and very locally in summer on eastern plains, with nesting recorded at two sites. Although nests have been found in Colorado (Bailey and Niedrach 1965), Davis (1976) suggested that most of the birds which occur in Colorado in summer are nonbreeders.

Accidental in **winter** (two records*). Because of the possibility of confusion with the common winter raptors, some of which show wide variability in plumage, all winter reports should be carefully documented.

Habitat: Migrants and foraging birds occur over most open habitats such as grasslands, shrublands, and agricultural areas; nests are placed on cliffs.

Records: **Summer in high mountains:** nest at 12,000 ft. in the La Plata Mountains, La Plata/Montezuma counties (Morrison 1889); observed at 12,000 ft. in the Wet Mountains, Huerfano County (Lowe 1894); 6 Aug 1960, Echo Lake, Clear Creek County. **Breeding on eastern plains:** nest 30 June 1963, Pawnee Buttes, Weld County (Bailey and Niedrach 1965); nests regularly at Two Buttes Reservoir, Baca County. **Winter*:** 13 Jan 1974, Ft. Collins, Larimer County; three on 21 Dec 1986, Grand Junction, Mesa County.

Order Falconiformes
Family Accipitridae

Osprey
Pandion haliaetus

Rare; locally in mountains during the summer and statewide in migration.

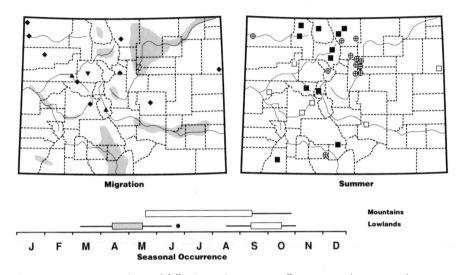

Migration **Summer**

Mountains
Lowlands

Seasonal Occurrence

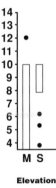

Elevation

Status (SP) (B): Rare to uncommon **spring** and **fall** migrant in western valleys, mountains, mountain parks, and on eastern plains. At the Dinosaur Ridge hawk watch, Jefferson County, 17 were seen in spring 1990 and 45 in spring 1991 (Nelson 1990, D. Nelson, pers. comm.). Accidental above timberline (one record).

Rare to uncommon local **summer** resident in mountains and mountain parks. Bailey and Niedrach (1965) listed two confirmed breeding records, and two other records that they considered as "unsatisfactory" and "indefinite." There are now confirmed or probable breeding records from at least 15 sites in the mountains nearly statewide, but concentrated in the northern half of the state. The largest concentration is at the reservoirs of eastern Grand County, where at least 22 pairs nested in 1989 and 25 in 1990 (D. Jasper, pers. comm.). Such a large population is very recent; as recently as 1986 there were only eight nesting pairs there. There are also many observations of apparent nonbreeders in the mountains and mountain parks. Casual nonbreeder in summer on eastern plains (eight records) and two possible breeding records. The increase in breeding in Colorado may be due to the proliferation of mountain reservoirs in conjunction with this species' continuing population recovery.

There are 20 **winter** reports of this species, but none have the exhaustive and rigorous documentation such reports would need in order to distinguish the Osprey from immature Bald Eagles in a similar plumage.

Habitat: Reservoirs and large lakes.

Records: **Above timberline:** 8 Sep 1956, Summit Lake on Mt. Evans, Clear Creek County. **Possible breeding on eastern plains:** pair carrying nesting material 19–20 May 1983, Bonny Reservoir, Yuma County; pair abandoned a nest in 1990 and 1991, at Pueblo Reservoir, Pueblo County.

American Swallow-tailed Kite
Elanoides forficatus

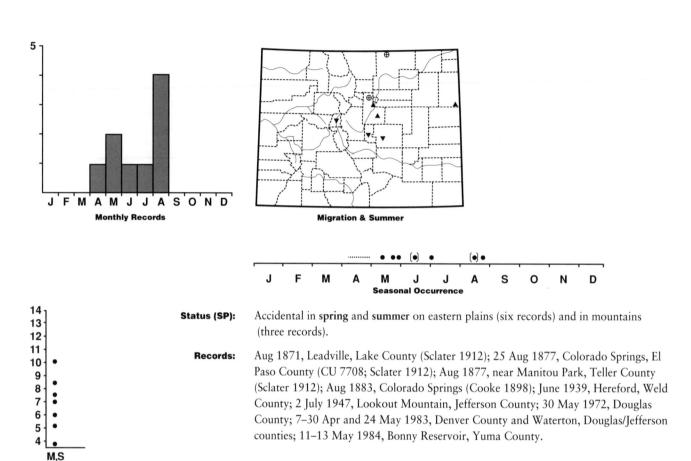

Status (SP): Accidental in **spring** and **summer** on eastern plains (six records) and in mountains (three records).

Records: Aug 1871, Leadville, Lake County (Sclater 1912); 25 Aug 1877, Colorado Springs, El Paso County (CU 7708; Sclater 1912); Aug 1877, near Manitou Park, Teller County (Sclater 1912); Aug 1883, Colorado Springs (Cooke 1898); June 1939, Hereford, Weld County; 2 July 1947, Lookout Mountain, Jefferson County; 30 May 1972, Douglas County; 7–30 Apr and 24 May 1983, Denver County and Waterton, Douglas/Jefferson counties; 11–13 May 1984, Bonny Reservoir, Yuma County.

Mississippi Kite

Ictinia mississippiensis

Fairly common in summer in southeastern Colorado.

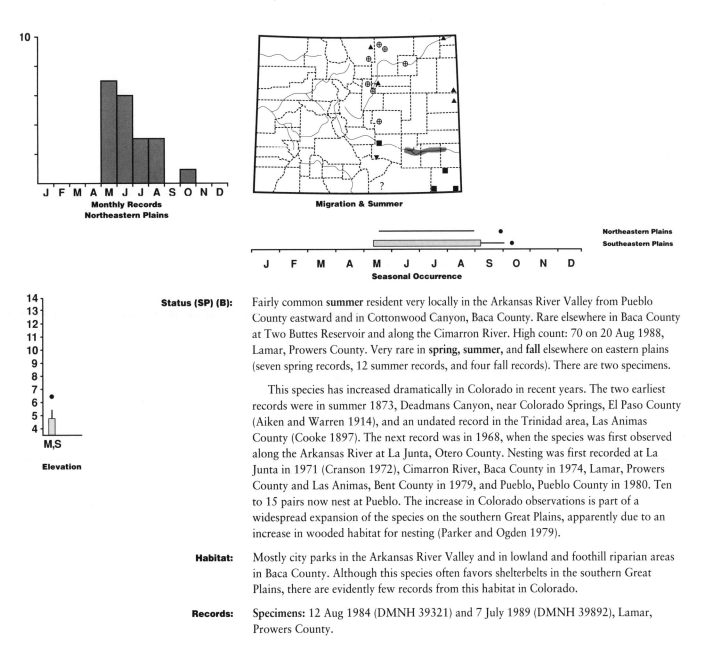

Status (SP) (B):

Fairly common **summer** resident very locally in the Arkansas River Valley from Pueblo County eastward and in Cottonwood Canyon, Baca County. Rare elsewhere in Baca County at Two Buttes Reservoir and along the Cimarron River. High count: 70 on 20 Aug 1988, Lamar, Prowers County. Very rare in **spring, summer,** and **fall** elsewhere on eastern plains (seven spring records, 12 summer records, and four fall records). There are two specimens.

This species has increased dramatically in Colorado in recent years. The two earliest records were in summer 1873, Deadmans Canyon, near Colorado Springs, El Paso County (Aiken and Warren 1914), and an undated record in the Trinidad area, Las Animas County (Cooke 1897). The next record was in 1968, when the species was first observed along the Arkansas River at La Junta, Otero County. Nesting was first recorded at La Junta in 1971 (Cranson 1972), Cimarron River, Baca County in 1974, Lamar, Prowers County and Las Animas, Bent County in 1979, and Pueblo, Pueblo County in 1980. Ten to 15 pairs now nest at Pueblo. The increase in Colorado observations is part of a widespread expansion of the species on the southern Great Plains, apparently due to an increase in wooded habitat for nesting (Parker and Ogden 1979).

Habitat:

Mostly city parks in the Arkansas River Valley and in lowland and foothill riparian areas in Baca County. Although this species often favors shelterbelts in the southern Great Plains, there are evidently few records from this habitat in Colorado.

Records:

Specimens: 12 Aug 1984 (DMNH 39321) and 7 July 1989 (DMNH 39892), Lamar, Prowers County.

Bald Eagle
Haliaeetus leucocephalus

Winter resident at low elevations and in mountain parks; very local in summer.

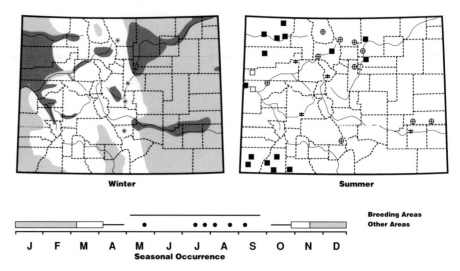

Winter   Summary

Breeding Areas
Other Areas

J F M A M J J A S O N D
Seasonal Occurrence

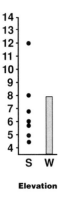

Elevation

Status (SP) (B): Uncommon to locally common **winter** resident in western valleys, in mountain parks, and on eastern plains. Statewide mid-winter counts conducted by the Colorado Division of Wildlife during the 1980s have ranged from 400 to almost 700 birds (Vaughan 1985, G. Craig, pers. comm.). Rare **summer** resident very locally. In the last several years, there have been 10 or more breeding pairs in Moffat, Rio Blanco, Mesa, Montezuma, La Plata, Archuleta, Adams, and Weld counties (Craig 1991a). In 1991, there were 13 territorial pairs, and nine pairs fledged 19 young (Craig 1991a). Historically, most breeding occurred in the northwest in Moffat, Rio Blanco and Garfield counties, and in the southwest in Montezuma, La Plata, and Archuleta counties. There is also an old breeding record from the Arkansas River, Bent County (Cooke 1897). Casual nonbreeder on eastern plains (five records).

Habitat: Reservoirs and rivers. In winter, may also occur locally in semideserts and grasslands (Enderson et al. 1970), especially near prairie dog towns.

Note: This species is considered to be endangered at both the state and federal levels.

Northern Harrier

Circus cyaneus

Resident in most of Colorado; most numerous in migration and least numerous in summer.

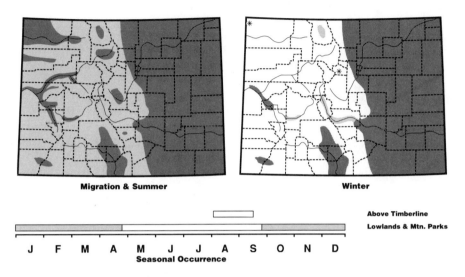

Migration & Summer   **Winter**

Above Timberline

Lowlands & Mtn. Parks

J F M A M J J A S O N D
Seasonal Occurrence

Elevation

14
13
12
11
10
9
8
7
6
5
4

M S W

Status (SP) (B): Uncommon to fairly common **spring** and **fall** migrant in western valleys, mountain parks, and on eastern plains. At the Dinosaur Ridge hawk watch, Jefferson County, 31 were seen in spring 1990 (Nelson 1990). Rare migrant in mountains outside parks, and rare to uncommon fall migrant above timberline. Uncommon to fairly common **winter** resident in western valleys, the San Luis Valley, and on eastern plains, and rare in other mountain parks and in mountains outside parks. Accidental above timberline (one record). Rare to locally uncommon **summer** resident in western valleys, mountains and mountain parks, and on eastern plains.

Habitat: Grasslands, agricultural areas, and marshes; also observed on alpine tundra in the fall. May also be seen in shrublands.

Record: **Winter above timberline:** 18 Feb 1979, Guanella Pass, Clear Creek County.

Note: This species has declined in North America, and is on the National Audubon Society Blue List (Tate 1986).

Sharp-shinned Hawk

Accipiter striatus

Resident in mountains, and in migration and winter at lower elevations.

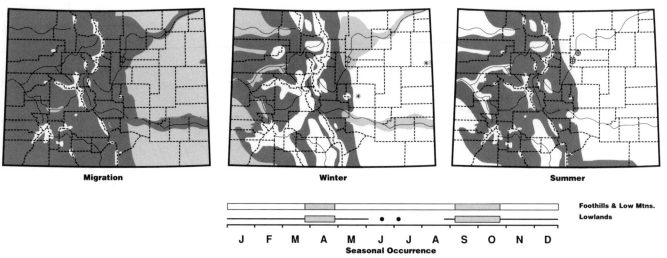

| Migration | Winter | Summer |

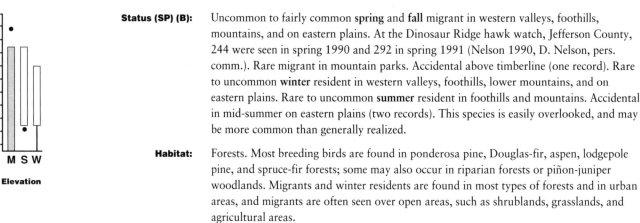

Foothills & Low Mtns.

Lowlands

J F M A M J J A S O N D

Seasonal Occurrence

Elevation

Status (SP) (B): Uncommon to fairly common **spring** and **fall** migrant in western valleys, foothills, mountains, and on eastern plains. At the Dinosaur Ridge hawk watch, Jefferson County, 244 were seen in spring 1990 and 292 in spring 1991 (Nelson 1990, D. Nelson, pers. comm.). Rare migrant in mountain parks. Accidental above timberline (one record). Rare to uncommon **winter** resident in western valleys, foothills, lower mountains, and on eastern plains. Rare to uncommon **summer** resident in foothills and mountains. Accidental in mid-summer on eastern plains (two records). This species is easily overlooked, and may be more common than generally realized.

Habitat: Forests. Most breeding birds are found in ponderosa pine, Douglas-fir, aspen, lodgepole pine, and spruce-fir forests; some may also occur in riparian forests or piñon-juniper woodlands. Migrants and winter residents are found in most types of forests and in urban areas, and migrants are often seen over open areas, such as shrublands, grasslands, and agricultural areas.

Records: **Fall above timberline:** 19 Sep 1969, Summit Lake, Clear Creek County. **Mid-summer on eastern plains:** 7 July 1978, Barr Lake, Adams County; 17 June 1984, Denver, Denver County.

Cooper's Hawk
Accipiter cooperii

Resident in mountains, and in migration and winter at lower elevations.

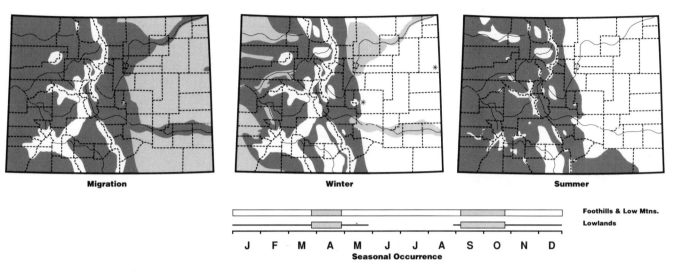

| Migration | Winter | Summer |

Foothills & Low Mtns.
Lowlands

J F M A M J J A S O N D
Seasonal Occurrence

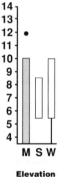

Elevation

Status (SP) (B): Uncommon to fairly common **spring** and **fall** migrant in western valleys, foothills, lower mountains, and on eastern plains. At the Dinosaur Ridge hawk watch, Jefferson County, 344 were seen in spring 1990 and 256 in spring 1991 (Nelson 1990, D. Nelson, pers. comm.). This species is generally believed to be less common in migration than the Sharp-shinned Hawk, but the data from the hawk watch show that it may be as common. Rare migrant in mountain parks. Accidental above timberline (one record).

Rare to uncommon **winter** resident in western valleys, foothills, lower mountains, and on eastern plains. Rare to uncommon **summer** resident in western valleys, foothills, and lower mountains. This species tends to breed at lower elevations than the Sharp-shinned Hawk. For example, in Mesa County it nests in lowland valleys and in piñon-juniper woodlands, which are never occupied in summer by Sharp-shinned Hawks (C. Dexter, R. Lambeth, R. Levad, pers. comm.).

Habitat: Forests. Most breeding birds are found in ponderosa pine, Douglas-fir, lodgepole pine, and aspen forests; some may also occur in riparian and spruce-fir forests and piñon-juniper woodlands. Migrants and winter residents are found in the same habitats as in summer, in addition to lowland riparian forests and urban areas, and migrants are often seen over open areas such as shrublands, grasslands, and agricultural areas.

Record: **Late summer above timberline:** 4 Aug 1988, Mt. Evans, Clear Creek County.

Note: There is concern about the population status of this species, and it is on the National Audubon Society Blue List (Tate 1986).

Northern Goshawk
Accipiter gentilis

Resident in foothills and mountains and occasional in migration and winter at lower elevations.

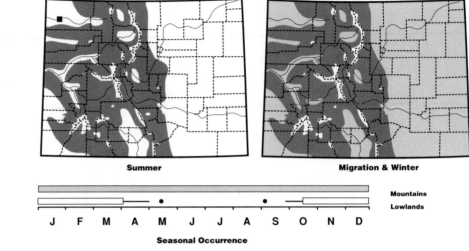

Summer   Migration & Winter

Mountains

Lowlands

J F M A M J J A S O N D

Seasonal Occurrence

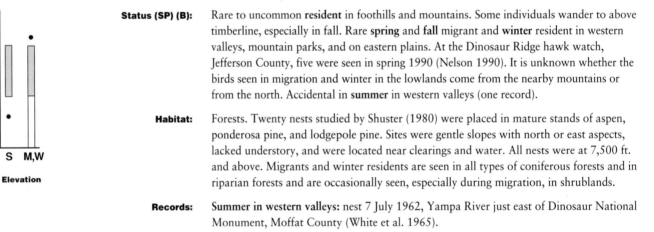

Elevation

Status (SP) (B): Rare to uncommon **resident** in foothills and mountains. Some individuals wander to above timberline, especially in fall. Rare **spring** and **fall** migrant and **winter** resident in western valleys, mountain parks, and on eastern plains. At the Dinosaur Ridge hawk watch, Jefferson County, five were seen in spring 1990 (Nelson 1990). It is unknown whether the birds seen in migration and winter in the lowlands come from the nearby mountains or from the north. Accidental in **summer** in western valleys (one record).

Habitat: Forests. Twenty nests studied by Shuster (1980) were placed in mature stands of aspen, ponderosa pine, and lodgepole pine. Sites were gentle slopes with north or east aspects, lacked understory, and were located near clearings and water. All nests were at 7,500 ft. and above. Migrants and winter residents are seen in all types of coniferous forests and in riparian forests and are occasionally seen, especially during migration, in shrublands.

Records: **Summer in western valleys:** nest 7 July 1962, Yampa River just east of Dinosaur National Monument, Moffat County (White et al. 1965).

References: Doerr and Enderson (1965), Shuster (1976).

Red-shouldered Hawk

Buteo lineatus

Occasional on eastern plains, mostly in migration.

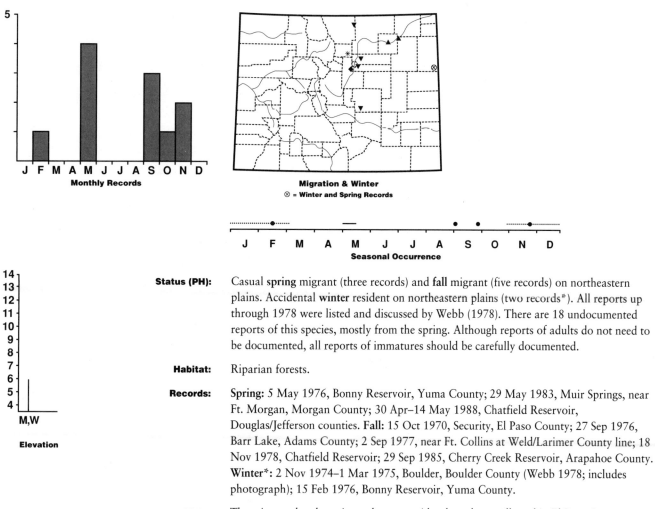

Monthly Records

Migration & Winter
⊗ = Winter and Spring Records

Seasonal Occurrence

Elevation

Status (PH): Casual **spring** migrant (three records) and **fall** migrant (five records) on northeastern plains. Accidental **winter** resident on northeastern plains (two records*). All reports up through 1978 were listed and discussed by Webb (1978). There are 18 undocumented reports of this species, mostly from the spring. Although reports of adults do not need to be documented, all reports of immatures should be carefully documented.

Habitat: Riparian forests.

Records: **Spring:** 5 May 1976, Bonny Reservoir, Yuma County; 29 May 1983, Muir Springs, near Ft. Morgan, Morgan County; 30 Apr–14 May 1988, Chatfield Reservoir, Douglas/Jefferson counties. **Fall:** 15 Oct 1970, Security, El Paso County; 27 Sep 1976, Barr Lake, Adams County; 2 Sep 1977, near Ft. Collins at Weld/Larimer County line; 18 Nov 1978, Chatfield Reservoir; 29 Sep 1985, Cherry Creek Reservoir, Arapahoe County. **Winter*:** 2 Nov 1974–1 Mar 1975, Boulder, Boulder County (Webb 1978; includes photograph); 15 Feb 1976, Bonny Reservoir, Yuma County.

Note: There is a undated specimen that was said to have been collected in El Paso County (Bailey and Niedrach 1965); however, we have been unable to verify this specimen record.

Broad-winged Hawk
Buteo platypterus

Rare migrant in eastern Colorado; one breeding record.

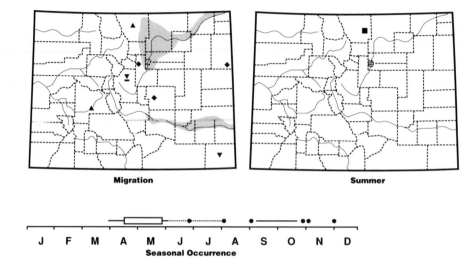

Migration	**Summer**

Seasonal Occurrence

J   F   M   A   M   J   J   A   S   O   N   D

Status (SP) (B): Rare **spring** migrant on eastern plains. At the Dinosaur Ridge hawk watch, Jefferson County, eight were seen in spring 1990 and 27 in spring 1991 (Nelson 1990, D. Nelson, pers. comm.). Accidental in lower mountains (two records) and in western valleys (one record). Very rare fall migrant on eastern plains (38 records). Accidental in lower mountains (two records). Most observations are of light morph birds. There are eight records of dark morph birds, six in spring and two in fall. Accidental in **summer** on northeastern plains (two records, including one confirmed **breeding** record).

Habitat: Riparian forests, and city parks and residential areas.

Records: **Spring in low mountains:** 1 May 1983, Evergreen, Jefferson County; 22 Apr 1989, Poudre Park, Larimer County. **Spring in western valleys:** 1 June 1978, Gunnison, Gunnison County. **Fall in low mountains:** 3 Sep 1977, Grant, Park County (DMNH 36714); 22–23 Sep 1977, Evergreen. **Summer:** pair bred successfully in 1978, Ft. Collins, Larimer County (Gent 1987); nonbreeder 24 June 1984, Denver County.

14
13
12
11
10
9
8
7
6
5
4

M

Elevation

Swainson's Hawk

Buteo swainsoni

Migrant and summer resident; most numerous in eastern Colorado and less in mountains and in western Colorado.

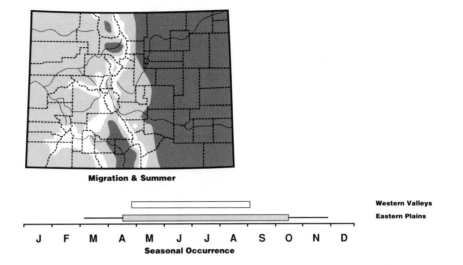

Migration & Summer

Western Valleys
Eastern Plains

J   F   M   A   M   J   J   A   S   O   N   D

Seasonal Occurrence

Elevation

Status (SP) (B): Fairly common to common **spring** and **fall** migrant on eastern plains; uncommon in mountain parks and rare in foothills, lower mountains, and in western valleys. Most migrants appear on the plains well out from the foothills; only 15 were seen in spring 1990 at the Dinosaur Ridge hawk watch, Jefferson County (Nelson 1990). Casual from mid-summer to early fall in high mountains and above timberline (four records). Flocks of up to 100 birds are regularly seen (occasionally up to 500 birds), primarily in late summer and early fall on eastern plains. High count: 1,325 in three hours on 28 Sep 1989, Washington County (B. Wheeler, pers. comm.). Uncommon to fairly common **summer** resident in North Park, Middle Park, San Luis Valley, and on eastern plains; rare in foothills, lower mountains, and western valleys.

Most birds are light morph individuals. Dark morph birds are seen regularly, especially in migration, and the large flocks that are occasionally seen in late summer and fall often have many dark individuals.

There are no valid **winter** records. The latest Colorado specimen is 22 Nov 1985, Denver County (DMNH 39183). The four winter specimens listed by Bailey and Niedrach (1965) can't be located and should be disregarded. None of the numerous subsequent sight reports was rigorously documented. There are a few records from the extreme southern United States; they are mostly immatures, while most winter sight reports are adults (Browning 1974). There are no valid winter (late Dec through Feb) records from temperate North America (Clark 1987). All sight reports in that period should be thoroughly documented.

Habitat: Grasslands, agricultural areas, shrublands, and riparian forests. Breeding birds nest in trees in or near open areas; migrants often appear in treeless areas. Large flocks are most often seen in agricultural areas near grasshopper infestations (Woffinden 1986, Johnson et al. 1987).

Note: Although it is common, there is some concern about this species. It is on the National Audubon Society Special Concern List (Tate 1986) and is a candidate for listing under the Endangered Species Act (Knopf 1988).

Red-tailed Hawk
Buteo jamaicensis

The several field-identifiable subspecies of this species are treated separately.

Eastern subspecies
B. j. borealis

Status (SR): Common **spring** and **fall** migrant and **winter** resident on eastern plains (B. Wheeler, pers. comm.).

Habitat: Riparian forests, and agricultural areas and grasslands with scattered trees.

Krider's subspecies
B. j. kriderii

Status uncertain, probably rare in migration and winter in eastern Colorado.

Status (SR): There are 28+ sight reports of this form on eastern plains, mostly in spring, fall, and winter but a few in summer. Most of these records are questionable because most identifications are based on the degree of pigmentation, and unusually light B. j. *calurus* could be misidentified as *kriderii* (C. Preston, pers. comm.). It can also be easily confused with the Ferruginous Hawk. There are several summer reports, including a set of three eggs collected at Greeley, Weld County (Dille 1887), but the occurrence of this race in Colorado in the summer is uncertain; such observations could be either light *calurus* or intergrades. The true status of this race in Colorado is unknown, but it probably occurs as a rare migrant and winter resident.

Habitat: Riparian forests, agricultural areas, and grasslands.

Note: There is one specimen (10 Oct 1981, Breckenridge, Summit County; DMNH 7002), but it is doubtful that it was in fact collected at Breckenridge.

Western subspecies

B. j. calurus

Resident throughout most of Colorado; most numerous in migration and winter.

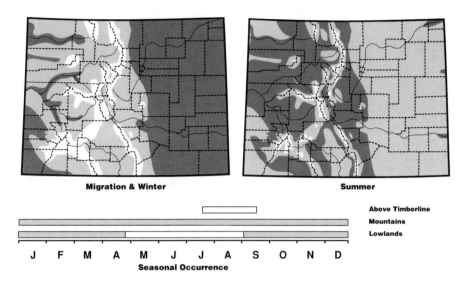

Migration & Winter   Summer

Above Timberline
Mountains
Lowlands

J   F   M   A   M   J   J   A   S   O   N   D
Seasonal Occurrence

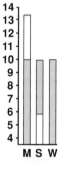

Elevation

Status (SP) (B): Uncommon to common **spring** and **fall** migrant in western valleys, foothills, lower mountains, mountain parks, and on eastern plains. At the Dinosaur Ridge hawk watch, Jefferson County, 421 were seen in spring 1990 (Nelson 1990). Rare, mostly from mid-summer to early fall, in higher mountains and above timberline. Uncommon to common **winter** resident in western valleys and on eastern plains; rare in mountain parks. This bird formerly wintered in greater numbers than at present due to the decline of prairie dogs (Bailey and Niedrach 1965). Uncommon to fairly common **summer** resident in western valleys, lower mountains, mountain parks, and on extreme eastern plains.

Most birds seen are light morph birds, but dark and rufous morph individuals and intergrades between morphs are seen regularly, especially in migration and winter.

Habitat: Breeding birds occur in forests or in open areas with scattered trees or groves. Migrant and winter birds are also found in agricultural areas, grasslands, and shrublands, but usually close to trees. Winter birds are more associated with riparian areas or agricultural areas with numerous scattered trees than other buteos.

References: Gatz and Hegdal (1986), McGovern and McNurney (1986).

Harlan's subspecies

B. j. harlani

Migrant and winter resident in eastern Colorado.

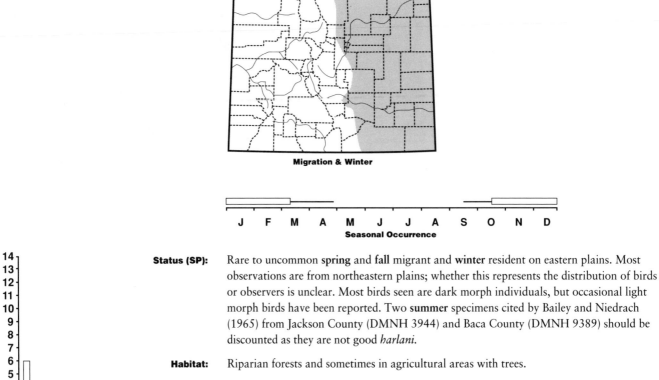

Migration & Winter

Seasonal Occurrence

J F M A M J J A S O N D

Elevation

M,W

Status (SP): Rare to uncommon **spring** and **fall** migrant and **winter** resident on eastern plains. Most observations are from northeastern plains; whether this represents the distribution of birds or observers is unclear. Most birds seen are dark morph individuals, but occasional light morph birds have been reported. Two **summer** specimens cited by Bailey and Niedrach (1965) from Jackson County (DMNH 3944) and Baca County (DMNH 9389) should be discounted as they are not good *harlani*.

Habitat: Riparian forests and sometimes in agricultural areas with trees.

Ferruginous Hawk

Buteo regalis

Resident; common in winter in eastern Colorado, and rare or uncommon in other areas and seasons.

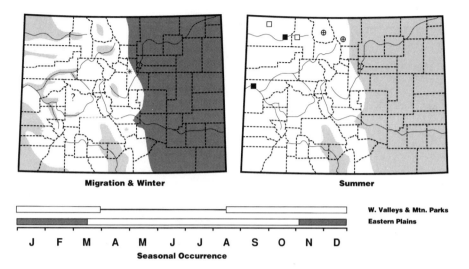

Migration & Winter   **Summer**

W. Valleys & Mtn. Parks
Eastern Plains

J F M A M J J A S O N D

Seasonal Occurrence

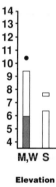

Elevation

Status (SP) (B): Fairly common to common **winter** resident on eastern plains; uncommon to rare in western valleys and mountain parks. Johnsgard (1990) estimated that about 1,200 birds winter in Colorado, second only to Arizona and comprising about 20 percent of the total winter population in the United States. This species has been increasing on Christmas Bird Counts in the Great Plains (Warkentin and James 1988). Rare to uncommon **summer** resident locally on eastern plains, and very locally in Moffat and Routt counties (Felger 1910, Hendee 1929, Martin et al. 1974), along the Book Cliffs and in the Grand Valley, Mesa County, and in the San Luis Valley. There are about 150 nest sites in Colorado, primarily on eastern plains (G. Craig, pers. comm.). Casual at all seasons in lower mountains outside parks (five records).

Habitat: Grasslands and semidesert shrublands, and rare in piñon-juniper woodlands. Breeding birds nest in isolated trees, on rock outcrops, structures such as windmills and power poles, or on the ground. Winter residents concentrate around prairie dog towns. Winter numbers and distribution fluctuate greatly according to the availability of prairie dogs; when a local prairie dog population dies off due to plague, hawk numbers decrease drastically. Migrants and winter residents may also occur in shrublands and agricultural areas.

Notes: (1) Birds raised in Colorado winter primarily in Texas (Harmata 1981). (2) Although this is still a common species in some areas, there is concern about it, and it is on the National Audubon Society Special Concern List (Tate 1986) and is a candidate for listing under the Endangered Species Act (Knopf 1988).

Reference: Lockhart and Craig (1985).

Rough-legged Hawk
Buteo lagopus

Winter resident throughout; most numerous in eastern Colorado.

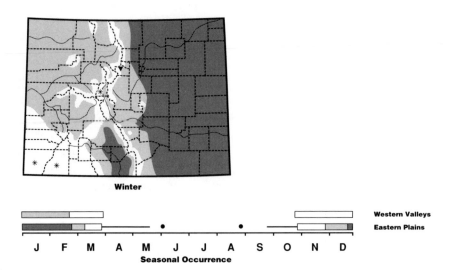

Winter

Western Valleys

Eastern Plains

J F M A M J J A S O N D

Seasonal Occurrence

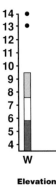

Elevation

Status (SP): Fairly common to common **winter** resident on eastern plains and in the San Luis Valley, and uncommon to fairly common in western valleys and mountain parks (primarily in the northern half of the state). Rare in foothills and lower mountains, and accidental above timberline (two records). Peak numbers are usually not reached until late Dec or early Jan, and by mid-Feb numbers are already declining as birds begin to move back north. Eastern Colorado is part of this species' core winter range in North America (Bock and Lepthien 1976a, Root 1988, Johnsgard 1990). This species is very variable in its plumages, and light and dark morph birds and adults and immatures are all seen frequently in Colorado.

Several sets of eggs purported to be of this species collected south of Canada include one set from Colorado, but Bechard and Houston (1984) showed that all such reports of breeding are invalid. Several local checklists incorrectly list this as a breeding species.

Habitat: Grasslands, shrublands, agricultural areas, and occasionally in riparian forests.

Records: **Above timberline:** 15 Sep 1977, near Silver Plume, Clear Creek County; 20 Feb 1978, Mt. Elbert, Lake County.

Reference: Gatz and Hegdal (1986).

Golden Eagle

Aquila chrysaetos

Resident throughout Colorado; most common in winter.

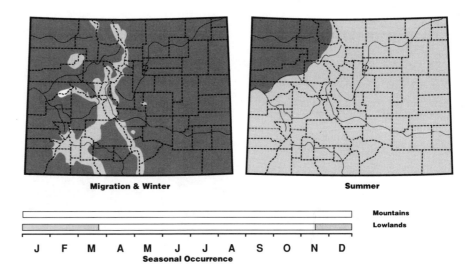

Migration & Winter   **Summer**

Mountains
Lowlands

J F M A M J J A S O N D
Seasonal Occurrence

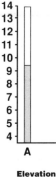

A

Elevation

Status (SP) (B): **Winter** resident, uncommon to locally fairly common or even common in western valleys, foothills, lower mountains, mountain parks, and eastern plains. The greatest winter concentrations occur in northwestern Colorado. Rare to uncommon **summer** resident in western valleys, foothills, mountains, mountain parks, and eastern plains. There are about 500 nest sites in the state, but only about half are used in any given year; for example, in 1979 there were 191 active nests (hatching 248 young and fledging 218) and 253 inactive nests (Craig 1981). The 1979 active nests were distributed as follows: 114 in northwestern Colorado, 39 in the southwest, 19 in the southeast, and 36 in the northeast (Craig 1981). Snow (1973) estimated there were 2,600 birds resident in Colorado.

Habitat: Grasslands, shrublands, piñon-juniper woodlands, and ponderosa pine forests; may occur in most other habitats occasionally, especially in migration and winter. Nests are placed on cliffs and sometimes in trees in rugged areas, and breeding birds range widely over surrounding habitats.

Reference: Enderson et al. (1970).

**Order Falconiformes
Family Falconidae**

American Kestrel

Falco sparverius

Resident throughout most of Colorado; most numerous in migration.

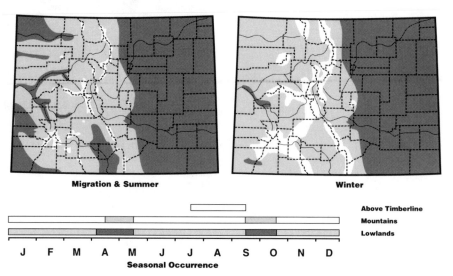

Migration & Summer / Winter

Above Timberline
Mountains
Lowlands

J F M A M J J A S O N D
Seasonal Occurrence

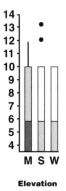

M S W

Elevation

Status (SP) (B): Common **spring** and **fall** migrant in western valleys, the San Luis Valley, and on eastern plains; uncommon to fairly common in mountain parks and uncommon in foothills and lower mountains. At the Dinosaur Ridge hawk watch, Jefferson County, 472 were seen in spring 1990 (Nelson 1990). Rare migrant during late summer and early fall in higher mountains and above timberline. Uncommon to fairly common **summer** resident in western valleys, the San Luis Valley, and on eastern plains, and uncommon in foothills, lower mountains, and mountain parks. Uncommon to fairly common **winter** resident in western valleys, the San Luis Valley, and on eastern plains and rare to uncommon in foothills, lower mountains, and mountain parks.

Habitat: Most often observed in agricultural areas, grasslands, riparian forest edges, and urban areas. It is also observed in virtually all other habitats, especially in migration.

Reference: Stahlecker and Griese (1977).

Merlin

Falco columbarius

Migrant and winter resident at low elevations and in mountain parks; two old breeding records.

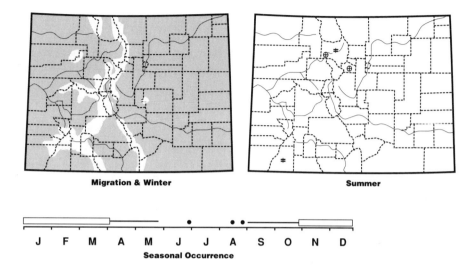

Migration & Winter   **Summer**

Seasonal Occurrence

J F M A M J J A S O N D

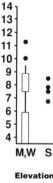

Elevation

M,W S

Status (SP) (FB): Rare to uncommon **spring** and **fall** migrant and **winter** resident in western valleys, mountain parks, and eastern plains; rare in foothills and lower mountains. At the Dinosaur Ridge hawk watch, Jefferson County, 14 were seen in spring 1990 (Nelson 1990). Accidental in higher mountains (two records). There are two confirmed **breeding** records: a pair and a set of four eggs 26 May 1877 along the Colorado River, Grand County (Bailey and Niedrach 1965) and a nest with five eggs 3 July 1887, Ft. Lewis, La Plata County (Morrison 1889). Also seen near Georgetown, Clear Creek County in June 1901 (Keyser 1902). There have been four recent summer records from Grand County (D. Jasper, pers. comm.). Merlins nest in southwestern and central Wyoming (Dorn and Dorn 1990), and additional breeding records are possible in northwestern or north-central Colorado.

Most Colorado birds belong the race *F. c. richardsoni* (Prairie Merlin) of the northern Great Plains (Clark 1987). There have been several sight reports of very dark birds that may belong to the race *F. c. suckleyi* (Black Merlin) of the Pacific Northwest; however, there are no specimens. There have also been sight reports of *F. c. columbarius* and *F. c. bendirei*, which breed in the taiga of Alaska and Canada. There is one specimen of *columbarius*: 14 Dec 1940, Weldona, Morgan County (DMNH 22319) (reported in Bailey and Niedrach 1965 as *suckleyi*, and incorrectly as DMNH 22391). Field identifications of races other than *richardsoni* should be made carefully and documented thoroughly.

Habitat: Observed mostly in grasslands, agricultural areas, riparian forests, and urban areas, but the species has been observed occasionally in most other habitats.

Records: **Higher mountains:** undated observation at 11,300 ft. on Berthoud Pass, Clear Creek/Grand counties (Coues 1874); in Sep at 10,000 ft. at Silver Lake, Boulder County (Henderson 1909).

Note: Birds banded as nestlings in Alberta and Saskatchewan have been recovered in Colorado during mid-winter (Schmutz et al. 1991).

Prairie Falcon
Falco mexicanus

Resident throughout Colorado.

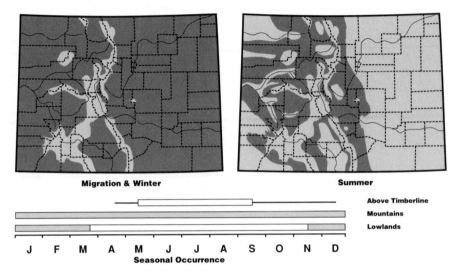

Migration & Winter   **Summer**

Above Timberline
Mountains
Lowlands

J F M A M J J A S O N D
Seasonal Occurrence

Status (SP) (B): Uncommon **spring** and **fall** migrant and **winter** resident in western valleys, foothills, lower mountains, mountain parks, and on eastern plains. Johnsgard (1990) estimated that 900 birds winter in Colorado, which was the third highest state count. At the Dinosaur Ridge hawk watch, Jefferson County, nine were seen in spring 1990 (Nelson 1990). Rare local **summer** resident in western valleys, foothills, mountains, mountain parks, and on eastern plains. Rare in migration and summer in higher mountains and above timberline (Marti and Braun 1975). The number of nesting pairs in Colorado has declined, probably because of the loss of nest sites due to urbanization and human disturbance. Webster (1944) estimated there were 400 nest sites, but Enderson (1964) believed there were no more than 300, which is probably a more accurate number (G. Craig, pers. comm.). There are now about 190 nest sites in the state (G. Craig, pers. comm.).

Habitat: Breeding birds nest on cliffs or bluffs in open areas, and range widely over surrounding grasslands, shrublands, and alpine tundra. Migrants and winter residents occur mostly in grasslands, shrublands, and agricultural areas. Winter distribution is correlated with that of Horned Larks (Enderson 1964).

Note: Birds banded as nestlings in Alberta and Saskatchewan have been recovered in Colorado during mid-winter (Schmutz et al. 1991).

Reference: Gatz and Hegdal (1986).

14
13
12
11
10
9
8
7
6
5
4

M,W S

Elevation

Peregrine Falcon
Falco peregrinus

Rare migrant throughout most of Colorado; local in summer in mountains, and a few in winter.

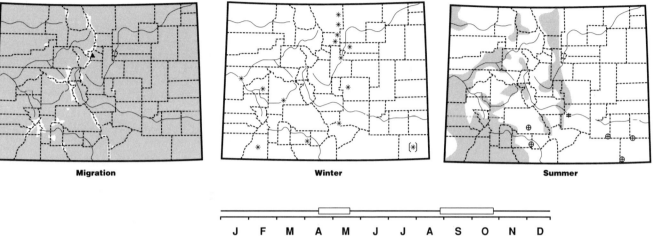

| Migration | Winter | Summer |

J F M A M J J A S O N D

Seasonal Occurrence

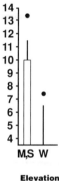

Elevation

Status (SP) (B): Rare **spring** and **fall** migrant in western valleys, foothills, lower mountains, mountain parks, and on eastern plains. At the Dinosaur Ridge hawk watch, Jefferson County, 10 were seen in both spring 1990 and spring 1991 (Nelson 1990, D. Nelson, pers. comm.). Accidental in higher mountains (one record). Rare **winter** resident at Monte Vista National Wildlife Refuge, Rio Grande County, and very rare in western valleys (16 records) and on eastern plains near foothills (25 records); accidental on far eastern plains (one record).

Rare **summer** resident in foothills and lower mountains. Formerly, the species nested in at least 15 counties (Enderson 1965), with only six nesting sites occupied in 1964 (Bailey and Niedrach 1965). There were 58 active nest sites in 1991, 42 on the western slope (fledging 75 young) and 16 on the eastern slope (fledging 16 young) (Craig 1991b). The number of active sites and young birds produced increases annually. Some summer birds are nonbreeders. Birds have been reintroduced into former nesting sites, and even into downtown Denver, and some former nesting sites have been reoccupied by wild birds.

This species suffered serious population declines in North America during this century, primarily due to pesticides. Many agencies have worked in North America to restore populations by breeding birds in captivity and releasing them at suitable nesting sites, and as can be seen from the above numbers of breeding birds, the population is rebounding in Colorado.

Habitat: Breeding pairs nest on cliffs and forage over adjacent coniferous and riparian forests, and at times other habitats. Migrants and winter residents occur mostly around reservoirs, rivers, and marshes, but may also be seen in grasslands, agricultural areas, and less often in other habitats.

Records: **Higher mountains:** 12 May 1974, Guanella Pass, Clear Creek/Park counties. **Winter on extreme eastern plains:** 19 Feb 1977, Baca County.

Note: This species is considered to be endangered at both the state and federal levels.

Gyrfalcon
Falco rusticolus

Status (SP): Casual **winter** resident on northeastern plains (four records*). Kingery (1991a) notes that falconers claim that this species occurs regularly in Colorado.

Habitat: Grasslands and agricultural areas.

Records: 11 Dec 1969, Horse Creek Reservoir, Adams/Weld counties (DMNH 36112) (Craig 1971, Bailey 1972); 2–4 Jan 1981, Prewitt Reservoir area, Logan County; 12 Oct 1986, Windsor Reservoir, Weld County; 2 December 1990–2 February 1991, western Pawnee National Grassland, Weld County.

Order Galliformes
Family Phasianidae

Chukar

Alectoris chukar

Local resident in western Colorado.

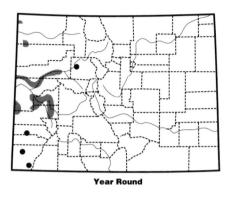

Year Round

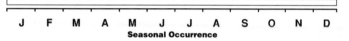

J F M A M J J A S O N D
Seasonal Occurrence

Elevation

Status (SP) (B): Rare to uncommon local **resident** in western valleys. It occurs primarily in west-central Colorado, but also is found locally in northwestern (Dunn and Ryder 1986, National Park Service 1988) and southwestern Colorado (Braun et al. 1991). This species was introduced into Colorado beginning in the 1930s, and releases were made in 52 counties, but self-sustaining populations have been established only in western Colorado (Braun et al. 1991).

Habitat: Steep, rocky, dry canyon slopes with cheat-grass where snow quickly melts (C. Braun, pers. comm.).

Ring-necked Pheasant

Phasianus colchicus

Resident in agricultural areas; most numerous in eastern Colorado.

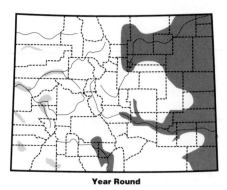

Year Round

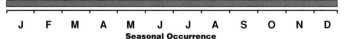

J F M A M J J A S O N D

Seasonal Occurrence

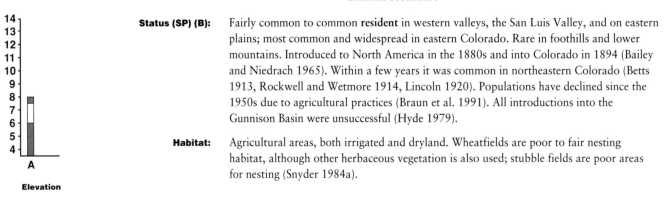

Elevation

Status (SP) (B): Fairly common to common **resident** in western valleys, the San Luis Valley, and on eastern plains; most common and widespread in eastern Colorado. Rare in foothills and lower mountains. Introduced to North America in the 1880s and into Colorado in 1894 (Bailey and Niedrach 1965). Within a few years it was common in northeastern Colorado (Betts 1913, Rockwell and Wetmore 1914, Lincoln 1920). Populations have declined since the 1950s due to agricultural practices (Braun et al. 1991). All introductions into the Gunnison Basin were unsuccessful (Hyde 1979).

Habitat: Agricultural areas, both irrigated and dryland. Wheatfields are poor to fair nesting habitat, although other herbaceous vegetation is also used; stubble fields are poor areas for nesting (Snyder 1984a).

Blue Grouse

Dendragapus obscurus

Resident in the foothills and mountains.

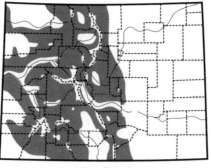

Year Round

J F M A M J J A S O N D

Seasonal Occurrence

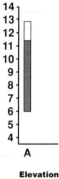

Elevation

Status (SP) (B): Common **resident** in foothills and mountains. Altitudinal movements are generally no more than 1,000–3,000 ft., with birds tending to move down in spring and back up to higher elevations in late summer and fall, although local variations exist depending upon vegetation. Statewide, the abundance and distribution has not changed much in the last 50 years and current populations are generally stable, although local declines may have occurred due to grazing (Braun et al. 1991, C. Braun and K. Giesen, pers. comm.).

Habitat: Breeds in open coniferous and aspen forests with a shrub understory or adjacent to shrublands. Winters in Douglas-fir and lodgepole pine forests (Cade and Hoffman 1990, Braun et al. 1991). They occur in all coniferous forest types, but are rare in piñon-juniper woodlands.

Reference: Rogers (1968).

White-tailed Ptarmigan
Lagopus leucurus

Resident above timberline.

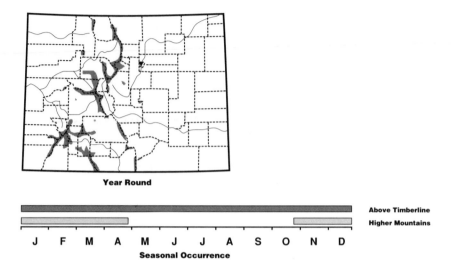

Year Round

Above Timberline

Higher Mountains

J F M A M J J A S O N D

Seasonal Occurrence

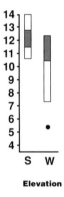

Elevation

Status (SP) (B): Common **summer** resident above timberline. Birds are widely distributed across the alpine tundra during the summer, when it occurs only at or above timberline. Common local **winter** resident above treeline and in higher mountains below treeline. During fall and winter, they are very concentrated, and large areas may be unoccupied. Females may winter below timberline in higher mountains, and in areas of western Colorado where snowfall is heavy, both sexes move below timberline. There are records into the lower mountains in late fall and winter (C. Braun, pers. comm.). Accidental on eastern plains (one record). This species was absent from the Spanish Peaks, Huerfano/Las Animas counties (due to lack of vegetation above timberline) and from Pikes Peak, El Paso County (due to distance from occupied areas), and was successfully introduced onto Pikes Peak in 1975 (Hoffman and Giesen 1983).

Habitat: Alpine tundra. Areas that are mostly snowfree early in the season are used for breeding, and females with broods generally occur on rocky, wet tundra. Males generally winter above timberline in areas of short willow thickets, while females often winter at or below timberline in taller, denser willow thickets and along willow-dominated watercourses (Hoffman and Braun 1977).

Record: **Eastern plains:** two on 20 Oct 1941, Denver, Denver County (Bailey and Niedrach 1965).

References: Braun and Rogers (1971), Hoffman and Braun (1975), Giesen et al. (1980).

Ruffed Grouse
Bonasa umbellus

Status (SP) (B): Casual in northwestern Colorado.

Records: Adult male 24 Oct 1988, Hoy Mountain, Moffat County (DMNH 39566) (Webb and Reddall 1989, which incorrectly states Rio Blanco County); several observed and two collected in same area in Oct 1990 (Braun et al. 1991) and one seen 28 Sep 1991 (Nelson 1992). The specimens collected in 1990 were an adult female and a juvenile male, and confirmed breeding at that site (Braun et al. 1991). There were numerous other reports from the state all believed by Hoffman and Braun (1978) to be Blue Grouse.

Habitat: Mesic conifer/aspen with dense shrub understory (K. Giesen and R. Hoffman, pers. comm.).

Sage Grouse
Centrocercus urophasianus

Resident locally, primarily in northwestern and west-central Colorado.

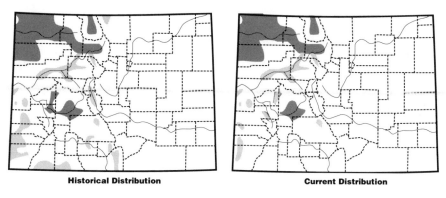

Historical Distribution   **Current Distribution**

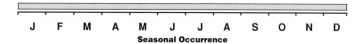

J F M A M J J A S O N D
Seasonal Occurrence

Status (SP) (B): Fairly common local **resident** in northwestern Colorado, especially in Moffat County, North Park, Middle Park, and in the Gunnison Basin, Gunnsion County. Small populations occur locally elsewhere in western Colorado, and in Saguache and Larimer counties (Braun et al. 1991). The greatest concentrations occur on wintering grounds; large numbers may also be seen at display sites in spring. Accidental above timberline (two records).

The primary areas where this species presently occurs were also the most important historic areas, but populations in other areas have declined (Braun et al. 1991). Some populations have been extirpated, especially in the San Luis Valley, the upper Arkansas River Valley in Chaffee and Lake counties, and around Dove Creek, Dolores County (Braun et al. 1991, C. Braun, pers. comm.). The main reduction came from the late 1800s to about 1910, and the population in Costilla County was extirpated sometime in the mid-1900s. It is unlikely this species was ever resident on the eastern plains (Rogers 1964, Braun et al. 1991), in spite of statements to that effect (Ridgway and Friedman 1946).

Habitat: Sagebrush shrublands. Prime habitat is large, contiguous, and gently rolling areas of sagebrush. In summer native or cultivated meadows, grasslands, aspen and willow thickets adjacent to or interspersed with sagebrush are frequently used, but sage mixed with piñon-juniper is rarely used.

Records: **Above timberline:** date unknown at 14,000 ft. near Breckenridge, Summit County (Cooke 1900); flock of three on 4 Aug 1981, Elliott Ridge, south of Kremmling, Grand County (Hoffman and Cade 1982).

Reference: Rogers (1964).

14
13
12
11
10
9
8
7
6
5
4

A

Elevation

Greater Prairie-Chicken

Tympanuchus cupido

Fairly common resident in sandhills of northeastern Colorado.

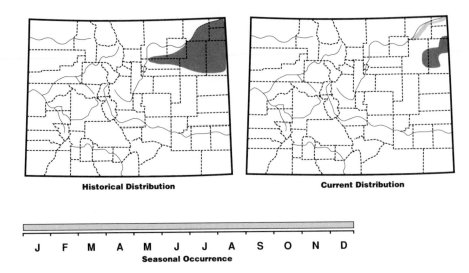

Historical Distribution   Current Distribution

| J | F | M | A | M | J | J | A | S | O | N | D |

Seasonal Occurrence

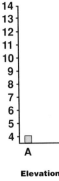

Elevation

Status (SP) (B): Fairly common local **resident** in sandhills of northern and central Yuma County, extreme eastern Washington County, and extreme southern Phillips County. There were at least 146 active leks and 3,000–6,000 birds in that area (Van Sant and Braun 1990). This species was released in sandhills on the south side of the South Platte River in Logan and Sedgwick counties in 1984 and 1985 (Van Sant and Braun 1990). Releases were made in 1991 in Weld, Morgan, and Washington counties (Braun et al. 1991).

This species did not occur in Colorado until about 1897, when its range expanded with grain cultivation; it reached the Denver area by 1907 and occurred locally through most of northeastern Colorado (Johnsgard and Wood 1968, Van Sant and Braun 1990). It occurred mostly in low numbers, but was apparently common in Yuma County in the 1920s and 1930s. Its newly expanded range began to contract starting in the mid-1930s due to excessive agricultural encroachment (Johnsgard and Wood 1968, Van Sant and Braun 1990). It nested in the Barr Lake area, Adams County as late as 1908 (Hersey and Rockwell 1909), and was observed there as late as 1936 (Bailey and Niedrach 1965). Flocks were seen in the Ft. Morgan area, Morgan County in 1932 (Bergtold 1932a). A report in 1847 in El Paso County (Marsh 1968) probably was either of Lesser Prairie-Chickens or Sharp-tailed Grouse (C. Braun, pers. comm.).

There are several records of Greater Prairie-Chicken X Sharp-tailed Grouse hybrids: a male in Apr 1963 and 1964, 10 mi. north of Wray, Yuma County (Evans 1966; includes photo), and hybrids are common at Tamarack Ranch, Logan and Sedgwick counties (Braun et al. 1992).

Habitat: Mid-grass sandsage grasslands on sandhills, mixed with cornfields (Evans and Gilbert 1969, Van Sant and Braun 1990).

Note: This is an endangered species (Van Sant and Braun 1990).

Reference: Tully (1974).

Lesser Prairie-Chicken
Tympanuchus pallidicinctus

Uncommon resident in extreme southeastern Colorado.

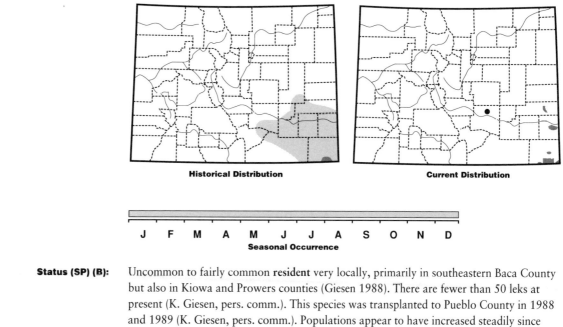

Historical Distribution   Current Distribution

J F M A M J J A S O N D
Seasonal Occurrence

Status (SP) (B): Uncommon to fairly common **resident** very locally, primarily in southeastern Baca County but also in Kiowa and Prowers counties (Giesen 1988). There are fewer than 50 leks at present (K. Giesen, pers. comm.). This species was transplanted to Pueblo County in 1988 and 1989 (K. Giesen, pers. comm.). Populations appear to have increased steadily since 1977 (Braun et al. 1991). Although it formerly occurred in 11 counties in southeastern Colorado, it was always a peripheral species in the state and was probably never numerous except near Campo, Baca County (Braun et al. 1991).

Habitat: Sandsage and sandsage-bluestem grasslands. May also occur at times in agricultural areas, especially in winter.

Reference: Hoffman (1963).

Elevation

Sharp-tailed Grouse
Tympanuchus phasianellus

The two native subspecies are treated separately.

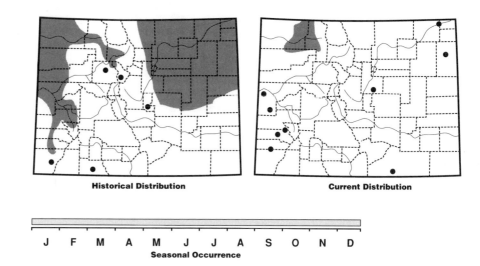

Historical Distribution   Current Distribution

J F M A M J J A S O N D
Seasonal Occurrence

Elevation

Columbian Sharp-tailed Grouse

T. p. columbianus

Local resident in northwestern Colorado.

Status (SP) (B): Uncommon local **resident** in Routt and eastern Moffat counties, with smaller and localized populations south to Montezuma County. Greatest concentrations occur at display grounds in spring. This bird has declined due to habitat changes since the turn of the century; many areas within the historic range are unoccupied or have low densities (Braun et al. 1991).

Habitat: Gambel oak and serviceberry shrublands, often interspersed with sagebrush shrublands, aspen forests, wheatfields, and irrigated meadows and alfalfa fields. Display grounds are on knolls or ridges.

Reference: Rogers (1969).

Plains Sharp-tailed Grouse

T. p. jamesii

Very local; primarily in Douglas County.

Status (SP) (B): Rare to uncommon **resident** in Douglas County. Birds wander from the Nebraska Sandhills to Logan and Sedgwick counties (Hoag and Braun 1990) and from Kansas to Yuma County (Braun et al. 1992). Birds were transplanted from 1987 to 1989 to the Raton Mesa and Fisher Peak area, Las Animas County (Hoag and Braun 1990).

This subspecies formerly occurred in eastern Colorado west to Larimer County and south to El Paso, Lincoln, and Kit Carson counties, and was most numerous along the edge of the foothills from Larimer to El Paso counties (Hoag and Braun 1990, Braun et al. 1992). Numbers declined dramatically due to habitat loss starting between 1877 and 1887, and by the 1960s, only about 200–300 occurred in Douglas and Elbert counties (Hoag and Braun 1990, Braun et al. 1992). At present there are three to six leks with a total of less than 225 birds (Hoag and Braun 1990, Braun et al. 1992). Hybrids between the Plains Sharp-tailed Grouse and the Greater Prairie-Chicken are regularly seen in Logan and Sedgwick counties (Braun et al. 1992).

Habitat: The historic habitat was shrub-prairie ecotone along the foothills and stream courses on the plains, and presently occurs in Gambel oak and other shrublands lacking conifers (Hoag and Braun 1990). Croplands and riparian areas are also used, especially in fall and winter (Braun et al. 1992). Leks are located in wet meadows, ridges and knolls, or recently burned areas (Braun et al. 1992).

Note: This subspecies is endangered (Hoag and Braun 1990).

Reference: Rogers (1969).

Wild Turkey

Meleagris gallopavo

Uncommon to fairly common resident in foothills, primarily in southern Colorado.

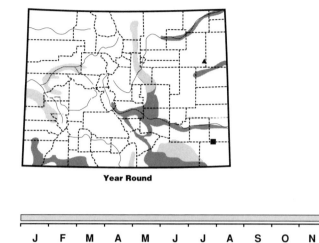

Year Round

| J | F | M | A | M | J | J | A | S | O | N | D |

Seasonal Occurrence

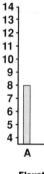

Elevation

Status (SP) (B): Fairly common **resident** in foothills and mesas of southern Colorado, primarily from Monte-zuma County east to Archuleta County and from Las Animas County east to southwestern Baca County and north to Fremont County. Rare to fairly common very locally north to Garfield and Eagle counties, rare in foothills of the southeastern San Luis Valley in Costilla County, and from El Paso County north to Larimer County. Garfield, Eagle, and Larimer counties are north of the historic range, and those populations resulted from introductions (Braun et al. 1991). The Merriam's subspecies (*M. g. merriami*) is the native form.

The Rio Grande subspecies (*M. g. intermedia*) was introduced on the eastern plains starting in 1981, where it is now common along the major rivers. This subspecies is not native to Colorado.

Habitat: Primarily ponderosa pine forests with an understory of Gambel oak. Tall pines are used at all seasons for roosting (Hoffman 1968). Eastern plains birds occur in lowland riparian forests. At times it may also be found in other foothill shrublands (mountain mahogany), piñon-juniper woodlands, foothill riparian forests, and in agricultural areas.

References: Burget (1957), Schmutz (1988).

Northern Bobwhite
Colinus virginianus

Resident in eastern Colorado.

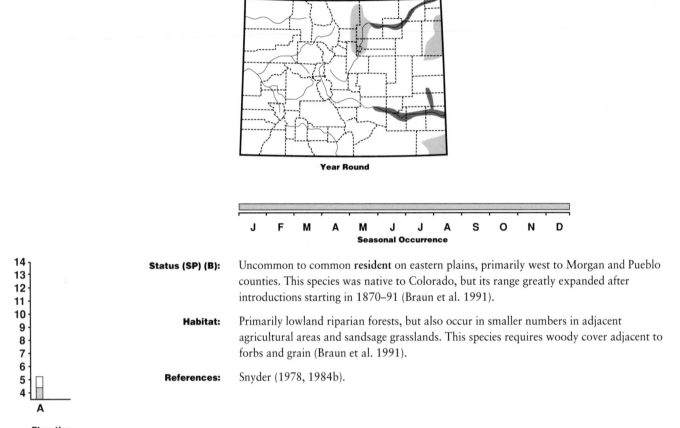

Year Round

J F M A M J J A S O N D
Seasonal Occurrence

Elevation

Status (SP) (B): Uncommon to common **resident** on eastern plains, primarily west to Morgan and Pueblo counties. This species was native to Colorado, but its range greatly expanded after introductions starting in 1870–91 (Braun et al. 1991).

Habitat: Primarily lowland riparian forests, but also occur in smaller numbers in adjacent agricultural areas and sandsage grasslands. This species requires woody cover adjacent to forbs and grain (Braun et al. 1991).

References: Snyder (1978, 1984b).

Scaled Quail

Callipepla squamata

Resident in southeastern Colorado.

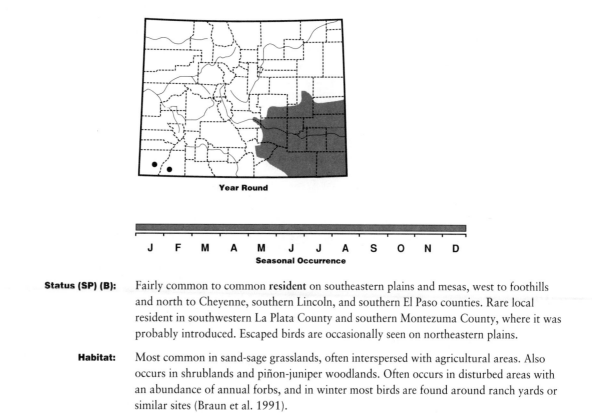

Year Round

J F M A M J J A S O N D

Seasonal Occurrence

14 13 12 11 10 9 8 7 6 5 4

A

Elevation

Status (SP) (B): Fairly common to common **resident** on southeastern plains and mesas, west to foothills and north to Cheyenne, southern Lincoln, and southern El Paso counties. Rare local resident in southwestern La Plata County and southern Montezuma County, where it was probably introduced. Escaped birds are occasionally seen on northeastern plains.

Habitat: Most common in sand-sage grasslands, often interspersed with agricultural areas. Also occurs in shrublands and piñon-juniper woodlands. Often occurs in disturbed areas with an abundance of annual forbs, and in winter most birds are found around ranch yards or similar sites (Braun et al. 1991).

References: Hoffman (1965), Rea (1975).

Gambel's Quail
Callipepla gambelii

Resident in western Colorado.

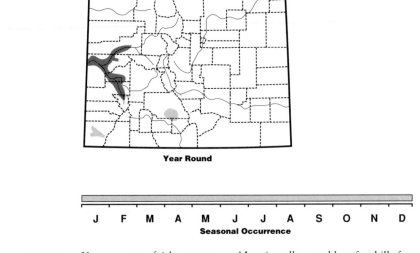

Year Round

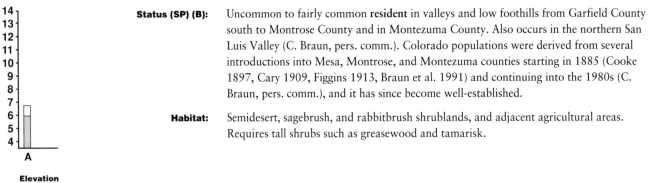

J   F   M   A   M   J   J   A   S   O   N   D
Seasonal Occurrence

Status (SP) (B): Uncommon to fairly common **resident** in valleys and low foothills from Garfield County south to Montrose County and in Montezuma County. Also occurs in the northern San Luis Valley (C. Braun, pers. comm.). Colorado populations were derived from several introductions into Mesa, Montrose, and Montezuma counties starting in 1885 (Cooke 1897, Cary 1909, Figgins 1913, Braun et al. 1991) and continuing into the 1980s (C. Braun, pers. comm.), and it has since become well-established.

Habitat: Semidesert, sagebrush, and rabbitbrush shrublands, and adjacent agricultural areas. Requires tall shrubs such as greasewood and tamarisk.

14
13
12
11
10
9
8
7
6
5
4

A

Elevation

Order Gruiformes
Family Rallidae

Yellow Rail

Coturnicops noveboracensis

Status (SP): Accidental in **summer** (one record*).

Record: July 1906, Barr Lake area, Adams County (DMNH 957).

Black Rail

Laterallus jamaicensis

Status (PH): Casual in **spring, early summer,** and **fall** (four records*).

Records: One taped 11–25 May 1975, Ft. Lyon, Bent County (Griese et al. 1980); one seen 30 Apr 1982, Ft. Collins, Larimer County; two seen 9 Sep 1987, near Ft. Collins; one or two seen and photographed 7 May–22 June 1991, Bent's Old Fort, Otero County (Bridges 1992a; photo published in that reference and on file with the RC). The birds seen in 1991 were territorial and may have nested. A specimen said to have been collected in the mid-1890s at or near Denver (Cooke 1898) is not extant and should be disregarded.

Habitat: Cattail marshes.

King Rail

Rallus elegans

Status (PH): Accidental in **spring** and **summer** (two records*).

Records: 12 June–3 July 1976, CF&I Lakes, Pueblo County (Griffiths 1976; photograph published in Andrews 1979); 12 May–2 June 1985, Lower Latham Reservoir, Weld County (Cairo 1985).

Habitat: Cattail marshes.

Virginia Rail
Rallus limicola

Summer resident at low elevations and in mountain parks; rare in winter.

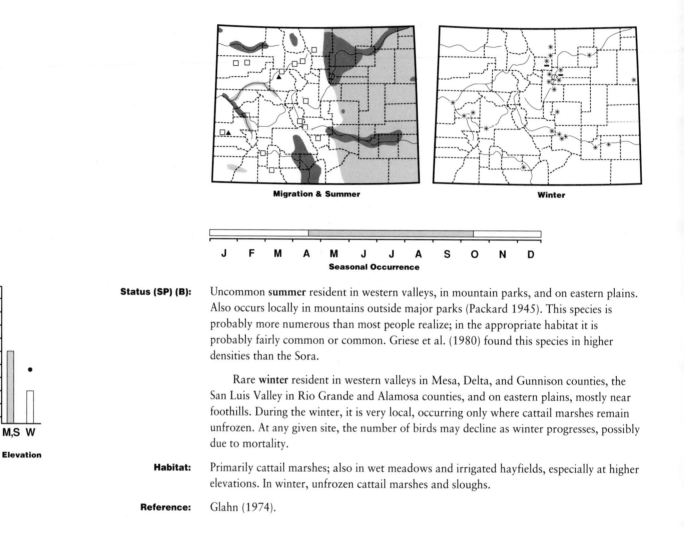

Migration & Summer   **Winter**

J   F   M   A   M   J   J   A   S   O   N   D
Seasonal Occurrence

Elevation

14
13
12
11
10
9
8
7
6
5
4

M,S W

Status (SP) (B): Uncommon **summer** resident in western valleys, in mountain parks, and on eastern plains. Also occurs locally in mountains outside major parks (Packard 1945). This species is probably more numerous than most people realize; in the appropriate habitat it is probably fairly common or common. Griese et al. (1980) found this species in higher densities than the Sora.

Rare **winter** resident in western valleys in Mesa, Delta, and Gunnison counties, the San Luis Valley in Rio Grande and Alamosa counties, and on eastern plains, mostly near foothills. During the winter, it is very local, occurring only where cattail marshes remain unfrozen. At any given site, the number of birds may decline as winter progresses, possibly due to mortality.

Habitat: Primarily cattail marshes; also in wet meadows and irrigated hayfields, especially at higher elevations. In winter, unfrozen cattail marshes and sloughs.

Reference: Glahn (1974).

Sora

Porzana carolina

Summer resident at low elevations and in mountain parks; very rare in winter.

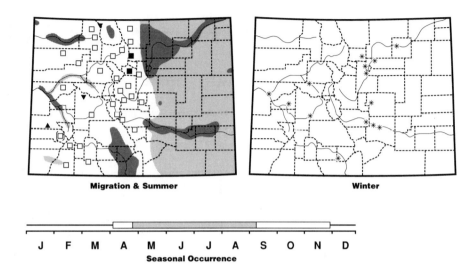

Migration & Summer **Winter**

Seasonal Occurrence

J F M A M J J A S O N D

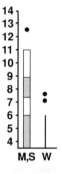

Elevation

Status (SP) (B): Uncommon **summer** resident in western valleys, in mountain parks, and on eastern plains. It is easily overlooked and may be fairly common, but it occurs in lower densities than the Virginia Rail (Griese et al. 1980). In addition to the major mountain parks, it occurs as a rare migrant and summer resident in many minor parks in the mountains. Accidental above timberline (one record).

Very rare **winter** resident on eastern plains (19 records), mostly near foothills. Casual in western valleys in Mesa, Pitkin, Delta, and Gunnison counties (seven records), and also recorded wintering in the San Luis Valley in Rio Grande and Alamosa counties. Although it may be overlooked in winter, it appears to occur less commonly in winter than the Virginia Rail. It may have increased as a winter bird, because Bailey and Niedrach (1965) listed only one winter record.

Habitat: Primarily cattail marshes; locally in grassy or sedge marshes, wet meadows, and irrigated hayfields, especially in mountain parks.

Record: Above timberline: 2 Sep 1903, at 12,500 ft. on Arapahoe Peak, Boulder County (Felger 1909).

Reference: Glahn (1974).

Purple Gallinule

Porphyrula martinica

Status (PH):   Accidental in **fall** (one record*).

Record: 6–7 Aug 1978, near Durango, La Plata County (photos in RC files). A specimen collected 17 June 1911, Florence, Fremont County (DMNH 4749) shows signs of having been in captivity, and is not a valid record.

Common Moorhen

Gallinula chloropus

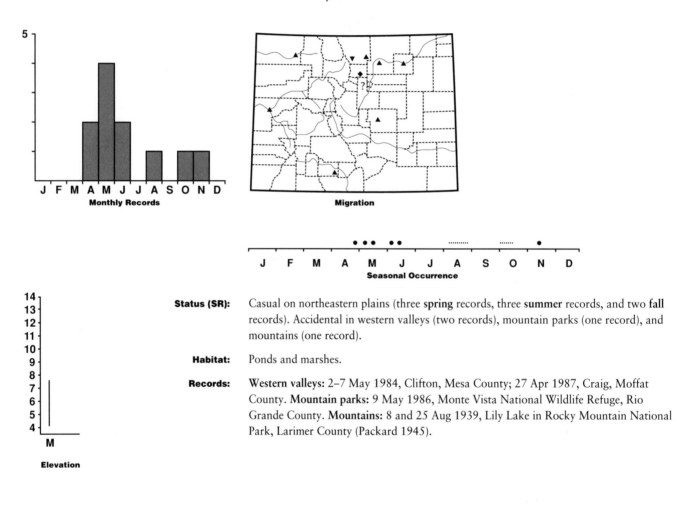

Status (SR):   Casual on northeastern plains (three **spring** records, three **summer** records, and two **fall** records). Accidental in western valleys (two records), mountain parks (one record), and mountains (one record).

Habitat: Ponds and marshes.

Records: **Western valleys:** 2–7 May 1984, Clifton, Mesa County; 27 Apr 1987, Craig, Moffat County. **Mountain parks:** 9 May 1986, Monte Vista National Wildlife Refuge, Rio Grande County. **Mountains:** 8 and 25 Aug 1939, Lily Lake in Rocky Mountain National Park, Larimer County (Packard 1945).

American Coot

Fulica americana

Migrant and summer resident at low elevations and in mountain parks; rare in winter.

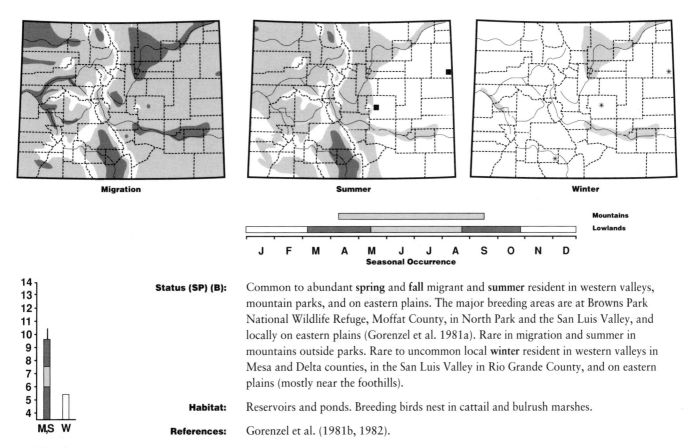

| Migration | Summer | Winter |

Seasonal Occurrence

Mountains
Lowlands

J F M A M J J A S O N D

Elevation

Status (SP) (B): Common to abundant **spring** and **fall** migrant and **summer** resident in western valleys, mountain parks, and on eastern plains. The major breeding areas are at Browns Park National Wildlife Refuge, Moffat County, in North Park and the San Luis Valley, and locally on eastern plains (Gorenzel et al. 1981a). Rare in migration and summer in mountains outside parks. Rare to uncommon local **winter** resident in western valleys in Mesa and Delta counties, in the San Luis Valley in Rio Grande County, and on eastern plains (mostly near the foothills).

Habitat: Reservoirs and ponds. Breeding birds nest in cattail and bulrush marshes.

References: Gorenzel et al. (1981b, 1982).

Order Gruiformes
Family Gruidae

Sandhill Crane
Grus canadensis

Abundant migrant in San Luis Valley, and irregular elsewhere; a few nest in the northern mountains.

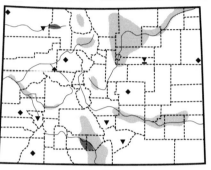

Migration

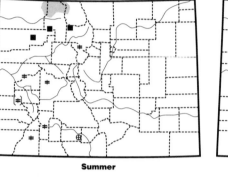

Summer

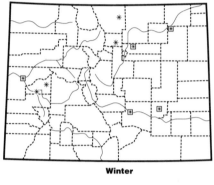

Winter

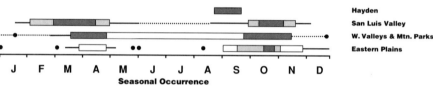

		Hayden
		San Luis Valley
		W. Valleys & Mtn. Parks
		Eastern Plains

J F M A M J J A S O N D

Seasonal Occurrence

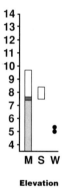

Elevation

Status (SP) (B): Abundant **spring** and **fall** migrant in the San Luis Valley. Peak migration counts may be as high as 17,000. Abundant in fall on staging grounds in the Hayden area, Routt County. Irregular common to abundant migrant, primarily in spring, in western valleys from Montrose County northward and east to Eagle and Gunnison counties. Rare in valleys of La Plata County. Irregular migrant on eastern plains, where it is often locally abundant in fall but is usually rare to uncommon in spring. In fall in both western valleys and eastern plains, large flocks sometimes stop at reservoirs, but flocks are frequently seen flying overhead in nonstop flight. Rare fall migrant (irregularly common) in North, Middle, and South Parks.

Rare **summer** resident in the parks of the Elkhead Mountains and Park Range in eastern Moffat, northern Routt, and western Jackson counties, and a few south to northeastern Rio Blanco and northwestern Grand counties. Also nests at Meeker, Rio Blanco County. In 1991, there were 118 active nest sites (Renner et al. 1991). The population is believed to be stable and possibly even increasing (Renner et al. 1991). It nested sparingly throughout the mountains of western Colorado south to La Plata County as late as 1905 (Drew 1881, Warren 1904, Rockwell 1908, Felger 1910, Sclater 1912, Bailey and Niedrach 1965). Nonbreeders very rarely summer in the San Luis Valley (Ryder 1965).

Casual in **mid-winter** (four records); a few formerly wintered in the San Luis Valley, but now only cripples winter there (Drewien and Bizeau 1974).

Habitat: Migrants occur on mudflats around reservoirs, in moist meadows, and in agricultural areas. Breeding birds are found in parks with grassy hummocks and watercourses, beaver ponds, and natural ponds lined with willows or aspens (Ellis and Haskins 1985, Renner et al. 1990).

Records: **Mid-winter:** Nov 1969–Mar 1970, Hotchkiss, Delta County (Davis 1970); mid-Dec 1979–5 Jan 1980, Wellington Reservoir, Larimer County; 22 Jan 1989, Delta, Delta County; 1 Jan 1991, Boulder County.

Note: Considered to be a state endangered breeding species (Stevens 1991).

Whooping Crane
Grus americana

Regular migrant in San Luis Valley and western valleys.

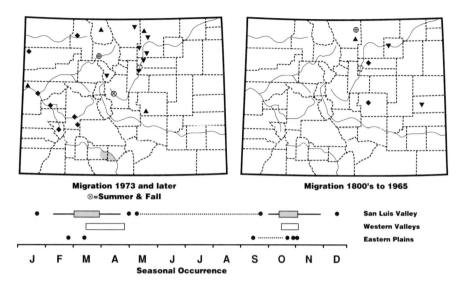

Migration 1973 and later
⊗=Summer & Fall

Migration 1800's to 1965

San Luis Valley
Western Valleys
Eastern Plains

J F M A M J J A S O N D
Seasonal Occurrence

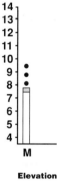

Elevation

Status (PH): Uncommon **spring** and **fall** migrant in the San Luis Valley. Rare migrant in western valleys; most records in Mesa, Delta, and Gunnison counties. Casual migrant on eastern plains (two spring records and eight fall records). Accidental in mountain parks in migration (two records) and in **summer** (two records). Colorado records since the early 1970s are of transplanted birds that summer in Idaho and winter in New Mexico. The transplantation effort has not been very successful and may soon be terminated; if so, this species will after a few years no longer occur as a regular migrant in Colorado.

Birds of the original wild population, which nests in Alberta and winters on the Texas coast, formerly occurred in migration on the eastern plains (Hersey and Rockwell 1909, Sclater 1912, Bergtold 1928), although never in great numbers. Most records were in the late 1800s, and there were only four records in this century prior to the transplantation efforts and hence which refer to the original flock. Although it is possible that individuals from the original flock may stray to eastern Colorado, recent individuals whose origin could be determined came from the transplanted flock (Dennis 1985).

Habitat: Mudflats around reservoirs and in agricultural areas.

Records: **Mid-20th century:** 20 June 1931, Ft. Collins, Larimer County (Bergtold 1931); 13–15 Oct 1941 and Oct 1942, near Kit Carson, Cheyenne County (Bailey and Niedrach 1965); 18 Oct 1965, Orchard, Morgan County (Bailey and Niedrach 1965). **Spring on eastern plains:** 12 Mar 1979, Fountain, El Paso County; 28 Feb 1982, Windsor, Weld County. **Migration in mountain parks:** 10 Apr 1988, Walden, Jackson County; 8 Oct 1989, Dillon Reservoir, Summit County. **Summer in mountain parks:** summer and fall 1980, Antero Reservoir, Park County; summer 1983, Kremmling, Grand County.

Reference: Shenk (1988).

Order Charadriiformes
Family Charadriidae

Black-bellied Plover
Pluvialis squatarola

Migrant in eastern Colorado; occasional elsewhere.

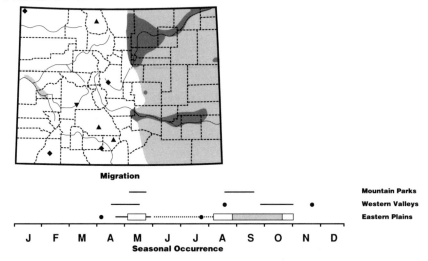

Migration

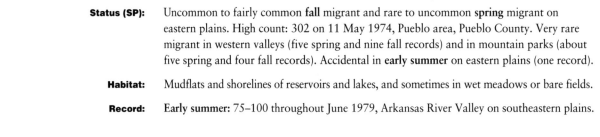

Mountain Parks
Western Valleys
Eastern Plains

J F M A M J J A S O N D
Seasonal Occurrence

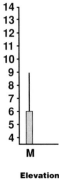

Elevation

Status (SP): Uncommon to fairly common **fall** migrant and rare to uncommon **spring** migrant on eastern plains. High count: 302 on 11 May 1974, Pueblo area, Pueblo County. Very rare migrant in western valleys (five spring and nine fall records) and in mountain parks (about five spring and four fall records). Accidental in **early summer** on eastern plains (one record).

Habitat: Mudflats and shorelines of reservoirs and lakes, and sometimes in wet meadows or bare fields.

Record: Early summer: 75–100 throughout June 1979, Arkansas River Valley on southeastern plains.

Lesser Golden-Plover
Pluvialis dominica

Migrant, primarily in fall; mostly in eastern Colorado.

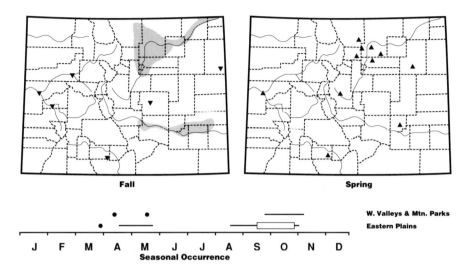

Fall   Spring

W. Valleys & Mtn. Parks

Eastern Plains

J F M A M J J A S O N D
Seasonal Occurrence

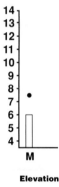

Elevation

Status (SP): Rare **fall** migrant on eastern plains. Very rare fall migrant in western valleys, mostly in Delta County (15 records). Accidental in San Luis Valley (one record). Very rare **spring** migrant on eastern plains (12 records) and accidental in mountain parks (two records) and in western valleys (one record). All Colorado records pertain to the subspecies *P. d. dominica;* there are no records of *P. d. fulva.*

Habitat: Mudflats and shorelines of reservoirs and lakes, and sometimes in wet meadows or bare fields.

Records: **Fall in San Luis Valley:** 20–21 Oct 1984, Monte Vista National Wildlife Refuge, Rio Grande County. **Spring in mountain parks:** 18 May (year unknown) Monte Vista National Wildlife Refuge; 21 May 1982, Antero Reservoir, Park County. **Spring in western valleys:** 11 Apr 1974, Fruita, Mesa County.

Snowy Plover
Charadrius alexandrinus

Uncommon in summer in southeastern Colorado; occasional elsewhere.

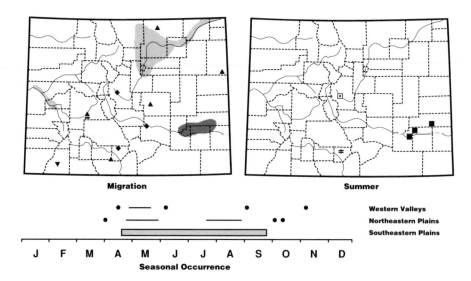

Migration   Summer

Western Valleys
Northeastern Plains
Southeastern Plains

J F M A M J J A S O N D

Seasonal Occurrence

Status (SP) (B): Uncommon **spring** and **fall** migrant and **summer** resident on southeastern plains from Otero County east to Kiowa County. The first state nesting record was in 1939 at Neegronda Reservoir, Kiowa County. Numbers fluctuate widely from year to year; in good years up to 40 nests have been found (Chase 1979). High count: 100 at Blue Lake, Kiowa/Bent counties and 50 at Cheraw Lake, Otero County on 12 Aug 1979. Uncommon at Antero Reservoir, Park County where it has been present in summer since 1971 and the first confirmed breeding was in 1983. Rare in the San Luis Valley. It nested in very small numbers from 1965 to 1984 at San Luis Lakes, Alamosa County, but there have been no nesting records since because the alkali flats were flooded by a water project.

Very rare spring migrant on northeastern plains (23 records) and in western valleys (13 records). Casual fall migrant on northeastern plains (10 records) and accidental in western valleys (two records).

Habitat: Breeding birds occur on alkali flats around reservoirs. Migrants also occur on mudflats and sandy shorelines.

Records: **Fall in western valleys:** 7 Nov 1964, Grand Junction, Mesa County (Davis 1969); 3 Sep 1981, Durango, La Plata County. **Specimen in western valleys:** May 1966, Gunnison, Gunnison County (DMNH 36722).

Note: This species is on the National Audubon Society Special Concern list (Tate 1986).

14
13
12
11
10
9
8
7
6
5
4

M,S

Elevation

Semipalmated Plover

Charadrius semipalmatus

Migrant in eastern Colorado; occasional elsewhere.

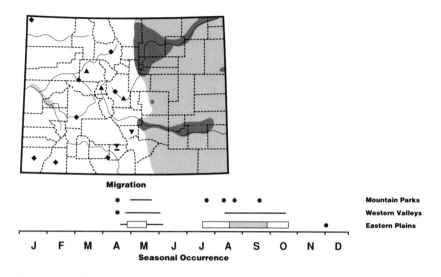

Migration

Mountain Parks
Western Valleys
Eastern Plains

J F M A M J J A S O N D

Seasonal Occurrence

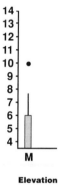

Elevation

Status (SP): Uncommon **fall** migrant and rare to uncommon **spring** migrant on eastern plains. High count: 33 on 14 May 1960, Ft. Collins, Larimer County. Very rare in western valleys, mostly in Mesa and Delta counties (about 24 records) and mountain parks (about 12 records).

Habitat: Mudflats and shorelines of reservoirs and lakes.

Piping Plover
Charadrius melodus

Very rare migrant in eastern Colorado; breeds in the southeast.

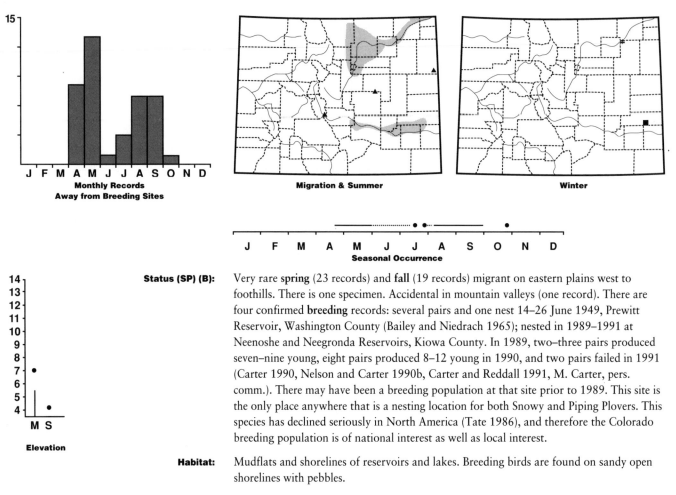

Migration & Summer   Winter

Monthly Records
Away from Breeding Sites

Seasonal Occurrence

Elevation

Status (SP) (B): Very rare **spring** (23 records) and **fall** (19 records) migrant on eastern plains west to foothills. There is one specimen. Accidental in mountain valleys (one record). There are four confirmed **breeding** records: several pairs and one nest 14–26 June 1949, Prewitt Reservoir, Washington County (Bailey and Niedrach 1965); nested in 1989–1991 at Neenoshe and Neegronda Reservoirs, Kiowa County. In 1989, two–three pairs produced seven–nine young, eight pairs produced 8–12 young in 1990, and two pairs failed in 1991 (Carter 1990, Nelson and Carter 1990b, Carter and Reddall 1991, M. Carter, pers. comm.). There may have been a breeding population at that site prior to 1989. This site is the only place anywhere that is a nesting location for both Snowy and Piping Plovers. This species has declined seriously in North America (Tate 1986), and therefore the Colorado breeding population is of national interest as well as local interest.

Habitat: Mudflats and shorelines of reservoirs and lakes. Breeding birds are found on sandy open shorelines with pebbles.

Records: **Mountain valleys:** 17 May 1986, Salida, Chaffee County. **Specimen:** 6 May 1939, Mile High Duck Club, Adams County (DMNH 20067); this record was also the first for Colorado.

Reference: Gray (1990).

Killdeer

Charadrius vociferus

Migrant and summer resident low elevations and in the mountain parks; rare in winter.

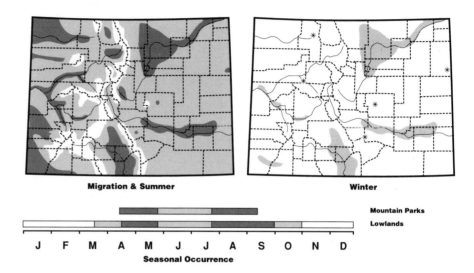

Migration & Summer   **Winter**

Mountain Parks
Lowlands

J   F   M   A   M   J   J   A   S   O   N   D

Seasonal Occurrence

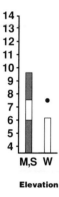

Elevation

Status (SP) (B): Common to abundant **spring** and **fall** migrant and fairly common to common **summer** resident in western valleys, mountain parks, and on eastern plains; rare to uncommon in foothills and mountains. Peak numbers occur during Aug and Sep around the large reservoirs on the eastern plains. Rare to fairly common local **winter** resident in western valleys, in the San Luis Valley, and on eastern plains.

Habitat: Shorelines, marsh edges, wet meadows, grasslands, and sparsely vegetated agricultural areas.

Mountain Plover
Charadrius montanus

Local summer resident on eastern plains; occasional elsewhere.

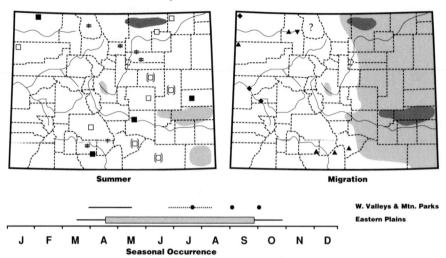

Summer   Migration

W. Valleys & Mtn. Parks
Eastern Plains

J F M A M J J A S O N D
Seasonal Occurrence

14
13
12
11
10
9
8
7
6
5
4

S M

Elevation

Status (SP) (B): Rare to fairly common **summer** resident locally on eastern plains. The greatest numbers occur in northern Weld County (Graul and Webster 1976), and smaller numbers occur locally in El Paso and Pueblo counties, along the northern edge of the Arkansas Valley in Crowley and Kiowa counties, and in Cheyenne and Baca counties. It also may occur very locally elsewhere. Rare in South Park. Accidental in the San Luis Valley (two records) and western valleys (three records). This species appears to be somewhat colonial when nesting, and breeding areas may shift locally from one year to the next (Leachman and Osmundson 1990).

Common to abundant **fall** migrant locally in Weld County and in the lower Arkansas Valley in Crowley, Bent, and Kiowa counties. High counts: 2,500 on 23 Sep 1972, Pawnee National Grassland, Weld County; 500 in Aug 1990, Neesopah Reservoir, Kiowa County. Rare spring and fall migrant elsewhere on eastern plains (primarily fall). Casual migrant (three **spring** records and four **fall** records) in northwestern and west-central valleys and in the San Luis Valley (three spring records).

This species was once widespread in eastern Colorado, but the conversion of the prairies to croplands drastically reduced available habitat. It nested in Boulder County in the 1880s (Betts 1913), in the Barr Lake area, Adams County, until the early 1900s (Hersey and Rockwell 1909), and in Larimer and Arapahoe counties early in the century (Graul and Webster 1976). There have been no recent records from Boulder County, and the species is a casual fall migrant in the Barr Lake area (Andrews and Carter 1992). In the late 1800s and early 1900s this species also occurred commonly and nested around the periphery of the San Luis Valley (Henshaw 1875, Warren 1910, Sclater 1912). There was one nesting record in Jackson County in 1911 (Warren 1912).

In recent years the stronghold of this species in Colorado has been in Weld County, which had an estimated population of 21,000 birds in 1967–68 (Graul and Webster 1976). By 1991 there were approximately 1,971 in Weld County, and perhaps 1,000 elsewhere in Colorado for a statewide population of about 3,000 birds (Knopf 1991). Weld County, Colorado and Phillips County, Montana hold about half of the breeding population of this species (Knopf 1991), which is proposed for listing under the Endangered Species Act (F. Knopf, pers. comm.).

Habitat: Short-grass grassland, occurring primarily on level areas with very short grass and scattered cactus and avoiding taller grass and hillsides (Graul 1975). Suitable areas occur where grazing is intensive. In other states active prairie dog towns are an important habitat (Knowles et al. 1982) and this also appears to be true in Colorado (F. Knopf, pers. comm.). Migrants sometimes occur on dry mudflats and shorelines of dry reservoirs.

Records: **Summer in San Luis Valley:** adult with downy young 26 June 1978 near Capulin, Conejos County; three birds courting 11 May 1991, near Saguache, Saguache County. **Summer in western valleys:** observed and possibly nesting in 1979 and 1980 near Rangely, Rio Blanco County; adult with chicks 12 July 1989, Moffat County near Wyoming border (Leachman and Osmundson 1990).

References: Graul (1973, 1976a, b), McCaffery et al. (1984).

Order Charadriiformes
Family Recurvirostridae

Black-necked Stilt
Himantopus mexicanus

Summer resident in southeastern Colorado; occasional elsewhere, mostly in migration.

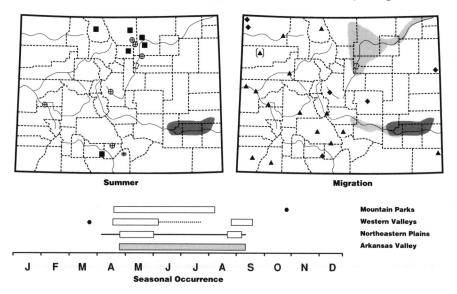

Summer   Migration

Mountain Parks
Western Valleys
Northeastern Plains
Arkansas Valley

J   F   M   A   M   J   J   A   S   O   N   D
Seasonal Occurrence

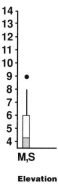

Elevation

Status (SP) (B): Uncommon to fairly common **summer** resident on southeastern plains in Crowley, Otero, Kiowa, and Bent counties. Rare breeder in San Luis Valley in Rio Grande and Alamosa counties and in North Park at Arapaho National Wildlife Refuge, Jackson County (USFWS 1989, 1990). Casual on northeastern plains, with four confirmed breeding records at Windsor and Lower Latham reservoirs, Weld County, near Boulder, Boulder County, and at Ft. Collins, Larimer County. Birds seen at other sites in June and July were suspected of breeding, but without confirmation. Casual nonbreeder in western valleys (three records) and in South Park (one record). Nesting in southeastern Colorado appears to be a recent phenomenon as the only breeding record mentioned by Bailey and Niedrach (1965) was in the last century in Alamosa County. It is not clear when they first nested in southeastern Colorado; birds were seen in the summer of 1978 but no nests were found (Chase 1979); there was one nest found in 1979.

Rare **spring** and **fall** migrant in western valleys and on eastern plains. Casual in mountain parks (five spring records and one fall record).

Habitat: Breeding birds occur on alkaline flats around lakes and ponds. Migrants occur on lake, pond, and marsh shorelines and edges.

Records: **Summer in western valleys:** 2 July 1984, 18 July 1985, and 10–11 June 1986, near Delta, Delta County. **Summer in mountain parks:** 14 June 1975, Antero Reservoir, Park County.

American Avocet

Recurvirostra americana

Migrant and summer resident at low elevations and in the mountain parks.

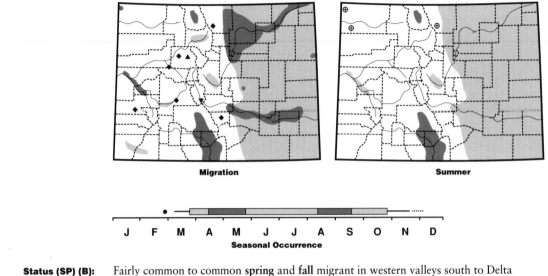

Migration   Summer

Seasonal Occurrence

J F M A M J J A S O N D

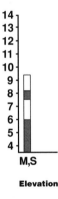

M,S

Elevation

Status (SP) (B): Fairly common to common **spring** and **fall** migrant in western valleys south to Delta County, in North Park, the San Luis Valley, and on eastern plains. High count: 400+ on 12 Aug 1956, Barr Lake, Adams County. Rare to uncommon in southwestern valleys and in other mountain parks. Fairly common **summer** resident in North Park and the San Luis Valley, and uncommon locally in western valleys south to Delta County and on eastern plains. Breeding in western valleys is a recent development: nesting was first recorded at Delta, Delta County in 1986 and at Grand Junction, Mesa County in 1987.

Habitat: Breeding birds occur around lake and marsh shorelines, especially those with alkali flats. Migrants are found around most reservoir and lake shorelines.

Order Charadriiformes
Family Scolopacidae

Greater Yellowlegs
Tringa melanoleuca

Migrant at low elevations and in the mountain parks; occasional in winter.

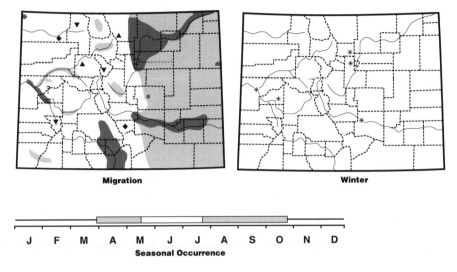

Migration   Winter

J F M A M J J A S O N D
Seasonal Occurrence

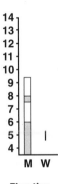

Elevation

Status (SP): Uncommon **spring** and **fall** migrant in northwestern and west-central valleys, in the San Luis Valley, and on eastern plains. Rare in southwestern valleys and in other mountain parks. Casual in mountains outside parks (five records) in Mesa, Summit, and Larimer Counties. Rare in **early summer** in western valleys, in North Park, the San Luis Valley, and on eastern plains; these birds would be either late spring migrants or early fall migrants. Casual **winter** resident, recorded in Mesa and Delta counties and from Boulder County south to Pueblo County. A single individual was observed annually at Wheat Ridge, Jefferson County from 1982–1988; there are 10 records from other sites.

Habitat: Reservoir and lake shorelines and wet grassy meadows.

Lesser Yellowlegs

Tringa flavipes

Migrant at low elevations and in mountain parks.

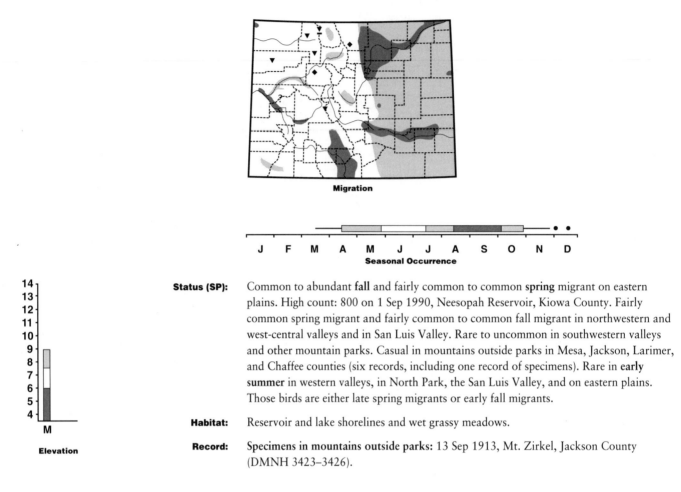

Migration

J F M A M J J A S O N D
Seasonal Occurrence

Elevation

Status (SP): Common to abundant **fall** and fairly common to common **spring** migrant on eastern plains. High count: 800 on 1 Sep 1990, Neesopah Reservoir, Kiowa County. Fairly common spring migrant and fairly common to common fall migrant in northwestern and west-central valleys and in San Luis Valley. Rare to uncommon in southwestern valleys and other mountain parks. Casual in mountains outside parks in Mesa, Jackson, Larimer, and Chaffee counties (six records, including one record of specimens). Rare in **early summer** in western valleys, in North Park, the San Luis Valley, and on eastern plains. Those birds are either late spring migrants or early fall migrants.

Habitat: Reservoir and lake shorelines and wet grassy meadows.

Record: Specimens in mountains outside parks: 13 Sep 1913, Mt. Zirkel, Jackson County (DMNH 3423–3426).

Solitary Sandpiper

Tringa solitaria

Migrant in eastern Colorado and occasional elsewhere.

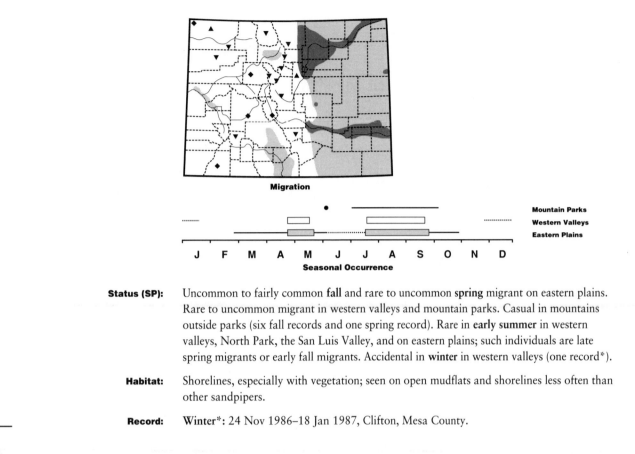

Migration

Seasonal Occurrence

Mountain Parks
Western Valleys
Eastern Plains

Elevation

Status (SP): Uncommon to fairly common **fall** and rare to uncommon **spring** migrant on eastern plains. Rare to uncommon migrant in western valleys and mountain parks. Casual in mountains outside parks (six fall records and one spring record). Rare in **early summer** in western valleys, North Park, the San Luis Valley, and on eastern plains; such individuals are late spring migrants or early fall migrants. Accidental in **winter** in western valleys (one record*).

Habitat: Shorelines, especially with vegetation; seen on open mudflats and shorelines less often than other sandpipers.

Record: Winter*: 24 Nov 1986–18 Jan 1987, Clifton, Mesa County.

Willet

Catoptrophorus semipalmatus

Migrant in lowlands and mountain parks; breeds in North Park.

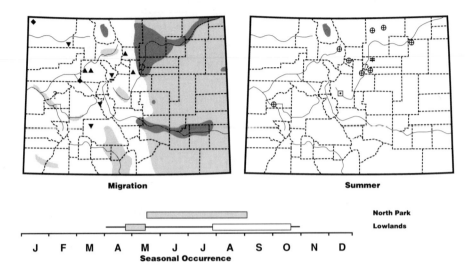

Migration   Summer

North Park

Lowlands

J F M A M J J A S O N D
Seasonal Occurrence

Elevation

Status (SP) (B):   Uncommon to fairly common **spring** migrant and rare to uncommon **fall** migrant on eastern plains. High count: 200 on 28 Apr 1984, Pawnee National Grassland, Weld County. Rare to uncommon spring migrant and rare fall migrant in western valleys and mountain parks. Casual in mountains outside parks (five records).

Uncommon to fairly common **summer** resident in North Park. It nested in the Barr Lake area, Adams County in 1931 and 1936 (Bailey and Niedrach 1965) and at Antero Reservoir, Park County in 1982–83 and probably in 1981. Rare in early summer on eastern plains and also recorded in Delta County (five records) and in Middle Park (one record); some of those birds were suspected of nesting, although many were probably nonbreeders.

Habitat: Breeds in grassy marshes. Migrants occur along reservoir and lake shorelines and in wet grassy meadows and marshes.

Spotted Sandpiper
Actitis macularia

Migrant and summer resident throughout state below timberline.

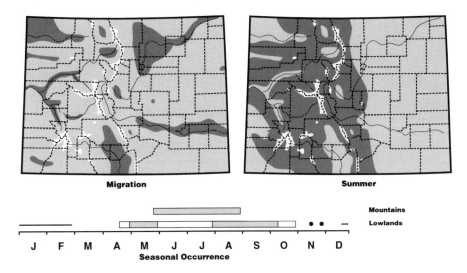

Migration   Summer

Mountains
Lowlands

J   F   M   A   M   J   J   A   S   O   N   D
Seasonal Occurrence

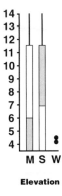

Elevation

Status (SP) (B): Uncommon to fairly common **spring** and **fall** migrant in western valleys, mountains, mountain parks, and on eastern plains. Uncommon to fairly common **summer** resident in western valleys, mountains and mountain parks, and rare to uncommon on eastern plains. Rare above timberline in summer and fall. Casual **winter** resident in west-central valleys in Mesa County (six records); accidental on northeastern plains in early winter (one record).

Habitat: Shorelines of reservoirs, ponds, rivers, and streams.

Record: Early winter on northeastern plains: 21 Dec 1970, Brush, Morgan County.

Upland Sandpiper

Bartramia longicauda

Summer resident in extreme northeastern Colorado; occasional elsewhere.

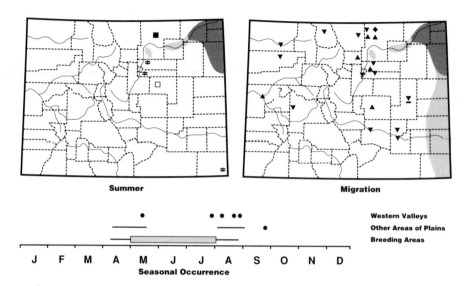

Summer   Migration

Western Valleys
Other Areas of Plains
Breeding Areas

J   F   M   A   M   J   J   A   S   O   N   D
Seasonal Occurrence

Elevation

Status (SP) (B): Uncommon to fairly common **summer** resident on northeastern plains west to Logan County and south to Yuma County; rare to uncommon west to Morgan County. There is a small population between Hudson and Kersey, southwestern Weld County, and there is one recent breeding record near Briggsdale, Weld County. The species occurred as a breeder west to the Barr Lake area, Adams County as late as 1908 (Hersey and Rockwell 1909, Rockwell 1912) and up to 1924 in western Arapahoe County (Bailey and Niedrach 1965). Accidental on southeastern plains (one breeding record).

Very rare **spring** and **fall** migrant on southeastern plains (16 records). This species is a common migrant in July and Aug in western Kansas, when it is often heard at night (S. Seltman, pers. comm.); it is probably more common in eastern Colorado than most observers realize. Casual on northeastern plains near the foothills (nine records since 1969); apparently it was more common earlier in the century, when many specimens were brought to market in Colorado Springs, El Paso County (Sclater 1912), and Bergtold (1928) considered it an abundant migrant. Casual migrant in western valleys (one spring record and five fall records). Accidental in mountains (two records) and mountain parks (one record).

Habitat: Tall-grass sandhill grassland and moist meadows. Migrants have also been recorded in short-grass grassland and cropland.

Records: **Breeding in Weld County (outside Hudson area):** downy young 28 June 1969, near Briggsdale. **Breeding on southeastern plains:** nest with eggs 20 May 1923, Baca County (Bailey and Niedrach 1965). **Migration in western valleys:** 6 Aug 1905, Lay, Moffat County and 9 Aug 1905, Meeker, Rio Blanco County (Cary 1909); 10 Aug 1909 near Meeker, Rio Blanco County and 28 Aug 1909, Buford, Rio Blanco County (Felger 1910); 12 May 1986, Clifton, Mesa County. **Migration in mountains:** unknown date at 6,800 ft. in Plateau Creek Valley, Mesa County (Rockwell 1908); 9 Aug 1907, West Elk Mountains, Gunnison County (Cary 1909). **Fall in mountain parks:** 22 Aug 1987, Arapaho National Wildlife Refuge, Jackson County.

Note: This species is on the National Audubon Society Blue List (Tate 1986).

Eskimo Curlew
Numenius borealis

Status (SP): Accidental **spring** migrant (one record*).

Record: Two collected on 29 Apr 1882, Denver, Denver County (FMNH 406960, SDNHM 20936). This species is near extinction, and additional records are unlikely.

Whimbrel
Numenius phaeopus

Rare in spring in eastern Colorado; occasional in fall.

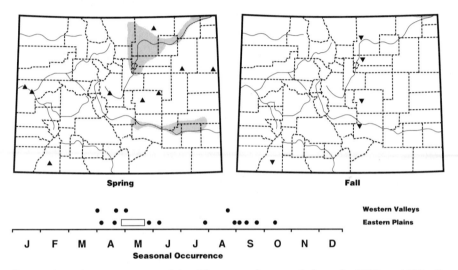

Spring   Fall

Western Valleys
Eastern Plains

J F M A M J J A S O N D
Seasonal Occurrence

Elevation

Status (SP): Rare **spring** migrant on eastern plains. There were five records from the 1880s to 1909; all of the remaining 90+ records were 1952 and later. During the late 1980s, up to 50 birds were reported each year; many observations were of flocks of 5–10 individuals. High count: 90+ from 10–13 May 1976, Union Reservoir, Weld County. Casual spring migrant in western valleys; recorded only from Mesa and La Plata counties (seven records). Accidental in mountain parks (one record). Casual **fall** migrant on eastern plains (seven records) and accidental in western valleys (one record). There is one specimen.

Habitat: Shorelines of reservoirs, lakes, and rain ponds.

Records: **Spring in mountain parks:** 18 May 1986, Antero Reservoir, Park County. **Fall in western valleys:** 21 Aug 1984, Durango, La Plata County. **Specimen:** 15 May 1953, Union Reservoir, Weld County (DMNH 26738).

Long-billed Curlew

Numenius americanus

Local summer resident in southeastern Colorado; occasional elsewhere.

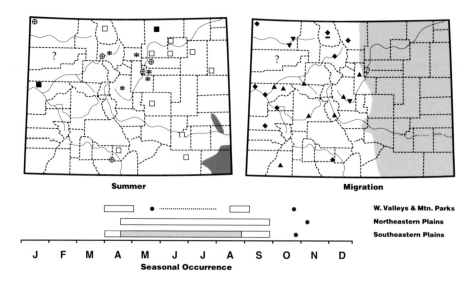

Summer   **Migration**

W. Valleys & Mtn. Parks

Northeastern Plains

Southeastern Plains

J F M A M J J A S O N D

Seasonal Occurrence

Elevation

Status (SP) (B): Uncommon to fairly common local **summer** resident on southeastern plains. This species is most common in Baca County (McCallum et al. 1977), and also breeds in Prowers and Kiowa counties. Rare elsewhere on eastern plains, such as in Yuma County and at the Pawnee National Grassland, Weld County, where the only recent nest was one in 1969 (Graul 1971). High count: 64 on 8 July 1988, Neeskah Reservoir, Kiowa County. Accidental breeder in western valleys (two records), and probably nests in North Park and the San Luis Valley.

Rare **spring** and **fall** migrant in western valleys, mountain parks, and on eastern plains. Accidental in mountains outside parks (one record).

This species was formerly abundant throughout eastern Colorado (Bergtold 1928), and also nested in Middle and South Parks in the 1870s (Sclater 1912, McCallum et al. 1977). In the early 1900s it still occurred throughout the eastern plains west to Boulder and Adams counties (Felger 1909, Hersey and Rockwell 1909, Betts 1913). Nesting was recorded as late as 1931 in Douglas County (Niedrach and Rockwell 1939) and in 1956 in Arapahoe County (Bailey and Niedrach 1965). This species is on the National Audubon Society Special Concern List (Tate 1986) and is a candidate for listing under the Endangered Species Act (Knopf 1988).

Habitat: Short-grass grasslands and sometimes in wheatfields or fallow fields. Most nests are close to standing water, so that many otherwise suitable areas may be unoccupied (McCallum et al. 1977). Migrants also are seen on shorelines and in meadows and fields.

Records: **Summer in western valleys:** two adults and one young 18 July 1982, Fruita, Mesa County; nesting 12 July 1985, north of Highline Canal, Mesa County. **Summer in North Park:** 1974 or 1975 (McCallum et al. 1977); 16–18 June 1984; June–July 1988 and 23 June 1989, Arapaho National Wildlife Refuge, Jackson County. **Summer in San Luis Valley:** 15 June 1975, San Luis Lake, Alamosa County (McCallum et al. 1977). **Mountains outside parks:** 1 May 1973, Evergreen, Jefferson County.

Hudsonian Godwit

Limosa haemastica

Very rare in spring in eastern Colorado.

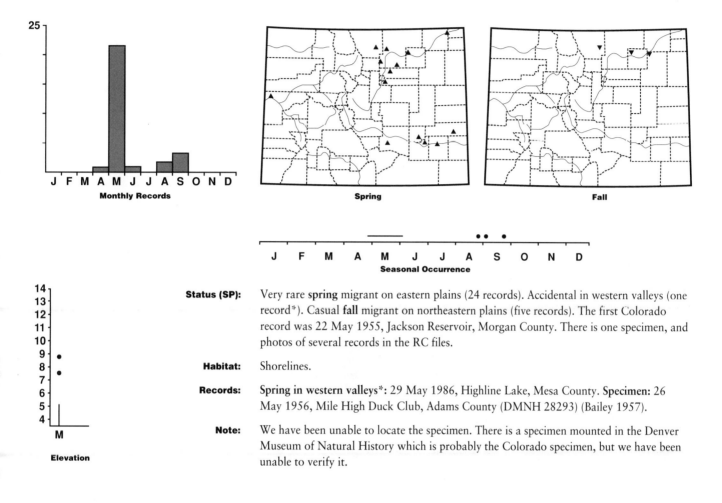

Monthly Records

Spring

Fall

Seasonal Occurrence

Elevation

Status (SP): Very rare **spring** migrant on eastern plains (24 records). Accidental in western valleys (one record*). Casual **fall** migrant on northeastern plains (five records). The first Colorado record was 22 May 1955, Jackson Reservoir, Morgan County. There is one specimen, and photos of several records in the RC files.

Habitat: Shorelines.

Records: **Spring in western valleys***: 29 May 1986, Highline Lake, Mesa County. **Specimen:** 26 May 1956, Mile High Duck Club, Adams County (DMNH 28293) (Bailey 1957).

Note: We have been unable to locate the specimen. There is a specimen mounted in the Denver Museum of Natural History which is probably the Colorado specimen, but we have been unable to verify it.

Marbled Godwit

Limosa fedoa

Migrant at low elevations and in mountain parks; more common in spring than in fall.

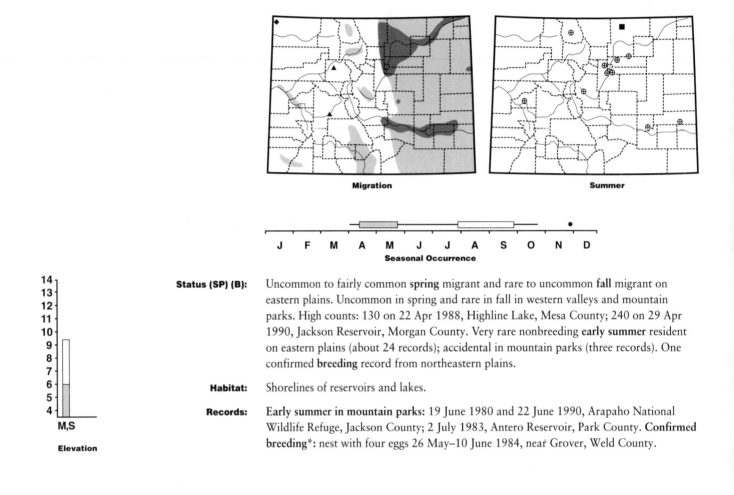

Migration   Summer

Seasonal Occurrence

Elevation

Status (SP) (B): Uncommon to fairly common **spring** migrant and rare to uncommon **fall** migrant on eastern plains. Uncommon in spring and rare in fall in western valleys and mountain parks. High counts: 130 on 22 Apr 1988, Highline Lake, Mesa County; 240 on 29 Apr 1990, Jackson Reservoir, Morgan County. Very rare nonbreeding **early summer** resident on eastern plains (about 24 records); accidental in mountain parks (three records). One confirmed **breeding** record from northeastern plains.

Habitat: Shorelines of reservoirs and lakes.

Records: **Early summer in mountain parks:** 19 June 1980 and 22 June 1990, Arapaho National Wildlife Refuge, Jackson County; 2 July 1983, Antero Reservoir, Park County. **Confirmed breeding*:** nest with four eggs 26 May–10 June 1984, near Grover, Weld County.

Ruddy Turnstone
Arenaria interpres

Very rare in migration in eastern Colorado.

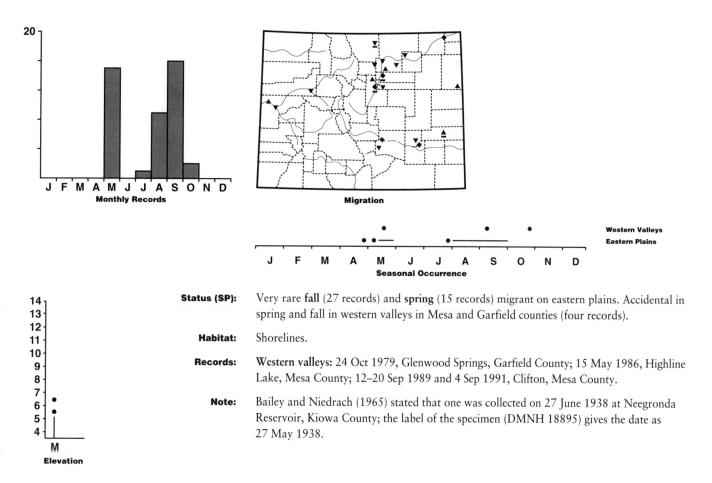

Status (SP): Very rare **fall** (27 records) and **spring** (15 records) migrant on eastern plains. Accidental in spring and fall in western valleys in Mesa and Garfield counties (four records).

Habitat: Shorelines.

Records: **Western valleys:** 24 Oct 1979, Glenwood Springs, Garfield County; 15 May 1986, Highline Lake, Mesa County; 12–20 Sep 1989 and 4 Sep 1991, Clifton, Mesa County.

Note: Bailey and Niedrach (1965) stated that one was collected on 27 June 1938 at Neegronda Reservoir, Kiowa County; the label of the specimen (DMNH 18895) gives the date as 27 May 1938.

Red Knot
Calidris canutus

Migrant in eastern Colorado.

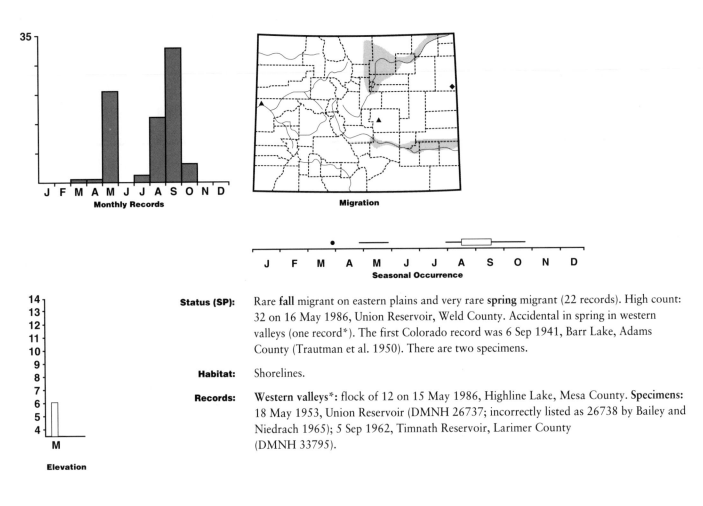

Monthly Records

Migration

Seasonal Occurrence

Elevation

Status (SP): Rare **fall** migrant on eastern plains and very rare **spring** migrant (22 records). High count: 32 on 16 May 1986, Union Reservoir, Weld County. Accidental in spring in western valleys (one record*). The first Colorado record was 6 Sep 1941, Barr Lake, Adams County (Trautman et al. 1950). There are two specimens.

Habitat: Shorelines.

Records: Western valleys*: flock of 12 on 15 May 1986, Highline Lake, Mesa County. **Specimens:** 18 May 1953, Union Reservoir (DMNH 26737; incorrectly listed as 26738 by Bailey and Niedrach 1965); 5 Sep 1962, Timnath Reservoir, Larimer County (DMNH 33795).

Sanderling
Calidris alba

Migrant in eastern Colorado; occasional elsewhere.

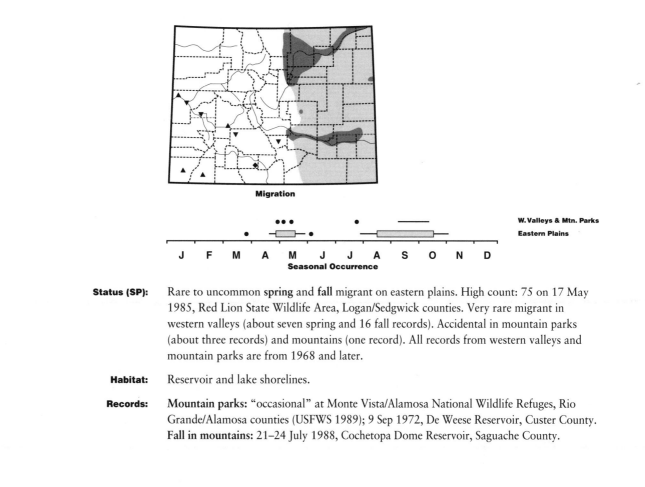

Status (SP): Rare to uncommon **spring** and **fall** migrant on eastern plains. High count: 75 on 17 May 1985, Red Lion State Wildlife Area, Logan/Sedgwick counties. Very rare migrant in western valleys (about seven spring and 16 fall records). Accidental in mountain parks (about three records) and mountains (one record). All records from western valleys and mountain parks are from 1968 and later.

Habitat: Reservoir and lake shorelines.

Records: **Mountain parks:** "occasional" at Monte Vista/Alamosa National Wildlife Refuges, Rio Grande/Alamosa counties (USFWS 1989); 9 Sep 1972, De Weese Reservoir, Custer County. **Fall in mountains:** 21–24 July 1988, Cochetopa Dome Reservoir, Saguache County.

Semipalmated Sandpiper
Calidris pusilla

Migrant in eastern Colorado; occasional elsewhere.

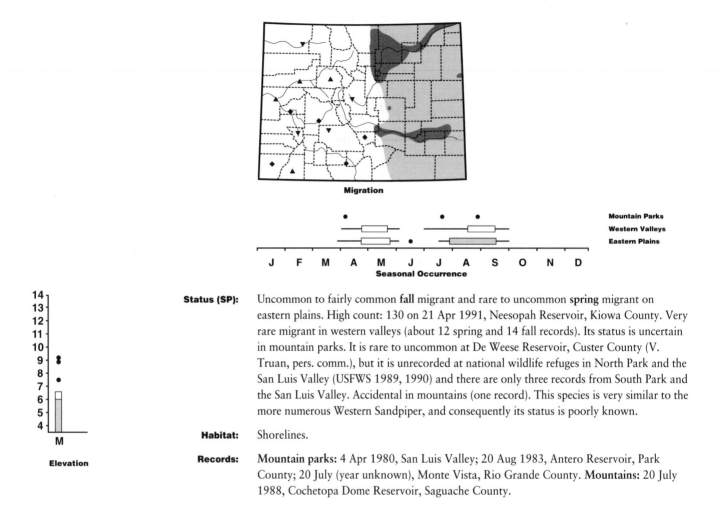

Migration

Mountain Parks
Western Valleys
Eastern Plains

J F M A M J J A S O N D

Seasonal Occurrence

Elevation

Status (SP): Uncommon to fairly common **fall** migrant and rare to uncommon **spring** migrant on eastern plains. High count: 130 on 21 Apr 1991, Neesopah Reservoir, Kiowa County. Very rare migrant in western valleys (about 12 spring and 14 fall records). Its status is uncertain in mountain parks. It is rare to uncommon at De Weese Reservoir, Custer County (V. Truan, pers. comm.), but it is unrecorded at national wildlife refuges in North Park and the San Luis Valley (USFWS 1989, 1990) and there are only three records from South Park and the San Luis Valley. Accidental in mountains (one record). This species is very similar to the more numerous Western Sandpiper, and consequently its status is poorly known.

Habitat: Shorelines.

Records: **Mountain parks:** 4 Apr 1980, San Luis Valley; 20 Aug 1983, Antero Reservoir, Park County; 20 July (year unknown), Monte Vista, Rio Grande County. **Mountains:** 20 July 1988, Cochetopa Dome Reservoir, Saguache County.

Western Sandpiper

Calidris mauri

Migrant at low elevations and in mountain parks; most common in fall.

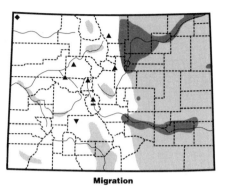

Migration

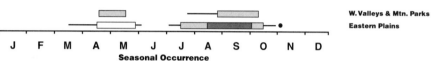

W. Valleys & Mtn. Parks

Eastern Plains

J F M A M J J A S O N D

Seasonal Occurrence

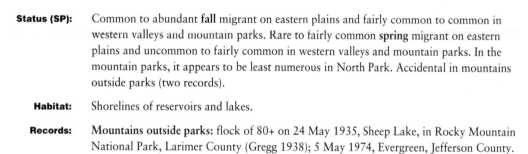

M

Elevation

Status (SP): Common to abundant **fall** migrant on eastern plains and fairly common to common in western valleys and mountain parks. Rare to fairly common **spring** migrant on eastern plains and uncommon to fairly common in western valleys and mountain parks. In the mountain parks, it appears to be least numerous in North Park. Accidental in mountains outside parks (two records).

Habitat: Shorelines of reservoirs and lakes.

Records: **Mountains outside parks:** flock of 80+ on 24 May 1935, Sheep Lake, in Rocky Mountain National Park, Larimer County (Gregg 1938); 5 May 1974, Evergreen, Jefferson County.

Reference: Senner and Martinez (1982).

Least Sandpiper

Calidris minutilla

Migrant at low elevations and in mountain parks; most numerous in fall.

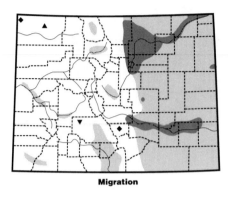

Migration

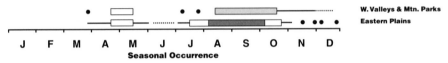

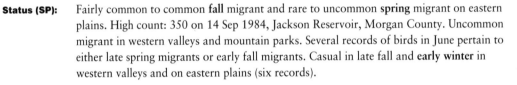

W. Valleys & Mtn. Parks

Eastern Plains

J F M A M J J A S O N D

Seasonal Occurrence

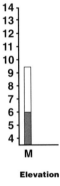

Elevation

Status (SP): Fairly common to common **fall** migrant and rare to uncommon **spring** migrant on eastern plains. High count: 350 on 14 Sep 1984, Jackson Reservoir, Morgan County. Uncommon migrant in western valleys and mountain parks. Several records of birds in June pertain to either late spring migrants or early fall migrants. Casual in late fall and **early winter** in western valleys and on eastern plains (six records).

Habitat: Reservoir and lake shorelines and wet meadows.

White-rumped Sandpiper

Calidris fuscicollis

Late spring migrant in extreme eastern Colorado.

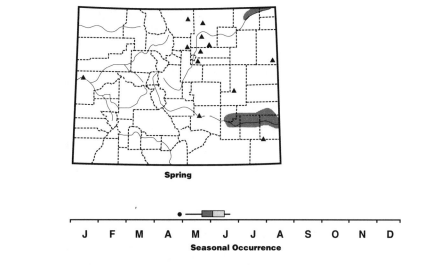

Spring

Seasonal Occurrence

J F M A M J J A S O N D

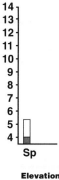

Elevation

Status (SP): Fairly common to common **spring** migrant on extreme eastern plains. High count: 121 on 1 June 1989, Red Lion State Wildlife Area, Logan/Sedgwick counties and 120 on 26 May 1991, Horse Creek Reservoir, Otero/Bent counties. Rare west to near foothills. It was apparently more common formerly, as Hersey and Rockwell (1909) found it fairly common in the Barr Lake area, Adams County, where it is now rare. Accidental in western valleys (one record*).

There are 27 **fall** reports, but they either lack documentation or have only minimal details. Whereas the main spring migration route of this species is on the Great Plains, the fall migration route is primarily along the east coast, and it would be very unusual in Colorado in fall. Therefore, all fall reports should be carefully documented.

Habitat: Reservoir and lake shorelines.

Record: **Spring in western valleys*:** 3 June 1986, Highline Lake, Mesa County.

Baird's Sandpiper
Calidris bairdii

Migrant at low elevations and in the mountain parks; most abundant in fall in eastern Colorado.

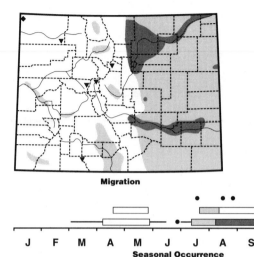

Migration

Above Timberline
W. Valleys & Mtn. Parks
Eastern Plains

J F M A M J J A S O N D
Seasonal Occurrence

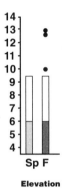

Sp F

Elevation

Status (SP): Common to abundant **fall** migrant on eastern plains. High count: 3,000 on 4 Sep 1977, Jackson Reservoir, Morgan County. Uncommon to fairly common in western valleys and mountain parks. Casual above timberline (five records). Rare to uncommon **spring** migrant on eastern plains and rare to uncommon in western valleys and mountain parks. Accidental above timberline (one record). Several records of birds in June pertain to either late spring migrants or early fall migrants. There is a **mid-winter** specimen (2 Jan 1942, Barr Lake, Adams County, DMNH 23966). However, Jehl (1979) thought the date "unbelievable."

Habitat: Reservoir and lake shorelines; often found on the drier parts of mudflats.

Record: Spring above **timberline:** June (year unknown), Trail Ridge Road in Rocky Mountain National Park, Larimer County (Bailey and Niedrach 1965).

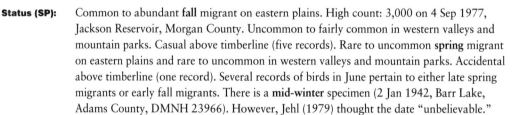

Pectoral Sandpiper

Calidris melanotos

Migrant in eastern Colorado; occasional elsewhere.

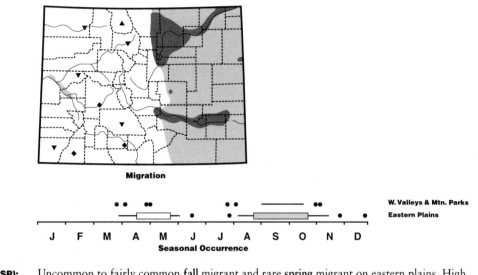

Migration

W. Valleys & Mtn. Parks

Eastern Plains

J F M A M J J A S O N D

Seasonal Occurrence

Status (SP): Uncommon to fairly common **fall** migrant and rare **spring** migrant on eastern plains. High count: 150 on 5 Sep 1981 and 23 Sep 1984, Jackson Reservoir, Morgan County. Very rare fall migrant in western valleys (about 17 fall records) and casual in spring (six records). Most records in western valleys are in Mesa and Delta counties. Apparently a casual migrant in mountain parks (about six records), probably mostly in fall. Accidental in **early winter** on northeastern plains (one record*).

Habitat: Shorelines of reservoirs and lakes and wet meadows.

Record: **Early winter on plains***: 26 Dec 1981, near Barr Lake, Adams County.

14
13
12
11
10
9
8
7
6
5
4

M

Elevation

Sharp-tailed Sandpiper
Calidris acuminata

Status (PH): Accidental **fall** migrant (one record*).

Record: 26 Oct–6 Nov 1975, near Lafayette, Boulder County (Webb and Conry 1979, includes color photo).

Dunlin
Calidris alpina

Very rare in migration in eastern Colorado; occasional elsewhere.

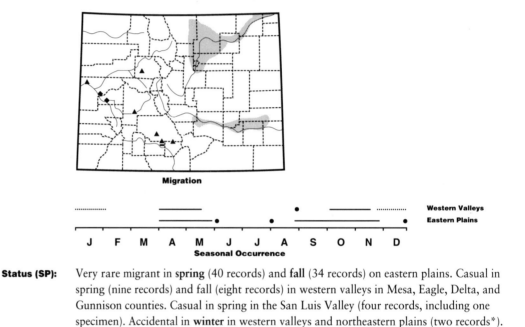

Migration

Seasonal Occurrence

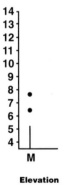

Elevation

Status (SP): Very rare migrant in **spring** (40 records) and **fall** (34 records) on eastern plains. Casual in spring (nine records) and fall (eight records) in western valleys in Mesa, Eagle, Delta, and Gunnison counties. Casual in spring in the San Luis Valley (four records, including one specimen). Accidental in **winter** in western valleys and northeastern plains (two records*). There are three specimens.

Habitat: Shorelines of reservoirs and lakes.

Records: Winter*: 30 Dec 1958, St. Vrain Creek, east of Longmont in Weld County (DMNH 33715); flock of four–five from 19 Oct 1985–2 Feb 1986, near Delta, Delta County. **Specimens:** 2 May 1937, Barr Lake area, Adams County (DMNH 17172); 5 May 1950, Center, Saguache County (DMNH 26132); 30 Dec 1958, St. Vrain Creek, east of Longmont in Weld County (DMNH 33715).

Stilt Sandpiper
Calidris himantopus

Migrant in eastern Colorado; occasional elsewhere.

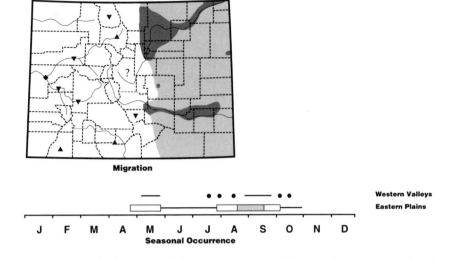

Migration

Western Valleys
Eastern Plains

J F M A M J J A S O N D
Seasonal Occurrence

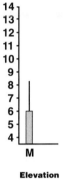

Elevation

Status (SP): Uncommon to fairly common **fall** migrant on eastern plains; may be common or abundant locally. High count: 2,000 on 4 Sep 1977, Jackson Reservoir, Morgan County. This species has increased in eastern Colorado; Bergtold (1928) regarded it as a rare migrant. Very rare in western valleys (about 18 records). Accidental in mountain parks (two records). Rare to uncommon **spring** migrant on eastern plains. Casual in western valleys (five records) and accidental in mountain parks (two records). Several records in June pertain to late spring migrants and early fall migrants. All western valley records were from 1969 and later.

Habitat: Shorelines of reservoirs and lakes.

Records: **Fall in mountain parks:** 26 Aug 1989, De Weese Reservoir, Custer County; 27 Sep 1989, Walden Reservoir, Jackson County. **Spring in mountain parks.** 9 May 1884, Grand County; 28 May 1978, Monte Vista National Wildlife Refuge, Rio Grande County.

Note: A specimen listed for 13 Dec at Barr Lake, Adams County (DMNH 977) by Bailey and Niedrach (1965) was actually collected on 13 Oct.

Buff-breasted Sandpiper

Tryngites subruficollis

Very rare in fall in eastern Colorado.

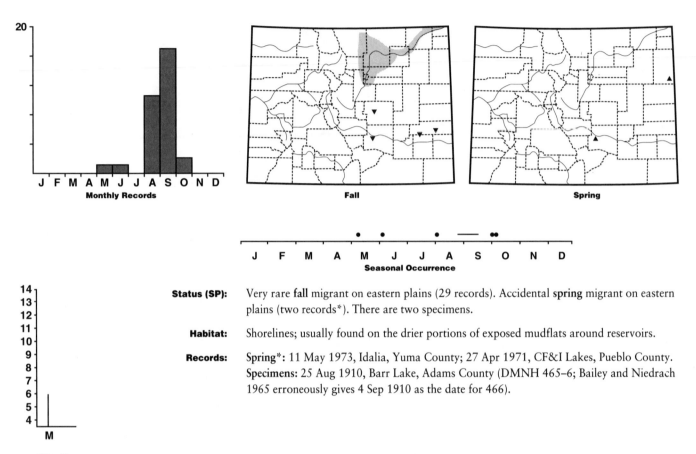

Fall

Spring

Monthly Records

Seasonal Occurrence

Elevation

Status (SP):	Very rare **fall** migrant on eastern plains (29 records). Accidental **spring** migrant on eastern plains (two records*). There are two specimens.
Habitat:	Shorelines; usually found on the drier portions of exposed mudflats around reservoirs.
Records:	**Spring***: 11 May 1973, Idalia, Yuma County; 27 Apr 1971, CF&I Lakes, Pueblo County. **Specimens**: 25 Aug 1910, Barr Lake, Adams County (DMNH 465–6; Bailey and Niedrach 1965 erroneously gives 4 Sep 1910 as the date for 466).

Ruff
Philomachus pugnax

Status (SR): Accidental in **spring** and **fall** on northeastern plains (two records*).

Records: 30 May–1 June 1977, near Prospect Reservoir, Weld County; 21 Aug 1983, Lower Latham Reservoir, Weld County.

Short-billed Dowitcher
Limnodromus griseus

Migrant in eastern Colorado; status still uncertain.

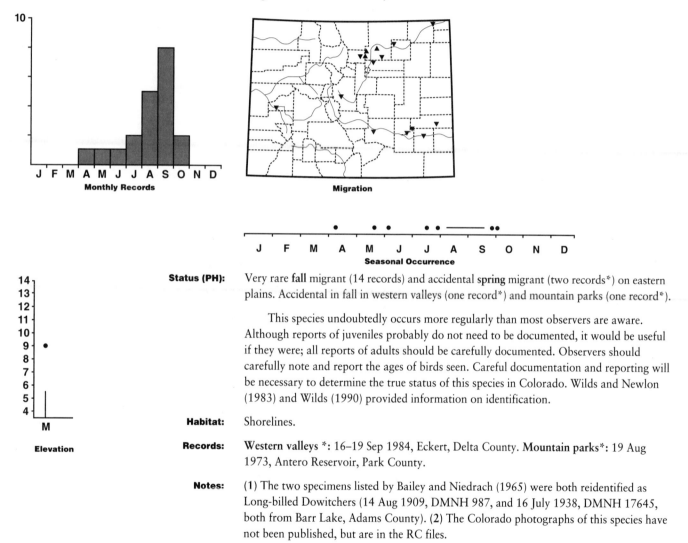

Status (PH): Very rare **fall** migrant (14 records) and accidental **spring** migrant (two records*) on eastern plains. Accidental in fall in western valleys (one record*) and mountain parks (one record*).

This species undoubtedly occurs more regularly than most observers are aware. Although reports of juveniles probably do not need to be documented, it would be useful if they were; all reports of adults should be carefully documented. Observers should carefully note and report the ages of birds seen. Careful documentation and reporting will be necessary to determine the true status of this species in Colorado. Wilds and Newlon (1983) and Wilds (1990) provided information on identification.

Habitat: Shorelines.

Records: **Western valleys** *: 16–19 Sep 1984, Eckert, Delta County. **Mountain parks***: 19 Aug 1973, Antero Reservoir, Park County.

Notes: (1) The two specimens listed by Bailey and Niedrach (1965) were both reidentified as Long-billed Dowitchers (14 Aug 1909, DMNH 987, and 16 July 1938, DMNH 17645, both from Barr Lake, Adams County). (2) The Colorado photographs of this species have not been published, but are in the RC files.

Long-billed Dowitcher
Limnodromus scolopaceus

Migrant, most common in eastern Colorado.

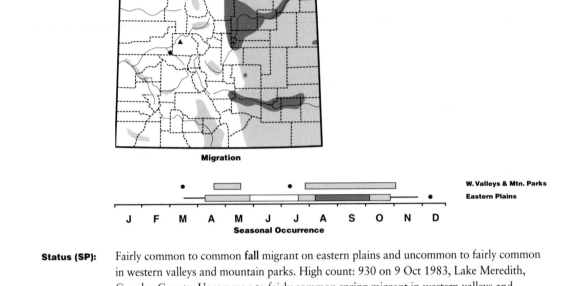

Migration

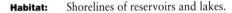

W. Valleys & Mtn. Parks

Eastern Plains

J F M A M J J A S O N D

Seasonal Occurrence

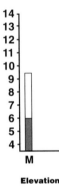

M

Elevation

Status (SP): Fairly common to common **fall** migrant on eastern plains and uncommon to fairly common in western valleys and mountain parks. High count: 930 on 9 Oct 1983, Lake Meredith, Crowley County. Uncommon to fairly common **spring** migrant in western valleys and mountain parks and on eastern plains. All records from the mountain parks and western valleys are recent because Bailey and Niedrach (1965) listed no records. Rare in **early summer**; such birds would be either late spring or early fall migrants. There is a **mid-winter** observation, but the bird was unable to fly and thus should not be considered a valid record.

Although this species is undoubtedly far more common than the Short-billed Dowitcher, observers should not assume that all dowitchers are Long-billeds; this is especially true early in the fall migration (July and early Aug), when Short-billeds may be as likely as Long-billeds.

Habitat: Shorelines of reservoirs and lakes.

Common Snipe
Gallinago gallinago

Migrant and summer resident throughout Colorado; local in winter.

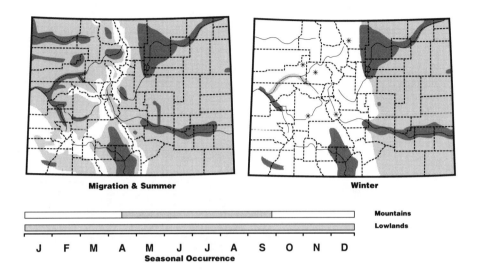

Migration & Summer **Winter**

Mountains
Lowlands

J F M A M J J A S O N D
Seasonal Occurrence

Elevation

Status (SP) (B): Uncommon to fairly common **spring** and **fall** migrant throughout the state below timberline; accidental above timberline (one record). High count: 60 on 31 Aug 1985, Lower Latham Reservoir, Weld County. Uncommon to fairly common **winter** resident in western valleys from Garfield County southward, in the San Luis Valley, and on eastern plains. Rare in foothills and low mountains. Uncommon **summer** resident statewide below timberline. Johnson and Ryder (1977) found densities to be highest on the northeastern plains, and the northwestern valleys also seem to support sizable breeding populations (Martin et al. 1974).

Habitat: Moist areas with vegetation, such as streambanks, marshes, and wet meadows.

Record: **Above timberline:** 3 Aug 1985, at the summit of Guanella Pass (11,665 ft.), Clear Creek County.

American Woodcock
Scolopax minor

Status (SP): Casual in **spring, summer,** and **fall** on northeastern plains (five records*).

Records: 9 Aug 1885, near Denver (DMNH 14760); 16 Sep 1945, Bennett, Adams County (DMNH 24766); 5 July 1974, near Ft. Collins, Larimer County; 26 Oct 1980, Colorado Springs, El Paso County (DMNH 37309); 28–30 Nov 1990, Boulder, Boulder County.

Wilson's Phalarope
Phalaropus tricolor

Migration and summer resident at low elevations and in mountain parks.

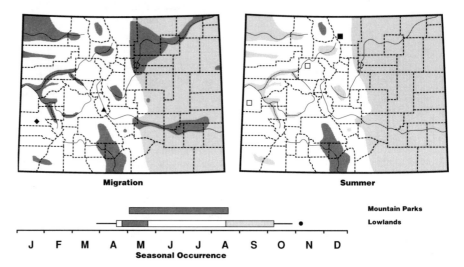

Migration   Summer

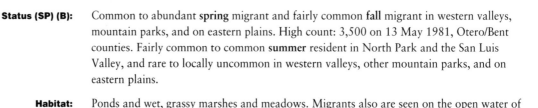

Mountain Parks
Lowlands

J F M A M J J A S O N D
Seasonal Occurrence

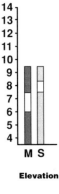

M S

Elevation

Status (SP) (B): Common to abundant **spring** migrant and fairly common **fall** migrant in western valleys, mountain parks, and on eastern plains. High count: 3,500 on 13 May 1981, Otero/Bent counties. Fairly common to common **summer** resident in North Park and the San Luis Valley, and rare to locally uncommon in western valleys, other mountain parks, and on eastern plains.

Habitat: Ponds and wet, grassy marshes and meadows. Migrants also are seen on the open water of reservoirs and on mudflats.

Red-necked Phalarope

Phalaropus lobatus

Migrant at low elevations and in mountain parks.

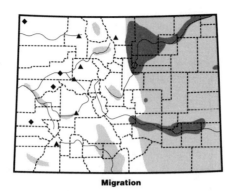

Migration

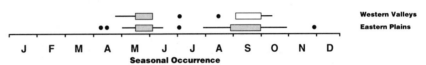

Western Valleys

Eastern Plains

Seasonal Occurrence

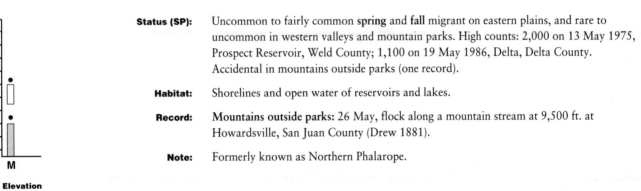

Elevation

Status (SP): Uncommon to fairly common **spring** and **fall** migrant on eastern plains, and rare to uncommon in western valleys and mountain parks. High counts: 2,000 on 13 May 1975, Prospect Reservoir, Weld County; 1,100 on 19 May 1986, Delta, Delta County. Accidental in mountains outside parks (one record).

Habitat: Shorelines and open water of reservoirs and lakes.

Record: **Mountains outside parks:** 26 May, flock along a mountain stream at 9,500 ft. at Howardsville, San Juan County (Drew 1881).

Note: Formerly known as Northern Phalarope.

Red Phalarope

Phalaropus fulicaria

Very rare in eastern Colorado (mostly fall); occasional elsewhere.

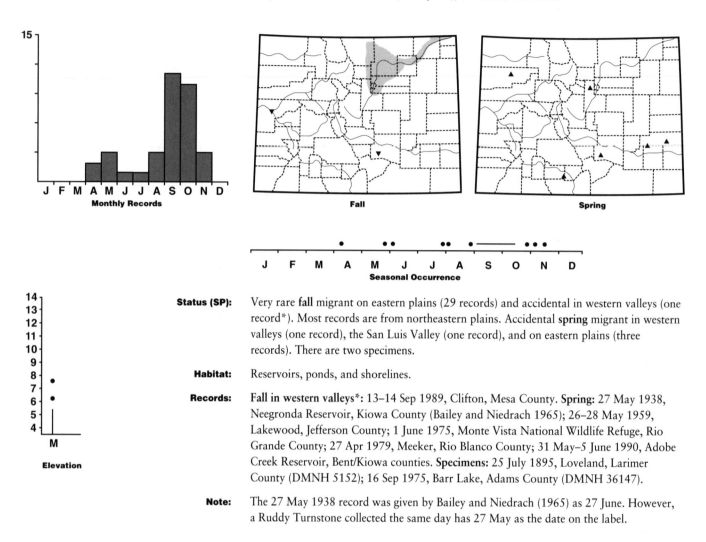

Fall

Spring

Monthly Records

Seasonal Occurrence

Elevation

Status (SP): Very rare **fall** migrant on eastern plains (29 records) and accidental in western valleys (one record*). Most records are from northeastern plains. Accidental **spring** migrant in western valleys (one record), the San Luis Valley (one record), and on eastern plains (three records). There are two specimens.

Habitat: Reservoirs, ponds, and shorelines.

Records: **Fall in western valleys*:** 13–14 Sep 1989, Clifton, Mesa County. **Spring:** 27 May 1938, Neegronda Reservoir, Kiowa County (Bailey and Niedrach 1965); 26–28 May 1959, Lakewood, Jefferson County; 1 June 1975, Monte Vista National Wildlife Refuge, Rio Grande County; 27 Apr 1979, Meeker, Rio Blanco County; 31 May–5 June 1990, Adobe Creek Reservoir, Bent/Kiowa counties. **Specimens:** 25 July 1895, Loveland, Larimer County (DMNH 5152); 16 Sep 1975, Barr Lake, Adams County (DMNH 36147).

Note: The 27 May 1938 record was given by Bailey and Niedrach (1965) as 27 June. However, a Ruddy Turnstone collected the same day has 27 May as the date on the label.

**Order Charadriiformes
Family Laridae**

Jaegers
Stercorarius spp.

Rare in fall in eastern Colorado.

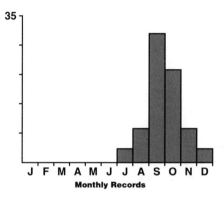

Monthly Records

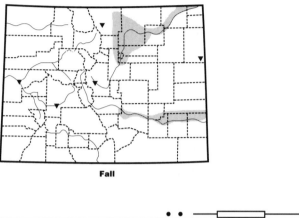

Fall

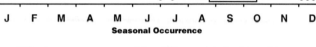

Seasonal Occurrence

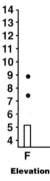

Elevation

Status: Rare **fall** migrant on eastern plains (77 records). Accidental in mountains and mountain parks (three records) and in western valleys (two records).

Habitat: Reservoirs.

Records: **Mountains and mountain parks:** 9 Nov 1957, Estes Park, Larimer County; 30 Aug 1987, Antero Reservoir, Park County; 12–22 July 1988, Antero Reservoir. **Western valleys:** 15 Oct 1965, Grand Junction, Mesa County; 25 Sep 1985, Blue Mesa Reservoir, Gunnison County.

Note: There are 91 records of jaegers in Colorado, primarily of juveniles and immatures. Virtually all were identified to the species level by the observers (about half Pomarine and half Parasitic). Although it is possible to identify jaegers to the species level, it is very difficult and requires considerable experience with known-identity birds, knowledge of the wide variation in plumages of each species, and is best done with other birds for comparison. These criteria are almost never met in Colorado. Therefore, we believe that most jaeger records should be regarded as jaeger spp. rather than listed at the species level. In the individual species accounts that follow we have included only specimens and documented photographic and sight records that meet identification criteria such as given by Olsen (1989) and Kaufman (1990).

Pomarine Jaeger
Stercorarius pomarinus

Status (SP): Accidental **fall** migrant on eastern plains (three records*) and **spring** migrant in mountain parks (one record*).

Records: Fall*: three immatures, and one collected 30 Sep 1963, Cherry Creek Reservoir, Arapahoe County (DMNH 33798); light adult 17–30 Nov 1985, Cherry Creek Reservoir; light adult 30 June–6 July 1991, Barr Lake, Adams County. **Spring***: light adult 12–13 May 1973, De Weese Reservoir, Custer County.

Parasitic Jaeger
Stercorarius parasiticus

Status (PH): Accidental **fall** migrant on eastern plains (three records*).

Records: Juvenile 16–24 Sep 1973, Cherry Creek Reservoir, Arapahoe County (photos in RC files); light adult 13 Aug–14 Sep 1977, Union Reservoir, Weld County; light adult 14–15 Sep 1989, Holbrook Reservoir, Otero County.

Long-tailed Jaeger
Stercorarius longicaudus

Status (SP): Accidental **fall** migrant (one record*) and **spring** migrant (one record*) on eastern plains.

Records: 8 Oct 1902, Windsor Reservoir, Weld County (DMNH 20153); light adult 29 May 1963, Rocky Ford, Otero County (photo in Bailey and Niedrach 1965).

Laughing Gull

Larus atricilla

Occasional in eastern Colorado, mostly in spring.

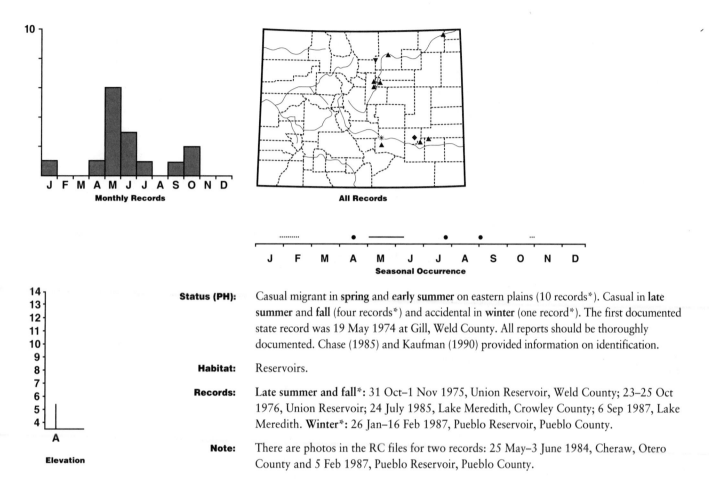

Status (PH): Casual migrant in **spring** and **early summer** on eastern plains (10 records*). Casual in **late summer** and **fall** (four records*) and accidental in **winter** (one record*). The first documented state record was 19 May 1974 at Gill, Weld County. All reports should be thoroughly documented. Chase (1985) and Kaufman (1990) provided information on identification.

Habitat: Reservoirs.

Records: **Late summer and fall***: 31 Oct–1 Nov 1975, Union Reservoir, Weld County; 23–25 Oct 1976, Union Reservoir; 24 July 1985, Lake Meredith, Crowley County; 6 Sep 1987, Lake Meredith. **Winter***: 26 Jan–16 Feb 1987, Pueblo Reservoir, Pueblo County.

Note: There are photos in the RC files for two records: 25 May–3 June 1984, Cheraw, Otero County and 5 Feb 1987, Pueblo Reservoir, Pueblo County.

Franklin's Gull

Larus pipixcan

Migrant at low elevations and in mountain parks; most common in eastern Colorado.

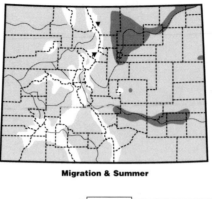

Migration & Summer

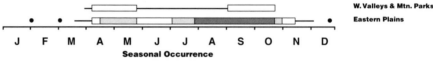

W. Valleys & Mtn. Parks

Eastern Plains

J F M A M J J A S O N D

Seasonal Occurrence

M,S

Elevation

Status (SP): Abundant **fall** migrant and fairly common to common **spring** migrant on eastern plains. High count: estimated 21,500 on 21 Sep 1974 in the lower Arkansas River Valley. Numbers fluctuate widely from year to year. Rare to uncommon migrant in western valleys, mountain parks, and (in flight overhead) in foothills and lower mountains; more regular in fall than in spring. Accidental in fall above timberline (two records). Rare to uncommon nonbreeder in **early summer** in western valleys, mountain parks, and eastern plains. In some years, can be common or abundant in June on eastern plains. High count: 750 on 26 June 1977, Barr Lake, Adams County.

This species has increased dramatically in numbers in Colorado since the 1920s. Sclater (1912) noted that the species was "hardly known from Colorado" and listed only three records. Only one was observed in several years in the Barr Lake area, Adams County (Hersey and Rockwell 1909). When a flock of several thousand was attracted to a grasshopper infestation in the Barr Lake area in late Aug and early Sep 1925, the number of birds seen so exceeded all previous Colorado reports that details were published (Bailey and Niedrach 1926). It appears that by the 1950s, this species had become common. The increase of reservoirs and croplands in Colorado probably is responsible for the increased numbers.

Habitat: Reservoirs and lakes, croplands (especially recently plowed fields). Often seen in flight over urban areas.

Records: **Fall above timberline:** 20 on 8 Sep 1968, summit of Mt. Evans, Clear Creek County; 100 on 27 Sep 1975, Trail Ridge Road in Rocky Mountain National Park, Larimer County.

Little Gull
Larus minutus

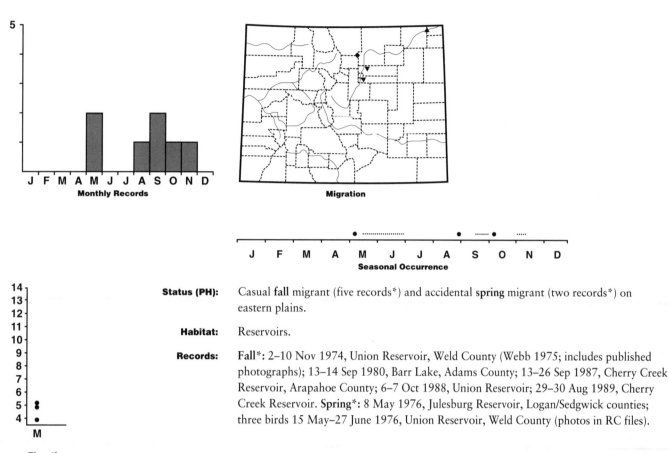

Status (PH): Casual **fall** migrant (five records*) and accidental **spring** migrant (two records*) on eastern plains.

Habitat: Reservoirs.

Records: **Fall***: 2–10 Nov 1974, Union Reservoir, Weld County (Webb 1975; includes published photographs); 13–14 Sep 1980, Barr Lake, Adams County; 13–26 Sep 1987, Cherry Creek Reservoir, Arapahoe County; 6–7 Oct 1988, Union Reservoir; 29–30 Aug 1989, Cherry Creek Reservoir. **Spring***: 8 May 1976, Julesburg Reservoir, Logan/Sedgwick counties; three birds 15 May–27 June 1976, Union Reservoir, Weld County (photos in RC files).

Common Black-headed Gull

Larus ridibundus

Status (PH):   Accidental **spring** and **fall** migrant (two records*).

Records: 8–9 Oct 1988, Cherry Creek Reservoir, Arapahoe County; 9–15 Apr 1990, Jim Hamm Pond, Boulder County and Union Reservoir, Weld County (photos published in Kingery 1990c).

Bonaparte's Gull

Larus philadelphia

Migrant at low elevations and in mountain parks.

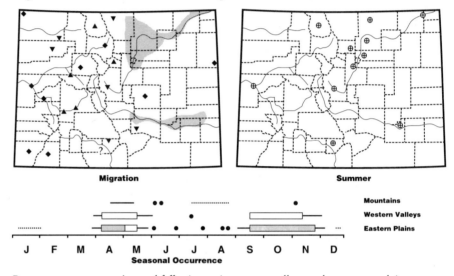

Migration   Summer

J	F	M	A	M	J	J	A	S	O	N	D	

Seasonal Occurrence

Mountains
Western Valleys
Eastern Plains

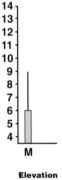

Elevation

Status (SP):   Rare to uncommon **spring** and **fall** migrant in western valleys and on eastern plains; locally it may be fairly common. High count: 200 on 6 Oct 1974, Holbrook Reservoir, Otero County. Accidental in spring in mountain parks (three records). Accidental in mountains outside parks (two spring records and one fall record). Casual in **winter** (six records from 1983 and later) at Pueblo Reservoir, Pueblo County. High count: 34 on 20 Dec 1986. In **summer**, casual on eastern plains (seven records) and in mountain parks (five records) and accidental in western valleys (two records).

Habitat: Reservoirs and lakes.

Records: **Mountains outside parks:** 2 Nov 1924, Red Feather Lakes, Larimer County (DMNH 11143); 16 Apr 1939 and 15 Apr 1940, Georgetown, Clear Creek County (Bailey and Niedrach 1965).

Mew Gull
Larus canus

Status (PH): Casual **spring** migrant on northeastern plains (five records*). Accidental **fall** migrant on southeastern plains (one record*). Accidental in **winter** on eastern plains (two records*).

Habitat: Reservoirs and lakes.

Records: **Spring*:** 7–12 Mar 1980, Denver County (photos published in Chase 1983 and Gent 1987); 28 Apr 1981, Union Reservoir, Weld County; 22 Mar 1982, Denver (photos published in Chase 1983 and Gent 1987); 6–15 Mar 1986, Cherry Creek Reservoir, Arapahoe County; 28 Apr 1991, Union Reservoir. **Fall*:** 27–30 Sep 1990, Pueblo, Pueblo County. **Winter*:** 27 Jan–26 Feb 1985, Cherry Creek Reservoir; 2 Jan–8 Feb 1990, Pueblo (photo published in Kingery 1990b).

Ring-billed Gull
Larus delawarensis

Observed all year at low elevations and in summer in mountain parks.

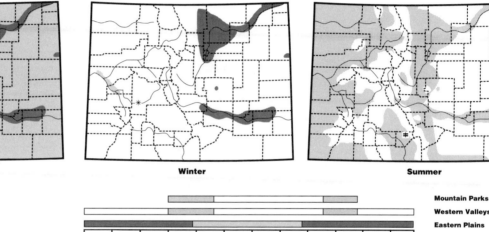

Migration   Winter   Summer

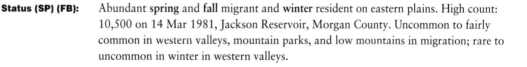

Mountain Parks
Western Valleys
Eastern Plains

J F M A M J J A S O N D
Seasonal Occurrence

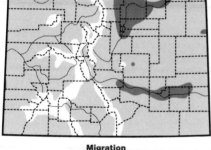

Elevation

Status (SP) (FB): Abundant **spring** and **fall** migrant and **winter** resident on eastern plains. High count: 10,500 on 14 Mar 1981, Jackson Reservoir, Morgan County. Uncommon to fairly common in western valleys, mountain parks, and low mountains in migration; rare to uncommon in winter in western valleys.

Uncommon (locally common to abundant) nonbreeding **summer** resident on eastern plains, and rare to uncommon in western valleys, mountain parks, and low mountains. One former **breeding** record 18 June 1898 at San Luis Lakes, Alamosa County (Cooke 1900). This species does breed in central and northwestern Wyoming (Findholt 1986, Dorn and Dorn 1990), so there is a possibility that this species could breed again in Colorado, especially because populations are increasing (Conover 1983).

Habitat: Reservoirs, lakes, and croplands (especially recently plowed fields).

References: Ryder (1967b, 1978).

California Gull

Larus californicus

Migrant and summer resident at low elevations and mountain parks, with five nesting colonies; rare in winter.

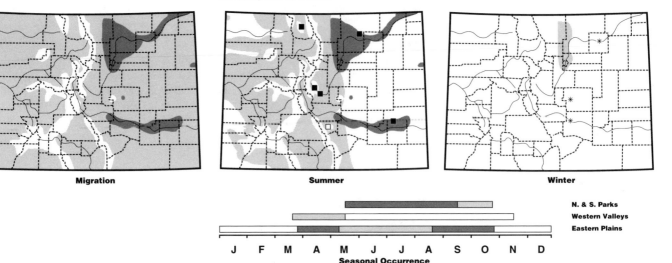

| | Migration | Summer | Winter |

Elevation

Status (SP) (B): Common to abundant **spring** and **fall** migrant on eastern plains, and uncommon to fairly common in western valleys, mountain parks, and mountains.

Fairly common to common nonbreeding **summer** resident on eastern plains, and uncommon to fairly common in western valleys and mountains. There are confirmed **breeding** records from five sites: Riverside Reservoir, Weld County (up to 1,500 pairs; R. Ryder, pers. comm.); Adobe Creek Reservoir, Bent/Kiowa counties (in some years up to 65 pairs; D. Nelson, pers. comm.), Walden Reservoir, Jackson County (100 pairs; B. Howe, pers. comm.), Antero Reservoir (1,200 pairs; C. Chase, pers. comm.) and Eleven Mile Reservoir (2,000 pairs; R. Ryder, pers comm.), Park County.

Rare **winter** resident on eastern plains, mostly near foothills; may be locally uncommon to fairly common.

This species has increased dramatically in Colorado in the past half-century, as it has throughout its range (Conover 1983). It was a very rare spring and fall migrant in Colorado prior to the 1950s. Sclater (1912) listed only four records. The first specimen was collected 27 Mar 1938 at Barr Lake, Adams County (DMNH 18802). The first nesting was recorded in 1963 at Riverside Reservoir (Ryder 1964). Subsequently, birds began nesting in 1965 at Antero Reservoir (Ryder 1978), in 1977 at Eleven Mile Reservoir (Loeffler 1977), in 1988 at Adobe Creek Reservoir (M. Janos, pers. comm.), and in 1990 (and possibly as early as 1988) at Walden Reservoir (B. Howe, pers. comm.). There were no winter records from Colorado until 1960, and the species was not observed regularly until the mid-1970s.

Habitat: Reservoirs and lakes, and croplands (especially recently plowed fields). Breeding birds nest on islands in reservoirs.

Note: Hybridization occurred between California and Herring Gulls at Antero Reservoir in 1982 and 1983 (Chase 1984). Three specimens were collected 8 June 1983: one adult (DMNH 38801) and two chicks (DMNH 38802–03).

Reference: Ryder (1967b).

Herring Gull
Larus argentatus

Common in winter in eastern Colorado; rare in western Colorado.

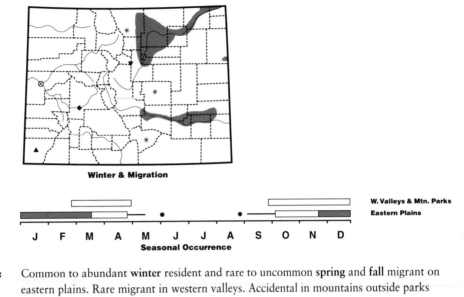

Winter & Migration

W. Valleys & Mtn. Parks
Eastern Plains

J F M A M J J A S O N D
Seasonal Occurrence

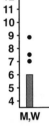

Elevation

Status (SP): Common to abundant **winter** resident and rare to uncommon **spring** and **fall** migrant on eastern plains. Rare migrant in western valleys. Accidental in mountains outside parks (one record). Accidental in summer in South Park (three records). This species has evidently increased in Colorado, because Bergtold (1928) considered it to be only a rare migrant.

Habitat: Reservoirs and lakes.

Records: **Mountains outside parks:** 13 Oct 1979, Evergreen, Jefferson County. **Summer:** hybridized with California Gulls in 1982 and 1983, Antero Reservoir (see California Gull account); also observed at Antero 25 July 1981.

Thayer's Gull

Larus thayeri

Winter resident in northeastern Colorado.

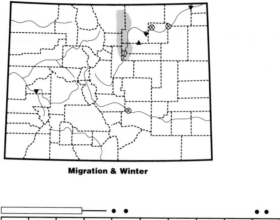

Migration & Winter

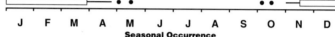

J F M A M J J A S O N D

Seasonal Occurrence

Elevation

Status (SP): Apparently a rare **winter** resident on northeastern plains, primarily near foothills. High count: 7 on 15 Feb 1985 in the Denver metropolitan area. Accidental in western valleys (one record*).

The status of this bird in Colorado remains uncertain. Some early specimens were misidentified. The first state specimen (3 Nov 1912, La Salle, Weld County; DMNH 880) was originally reported as a Glaucous-winged Gull (Bailey and Niedrach 1937). A specimen collected 20 Apr 1938 at Barr Lake, Adams County (DMNH 18886) was listed twice by Bailey and Niedrach (1965): once as Iceland and once as Thayer's. Starting in the mid-1950s, there were occasional sight records of first-year gulls that were probably this species, although usually identified as Glaucous-winged Gulls. By the mid-1970s, observations of these birds, by then being called Thayer's Gull, started to increase dramatically. Since the mid-1970s, there have been 140+ sight reports of Thayer's Gulls. Most records are of first-year birds, but older birds (including adults) have been seen. Identification of this bird should still be made very carefully, in spite of the large number of observations; identification was discussed by Lehman (1980) and Kaufman (1990).

Habitat: Reservoirs and lakes.

Record: **Western valleys***: 8 Dec 1986, Sweitzer Lake, Delta County.

Lesser Black-backed Gull
Larus fuscus

Status (PH): Accidental in **fall** and **winter** (three records*).

Records: 11 Dec 1976–1 Jan 1977, Lake Sangraco, Adams County (Webb and Conry 1978; includes photograph); 6 Feb–10 Mar 1988, Hamilton Reservoir, Larimer County; 17–23 Nov 1990, Cherry Creek Reservoir, Arapahoe County.

Glaucous-winged Gull
Larus glaucescens

Status (PH): Accidental in **spring** and **summer** (three records*).

Records: 25 July 1981, Antero Reservoir, Park County (photographs published in Chase 1983); 31 Mar–6 Apr 1989, Julesburg Reservoir, Logan/Sedgwick counties; 11–19 Apr 1989, Cherry Creek Reservoir, Arapahoe County.

Glaucous Gull
Larus hyperboreus

Rare in winter in northeastern Colorado.

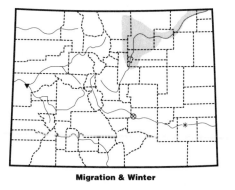

Migration & Winter

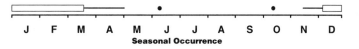

J F M A M J J A S O N D

Seasonal Occurrence

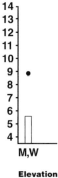

Elevation

Status (SP): Rare **winter** resident on northeastern plains, mostly near foothills; south to Pueblo County. Accidental on far southeastern plains (one record) and in western valleys (one record*). The first records were two specimens collected in 1938, and Bailey and Niedrach (1965) listed only seven records; most records are from the late 1960s and later.

Habitat: Reservoirs and lakes.

Records: **Southeastern plains:** 26 Feb 1989, John Martin Reservoir, Bent County. **Western valleys*:** 2 Nov 1991, Clifton, Mesa County. **Specimens:** 28 Mar 1938 (DMNH 18799) and 1 Apr 1938 (DMNH 18800), both at Barr Lake, Adams County (Bailey and Niedrach 1939).

Great Black-backed Gull
Larus marinus

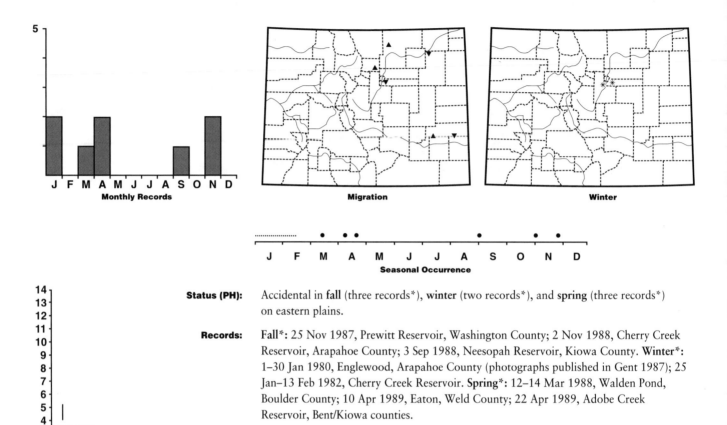

Migration **Winter**

Monthly Records

Seasonal Occurrence

Elevation

Status (PH): Accidental in **fall** (three records*), **winter** (two records*), and **spring** (three records*) on eastern plains.

Records: Fall*: 25 Nov 1987, Prewitt Reservoir, Washington County; 2 Nov 1988, Cherry Creek Reservoir, Arapahoe County; 3 Sep 1988, Neesopah Reservoir, Kiowa County. **Winter***: 1–30 Jan 1980, Englewood, Arapahoe County (photographs published in Gent 1987); 25 Jan–13 Feb 1982, Cherry Creek Reservoir. **Spring***: 12–14 Mar 1988, Walden Pond, Boulder County; 10 Apr 1989, Eaton, Weld County; 22 Apr 1989, Adobe Creek Reservoir, Bent/Kiowa counties.

Black-legged Kittiwake

Rissa tridactyla

Very rare in eastern Colorado from late fall to early spring.

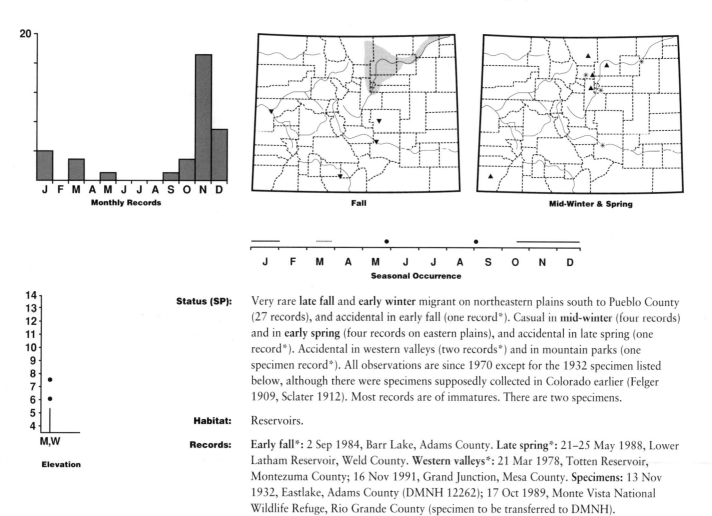

Status (SP): Very rare **late fall** and **early winter** migrant on northeastern plains south to Pueblo County (27 records), and accidental in early fall (one record*). Casual in **mid-winter** (four records) and in **early spring** (four records on eastern plains), and accidental in late spring (one record*). Accidental in western valleys (two records*) and in mountain parks (one specimen record*). All observations are since 1970 except for the 1932 specimen listed below, although there were specimens supposedly collected in Colorado earlier (Felger 1909, Sclater 1912). Most records are of immatures. There are two specimens.

Habitat: Reservoirs.

Records: **Early fall***: 2 Sep 1984, Barr Lake, Adams County. **Late spring***: 21–25 May 1988, Lower Latham Reservoir, Weld County. **Western valleys***: 21 Mar 1978, Totten Reservoir, Montezuma County; 16 Nov 1991, Grand Junction, Mesa County. **Specimens:** 13 Nov 1932, Eastlake, Adams County (DMNH 12262); 17 Oct 1989, Monte Vista National Wildlife Refuge, Rio Grande County (specimen to be transferred to DMNH).

Ross' Gull

Rhodostethia rosea

Status (PH): Accidental **spring** migrant (one record*).

Record: 28 Apr–7 May 1983, Julesburg Reservoir, Logan/Sedgwick counties (Anonymous 1983; photographs published in that reference and in Gent 1987).

Sabine's Gull
Xema sabini

Rare in fall in eastern Colorado; occasional elsewhere.

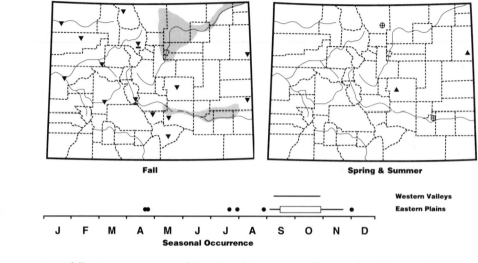

Fall   Spring & Summer

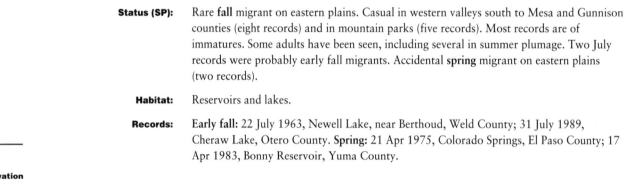

Western Valleys
Eastern Plains

J F M A M J J A S O N D
Seasonal Occurrence

14
13
12
11
10
9
8
7
6
5
4

F

Elevation

Status (SP):   Rare **fall** migrant on eastern plains. Casual in western valleys south to Mesa and Gunnison counties (eight records) and in mountain parks (five records). Most records are of immatures. Some adults have been seen, including several in summer plumage. Two July records were probably early fall migrants. Accidental **spring** migrant on eastern plains (two records).

Habitat: Reservoirs and lakes.

Records: **Early fall:** 22 July 1963, Newell Lake, near Berthoud, Weld County; 31 July 1989, Cheraw Lake, Otero County. **Spring:** 21 Apr 1975, Colorado Springs, El Paso County; 17 Apr 1983, Bonny Reservoir, Yuma County.

Ivory Gull
Pagophila eburnea

Status (SP):   Accidental in **winter** (one record*).

Record: 2 Jan 1926, near Strasburg, Adams County (DMNH 11700) (Bailey 1926).

Caspian Tern
Sterna caspia

Occasional at low elevations and in mountain parks in spring, summer, and fall.

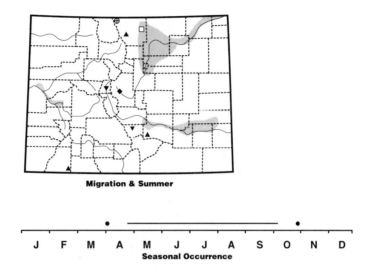

Migration & Summer

J F M A M J J A S O N D

Seasonal Occurrence

Status (PH): Very rare **spring** and **fall** migrant and nonbreeding **summer** resident on eastern plains (12 spring records, 38 summer records, and nine fall records). One possible breeding record. Very rare spring migrant in west-central valleys in Mesa, Delta and La Plata counties (12 records) and accidental in summer (three records) and fall (one record). Casual in mountain parks (five records). The first Colorado record was 27–28 May 1974, Lake Henry, Crowley County (photographs published in Andrews 1979). In 1990 there were 15 records.

Habitat: Reservoirs and lakes.

Records: **Possible breeding:** pair carrying food in courtship behavior, May and June 1990, Ft. Collins, Larimer County. **Mountain parks:** 16 Aug 1981 and 22 May 1983, Antero Reservoir, Park County; 3 Aug 1986, De Weese Reservoir, Custer County; 2–3 Aug 1987, Twin Lakes, Lake County; 7 May 1990, Lake Estes, Larimer County.

14
13
12
11
10
9
8
7
6
5
4

M,S
Elevation

Common Tern
Sterna hirundo

Rare at low elevations in migration; occasional nonbreeder in summer.

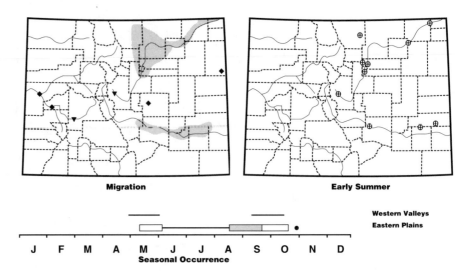

Migration | Early Summer

Western Valleys
Eastern Plains

J F M A M J J A S O N D
Seasonal Occurrence

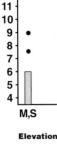

Elevation

Status (SP): Rare to uncommon **fall** migrant on eastern plains. Very rare in west-central valleys in Mesa, Delta, and Gunnison counties (about 15 records). Accidental in mountain parks (one record). Rare **spring** migrant on eastern plains and casual in west-central valleys in Mesa and Delta counties (eight records). Casual nonbreeding **early summer** visitor on eastern plains (eight records); accidental in mountain parks (one record).

The number of reports has proliferated rapidly during the 1980s; by the late 1980s as many as 30 were reported in a single fall. Although this species undoubtedly occurs regularly in small numbers, observers should continue to be very cautious about identifying Common Terns; Zimmer (1985) and Kaufman (1990) provided identification material.

Habitat: Reservoirs and lakes.

Records: Mountain parks: 19 Sep 1982 and 12 June 1983, Antero Reservoir, Park County.

Arctic Tern
Sterna paradisaea

Status (SP): Accidental **fall** migrant (two records*) and **late spring** migrant (one record*) on eastern plains.

Records: Fall*: 16 Sep 1912, Windsor, Weld County (formerly CU 8108, now DMNH 39080) (Conry and Webb 1982; includes photo of primaries); 11–12 Sep 1979, Union Reservoir, Weld County. **Late spring**: 12 June 1991, Adobe Creek Reservoir, Kiowa/Bent counties. The two specimens listed by Bailey and Niedrach (1965) are not extant and should be disregarded.

Forster's Tern
Sterna forsteri

Migrant and summer resident at low elevations and in mountain parks.

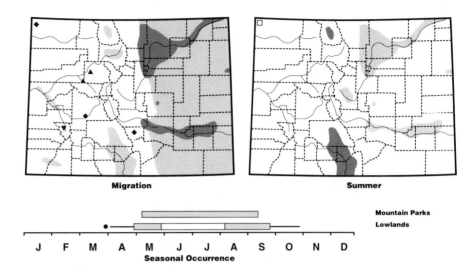

Migration **Summer**

Mountain Parks
Lowlands

J F M A M J J A S O N D
Seasonal Occurrence

Elevation

M,S

Status (SP) (B): Uncommon to fairly common **spring** and **fall** migrant on eastern plains, and rare to uncommon in western valleys and mountain parks. High count: 112 on 6–7 May 1967, Bonny Reservoir, Yuma County. Uncommon to fairly common local **summer** resident in North Park and the San Luis Valley and on eastern plains. Some summer birds may be nonbreeders. This species has declined as a breeder in some areas. Up to 100 pairs formerly nested in the Barr Lake area, Adams County (Hersey and Rockwell 1909), but now there are probably only a few nesting pairs.

Habitat: Nests in cattail marshes near open water. Migrants occur on lakes and reservoirs.

Reference: Gorenzel (1977).

Least Tern

Sterna antillarum

Uncommon in migration and summer in southeastern Colorado; occasional elsewhere.

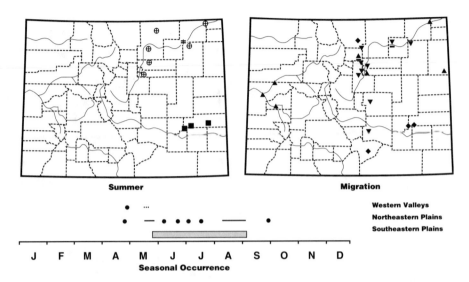

Summer   **Migration**

Western Valleys
Northeastern Plains
Southeastern Plains

J F M A M J J A S O N D

Seasonal Occurrence

Elevation
M,S

Status (SP) (B): Local uncommon **summer** resident on southeastern plains in the Arkansas River Valley. The species breeds in most years at Adobe Creek Reservoir, Kiowa County, and Horse Creek Reservoir, Otero County; nesting was first recorded at both sites in 1978 (Chase 1979). They also nested at Neenoshe Reservoir, Kiowa County in 1989 and 1990 (Carter 1990, Nelson and Carter 1990b). In 1991, there were 19 nests at Adobe Creek Reservoir and four at Neenoshe Reservoir (M. Carter, pers. comm.). Breeding may not be attempted or may fail in some years due to water levels that are either too high or that fluctuate too much. Migrants or nonbreeding individuals also occur at other reservoirs on the southeastern plains. Casual nonbreeding summer visitor on northeastern plains (eight records). A flock of 14 birds nested successfully in June 1949 on sandbars of the South Platte River at Beetland, Washington County, and in the same month a group of 30 birds attempted to nest but were unsuccessful at nearby Prewitt Reservoir, Washington County (Lamb 1950).

Casual to very rare **spring** and **fall** migrant on northeastern plains (seven spring records and 11 fall records). Casual spring migrant in west-central valleys in Mesa and Delta counties (seven records) (Janos 1985b).

Habitat: Breeding birds nest on bare sandy shorelines of islands in reservoirs. Migrants occur at reservoirs, lakes, and rivers with bare sandy shorelines.

Records: Specimens: 26 May 1935, Boulder, Boulder County (CU 3351); three on 10 Aug 1940, Jackson Reservoir, Morgan County (DMNH 21696-98).

Note: This is an endangered species.

Black Tern
Chlidonias niger

Migrant and breeder at low elevations and in mountain parks; most numerous in spring.

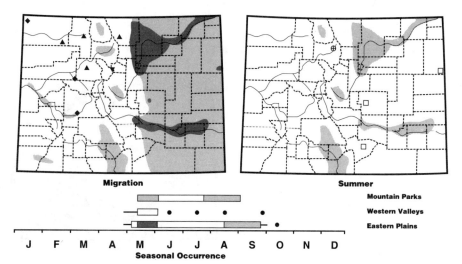

Migration

Summer

Mountain Parks

Western Valleys

Eastern Plains

J F M A M J J A S O N D
Seasonal Occurrence

Status (SP) (B):	Common to abundant **spring** migrant and uncommon to fairly common **fall** migrant on eastern plains. High count: 1,200 on 17 May 1957, Bonny Reservoir, Yuma County. Rare to uncommon migrant in western valleys and mountain parks. Accidental in mountains outside parks (one record). Rare to uncommon **summer** resident locally in mountain parks and on eastern plains. It was once more common as a breeder, at least in some localities: Hersey and Rockwell (1909) and Rockwell (1911) considered it a common nester in the Barr Lake area, Adams County, but it now breeds there only rarely. This species is on the National Audubon Society Blue List (Tate 1986). There have been widespread declines, probably due to loss of habitat but perhaps also due to pesticides (McDonald 1991).
Habitat:	Reservoirs and lakes. Breeding birds nest in large cattail marshes adjacent to open water.
Record:	**Mountains outside parks:** several dozen in a flock 14 Sep 1977 at 13,000 ft. on Loveland Pass, Clear Creek/Summit counties.

14
13
12
11
10
9
8
7
6
5
4

M,S

Elevation

Order Charadriiformes
Family Alcidae

Marbled Murrelet
Brachyramphus marmoratus

Status (SP):	Accidental **fall** migrant (one record*).
Record:	22 Aug 1982, Aspen, Pitkin County (DMNH 37691) (Webb and Reddall 1989). The bird was of the Asiatic race *B. m. perdix*; Sealy et al. (1982) discussed the occurrence of this subspecies in North America.

Ancient Murrelet
Synthliboramphus antiquus

Status (SP):	Accidental **fall** migrant (two records*).
Records:	28 Nov 1957, Lafayette, Boulder County (DMNH 6282) (Douglass and Douglass 1958); 14 Oct 1965, Union Reservoir, Weld County (DMNH 33827).

Order Columbiformes
Family Columbidae

Rock Dove

Columba livia

Common year round at low elevations.

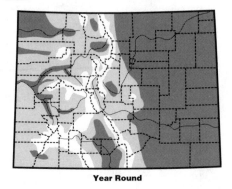

Year Round

| J | F | M | A | M | J | J | A | S | O | N | D |

Seasonal Occurrence

Elevation

Status (SP) (B): Common to abundant **resident** in western valleys, in foothills, and on eastern plains; local and uncommon in mountain parks and lower mountains.

Habitat: Urban areas and farmland, and locally around cliffs and bridges and in canyons.

Band-tailed Pigeon
Columba fasciata

Summer resident in foothills and lower mountains; most numerous in southern Colorado.

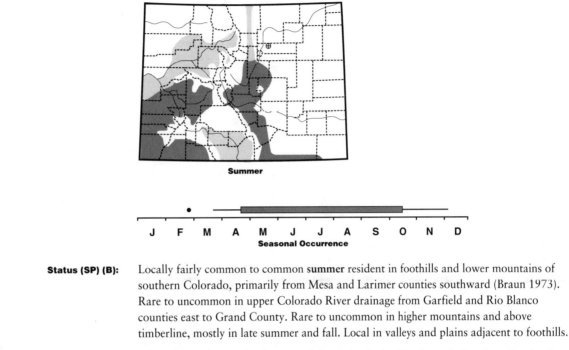

Summer

Seasonal Occurrence

J F M A M J J A S O N D

14
13
12
11
10
9
8
7
6
5
4

M,S

Elevation

Status (SP) (B): Locally fairly common to common **summer** resident in foothills and lower mountains of southern Colorado, primarily from Mesa and Larimer counties southward (Braun 1973). Rare to uncommon in upper Colorado River drainage from Garfield and Rio Blanco counties east to Grand County. Rare to uncommon in higher mountains and above timberline, mostly in late summer and fall. Local in valleys and plains adjacent to foothills.

Habitat: Primarily ponderosa pine forests and Gambel oak shrublands, and often found in riparian and agricultural areas in the foothills adjacent to those habitats (Braun 1973). Less frequently occurs in other types of coniferous forests. Often seen in flight over other habitats.

References: Neff and Culbreath (1946), Gutiérrez et al. (1975).

White-winged Dove
Zenaida asiatica

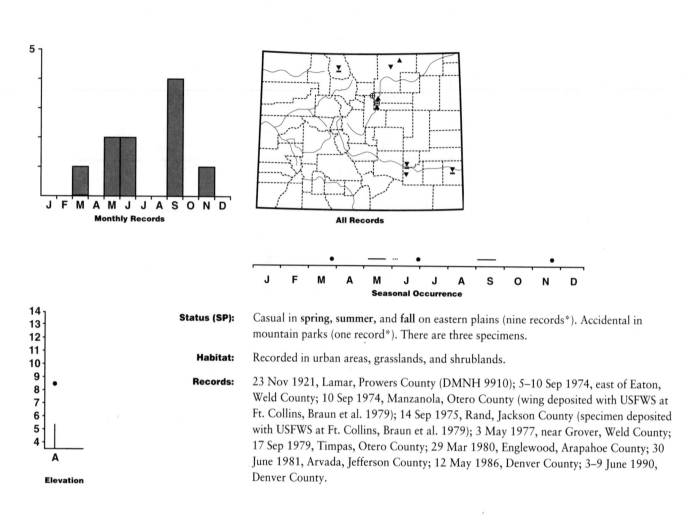

Status (SP): Casual in **spring**, **summer**, and **fall** on eastern plains (nine records*). Accidental in mountain parks (one record*). There are three specimens.

Habitat: Recorded in urban areas, grasslands, and shrublands.

Records: 23 Nov 1921, Lamar, Prowers County (DMNH 9910); 5–10 Sep 1974, east of Eaton, Weld County; 10 Sep 1974, Manzanola, Otero County (wing deposited with USFWS at Ft. Collins, Braun et al. 1979); 14 Sep 1975, Rand, Jackson County (specimen deposited with USFWS at Ft. Collins, Braun et al. 1979); 3 May 1977, near Grover, Weld County; 17 Sep 1979, Timpas, Otero County; 29 Mar 1980, Englewood, Arapahoe County; 30 June 1981, Arvada, Jefferson County; 12 May 1986, Denver County; 3–9 June 1990, Denver County.

Mourning Dove
Zenaida macroura

Abundant in migration and summer at low elevations and fairly common in mountains; rare in winter.

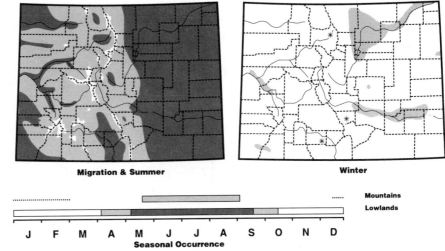

Migration & Summer | **Winter**

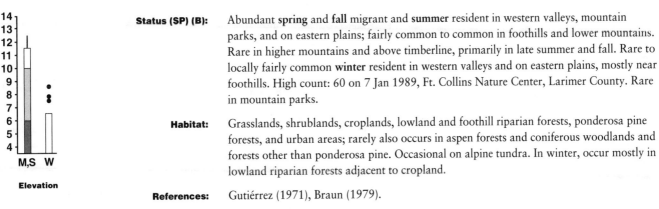

Mountains
Lowlands

J F M A M J J A S O N D
Seasonal Occurrence

Status (SP) (B): Abundant **spring** and **fall** migrant and **summer** resident in western valleys, mountain parks, and on eastern plains; fairly common to common in foothills and lower mountains. Rare in higher mountains and above timberline, primarily in late summer and fall. Rare to locally fairly common **winter** resident in western valleys and on eastern plains, mostly near foothills. High count: 60 on 7 Jan 1989, Ft. Collins Nature Center, Larimer County. Rare in mountain parks.

Habitat: Grasslands, shrublands, croplands, lowland and foothill riparian forests, ponderosa pine forests, and urban areas; rarely also occurs in aspen forests and coniferous woodlands and forests other than ponderosa pine. Occasional on alpine tundra. In winter, occur mostly in lowland riparian forests adjacent to cropland.

References: Gutiérrez (1971), Braun (1979).

Elevation (M,S / W)

Order Psittaciformes
Family Psittacidae

Carolina Parakeet
Conuropsis carolinensis

Status (SR): Former visitor to eastern plains. There were several observations of this species in eastern Colorado from 1860 to 1864, after which it disappeared except for a single sighting in 1877. In the 1860s it was considered to be "not uncommon" along the Arkansas and Huerfano rivers in Pueblo County (McKinley 1964). There were records from Larimer, Boulder, Jefferson, Denver, Pueblo, and Bent counties. There were no breeding records. This species is now extinct.

Order Cuculiformes
Family Cuculidae

Black-billed Cuckoo
Coccyzus erythropthalmus

Rare in migration and in summer in extreme northeastern Colorado; occasional elsewhere.

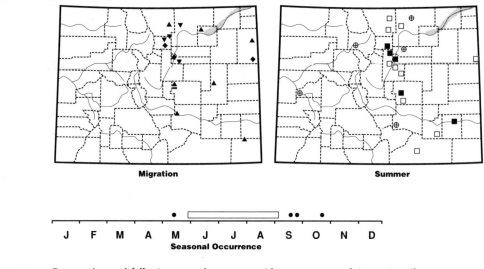

Migration   Summer

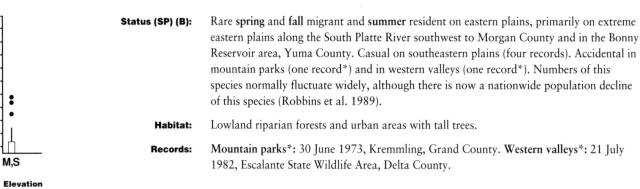

Seasonal Occurrence

Elevation

Status (SP) (B): Rare **spring** and **fall** migrant and **summer** resident on eastern plains, primarily on extreme eastern plains along the South Platte River southwest to Morgan County and in the Bonny Reservoir area, Yuma County. Casual on southeastern plains (four records). Accidental in mountain parks (one record*) and in western valleys (one record*). Numbers of this species normally fluctuate widely, although there is now a nationwide population decline of this species (Robbins et al. 1989).

Habitat: Lowland riparian forests and urban areas with tall trees.

Records: **Mountain parks***: 30 June 1973, Kremmling, Grand County. **Western valleys***: 21 July 1982, Escalante State Wildlife Area, Delta County.

Yellow-billed Cuckoo

Coccyzus americanus

Migrant and summer resident at low elevations, mostly in extreme eastern Colorado.

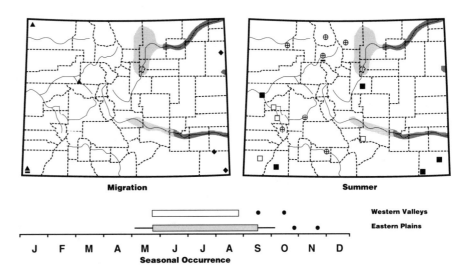

Migration   **Summer**

Western Valleys

Eastern Plains

J F M A M J J A S O N D

Seasonal Occurrence

Elevation

Status (SP) (B): Rare to uncommon **spring** and **fall** migrant and **summer** resident on eastern plains west to Morgan and Otero counties, and rare west to foothills. Rare local summer resident in western valleys, primarily from Mesa County southward. Casual in mountain parks (four records) and in foothills and lower mountains (four records). Numbers of this species fluctuate widely from year to year.

North American populations of this species are declining significantly (Robbins et al. 1989), and it is on the National Audubon Society Blue List (Tate 1986). The range of the western subspecies of this bird has contracted, and populations have declined dramatically within the remaining range, due to loss of mature closed-canopy riparian forests (Laymon and Halterman 1987). Western Colorado is part of the range of that subspecies, but it appears that it was never common in Colorado. Neither Gilman (1907) or Warren (1908) observed the species in western Colorado. Rockwell (1908) mentioned a single pair that nested at Grand Junction, Mesa County, and Bergtold (1928) indicated that it was "infrequent."

Habitat: Lowland riparian forests and urban areas with tall trees.

Records: **Mountain parks:** 18 July 1980, Monte Vista, Rio Grande County; 15 June 1982 and early July 1988, Arapaho National Wildlife Refuge, Jackson County; 14 June 1984, Kremmling, Grand County (DMNH 39325). **Foothills and low mountains:** 31 July 1940, Rocky Mountain National Park, Larimer County (Packard 1945); 9 July 1967, Devil's Head, Douglas County; 16 June 1977, Rocky Mountain National Park; 7 June 1980, Estes Park, Larimer County.

Greater Roadrunner

Geococcyx californianus

Rare year-round in foothills and mesas of southeastern Colorado; occasional elsewhere.

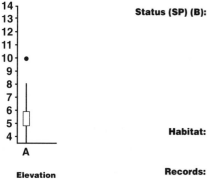

**Monthly Records
Outside Southeastern Colorado**

Elevation

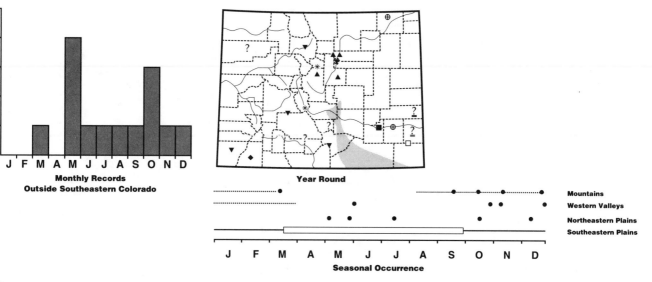

Year Round

Mountains
Western Valleys
Northeastern Plains
Southeastern Plains

J F M A M J J A S O N D

Seasonal Occurrence

Status (SP) (B): Rare to uncommon **resident** in southeastern foothills and mesas from eastern Fremont and southwestern El Paso counties southward and east to southwestern Baca County, and also occurs at Two Buttes Reservoir in northern Baca County. Casual on southeastern plains north to Kiowa County (six records). Casual visitor on eastern plains near foothills north to Jefferson County (nine records); accidental on extreme northeastern plains (one record). Casual in foothills and lower mountains (four records) and in western valleys (five records). Accidental in mountain parks (three records).

Habitat: Shrublands and piñon-juniper woodlands; may also occur at times in grasslands, especially cholla grasslands.

Records: **Extreme northeastern plains:** 15 July 1946, Peetz, Logan County (Bailey and Niedrach 1965). **Foothills and low mountains:** at 8,000 ft. on west side of Wet Mountains, Custer County (Lowe 1894); 12 Oct 1908, at 10,000 ft. on Marshall Pass, Saguache County (Cooke 1909); 19 Aug 1956–11 Mar 1957, Squaw Mountain, Clear Creek Valley and Idaho Springs area, Clear Creek County; 19 Sep 1958, at 7,500 ft. on La Veta Pass, Costilla/ Huerfano counties. **Mountain parks:** 25 Dec 1806, northwest of Salida, Chaffee County (Aiken and Warren 1914); 10 Nov 1875, Williams Fork River in Middle Park, Grand County; 15 Mar 1907, Park County (Cooke 1909). **Western valleys:** date unknown at Meeker, Rio Blanco County (Felger 1910); 23 Oct 1954, Cortez, Montezuma County; 10 Nov 1960, 3 June 1979, and from 31 Dec 1989 through rest of winter, Durango, La Plata County.

Groove-billed Ani
Crotophaga sulcirostris

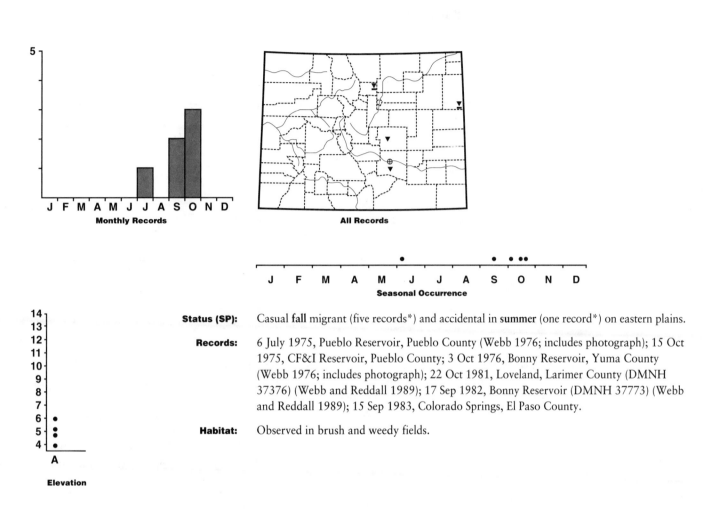

Monthly Records

All Records

Seasonal Occurrence

Elevation

Status (SP):	Casual **fall** migrant (five records*) and accidental in **summer** (one record*) on eastern plains.
Records:	6 July 1975, Pueblo Reservoir, Pueblo County (Webb 1976; includes photograph); 15 Oct 1975, CF&I Reservoir, Pueblo County; 3 Oct 1976, Bonny Reservoir, Yuma County (Webb 1976; includes photograph); 22 Oct 1981, Loveland, Larimer County (DMNH 37376) (Webb and Reddall 1989); 17 Sep 1982, Bonny Reservoir (DMNH 37773) (Webb and Reddall 1989); 15 Sep 1983, Colorado Springs, El Paso County.
Habitat:	Observed in brush and weedy fields.

Order Strigiformes
Family Tytonidae

Barn Owl

Tyto alba

Migrant and summer resident at low elevations; occasional in winter.

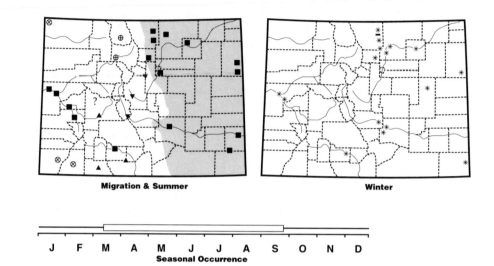

Migration & Summer	**Winter**

Seasonal Occurrence

J F M A M J J A S O N D

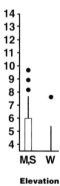

Elevation

Status (SP) (B):   Rare, and probably locally uncommon, **spring** and **fall** migrant and **summer** resident in western valleys and on eastern plains. In at least some areas, it may be more common than the records available seem to indicate. Bailey and Niedrach (1965) included only one record for western Colorado, but it is not known whether this species has increased or has been found more often due to more observers. Casual in mountain parks (seven records, including one breeding record) and accidental in lower mountains outside parks (two records). In **winter**, very rare on eastern plains (21 records), casual in western valleys (nine records), and accidental in San Luis Valley (two records).

Habitat: Cliffs, dirt banks, buildings, and dead trees in riparian, agricultural, and grassland areas. In Larimer and Weld counties, most nests were found in the walls of arroyos, even where other nesting sites were available (Millsap and Millsap 1987).

Records: Breeding in mountain parks: nested about 1985 at Del Norte, Rio Grande County (J. Rawinski, pers. comm.). **Mountains outside parks:** 13 Sep 1979, Evergreen, Jefferson County; 30 Apr 1990, Echo Canyon Reservoir, Archuleta County. **Winter in San Luis Valley:** 22 Dec 1961 and 21 Dec 1965, Monte Vista, Rio Grande County.

Note: There is widespread concern that this species is declining, and it is on the National Audubon Society Special Concern list (Tate 1986).

References: Marti (1968, 1973a, b, 1974).

Order Strigiformes
Family Strigidae

Flammulated Owl
Otus flammeolus

Occurs in summer in foothills and lower mountains; more common than the records indicate.

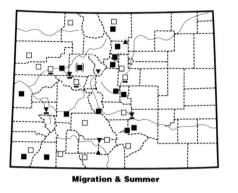

Migration & Summer

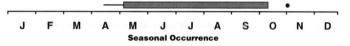

J F M A M J J A S O N D
Seasonal Occurrence

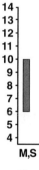

M,S

Elevation

Status (SP) (B): Uncommon to common **summer** resident in foothills and lower mountains. This species appears to be more common than most observers have realized; Richmond et al. (1980) concluded that "their obscurity is probably attributable more to behavior than scarcity." The species appears to be most common in western and southern Colorado. This owl apparently migrates through the mountains, as indicated by the discovery of five individuals during a severe snowstorm 8–9 May 1979 in the Aspen area, Pitkin County.

Accidental in **spring** and **fall** in lowlands and the San Luis Valley (four records). In Arizona and New Mexico, Balda et al. (1975) found that this species tends to migrate through lowlands in the spring and in the fall migrates south primarily through mountains, but there are too few migration records to determine if this is also true in Colorado.

Habitat: Old-growth (>200 yrs) or mature (>150 yrs) ponderosa pine and ponderosa-Douglas-fir forests, often mixed with mature aspen (Richmond et al. 1980, Webb 1982a, Reynolds and Linkhart 1987a, Jones 1987, 1991). In some areas, birds are seen in pure aspen. Some also occur in old-growth piñon-juniper woodlands (R. Reynolds, pers. comm.).

Records: **Lowlands:** 16 Apr 1959, Longmont, Boulder County (Bailey and Niedrach 1965); six during Apr and May 1962, Monte Vista National Wildlife Refuge, Rio Grande County (Bailey and Niedrach 1965); 1 Nov 1972, Montrose, Montrose County (WSC); spring 1983, Monte Vista National Wildlife Refuge.

References: Winn (1970), Linkhart and Reynolds (1987), Reynolds and Linkhart (1987b).

Eastern Screech-Owl
Otus asio

Year round in northeastern Colorado.

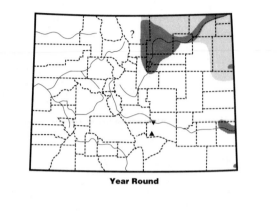

Year Round

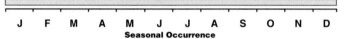

| J | F | M | A | M | J | J | A | S | O | N | D |

Seasonal Occurrence

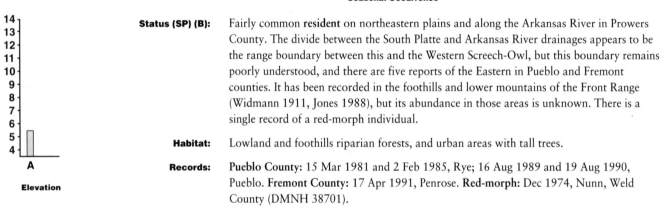

Elevation

Status (SP) (B): Fairly common **resident** on northeastern plains and along the Arkansas River in Prowers County. The divide between the South Platte and Arkansas River drainages appears to be the range boundary between this and the Western Screech-Owl, but this boundary remains poorly understood, and there are five reports of the Eastern in Pueblo and Fremont counties. It has been recorded in the foothills and lower mountains of the Front Range (Widmann 1911, Jones 1988), but its abundance in those areas is unknown. There is a single record of a red-morph individual.

Habitat: Lowland and foothills riparian forests, and urban areas with tall trees.

Records: **Pueblo County:** 15 Mar 1981 and 2 Feb 1985, Rye; 16 Aug 1989 and 19 Aug 1990, Pueblo. **Fremont County:** 17 Apr 1991, Penrose. **Red-morph:** Dec 1974, Nunn, Weld County (DMNH 38701).

Western Screech-Owl
Otus kennicottii

Year round in western and southeastern Colorado.

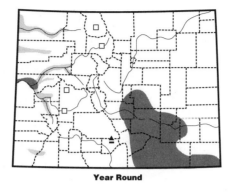

Year Round

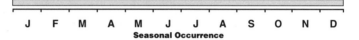

J F M A M J J A S O N D
Seasonal Occurrence

Elevation

Status (SP) (B): Uncommon to fairly common **resident** in western valleys and on southeastern plains and foothills north to El Paso and Fremont counties and east to western Bent County and southern Baca County. On the eastern plains, the northern boundary appears to be the divide between the South Platte and Arkansas River drainages, but this boundary is still poorly delineated (Jones 1988). Occurs in foothills and lower mountains (Cooke 1897). Its abundance in those areas is uncertain, but it may be less common than at lower elevations. Rare summer resident in Grand County (Jasper and Collins 1987), and accidental in North Park (one record) and the San Luis Valley (one record). This species may be more widespread in foothills and mountains than shown on the map, but its distribution in most of Colorado remains poorly known.

Habitat: Mature lowland and foothill riparian forests with shrubby undergrowth and rural woodlots (Levad 1989); also recorded from aspen and coniferous forests in Grand County (Jasper and Collins 1987), and from piñon-juniper woodlands in Las Animas County (latilong files).

Records: **North Park:** 4–5 July 1987. **San Luis Valley:** specimen found dead late May 1990, Great Sand Dunes National Monument, Alamosa County (Rawinski and Ryder 1991; specimen to be mounted at monument visitor center).

Great Horned Owl

Bubo virginianus

Year round throughout Colorado; most numerous at lower elevations.

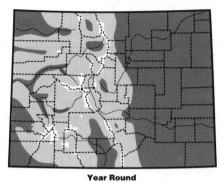

Year Round

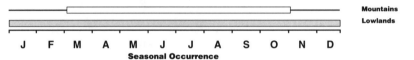

Mountains
Lowlands

J F M A M J J A S O N D

Seasonal Occurrence

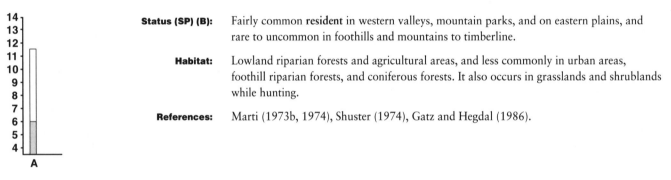

Elevation

Status (SP) (B): Fairly common **resident** in western valleys, mountain parks, and on eastern plains, and rare to uncommon in foothills and mountains to timberline.

Habitat: Lowland riparian forests and agricultural areas, and less commonly in urban areas, foothill riparian forests, and coniferous forests. It also occurs in grasslands and shrublands while hunting.

References: Marti (1973b, 1974), Shuster (1974), Gatz and Hegdal (1986).

Snowy Owl

Nyctea scandiaca

Occasional in winter, mostly in northeastern Colorado.

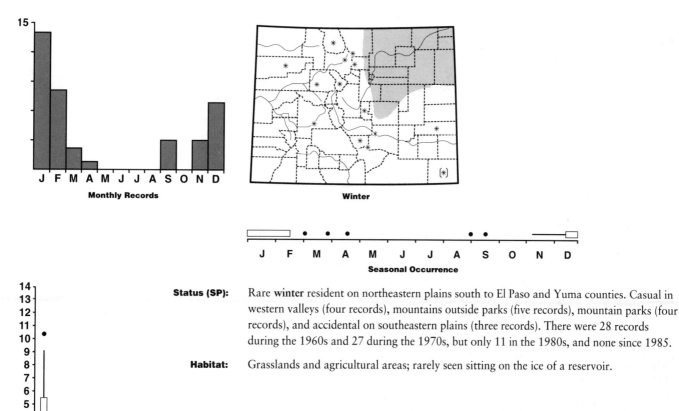

Monthly Records

Winter

Seasonal Occurrence

Elevation

Status (SP): Rare **winter** resident on northeastern plains south to El Paso and Yuma counties. Casual in western valleys (four records), mountains outside parks (five records), mountain parks (four records), and accidental on southeastern plains (three records). There were 28 records during the 1960s and 27 during the 1970s, but only 11 in the 1980s, and none since 1985.

Habitat: Grasslands and agricultural areas; rarely seen sitting on the ice of a reservoir.

Northern Pygmy-Owl

Glaucidium gnoma

Rare year round in the foothills and mountains.

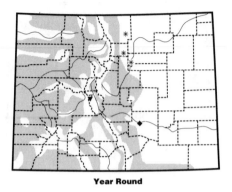

Year Round

J   F   M   A   M   J   J   A   S   O   N   D

Seasonal Occurrence

Status (SP) (B): Apparently a rare **resident** in foothills and mountains. Most summer observations are in higher foothills and mountains, and most winter observations are in foothills and lower mountains. This could suggest that there may be some altitudinal movement during the year, although it may also reflect observer distribution. In winter, some individuals may move into lowlands but are casual (six records) more than a few miles from the foothills. Accidental in fall above timberline (one record).

The true status of this species in Colorado is uncertain. Most observers have believed that this species was rare (Bailey and Niedrach 1965, Bridges 1992b). During two years of summer field work throughout the Colorado mountains, Webb (1982b) found only two. However, Rees (1977) described the species as "relatively common" in Gunnison County. An owl survey in Boulder County found 16 birds in 1985, suggesting that the species may be much more common than generally realized (Jones 1991). However, many fewer were found in the same area in subsequent years (Jones 1991).

Habitat: Coniferous forests, piñon-juniper woodlands, aspen forests, and foothills and montane riparian forests. It seems to prefer canyons with running water and ecotonal areas (Jones 1988).

Record: **Above timberline:** 2 Sep 1984, Mt. Shavano summit (14,229 ft.), Chaffee County (Gent 1984b).

Reference: Jones (1987).

14
13
12
11
10
9
8
7
6
5
4

A

Elevation

Burrowing Owl
Athene cunicularia

Summer resident, mostly in eastern Colorado.

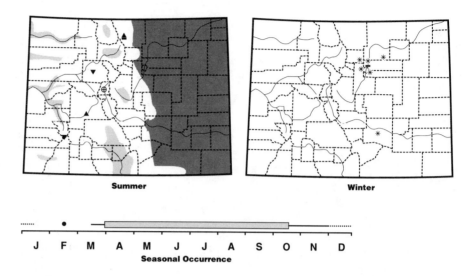

Summer   Winter

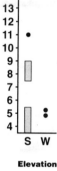

Elevation

| | | | | | | | | | | | |
|J|F|M|A|M|J|J|A|S|O|N|D|

Seasonal Occurrence

Status (SP) (B): Locally uncommon to fairly common **summer** resident on eastern plains. Uncommon in the Grand Valley, Mesa County and rare to uncommon in other western valleys and mountain parks. Accidental in mountains outside parks (two records). Casual **winter** resident on eastern plains (six records, including one specimen).

This species is declining in Colorado. In some areas, it has been completely or nearly extirpated. Although loss of habitat may be responsible in some areas, there are sites with suitable habitat that no longer have owls, so other factors appear to be involved as well.

Habitat: Grasslands and rarely semidesert shrublands; usually in or near prairie dog towns.

Records: **Mountains outside parks:** 20 Oct 1980, at 10,800 ft. on Red Mountain Pass, Ouray/San Juan counties; 16 May 1983, northeast entrance to Rocky Mountain National Park, Larimer County (DMNH 39271). **Winter specimen:** 29 Dec 1961, 5 mi. north of Brighton, in Weld County (DMNH 34436).

References: Marti (1973b, 1974).

Spotted Owl
Strix occidentalis

Resident in foothills and mountains, mostly in southern Colorado.

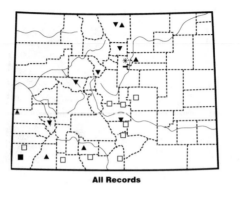

All Records

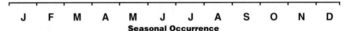

J   F   M   A   M   J   J   A   S   O   N   D
Seasonal Occurrence

14
13
12
11
10
9
8
7
6
5
4

A

Elevation

Status (SP) (B): Very rare **resident** in foothills and mountains (about 30 records). Survey work in 1989 and 1990 located pairs or individual birds at ten sites in two main areas: southwestern canyons in Montezuma, Archuleta and Conejos counties, and on the east side of the Wet Mountains in Custer and Huerfano counties (Reynolds 1990). The only confirmed breeding site is at Mesa Verde National Park, Montezuma County. A young bird was said to have been taken in 1941 near Hartsel, Park County (Gadd 1942). Most Colorado records are in the southern part of the state, but it has been recorded north to Pitkin, Summit, and Larimer counties (Webb 1983, Kingery 1991b). Most records are in summer, but that may reflect observer bias more than the seasonal distribution of the bird. Large areas of Colorado have not yet been surveyed for this species, and its status in Colorado remains poorly known. Accidental on eastern plains (two records*).

Habitat: This species occupies two distinct habitats in Colorado (Reynolds 1990): large, steep canyons with exposed cliffs and dense old-growth mixed forest of Douglas-fir, white fir, and ponderosa pine, and canyons in piñon-juniper areas with small and widely scattered patches of old Douglas-firs. Summer roost sites are in a cool microclimate, generally with a closed canopy and/or on a north-facing slope (Barrows 1981).

Records: Eastern plains*: 31 Dec 1958, Lakewood, Jefferson County (DMNH 34437); 3–5 June 1975, Rocky Mountain Arsenal, Adams County.

Long-eared Owl

Asio otus

Year round throughout Colorado, but mostly at low elevations.

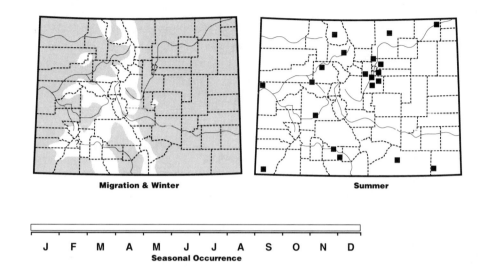

Migration & Winter   **Summer**

J F M A M J J A S O N D
Seasonal Occurrence

A
Elevation

Status (SP) (B): Rare **resident** in western valleys, foothills, lower mountains, mountain parks, and on eastern plains. Apparently very rare in higher mountains. May be locally uncommon in the winter around roosts. Very local in summer, and at many sites apparently does not occur in summer. At some mountain sites it is apparently absent in winter. Rare migrant and summer resident in North Park (USFWS 1990) and Middle Park (Jasper and Collins 1987); occurs primarily in fall and winter in the San Luis Valley (USFWS 1989). This species is declining in Colorado (Jones 1988), and its current status and distribution are rather poorly known, especially at higher altitudes.

Habitat: In lowlands, occurs primarily in riparian forest and windbreaks, but also in urban areas and tamarisk thickets. In mountains, occurs primarily in dense Douglas-fir forest (Jones 1988). In all areas, it is found primarily where there are dense tall shrubs and/or trees. Also recorded from foothill shrublands, piñon-juniper woodlands, aspen forests, and spruce-fir forests (Kingery 1988, J. Rawinski, pers. comm.).

References: Catlett et al. (1958), Marti (1973b, 1974), Moulton et al. (1976).

Short-eared Owl

Asio flammeus

Year round at low elevations and in mountain parks; most numerous in winter.

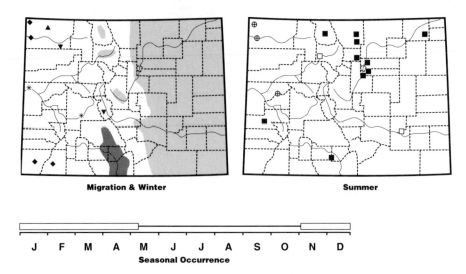

Migration & Winter   Summer

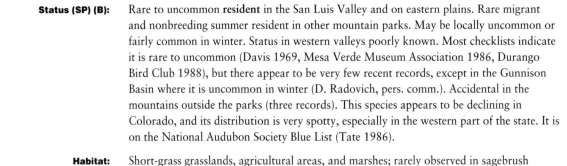

J   F   M   A   M   J   J   A   S   O   N   D

Seasonal Occurrence

Status (SP) (B): Rare to uncommon **resident** in the San Luis Valley and on eastern plains. Rare migrant and nonbreeding summer resident in other mountain parks. May be locally uncommon or fairly common in winter. Status in western valleys poorly known. Most checklists indicate it is rare to uncommon (Davis 1969, Mesa Verde Museum Association 1986, Durango Bird Club 1988), but there appear to be very few recent records, except in the Gunnison Basin where it is uncommon in winter (D. Radovich, pers. comm.). Accidental in the mountains outside the parks (three records). This species appears to be declining in Colorado, and its distribution is very spotty, especially in the western part of the state. It is on the National Audubon Society Blue List (Tate 1986).

Habitat: Short-grass grasslands, agricultural areas, and marshes; rarely observed in sagebrush shrubland or piñon-juniper woodland.

Records: **Mountains outside parks:** 4 Sep 1988, Mt. Antero, Chaffee County; 3 June 1989, Grand Mesa, Mesa County; nest on 17 July 1990, Uncompahgre Plateau, Montrose County.

Elevation

Boreal Owl

Aegolius funereus

Rare year round in high mountains.

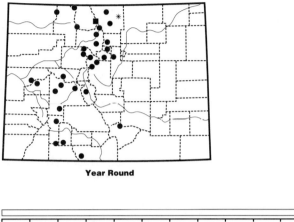

Year Round

| J | F | M | A | M | J | J | A | S | O | N | D |

Seasonal Occurrence

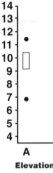

A

Elevation

Status (SP) (B): Rare to locally uncommon **resident** in higher mountains. Accidental in lower mountains (one record). The first confirmed **breeding** records were in 1981 and 1982, Cameron Pass, Larimer County (Palmer and Ryder 1984), although juveniles were observed 14 Aug 1963, Deadman Mountain Lookout, Larimer County (Baldwin and Koplin 1966) and 31 Aug 1971, Rocky Mountain Biological Lab, Gunnison County. Intensive work has shown that the species is widely distributed in the proper habitat and elevations, with records from most of the higher ranges of the state (Webb 1982b, Palmer 1984, Ryder et al. 1987, Stahlecker and Rawinski 1990, Ryder 1991b). There are no records from the Rampart Range, the Pikes Peak area, the Sangre de Cristo and Culebra Ranges, or the Spanish Peaks area, and there is only a probable record from the Wet Mountains. This species has probably always been present in Colorado; the recent increase in records is due to more intensive and knowledgeable searching.

Habitat: Mature spruce-fir or spruce-fir/lodgepole pine forest interspersed with meadows (Palmer 1984, Ryder et al. 1987).

Record: Low mountains: 22 Dec 1990, Lory State Park, Larimer County.

References: Palmer (1987), Reynolds et al. (1990, Bridges 1992c).

Northern Saw-whet Owl

Aegolius acadicus

Year round in the foothills and low mountains; occasional in migration and winter at lower elevations.

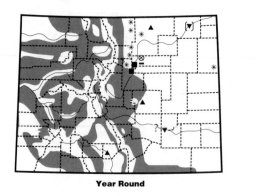

Year Round

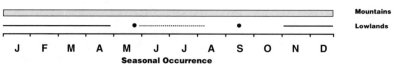

Seasonal Occurrence

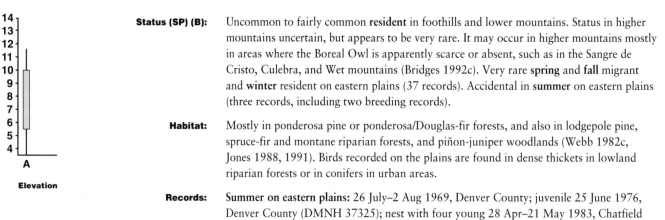

Elevation

Status (SP) (B): Uncommon to fairly common **resident** in foothills and lower mountains. Status in higher mountains uncertain, but appears to be very rare. It may occur in higher mountains mostly in areas where the Boreal Owl is apparently scarce or absent, such as in the Sangre de Cristo, Culebra, and Wet mountains (Bridges 1992c). Very rare **spring** and **fall** migrant and **winter** resident on eastern plains (37 records). Accidental in **summer** on eastern plains (three records, including two breeding records).

Habitat: Mostly in ponderosa pine or ponderosa/Douglas-fir forests, and also in lodgepole pine, spruce-fir and montane riparian forests, and piñon-juniper woodlands (Webb 1982c, Jones 1988, 1991). Birds recorded on the plains are found in dense thickets in lowland riparian forests or in conifers in urban areas.

Records: **Summer on eastern plains:** 26 July–2 Aug 1969, Denver County; juvenile 25 June 1976, Denver County (DMNH 37325); nest with four young 28 Apr–21 May 1983, Chatfield Reservoir, Jefferson County (Palmer 1983).

Order Caprimulgiformes
Family Caprimulgidae

Lesser Nighthawk
Chordeiles acutipennis

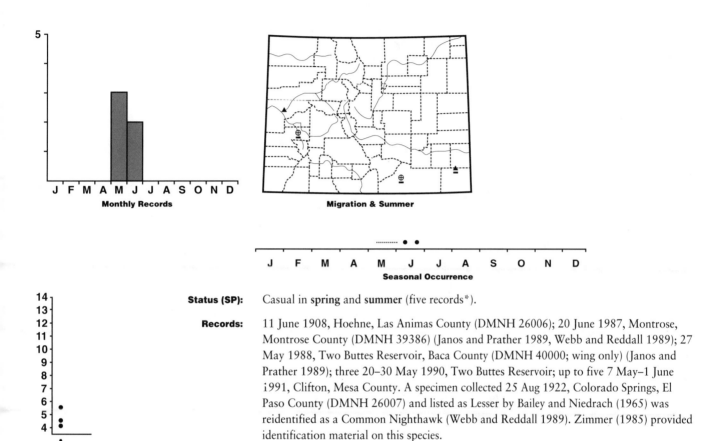

Monthly Records

Migration & Summer

Seasonal Occurrence

Elevation

Status (SP): Casual in **spring** and **summer** (five records*).

Records: 11 June 1908, Hoehne, Las Animas County (DMNH 26006); 20 June 1987, Montrose, Montrose County (DMNH 39386) (Janos and Prather 1989, Webb and Reddall 1989); 27 May 1988, Two Buttes Reservoir, Baca County (DMNH 40000; wing only) (Janos and Prather 1989); three 20–30 May 1990, Two Buttes Reservoir; up to five 7 May–1 June 1991, Clifton, Mesa County. A specimen collected 25 Aug 1922, Colorado Springs, El Paso County (DMNH 26007) and listed as Lesser by Bailey and Niedrach (1965) was reidentified as a Common Nighthawk (Webb and Reddall 1989). Zimmer (1985) provided identification material on this species.

Common Nighthawk

Chordeiles minor

Summer resident throughout Colorado below 10,000 ft.

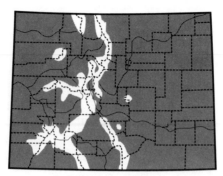

Migration & Summer

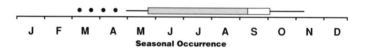

Seasonal Occurrence

J F M A M J J A S O N D

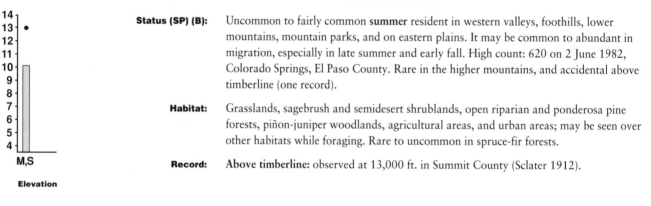

Elevation

Status (SP) (B): Uncommon to fairly common **summer** resident in western valleys, foothills, lower mountains, mountain parks, and on eastern plains. It may be common to abundant in migration, especially in late summer and early fall. High count: 620 on 2 June 1982, Colorado Springs, El Paso County. Rare in the higher mountains, and accidental above timberline (one record).

Habitat: Grasslands, sagebrush and semidesert shrublands, open riparian and ponderosa pine forests, piñon-juniper woodlands, agricultural areas, and urban areas; may be seen over other habitats while foraging. Rare to uncommon in spruce-fir forests.

Record: **Above timberline:** observed at 13,000 ft. in Summit County (Sclater 1912).

Common Poorwill
Phalaenoptilus nuttallii

Summer resident in foothills; rare in migration at low elevations.

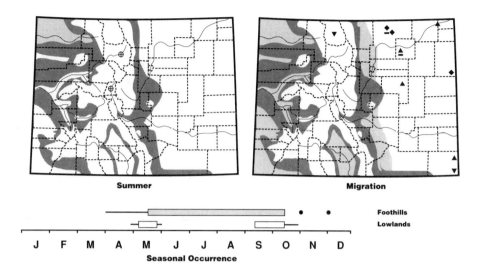

| Summer | Migration |

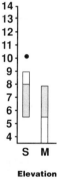

Elevation

Status (SP) (B): Uncommon to fairly common **summer** resident in foothills and mesas, including the foothills around the San Luis Valley; rare in lower mountains. Recorded in higher mountains by Bergtold (1928), but no recent records. Rare nonbreeding summer resident in Middle Park (Jasper and Collins 1987). Accidental in the upper Arkansas River Valley (one record). Migrates primarily through the foothills. Rare migrant in western valleys, in the mountain parks and on eastern plains near foothills; very rare on extreme eastern plains (21+ records).

Bergtold (1928) thought it may occasionally **winter** in southern Colorado, but he did not provide any records. A dead bird was found 18 Jan 1975 near Livermore, Larimer County (CSU 9857). The bird had not been dead for long; it may have been hibernating and came out during a warm spell and subsequently died when colder weather resumed (Ryder 1975).

Habitat: Breeds in foothill shrublands (Gambel oak, mountain mahogany, serviceberry, etc.), piñon-juniper woodlands, and ponderosa pine forests. It often forages over adjacent grasslands. In migration, may be found in lowland riparian forests or in short-grass grasslands.

Whip-poor-will
Caprimulgus vociferus

Status (SP): Casual migrant on eastern plains (four **spring** records and three **fall** records*). Accidental in **summer** in foothills (one record*).

Habitat: Migrants were seen in lowland riparian forest. The summer bird was singing in foothill riparian forest with a Gambel oak understory.

Records: **Spring***: 13 May 1982, Colorado Springs State Wildlife Area, El Paso County; 13 May 1982, Cache La Poudre River, Larimer County; 26 May 1986, Mesa de Maya, Las Animas County; 13 May 1989, Lake Henry, Crowley County. **Fall***: 14 Sep 1903, Ft. Collins, Larimer County (DMNH 6399) (Burnett 1904); 21 Sep 1985, Bonny Reservoir, Yuma County; 27 Sep 1987, Julesburg, Sedgwick County. **Summer***: singing male 15–30 July 1981, South Cheyenne Canyon, El Paso County; based on the song, this bird was identified as the southwestern race *C. v. arizonae*.

Order Apodiformes
Family Apodidae

Black Swift

Cypseloides niger

Local in summer in the mountains; most numerous in southwestern Colorado.

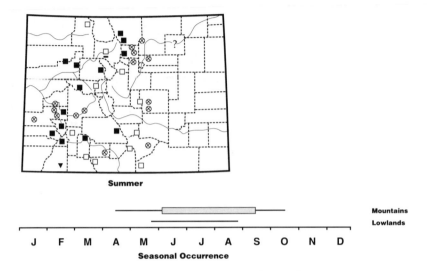

Summer

Mountains
Lowlands

J F M A M J J A S O N D
Seasonal Occurrence

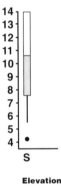

Elevation

Status (SP) (B): Locally uncommon to fairly common **summer** resident in the San Juan Mountains, and rare to uncommon very locally in most other mountain ranges in the state, north to the Park Range and the Front Range. Breeding was first confirmed in the state in 1949 (Knorr and Baily 1950).

Very rare in foothills, and in western valleys, mountain parks, and on eastern plains, mostly within 10 mi. of foothills. Most such observations are in western Colorado in Delta, Montrose, and Gunnison counties, and in northeastern Colorado in Boulder and El Paso counties. Accidental on extreme eastern plains (one record). Low elevation observations probably represent widely foraging birds from the higher mountains; they seem to be forced to forage lower during stormy weather at higher elevations. Some of the June and Aug observations could represent migrants.

Habitat: Nest on precipitous cliffs near or behind high waterfalls. Foraging birds range at high elevations widely over most montane and adjacent lowland habitats.

Record: Extreme eastern plains: date unknown in 1923, Ft. Morgan, Morgan County (Bailey and Niedrach 1965).

Reference: Knorr (1961).

Chimney Swift
Chaetura pelagica

Fairly common in summer in eastern Colorado, especially in the extreme east.

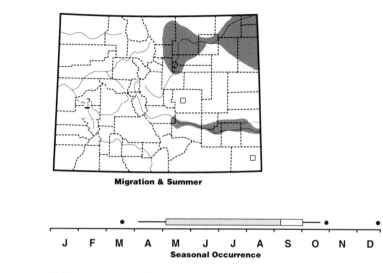

Migration & Summer

J F M A M J J A S O N D

Seasonal Occurrence

Status (SP) (B): Fairly common local **summer** resident on eastern plains. Observed mostly along the South Platte and Arkansas rivers, and in the towns and cities at the base of the Front Range. This species has become more common in Colorado in recent decades. The first record from the state was in June 1917, and the first nesting in 1938, both in Denver County (Bailey and Niedrach 1965). Accidental in western valleys (one record*). There are two specimens.

Habitat: Towns and cities; rarely over riparian areas away from towns.

Records: **Western valleys***: desiccated bird found in 1988 at Delta, Delta County (DMNH 39749). **Specimen:** 27 Sep 1963, Denver County (DMNH 33799).

14
13
12
11
10
9
8
7
6
5
4

M,S

Elevation

Chimney/Vaux's Swift
Chaetura pelagica/vauxi

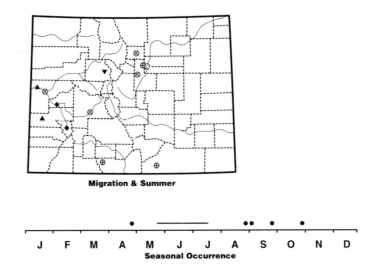

Migration & Summer

Seasonal Occurrence

J F M A M J J A S O N D

Elevation

14
13
12
11
10
9
8
7
6
5
4

M,S

Status (SR): There are 20 records of *Chaetura* swifts away from the eastern plains: 13 from western valleys, four from mountains, and three from eastern foothills. Some were reported as possible Vaux's Swifts, some as Chimney Swifts, and others were unidentified to species. There are no confirmed records of Vaux's Swift from Colorado. There have been several documented reports that were strongly suggestive of Vaux's, but the CFO Records Committee has been reluctant to include the species on the state list without specimens. Some records of western Chimney Swifts were considered as Chimney by the Records Committee, but we have included these as of uncertain identity. All sight reports of *Chaetura* swifts away from the eastern plains should be rigorously documented.

White-throated Swift

Aeronautes saxatalis

Common in summer around foothill cliffs and canyons.

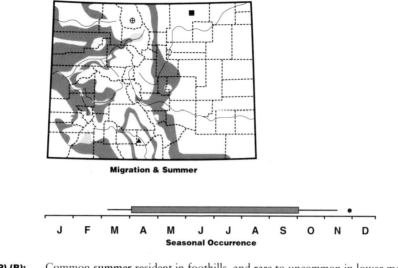

Migration & Summer

Seasonal Occurrence

J F M A M J J A S O N D

Elevation

14
13 •
12
11
10
9
8
7
6
5
4

M,S

Status (SP) (B): Common **summer** resident in foothills, and rare to uncommon in lower mountains. High count: 300 to 400 on 7 Oct 1990, Clifton, Mesa County. Often wanders, especially in stormy weather, to adjacent lowlands, but rarely occurs more than a few miles away from cliffs. Although recorded from the lower mountains around the periphery of Middle Park and the San Luis Valley, it is apparently unrecorded from South Park and accidental in North Park (one record). There is a small isolated breeding population (at least in some years) on the eastern plains at the Pawnee Buttes, Weld County. Accidental at or above timberline (one record).

Habitat: Cliffs; while foraging often occurs over other habitats.

Records: **North Park:** 17 June 1980. **Above timberline:** observed to 13,100 ft. on Upper Sand Creek, Saguache County (Gutiérrez 1970).

Order Apodiformes
Family Trochilidae

Blue-throated Hummingbird
Lampornis clemenciae

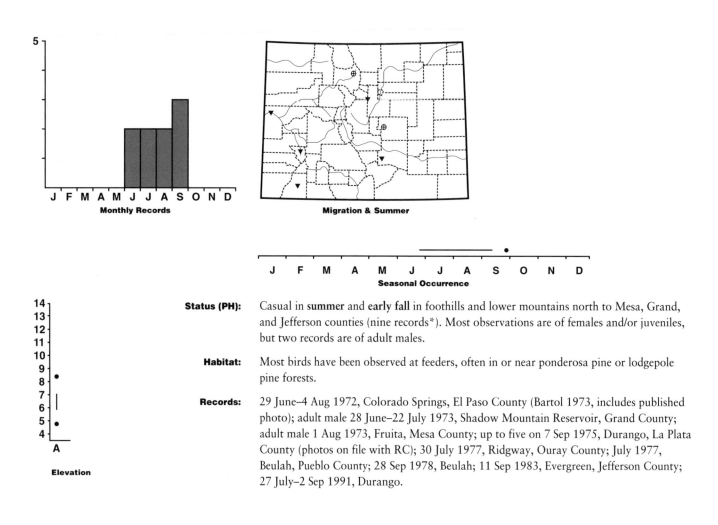

Monthly Records

Migration & Summer

Seasonal Occurrence

Elevation

Status (PH): Casual in **summer** and **early fall** in foothills and lower mountains north to Mesa, Grand, and Jefferson counties (nine records*). Most observations are of females and/or juveniles, but two records are of adult males.

Habitat: Most birds have been observed at feeders, often in or near ponderosa pine or lodgepole pine forests.

Records: 29 June–4 Aug 1972, Colorado Springs, El Paso County (Bartol 1973, includes published photo); adult male 28 June–22 July 1973, Shadow Mountain Reservoir, Grand County; adult male 1 Aug 1973, Fruita, Mesa County; up to five on 7 Sep 1975, Durango, La Plata County (photos on file with RC); 30 July 1977, Ridgway, Ouray County; July 1977, Beulah, Pueblo County; 28 Sep 1978, Beulah; 11 Sep 1983, Evergreen, Jefferson County; 27 July–2 Sep 1991, Durango.

Magnificent Hummingbird

Eugenes fulgens

Occasional in summer and fall in foothills and low mountains; one nesting record.

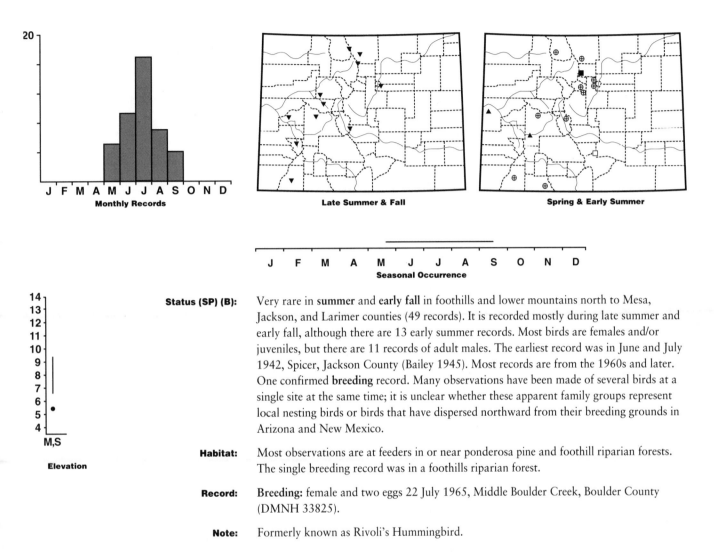

Monthly Records

Late Summer & Fall

Spring & Early Summer

J F M A M J J A S O N D
Seasonal Occurrence

Elevation

Status (SP) (B): Very rare in **summer** and **early fall** in foothills and lower mountains north to Mesa, Jackson, and Larimer counties (49 records). It is recorded mostly during late summer and early fall, although there are 13 early summer records. Most birds are females and/or juveniles, but there are 11 records of adult males. The earliest record was in June and July 1942, Spicer, Jackson County (Bailey 1945). Most records are from the 1960s and later. One confirmed **breeding** record. Many observations have been made of several birds at a single site at the same time; it is unclear whether these apparent family groups represent local nesting birds or birds that have dispersed northward from their breeding grounds in Arizona and New Mexico.

Habitat: Most observations are at feeders in or near ponderosa pine and foothill riparian forests. The single breeding record was in a foothills riparian forest.

Record: **Breeding:** female and two eggs 22 July 1965, Middle Boulder Creek, Boulder County (DMNH 33825).

Note: Formerly known as Rivoli's Hummingbird.

Black-chinned Hummingbird

Archilochus alexandri

Summer resident in foothills of western and southern Colorado; occasional elsewhere.

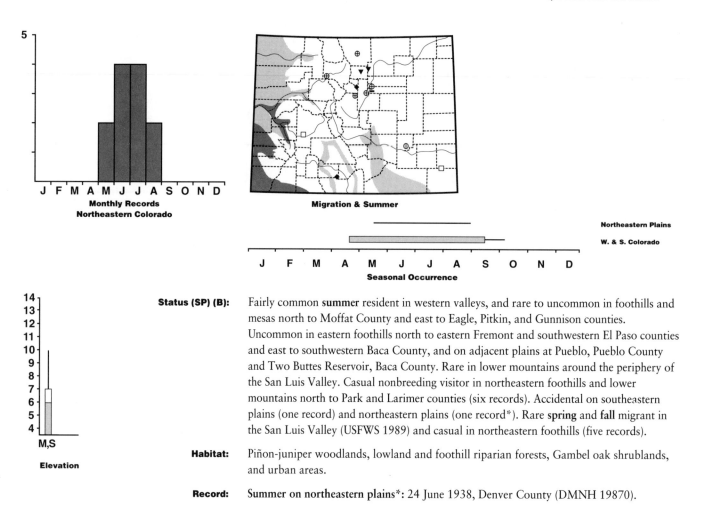

Monthly Records
Northeastern Colorado

Migration & Summer

Northeastern Plains

W. & S. Colorado

Seasonal Occurrence

Elevation

Status (SP) (B): Fairly common **summer** resident in western valleys, and rare to uncommon in foothills and mesas north to Moffat County and east to Eagle, Pitkin, and Gunnison counties. Uncommon in eastern foothills north to eastern Fremont and southwestern El Paso counties and east to southwestern Baca County, and on adjacent plains at Pueblo, Pueblo County and Two Buttes Reservoir, Baca County. Rare in lower mountains around the periphery of the San Luis Valley. Casual nonbreeding visitor in northeastern foothills and lower mountains north to Park and Larimer counties (six records). Accidental on southeastern plains (one record) and northeastern plains (one record*). Rare **spring** and **fall** migrant in the San Luis Valley (USFWS 1989) and casual in northeastern foothills (five records).

Habitat: Piñon-juniper woodlands, lowland and foothill riparian forests, Gambel oak shrublands, and urban areas.

Record: **Summer on northeastern plains***: 24 June 1938, Denver County (DMNH 19870).

Anna's Hummingbird
Calypte anna

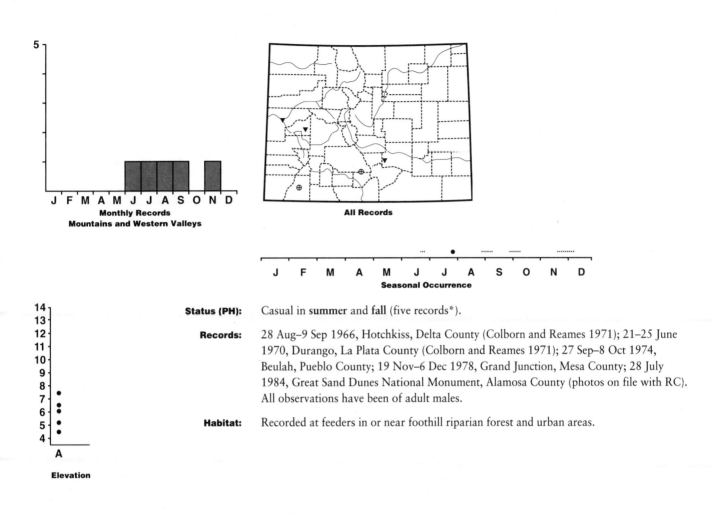

Monthly Records
Mountains and Western Valleys

All Records

Seasonal Occurrence

Elevation

Status (PH): Casual in **summer** and **fall** (five records*).

Records: 28 Aug–9 Sep 1966, Hotchkiss, Delta County (Colborn and Reames 1971); 21–25 June 1970, Durango, La Plata County (Colborn and Reames 1971); 27 Sep–8 Oct 1974, Beulah, Pueblo County; 19 Nov–6 Dec 1978, Grand Junction, Mesa County; 28 July 1984, Great Sand Dunes National Monument, Alamosa County (photos on file with RC). All observations have been of adult males.

Habitat: Recorded at feeders in or near foothill riparian forest and urban areas.

Calliope Hummingbird
Stellula calliope

Migrant in late summer and early fall in foothills and low mountains.

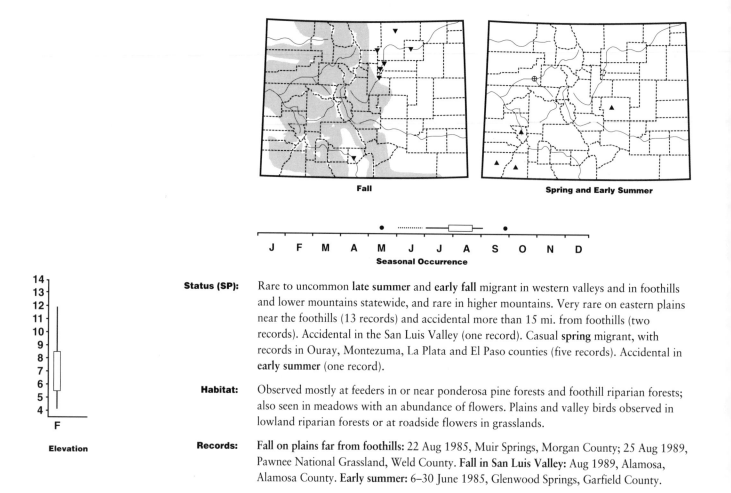

Fall

Spring and Early Summer

J F M A M J J A S O N D

Seasonal Occurrence

14
13
12
11
10
9
8
7
6
5
4

F

Elevation

Status (SP): Rare to uncommon **late summer** and **early fall** migrant in western valleys and in foothills and lower mountains statewide, and rare in higher mountains. Very rare on eastern plains near the foothills (13 records) and accidental more than 15 mi. from foothills (two records). Accidental in the San Luis Valley (one record). Casual **spring** migrant, with records in Ouray, Montezuma, La Plata and El Paso counties (five records). Accidental in **early summer** (one record).

Habitat: Observed mostly at feeders in or near ponderosa pine forests and foothill riparian forests; also seen in meadows with an abundance of flowers. Plains and valley birds observed in lowland riparian forests or at roadside flowers in grasslands.

Records: **Fall on plains far from foothills:** 22 Aug 1985, Muir Springs, Morgan County; 25 Aug 1989, Pawnee National Grassland, Weld County. **Fall in San Luis Valley:** Aug 1989, Alamosa, Alamosa County. **Early summer:** 6–30 June 1985, Glenwood Springs, Garfield County.

Broad-tailed Hummingbird
Selasphorus platycercus

Summer resident in foothills and low mountains; occasional in high mountains and at low elevations.

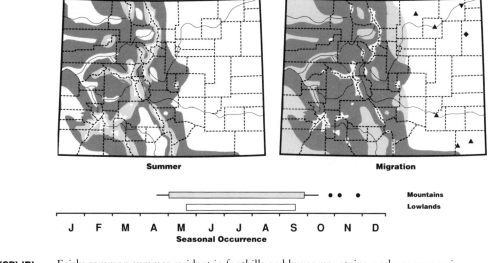

| Summer | Migration |

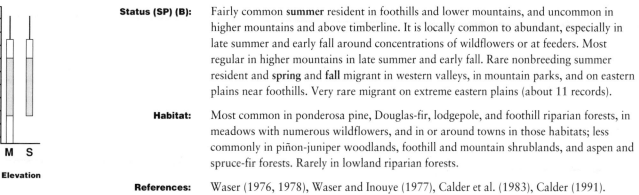

Mountains
Lowlands

J F M A M J J A S O N D
Seasonal Occurrence

Elevation
M   S

Status (SP) (B): Fairly common **summer** resident in foothills and lower mountains, and uncommon in higher mountains and above timberline. It is locally common to abundant, especially in late summer and early fall around concentrations of wildflowers or at feeders. Most regular in higher mountains in late summer and early fall. Rare nonbreeding summer resident and **spring** and **fall** migrant in western valleys, in mountain parks, and on eastern plains near foothills. Very rare migrant on extreme eastern plains (about 11 records).

Habitat: Most common in ponderosa pine, Douglas-fir, lodgepole, and foothill riparian forests, in meadows with numerous wildflowers, and in or around towns in those habitats; less commonly in piñon-juniper woodlands, foothill and mountain shrublands, and aspen and spruce-fir forests. Rarely in lowland riparian forests.

References: Waser (1976, 1978), Waser and Inouye (1977), Calder et al. (1983), Calder (1991).

Rufous Hummingbird
Selasphorus rufus

Migrant in late summer and early fall in mountains; occasional in spring and at low elevations.

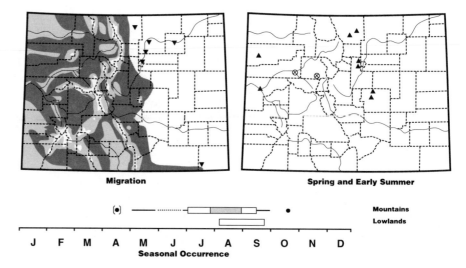

| Migration | Spring and Early Summer |

Mountains
Lowlands

J F M A M J J A S O N D
Seasonal Occurrence

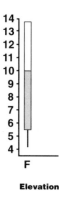

Elevation

Status (SP): Fairly common to common **summer** and **early fall** migrant in foothills, lower mountains, and mountain parks; rare to uncommon in higher mountains to timberline. Adult males arrive first, followed by adult females, and lastly by juveniles (Calder 1987). Uncommon fall migrant in western valleys and rare on eastern plains near foothills. Casual on northeastern plains more than five mi. from the foothills east to Morgan County (six records). Casual **spring** migrant in foothills and lower mountains (eight records).

Accidental in **early summer** (two records); it is unclear whether these were late spring migrants, early fall migrants, or nonbreeding summer residents. Although Drew (1881) and Bergtold (1928) claimed it nested in Colorado, there are no confirmed breeding records. Birds seen in late June should be considered fall migrants as this is one of the earliest returning fall migrants.

Habitat: Coniferous forests, foothill and mountain riparian forests and shrublands, foothill shrublands, meadows with abundant wildflowers, and in towns in or around those habitats; most common at feeders.

Records: **Early summer:** two males and two females 23 May–1 Aug 1973, Minturn, Eagle County; 14 June (year unknown), Glenwood Springs, Garfield County.

Order Coraciiformes
Family Alcedinidae

Belted Kingfisher
Ceryle alcyon

Year round at low elevations and in mountain parks.

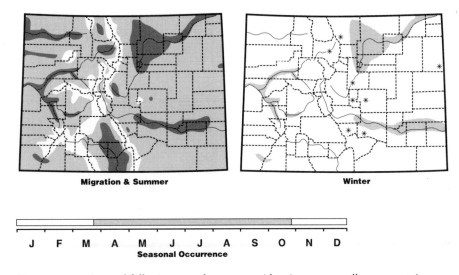

Migration & Summer   **Winter**

J F M A M J J A S O N D
Seasonal Occurrence

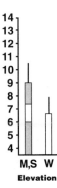

M,S W
Elevation

Status (SP) (B): Uncommon **spring** and **fall** migrant and **summer** resident in western valleys, mountain parks, and on eastern plains; rare in foothills and lower mountains. Rare to uncommon **winter** resident in western valleys, foothills, mountain parks, and on eastern plains.

Habitat: Lakes and slow-moving rivers.

Order Piciformes
Family Picidae

Lewis' Woodpecker

Melanerpes lewis

Year round in the foothills of southern Colorado; occasional elsewhere.

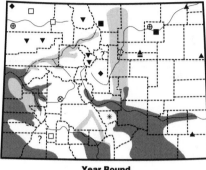

Year Round

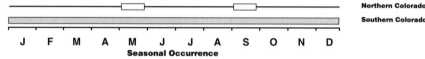

Northern Colorado

Southern Colorado

J   F   M   A   M   J   J   A   S   O   N   D
Seasonal Occurrence

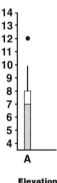

Elevation

Status (SP) (B):   Uncommon to locally fairly common **resident** in valleys, plains, foothills, and mesas in southern Colorado from Mesa, Chaffee, southwestern El Paso, and Prowers counties southward. On the southeastern plains, about half of the birds were resident and half wintered to the west in the southern foothills (Hadow 1973). It seems to be especially common in the Durango area, La Plata County and in southwestern Baca County. The occurrence of this species on the southeastern plains is recent, beginning about 1910 and accelerating since the 1950s, due to the maturation of cottonwoods in farmland areas and cultivation of corn, which they use for food (Hadow 1973).

Rare and local in valleys and foothills north to Moffat County and east to Grand County in western Colorado and north to Larimer County in eastern Colorado. In the northeastern foothills, at least in Larimer and Douglas counties, it formerly was more common (Packard 1946, Bailey and Niedrach 1965). Rare resident on northeastern plains, observed mostly from Weld and Adams counties west, and casual on extreme northeastern plains to Logan and Yuma counties (eight records). Uncommon summer resident in foothills around the periphery of the San Luis Valley and in the southern half of the valley proper (Ryder 1965, Simmons 1986). Very rare, mostly in spring and fall but also recorded in summer and winter, in lower mountains and mountain parks north to Jackson and Larimer counties (about 15 records). Accidental in higher mountains (two records).

Habitat: Lowland and foothill riparian forests, agricultural areas, and urban areas with tall deciduous trees; rarely in piñon-juniper woodlands. On the southeastern plains, it occurs mostly in open farmland with scattered tall cottonwoods and avoids riparian forests which are used primarily by Red-headed Woodpeckers (Bock et al. 1971).

Records: **High mountains:** observed to 12,000 ft. in La Plata County (Morrison 1886) and in the Wet Mountains, Custer/Pueblo counties (Lowe 1894).

Red-headed Woodpecker
Melanerpes erythrocephalus

Summer resident in extreme eastern Colorado, and less common west to the foothills; occasional elsewhere.

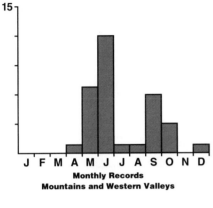

**Monthly Records
Mountains and Western Valleys**

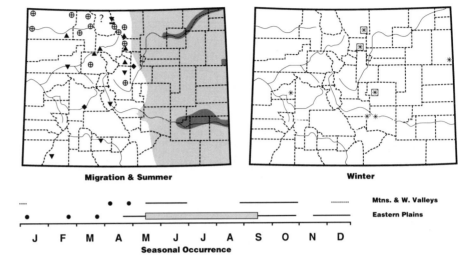

Migration & Summer   Winter

Mtns. & W. Valleys
Eastern Plains

Seasonal Occurrence

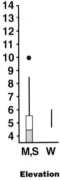

Elevation

Status (SP) (B): Uncommon to fairly common **spring** and **fall** migrant and **summer** resident on extreme eastern plains from Morgan and Otero counties eastward; rare west to foothills. Very rare spring, summer, and fall visitor in foothills and mountains east of the Continental Divide from Jackson and Larimer counties south to Chaffee and Jefferson counties (17 records, including one specimen). Widmann (1911) observed three pairs in June and July 1910 at Estes Park, Larimer County, but did not specifically mention breeding. Casual in mountain parks (nine records) and in the western valleys, mostly in northwestern Colorado (eight records). Accidental in mountains west of the Continental Divide (two records). Very rare in **early winter** on eastern plains near foothills (11 records). Accidental in **mid-winter** on eastern plains (three records) and in western valleys (one record*).

This species formerly was a common breeder on the plains near the foothills in the Denver area and Adams County (Dille 1903, Hersey and Rockwell 1909), but is now very rare. It also appears to have been more common formerly in southeastern Colorado than at present (Warren 1906), perhaps due to range expansion by Lewis' Woodpecker (Hadow 1973).

Habitat: Lowland riparian forests, and rarely in agricultural and urban areas with tall trees.

Records: **Mountain specimen:** 31 Aug 1913, Medicine Bow Range, Jackson County (DMNH 3457). **Mid-winter on eastern plains:** 19 Feb 1972, Pueblo, Pueblo County; 7 Jan 1978, Wetmore, Pueblo County; 20 Feb 1991, Bonny Reservoir, Yuma County. **Mid-winter in western valleys*:** 8 Dec 1973–9 Jan 1974, Hotchkiss, Delta County.

Red-bellied Woodpecker
Melanerpes carolinus

Year round in extreme northeastern Colorado; occasional west to the foothills.

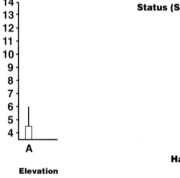

**Monthly Records
Away from Northeastern Corner**

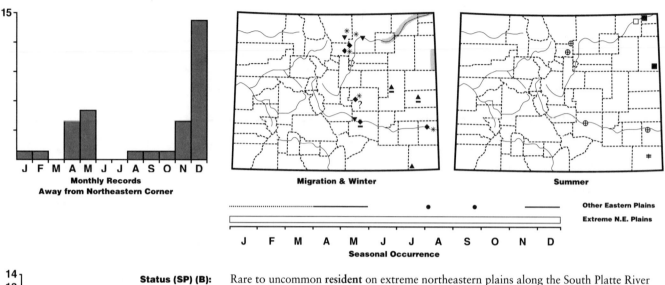

Elevation

Status (SP) (B): Rare to uncommon **resident** on extreme northeastern plains along the South Platte River west to Morgan County and in the Bonny Reservoir area, Yuma County. Breeding has been confirmed at Bonny Reservoir and at Ovid, Sedgwick County, and they probably breed at Tamarack Ranch, Logan County. Elsewhere on eastern plains, west to foothills and south to Pueblo and Baca counties, it is very rare in fall and winter (31 records) and casual in spring (eight records). One former breeding record on southeastern plains in June 1937 at Springfield, Baca County (Bailey and Niedrach 1965). All Colorado breeding records (except the 1937 record) have been in the late 1960s and later; this species appears to be slowly expanding into eastern Colorado.

Habitat: Lowland riparian forests.

Yellow-bellied Sapsucker

Sphyrapicus varius

Occasional in fall and winter in northeastern Colorado, but status and distribution still uncertain.

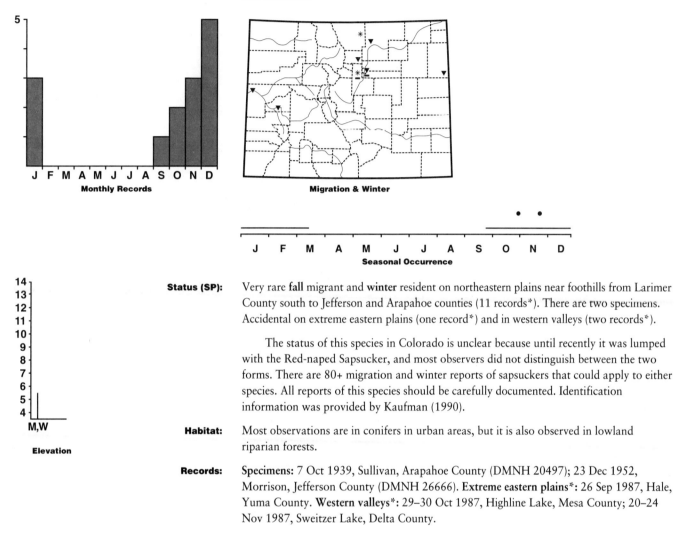

Monthly Records

Migration & Winter

Seasonal Occurrence

Elevation

Status (SP): Very rare **fall** migrant and **winter** resident on northeastern plains near foothills from Larimer County south to Jefferson and Arapahoe counties (11 records*). There are two specimens. Accidental on extreme eastern plains (one record*) and in western valleys (two records*).

The status of this species in Colorado is unclear because until recently it was lumped with the Red-naped Sapsucker, and most observers did not distinguish between the two forms. There are 80+ migration and winter reports of sapsuckers that could apply to either species. All reports of this species should be carefully documented. Identification information was provided by Kaufman (1990).

Habitat: Most observations are in conifers in urban areas, but it is also observed in lowland riparian forests.

Records: **Specimens:** 7 Oct 1939, Sullivan, Arapahoe County (DMNH 20497); 23 Dec 1952, Morrison, Jefferson County (DMNH 26666). **Extreme eastern plains*:** 26 Sep 1987, Hale, Yuma County. **Western valleys*:** 29–30 Oct 1987, Highline Lake, Mesa County; 20–24 Nov 1987, Sweitzer Lake, Delta County.

Red-naped Sapsucker
Sphyrapicus nuchalis

Summer resident in foothills and low mountains.

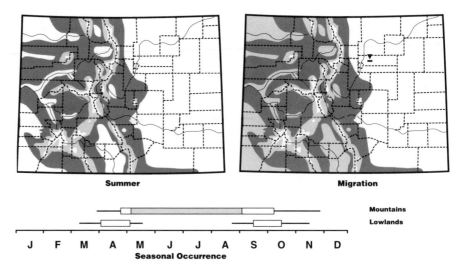

Summer   Migration

Mountains

Lowlands

| J | F | M | A | M | J | J | A | S | O | N | D |

Seasonal Occurrence

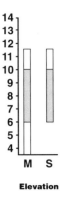

Elevation

Status (SP) (B): Uncommon to locally fairly common **summer** resident in foothills and lower mountains and rare in higher mountains. Rare **spring** and **fall** migrant in western valleys and mountain parks. Accidental on eastern plains (one record*). The **winter** status of this species is unclear. It is regular at Durango, La Plata County (K. Stranksy, pers. comm.). However, there are very few other winter records, and some of them may pertain to the Yellow-bellied Sapsucker. It seems best to document all winter records.

The status of this species on the eastern plains is unclear because most observers until recently have not distinguished between this and the Yellow-bellied Sapsucker. It probably occurs as a rare migrant near foothills (and perhaps farther east) and perhaps occasionally in winter, but the status of both sapsuckers on the eastern plains will require more information before definitive statements on their abundance and distribution can be made. Sapsuckers on the eastern plains in any season, and winter birds anywhere in the state could be either species, and therefore all such reports should be carefully documented.

Habitat: Breeds primarily in aspen forests, but also occurs less commonly in coniferous forests, especially where near or mixed with aspen. In migration and winter, found in lowland riparian forests and in urban areas (especially in conifers).

Record: Eastern plains*: 3 Oct 1936, Barr Lake, Adams County (DMNH 14639).

Reference: Crockett and Hadow (1975).

Williamson's Sapsucker
Sphyrapicus thyroideus

Summer resident in foothills and low mountains; occasional migrant at low elevations.

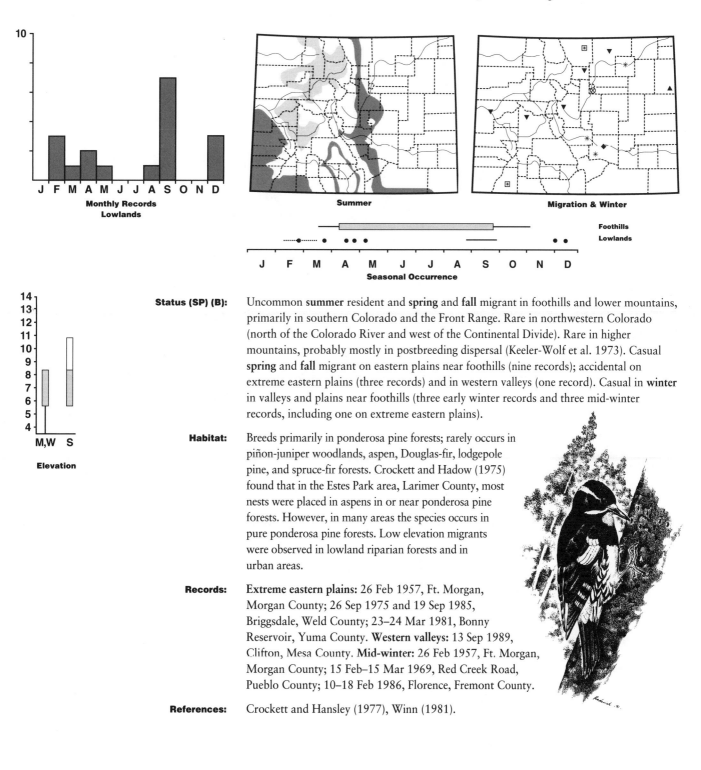

Monthly Records Lowlands

Summer

Migration & Winter

Seasonal Occurrence

Foothills

Lowlands

Elevation

Status (SP) (B): Uncommon **summer** resident and **spring** and **fall** migrant in foothills and lower mountains, primarily in southern Colorado and the Front Range. Rare in northwestern Colorado (north of the Colorado River and west of the Continental Divide). Rare in higher mountains, probably mostly in postbreeding dispersal (Keeler-Wolf et al. 1973). Casual **spring** and **fall** migrant on eastern plains near foothills (nine records); accidental on extreme eastern plains (three records) and in western valleys (one record). Casual in **winter** in valleys and plains near foothills (three early winter records and three mid-winter records, including one on extreme eastern plains).

Habitat: Breeds primarily in ponderosa pine forests; rarely occurs in piñon-juniper woodlands, aspen, Douglas-fir, lodgepole pine, and spruce-fir forests. Crockett and Hadow (1975) found that in the Estes Park area, Larimer County, most nests were placed in aspens in or near ponderosa pine forests. However, in many areas the species occurs in pure ponderosa pine forests. Low elevation migrants were observed in lowland riparian forests and in urban areas.

Records: Extreme eastern plains: 26 Feb 1957, Ft. Morgan, Morgan County; 26 Sep 1975 and 19 Sep 1985, Briggsdale, Weld County; 23–24 Mar 1981, Bonny Reservoir, Yuma County. **Western valleys:** 13 Sep 1989, Clifton, Mesa County. **Mid-winter:** 26 Feb 1957, Ft. Morgan, Morgan County; 15 Feb–15 Mar 1969, Red Creek Road, Pueblo County; 10–18 Feb 1986, Florence, Fremont County.

References: Crockett and Hansley (1977), Winn (1981).

Ladder-backed Woodpecker

Picoides scalaris

Year round in foothills and mesas of southeastern Colorado.

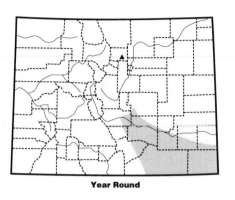

Year Round

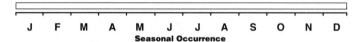

J   F   M   A   M   J   J   A   S   O   N   D

Seasonal Occurrence

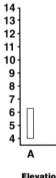

Elevation

Status (SP) (B): Rare to uncommon **resident** in southern foothills and mesas from eastern Fremont and southwestern El Paso counties southward and east to southwestern Baca County, and on adjacent plains of the Arkansas River Valley east to Otero County. It is most common in Baca County. Accidental on northeastern plains (one record*).

Habitat: Lowland and foothill riparian forests and foothill shrublands.

Record: **Northeastern plains*:** 27 Mar 1976, Boulder, Boulder County.

Downy Woodpecker
Picoides pubescens

Year round throughout Colorado except in the highest mountains.

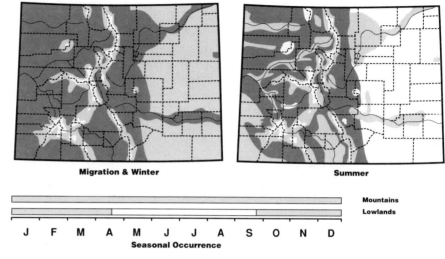

Migration & Winter   **Summer**

Mountains
Lowlands

J F M A M J J A S O N D
Seasonal Occurrence

Status (SP) (B): Uncommon **resident** in western valleys, foothills, lower mountains, mountain parks, and on eastern plains; rare in higher mountains. In western valleys and eastern plains, it is generally more common during the fall, winter, and spring than during the summer. The mountain race (*P. p. leucurus*), which is identifiable in the field from the northern and eastern races (*P. p. nelsoni* and *medianus*), occurs rarely in the fall, winter, and spring on eastern plains.

Habitat: Lowland and foothill riparian forests, urban areas with tall trees, ponderosa pine, Douglas-fir, lodgepole pine, and aspen forests. In mountains, it most often nests in aspens in areas where those trees are present (Crockett and Hadow 1975). Rarely in piñon-juniper woodland and spruce-fir forest.

Reference: Crockett and Hansley (1978).

14
13
12
11
10
9
8
7
6
5
4

S   W

Elevation

Hairy Woodpecker
Picoides villosus

Year round in the mountains; rare at low elevations, primarily in migration and winter.

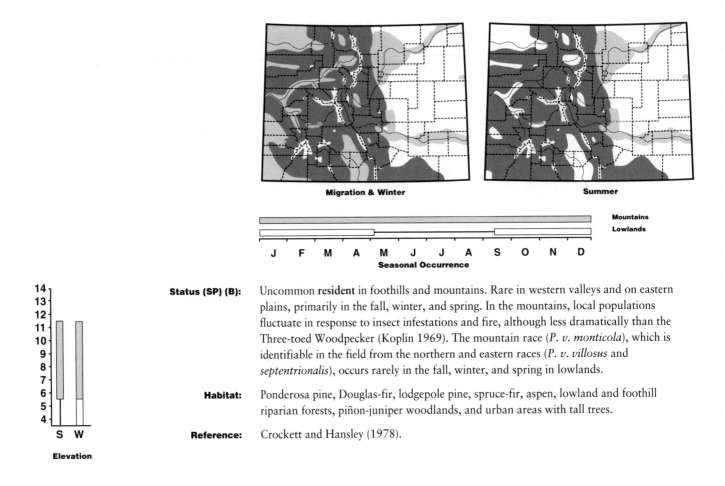

Status (SP) (B): Uncommon **resident** in foothills and mountains. Rare in western valleys and on eastern plains, primarily in the fall, winter, and spring. In the mountains, local populations fluctuate in response to insect infestations and fire, although less dramatically than the Three-toed Woodpecker (Koplin 1969). The mountain race (*P. v. monticola*), which is identifiable in the field from the northern and eastern races (*P. v. villosus* and *septentrionalis*), occurs rarely in the fall, winter, and spring in lowlands.

Habitat: Ponderosa pine, Douglas-fir, lodgepole pine, spruce-fir, aspen, lowland and foothill riparian forests, piñon-juniper woodlands, and urban areas with tall trees.

Reference: Crockett and Hansley (1978).

Three-toed Woodpecker
Picoides tridactylus

Year round in the high mountains.

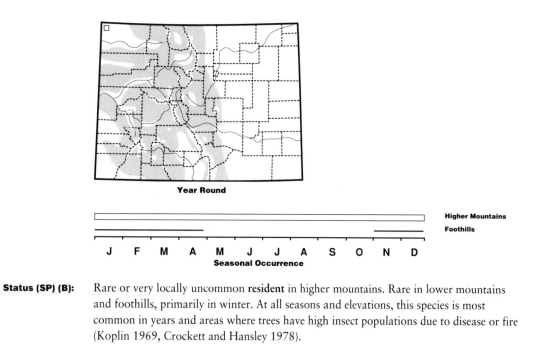

Year Round

Higher Mountains

Foothills

J F M A M J J A S O N D

Seasonal Occurrence

Elevation

Status (SP) (B): Rare or very locally uncommon **resident** in higher mountains. Rare in lower mountains and foothills, primarily in winter. At all seasons and elevations, this species is most common in years and areas where trees have high insect populations due to disease or fire (Koplin 1969, Crockett and Hansley 1978).

Habitat: Primarily spruce-fir forest, but where insect populations are high it may also occur in ponderosa pine, Douglas-fir, and lodgepole pine forests.

Note: Formerly known as Northern Three-toed Woodpecker.

Northern Flicker

Colaptes auratus

The two field-identifiable forms, formerly considered as separate species, are treated individually.

Yellow-shafted form and intergrades

Year round in extreme eastern Colorado; occasional elsewhere.

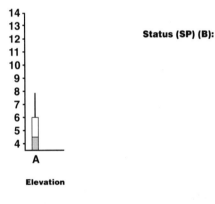

**Monthly Records
Mountains and Western Valleys**

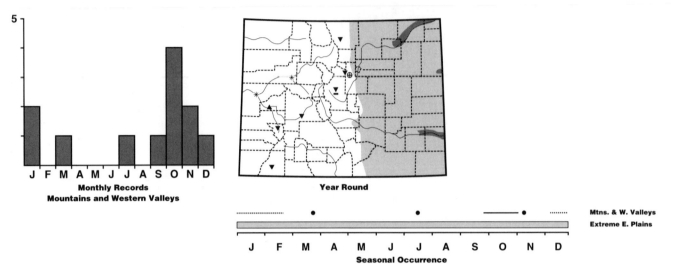

Year Round

Mtns. & W. Valleys
Extreme E. Plains

Seasonal Occurrence

Elevation

Status (SP) (B): Fairly common **resident** on extreme eastern plains from Morgan and Bent counties eastward. Rare to uncommon west to foothills; observed all year but most frequently during fall, winter, and spring. Accidental in foothills and lower mountains of Jefferson County (one summer record and two fall records) and Park County (one fall record). Casual in western valleys (five fall records, four winter records, and one spring record).

Eastern Colorado west to Morgan and Bent counties is part of the flicker hybrid zone, which has not shifted in historical times (Short 1965, Grudzien et al. 1987). Red-shafted, Yellow-shafted, and intergrade flickers in eastern Colorado mate randomly (Bock 1971). Although they are frequently called "Yellow-shafted Flickers" by observers, most flickers with yellow underwings seen in Colorado are intergrades. It is probable that pure Yellow-shafted birds occur in Colorado only rarely, mostly in migration and winter.

Habitat: Lowland riparian forests and urban areas.

Records: **Foothills and low mountains:** 24 Oct 1904, Hall Valley, Park County (DMNH 27416); 12 Oct 1968, Genesee Mountain, Jefferson County; 15 July 1972, Evergreen, Jefferson County; 19 Oct 1972, Estes Park, Larimer County.

Red-shafted form

Year round in most of Colorado except the extreme eastern border area.

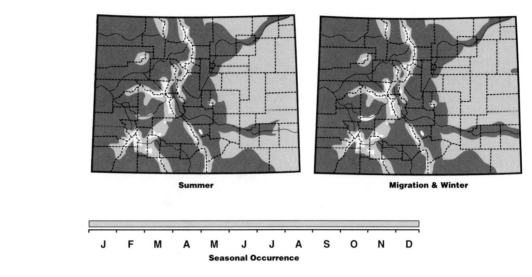

Summer

Migration & Winter

J F M A M J J A S O N D
Seasonal Occurrence

14
13
12
11
10
9
8
7
6
5
4

A

Elevation

Status (SP) (B): Resident, fairly common in western valleys and on eastern plains near foothills east to Morgan and Otero counties and uncommon to fairly common in foothills, lower mountains, and mountain parks. Rare to uncommon in higher mountains. Rare on extreme eastern plains in summer but fairly common in migration and winter. On eastern plains, it may be locally common during spring and fall migration.

Habitat: Primarily lowland and foothill riparian forests, ponderosa pine, Douglas-fir, lodgepole, and aspen forests, and in urban areas; rare in piñon-juniper woodlands and spruce-fir forests. In the mountains, they nest most frequently in aspens (Crockett and Hadow 1975).

**Order Passeriformes
Family Tyrannidae**

Olive-sided Flycatcher
Contopus borealis

Summer resident in mountains and migrant at lower elevations.

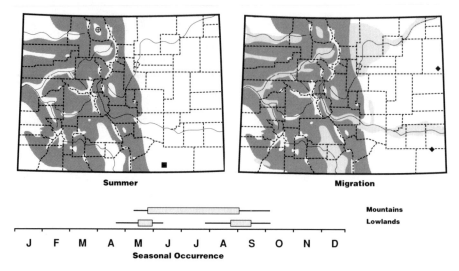

Summer   Migration

Mountains

Lowlands

J F M A M J J A S O N D

Seasonal Occurrence

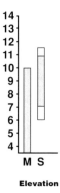

Elevation

Status (SP) (B): Uncommon **summer** resident in mountains, primarily in higher mountains. Rare to uncommon locally in lower mountains and foothills. Uncommon **spring** and **fall** migrant in western valleys, lower mountains, mountain parks, foothills, and on eastern plains. Occasional summer records on eastern plains in July and Aug probably refer to early migrants. Breeding Bird Survey data show that this species was "declining sharply" in western North America from 1965–1979 (Robbins et al. 1986).

Habitat: Breeds primarily in mature spruce-fir and Douglas-fir forests, especially on steep slopes or near cliffs, and less often in other types of coniferous forests, montane and foothill riparian, and aspen forests. In migration, occurs in all types of wooded habitats.

Western Wood-Pewee
Contopus sordidulus

Summer resident and migrant in lowlands, foothills, and lower mountains.

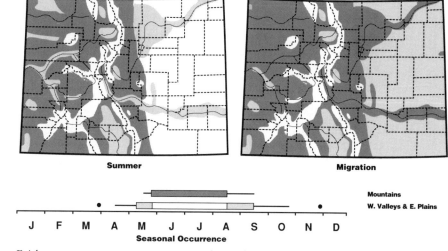

Summer   Migration

Mountains

W. Valleys & E. Plains

J F M A M J J A S O N D

Seasonal Occurrence

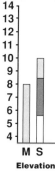

14
13
12
11
10
9
8
7
6
5
4

M S

Elevation

Status (SP) (B): Fairly common to common **summer** resident in foothills and lower mountains, and rare to uncommon in western valleys and on eastern plains. Fairly common **spring** and **fall** migrant in foothills and lowlands. In the western valleys and on eastern plains, it is usually more common as a migrant than as a summer resident.

Habitat: Breeds most commonly in aspen forests and also occurs in good numbers in ponderosa pine and foothill riparian forests. It is generally less common in lodgepole pine, Douglas-fir, and lowland riparian forests, and piñon-juniper woodlands. In migration, wooded riparian and urban areas.

References: Eckhardt (1976), Rising and Schueler (1980).

Eastern Wood-Pewee
Contopus virens

Status (SP): Accidental **spring** migrant (three records*) and **summer** resident (two records*).

Records: Spring*: 12 May 1905, Springfield, Baca County (CU 8691); 12 May 1982, Lake Henry, Crowley County; 24 May 1983, Colorado Springs State Wildlife Area, El Paso County. Summer*: one singing male 23 May-1 June 1989 and 21 May into July 1991 at Chatfield Reservoir, Jefferson County.

Notes: (1) A second specimen (26 Aug 1977, Limon, Lincoln County; DMNH 25851) is a chick, and the adult collected with it is not extant; it seems best to disregard this specimen (A. Phillips, pers. comm.). (2) There have been numerous other reports of this species in eastern Colorado, mostly singing individuals in spring and early summer. Undoubtedly this species occurs more regularly in eastern Colorado than our treatment suggests. It is believed to nest in southwestern Kansas only a few miles from Baca County (S. Seltman, pers. comm.). However, identification of this species by voice is not as simple as it first appears (Dunn and Garrett 1983, Kaufman 1990). The full song of the Eastern Wood-Pewee is very distinctive, but seems rarely to be given away from the breeding grounds, and hence is not likely to be heard very often in Colorado. The Western Wood-Pewee often gives clear notes that could be mistaken for the Eastern song. Therefore, observers should be very cautious about identifying this species, and written details (or better yet, tape recordings) of the vocalizations heard always should be made. Dunn and Garrett (1983a) and Kaufman (1990) discussed the identification of this species by voice.

Alder Flycatcher
Empidonax alnorum

Occasional spring migrant in eastern Colorado.

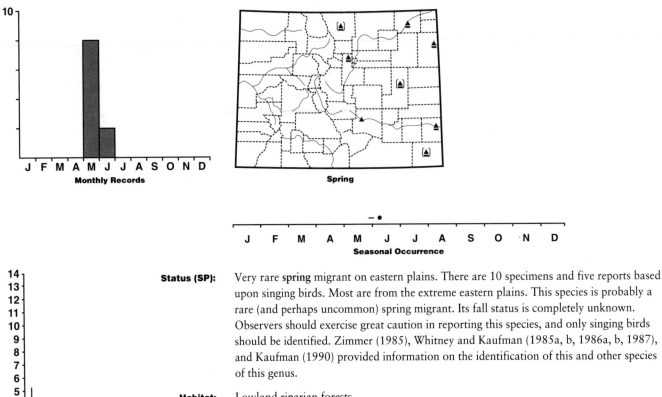

Monthly Records

Spring

Seasonal Occurrence

Elevation

Status (SP): Very rare **spring** migrant on eastern plains. There are 10 specimens and five reports based upon singing birds. Most are from the extreme eastern plains. This species is probably a rare (and perhaps uncommon) spring migrant. Its fall status is completely unknown. Observers should exercise great caution in reporting this species, and only singing birds should be identified. Zimmer (1985), Whitney and Kaufman (1985a, b, 1986a, b, 1987), and Kaufman (1990) provided information on the identification of this and other species of this genus.

Habitat: Lowland riparian forests.

Willow Flycatcher
Empidonax traillii

Summer resident in mountains and migrant in lowlands.

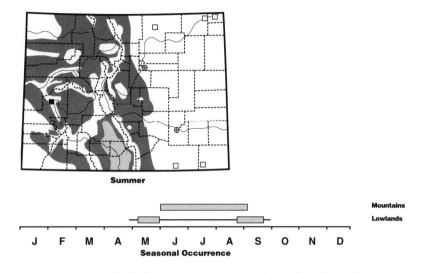

Summer

Mountains

Lowlands

J F M A M J J A S O N D

Seasonal Occurrence

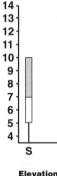

Elevation

Status (SP) (B): Uncommon to locally fairly common **summer** resident in foothills and lower mountains, generally in open valleys, and in mountain parks. Very rare in lowlands. It was observed annually from 1981–1986 at Escalante State Wildlife Area, Delta County, and breeding was confirmed in 1982 (M. Janos, pers. comm.). There are eight records on eastern plains, where breeding may occur but has never been proven. The species is recorded breeding in Nebraska along the South Platte River almost to the Colorado state line (Johnsgard 1979).

Spring and fall migrant in lowlands, but its status is difficult to determine (see account for *Empidonax* spp.). In western Kansas, migrates 12 May–12 June (but mostly 20–25 May) and 23 July–12 Sep (Ely 1970). Birds have been banded by the Colorado Bird Observatory in early June (M. Carter, pers. comm.).

Habitat: Breeds primarily in extensive foothill and montane riparian thickets (mostly willows), usually in areas distant from trees. In similar habitats adjacent to forests or in small thickets, this species is usually replaced by the Dusky Flycatcher. In migration, lowland riparian forests.

Notes: (1) This species is heavily parasitized by the Brown-headed Cowbird at Arapaho National Wildlife Refuge, Jackson County (Sedgwick and Knopf 1988), and probably elsewhere in Colorado. Because of declines due to loss of habitat and the impact of parasitism, this species is on the National Audubon Society Blue List (Tate 1986). (2) The southwestern subspecies (*E.t. extimus*) is declining seriously. It is uncertain whether this subspecies occurs in Colorado, but birds from south-central and southwestern Colorado may belong to this subspecies. There are recent records very close to Colorado in north-central and northwestern New Mexico (Unitt 1987).

Reference: Sedgwick and Knopf (1989).

Least Flycatcher
Empidonax minimus

Migrant in eastern Colorado; occasionally in summer.

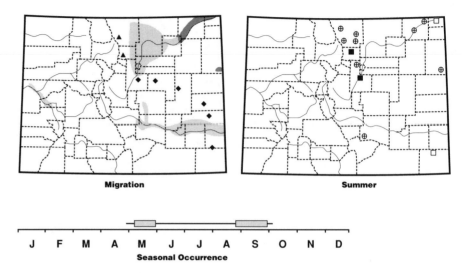

Migration   Summer

Seasonal Occurrence

J F M A M J J A S O N D

Elevation

14
13
12
11
10
9
8
7
6
5
4

M S

Status (SP) (B): Uncommon **spring** and **fall** migrant on extreme eastern plains, especially northeastern, and rare west to base of foothills. Most records are of singing males; therefore it is identified in spring more often than in fall. In western Kansas, migrants occur from 16 July–24 Sep (Ely 1970). High count: 16 on 14–15 May 1985, Bonny Reservoir, Yuma County. Accidental in lower mountains (three spring records).

Very rare **summer** resident (18 records of territorial males or pairs). The earliest was in 1927 (Bergtold 1927a), but all others are since 1971. The records come mostly from the plains near the foothills and in the lower foothills from Larimer County south to Jefferson County, but also at Beulah, Pueblo County, at several sites on the extreme eastern plains, in the mountains at Pennock Pass and Estes Park, Larimer County. There are three confirmed **breeding** records. A summer specimen (DMNH 4034) listed by Bailey and Niedrach (1965) is Hammond's Flycatcher (A. Phillips, pers. comm.). Birds seen in late May and early June and late July and August are as likely to be migrants as summer residents.

Habitat: Lowland and foothill riparian forests; also recorded once from aspen forest.

Records: **Spring in lower mountains:** 18 May (year unknown), Estes Park, Larimer County (Gregg 1938); 31 May 1988, Stapleton Park, Jefferson County; 5 June 1990, near Nederland, Boulder County. **Confirmed breeding:** nest in July 1988 at Lyons, Boulder County (Prather 1988); nested in 1990 and 1991 at Chatfield Reservoir, Douglas County (Anonymous 1990, Kingery 1991c).

Hammond's Flycatcher

Empidonax hammondii

Summer resident in high mountains and migrant at lower elevations.

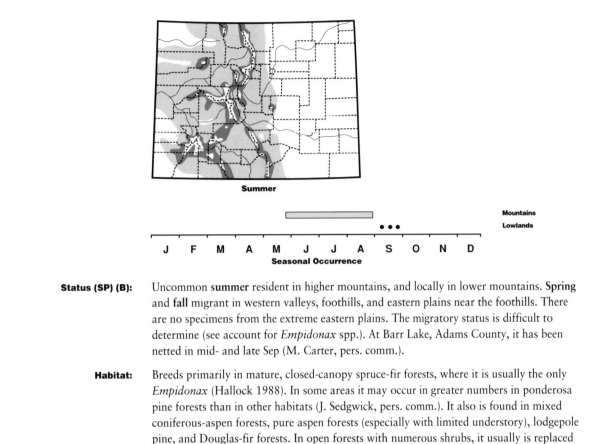

Summer

Mountains

Lowlands

J F M A M J J A S O N D

Seasonal Occurrence

Elevation

14
13
12
11
10
9
8
7
6
5
4

S

Status (SP) (B): Uncommon **summer** resident in higher mountains, and locally in lower mountains. **Spring** and **fall** migrant in western valleys, foothills, and eastern plains near the foothills. There are no specimens from the extreme eastern plains. The migratory status is difficult to determine (see account for *Empidonax* spp.). At Barr Lake, Adams County, it has been netted in mid- and late Sep (M. Carter, pers. comm.).

Habitat: Breeds primarily in mature, closed-canopy spruce-fir forests, where it is usually the only *Empidonax* (Hallock 1988). In some areas it may occur in greater numbers in ponderosa pine forests than in other habitats (J. Sedgwick, pers. comm.). It also is found in mixed coniferous-aspen forests, pure aspen forests (especially with limited understory), lodgepole pine, and Douglas-fir forests. In open forests with numerous shrubs, it usually is replaced by the Dusky Flycatcher. In migration, all wooded habitats.

Reference: Beaver and Baldwin (1975).

Dusky Flycatcher
Empidonax oberholseri

Summer resident in foothills and mountains, and migrant at lower elevations.

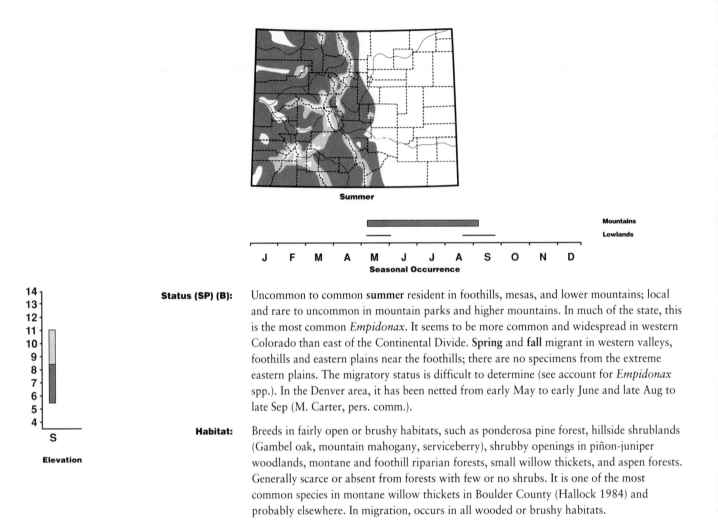

Summer

Mountains
Lowlands

J F M A M J J A S O N D

Seasonal Occurrence

Elevation

Status (SP) (B): Uncommon to common **summer** resident in foothills, mesas, and lower mountains; local and rare to uncommon in mountain parks and higher mountains. In much of the state, this is the most common *Empidonax*. It seems to be more common and widespread in western Colorado than east of the Continental Divide. **Spring** and **fall** migrant in western valleys, foothills and eastern plains near the foothills; there are no specimens from the extreme eastern plains. The migratory status is difficult to determine (see account for *Empidonax* spp.). In the Denver area, it has been netted from early May to early June and late Aug to late Sep (M. Carter, pers. comm.).

Habitat: Breeds in fairly open or brushy habitats, such as ponderosa pine forest, hillside shrublands (Gambel oak, mountain mahogany, serviceberry), shrubby openings in piñon-juniper woodlands, montane and foothill riparian forests, small willow thickets, and aspen forests. Generally scarce or absent from forests with few or no shrubs. It is one of the most common species in montane willow thickets in Boulder County (Hallock 1984) and probably elsewhere. In migration, occurs in all wooded or brushy habitats.

Reference: Eckhardt (1977).

Gray Flycatcher

Empidonax wrightii

Summer resident in mesas and foothills of western and southern Colorado.

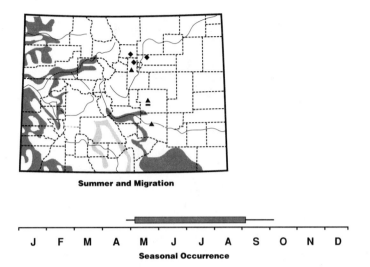

Summer and Migration

J F M A M J J A S O N D

Seasonal Occurrence

14
13
12
11
10
9
8
7
6
5
4

M,S

Elevation

Status (SP) (B): Uncommon to common **summer** resident on mesas and foothills. In western Colorado, occurs from Moffat County southward, and rare east to Eagle and southwestern Grand counties. In eastern Colorado, occurs from Fremont County southward and east to southern Las Animas County (and probably southwestern Baca County); rare west to southern Chaffee County and north to southern El Paso County. Rare (locally fairly common) around the periphery of the San Luis Valley. In northwestern Colorado north of the Colorado River, it is common and widespread, but it appears to be more local in southwestern Colorado.

Uncommon **spring** and **fall** migrant in western valleys. Casual migrant on eastern plains near foothills in Jefferson, Adams, and Boulder counties (eight spring records and two fall records, included four banded). Accidental in lower mountains (one record*).

Habitat: Breeds in piñon-juniper woodlands. In migration, also recorded from sagebrush and semidesert shrublands, and riparian areas.

Record: Mountains*: 4 May 1988, Evergreen, Jefferson County.

Cordilleran Flycatcher
Empidonax occidentalis

Summer resident in foothills and lower mountains, and migrant in adjacent lowlands.

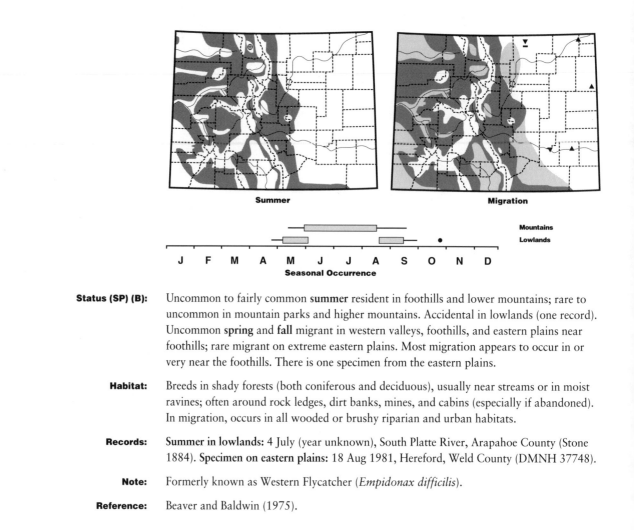

Summer **Migration**

Mountains
Lowlands

J F M A M J J A S O N D
Seasonal Occurrence

Elevation

Status (SP) (B): Uncommon to fairly common **summer** resident in foothills and lower mountains; rare to uncommon in mountain parks and higher mountains. Accidental in lowlands (one record). Uncommon **spring** and **fall** migrant in western valleys, foothills, and eastern plains near foothills; rare migrant on extreme eastern plains. Most migration appears to occur in or very near the foothills. There is one specimen from the eastern plains.

Habitat: Breeds in shady forests (both coniferous and deciduous), usually near streams or in moist ravines; often around rock ledges, dirt banks, mines, and cabins (especially if abandoned). In migration, occurs in all wooded or brushy riparian and urban habitats.

Records: **Summer in lowlands:** 4 July (year unknown), South Platte River, Arapahoe County (Stone 1884). **Specimen on eastern plains:** 18 Aug 1981, Hereford, Weld County (DMNH 37748).

Note: Formerly known as Western Flycatcher (*Empidonax difficilis*).

Reference: Beaver and Baldwin (1975).

Empidonax Flycatchers
Empidonax spp.

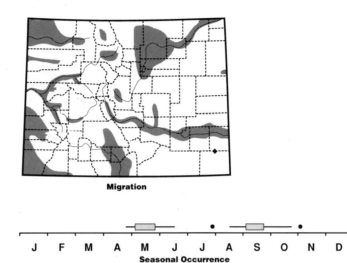

Migration

J   F   M   A   M   J   J   A   S   O   N   D

Seasonal Occurrence

Status: Fairly common **spring** and **fall** migrant, mostly in foothills and lowlands. Although many observers have made field identifications of non-singing migrant *Empidonax*, we feel that at present it is best to treat all such birds as *Empidonax* spp. The accompanying seasonal occurrence graph thus combines sight records of all species. The limited specimen and banding data available from Colorado show no significant differences in the timing of migration of the various species. Zimmer (1985), Whitney and Kaufman (1985a, b, 1986a, b, 1987), and Kaufman (1990) provided information on the identification of this group, but observers are urged to be cautious about identifying migrants until they have extensive experience with breeding birds.

Habitat: Wooded and brushy habitats.

14
13
12
11
10
9
8
7
6
5
4

M

Elevation

Black Phoebe
Sayornis nigricans

Occasional visitor; has nested in Pueblo County three times.

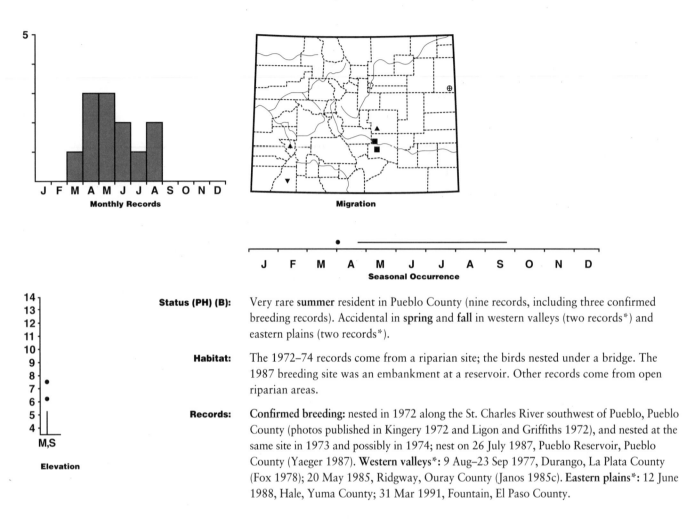

Status (PH) (B): Very rare **summer** resident in Pueblo County (nine records, including three confirmed breeding records). Accidental in **spring** and **fall** in western valleys (two records*) and eastern plains (two records*).

Habitat: The 1972–74 records come from a riparian site; the birds nested under a bridge. The 1987 breeding site was an embankment at a reservoir. Other records come from open riparian areas.

Records: **Confirmed breeding:** nested in 1972 along the St. Charles River southwest of Pueblo, Pueblo County (photos published in Kingery 1972 and Ligon and Griffiths 1972), and nested at the same site in 1973 and possibly in 1974; nest on 26 July 1987, Pueblo Reservoir, Pueblo County (Yaeger 1987). **Western valleys*:** 9 Aug–23 Sep 1977, Durango, La Plata County (Fox 1978); 20 May 1985, Ridgway, Ouray County (Janos 1985c). **Eastern plains*:** 12 June 1988, Hale, Yuma County; 31 Mar 1991, Fountain, El Paso County.

Eastern Phoebe
Sayornis phoebe

Migrant and local summer resident locally in eastern Colorado.

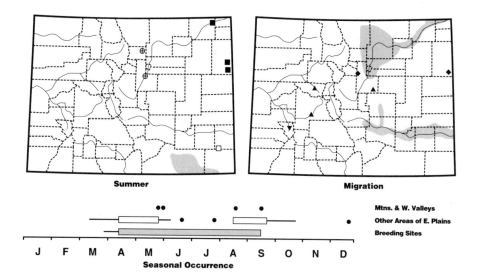

Summer **Migration**

Mtns. & W. Valleys
Other Areas of E. Plains
Breeding Sites

J F M A M J J A S O N D

Seasonal Occurrence

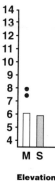

Elevation

Status (SP) (B): Rare to uncommon local **summer** resident in eastern Colorado. The main nesting area is in the canyons of southeastern Colorado from central Las Animas County to southwestern Baca County. The first nesting was in Baca County in 1914 (Bailey and Niedrach 1965). Also nests at Tamarack Ranch, Logan County and in the Bonny Reservoir area, Yuma County, and possibly at Two Buttes Reservoir, Baca County. Accidental (two records of nonbreeders) on the northeastern plains near foothills.

Rare **spring** and **fall** migrant on eastern plains. Accidental in western valleys (two records) and in mountains (two records). Accidental in **early winter** on northeastern plains (one record*). There are no winter records from southeastern Colorado, but it may occur rarely in the canyons where it breeds.

Habitat: In southeastern Colorado, breeds in moist, rocky ravines in canyons and mesas, often around abandoned buildings. Other records are from lowland riparian forests.

Records: **Summer near northeastern foothills:** 19 June 1961, Longmont, Boulder County; 23 July 1978, Chatfield Reservoir, Douglas/Jefferson counties. **Western valleys:** 22 May 1978, near Gunnison, Gunnison County; 11 Sep 1988, Ridgway, Ouray County. **Mountains:** 30 May 1976, Aspen, Pitkin County; 18 Aug 1979 and 13 Apr 1991, Evergreen, Jefferson County. **Early winter*:** 21 Dec 1975, Boulder, Boulder County.

Say's Phoebe

Sayornis saya

Summer resident and migrant at low elevations throughout Colorado, and rare in winter.

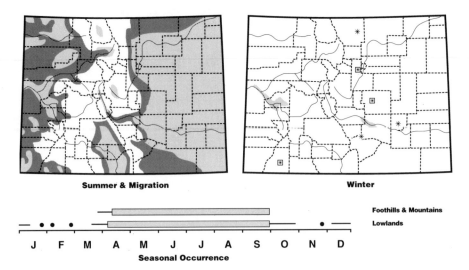

Summer & Migration   **Winter**

Foothills & Mountains
Lowlands

J F M A M J J A S O N D

Seasonal Occurrence

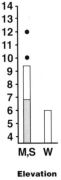

Elevation

Status (SP) (B): Uncommon to fairly common **summer** resident in foothills and mesas and in dry western valleys. Rare to uncommon locally on eastern plains away from the river valleys. On the eastern plains, it is most frequent north of the South Platte River in Weld and Logan counties. Rare to uncommon in lower mountains. It is fairly common in appropriate habitats in the San Luis Valley, but it is rare or uncommon in other mountain parks. This species may be increasing; its numbers rose significantly on Breeding Bird Survey routes in the western United States from 1965–1979 (Robbins et al. 1986).

Uncommon **spring** and **fall** migrant in western valleys and on eastern plains. Rare to uncommon in mountains and mountain parks, especially in late summer and fall. Accidental above timberline (one record). Rare to uncommon **winter** resident in valleys and adjacent lower foothills in southern Colorado, mostly in Mesa, Delta, Fremont, and Pueblo counties. Often becomes scarcer during late winter. Accidental in mid-winter in northern Colorado (one record).

Habitat: Breeds in most open habitats such as grasslands and shrublands, often near buildings (especially if abandoned) and bridges. It generally does not breed in agricultural areas except adjacent to uncultivated areas. In migration, it occurs in all open habitats, including cultivated and riparian areas. Winter birds are usually found around the open water of streams and sewage ponds.

Records: Above timberline: 26 July 1978 at 12,000 ft. in Rocky Mountain National Park, Larimer County. Mid-winter in northern Colorado: 9 Feb 1980, Ft. Collins, Larimer County.

Vermilion Flycatcher
Pyrocephalus rubinus

Occasional migrant, mostly in eastern Colorado.

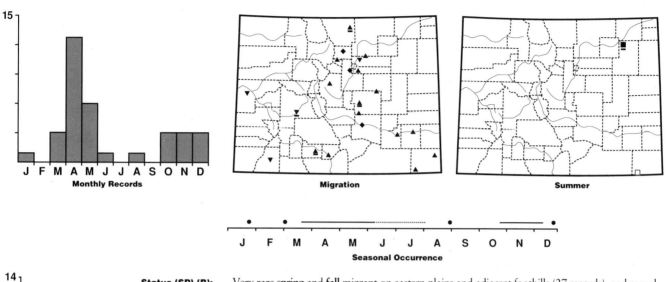

Migration   Summer

Seasonal Occurrence

Status (SP) (B): Very rare **spring** and **fall** migrant on eastern plains and adjacent foothills (27 records), and casual in mountains and western valleys (seven records). Occurs mostly in early spring and late fall.

There is one **breeding** record: one pair with nest and young 29 Apr–13 July 1981 at a farmhouse and shelterbelt in extreme northern Washington County (Downing 1981). The female and two nestlings were killed by hail on 13 July and were collected (DMNH 37401). There is a breeding record in extreme northeastern New Mexico (Johnsgard 1979) and at least two summer sight records of pairs in Cimarron County, Oklahoma, only a few miles from Baca County (Holmgren 1981). Breeding should be looked for in southern Las Animas and Baca counties.

Habitat: Open riparian areas.

Elevation

Dusky-capped Flycatcher
Myiarchus tuberculifer

Status (SP): Accidental **spring** migrant (one record*).

Record: 11 May 1883, Ft. Lyon, Bent County (MCZ 225639) (Thorne 1889, Bailey and Niedrach 1965).

Ash-throated Flycatcher
Myiarchus cinerascens

Summer resident in southern and western Colorado.

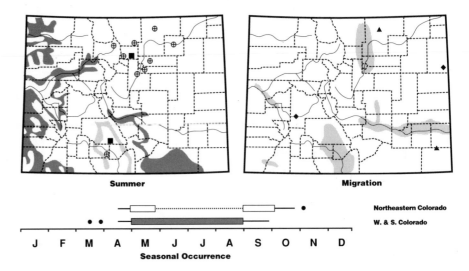

Summer   Migration

Northeastern Colorado

W. & S. Colorado

Seasonal Occurrence

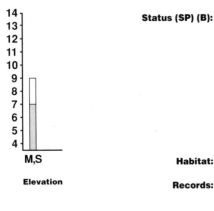

Elevation

Status (SP) (B): Uncommon to fairly common **summer** resident in foothills and mesas from Moffat County southward and from El Paso County southward and east to southwestern Baca County. In western Colorado, appears to be most common from Mesa County southward. Rare in the periphery of the San Luis Valley and accidental in valley proper (two records). Very rare nonbreeding summer visitor to northeastern plains (12 records), and one breeding record in northeastern foothills. Casual nonbreeder in mountains (five records).

Rare **spring** and **fall** migrant in western valleys east to Gunnison County, on southeastern plains, and on northeastern plains near foothills.

Habitat: Piñon-juniper woodlands and open riparian forests.

Records: **Summer in San Luis Valley:** 16 July 1989, Monte Vista, Rio Grande County; nest 4 July 1991 in southern Saguache County near Hooper, Alamosa County. **Breeding in northeastern foothills:** nest in summer 1986 near Boulder, Boulder County.

Great Crested Flycatcher
Myiarchus crinitus

Summer resident in extreme northeastern corner; occasional elsewhere.

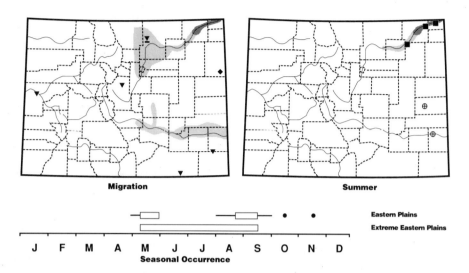

| Migration | Summer |

Eastern Plains
Extreme Eastern Plains

J F M A M J J A S O N D
Seasonal Occurrence

14 13 12 11 10 9 8 7 6 5 4
M,S

Elevation

Status (SP) (B): Uncommon **spring** and **fall** migrant on extreme northeastern plains, and rare west to foothills and on southeastern plains. Recorded more often in spring than in fall. Accidental in mountains (one record*) and western valleys (one record*). There are three specimens.

Uncommon **summer** resident along the South Platte River southwest to Masters, Weld County, but mostly in Logan and Sedgwick counties. Breeding confirmed southwest to Prewitt Reservoir, Washington County. All summer records were from the early 1970s and later, and breeding was first recorded in 1988. This species is definitely increasing in numbers and expanding into northeastern Colorado. Accidental on southeastern plains (two records).

Habitat: Lowland riparian forests.

Records: **Specimens:** 17 Aug 1911, Windsor, Weld County (DMNH 16419); 24 May 1960 (site unknown) (DMNH 34620); 16 Sep 1982, Bonny Reservoir, Yuma County (DMNH 37781). **Mountains*:** 13 Oct 1991, near Jefferson, Park County. **Western valleys*:** 25 Sep 1988, Fruita, Mesa County. **Summer on southeastern plains:** exploring nest hole but not nesting in 1990, Kit Carson, Cheyenne County; 21 June–10 July 1991, Lamar, Prowers County.

Cassin's Kingbird

Tyrannus vociferans

Summer resident in southeastern foothills, and occasional elsewhere.

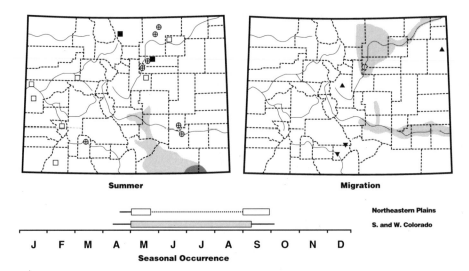

Northeastern Plains

S. and W. Colorado

Seasonal Occurrence

J F M A M J J A S O N D

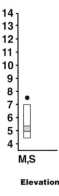

Elevation

Status (SP) (B): Uncommon to fairly common local **summer** resident of low foothills, mesas, and valleys in southeastern Colorado from Fremont and Pueblo counties southward and east to southwestern Baca County. Rare to uncommon and very local in western Colorado north to Mesa County. Casual in summer on northeastern plains (six nonbreeding records, including one specimen) and one breeding record. Accidental in mountains (three records, including one breeding record).

Rare **spring** and **fall** migrant on eastern plains and adjacent foothills, where it occurs more often in fall than in spring (and usually after Western Kingbirds have left). Accidental in mountain parks (three records).

Habitat: In Baca County, occurs in or near open foothill riparian forests, cholla grasslands, and agricultural areas. In the southeastern foothills and in western Colorado, it occurs in open piñon-juniper woodlands and isolated juniper stands. Migrants are seen in agricultural areas.

Records: Specimen on northeastern plains: 5 June 1900, Denver County (DMNH 13098). **Breeding on northeastern plains:** nested in June 1923 at Bootleg Reservoir, Adams County. **Summer in mountains:** nested Estes Park, Larimer County (Sclater 1912); 21 July 1988, near Creede, Mineral County; mid-June 1989, Estes Park. **Migration in mountain parks:** 13 Aug 1950, near Alamosa, Alamosa County (Ryder 1965); 3 June 1967, South Park, Park County; 31 Aug 1974, Great Sand Dunes National Monument, Alamosa County.

Western Kingbird

Tyrannus verticalis

Common summer resident at low elevations.

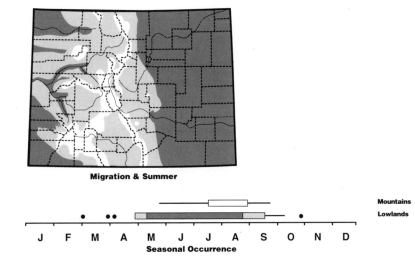

Migration & Summer

Mountains

Lowlands

J F M A M J J A S O N D

Seasonal Occurrence

14
13
12
11
10
9
8
7
6
5
4

M,S

Elevation

Status (SP) (B): **Summer** resident in lowlands; common on eastern plains and fairly common to common in western valleys. High count: 272 on 10 May 1975 in Pueblo County. Rare to uncommon in foothills, mountain parks, and lower mountains, mostly in late summer and fall. This species increased significantly on Breeding Bird Survey routes from 1965–1979 (Robbins et al. 1986).

Habitat: Breeds mostly in open riparian and agricultural areas, but also in piñon-juniper woodlands adjacent to fields and in urban areas. Occurs in grasslands or desert shrublands mostly in the vicinity of streams, isolated trees, shelterbelts, and houses.

Eastern Kingbird
Tyrannus tyrannus

Summer resident in lowlands, mostly in eastern Colorado.

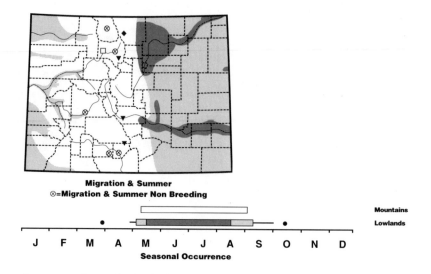

Migration & Summer
⊗=Migration & Summer Non Breeding

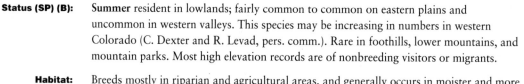

Mountains
Lowlands

J F M A M J J A S O N D

Seasonal Occurrence

Status (SP) (B): **Summer** resident in lowlands; fairly common to common on eastern plains and uncommon in western valleys. This species may be increasing in numbers in western Colorado (C. Dexter and R. Levad, pers. comm.). Rare in foothills, lower mountains, and mountain parks. Most high elevation records are of nonbreeding visitors or migrants.

Habitat: Breeds mostly in riparian and agricultural areas, and generally occurs in moister and more densely wooded areas than the Western Kingbird. Occasionally in piñon-juniper woodlands, shrublands, and urban areas.

14
13
12
11
10
9
8
7
6
5
4

M,S

Elevation

Scissor-tailed Flycatcher

Tyrannus forficatus

Rare in summer in Baca County; occasional migrant elsewhere.

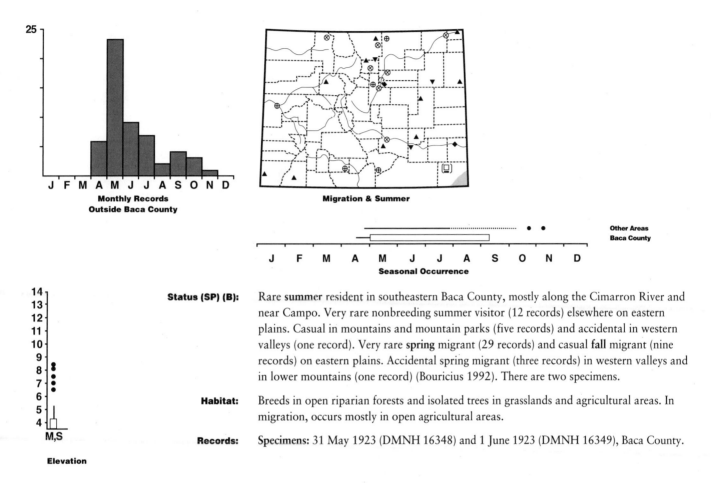

Monthly Records
Outside Baca County

Migration & Summer

Seasonal Occurrence

Other Areas
Baca County

Elevation

Status (SP) (B): Rare **summer** resident in southeastern Baca County, mostly along the Cimarron River and near Campo. Very rare nonbreeding summer visitor (12 records) elsewhere on eastern plains. Casual in mountains and mountain parks (five records) and accidental in western valleys (one record). Very rare **spring** migrant (29 records) and casual **fall** migrant (nine records) on eastern plains. Accidental spring migrant (three records) in western valleys and in lower mountains (one record) (Bouricius 1992). There are two specimens.

Habitat: Breeds in open riparian forests and isolated trees in grasslands and agricultural areas. In migration, occurs mostly in open agricultural areas.

Records: Specimens: 31 May 1923 (DMNH 16348) and 1 June 1923 (DMNH 16349), Baca County.

Order Passeriformes
Family Alaudidae

Horned Lark
Eremophila alpestris

Resident at low elevations and in mountain parks, and summer resident above timberline.

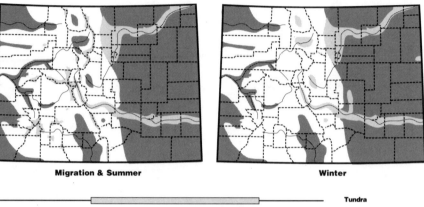

Migration & Summer   **Winter**

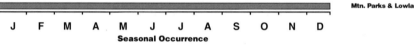

Tundra

Mtn. Parks & Lowlands

J F M A M J J A S O N D

Seasonal Occurrence

Elevation

Status (SP) (B): Common to abundant **resident** in western valleys, mountain parks, and on eastern plains. At low elevations, it is most common in winter, with large flocks occurring from Oct to Feb, and is more abundant on the eastern plains than elsewhere in the state. It is always abundant in winter, but numbers fluctuate widely within that range. High count: 15,580 on 18 Jan 1984 on Pawnee National Grassland, Weld County. The central Great Plains (including eastern Colorado) is a center of abundance in this species' North American range in summer (Robbins et al. 1986) and winter (Root 1988). Uncommon **summer** resident above timberline.

Habitat: Breeds in grasslands, sagebrush and semidesert shrublands, and alpine tundra. In migration and winter it occurs in the same habitats (except tundra), and also in agricultural areas; it is especially common in stubble and fallow fields. Also found around feedlots and farm yards in winter. Larks almost always occur where plant density is low and there is exposed soil.

Order Passeriformes
Family Hirundinidae

Purple Martin
Progne subis

Local summer resident in mountains in western Colorado; occasional elsewhere.

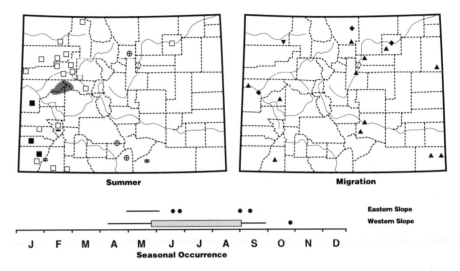

	Summer		Migration

Eastern Slope
Western Slope

J F M A M J J A S O N D
Seasonal Occurrence

Status (SP) (B): Common **summer** resident in lower mountains of northeastern Mesa, northeastern Delta, and northwestern Gunnison counties (Zerbi 1985, Reynolds et al. 1991). Rare to uncommon north to southeastern Moffat and northern Routt counties, east to Pitkin County, and south to Montezuma, La Plata, and southwestern Archuleta counties (Svoboda et al. 1980). Accidental in east slope mountains (three records) and on eastern plains (three records).

Rare **spring** and **fall** migrant in western valleys. Very rare spring migrant on eastern plains, mostly northeastern plains (11 records). Accidental fall migrant on northeastern plains (two records).

Habitat: Breeds in loose colonies in old-growth aspen forests near parks and generally near water (Reynolds et al. 1991), and sometimes also seen in mixed aspen/ponderosa pine or aspen/Douglas-fir forests. In some areas nests in dead trees near or standing in reservoirs. In migration, occurs over riparian areas, open agricultural areas, and reservoirs.

Records: **Summer in east slope mountains:** nested June 1872, Apishapa Creek, western Las Animas County (Sclater 1912); 19 July 1950, southeast of Ft. Garland, Costilla County (Ryder 1965); 14 July 1981, Great Sand Dunes National Monument, Alamosa County. **Summer on eastern plains:** pair collecting nest material but not known to have nested, 5 June 1971, Muir Springs, Morgan County; female 26 June 1974, Boulder, Boulder County; female 18 June 1976, Ft. Morgan, Morgan County. **Fall on eastern plains:** 1 Sep 1965, Ft. Collins, Larimer County; 11 Sep 1985, Ft. Morgan.

Elevation

14
13
12
11
10
9
8
7
6
5
4

M,S

Tree Swallow
Tachycineta bicolor

Summer resident, mostly in mountains but some on the plains, and widespread migrant.

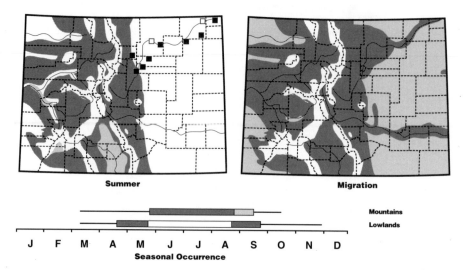

Seasonal Occurrence

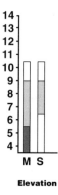

Elevation

Status (SP) (B): Fairly common **summer** resident in foothills and mountains, primarily in lower mountains. Local in mountain parks, usually around their periphery adjacent to wooded mountains. Uncommon and local summer resident in western valleys and on northeastern plains. The first plains breeding was recorded in 1963 at Cherry Creek Reservoir, Arapahoe County. At other sites breeding was first recorded from the mid-1970s or later, and breeding is now confirmed at nine sites.

Fairly common to common **spring** and **fall** migrant in western valleys, foothills, lower mountains, mountain parks, and on eastern plains. This is the most abundant migrant swallow in the Grand Valley, Mesa County (C. Dexter, pers. comm.), and at times is also abundant on the eastern plains, especially near the foothills. High count: 5,000 on 30 Apr 1989 at Chatfield Reservoir, Douglas/Jefferson counties.

Habitat: Breeds primarily in aspen forests, and sometimes in coniferous and montane riparian forests. In many areas, it uses nest boxes, and in areas where boxes have been provided local populations have increased and spread farther from wooded areas into parks and valleys. On the plains, nests in lowland riparian forests (mostly around reservoirs), but uses nest boxes at Walden Pond, Boulder County. In migration, occurs mostly around lakes and riparian areas.

References: Cohen (1976, 1977, 1978, 1982, 1984).

Violet-green Swallow

Tachycineta thalassina

Summer resident in mountains and migrant in adjacent lowlands.

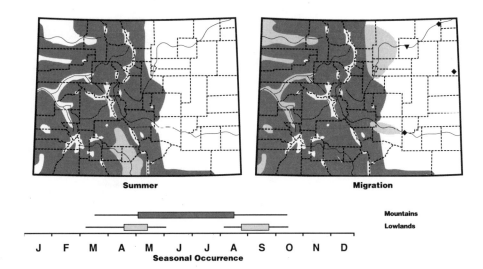

Summer **Migration**

Mountains
Lowlands

J F M A M J J A S O N D
Seasonal Occurrence

Elevation

Status (SP) (B): **Summer** resident; common in foothills and lower mountains, and uncommon to fairly common in higher mountains. Local in mountain parks, usually around their periphery or near buildings. Common **spring** and **fall** migrant in western valleys, and foothills throughout; fairly common on eastern plains near foothills and rare on extreme eastern plains. High count: 5,000 on 13 May 1989 at Chatfield Reservoir, Douglas/Jefferson counties.

Habitat: Breeds mostly in aspen forests, around cliffs, and in towns, but also in coniferous and montane riparian forests and in embankments. It forages along streams and over open mountain valleys. In migration, occurs mostly around lakes and in riparian areas.

Reference: Cohen (1982).

Northern Rough-winged Swallow
Stelgidopteryx serripennis

Summer resident and migrant at low elevations, and locally in mountain parks.

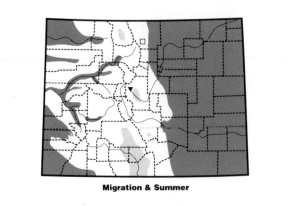

Migration & Summer

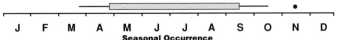

J F M A M J J A S O N D
Seasonal Occurrence

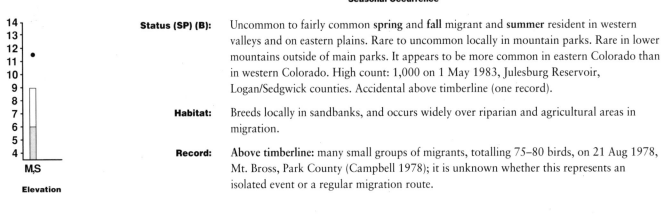

M,S

Elevation

Status (SP) (B): Uncommon to fairly common **spring** and **fall** migrant and **summer** resident in western valleys and on eastern plains. Rare to uncommon locally in mountain parks. Rare in lower mountains outside of main parks. It appears to be more common in eastern Colorado than in western Colorado. High count: 1,000 on 1 May 1983, Julesburg Reservoir, Logan/Sedgwick counties. Accidental above timberline (one record).

Habitat: Breeds locally in sandbanks, and occurs widely over riparian and agricultural areas in migration.

Record: **Above timberline:** many small groups of migrants, totalling 75–80 birds, on 21 Aug 1978, Mt. Bross, Park County (Campbell 1978); it is unknown whether this represents an isolated event or a regular migration route.

Bank Swallow

Riparia riparia

Local summer resident and migrant, mostly at low elevations but also in mountain parks.

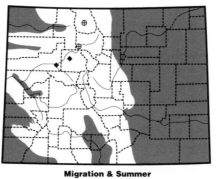

Migration & Summer

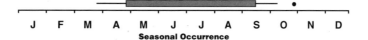

J   F   M   A   M   J   J   A   S   O   N   D

Seasonal Occurrence

14
13
12
11
10
9
8
7
6
5
4

M,S

Elevation

Status (SP) (B): Common to abundant local **summer** resident and **spring** and **fall** migrant in western valleys, the San Luis Valley, and on eastern plains. It may be more common in western Colorado than in eastern Colorado (M. Janos, pers. comm.). Very local in North and Middle Parks. High counts: 1,500 on 10 Aug 1985, Harts Basin, Delta County; about 800 on several dates in several years in late July and Aug at Lower Latham Reservoir, Weld County.

Habitat: Breeds in colonies locally in sandbanks, and occurs widely over riparian and agricultural areas in migration. The exact sites of colonies shifts from year to year.

Cliff Swallow
Hirundo pyrrhonota

Local summer resident and migrant at low elevations and in mountain parks.

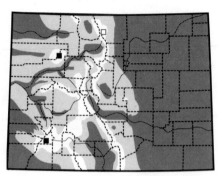

Migration & Summer

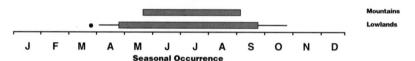

Mountains

Lowlands

J F M A M J J A S O N D

Seasonal Occurrence

Elevation

Status (SP) (B): Abundant local **summer** resident and **spring** and **fall** migrant in western valleys, mountain parks, and on eastern plains. Rare to uncommon in lower mountains outside the main parks. Rare in higher mountains to above timberline as a migrant, nonbreeding summer visitor, or local breeder. Populations of this species are increasing (Robbins et al. 1986).

Habitat: Breeds on cliffs and man-made structures such as buildings, bridges, culverts, and dams (mostly in or near open habitats). In migration, occurs widely over and around lakes, marshes and open agricultural areas.

Barn Swallow

Hirundo rustica

Summer resident and migrant at low elevations and in mountain parks.

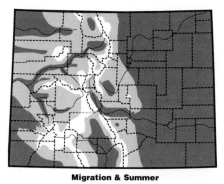

Migration & Summer

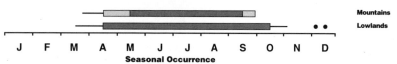

Mountains

Lowlands

J   F   M   A   M   J   J   A   S   O   N   D

Seasonal Occurrence

Elevation

Status (SP) (B): Abundant to common **summer** resident and **spring** and **fall** migrant in western valleys, foothills, mountain parks, and on eastern plains. Rare to uncommon in lower mountains outside the main parks. Populations of this species are increasing (Robbins et al. 1986).

Habitat: Breeds on structures such as buildings, culverts, and bridges in open riparian, agricultural, and aquatic habitats, and sometimes on cliffs and canyon walls. Ranges widely over most open areas while foraging and during migration. This is the most common swallow in urban areas.

Order Passeriformes
Family Corvidae

Gray Jay
Perisoreus canadensis

Resident in high mountains.

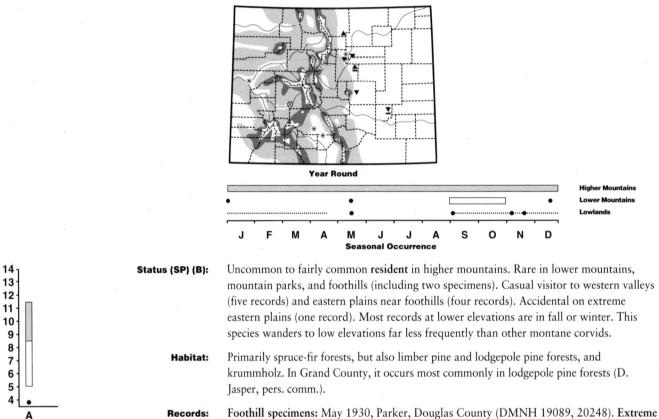

Year Round

Higher Mountains
Lower Mountains
Lowlands

J   F   M   A   M   J   J   A   S   O   N   D
Seasonal Occurrence

14
13
12
11
10
9
8
7
6
5
4

A

Elevation

Status (SP) (B): Uncommon to fairly common **resident** in higher mountains. Rare in lower mountains, mountain parks, and foothills (including two specimens). Casual visitor to western valleys (five records) and eastern plains near foothills (four records). Accidental on extreme eastern plains (one record). Most records at lower elevations are in fall or winter. This species wanders to low elevations far less frequently than other montane corvids.

Habitat: Primarily spruce-fir forests, but also limber pine and lodgepole pine forests, and krummholz. In Grand County, it occurs most commonly in lodgepole pine forests (D. Jasper, pers. comm.).

Records: Foothill specimens: May 1930, Parker, Douglas County (DMNH 19089, 20248). **Extreme eastern plains:** 2 Sep 1931, Crowley County (KU 18940, 191915).

References: Burnell and Tomback (1985), Ha and Lehner (1990).

Steller's Jay
Cyanocitta stelleri

Resident in foothills and lower mountains, and irregular fall and winter visitor to adjacent lowlands.

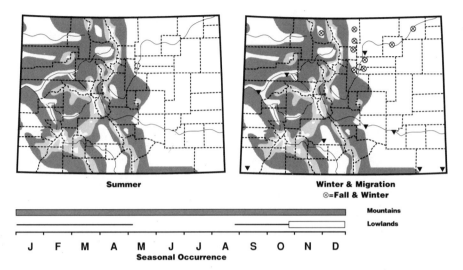

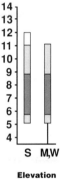

Elevation

Status (SP) (B): Fairly common to common **resident** in foothills and lower mountains. Rare to uncommon (locally fairly common to common) in higher mountains. In some areas, it occurs in the higher mountains most often in late summer and fall (Packard 1946). It seems to occur more commonly at higher elevations west of the Continental Divide than east.

Rare to uncommon irregular visitor in western valleys and mountain parks. Very rare in western semideserts and eastern plains, mostly near foothills but east to Sterling, Logan County, Rocky Ford, Otero County, and Cimarron River, Baca County. This altitudinal movement occurs mostly in fall and winter as birds withdraw from the highest parts of their range and move into the lowest foothills and adjacent valleys. These movements occur especially after heavy mountain snowfalls and during periods of food shortage. Some latitudinal movement also occurs, as suggested by an individual banded in Boulder, Boulder County on 15 Sep 1976 and recovered 215 mi. south at Stonewall, Las Animas County on 28 Nov 1976 (Webb 1981). However, Morrison and Yoders-Williams (1984) found no evidence for regular, long-distance migration in this species.

The westward expansion of the Blue Jay has brought it into contact with the Steller's Jay. Hybridization occurred at Boulder in 1969, which was the first known hybridization of the two species, and offspring and backcross individuals were observed until 1978 (Williams and Wheat 1971, Wheat 1980; see also color photo in Andrews 1979). Single hybrids were observed at Granby, Grand County in the winter of 1977–78, 18 Aug 1979–23 Mar 1980, and in Mar 1982, but their origin is unknown.

Habitat: In southern Colorado and along the Front Range, it is most common in ponderosa pine and Douglas-fir forests. In other parts of the state, it also occurs commonly in piñon-juniper, lodgepole pine, and even locally in spruce-fir forests. Wanderers to lower elevations occur in Gambel oak shrublands, lowland riparian forests, and in urban areas.

Reference: Burnell and Tomback (1985).

Blue Jay
Cyanocitta cristata

Resident on eastern plains, and wanders to mountains and west slope.

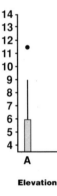

**Monthly Records
Mountains and Western Valleys**

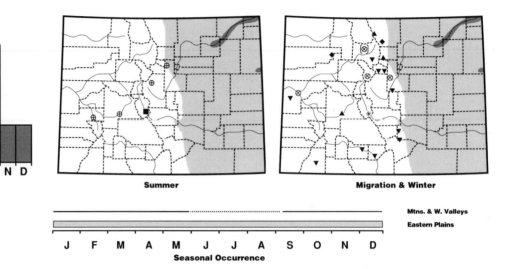

Summer

Migration & Winter

Mtns. & W. Valleys

Eastern Plains

J F M A M J J A S O N D

Seasonal Occurrence

Elevation

Status (SP) (B): Fairly common **resident** throughout eastern plains, but most common on extreme eastern plains, and somewhat more common in fall and winter. Many individuals are resident as long as local food supplies are sufficient, but some individuals do migrate along a southeast-northwest axis (Smith 1979).

This species has been expanding westward across the Great Plains (Bock and Lepthien 1976b, Smith 1978). The first record in Colorado was in 1903 at Yuma, Yuma County (Henderson 1905), and it first nested in the state in 1905 at Wray, Yuma County (Smith 1905). Since then, it has spread throughout the eastern plains. It was first recorded in the Denver area in 1917 (Felger 1917), but Niedrach and Rockwell (1939) listed it only as a "rare straggler" and gave no breeding records; it is uncertain when it first bred in that area. Breeding was first recorded at Pueblo, Pueblo County in 1970 and at Salida, Chaffee County in 1987.

The first mountain record was 11 Oct 1950, Evans Ranch (9,000 ft.), Clear Creek County. No west slope records were listed by Bailey and Niedrach (1965) or Davis (1969); the first was 29 May–19 Sep 1967 at Montrose, Montrose County. It is now a very rare visitor, mostly in fall, winter, and spring (casually in summer) to the mountains east of the Continental Divide to near timberline (25 records, three in summer), mountains west of the Continental Divide (20 records, one in summer) and western valleys (15 records, three in summer). There are no mountain or western breeding records, but it may eventually be found breeding in the western valleys.

See the Steller's Jay account for discussion of hybridization.

Habitat: Lowland riparian forests and urban areas. Montane visitors have been recorded in all types of coniferous forests and aspen forests.

Scrub Jay
Aphelocoma coerulescens

Resident in foothills and mesas; wanders down to lower valleys and plains, and up into mountains.

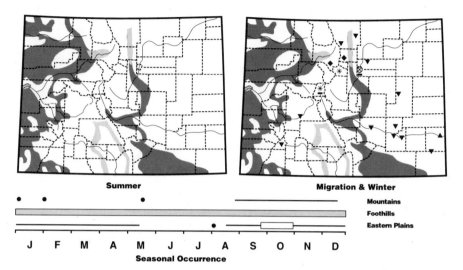

Summer   Migration & Winter

Mountains
Foothills
Eastern Plains

J F M A M J J A S O N D

Seasonal Occurrence

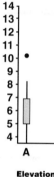

14
13
12
11
10
9
8
7
6
5
4

A

Elevation

Status (SP) (B): Fairly common **resident** in foothills and mesas of western and southern Colorado from Moffat County southward, east to Eagle County and the Blue Mesa Reservoir area, Gunnison County and from central Jefferson County southward and east through Las Animas County to southwestern Baca County. Uncommon locally in Grand County, in the foothills around the San Luis Valley, and from northern Jefferson County to Larimer County.

Rare to uncommon (locally fairly common) irregular visitor, mostly in fall but also in winter and spring, in western valleys and on eastern plains, mostly near foothills but east to Adams, Lincoln, Prowers, and Baca counties. It is regular on the southeastern plains but unrecorded on most of the northeastern plains. Casual visitor (five records) in low mountains, mostly in fall and winter. Accidental in high mountains (two records).

Habitat: Primarily Gambel oak shrublands, generally where interspersed with openings. Also occurs in mountain mahogany shrublands and piñon-juniper woodlands. Vagrants occur in most other wooded or brushy habitats.

Records: **High mountains:** San Juan County (Drew 1881); 1 Feb 1954, Lake County (KU 32011).

Pinyon Jay
Gymnorhinus cyanocephalus

Resident in foothills and mesas of western and southern Colorado, and wanders elsewhere, mostly in fall and winter.

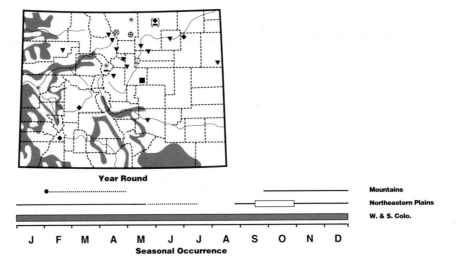

Year Round

Mountains

Northeastern Plains

W. & S. Colo.

J   F   M   A   M   J   J   A   S   O   N   D

Seasonal Occurrence

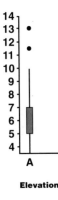

Elevation

Status (SP) (B): Common to abundant **resident** on mesas and foothills throughout western Colorado (east to southwestern Grand County), the periphery of the San Luis Valley, and in southeastern Colorado north to Chaffee and southern El Paso Counties and east to southwestern Baca County. Numbers fluctuate widely in response to cone crops, and it may be absent from suitable habitat in some years or seasons. Wanders irregularly and widely (usually in flocks) throughout the foothills and western valleys, mostly in fall and winter. Rare in Gunnison County.

Irregular visitor in northeastern foothills and adjacent plains. It is absent in most years, but in some years may be common, usually occurring in flocks. There are records throughout the year but mostly fall (especially Sep) and winter. Very rare visitor (18 records) on eastern plains east to Yuma County, mostly in fall (especially Sep-Oct) and early winter, but with records in Apr, June, and July. There are two plains specimens. Very rare visitor (10+ records) to mountains up to timberline, primarily in fall and early winter. There are two mountain specimens.

Habitat: Piñon-juniper woodlands. Wandering birds occur in or flying over riparian areas, grasslands, shrublands, coniferous forests, isolated aspen stands, and alpine tundra.

Records: **Plains specimens:** 29 Sep 1907, Weld County (KU 25663); Apr 1931, Weld County (DMNH 38011). **Mountain specimens:** 1 Feb 1954, Summit County (KU 32017, 32018).

Clark's Nutcracker
Nucifraga columbiana

Resident in higher mountains, and wanders irregularly to lower elevations, mostly in fall and winter.

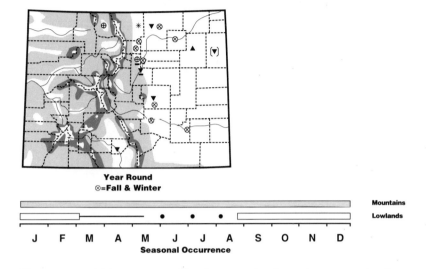

Year Round
⊗=Fall & Winter

Mountains
Lowlands

J F M A M J J A S O N D
Seasonal Occurrence

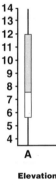

A

Elevation

Status (SP) (B): Uncommon to fairly common **resident** in mountains. It may be common locally, especially around human activity. This species wanders widely, both latitudinally and altitudinally. Flocks have been observed moving south in fall in the high mountains of Park County (Campbell 1978) and in northeastern Utah (Hoffman et al. 1978), indicating that there is latitudinal movement, at least in some years. In winter it generally withdraws from the highest portions of its breeding range, and often moves into the piñon-juniper zone (Vander Wall et al. 1981). In summer, individuals wander to above timberline.

Irregular visitor (very rare to common) to low elevations, with records all year but mostly in late summer, fall, and winter. Recorded at low elevations most often in the foothills of western Colorado and in eastern Colorado from El Paso County southward, primarily in the piñon-juniper zone in years when piñon cone crops are excellent. Uncommon to fairly common locally in summer in piñon-juniper zone, but not confirmed breeding in that habitat, although it is suspected and has nested at comparable elevations in Douglas-fir. It has been confirmed breeding in piñon-juniper in Utah (Vander Wall et al. 1981). Casual in northeastern foothills, mostly in fall and winter (five records).

Very rare visitor, mostly in fall and early winter, to northeastern plains near foothills. Casual fall and winter visitor (four records) on eastern plains, east to Yuma and Otero counties. There are two low elevation specimens.

Habitat: Breeds in spruce-fir, Douglas-fir, and limber pine forests, and also is seen in aspen forests at all seasons and krummholz in summer and fall. Wanders to alpine tundra in spring, summer, and fall, and to Gambel oak and mountain mahogany shrublands, riparian, and agricultural areas in fall and early winter. In years of large cone crops often occurs in large numbers in ponderosa pine forests and piñon-juniper woodlands. There are also summer records in piñon-juniper woodlands, but it is not known to breed in that habitat in Colorado (see above).

Records: Low elevation specimens: 2 Aug 1913, Chatfield Reservoir, Douglas/Jefferson counties (CU 2464); 7 July 1966, Lookout Mtn., Jefferson County (DMNH 35792).

Black-billed Magpie

Pica pica

Resident, primarily in lowlands, lower mountains, and mountain parks.

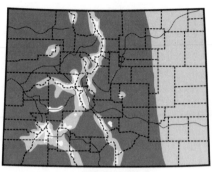

Year Round

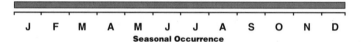

J F M A M J J A S O N D

Seasonal Occurrence

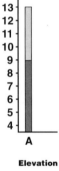

Elevation

Status (SP) (B): Common to abundant **resident** in western valleys, mountain parks, and on western portion of eastern plains. Uncommon to fairly common locally in foothills and lower mountains outside the main parks and valleys. Rare, mostly in summer and fall, in higher mountains. Uncommon to fairly common on extreme eastern plains. Central and western Colorado are part of this species' center of abundance, which extends northwestward through the northern Great Basin (Robbins et al. 1986, Root 1988). This species is heat-intolerant, and high temperatures and humidities restrict its distribution to west of the 100th meridian (Bock and Lepthien 1975, Hayworth and Weathers 1984).

Habitat: Occurs in all open habitats with scattered trees; avoids both treeless grasslands and deserts and dense forested areas. Most common in riparian forests, agricultural, and urban areas, but also occurs regularly in shrublands, piñon-juniper woodlands, and cholla grasslands.

American Crow
Corvus brachyrhynchos

Resident at low and middle elevations.

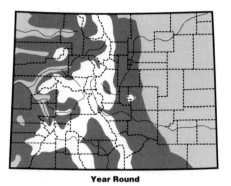

Year Round

J F M A M J J A S O N D
Seasonal Occurrence

Elevation

Status (SP) (B): Local **resident**, fairly common in summer and locally common to abundant Sep-Mar, in western valleys, foothills, and lower mountains, mountain parks, and on eastern plains near foothills. It seems to be quite local, and abundance varies widely from site to site. Rare to uncommon on plains away from foothills. Large migratory flocks are sometimes seen in fall (mostly Oct), and large winter roosts occur locally.

The distribution of this species has changed in recent years. Bailey and Niedrach (1965) considered it common only in northeastern Colorado and casual elsewhere. It is now more common in the foothills, lower mountains, and plains near foothills, and is rare in summer on most of the eastern plains (Andrews and Carter 1992, B. Howe, pers. comm.).

Habitat: Most common in riparian, agricultural and urban areas, but also occurs in coniferous forests (especially ponderosa pine and lodgepole pine), shrublands, and cholla grasslands.

Chihuahuan Raven
Corvus cryptoleucus

Resident on southeastern plains.

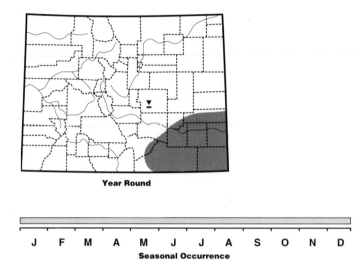

Year Round

J F M A M J J A S O N D

Seasonal Occurrence

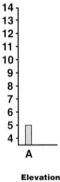

Elevation

Status (SP) (B): Uncommon (locally fairly common) **resident** on southeastern plains, mostly from Crowley, Kit Carson, and eastern Pueblo counties southward. High count: 100+ on 14 June 1988 near Villegreen, Las Animas County. It may occur in smaller numbers north to El Paso and Yuma counties, but its status in those areas is unclear. Although there are recent reports from the northeastern plains and southwestern Colorado, there are no documented records. Observers should be very cautious about identifying this species outside of southeastern Colorado.

This species was abundant throughout eastern Colorado in the 1800s and nested in huge colonies in the trees along watercourses (Henshaw 1875). By the early 1900s, it apparently no longer occurred in northeastern Colorado, but remained common in the southeast up to the 1930s. Aiken and Warren (1914) speculated that the species spread north during the late 1800s when the huge bison herds were being slaughtered, and withdrew after the bison had become extirpated. The species now has a much reduced range and is much less common within the range still occupied. Competition from American Crows may also have played a role in the last 20 years as the latter species expanded its range into southeastern Colorado (Chase 1980). Due to its population decline, this species is a Colorado Species of Special Concern (Webb 1985b).

Habitat: Arid or semiarid grasslands and semideserts such as shortgrass, cholla, and sandsage grasslands; also in tallgrass prairie or introduced grasslands. It nests on isolated trees and structures such as windmills and telephone poles.

Note: Formerly known as White-necked Raven.

Common Raven
Corvus corax

Resident throughout Colorado except on eastern plains.

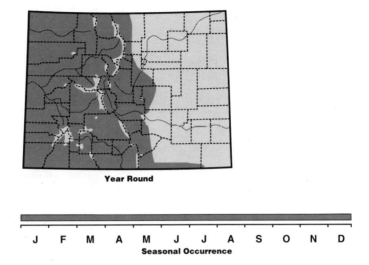

Year Round

Seasonal Occurrence

J F M A M J J A S O N D

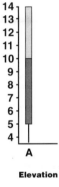

Elevation

Status (SP) (B): Fairly common to common **resident** in semideserts, foothills, mesas, and mountains to above timberline throughout Colorado. High counts: 370 on 16 Feb 1978, Shadow Mountain Reservoir, Grand County; 400 on 17 Nov 1990, Redlands, Mesa County. Generally most common in canyons and around cliffs in foothills and lower mountains. Uncommon to locally fairly common visitor all year, but mostly in fall, winter, and spring on eastern plains near foothills. Rare on eastern plains away from foothills; a few may breed locally around escarpments, especially in northern Weld County.

Habitat: Breeds on cliffs, and wanders (mostly outside of the breeding season) to adjacent lowlands, mostly in grasslands and shrublands, but also riparian and agricultural areas. Sometimes found at dumps.

Order Passeriformes
Family Paridae

Black-capped Chickadee
Parus atricapillus

Resident in lowlands and locally in the mountains.

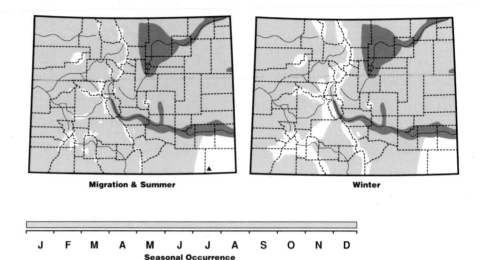

Migration & Summer   Winter

J   F   M   A   M   J   J   A   S   O   N   D
Seasonal Occurrence

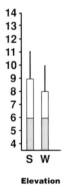

S   W

Elevation

Status (SP) (B): Resident in western valleys and on eastern plains, uncommon to fairly common in summer and fairly common to common at other seasons. Fairly common summer resident and rare winter resident on mesas, in foothills, and lower mountains in western Colorado but usually rare to uncommon locally (mostly in riparian areas) in similar areas along the Front Range. Uncommon in mountain parks and rare in high mountains, mostly in summer. There are two high elevation specimens. Accidental in Baca County (two records).

Habitat: In eastern Colorado, breeds primarily in riparian forests and in towns, and is rare in aspen and coniferous forests. In western Colorado, breeds in foothill and montane riparian forests, aspen forests, and Gambel oak shrublands, and rarely occurs in those habitats in winter but moves primarily down to lowland riparian forests. Uncommon to fairly common in mature piñon-juniper woodlands. Rare in spruce-fir forests and subalpine riparian shrublands. Also occurs in foothill and montane shrublands outside breeding season.

Records: High elevation specimens: 22 Sep 1942, Silver Plume (9,100 ft.), Clear Creek County (DMNH 23866); 30 Jan 1954, Lake County (KU 32020). **Baca County:** 28 Mar 1983 and 6–7 May 1989, Cottonwood Canyon.

Mountain Chickadee

Parus gambeli

Resident in foothills and mountains; irregular fall and winter visitor to lower elevations near foothills.

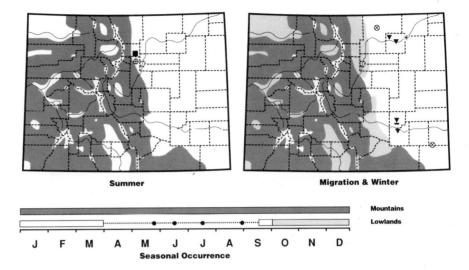

Summer   Migration & Winter

Mountains

Lowlands

J F M A M J J A S O N D

Seasonal Occurrence

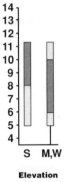

Elevation

Status (SP) (B): Fairly common to common **resident** in foothills and mountains. In fall and winter, there is altitudinal movement, as many birds withdraw from the highest parts of the breeding range and the numbers in the foothills increases. Irregular visitor, mostly **fall** and **early winter**, to western valleys and eastern plains (mostly near foothills) and in mountain parks. Usually rare or uncommon, but in some years may be fairly common and in exceptional years outnumbers Black-capped Chickadees. Very rare in fall and winter on extreme eastern plains. One eastern plains specimen. Casual in summer on eastern plains near foothills.

Habitat: Coniferous and aspen forests. It is one of the most common breeding species in old-growth spruce-fir forests (Scott et al. 1982, Hallock 1988). In winter, wandering birds also occur in shrublands, urban areas, and lowland riparian forests.

Records: **Eastern plains specimen:** 2 Sep 1931, Crowley County (KU 18593). **Breeding on eastern plains:** nested in eastern Boulder County several years in 1970s; 8-9 July 1982, Wheat Ridge, Jefferson County.

Plain Titmouse

Parus inornatus

Resident in foothills of western and southern Colorado.

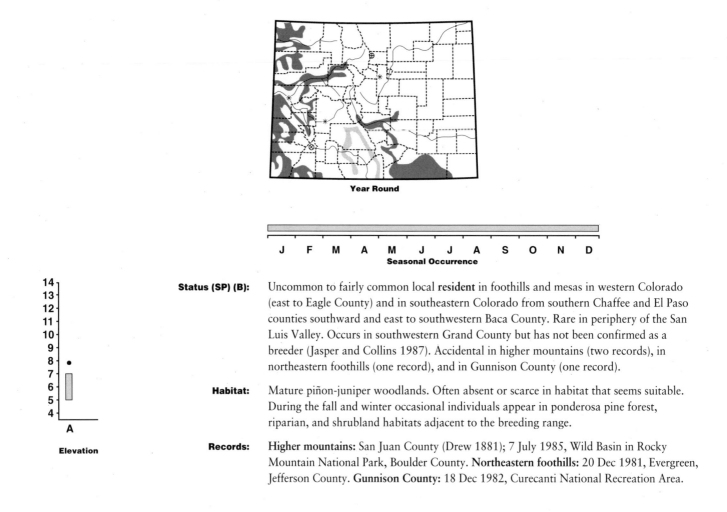

Year Round

J F M A M J J A S O N D

Seasonal Occurrence

Elevation

Status (SP) (B): Uncommon to fairly common local **resident** in foothills and mesas in western Colorado (east to Eagle County) and in southeastern Colorado from southern Chaffee and El Paso counties southward and east to southwestern Baca County. Rare in periphery of the San Luis Valley. Occurs in southwestern Grand County but has not been confirmed as a breeder (Jasper and Collins 1987). Accidental in higher mountains (two records), in northeastern foothills (one record), and in Gunnison County (one record).

Habitat: Mature piñon-juniper woodlands. Often absent or scarce in habitat that seems suitable. During the fall and winter occasional individuals appear in ponderosa pine forest, riparian, and shrubland habitats adjacent to the breeding range.

Records: **Higher mountains:** San Juan County (Drew 1881); 7 July 1985, Wild Basin in Rocky Mountain National Park, Boulder County. **Northeastern foothills:** 20 Dec 1981, Evergreen, Jefferson County. **Gunnison County:** 18 Dec 1982, Curecanti National Recreation Area.

Order Passeriformes
Family Aegithalidae

Bushtit

Psaltriparus minimus

Resident in foothills of western and southern Colorado, and wanders irregularly elsewhere.

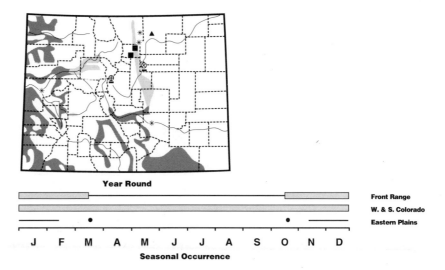

Year Round

Front Range
W. & S. Colorado
Eastern Plains

J F M A M J J A S O N D

Seasonal Occurrence

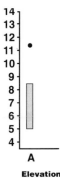

A

Elevation

Status (SP) (B): Rare to fairly common irregular **resident** in foothills and mesas of western Colorado, rarely east to western Eagle and Gunnison counties, in the periphery of the San Luis Valley, and in southeastern Colorado from southern Chaffee and El Paso counties southward and east to southwestern Baca County. In western Colorado, it appears to be most numerous south of the Colorado River. Numbers and local distribution of this species is quite irregular. It is often absent from apparently suitable habitat, and tends to appear and disappear unpredictably at any given site.

Rare to fairly common irregular **visitor** to riparian areas and shrublands in eastern foothills north to Larimer County; throughout year but mostly late Oct to mid-Mar. Casual breeder (four records since 1977) in low foothills of Boulder County. Irregular winter resident in western valleys. Very rare fall and winter visitor (11 records, including three specimens) on eastern plains. Accidental in higher mountains (one record).

Habitat: Primarily piñon-juniper woodlands, but also shrublands (both upland and riparian) and rarely orchards. Often in rabbitbrush in fall (C. Dexter, pers. comm.).

Records: **Higher mountains:** four collected 12 July 1922 at 11,500 ft. on Mt. Bross, Park County (DMNH 9964–67).

Order Passeriformes
Family Sittidae

Red-breasted Nuthatch
Sitta canadensis

Resident in mountains and migrant and winter resident at lower elevations; numbers highly variable.

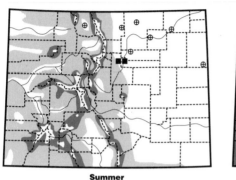

Summer

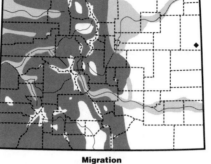

Migration

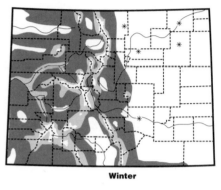

Winter

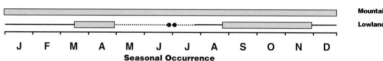

Mountains

Lowlands

J F M A M J J A S O N D
Seasonal Occurrence

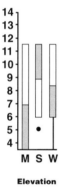

Elevation

Status (SP) (B): Rare to fairly common irregular **resident** in foothills and mountains. In summer, occurs mostly in higher mountains. In fall and winter, altitudinal movements occur, with most birds found in foothills and lower mountains. High count: 85 in two hours on 27 Feb 1982 in the Boulder County foothills. Rare to fairly common irregular **spring** and **fall** migrant in western valleys and on eastern plains. Rare to uncommon irregular **winter** visitor in western valleys and on eastern plains very near foothills; rare to very rare on eastern plains more than 10 mi. from foothills. Movements and numbers are usually correlated with local food supply; numbers increase whenever and wherever there are excellent conifer seed crops. Casual on eastern plains in **early summer** (nine records, including two breeding records).

Habitat: Primarily coniferous forests (and less often in aspen and riparian forests). Breeds most commonly in high mountain forests, especially spruce-fir but also lodgepole pine and Douglas-fir forests. Rare in summer, and more commonly in fall and winter (especially in years of good cone crops), in lower coniferous forests (Douglas-fir, ponderosa pine, piñon-juniper). Also occurs in Gambel oak shrublands, mostly in fall and winter. In migration and winter, also appears in lowland riparian forests and urban areas (especially around conifers in parks, cemeteries, and residential areas).

Records: **Breeding on eastern plains:** nested 1983 in Denver County and Golden, Jefferson County.

White-breasted Nuthatch
Sitta carolinensis

Resident in foothills and lower mountains, and at lower elevations mostly in migration and winter.

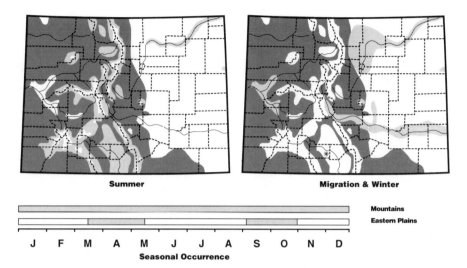

Summer   Migration & Winter

Mountains
Eastern Plains

J F M A M J J A S O N D
Seasonal Occurrence

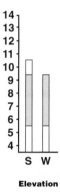

Elevation

Status (SP) (B): Fairly common **resident** in foothills and lower mountains; rarely in higher mountains, mostly in summer. Uncommon to fairly common migrant and winter resident in western valleys and eastern plains near foothills, and rare in summer. Uncommon migrant on eastern plains away from foothills and very rare to rare in winter and summer. Although numbers of this species do fluctuate, it does not seem to be as irregular as the Red-breasted Nuthatch.

Habitat: Most common in ponderosa pine forests (McEllin 1979) and piñon-juniper woodlands. Also regularly in foothill and lowland riparian forests. In the Front Range, common in aspen forests (Crockett and Hadow 1975) but rare in Gambel oak shrublands, while the situation is reversed in western Colorado (R. Lambeth, pers. comm.). Also in urban areas, especially in fall and winter. Rare in spruce-fir forests.

Pygmy Nuthatch

Sitta pygmaea

Resident in foothills and low mountains.

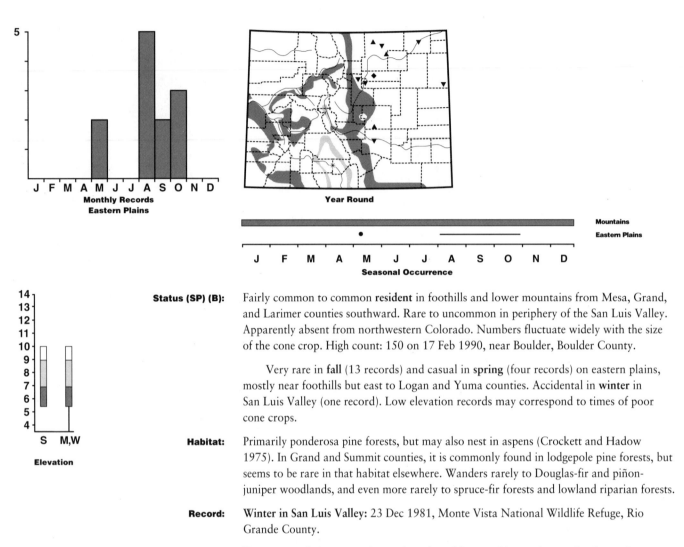

**Monthly Records
Eastern Plains**

Year Round

Seasonal Occurrence

Mountains

Eastern Plains

Elevation

Status (SP) (B): Fairly common to common **resident** in foothills and lower mountains from Mesa, Grand, and Larimer counties southward. Rare to uncommon in periphery of the San Luis Valley. Apparently absent from northwestern Colorado. Numbers fluctuate widely with the size of the cone crop. High count: 150 on 17 Feb 1990, near Boulder, Boulder County.

Very rare in **fall** (13 records) and casual in **spring** (four records) on eastern plains, mostly near foothills but east to Logan and Yuma counties. Accidental in **winter** in San Luis Valley (one record). Low elevation records may correspond to times of poor cone crops.

Habitat: Primarily ponderosa pine forests, but may also nest in aspens (Crockett and Hadow 1975). In Grand and Summit counties, it is commonly found in lodgepole pine forests, but seems to be rare in that habitat elsewhere. Wanders rarely to Douglas-fir and piñon-juniper woodlands, and even more rarely to spruce-fir forests and lowland riparian forests.

Record: **Winter in San Luis Valley:** 23 Dec 1981, Monte Vista National Wildlife Refuge, Rio Grande County.

Note: Human population expansion and cutting of firewood in ponderosa pine forests have caused a loss of trees with suitable nest sites, resulting in population declines. For this reason, and because the species is an excellent indicator species for the ponderosa pine forest, the Pygmy Nuthatch is a Colorado Species of Special Concern (Webb 1985b).

Reference: McEllin (1979).

Order Passeriformes
Family Certhiidae

Brown Creeper
Certhia americana

Resident in mountains and winter resident at low elevations.

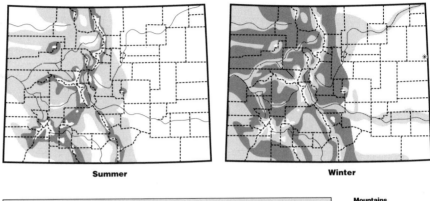

Summer   Winter

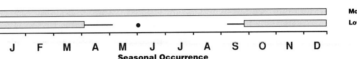

Mountains
Lowlands

J F M A M J J A S O N D
Seasonal Occurrence

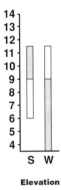

S W

Elevation

Status (SP) (B): Uncommon **resident** in mountains. In summer, occurs mostly in higher mountains, and in winter primarily in lower mountains and foothills. Uncommon **winter** resident in western valleys and on eastern plains.

Habitat: Breeds in coniferous forest, primarily spruce-fir, but also other forests such as limber pine, lodgepole pine, and Douglas-fir, and rarely in ponderosa pine. In winter, occurs in all types of coniferous forests (but rare in piñon-juniper), aspen and lowland riparian forests, and urban areas.

255

Order Passeriformes
Family Troglodytidae

Rock Wren
Salpinctes obsoletus

Summer resident in foothills and low mountains and migrant at low elevations; rare in winter.

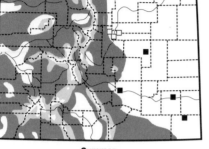

Summer   Migration   Winter

Mountains
Foothills
Lowlands

J F M A M J J A S O N D
Seasonal Occurrence

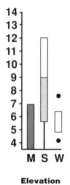

Elevation

Status (SP) (B): Uncommon to fairly common **summer** resident in foothills and lower mountains; local in mountain parks. Rare in higher mountains to just above timberline. Rare to uncommon very locally on rocky escarpments and rocky dams on eastern plains. Fairly common to common **spring** and **fall** migrant in western valleys and eastern plains near foothills; rare to uncommon on extreme eastern plains. High count: 500 on 11 May 1984, Pawnee National Grassland, Weld County. Rare migrant in mountains and mountain parks. Rare to uncommon local **winter** resident in valleys and low foothills, primarily from Mesa, Fremont, and southern El Paso counties southward and east to Baca County. Accidental on northeastern plains (three records).

Habitat: Open, rocky slopes and around cliffs. In migration, in grasslands, brushy slopes, riparian areas, and urban areas.

Records: **Winter on northeastern plains:** 20 Dec 1971 and 21 Dec 1982, Nunn CBC, Weld County; 23 Dec 1985, Weldona CBC, Morgan County.

Canyon Wren

Catherpes mexicanus

Resident in foothills; most common in summer.

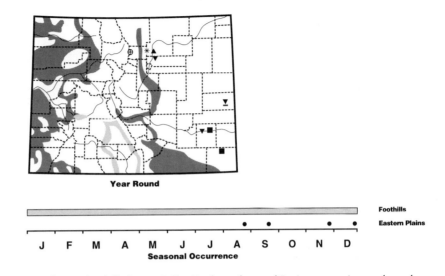

Year Round

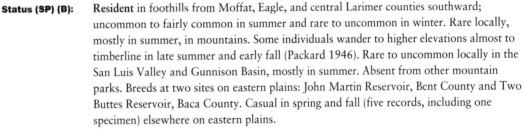

Foothills

Eastern Plains

J F M A M J J A S O N D

Seasonal Occurrence

Status (SP) (B): **Resident** in foothills from Moffat, Eagle, and central Larimer counties southward; uncommon to fairly common in summer and rare to uncommon in winter. Rare locally, mostly in summer, in mountains. Some individuals wander to higher elevations almost to timberline in late summer and early fall (Packard 1946). Rare to uncommon locally in the San Luis Valley and Gunnison Basin, mostly in summer. Absent from other mountain parks. Breeds at two sites on eastern plains: John Martin Reservoir, Bent County and Two Buttes Reservoir, Baca County. Casual in spring and fall (five records, including one specimen) elsewhere on eastern plains.

Habitat: Cliffs and rocky slopes.

Record: **Eastern plains specimen:** 23 Nov 1906, near Cheyenne Wells, Cheyenne County (CU 9846) (Warren 1907).

Note: This species has declined recently for unknown reasons, and therefore is a Colorado Species of Special Concern (Webb 1985b).

Elevation

14
13
12
11
10
9
8
7
6
5
4

A

Carolina Wren
Thryothorus ludovicianus

Occasional in eastern Colorado.

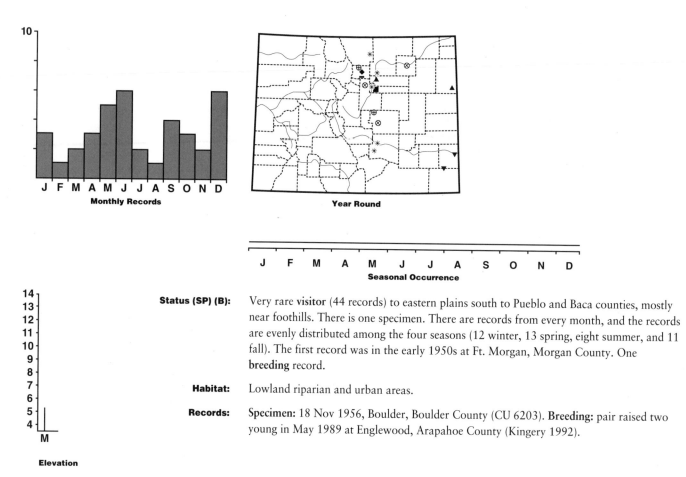

Monthly Records

Year Round

Seasonal Occurrence

Elevation

Status (SP) (B): Very rare **visitor** (44 records) to eastern plains south to Pueblo and Baca counties, mostly near foothills. There is one specimen. There are records from every month, and the records are evenly distributed among the four seasons (12 winter, 13 spring, eight summer, and 11 fall). The first record was in the early 1950s at Ft. Morgan, Morgan County. One **breeding** record.

Habitat: Lowland riparian and urban areas.

Records: **Specimen:** 18 Nov 1956, Boulder, Boulder County (CU 6203). **Breeding:** pair raised two young in May 1989 at Englewood, Arapahoe County (Kingery 1992).

Bewick's Wren

Thryomanes bewickii

Resident in western and southern Colorado.

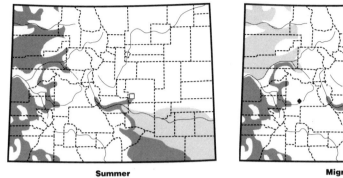

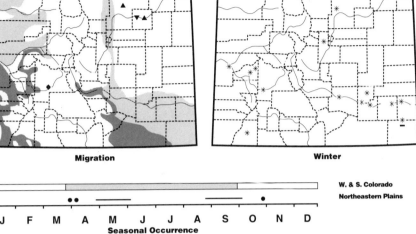

Summer   Migration   Winter

W. & S. Colorado
Northeastern Plains

J F M A M J J A S O N D

Seasonal Occurrence

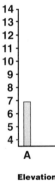

Elevation

Status (SP) (B): **Resident,** fairly common in summer and rare to fairly common in winter, in foothills and mesas from Moffat and southwestern El Paso counties southward and east to southwestern Baca County, and on southeastern plains in the Arkansas River Valley. Populations of this species fluctuate widely. This species is most common in western Colorado. In Mesa County, it is fairly common in winter (Lambeth and Armstrong 1985), but in most other areas it seems to be much less common in winter. There is one winter specimen.

Rare to uncommon **spring** and **fall** migrant in Gunnison County (D. Radovich, pers. comm.). Irregular fall migrant in western valleys; absent in some years but fairly common in others (C. Dexter, pers. comm.). Very rare spring migrant (18 records) and casual fall migrant (five records) on northeastern plains, mostly near foothills north to Larimer County and east to Morgan County; accidental in winter (one record).

Habitat: Piñon-juniper woodlands and semidesert shrublands; occasionally in sagebrush shrublands away from trees. In southeastern Colorado, also in lowland riparian forests, and occurs in that habitat in migration in western Colorado. Often found in tamarisk in summer (D. Nelson, pers. comm.), and occurs mostly in tamarisk in winter in Mesa County (R. Lambeth, pers. comm.).

Records: **Winter specimen:** 11 Feb 1941, Two Buttes Reservoir, Baca County (DMNH 22367). **Winter in northeastern foothills:** 9 Oct 1960–5 Mar 1961, Red Rocks, Jefferson County.

House Wren
Troglodytes aedon

Summer resident statewide except in higher mountains.

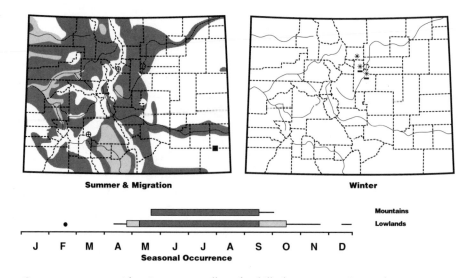

Summer & Migration **Winter**

Mountains
Lowlands

J F M A M J J A S O N D
Seasonal Occurrence

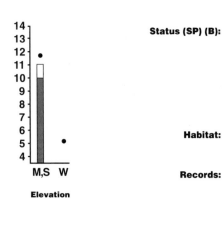

Elevation

Status (SP) (B): Common **summer** resident in western valleys, foothills, lower mountains, and on eastern plains. Absent in the Grand Valley in summer (C. Dexter, pers. comm.), but fairly common in migration (M. Janos, pers. comm.). Rare in higher mountains, and accidental at or above timberline (two records). One of the centers of abundance of this species in North America is in the Colorado mountains (Robbins et al. 1986). Casual in **winter** (four records*) on northeastern plains near foothills. All winter records should be carefully documented.

Habitat: All wooded habitats, most commonly riparian, aspen, and ponderosa pine forests; also other coniferous forests and Gambel oak shrublands. Rare in urban areas in summer.

Records: **Above timberline:** 31 July 1960, at 11,700 ft. on Mt. Goliath, Clear Creek County; 19 June 1989, at 11,800 ft. on Boot Mtn. in La Garita Mountains, Saguache County (Righter et al. 1989). **Winter*:** 19 Feb 1906, Arvada, Jefferson County (DMNH 13245); 28 Dec 1934, Littleton, Arapahoe County (DMNH 14326); 15 Dec 1973, Boulder, Boulder County; 20 Dec 1975, Littleton, Arapahoe County.

Winter Wren
Troglodytes troglodytes

Fall migrant and winter resident, mostly in eastern Colorado.

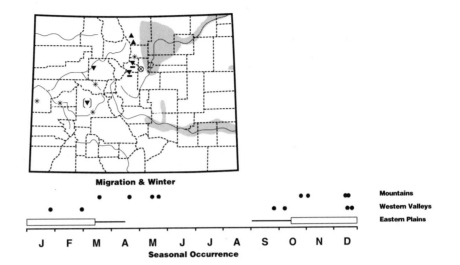

Migration & Winter

Mountains

Western Valleys

Eastern Plains

J F M A M J J A S O N D

Seasonal Occurrence

Status (SP): Rare fall migrant and winter resident on eastern plains; most records are near the edge of the foothills. Recorded annually; in most winters there are <10 records, but in exceptional years there may be many more (especially in fall). High count: 5 on 24 Oct 1987, Hale, Yuma County. Casual in foothills and lower mountains (10 records, including two specimens), mostly in northeast from Larimer to Jefferson counties. Casual (six records) in western valleys from Eagle County to Mesa and Gunnison counties. There are 10 summer records from the mountains, but they are undocumented.

Habitat: Dense thickets in riparian areas.

Records: Mountain specimens: 31 Oct 1964, Moon Gulch, Gilpin County (CU 8911); 8 Dec 1979, Guanella Pass, Clear Creek/Park counties (DMNH 39578).

14
13
12
11
10
9
8
7
6
5
4

M,W

Elevation

Sedge Wren
Cistothorus platensis

Occasional migrant, mostly in eastern Colorado, and several summer records.

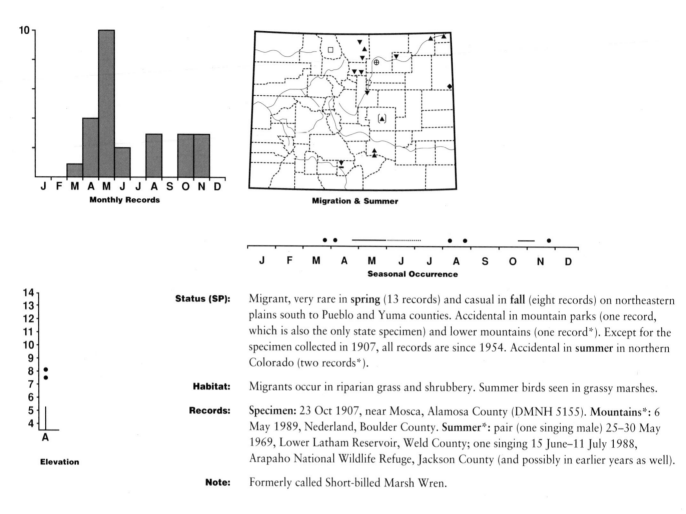

Monthly Records

Migration & Summer

Seasonal Occurrence

Elevation

Status (SP):	Migrant, very rare in **spring** (13 records) and casual in **fall** (eight records) on northeastern plains south to Pueblo and Yuma counties. Accidental in mountain parks (one record, which is also the only state specimen) and lower mountains (one record*). Except for the specimen collected in 1907, all records are since 1954. Accidental in **summer** in northern Colorado (two records*).
Habitat:	Migrants occur in riparian grass and shrubbery. Summer birds seen in grassy marshes.
Records:	**Specimen:** 23 Oct 1907, near Mosca, Alamosa County (DMNH 5155). **Mountains***: 6 May 1989, Nederland, Boulder County. **Summer***: pair (one singing male) 25–30 May 1969, Lower Latham Reservoir, Weld County; one singing 15 June–11 July 1988, Arapaho National Wildlife Refuge, Jackson County (and possibly in earlier years as well).
Note:	Formerly called Short-billed Marsh Wren.

Marsh Wren

Cistothorus palustris

Local in both summer and winter, mostly in northern Colorado and the San Luis Valley.

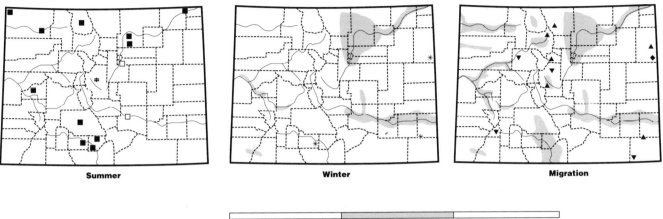

| Summer | Winter | Migration |

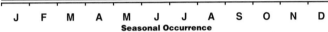

| J | F | M | A | M | J | J | A | S | O | N | D |

Seasonal Occurrence

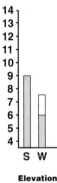

Elevation

Status (SP) (B): Local **resident**, uncommon to common in summer and rare to uncommon in winter. In summer, occurs in western valleys, mountain parks, and on eastern plains. The main breeding areas are in the San Luis Valley, and at scattered locations in the Yampa and South Platte River valleys. In winter, occurs in western valleys and eastern plains and rarely in the San Luis Valley. Recorded from every month, but the pattern of residency varies at different sites: some have breeders, others only winter residents, and other sites have birds all year. The factors controlling this are not clear, as many evidently suitable marshes do not have breeders. However, most large marshes have breeding populations while smaller marshes often lack them, and most marshes which remain unfrozen all winter support wintering individuals.

Very rare **spring** and **fall** migrant outside of marshes. Accidental migrant in mountains outside of main parks (three records).

Habitat: Cattail marshes; migrants may occur in riparian areas.

Records: **Mountains:** Sep (year unknown) in San Juan County (Drew 1881); 6–11 May 1933, Georgetown, Clear Creek County; 18 Apr 1972, Lake Estes, Larimer County; 1 June 1978, west side of Rocky Mountain National Park, Grand County.

Note: Formerly called Long-billed Marsh Wren.

**Order Passeriformes
Family Cinclidae**

American Dipper
Cinclus mexicanus

Resident in mountains, a few in winter at lower elevations.

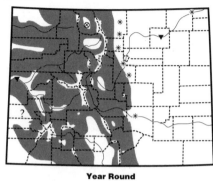

Year Round
⊗=Migration & Summer Non-Breeding

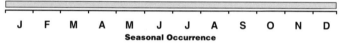

J F M A M J J A S O N D
Seasonal Occurrence

14	
13	
12	
11	
10	
9	
8	
7	
6	
5	
4	

S W

Elevation

Status (SP) (B): Uncommon **resident** in foothills and mountains, breeding mostly at middle elevations. In winter, birds withdraw from highest parts of the breeding range and occur mostly in lower mountains and foothills, but some individuals remain as high as open water is available. Fairly common to common **winter** resident in western valleys and rare to uncommon on eastern plains, mostly within five mi. of foothills and very rarely out to 20 mi. Rare visitor in mountain parks. Accidental on extreme northeastern plains (two records).

Habitat: Mountain streams and rivers. In summer, mostly around bridges, which have extensively supplanted natural nesting sites.

Records: **Extreme northeastern plains:** 31 Dec 1983, Julesburg Reservoir, Logan/Sedgwick counties; 1 Nov 1988, Muir Springs, Morgan County.

Note: This species is a Colorado Species of Special Concern because it is an excellent indicator species for stream quality (Webb 1985b).

References: Price and Bock (1973, 1983), Price (1979).

Order Passeriformes
Family Muscicapidae

Golden-crowned Kinglet

Regulus satrapa

Irregular resident in mountains, and in migration and winter at low elevations.

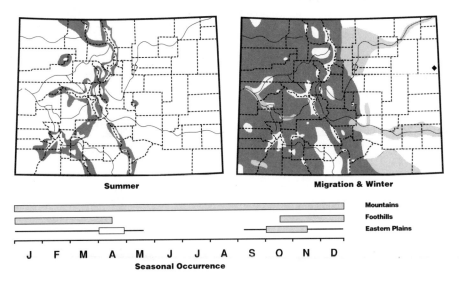

Summer   Migration & Winter

Mountains
Foothills
Eastern Plains

J F M A M J J A S O N D
Seasonal Occurrence

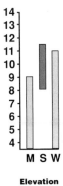

M S W

Elevation

Status (SP) (B): **Resident** in higher mountains; uncommon to fairly common in summer and rare in winter. In some high elevation areas, it may withdraw completely in the winter. It seems to be more common west of the Continental Divide than to the east. Uncommon to fairly common irregular **winter** resident in lower mountains and foothills. Rare in western valleys and eastern plains near foothills and very rare on plains away from foothills. Irregular migrant, rare to fairly common in **fall** and rare in **spring**, on eastern plains. In all areas and seasons, its numbers fluctuate widely.

Habitat: Breeds primarily in mature, dense spruce-fir forest, and rarely in limber pine and Douglas-fir forests. In winter, occurs in coniferous forests (especially Douglas-fir or ponderosa pine) but also in other types such as piñon-juniper woodlands, foothill and lowland riparian forests, and in planted conifers in parks, cemeteries, and residential areas in the lowlands. In migration, occurs in most wooded habitats.

Ruby-crowned Kinglet

Regulus calendula

Summer resident in higher mountains, and migrant and occasional winter resident at lower elevations.

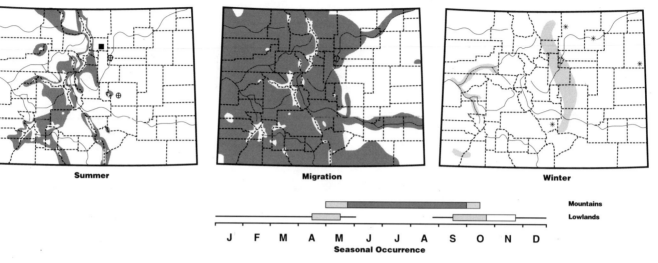

Summer   Migration   Winter

Mountains

Lowlands

J F M A M J J A S O N D

Seasonal Occurrence

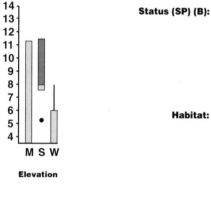

Elevation

Status (SP) (B):   Common **summer** resident in higher mountains, and uncommon to fairly common locally in lower mountains. One breeding record on eastern plains near foothills. Fairly common **spring** and **fall** migrant in western valleys, foothills, mountains, mountain parks, and on eastern plains. Rare to uncommon **winter** resident in foothills, western valleys, and on eastern plains near foothills, mostly from Mesa and El Paso counties southward. Accidental on extreme eastern plains (three records). There is one winter specimen.

Habitat: Breeds in coniferous forests, primarily in spruce-fir, and commonly in lodgepole pine forests in some areas (D. Jasper, pers. comm.). Less frequently nests in Douglas-fir forests. In most areas where censuses have been conducted, this bird was the most common breeding species in old-growth spruce-fir forests (Scott et al. 1982, Alles 1985, Hallock 1988). In migration, all wooded habitats. In winter, piñon-juniper woodlands, ponderosa pine forests, planted conifers, urban areas, and lowland riparian forests.

Records: **Breeding on plains:** one pair nested in 1973 at Boulder (5,350 ft.), Boulder County. **Winter on extreme eastern plains:** 1982 and 1985 on Weldona CBC, Morgan County; 1984 on Bonny Reservoir CBC, Yuma County. **Winter specimen:** 31 Dec 1982, Lakewood, Jefferson County (LSU 109220).

Blue-gray Gnatcatcher

Polioptila caerulea

Summer resident and migrant, mostly in western and southern Colorado.

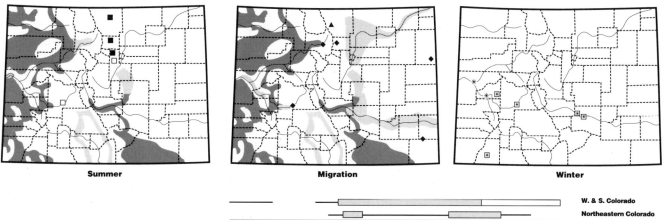

Summer   Migration   Winter

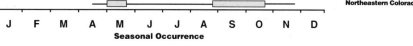

W. & S. Colorado
Northeastern Colorado

J   F   M   A   M   J   J   A   S   O   N   D

Seasonal Occurrence

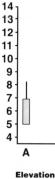

A

Elevation

Status (SP) (B): Fairly common to common **summer** resident in foothills and mesas from Moffat County southward, and rare east to southwestern Grand County, and from Douglas County southward. Rare in the periphery of the San Luis Valley. Rare to fairly common very locally in northeastern foothills from Jefferson County north to Larimer County (breeding confirmed or suspected at four sites). Suspected breeder at Gunnison, Gunnison County in 1975 (Hyde 1979).

  Spring and **fall** migrant, fairly common in western valleys and in western and southern foothills, and rare in lower mountains. Rare to uncommon in northeastern foothills, and rare on eastern plains and in the periphery of the San Luis Valley. Rare to uncommon in **early winter** and casual in **mid-winter** (seven records) in Mesa and Delta counties, and casual in lower foothills and valleys in Gunnison, La Plata, and Pueblo counties (five records). High count: 9 on 20 Dec 1981, Gunnison, Gunnison Co. All winter records are since 1970, but it is now recorded annually, at least in west-central Colorado.

Habitat: Breeds in piñon-juniper woodlands, Gambel oak, mountain mahogany and riparian shrublands; rarely sagebrush shrublands. In migration, occurs in most wooded or brushy habitats. Winter birds occur in shrublands on dry, sunny slopes or along open streams.

Eastern Bluebird
Sialia sialis

Resident in extreme eastern Colorado, and irregular and local west to foothills.

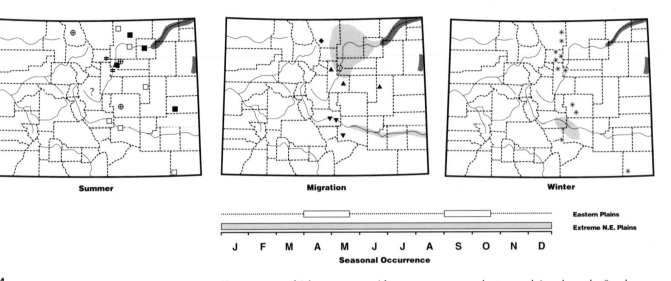

| Summer | Migration | Winter |

Eastern Plains
Extreme N.E. Plains

J F M A M J J A S O N D

Seasonal Occurrence

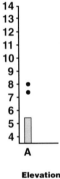

Elevation

Status (SP) (B): Uncommon to fairly common **resident** on extreme northeastern plains along the South Platte River west to Prewitt Reservoir, Washington County and in eastern Yuma County.

Uncommon **spring** and **fall** migrant in the Arkansas River Valley and uncommon **winter** resident in eastern Fremont, northeastern Custer, and western Pueblo counties. Rare migrant and very rare winter resident (about 13 records) on northeastern plains near foothills. Casual, mostly in spring and fall, in eastern foothills and lower mountains (seven records, including one breeding record). Accidental in mountain parks (two records).

Nested in Boulder, Boulder County in 1887 and many occurred in Denver County parks and residential areas in the 1920s, but the species had become much less common by the 1950s and 1960s (Bailey and Niedrach 1965). The species attempted to nest at Boulder in 1977, and in 1990 and 1991, nesting was confirmed west to the Rocky Mountain Arsenal, Adams County and suspected south and west to Penrose, Fremont County, Pueblo, Pueblo County, and Cottonwood Canyon, Baca County. This species is clearly, although slowly, expanding its range through eastern Colorado west to the base fo the foothills.

Habitat: Lowland riparian forests, mostly around farmhouses and adjacent open areas.

Records: **Breeding in eastern foothills:** nest 3 June 1931 at Evans Ranch (8,000 ft.), Clear Creek County (Bailey and Niedrach 1965). **Mountain parks:** Park County (Tresz 1881 in Bailey and Niedrach 1965); summer 1938, Jackson County (Bailey and Niedrach 1965).

Note: There is a hybrid specimen, *S. sialis* X *S. currucoides*: 25 May 1945, Deer Tail, Arapahoe County (DMNH 24715).

Western Bluebird

Sialia mexicana

Resident in foothills and lower mountains, mostly in southern Colorado.

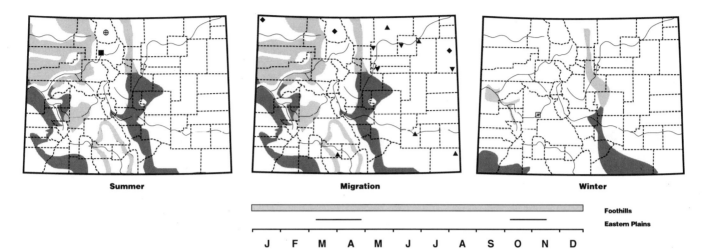

Summer				**Migration**				**Winter**			

Foothills

Eastern Plains

J F M A M J J A S O N D

Seasonal Occurrence

Elevation

Status (SP) (B): **Summer** resident in foothills and lower mountains; fairly common in southern Colorado south of the Colorado River and the Arkansas-Platte River divide. Uncommon locally northward in Front Range to Larimer County and in the periphery of the San Luis Valley, mostly in the southern part of the Valley. Appears to be rare and very local in northwestern Colorado. Rare summer resident in North Park, Middle Park, and the Gunnison Basin.

Uncommon to common **migrant** in western valleys, foothills, lower mountains, and mountain parks; most common in southern half of the state. Rare migrant on eastern plains within a few miles of foothills. Very rare migrant on eastern plains east to Yuma and Baca counties (12 records). Uncommon to fairly common local **winter** resident in foothills and mesas from Mesa and Fremont counties southward; very rare north to Larimer County.

Habitat: Breeds primarily in ponderosa pine forests (or mixed ponderosa pine/aspen) and less often in piñon-juniper woodlands and in Gambel oak shrublands. In migration, occurs in most open forest types and adjacent open areas. In winter, primarily piñon-juniper woodlands, but also riparian areas and shrublands, generally where fruits are abundant.

Mountain Bluebird

Sialia currucoides

Migrant and summer resident in foothills and mountains statewide, and winter resident primarily in southern Colorado.

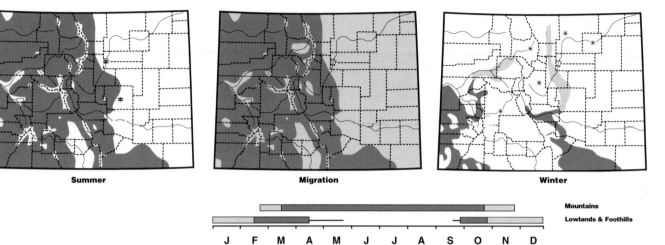

Summer   Migration   Winter

Mountains

Lowlands & Foothills

J F M A M J J A S O N D

Seasonal Occurrence

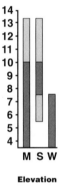

Elevation

Status (SP) (B):   **Summer** resident in foothills, mountains, and mountain parks. Common in lower mountains and mountain parks, uncommon to fairly common in foothills and rare to uncommon in higher mountains. Arrives on breeding grounds Feb–June, and departs Sep–Nov, depending on elevation and local weather conditions. Early arrivals often are pushed down into adjacent lowlands during cold, snowy spring weather. Formerly recorded as a breeder on the eastern plains near the foothills at Colorado Springs and Denver, but it was eliminated from those areas by competition with House Sparrows (Sclater 1912, Aiken and Warren 1914).

Common to abundant **spring** and **fall** migrant in western valleys, foothills, lower mountains, mountain parks, and on eastern plains near foothills. Uncommon above timberline (mostly fall), and rare on extreme eastern plains. On the eastern plains, it is more common in spring than in fall. High count: 4,000 on 22 Sep 1978 in northern Fremont County.

Fairly common to locally abundant **winter** resident in foothills and mesas (and sometimes adjacent valleys and plains) from Mesa and Fremont counties southward. High count: 740 on 7 Jan 1978, Burnt Mill Road, Pueblo County. Rare to uncommon north to Larimer County and in lower mountains. The east slope of the mountains and adjacent plains in southern Colorado, New Mexico, and western Texas is the species' primary winter range (Root 1988). Probably casual in winter on extreme eastern plains, but most winter records probably pertain to early spring migrants.

Habitat: In summer, mountain grasslands and sage shrublands adjacent to open coniferous forest (especially ponderosa pine and piñon-juniper) and aspen forests. Also alpine tundra adjacent to krummholz, and Gambel oak and mountain mahogany shrublands. Local breeding distribution is affected by nest hole availability, and the species has become more common locally where nest boxes are erected (especially in treeless parks). In migration, in grasslands, open shrublands, and agricultural areas. In winter, most common in piñon-juniper woodlands but also in shrublands and agricultural areas. Winter distribution and abundance is strongly influenced by the availability of fruits (especially juniper).

Note: This species is a Colorado Species of Special Concern due to population declines resulting from a decrease of snags, which are an important source of nest holes (Webb 1985b).

Townsend's Solitaire

Myadestes townsendi

Resident in mountains; moves upward in summer and downward in winter.

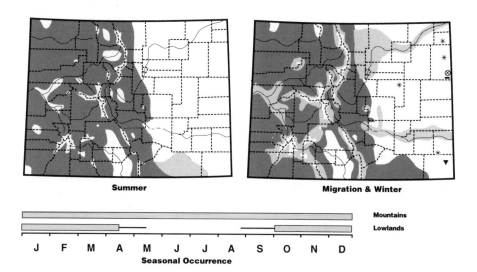

Summer   Migration & Winter

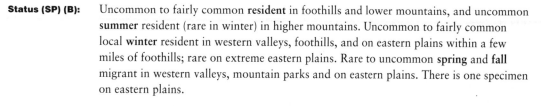

Mountains
Lowlands

J F M A M J J A S O N D

Seasonal Occurrence

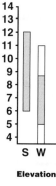

S W

Elevation

Status (SP) (B): Uncommon to fairly common **resident** in foothills and lower mountains, and uncommon **summer** resident (rare in winter) in higher mountains. Uncommon to fairly common local **winter** resident in western valleys, foothills, and on eastern plains within a few miles of foothills; rare on extreme eastern plains. Rare to uncommon **spring** and **fall** migrant in western valleys, mountain parks and on eastern plains. There is one specimen on eastern plains.

Habitat: In summer, coniferous forests. Nests on the ground, mostly on rocky slopes or embankments; also recorded nesting in abandoned mine-shafts (Swanson 1971). In migration, most wooded habitats and brushy riparian areas. In winter, mostly in coniferous forests (especially piñon-juniper), riparian areas, urban areas; primarily around native or planted berry-producing trees and shrubs such as junipers and Russian-olives. Winter distribution and abundance is greatly influenced by berry crops, primarily junipers (Bock 1982).

References: Benedict and Williams (1981), Strong (1983).

Veery

Catharus fuscescens

Migrant on eastern plains, and local summer resident in mountains.

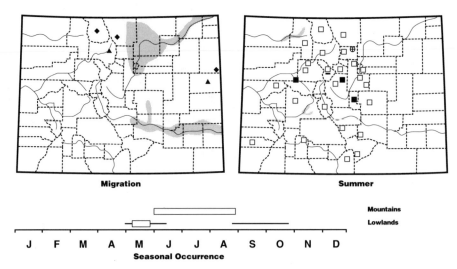

	Migration	Summer

Seasonal Occurrence

J F M A M J J A S O N D

Mountains

Lowlands

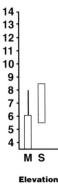

Elevation

Status (SP) (B): Uncommon **spring** migrant and rare **fall** migrant on eastern plains; rare in foothills. Local **summer** resident in foothills, lower mountains, and mountain parks, mostly in northern and central Colorado, south to Dolores, Mineral, Costilla, and Huerfano counties. It appears to be uncommon to fairly common along the Yampa and Elk rivers in eastern Moffat and northern Routt counties, along the Michigan River at Walden, Jackson County, and along the Taylor River and Quartz Creek in eastern Gunnison County. Elsewhere the species seems to be rare, but there are summer sightings from 15 sites and confirmed nesting at three sites. The distribution of this species in summer remains poorly known. Casual on eastern plains near foothills (three-four records, including one probable breeding record).

Habitat: In summer, moist, dense riparian thickets such as willow, dogwood, or cottonwood saplings; also recorded on drier, hillside brush near streams and in aspen forests. In migration, lowland riparian forests and shrublands.

Records: **Summer on eastern plains:** 7 July 1976, Lykin's Gulch, Boulder County; 11 June 1979, Lykin's Gulch (DMNH 36804)(perhaps a late migrant); pair (carrying food; nest or young not seen) 3–30 June 1986, Wheat Ridge Greenbelt, Jefferson County; 13–23 June 1991, Cherry Creek Reservoir, Arapahoe County.

Gray-cheeked Thrush
Catharus minimus

Occasional spring migrant on northeastern plains.

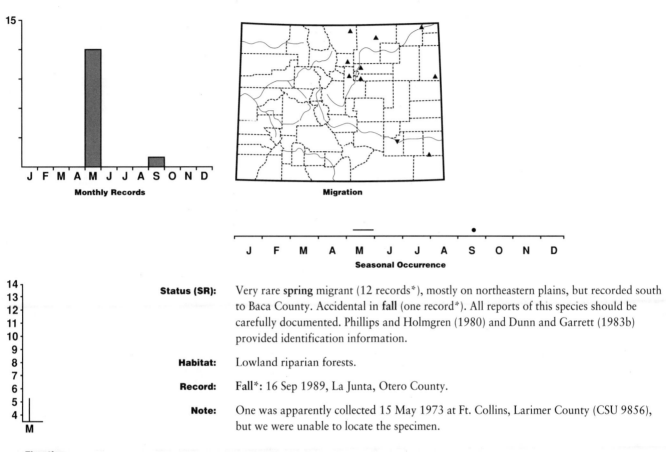

Status (SR): Very rare **spring** migrant (12 records*), mostly on northeastern plains, but recorded south to Baca County. Accidental in **fall** (one record*). All reports of this species should be carefully documented. Phillips and Holmgren (1980) and Dunn and Garrett (1983b) provided identification information.

Habitat: Lowland riparian forests.

Record: Fall*: 16 Sep 1989, La Junta, Otero County.

Note: One was apparently collected 15 May 1973 at Ft. Collins, Larimer County (CSU 9856), but we were unable to locate the specimen.

Swainson's Thrush
Catharus ustulatus

Local summer resident in mountains, and migrant in eastern Colorado.

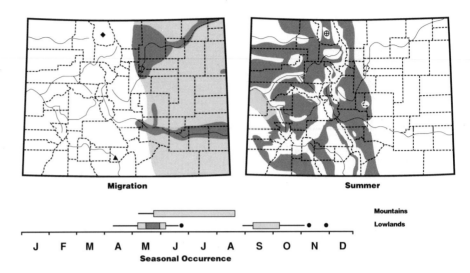

Migration   **Summer**

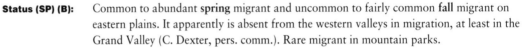

Mountains

Lowlands

J F M A M J J A S O N D
Seasonal Occurrence

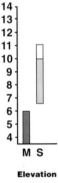

Elevation

Status (SP) (B): Common to abundant **spring** migrant and uncommon to fairly common **fall** migrant on eastern plains. It apparently is absent from the western valleys in migration, at least in the Grand Valley (C. Dexter, pers. comm.). Rare migrant in mountain parks.

Uncommon to fairly common local **summer** resident in mountains. This species is quite local, and is sometimes absent from seemingly suitable habitat. Rare on the Uncompahgre Plateau (R. Levad, pers. comm.). This species may have declined recently; at Eldora, Boulder County it was fairly common in the 1950s but much rarer and sometimes absent by the early 1970s (Kingery 1971).

Habitat: In summer, foothill and montane and riparian thickets and riparian (sometimes upland) spruce-fir forests. Often in moist, steep ravines. In migration, riparian and urban areas.

Hermit Thrush
Catharus guttatus

Summer resident in mountains and migrant in lowlands; a few in winter.

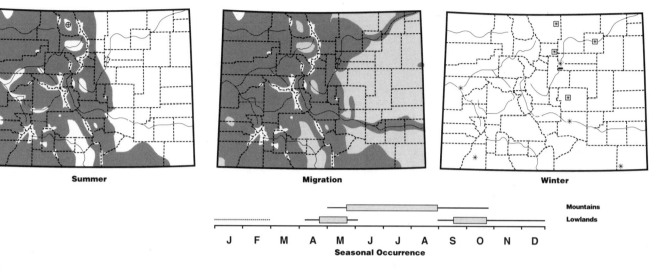

Summer   Migration   Winter

Mountains
Lowlands

J F M A M J J A S O N D
Seasonal Occurrence

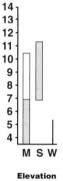

Elevation

Status (SP) (B): Fairly common to common **summer** resident in foothills and mountains; most common in higher mountains. More common and widespread than the Swainson's Thrush. Uncommon **spring** and **fall** migrant in western valleys, foothills, mountain parks, and on eastern plains. High count: 67 on 18 Oct 1969, Waterton, Douglas/Jefferson counties.

Very rare in **early winter** (16 records) and casual in **mid-winter** (five records) in low foothills and adjacent valleys and plains from Mesa and Larimer counties southward, and east to Morgan and Baca counties. There is one specimen. Some early winter records probably pertain to late fall migrants. There are few winter records in southern Colorado, where it is most likely to occur.

Habitat: In summer, primarily spruce-fir forests, but also all other coniferous forest types; in some areas, most common in lodgepole pine forests. Generally rare in piñon-juniper woodlands, but may be fairly common in dense upper elevation piñon-juniper woodlands. Locally may occur also in Gambel oak shrublands, especially those with scattered conifers. One of the most common breeding species in old-growth spruce-fir forest (Scott et al. 1982, Hallock 1988). In migration, all wooded habitats.

Record: Winter specimen: 8 Feb 1939, Denver County (DMNH 19869).

Wood Thrush

Hylocichla mustelina

Occasional migrant on eastern plains.

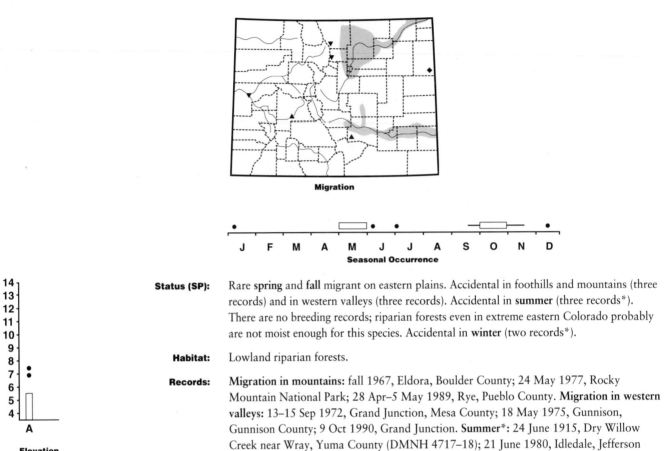

Migration

Seasonal Occurrence

J F M A M J J A S O N D

Elevation

14
13
12
11
10
9
8
7
6
5
4

A

Status (SP): Rare **spring** and **fall** migrant on eastern plains. Accidental in foothills and mountains (three records) and in western valleys (three records). Accidental in **summer** (three records*). There are no breeding records; riparian forests even in extreme eastern Colorado probably are not moist enough for this species. Accidental in **winter** (two records*).

Habitat: Lowland riparian forests.

Records: **Migration in mountains:** fall 1967, Eldora, Boulder County; 24 May 1977, Rocky Mountain National Park; 28 Apr–5 May 1989, Rye, Pueblo County. **Migration in western valleys:** 13–15 Sep 1972, Grand Junction, Mesa County; 18 May 1975, Gunnison, Gunnison County; 9 Oct 1990, Grand Junction. **Summer***: 24 June 1915, Dry Willow Creek near Wray, Yuma County (DMNH 4717–18); 21 June 1980, Idledale, Jefferson County; 4 July 1988, Barr Lake, Adams County. **Winter***: 8 Jan 1975, Boulder, Boulder County; 15 Dec 1984, Waterton, Jefferson County.

American Robin
Turdus migratorius

Statewide in migration and summer, and at low elevations in winter.

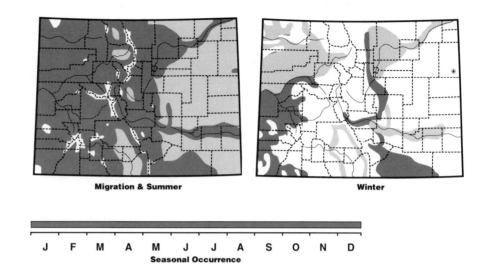

Migration & Summer   Winter

J   F   M   A   M   J   J   A   S   O   N   D
Seasonal Occurrence

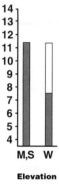

Elevation

Status (SP) (B): Common to abundant in **spring**, **summer**, and **fall** in western valleys, foothills, and on eastern plains. Fairly common to common, primarily in summer, in mountains. Some individuals move to higher elevations in late summer and fall (Packard 1946). Fairly common to abundant local **winter** resident, mostly in western valleys, foothills, and on eastern plains. Rare in mountains to timberline. In winter, most common in the southern half of Colorado.

Habitat: In summer, urban areas, around farmhouses and windbreaks, riparian, coniferous, and aspen forests, and krummholz. It is one of the most common breeding birds in old-growth spruce-fir forests in Boulder County (Hallock 1988). In migration, occurs in most wooded habitats, and also often in bare or sparsely vegetated fields. In winter, urban, riparian, and agricultural areas, and in piñon-juniper woodlands and ponderosa pine forests (rarely in other coniferous forests). Occurs primarily where wild or planted juniper, Russian-olive, crabapple and other trees and shrubs have ample berry crops. In many parts of the state, it is most common in winter in piñon-juniper woodlands.

Varied Thrush
Ixoreus naevius

Migrant and winter resident, mostly at lower edge of eastern foothills.

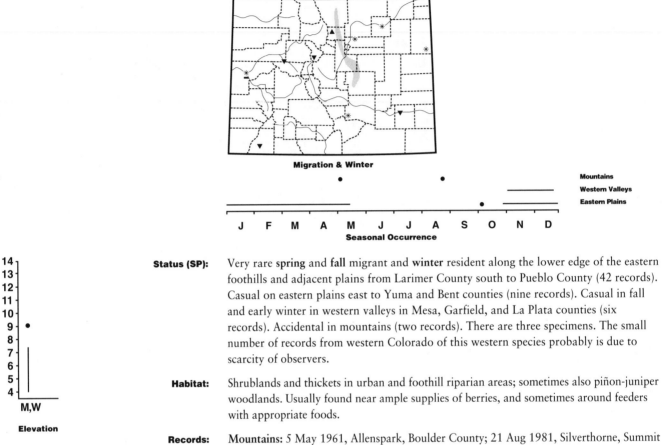

Migration & Winter

Mountains
Western Valleys
Eastern Plains

J   F   M   A   M   J   J   A   S   O   N   D

Seasonal Occurrence

Elevation

M,W

Status (SP): Very rare **spring** and **fall** migrant and **winter** resident along the lower edge of the eastern foothills and adjacent plains from Larimer County south to Pueblo County (42 records). Casual on eastern plains east to Yuma and Bent counties (nine records). Casual in fall and early winter in western valleys in Mesa, Garfield, and La Plata counties (six records). Accidental in mountains (two records). There are three specimens. The small number of records from western Colorado of this western species probably is due to scarcity of observers.

Habitat: Shrublands and thickets in urban and foothill riparian areas; sometimes also piñon-juniper woodlands. Usually found near ample supplies of berries, and sometimes around feeders with appropriate foods.

Records: **Mountains:** 5 May 1961, Allenspark, Boulder County; 21 Aug 1981, Silverthorne, Summit County. **Specimens:** 25 Apr 1968, Loveland, Larimer County (DMNH 36057); 19 Dec 1988, Grand Junction, Mesa County (DMNH 39555); 13-17 Jan 1990, Ft. Collins, Larimer County (DMNH).

Order Passeriformes
Family Mimidae

Gray Catbird
Dumetella carolinensis

Migrant in lowlands, and local summer resident in lowlands and foothills.

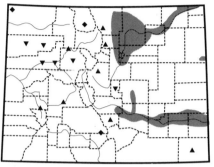

Migration

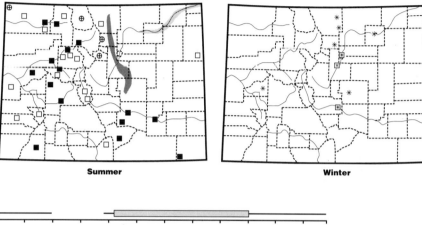

Summer

Winter

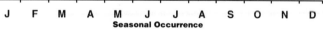

J   F   M   A   M   J   J   A   S   O   N   D
Seasonal Occurrence

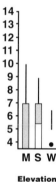

Elevation

Status (SP) (B): Uncommon **spring** migrant and rare to uncommon **fall** migrant on eastern plains. Rare in western valleys, foothills, lower mountains, and mountain parks.

Rare to uncommon very local **summer** resident. Occurs primarily in foothill canyons and ravines at the base of the eastern foothills from Larimer County south to Huerfano County and in western Colorado from the Colorado River south to La Plata County, and in the Yampa River Valley (Martin et al. 1974). Also recorded in Chaffee County and in southwestern Baca County. In eastern Colorado, also in the South Platte River Valley in northeastern Colorado, the Bonny Reservoir area, Yuma County, and less often in the Arkansas River Valley in southeastern Colorado. In mountain parks recorded in southwestern Grand County and in northern Costilla County, and nonbreeders seen in summer at Arapaho National Wildlife Refuge, Jackson County.

Very rare **winter** resident (11 records) along base of northeastern foothills and adjacent plains from Larimer County south to Fremont County. Some of those records may pertain to late fall migrants, but there are seven mid-winter records. Accidental on eastern plains (one record) and in western valleys (one record).

Habitat: Dense riparian thickets, and also in foothill shrublands in summer.

Records: **Winter on eastern plains:** 6 Feb 1982, Muir Springs, Morgan County. **Winter in western valleys:** 31 Dec 1987–1 Jan 1988, Hotchkiss, Delta County.

Northern Mockingbird
Mimus polyglottos

Migrant and summer resident, most common in southeastern Colorado.

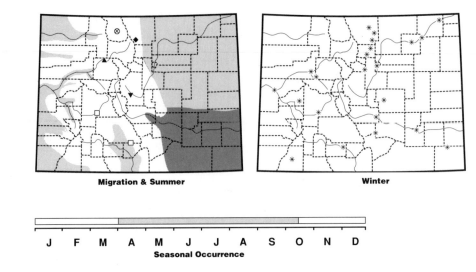

Migration & Summer   Winter

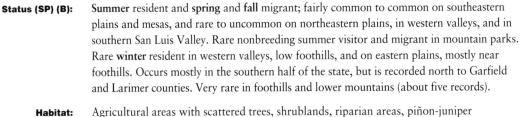

J F M A M J J A S O N D
Seasonal Occurrence

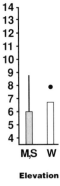

Elevation

Status (SP) (B): **Summer** resident and **spring** and **fall** migrant; fairly common to common on southeastern plains and mesas, and rare to uncommon on northeastern plains, in western valleys, and in southern San Luis Valley. Rare nonbreeding summer visitor and migrant in mountain parks. Rare **winter** resident in western valleys, low foothills, and on eastern plains, mostly near foothills. Occurs mostly in the southern half of the state, but is recorded north to Garfield and Larimer counties. Very rare in foothills and lower mountains (about five records).

Habitat: Agricultural areas with scattered trees, shrublands, riparian areas, piñon-juniper woodlands, and cholla grassland.

Sage Thrasher

Oreoscoptes montanus

Summer resident in sagebrush, and widespread migrant.

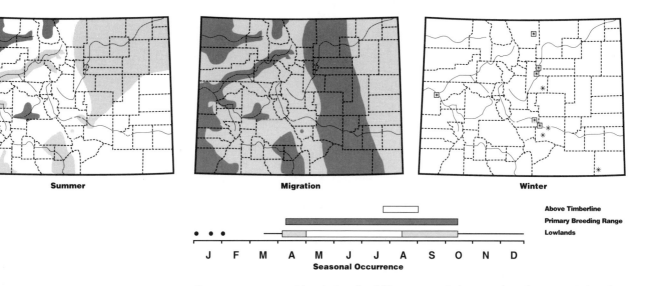

Summer   Migration   Winter

Above Timberline
Primary Breeding Range
Lowlands

J F M A M J J A S O N D

Seasonal Occurrence

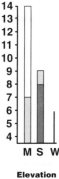

Elevation

Status (SP) (B): Common **summer** resident in low foothills, mesas and plateaus of northwestern Colorado, in North Park, parts of the San Luis Valley, and in the Gunnison Basin. Rare to uncommon locally in mesas and low valleys of west-central and southwestern Colorado, in San Juan County (Drew 1881), in Middle Park, the Wet Mountain Valley, in low eastern foothills, and on eastern plains south to Pueblo and Yuma counties.

Uncommon to fairly common irregular **spring** and **fall** migrant in western valleys, lower foothills, mountain parks, and eastern plains near foothills. Rare in mountains outside parks and on extreme eastern plains. Rare in fall above timberline. Very rare **winter** resident (about 14 records) in western valleys, lower foothills, and on eastern plains near foothills, mostly in southern Colorado and north to Mesa and Larimer counties. Most records are from Fremont and Pueblo counties.

Habitat: Breeds in sagebrush shrublands and occasionally in other shrublands or cholla grassland. In migration and winter, open agricultural areas, pastures, grasslands, shrublands, open riparian areas, and piñon-juniper woodlands.

Reference: Killpack (1970).

Brown Thrasher
Toxostoma rufum

Summer resident and migrant on eastern plains, especially in extreme east, and occasionally elsewhere.

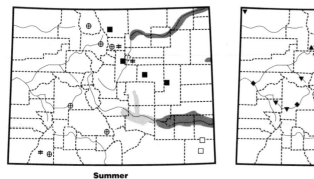

Summer

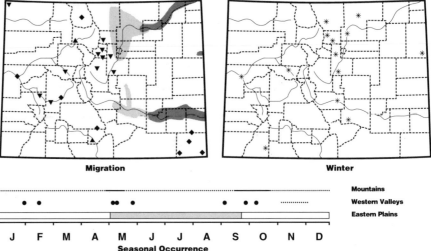

Migration   Winter

Seasonal Occurrence

Status (SP) (B): Fairly common (locally common) **summer** resident on eastern plains west to Morgan and Otero counties; rare to locally uncommon west to base of foothills. Casual in mountains (four records, including one nesting record) and in western valleys (four records, including one nesting record).

Fairly common **spring** and **fall** migrant on extreme eastern plains and uncommon west to base of foothills. Very rare in foothills, mountains, and mountain parks (25 records), mostly east of the Continental Divide. Casual in western valleys (eight records). Rare **winter** resident along base of eastern foothills and adjacent plains from Larimer County south to Pueblo County and east to Yuma County. Casual in foothills and mountains east of the Continental Divide, mostly at Estes Park, Larimer County and Evergreen, Jefferson County (seven records). Accidental in western valleys (two records).

Habitat: Lowland riparian forests and shrublands, and windbreaks; in winter also in urban areas.

Records: **Summer in mountains:** 19 July 1963, Moraine Park, Rocky Mountain National Park, Larimer County; June 1977, Grand Lake, Grand County; 2 July 1982, Eldora, Boulder County; has nested at Estes Park, Larimer County (W. Reeser, pers. comm.). **Summer in western valleys:** nested in 1904 in La Plata County (Gilman 1907); 10 July 1961, site unknown (Davis 1969); 9 June 1971, Bayfield, La Plata County; 21 June 1981, Gunnison, Gunnison County. **Winter in western valleys:** 10–14 Feb 1974, Grand Junction, Mesa County; 31 Jan 1982, Bayfield, La Plata County.

Elevation

Long-billed Thrasher
Toxostoma longirostre

Status (SP): Accidental in **spring** (one record*).

Record: May 1906, Barr Lake, Adams County (DMNH 2359) (Lincoln 1919).

Bendire's Thrasher
Toxostoma bendirei

Local summer resident in southern Colorado.

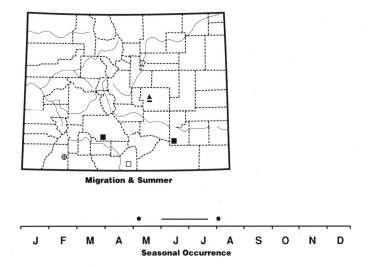

Migration & Summer

Seasonal Occurrence

J F M A M J J A S O N D

14
13
12
11
10
9
8
7
6
5
4

M,S

Elevation

Status (SP) (B): Local **summer** resident in the foothills of the San Luis Valley. Birds have been seen each summer from 1984 and later near La Garita, southwestern Saguache County. Up to six singing birds have been seen, and in 1989 a nest was found, and young birds were seen in 1990. In 1991, birds were found near San Luis, Costilla County. Accidental on southeastern plains (two records, including one specimen and one nest*) and in southwestern valleys (one record*).

This species has been expanding northward in northwestern and north-central New Mexico, probably in response to expansion of piñon pine due to overgrazing (Darling 1970). Thus, its recent appearance in southern Colorado is not surprising, and birds are likely to be found at additional sites, especially in the San Luis Valley and southwestern Colorado. Nevertheless, observers should still be very cautious identifying this species as it can be confused with Sage and Curve-billed Thrashers (Phillips and Holmgren 1980, Zimmer 1985, Kaufman 1990).

Habitat: Observed in open piñon-juniper woodlands in the San Luis Valley. The nest in Otero County was in cholla grassland.

Records: **Southeastern plains***: 8 May 1882, Austin's Bluff, El Paso County (DMNH 6729); nest photographed 9 June 1970, near Timpas, Otero County (Buttery 1971). **Southwestern valleys***: 2–3 Aug 1974, near Bayfield, La Plata County.

Curve-billed Thrasher

Toxostoma curvirostre

Resident on southeastern plains.

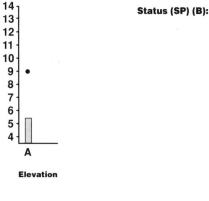

**Monthly Records
Northern Colorado**

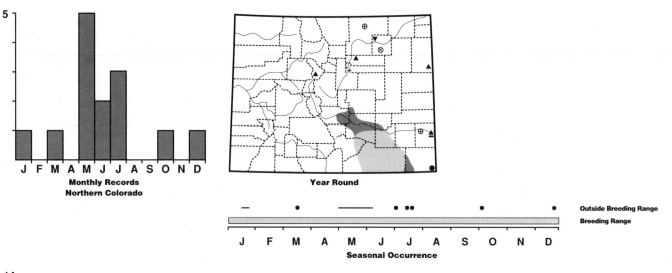

Year Round

Outside Breeding Range

Breeding Range

Seasonal Occurrence

Elevation

Status (SP) (B): Uncommon local **resident** on southeastern plains and mesas northwest to eastern Fremont and southern El Paso counties. Most records come from an arc along Fountain Creek and the Arkansas River from Fountain, El Paso County to Pueblo and east to southwestern Crowley County, and in southwestern Baca County. This may reflect the pattern of the best-known and most accessible suitable habitat. There are two specimens.

This species has spread into Colorado in recent years. The first state record was 25 Mar 1951 at Granada, Prowers County, but all other records have been since 1967. The first record in Baca County was in 1967 and in Pueblo County in 1970. The first nesting in the state was in Baca County in 1972 (Kingery 1973b). This is consistent with the pattern in New Mexico, where it has spread north and first appeared in northeastern New Mexico in 1968, probably as cholla became more common due to grazing (Darling 1970).

Very rare **visitor** (13 records) on northeastern plains north to Weld, Morgan and Yuma counties. Most records are in spring (five records) or summer (five records), but also recorded in fall (one record) and winter (two records). Accidental in mountains (one record*).

Habitat: Primarily cholla grassland; sometimes also open piñon-juniper woodlands, and riparian areas. Vagrant in shortgrass prairie, agricultural areas, and riparian areas.

Records: Specimens: 25 Mar 1951, Granada, Prowers County (WSC); 14 Dec 1981, Baculite Mesa, northeast of Pueblo, Pueblo County (DMNH 37660). **Mountains***: 30 Apr–7 May 1976, Silverthorne, Summit County.

Order Passeriformes
Family Motacillidae

American Pipit
Anthus rubescens

Summer resident above timberline, and migrant and local winter resident at low elevations.

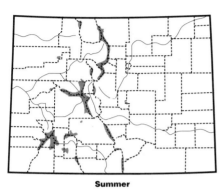

Summer

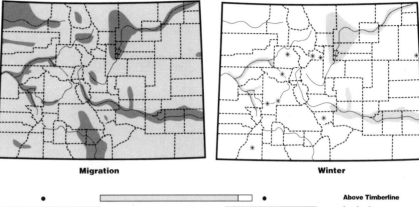

Migration   Winter

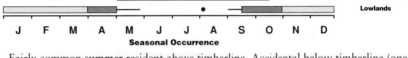

Above Timberline

Lowlands

Seasonal Occurrence

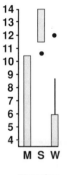

Elevation

Status (SP) (B): Fairly common **summer** resident above timberline. Accidental below timberline (one breeding record). The arrival and departure from the breeding grounds is determined by weather. Birds may be forced back down into the mountain parks by late storms, and they remain above timberline until the first fall storms, when they suddenly move in large numbers down into the parks and valleys.

Uncommon to common **spring** and **fall** migrant in western valleys, mountain parks, and on eastern plains. High count: 300 on 18 May 1957, Weldona, Morgan County. Rare to uncommon local **winter** resident in western valleys and on eastern plains (mostly near foothills). High count: 200 during the winter of 1988–89, Grand Junction, Mesa County.

Habitat: Breeds on alpine tundra, often where moist or wet (Braun 1980). In migration, open shorelines of lakes and reservoirs, and sometimes in open fields. In winter, shorelines (especially bare, sandy areas) of ice-free rivers, streams, and irrigation ditches (sometimes lakes), and sometimes around farmyards.

Record: Breeding below timberline: 19 July 1991, at 10,500 ft. on Buffalo Pass, Routt County.

Note: Formerly known as Water Pipit (*Anthus spinoletta*).

Sprague's Pipit
Anthus spragueii

Status (SP): Uncommon and very local **fall** migrant (several records*, including one specimen). Occurred in 1989 and 1991 near Julesburg, Sedgwick County. It probably occurs almost annually in small numbers there and elsewhere on the extreme northeastern plains. Based upon recent observations and migration patterns in Kansas (S. Seltman, pers. comm.) and New Mexico (B. Howe, pers. comm.), this species is most likely to occur in fall from late Sep and later. Until the status and distribution of this species can be better worked out, all observations should be carefully documented. Zimmer (1985) provided information on the identification of this species.

Habitat: Observed in sprouting winter wheat, volunteer wheat, and fallow wheat fields (Bridges and Leatherman 1991).

Records: Fall 1982, Lake George, Fremont County (DMNH 39897) (Webb and Phillips 1992); up to ten individuals 30 Sep–31 Oct 1989 (Bridges and Leatherman 1991) and about four individuals 12–19 Oct 1991, just south of Julesburg.

Order Passeriformes
Family Bombycillidae

Bohemian Waxwing
Bombycilla garrulus

Irregular (often abundant) winter visitor, mostly in northern half of Colorado.

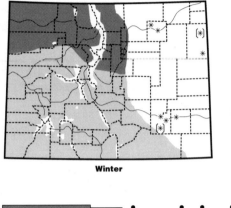

Winter

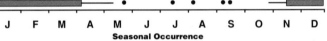

J F M A M J J A S O N D

Seasonal Occurrence

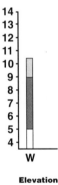

W

Elevation

Status (SP): Irregular in **winter**; abundant in major flight years and very rare or absent in other years. Occurs mostly in western valleys, lower mountains, foothills, and on eastern plains near foothills; very rare on extreme eastern plains (even in flight years). Recorded throughout the state, but most records are from the northern half of the state. This species may occur annually in the mountains, and several observations of large flocks in the higher mountains suggest it may occur there in larger numbers than generally recognized. Birds are often seen in the mountains in winters when it is absent at lower elevations, and it may be present at low elevations mostly in major flight years, in years when mountain food supplies are poor, and especially when those two factors coincide. This species generally does not mix with Cedar Waxwings. Accidental in **summer** (two records).

Habitat: Urban, riparian, and agricultural areas, and coniferous forests; mostly in areas where there are abundant crops of wild or ornamental berries (especially Russian-olive, but also others such as crabapples or junipers).

Records: Summer: 5 Aug 1917, Denver County (CU 10180); 13 July 1924, Lost Park (12,000 ft.), Park County (Bergtold 1924).

Cedar Waxwing
Bombycilla cedrorum

Irregular visitor in lowlands and foothills, mostly in migration and winter.

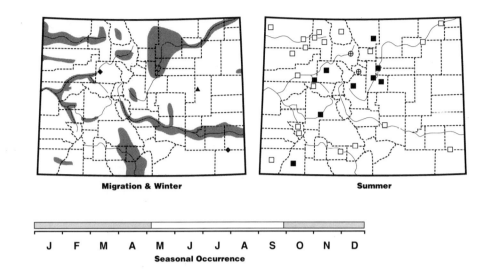

Migration & Winter   **Summer**

J F M A M J J A S O N D

Seasonal Occurrence

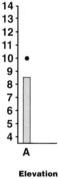

Elevation

Status (SP) (B): Irregular in western valleys, foothills, lower mountains, mountain parks, and on eastern plains. Most common in **spring** and **fall** (but especially fall) and **winter**. In most years, it is rare to uncommon, but can be fairly common to abundant in some years, and in other years is absent. Movements of this species do not appear to coincide with those of the Bohemian Waxwing. High count: 800 on 11–13 May 1984, Bonny Reservoir, Yuma County. Rare to uncommon very local **summer** resident, mostly in lower foothills and adjacent lowlands, but also very locally on eastern plains. Many, and perhaps most, summer birds may be nonbreeders, but there are many widely scattered breeding records. However, the relative scarcity of breeding records may be due to this species' inconspicuousness during nesting.

Habitat: Primarily riparian, urban, and agricultural areas, but also in piñon-juniper woodlands (and sometimes other coniferous forests) in migration and winter. Most often in areas with abundant crops of wild or ornamental berries (especially in fall and winter).

Order Passeriformes
Family Ptilogonatidae

Phainopepla
Phainopepla nitens

Occasional visitor, mostly in fall.

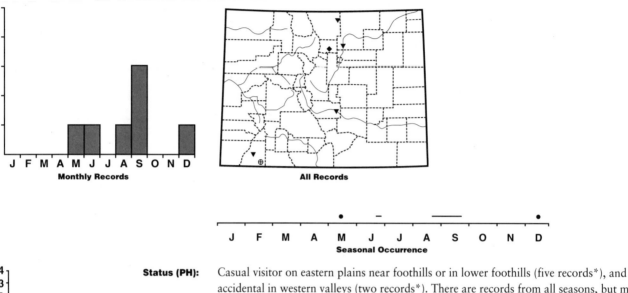

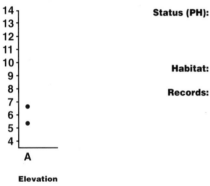

Status (PH): Casual visitor on eastern plains near foothills or in lower foothills (five records*), and accidental in western valleys (two records*). There are records from all seasons, but most are in fall. All records are of single birds, and all but one were immatures or females.

Habitat: Most records are from urban areas; also seen in piñon-juniper woodland.

Records: **Eastern Colorado***: 29–30 Aug 1965, Platteville, Weld County (photo in Bailey and Niedrach 1965); 15–18 Dec 1973, Boulder, Boulder County (Hubbard et al. 1975); 16–17 Sep 1978, Wellington, Larimer County; male 13–16 May 1982, Boulder, Boulder County; 8–12 Sep 1989, Penrose, Fremont County. **Western valleys***: 25–26 Sep 1978, Durango, La Plata County; 20–28 June 1986, Ignacio, La Plata County (photos in RC files).

Order Passeriformes
Family Laniidae

Northern Shrike

Lanius excubitor

Winter resident, mostly at low elevations and in northern Colorado.

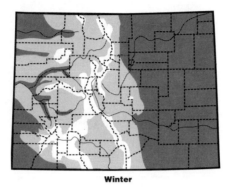

Winter

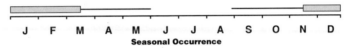

J F M A M J J A S O N D
Seasonal Occurrence

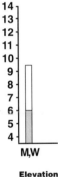

Elevation

Status (SP): Rare to uncommon **winter** resident in western valleys, foothills, lower mountains, mountain parks, and on eastern plains. Most common in the northern half of the state, especially on the eastern plains. Numbers of this species fluctuate widely from year to year. There are several summer and early fall records which almost certainly pertain to immature Loggerhead Shrikes.

Habitat: Open areas, such as agricultural areas, grasslands, and riparian edges, and sometimes in piñon-juniper woodlands and shrublands.

Loggerhead Shrike
Lanius ludovicianus

Migrant and summer resident, mostly at low elevations, and winter resident in western and southern Colorado.

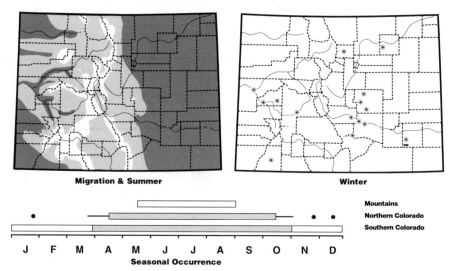

Migration & Summer **Winter**

Mountains
Northern Colorado
Southern Colorado

J F M A M J J A S O N D

Seasonal Occurrence

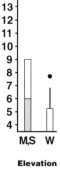

Elevation

Status (SP) (B): Fairly common **spring** and **fall** migrant in western valleys and eastern plains. Fairly common **summer** resident in western valleys and in the San Luis Valley. Rare to uncommon locally on eastern plains. Rare to uncommon in mountain parks and rare in mountains, mostly in lower mountains. Most regular in mountains in late summer and fall. There are no confirmed breeding records in the mountain parks (except the San Luis Valley) or mountains.

Rare to uncommon **winter** resident in western valleys north to Mesa County and on southeastern plains north to southern El Paso County. In those areas, it may equal or outnumber the Northern Shrike in some winters. Accidental on northeastern plains (two records*). There are numerous winter reports of this species from northern Colorado, but most lack details. All winter observations in northern Colorado and in the mountains should be carefully documented. Balch (1979) and Phillips et al. (1984) provided information on separating the two shrikes.

This species has shown significant population declines over much of North America (Robbins et al. 1986), and for that reason is listed on the National Audubon Society Blue List (Tate 1986) and is a Colorado Species of Special Concern (Webb 1985b). This species apparently has been extirpated from some areas of eastern Colorado as a breeding species, but it does not appear to have declined in western Colorado (R. Lambeth, pers. comm.).

Habitat: Open riparian areas, agricultural areas, grasslands, and shrublands, especially semidesert shrublands, and sometimes open piñon-juniper woodlands. Breeding birds are usually near isolated trees or large shrubs. Primarily greasewood draws in both summer and winter in Mesa County (R. Lambeth and R. Levad, pers. comm.) and probably elsewhere in western Colorado.

Records: **Winter on northeastern plains***: 24 Jan 1976, near Wiggins, Morgan County; 17–19 Dec 1976, Boulder, Boulder county.

Reference: Porter et al. (1975).

Order Passeriformes
Family Sturnidae

European Starling
Sturnus vulgaris

Resident in lowlands, and locally in mountains.

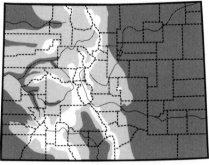

Year Round

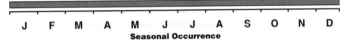

| J | F | M | A | M | J | J | A | S | O | N | D |

Seasonal Occurrence

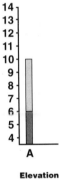

Elevation

Status (SP) (B): Abundant **resident** in western valleys and on eastern plains, and locally in foothills, lower mountains, and mountain parks. The first record from the state was a flock of several hundred on 16 Feb 1937 at Sterling, Logan County, and the first specimen was collected at Mile High Duck Club, Adams County on 17 Dec 1938 (Bailey and Niedrach 1965). Most of the earliest records were in fall and winter. The first breeding occurred in the state 16 May 1943 in Denver County (Breiding 1943). By 1953, there was a breeding record at 9,000 ft. at the Evans Ranch, Clear Creek County in the eastern mountains, and by 1955 in Moffat County in western Colorado (Bailey and Niedrach 1965). Populations in north-central Colorado appear to be primarily nonmigratory, but some birds that breed north of Colorado winter in Colorado or migrate through the state (Royall and Guarino 1976).

Habitat: Agricultural and urban areas, and riparian areas at low elevations.

Note: This species is a Colorado Species of Special Concern due to its negative impact on native cavity-nesting species such as woodpeckers and bluebirds (Webb 1985b).

Reference: DeHaven and Guarino (1970).

Order Passeriformes
Family Vireonidae

White-eyed Vireo
Vireo griseus

Occasional migrant on eastern plains.

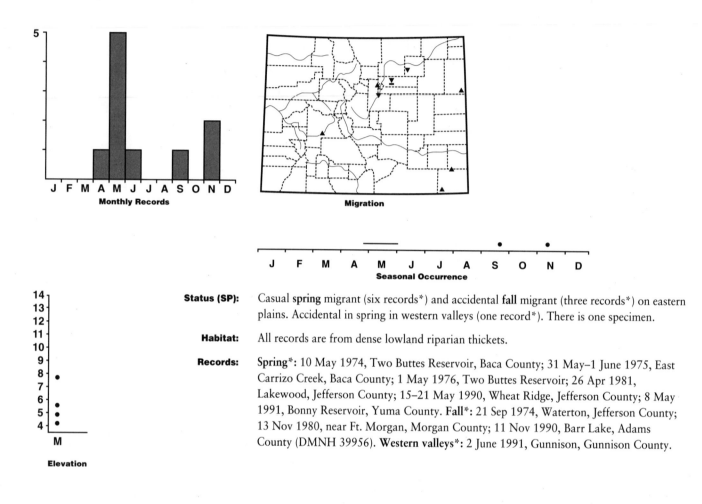

Monthly Records

Migration

Seasonal Occurrence

Elevation

Status (SP): Casual **spring** migrant (six records*) and accidental **fall** migrant (three records*) on eastern plains. Accidental in spring in western valleys (one record*). There is one specimen.

Habitat: All records are from dense lowland riparian thickets.

Records: **Spring***: 10 May 1974, Two Buttes Reservoir, Baca County; 31 May–1 June 1975, East Carrizo Creek, Baca County; 1 May 1976, Two Buttes Reservoir; 26 Apr 1981, Lakewood, Jefferson County; 15–21 May 1990, Wheat Ridge, Jefferson County; 8 May 1991, Bonny Reservoir, Yuma County. **Fall***: 21 Sep 1974, Waterton, Jefferson County; 13 Nov 1980, near Ft. Morgan, Morgan County; 11 Nov 1990, Barr Lake, Adams County (DMNH 39956). **Western valleys***: 2 June 1991, Gunnison, Gunnison County.

Bell's Vireo
Vireo bellii

Summer resident along eastern border; occasionally elsewhere in migration.

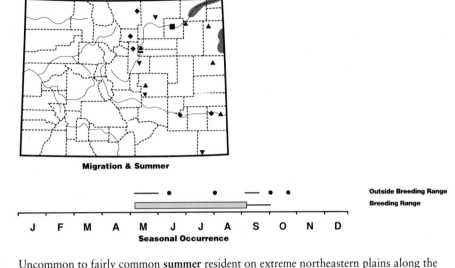

Migration & Summer

Outside Breeding Range
Breeding Range

J F M A M J J A S O N D
Seasonal Occurrence

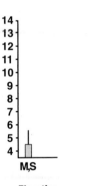

Elevation

Status (SP) (B): Uncommon to fairly common **summer** resident on extreme northeastern plains along the South Platte River in Sedgwick and Logan counties and in eastern Yuma County. Elsewhere on the eastern plains west to the lower foothills, it is a very rare **spring** migrant (16 records) and casual **fall** migrant (nine records). There is one specimen.

Habitat: In summer, dense lowland riparian shrublands. In migration, wooded riparian and urban areas.

Record: Specimen: 12 June 1903, Denver County (DMNH 13899) (this would be the only summer record from near the foothills, but it may represent a late spring migrant).

Note: This species showed a "sharp decline" in the central United States (Robbins et al. 1986) and is on the National Audubon Society list of species of special concern (Tate 1986). Although evidence of this decline has come mostly from Kansas and Oklahoma, the populations in Colorado should be monitored.

Gray Vireo

Vireo vicinior

Local summer resident in western and southern Colorado.

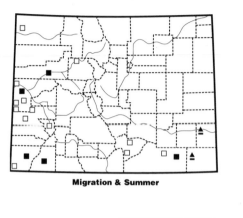

Migration & Summer

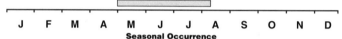

J F M A M J J A S O N D

Seasonal Occurrence

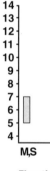

Elevation

Status (SP) (B): Uncommon and very local **summer** resident on mesas and low foothills. It is recorded primarily from Mesa County, and has also been seen in western Colorado north to Moffat County and south to La Plata County. There are few records in northwestern Colorado, but it should be looked for there as it occurs rarely in adjacent southwestern Wyoming (Fitton and Scott 1984, Dorn and Dorn 1990). It also occurs locally in the southeastern foothills from western Huerfano County east to eastern Las Animas County (and perhaps in western Baca County and Fremont County). The only confirmed breeding record in southeastern Colorado was in 1990 near Kim, Las Animas County (Anonymous 1990, Kingery 1990a).

The earliest state records were four specimens collected from 1907 to 1914 in southeastern Colorado. The first record in western Colorado was in 1944.

Although this species may be somewhat more widely distributed in Colorado than the records suggest, observers should be very cautious about reporting this species from new localities and identifying it at known localities. It probably is truly very local, and the very similar Solitary Vireo is widely distributed and often numerous in piñon-juniper woodlands. The distribution of this species in Colorado is still poorly known, and careful field work on this species would be worthwhile.

Habitat: Open and very dry piñon-juniper woodlands on rocky slopes at the lower elevation range of piñon-juniper; seems to avoid denser and higher piñon-juniper woodlands, which are often occupied by Solitary Vireos (Janos 1989). The species is apparently quite local.

Records: Specimens: 16–20 May 1907, near Lamar, Prowers County (DMNH 12735, 14583–84); 20 May 1914, Jimmie Creek, Baca County (DMNH 3841).

Solitary Vireo
Vireo solitarius

The three subspecies that occur are treated separately.

Blue-headed subspecies
V. s. solitarius

Status (SP): Accidental in **fall** (one record*).

Record: 6 Oct 1982, Hale, Yuma County (DMNH 38518).

Plumbeous subspecies
V. s. plumbeus

Summer resident in foothills and migrant in lowlands.

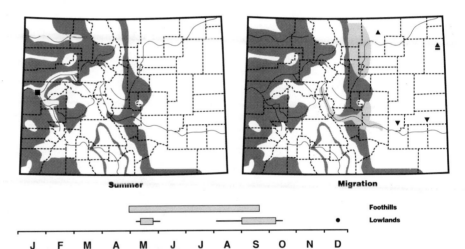

Summer   Migration

Foothills
Lowlands

J F M A M J J A S O N D
Seasonal Occurrence

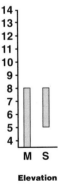

Elevation

Status (SP) (B): Fairly common **summer** resident in foothills and lower mountains. Uncommon **spring** and **fall** migrant in western valleys and on the eastern plains near foothills. Rare on extreme eastern plains.

This bird is heavily parasitized by Brown-headed Cowbirds in Boulder County (Marvil and Cruz 1989), and is considered to be a Colorado Species of Special Concern due to this parasitism (Webb 1985b).

Habitat: Ponderosa pine forests, piñon-juniper woodlands, especially denser woodlands at the upper elevational range of piñon-juniper (Janos 1989), aspen forests, foothill riparian forests, and Gambel oak shrublands with scattered tall trees. Occasionally breeds in lowland riparian forests adjacent to foothills in western Colorado.

Cassin's subspecies
V. s. cassinii

Migrant at low elevations.

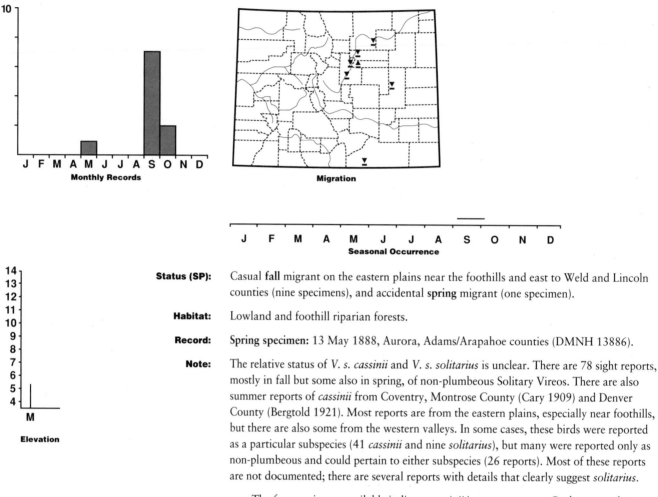

Monthly Records

Migration

Seasonal Occurrence

Elevation

Status (SP):	Casual **fall** migrant on the eastern plains near the foothills and east to Weld and Lincoln counties (nine specimens), and accidental **spring** migrant (one specimen).
Habitat:	Lowland and foothill riparian forests.
Record:	Spring specimen: 13 May 1888, Aurora, Adams/Arapahoe counties (DMNH 13886).
Note:	The relative status of *V. s. cassinii* and *V. s. solitarius* is unclear. There are 78 sight reports, mostly in fall but some also in spring, of non-plumbeous Solitary Vireos. There are also summer reports of *cassinii* from Coventry, Montrose County (Cary 1909) and Denver County (Bergtold 1921). Most reports are from the eastern plains, especially near foothills, but there are also some from the western valleys. In some cases, these birds were reported as a particular subspecies (41 *cassinii* and nine *solitarius*), but many were reported only as non-plumbeous and could pertain to either subspecies (26 reports). Most of these reports are not documented; there are several reports with details that clearly suggest *solitarius*.

The few specimens available indicate *cassinii* is more common. Both seem to be most regular in the fall. Most reports of *cassinii* are in Sep, while *solitarius* is reported mostly in Oct. Although *cassinii* is likely to be the more common of the two forms, many warbler species with a similar range as *solitarius* are regular in Colorado, and *solitarius* is likely to occur regularly in eastern Colorado.

Until recently, many observers have not been fully aware of the differences between the two non-plumbeous subspecies. They are at best difficult to separate in the field (A. Phillips and J. V. Remsen, pers. comm.) and may not be safely separable. Additional specimens and banding records will be necessary to clearly understand the relative distribution and abundance of these birds. Careful field observations will also be helpful if supported by details and with the recognition that many individuals may not be identifiable.

The maps and graphs on the next page combine all sight records of *V.s. solitarius* and *V.s. cassinii*.

Blue-headed/Cassin's subspecies

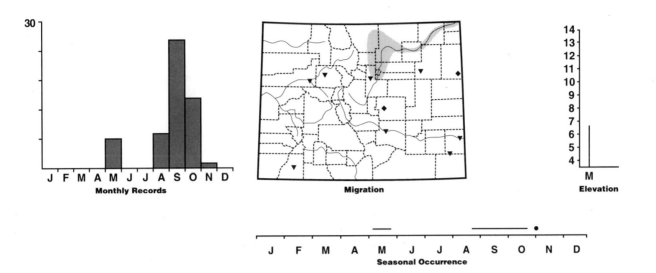

Yellow-throated Vireo

Vireo flavifrons

Occasional migrant in eastern Colorado.

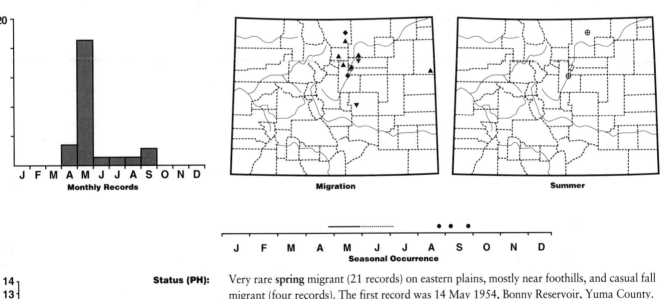

Status (PH): Very rare **spring** migrant (21 records) on eastern plains, mostly near foothills, and casual fall migrant (four records). The first record was 14 May 1954, Bonny Reservoir, Yuma County. Casual in **summer** (four records of territorial singing males, but no breeding records).

Habitat: Lowland riparian forests.

Records: Summer: 3–6 July 1979, Briggsdale, Weld County (Buechert 1980); 22 May–18 June 1990 and 13 May–into June 1991, Chatfield Reservoir, Douglas County (photos are on file with the RC); 20 June 1990, Briggsdale, Weld County.

Warbling Vireo
Vireo gilvus

Summer resident, mostly in mountains, and migrant at low elevations.

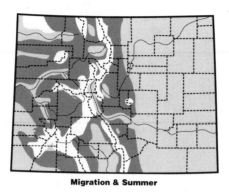

Migration & Summer

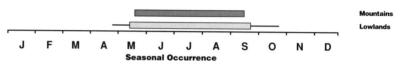

Mountains

Lowlands

J F M A M J J A S O N D

Seasonal Occurrence

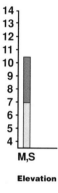

Elevation

Status (SP) (B): Fairly common to common **summer** resident in foothills and lower mountains. Uncommon to fairly common in western valleys and on eastern plains. Colorado is a center of abundance for this species (Robbins et al. 1986). Uncommon **spring** and **fall** migrant in western valleys, foothills, and on eastern plains. In the Grand Valley, it occurs in fall migration but not in spring (C. Dexter, pers. comm.).

Habitat: Most numerous in aspen forests, and also in lowland and foothill riparian forests, and sometimes in urban areas with tall trees. Rare in coniferous forests lacking deciduous trees. Recorded as the sixth most common breeding passerine (among 15 species) in montane willow shrublands in Boulder County (Hallock 1984).

Philadelphia Vireo

Vireo philadelphicus

Occasional migrant on eastern plains.

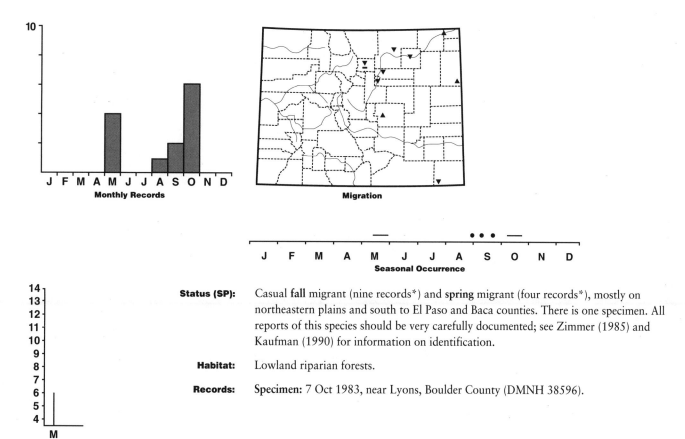

Status (SP): Casual **fall** migrant (nine records*) and **spring** migrant (four records*), mostly on northeastern plains and south to El Paso and Baca counties. There is one specimen. All reports of this species should be very carefully documented; see Zimmer (1985) and Kaufman (1990) for information on identification.

Habitat: Lowland riparian forests.

Records: Specimen: 7 Oct 1983, near Lyons, Boulder County (DMNH 38596).

Red-eyed Vireo
Vireo olivaceus

Migrant and local summer resident, mostly in eastern Colorado.

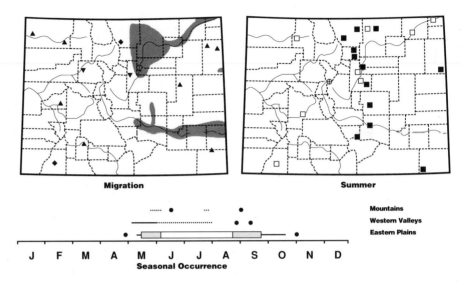

Migration   Summer

Mountains
Western Valleys
Eastern Plains

J F M A M J J A S O N D
Seasonal Occurrence

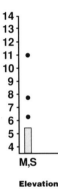

Elevation

Status (SP) (B): Uncommon **spring** migrant and rare **fall** migrant on eastern plains. Casual migrant in western valleys (four spring records and two fall records). Casual in lower mountains (several records). Rare to uncommon very local **summer** resident. Most records are at the base of the eastern foothills and adjacent plains from Larimer County south to Pueblo County, and also in southwestern Baca County. Very local on northeastern plains. Summer status at some localities is somewhat unclear because migrants are still moving through in late May and early June. Casual in western valleys (four records) and in mountains (several records).

Habitat: Lowland riparian forests and urban areas with tall trees.

Records: **Migration in mountains:** 3 Sep 1975, Evergreen, Jefferson County; recorded in migration in Rocky Mountain National Park (Packard 1945, Beidleman undated). **Summer in western valleys:** pair in 1967, Gunnison, Gunnison County (Hyde 1979); up to two singing males 28 May–8 July 1972 and 6 June–3 July 1973, near Hayden, Routt County (Martin et al. 1974); 7 July 1989, near Durango, La Plata County. **Summer in mountains:** 19–26 July 1871, at 11,000 ft. on Mt. Lincoln, Park County (Allen 1872); rare in summer in Rocky Mountain National Park (Beidleman undated); 16 June 1991, Creede, Rio Grande County (possibly a late spring migrant).

Order Passeriformes
Family Emberizidae

Subfamily Parulinae

Blue-winged Warbler
Vermivora pinus

Occasional migrant in eastern Colorado.

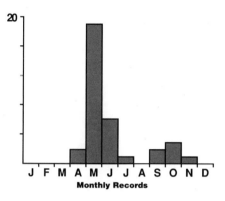

Monthly Records

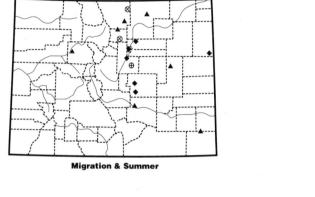

Migration & Summer

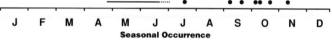

Seasonal Occurrence

Elevation
M,S

Status (PH): Very rare **spring** migrant (28 records) and casual **fall** migrant (eight records) on eastern plains. Accidental in western valleys (one spring record*). Accidental in **summer** (one record*); several records in early and mid-June probably pertain to late spring migrants. The first record was 23 May 1961, Golden, Jefferson County, and most are from the mid-1970s and later.

Habitat: Lowland riparian forests.

Records: **Western valleys***: 9 May 1988, Gypsum, Eagle County. **Summer***: pair (one singing) 4 June into early July 1991, Castlewood Canyon State Park, Douglas County.

Note: There are photos on file with the RC.

Brewster's Warbler
Vermivora pinus X *chrysoptera*

Status (SR): Accidental **spring** migrant (two records*).

Records: 30 Apr 1980 and 21–22 May 1987, Colorado Springs State Wildlife Area, El Paso County.

Golden-winged Warbler
Vermivora chrysoptera

Occasional migrant in eastern Colorado.

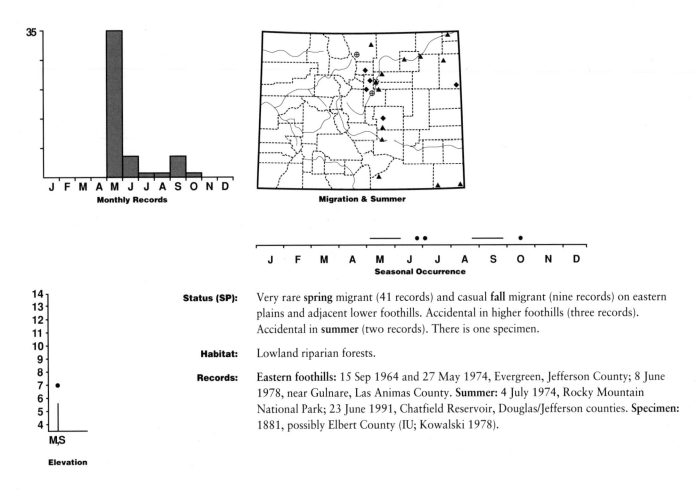

Monthly Records

Migration & Summer

Seasonal Occurrence

Elevation

Status (SP): Very rare **spring** migrant (41 records) and casual **fall** migrant (nine records) on eastern plains and adjacent lower foothills. Accidental in higher foothills (three records). Accidental in **summer** (two records). There is one specimen.

Habitat: Lowland riparian forests.

Records: **Eastern foothills:** 15 Sep 1964 and 27 May 1974, Evergreen, Jefferson County; 8 June 1978, near Gulnare, Las Animas County. **Summer:** 4 July 1974, Rocky Mountain National Park; 23 June 1991, Chatfield Reservoir, Douglas/Jefferson counties. **Specimen:** 1881, possibly Elbert County (IU; Kowalski 1978).

Tennessee Warbler
Vermivora peregrina

Migrant, mostly in eastern Colorado.

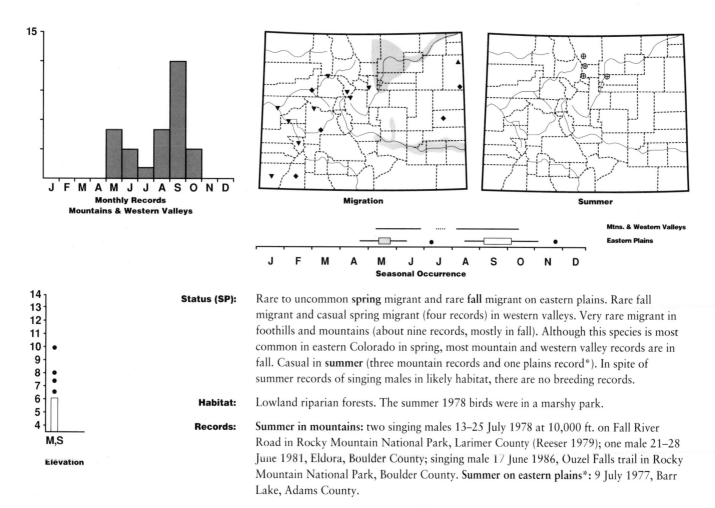

Monthly Records
Mountains & Western Valleys

Migration   Summer

Mtns. & Western Valleys
Eastern Plains

Seasonal Occurrence

Elevation

Status (SP): Rare to uncommon **spring** migrant and rare **fall** migrant on eastern plains. Rare fall migrant and casual spring migrant (four records) in western valleys. Very rare migrant in foothills and mountains (about nine records, mostly in fall). Although this species is most common in eastern Colorado in spring, most mountain and western valley records are in fall. Casual in **summer** (three mountain records and one plains record*). In spite of summer records of singing males in likely habitat, there are no breeding records.

Habitat: Lowland riparian forests. The summer 1978 birds were in a marshy park.

Records: **Summer in mountains:** two singing males 13–25 July 1978 at 10,000 ft. on Fall River Road in Rocky Mountain National Park, Larimer County (Reeser 1979); one male 21–28 June 1981, Eldora, Boulder County; singing male 17 June 1986, Ouzel Falls trail in Rocky Mountain National Park, Boulder County. **Summer on eastern plains*:** 9 July 1977, Barr Lake, Adams County.

Orange-crowned Warbler

Vermivora celata

Migrant in lowlands, and summer resident, primarily in western Colorado.

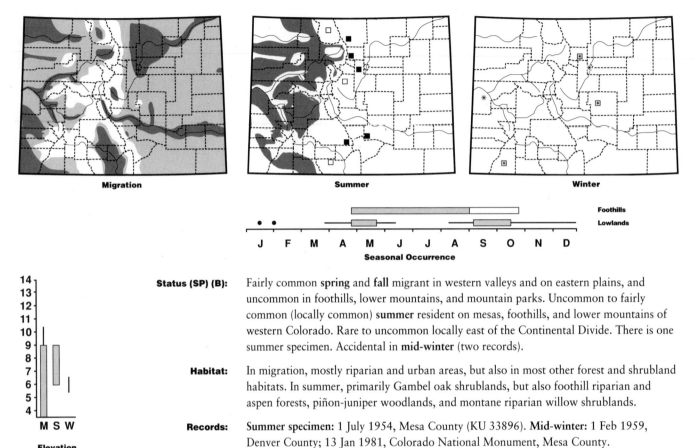

Migration   Summer   Winter

Foothills

Lowlands

J   F   M   A   M   J   J   A   S   O   N   D

Seasonal Occurrence

Elevation

Status (SP) (B): Fairly common **spring** and **fall** migrant in western valleys and on eastern plains, and uncommon in foothills, lower mountains, and mountain parks. Uncommon to fairly common (locally common) **summer** resident on mesas, foothills, and lower mountains of western Colorado. Rare to uncommon locally east of the Continental Divide. There is one summer specimen. Accidental in **mid-winter** (two records).

Habitat: In migration, mostly riparian and urban areas, but also in most other forest and shrubland habitats. In summer, primarily Gambel oak shrublands, but also foothill riparian and aspen forests, piñon-juniper woodlands, and montane riparian willow shrublands.

Records: Summer specimen: 1 July 1954, Mesa County (KU 33896). **Mid-winter:** 1 Feb 1959, Denver County; 13 Jan 1981, Colorado National Monument, Mesa County.

Nashville Warbler
Vermivora ruficapilla

Migrant at lower elevations.

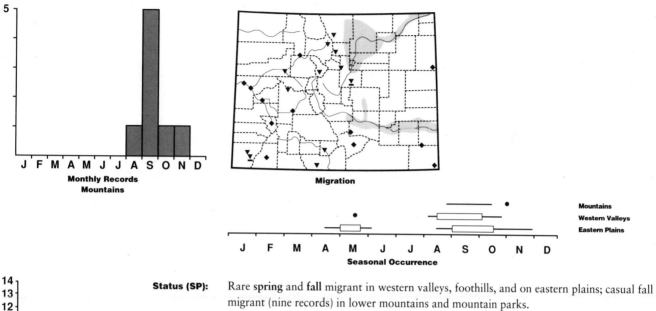

Monthly Records
Mountains

Migration

Seasonal Occurrence

Mountains
Western Valleys
Eastern Plains

Elevation

Status (SP): Rare **spring** and **fall** migrant in western valleys, foothills, and on eastern plains; casual fall migrant (nine records) in lower mountains and mountain parks.

Habitat: Lowland riparian and urban areas; also seen in ponderosa pine/Gambel oak and piñon-juniper in western Colorado.

Virginia's Warbler

Vermivora virginiae

Summer resident in foothills, and migrant in lowlands.

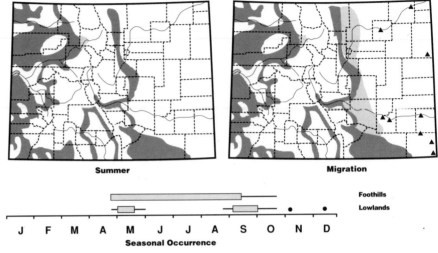

Summer	Migration

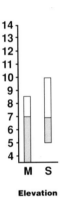

Elevation

Status (SP) (B): Fairly common **summer** resident on mesas and foothills and rare in lower mountains. Fairly common to common **spring** and **fall** migrant in western valleys, foothills, and on eastern plains near foothills. High count: 480+ on 20 May 1979, Chatfield Reservoir, Douglas/Jefferson counties. Very rare on extreme eastern plains (eight records). Accidental in **early winter** (one record*).

Habitat: Breeds in dry, dense hillside shrublands, especially Gambel oak. Also in mountain mahogany and riparian thickets, and in ponderosa pine forests and piñon-juniper woodlands, especially with shrubby understories. Occasionally in aspen or Douglas-fir forests, especially those with an understory of shrubs. In migration, in riparian and urban areas, and shrublands.

Record: Early winter*: 15 Dec 1973, Boulder, Boulder County.

Lucy's Warbler

Vermivora luciae

Status (SP) (FB): Accidental in **spring** (three records*). This species is rare in adjacent southeastern Utah (Behle and Perry 1975) and northeastern Arizona (Rosenberg and Terrill 1986), and may occur occasionally in summer and migration in southwestern Colorado.

Records: Three adults and nest with four eggs collected 13 and 19 May 1913, Four Corners area, Montezuma County (DMNH 3384–86); 11 May 1991, Grand Junction, Mesa County.

Northern Parula

Parula americana

Migrant in eastern Colorado.

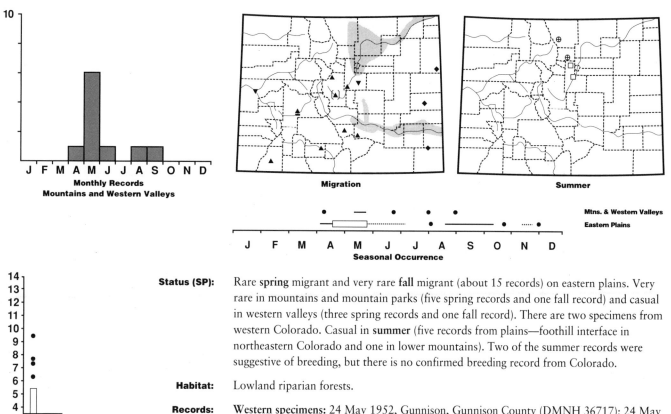

Monthly Records
Mountains and Western Valleys

Migration

Summer

Mtns. & Western Valleys

Eastern Plains

Seasonal Occurrence

Elevation

Status (SP): Rare **spring** migrant and very rare **fall** migrant (about 15 records) on eastern plains. Very rare in mountains and mountain parks (five spring records and one fall record) and casual in western valleys (three spring records and one fall record). There are two specimens from western Colorado. Casual in **summer** (five records from plains—foothill interface in northeastern Colorado and one in lower mountains). Two of the summer records were suggestive of breeding, but there is no confirmed breeding record from Colorado.

Habitat: Lowland riparian forests.

Records: **Western specimens:** 24 May 1952, Gunnison, Gunnison County (DMNH 36717); 24 May 1977, Gunnison (DMNH 36724). **Possible breeding:** one female and nest, which had no eggs and was destroyed in a storm, 11–16 June 1982, Golden, Jefferson County; possible fledgling 12–23 Aug 1987, Waterton, Douglas/Jefferson counties.

Yellow Warbler
Dendroica petechia

Summer resident and migrant throughout Colorado.

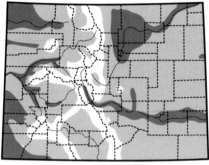

Migration & Summer

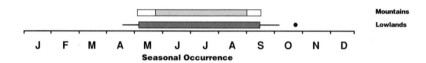

Mountains

Lowlands

J F M A M J J A S O N D

Seasonal Occurrence

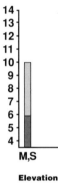

M,S

Elevation

Status (SP) (B): Fairly common to common **summer** resident and **spring** and **fall** migrant in western valleys, lower mountain valleys and parks, and on eastern plains; rare and local in higher mountains.

Populations of this species have declined in some parts of North America, and it is a Species of Special Concern, both nationally (Tate 1986) and in Colorado (Webb 1985b).

Habitat: Lowland and foothill riparian forests, urban areas, around farmhouses, and windbreaks; in mountains primarily in riparian willow shrublands.

Chestnut-sided Warbler
Dendroica pensylvanica

Migrant in eastern Colorado; occasionally breeds.

**Monthly Records
Mountains and Western Valleys**

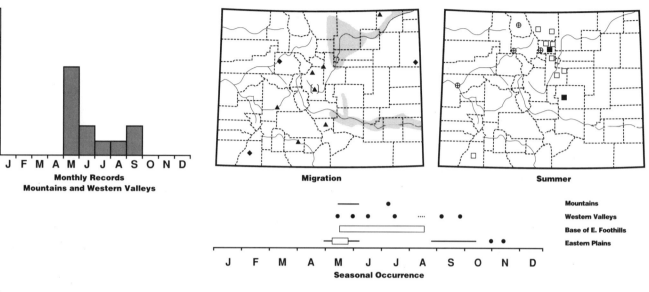

Migration   Summer

Mountains
Western Valleys
Base of E. Foothills
Eastern Plains

Seasonal Occurrence

Elevation

Status (SP) (B): Rare **spring** migrant on eastern plains; very rare **fall** migrant (about 18 records). Casual in eastern foothills, lower mountains, and mountain parks (six spring records) and in western valleys (two spring records and three fall records). All fall records are since 1964. There is one specimen from the state, which was also the first record.

Very rare **summer** resident in low northeastern foothill canyons and adjacent plains from Larimer County south to El Paso County (21 records); all records since 1964. There are two confirmed **breeding** records. Casual (four records) in lower mountains at Estes Park and adjacent Rocky Mountain National Park, Larimer County and Eldora, Boulder County. Accidental in mountain parks (two records) and in western valleys (two records).

Habitat: In migration, riparian and urban areas. In summer, in foothill riparian shrublands and adjacent hillside shrublands.

Records: Specimen: 16 May 1933, Barr Lake, Adams County (DMNH 12314). **Confirmed breeding:** 1968 in Bear Creek Canyon, near Colorado Springs, El Paso County (Gadd 1969, van Sickle and Thurlow 1971); 1975 at Boulder, Boulder County (Bosley 1975). **Summer in mountain parks:** 16–18 June 1987, Radium, Grand County; 7 July 1990, Arapaho National Wildlife Refuge, Jackson County. **Summer in western valleys:** 1977, Durango, La Plata County; 14 July 1991, Coal Canyon near Camco, Mesa County.

Magnolia Warbler
Dendroica magnolia

Occasional migrant in eastern Colorado.

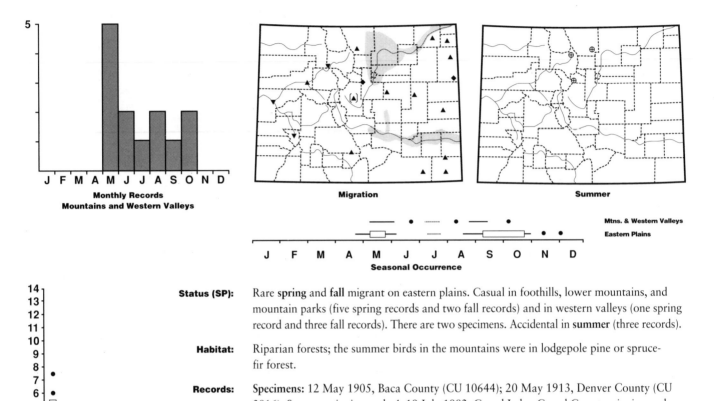

**Monthly Records
Mountains and Western Valleys**

Migration

Summer

Mtns. & Western Valleys

Eastern Plains

Seasonal Occurrence

Elevation

Status (SP): Rare **spring** and **fall** migrant on eastern plains. Casual in foothills, lower mountains, and mountain parks (five spring records and two fall records) and in western valleys (one spring record and three fall records). There are two specimens. Accidental in **summer** (three records).

Habitat: Riparian forests; the summer birds in the mountains were in lodgepole pine or spruce-fir forest.

Records: **Specimens:** 12 May 1905, Baca County (CU 10644); 20 May 1913, Denver County (CU 2816). **Summer:** singing male 4–19 July 1982, Grand Lake, Grand County; singing male 20 June 1983, Echo Lake, Clear Creek County; 10–20 July 1990, Boyd Lake State Recreation Area, Larimer County.

Cape May Warbler
Dendroica tigrina

Occasional migrant in eastern Colorado.

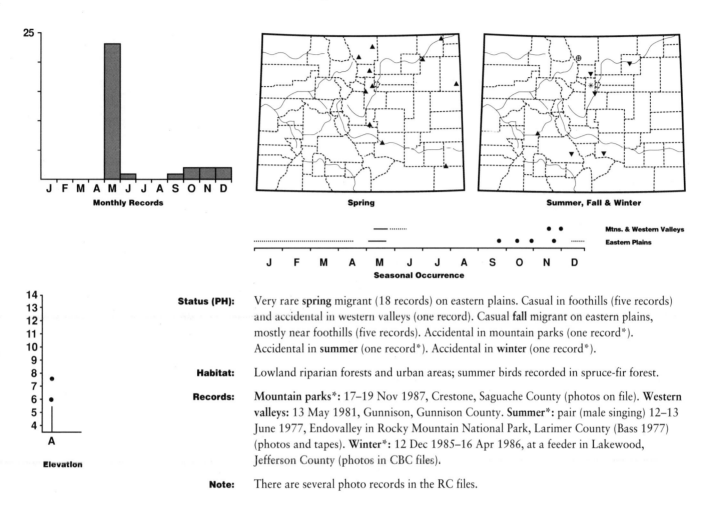

Monthly Records

Spring

Summer, Fall & Winter

Mtns. & Western Valleys

Eastern Plains

Seasonal Occurrence

Elevation

Status (PH): Very rare **spring** migrant (18 records) on eastern plains. Casual in foothills (five records) and accidental in western valleys (one record). Casual **fall** migrant on eastern plains, mostly near foothills (five records). Accidental in mountain parks (one record*). Accidental in **summer** (one record*). Accidental in **winter** (one record*).

Habitat: Lowland riparian forests and urban areas; summer birds recorded in spruce-fir forest.

Records: Mountain parks*: 17–19 Nov 1987, Crestone, Saguache County (photos on file). **Western valleys:** 13 May 1981, Gunnison, Gunnison County. **Summer*:** pair (male singing) 12–13 June 1977, Endovalley in Rocky Mountain National Park, Larimer County (Bass 1977) (photos and tapes). **Winter*:** 12 Dec 1985–16 Apr 1986, at a feeder in Lakewood, Jefferson County (photos in CBC files).

Note: There are several photo records in the RC files.

Black-throated Blue Warbler
Dendroica caerulescens

Occasional migrant in eastern Colorado.

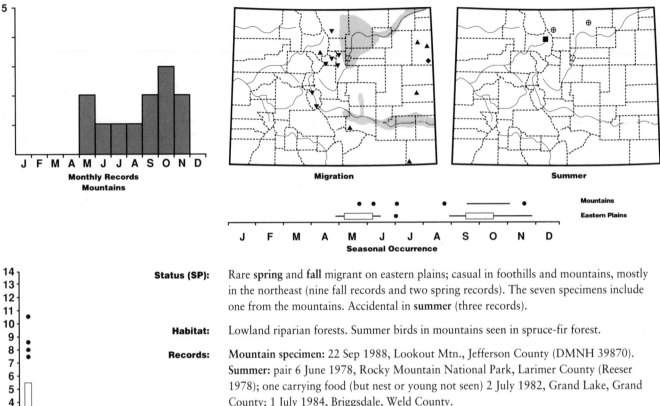

Monthly Records
Mountains

Migration

Summer

Mountains

Eastern Plains

Seasonal Occurrence

Elevation

Status (SP): Rare **spring** and **fall** migrant on eastern plains; casual in foothills and mountains, mostly in the northeast (nine fall records and two spring records). The seven specimens include one from the mountains. Accidental in **summer** (three records).

Habitat: Lowland riparian forests. Summer birds in mountains seen in spruce-fir forest.

Records: **Mountain specimen:** 22 Sep 1988, Lookout Mtn., Jefferson County (DMNH 39870). **Summer:** pair 6 June 1978, Rocky Mountain National Park, Larimer County (Reeser 1978); one carrying food (but nest or young not seen) 2 July 1982, Grand Lake, Grand County; 1 July 1984, Briggsdale, Weld County.

Yellow-rumped Warbler

Dendroica coronata

The two field-identifiable forms are treated separately.

Myrtle form

Migrant, mostly in eastern Colorado, and occasionally in winter.

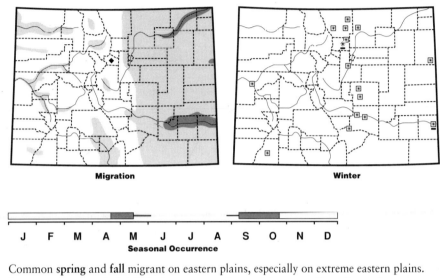

Migration   Winter

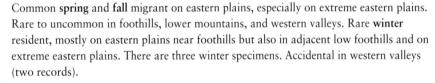

J F M A M J J A S O N D
Seasonal Occurrence

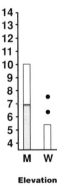

M   W

Elevation

Status (SP): Common **spring** and **fall** migrant on eastern plains, especially on extreme eastern plains. Rare to uncommon in foothills, lower mountains, and western valleys. Rare **winter** resident, mostly on eastern plains near foothills but also in adjacent low foothills and on extreme eastern plains. There are three winter specimens. Accidental in western valleys (two records).

Habitat: Lowland riparian forests and wooded urban areas.

Records: **Winter in western valleys:** Jan–Mar 1970, Durango, La Plata County (Davis 1970); 3 Jan 1982, Grand Junction, Mesa County.

Audubon's form

Summer resident in mountains and widespread migrant; locally in winter.

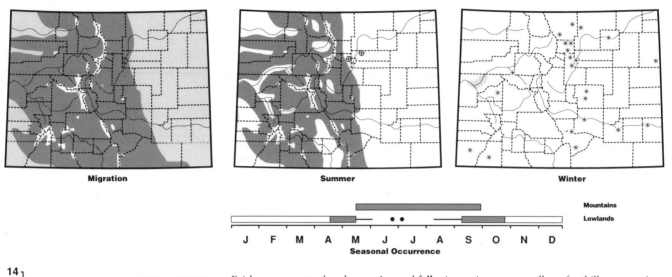

Migration   Summer   Winter

	J F M A M J J A S O N D
Mountains	
Lowlands	

Seasonal Occurrence

Elevation

Status (SP) (B): Fairly common to abundant **spring** and **fall** migrant in western valleys, foothills, mountains, mountain parks, and on eastern plains near foothills. Fairly common on southeastern plains and rare to uncommon on extreme northeastern plains. High count: 1,000 on 13 May 1967, northern Eagle County. Fairly common to common **summer** resident in mountains; most numerous at middle and higher elevations. Accidental on eastern plains (two records). Rare to uncommon **winter** resident in western valleys and lower eastern foothills and adjacent plains, Mesa and El Paso counties southward. In some years, it may be fairly common. Very rare in mountains, north to Garfield and Larimer counties, and on eastern plains east to Yuma and Prowers counties. There is one winter specimen.

Habitat: Breeds in coniferous forests. It is most common in mature spruce-fir forests, in which it is one of the most common breeding species (Scott et al. 1982, Alles 1985, Hallock 1988). Also found in all other coniferous forest types and in aspen forests, especially adjacent to or mixed with coniferous forests. In migration, most wooded areas. Winters in lowland and foothill riparian forests.

Records: **Summer on eastern plains:** 25 June 1976, Barr Lake, Adams County; 4 July 1988, Wheat Ridge, Jefferson County. **Winter specimen:** 11 Dec 1981, Grand Junction, Mesa County (DMNH 37433).

Black-throated Gray Warbler
Dendroica nigrescens

Summer resident in western and southern Colorado.

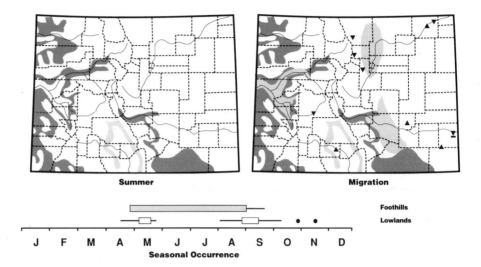

Summer   Migration

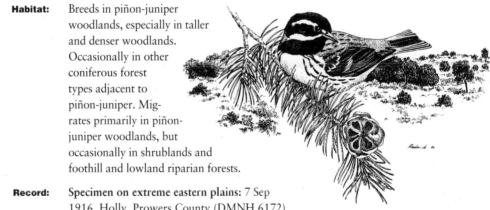

Foothills

Lowlands

J   F   M   A   M   J   J   A   S   O   N   D

Seasonal Occurrence

Elevation

Status (SP) (B): Fairly common **summer** resident in foothills and mesas from Moffat County southward and east to southwestern Grand County, and from southern Chaffee and southwestern El Paso counties southward. Rare in the periphery of the San Luis Valley. Rare **spring** and **fall** migrant in valleys and plains adjacent to breeding range. Rare migrant in northeastern foothills and adjacent plains. Casual on extreme eastern plains (six records, including one specimen).

Habitat: Breeds in piñon-juniper woodlands, especially in taller and denser woodlands. Occasionally in other coniferous forest types adjacent to piñon-juniper. Migrates primarily in piñon-juniper woodlands, but occasionally in shrublands and foothill and lowland riparian forests.

Record: Specimen on extreme eastern plains: 7 Sep 1916, Holly, Prowers County (DMNH 6172).

315

Townsend's Warbler
Dendroica townsendi

Migrant, primarily in fall.

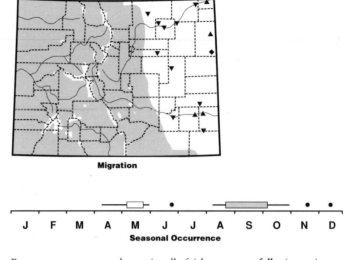

Migration

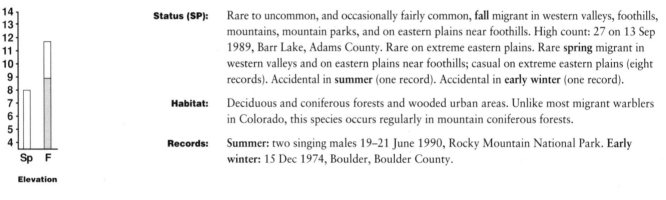

J F M A M J J A S O N D

Seasonal Occurrence

Elevation

14
13
12
11
10
9
8
7
6
5
4

Sp   F

Status (SP): Rare to uncommon, and occasionally fairly common, **fall** migrant in western valleys, foothills, mountains, mountain parks, and on eastern plains near foothills. High count: 27 on 13 Sep 1989, Barr Lake, Adams County. Rare on extreme eastern plains. Rare **spring** migrant in western valleys and on eastern plains near foothills; casual on extreme eastern plains (eight records). Accidental in **summer** (one record). Accidental in **early winter** (one record).

Habitat: Deciduous and coniferous forests and wooded urban areas. Unlike most migrant warblers in Colorado, this species occurs regularly in mountain coniferous forests.

Records: **Summer:** two singing males 19–21 June 1990, Rocky Mountain National Park. **Early winter:** 15 Dec 1974, Boulder, Boulder County.

Hermit Warbler
Dendroica occidentalis

Occasional spring migrant.

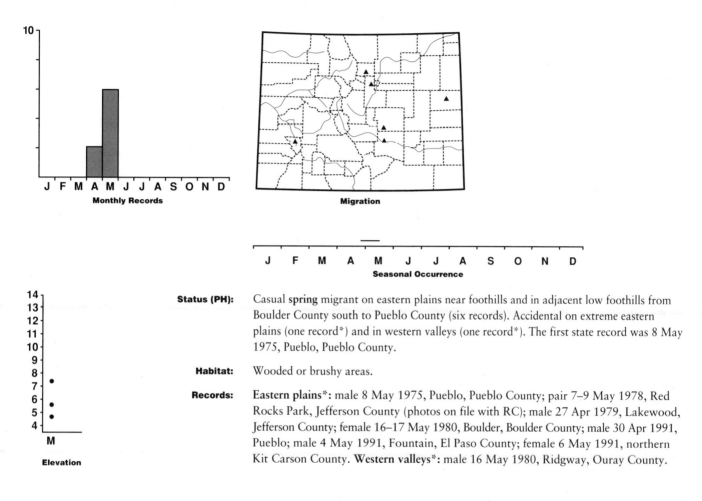

Monthly Records

Migration

Seasonal Occurrence

Elevation

Status (PH): Casual **spring** migrant on eastern plains near foothills and in adjacent low foothills from Boulder County south to Pueblo County (six records). Accidental on extreme eastern plains (one record*) and in western valleys (one record*). The first state record was 8 May 1975, Pueblo, Pueblo County.

Habitat: Wooded or brushy areas.

Records: **Eastern plains***: male 8 May 1975, Pueblo, Pueblo County; pair 7–9 May 1978, Red Rocks Park, Jefferson County (photos on file with RC); male 27 Apr 1979, Lakewood, Jefferson County; female 16–17 May 1980, Boulder, Boulder County; male 30 Apr 1991, Pueblo; male 4 May 1991, Fountain, El Paso County; female 6 May 1991, northern Kit Carson County. **Western valleys***: male 16 May 1980, Ridgway, Ouray County.

Black-throated Green Warbler
Dendroica virens

Occasional migrant in eastern Colorado.

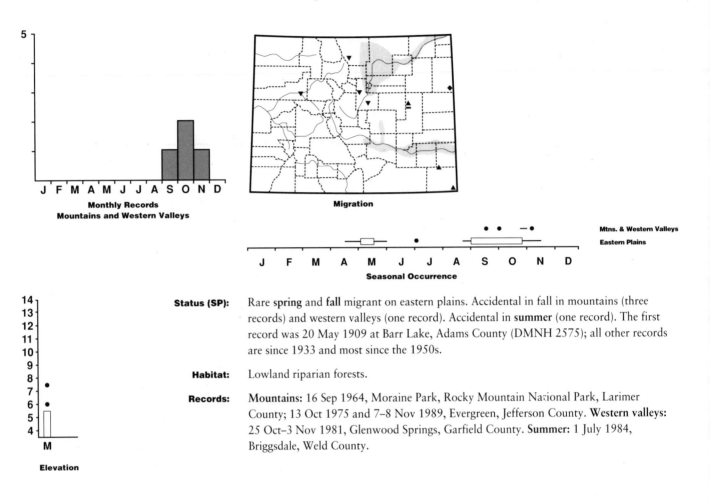

Monthly Records
Mountains and Western Valleys

Migration

Mtns. & Western Valleys

Eastern Plains

Seasonal Occurrence

Elevation

Status (SP): Rare **spring** and **fall** migrant on eastern plains. Accidental in fall in mountains (three records) and western valleys (one record). Accidental in **summer** (one record). The first record was 20 May 1909 at Barr Lake, Adams County (DMNH 2575); all other records are since 1933 and most since the 1950s.

Habitat: Lowland riparian forests.

Records: **Mountains:** 16 Sep 1964, Moraine Park, Rocky Mountain National Park, Larimer County; 13 Oct 1975 and 7–8 Nov 1989, Evergreen, Jefferson County. **Western valleys:** 25 Oct–3 Nov 1981, Glenwood Springs, Garfield County. **Summer:** 1 July 1984, Briggsdale, Weld County.

Blackburnian Warbler

Dendroica fusca

Occasional migrant in eastern Colorado.

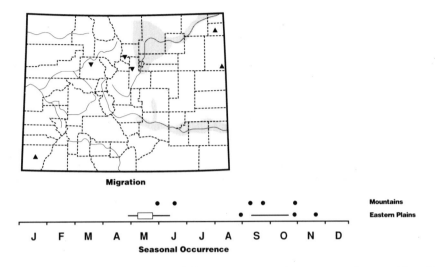

Migration

Seasonal Occurrence

Mountains

Eastern Plains

J F M A M J J A S O N D

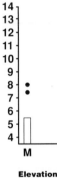

Elevation

Status (SP): Rare **spring** migrant and very rare **fall** migrant (18 records) on eastern plains; accidental in adjacent foothills (one spring record, two fall records). There are two specimens. Accidental in western valleys (three records). Accidental in **summer** in mountains (two records).

Habitat: Lowland riparian forests.

Records: **Specimens:** 3 June 1975, Lakewood, Jefferson County (DMNH 36144); 14 Sep 1975, Wheat Ridge, Jefferson County (DMNH 37436). **Western valleys*:** 20 Sep 1988, near Edwards, Eagle County; 7 May 1991, 10 mi. northwest of Cortez, Montezuma County; 10–13 May 1991, Cortez. **Summer:** pair 12 June 1962, Boulder County; male 17 June 1970, Moraine Park, Rocky Mountain National Park, Larimer County (Franks et al. 1971).

Yellow-throated Warbler
Dendroica dominica

Occasional migrant in eastern Colorado.

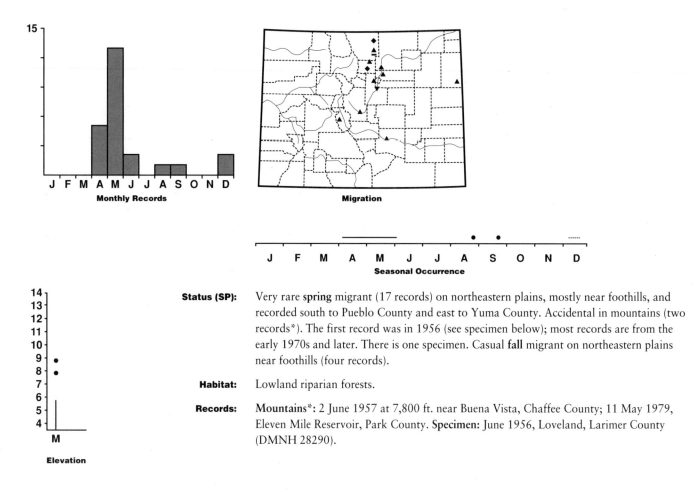

Monthly Records

Migration

Seasonal Occurrence

Elevation

Status (SP): Very rare **spring** migrant (17 records) on northeastern plains, mostly near foothills, and recorded south to Pueblo County and east to Yuma County. Accidental in mountains (two records*). The first record was in 1956 (see specimen below); most records are from the early 1970s and later. There is one specimen. Casual **fall** migrant on northeastern plains near foothills (four records).

Habitat: Lowland riparian forests.

Records: Mountains*: 2 June 1957 at 7,800 ft. near Buena Vista, Chaffee County; 11 May 1979, Eleven Mile Reservoir, Park County. **Specimen:** June 1956, Loveland, Larimer County (DMNH 28290).

Grace's Warbler
Dendroica graciae

Summer resident in southwestern mountains.

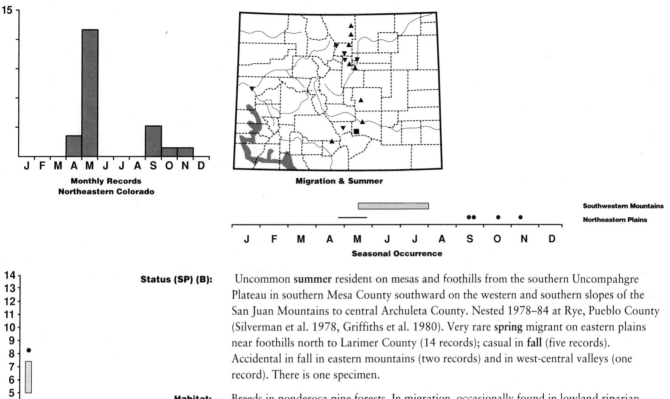

**Monthly Records
Northeastern Colorado**

Migration & Summer

Southwestern Mountains

Northeastern Plains

Seasonal Occurrence

Elevation

Status (SP) (B): Uncommon **summer** resident on mesas and foothills from the southern Uncompahgre Plateau in southern Mesa County southward on the western and southern slopes of the San Juan Mountains to central Archuleta County. Nested 1978–84 at Rye, Pueblo County (Silverman et al. 1978, Griffiths et al. 1980). Very rare **spring** migrant on eastern plains near foothills north to Larimer County (14 records); casual in **fall** (five records). Accidental in fall in eastern mountains (two records) and in west-central valleys (one record). There is one specimen.

Habitat: Breeds in ponderosa pine forests. In migration, occasionally found in lowland riparian forests or other wooded areas.

Records: **Eastern mountains:** 14 Sep 1958, Wild Basin in Rocky Mountain National Park, Boulder County; 24 Aug 1991, Westcliffe, Custer County. **West-central valleys:** 22 Oct 1971, Grand Junction, Mesa County. **Specimen:** undated, Paradox Valley, Montrose County (DMNH 4521).

Note: One hybrid specimen, *D. graciae* X *D. coronata memorabilis*: 20 Apr 1977, Aurora, Adams County (DMNH 36657).

Pine Warbler

Dendroica pinus

Occasional migrant in eastern Colorado.

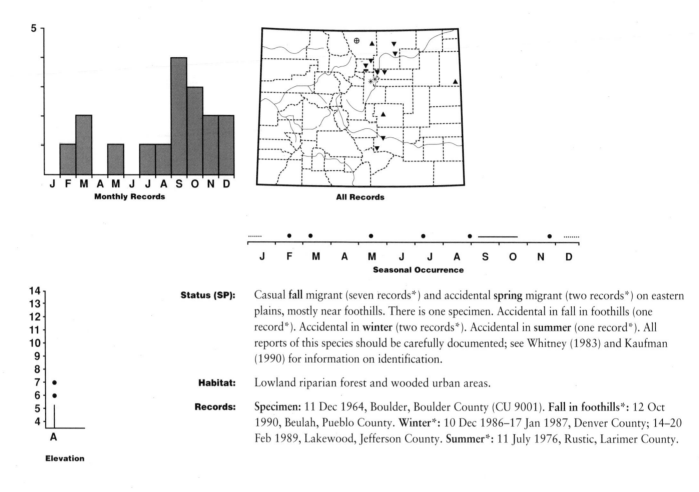

Monthly Records

All Records

Seasonal Occurrence

Elevation

Status (SP): Casual **fall** migrant (seven records*) and accidental **spring** migrant (two records*) on eastern plains, mostly near foothills. There is one specimen. Accidental in fall in foothills (one record*). Accidental in **winter** (two records*). Accidental in **summer** (one record*). All reports of this species should be carefully documented; see Whitney (1983) and Kaufman (1990) for information on identification.

Habitat: Lowland riparian forest and wooded urban areas.

Records: Specimen: 11 Dec 1964, Boulder, Boulder County (CU 9001). **Fall in foothills*:** 12 Oct 1990, Beulah, Pueblo County. **Winter*:** 10 Dec 1986–17 Jan 1987, Denver County; 14–20 Feb 1989, Lakewood, Jefferson County. **Summer*:** 11 July 1976, Rustic, Larimer County.

Prairie Warbler
Dendroica discolor

Occasional migrant in eastern Colorado.

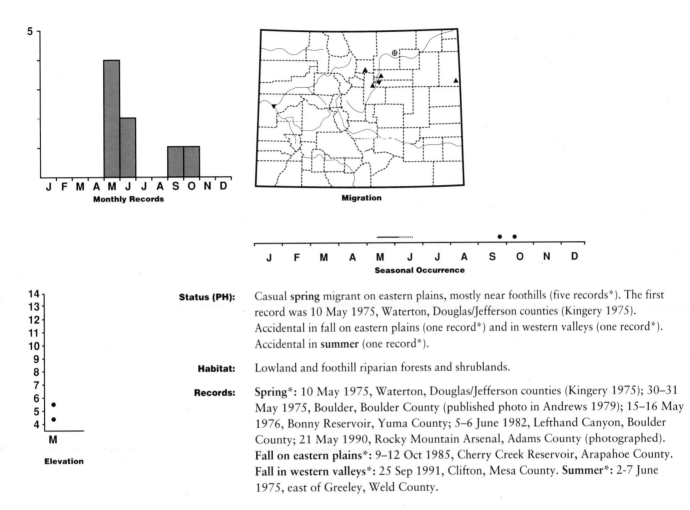

Monthly Records

Migration

Seasonal Occurrence

Elevation

Status (PH): Casual **spring** migrant on eastern plains, mostly near foothills (five records*). The first record was 10 May 1975, Waterton, Douglas/Jefferson counties (Kingery 1975). Accidental in fall on eastern plains (one record*) and in western valleys (one record*). Accidental in **summer** (one record*).

Habitat: Lowland and foothill riparian forests and shrublands.

Records: **Spring***: 10 May 1975, Waterton, Douglas/Jefferson counties (Kingery 1975); 30–31 May 1975, Boulder, Boulder County (published photo in Andrews 1979); 15–16 May 1976, Bonny Reservoir, Yuma County; 5–6 June 1982, Lefthand Canyon, Boulder County; 21 May 1990, Rocky Mountain Arsenal, Adams County (photographed). **Fall on eastern plains***: 9–12 Oct 1985, Cherry Creek Reservoir, Arapahoe County. **Fall in western valleys***: 25 Sep 1991, Clifton, Mesa County. **Summer***: 2-7 June 1975, east of Greeley, Weld County.

Palm Warbler
Dendroica palmarum

Occasional migrant in eastern Colorado.

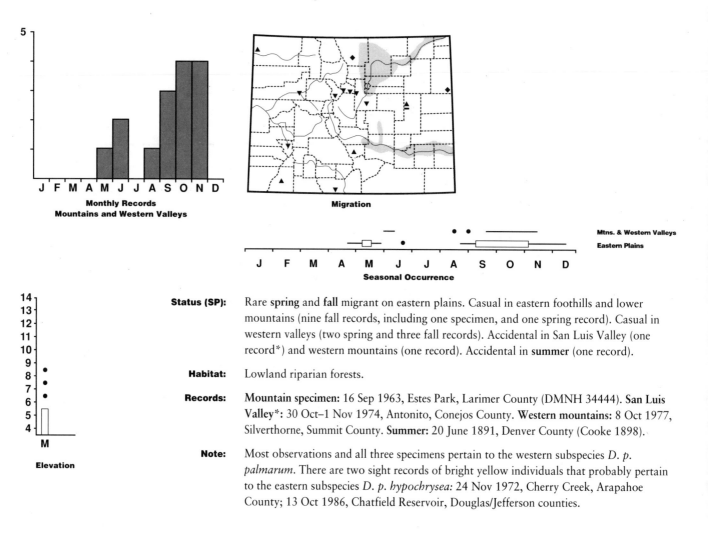

Monthly Records
Mountains and Western Valleys

Migration

Seasonal Occurrence

Mtns. & Western Valleys

Eastern Plains

Elevation

Status (SP): Rare **spring** and **fall** migrant on eastern plains. Casual in eastern foothills and lower mountains (nine fall records, including one specimen, and one spring record). Casual in western valleys (two spring and three fall records). Accidental in San Luis Valley (one record*) and western mountains (one record). Accidental in **summer** (one record).

Habitat: Lowland riparian forests.

Records: **Mountain specimen:** 16 Sep 1963, Estes Park, Larimer County (DMNH 34444). **San Luis Valley*:** 30 Oct–1 Nov 1974, Antonito, Conejos County. **Western mountains:** 8 Oct 1977, Silverthorne, Summit County. **Summer:** 20 June 1891, Denver County (Cooke 1898).

Note: Most observations and all three specimens pertain to the western subspecies *D. p. palmarum*. There are two sight records of bright yellow individuals that probably pertain to the eastern subspecies *D. p. hypochrysea*: 24 Nov 1972, Cherry Creek, Arapahoe County; 13 Oct 1986, Chatfield Reservoir, Douglas/Jefferson counties.

Bay-breasted Warbler
Dendroica castanea

Occasional migrant in eastern Colorado.

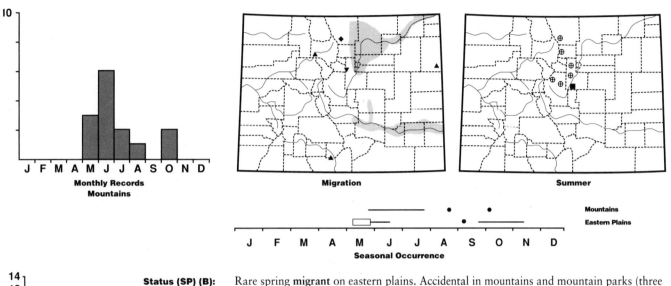

Migration	Summer

Monthly Records Mountains

Seasonal Occurrence

Mountains

Eastern Plains

Elevation M,S

Status (SP) (B): Rare spring **migrant** on eastern plains. Accidental in mountains and mountain parks (three records). Very rare **fall** migrant on eastern plains (13 records). Accidental in mountains (two records). There are two specimens.

Casual **summer** resident (seven records) in foothills and low mountains east of the Continental Divide. There is one confirmed **breeding** record, and other summer records were of pairs and also have been suggestive of breeding (Reeser 1979). This species is opportunistic, and may breed in extralimital areas where food supplies are abundant (Sealy 1979).

Habitat: In migration, lowland riparian forests. Summer birds have been recorded in coniferous forests.

Records: **Spring in mountains and mountain parks:** 20 May 1973, Estes Park, Larimer County; 20 May 1976, Kremmling, Grand County; 23 May 1984, Lasauses, Conejos County. **Fall in mountains:** 1 Oct 1960, Genesee Park, Jefferson County; 22–23 Aug 1963, Moraine Park, Rocky Mountain National Park, Larimer County. **Specimens:** 8 Nov 1971, Boulder, Boulder County (CU 7746); Nov 1978, Boulder, Boulder County (DMNH 38670). **Confirmed breeding:** a pair observed feeding young 24 July 1978, Westcreek, Douglas County (Winn 1979).

Blackpoll Warbler
Dendroica striata

Occasional migrant in eastern Colorado.

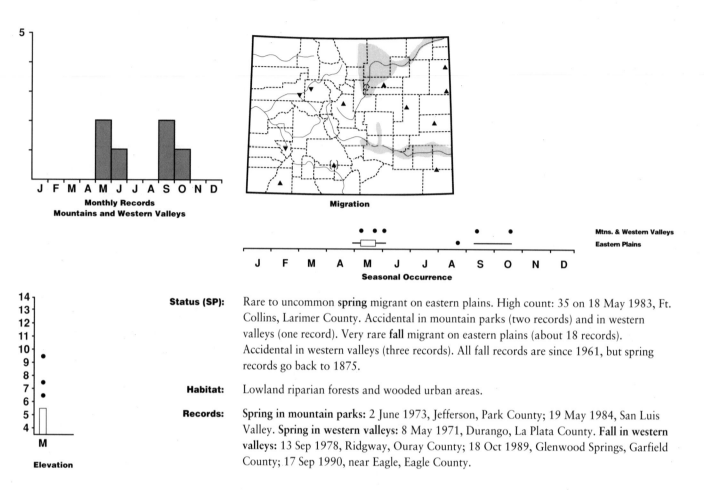

Monthly Records
Mountains and Western Valleys

Migration

Mtns. & Western Valleys
Eastern Plains

Seasonal Occurrence

Elevation

Status (SP): Rare to uncommon **spring** migrant on eastern plains. High count: 35 on 18 May 1983, Ft. Collins, Larimer County. Accidental in mountain parks (two records) and in western valleys (one record). Very rare **fall** migrant on eastern plains (about 18 records). Accidental in western valleys (three records). All fall records are since 1961, but spring records go back to 1875.

Habitat: Lowland riparian forests and wooded urban areas.

Records: Spring in mountain parks: 2 June 1973, Jefferson, Park County; 19 May 1984, San Luis Valley. **Spring in western valleys:** 8 May 1971, Durango, La Plata County. **Fall in western valleys:** 13 Sep 1978, Ridgway, Ouray County; 18 Oct 1989, Glenwood Springs, Garfield County; 17 Sep 1990, near Eagle, Eagle County.

Cerulean Warbler
Dendroica cerulea

Status (SP): Accidental **spring** and **fall** migrant (two records*).

Records: 20 Sep 1936, Parker, Douglas County (DMNH 15073); 4 Sep 1989, Two Buttes Reservoir, Baca County. There are two additional specimens that are apparently from Colorado, but the date and locality are uncertain. They are said to have been collected sometime between 1881–1885 at Silverton, San Juan County (Thompson 1971). A high mountain valley in southwestern Colorado would be one of the least likely sites for this species to occur (especially twice), and so these records seem doubtful.

Habitat: Lowland riparian areas.

Black-and-white Warbler

Mniotilta varia

Migrant in eastern Colorado; occasional elsewhere.

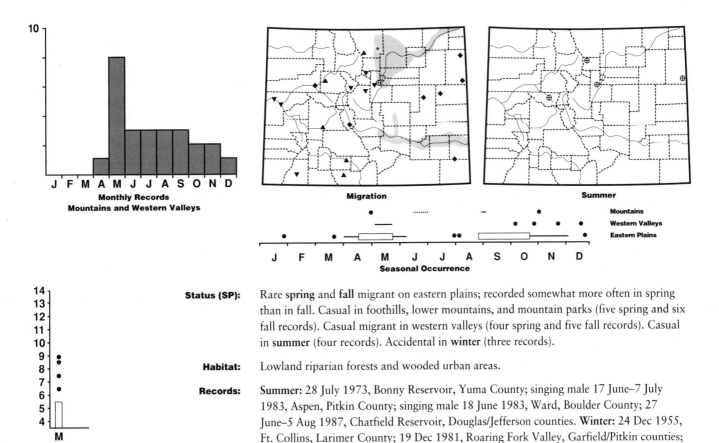

Monthly Records
Mountains and Western Valleys

Migration   **Summer**

Seasonal Occurrence

Mountains
Western Valleys
Eastern Plains

Elevation

Status (SP): Rare **spring** and **fall** migrant on eastern plains; recorded somewhat more often in spring than in fall. Casual in foothills, lower mountains, and mountain parks (five spring and six fall records). Casual migrant in western valleys (four spring and five fall records). Casual in **summer** (four records). Accidental in **winter** (three records).

Habitat: Lowland riparian forests and wooded urban areas.

Records: **Summer:** 28 July 1973, Bonny Reservoir, Yuma County; singing male 17 June–7 July 1983, Aspen, Pitkin County; singing male 18 June 1983, Ward, Boulder County; 27 June–5 Aug 1987, Chatfield Reservoir, Douglas/Jefferson counties. **Winter:** 24 Dec 1955, Ft. Collins, Larimer County; 19 Dec 1981, Roaring Fork Valley, Garfield/Pitkin counties; 24 Jan 1984, Ft. Collins.

American Redstart
Setophaga ruticilla

Migrant and local summer resident, mostly in eastern Colorado.

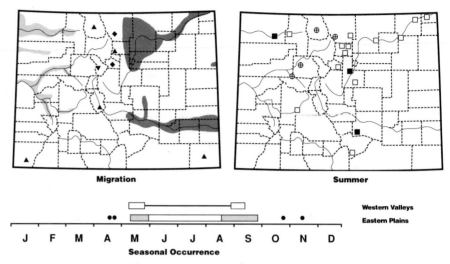

| Migration | Summer |

Seasonal Occurrence

Western Valleys
Eastern Plains

J F M A M J J A S O N D

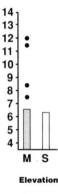

Elevation

Status (SP) (B): Uncommon **spring** and **fall** migrant on eastern plains. Rare in western valleys. Casual in foothills, lower mountains, and mountain parks (about seven records). Accidental in higher mountains (one record). Rare **summer** resident in canyons at the base of eastern foothills and immediately adjacent plains, Larimer County south to Huerfano County. Most confirmed breeding records are from this area. Also locally along the South Platte River from eastern Weld County northeast to Sedgwick County and along the Yampa River in Routt County (Martin et al. 1974). Elsewhere in the western valleys, there are summer records from Moffat, Eagle, and Gunnison counties, and in the Roaring Fork Valley. This species is a fairly late migrant, and birds seen in early June could still be migrants rather than summer residents.

Habitat: Lowland and foothill riparian forests and wooded urban areas.

Records: **Migration in high mountains:** 31 Aug 1972, at 12,000 ft. on Mt. Goliath, Clear Creek County. **Summer in mountains:** July (year unknown), at timberline near Idaho Springs, Clear Creek County; several records in Rocky Mountain National Park.

Prothonotary Warbler

Protonotaria citrea

Occasional migrant in eastern Colorado.

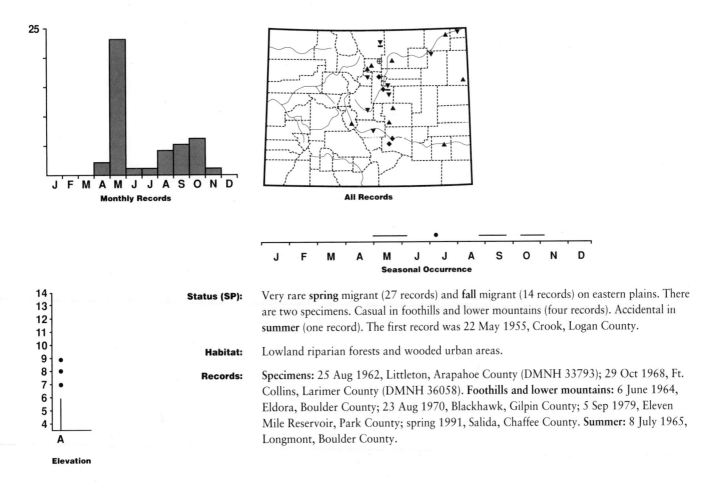

Monthly Records

All Records

Seasonal Occurrence

Elevation

Status (SP): Very rare **spring** migrant (27 records) and **fall** migrant (14 records) on eastern plains. There are two specimens. Casual in foothills and lower mountains (four records). Accidental in **summer** (one record). The first record was 22 May 1955, Crook, Logan County.

Habitat: Lowland riparian forests and wooded urban areas.

Records: Specimens: 25 Aug 1962, Littleton, Arapahoe County (DMNH 33793); 29 Oct 1968, Ft. Collins, Larimer County (DMNH 36058). **Foothills and lower mountains:** 6 June 1964, Eldora, Boulder County; 23 Aug 1970, Blackhawk, Gilpin County; 5 Sep 1979, Eleven Mile Reservoir, Park County; spring 1991, Salida, Chaffee County. **Summer:** 8 July 1965, Longmont, Boulder County.

Worm-eating Warbler
Helmitheros vermivorus

Occasional migrant in eastern Colorado.

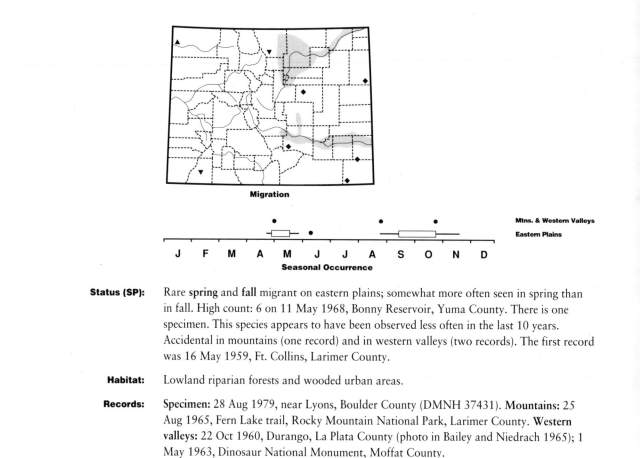

Migration

Mtns. & Western Valleys

Eastern Plains

J F M A M J J A S O N D

Seasonal Occurrence

Elevation

Status (SP):	Rare **spring** and **fall** migrant on eastern plains; somewhat more often seen in spring than in fall. High count: 6 on 11 May 1968, Bonny Reservoir, Yuma County. There is one specimen. This species appears to have been observed less often in the last 10 years. Accidental in mountains (one record) and in western valleys (two records). The first record was 16 May 1959, Ft. Collins, Larimer County.
Habitat:	Lowland riparian forests and wooded urban areas.
Records:	**Specimen:** 28 Aug 1979, near Lyons, Boulder County (DMNH 37431). **Mountains:** 25 Aug 1965, Fern Lake trail, Rocky Mountain National Park, Larimer County. **Western valleys:** 22 Oct 1960, Durango, La Plata County (photo in Bailey and Niedrach 1965); 1 May 1963, Dinosaur National Monument, Moffat County.

Swainson's Warbler
Limnothlypis swainsonii

Status (SP):	Casual **spring** migrant on eastern plains (four records*).
Records:	12 May 1913, Holly, Prowers County (DMNH 2806); 20–21 May 1975, Boulder, Boulder County; 17 May 1988, Colorado Springs State Wildlife Area, El Paso County; 27 May–8 June 1990, Ft. Collins, Larimer County (Howe and Leatherman 1991).
Habitat:	Lowland riparian forests.

Ovenbird
Seiurus aurocapillus

Migrant on eastern plains, and local summer resident in eastern foothills.

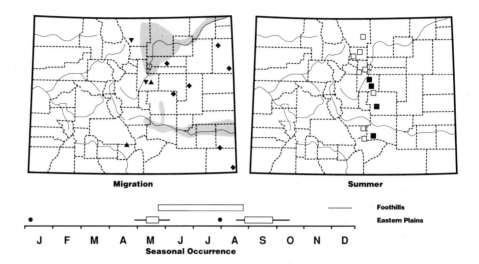

Migration   Summer

Foothills ....
Eastern Plains

J F M A M J J A S O N D
Seasonal Occurrence

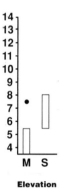

Elevation

Status (SP) (B): Rare **spring** and **fall** migrant on eastern plains. Accidental in lower mountains (two records). Rare to uncommon local **summer** resident in eastern foothills and lower mountains from southern Larimer County to northern Huerfano County; most records are from Jefferson and Douglas counties. Accidental in **winter** (one record*).

Habitat: Migrants occur in lowland riparian forests, shrublands, and wooded urban areas. Breeds in foothill riparian thickets, and in aspen or ponderosa pine forests with an understory of Gambel oak or other shrubs.

Records: **Migration in mountains:** 22 Nov–28 Dec 1970, Estes Park, Larimer County; recorded as a spring migrant at Great Sand Dunes National Monument, Alamosa County (Simmons 1986). **Winter*:** Jan 1982, Englewood, Arapahoe County (DMNH 37438).

Northern Waterthrush

Seiurus noveboracensis

Migrant at low elevations, mostly in eastern Colorado.

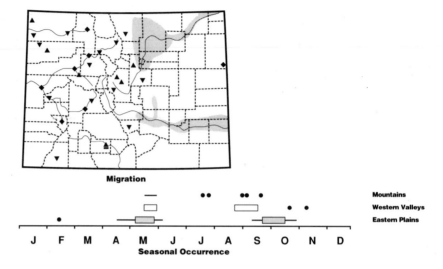

Migration

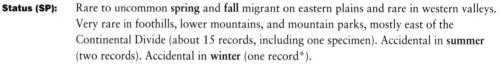

Mountains
Western Valleys
Eastern Plains

J F M A M J J A S O N D

Seasonal Occurrence

14		
13		
12		
11		
10		
9		
8		
7		
6		
5		
4		

M

Elevation

Status (SP): Rare to uncommon **spring** and **fall** migrant on eastern plains and rare in western valleys. Very rare in foothills, lower mountains, and mountain parks, mostly east of the Continental Divide (about 15 records, including one specimen). Accidental in **summer** (two records). Accidental in **winter** (one record*).

Habitat: Streambanks, lakeshores, and edges of marshes.

Records: **Mountain specimen:** 16 May 1950, Monte Vista, Rio Grande County (DMNH 26131). **Summer:** 25 July 1962, Rocky Mountain National Park (this record could be an early fall migrant); 16 July 1989, Arapaho National Wildlife Refuge, Jackson County. **Winter*:** 11 Feb 1973, Waterton, Douglas/Jefferson counties.

Louisiana Waterthrush

Seiurus motacilla

Status (SR): Accidental **spring** migrant (four records*) and **fall** migrant (one record*) on eastern plains. Zimmer (1985) and Kaufman (1990) provided information on the identification of waterthrushes.

Records: **Spring*:** 1–2 June 1975, Cottonwood Canyon, Baca County; 14 May 1977, 14–15 May 1983, and 20 May 1986, all at Bonny Reservoir, Yuma County. **Fall*:** 6 Sep 1989, near Walsh, Baca County.

Habitat: Streamsides and lakeshores.

Kentucky Warbler
Oporornis formosus

Occasional migrant in eastern Colorado.

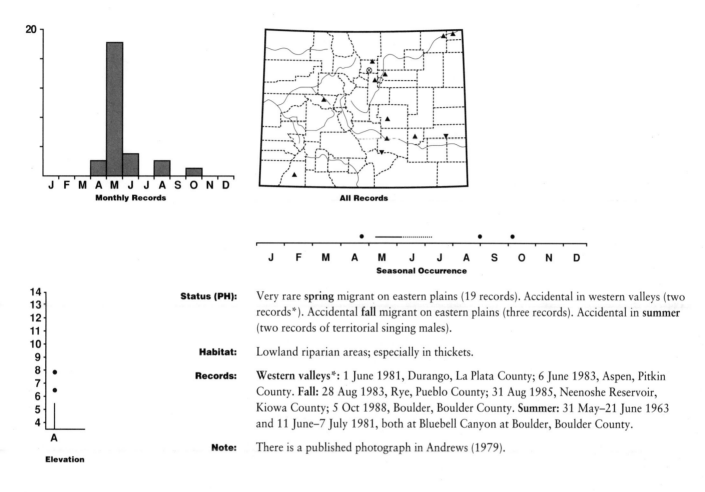

Monthly Records

All Records

Seasonal Occurrence

Elevation

Status (PH): Very rare **spring** migrant on eastern plains (19 records). Accidental in western valleys (two records*). Accidental **fall** migrant on eastern plains (three records). Accidental in **summer** (two records of territorial singing males).

Habitat: Lowland riparian areas; especially in thickets.

Records: Western valleys*: 1 June 1981, Durango, La Plata County; 6 June 1983, Aspen, Pitkin County. **Fall:** 28 Aug 1983, Rye, Pueblo County; 31 Aug 1985, Neenoshe Reservoir, Kiowa County; 5 Oct 1988, Boulder, Boulder County. **Summer:** 31 May–21 June 1963 and 11 June–7 July 1981, both at Bluebell Canyon at Boulder, Boulder County.

Note: There is a published photograph in Andrews (1979).

Connecticut Warbler
Oporornis agilis

Status (SP): Accidental **spring** migrant on eastern plains (two records*).

Records: 24 May 1899, Limon, Lincoln County (DMNH 26000); 24 May 1990, Ft. Lyon, Bent County. Observers should be cautious about identifying this species.

Habitat: Lowland riparian forests.

Mourning Warbler
Oporornis philadelphia

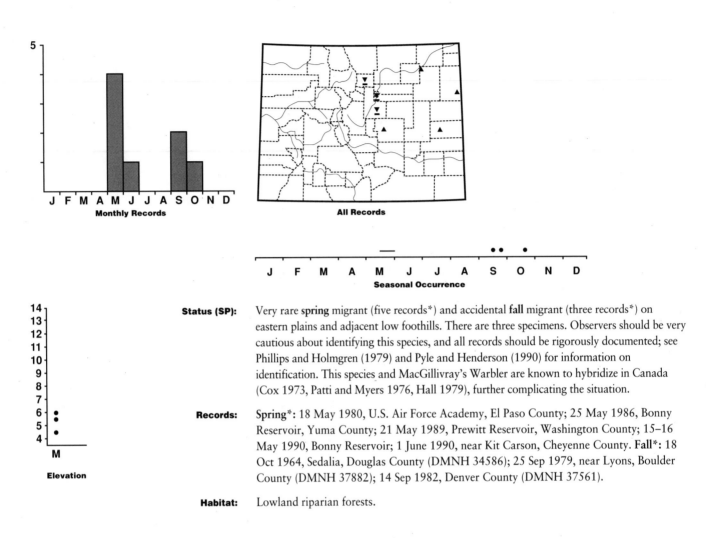

Monthly Records

All Records

Seasonal Occurrence

Elevation

Status (SP): Very rare **spring** migrant (five records*) and accidental **fall** migrant (three records*) on eastern plains and adjacent low foothills. There are three specimens. Observers should be very cautious about identifying this species, and all records should be rigorously documented; see Phillips and Holmgren (1979) and Pyle and Henderson (1990) for information on identification. This species and MacGillivray's Warbler are known to hybridize in Canada (Cox 1973, Patti and Myers 1976, Hall 1979), further complicating the situation.

Records: Spring*: 18 May 1980, U.S. Air Force Academy, El Paso County; 25 May 1986, Bonny Reservoir, Yuma County; 21 May 1989, Prewitt Reservoir, Washington County; 15–16 May 1990, Bonny Reservoir; 1 June 1990, near Kit Carson, Cheyenne County. **Fall**: 18 Oct 1964, Sedalia, Douglas County (DMNH 34586); 25 Sep 1979, near Lyons, Boulder County (DMNH 37882); 14 Sep 1982, Denver County (DMNH 37561).

Habitat: Lowland riparian forests.

MacGillivray's Warbler

Oporornis tolmiei

Summer resident in mountains, and migrant at lower elevations.

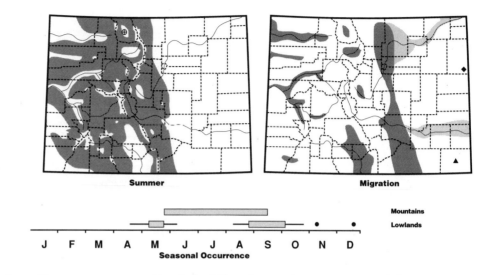

Seasonal Occurrence

Elevation

Status (SP) (B): Uncommon **summer** resident in foothills and mountains, most numerous in lower mountains; locally in mountain parks. Uncommon **spring** and **fall** migrant in western valleys, foothills, lower mountains, mountain parks, and on eastern plains near foothills; rare on extreme eastern plains. Accidental in **early winter** (one record*).

Habitat: Breeds in foothill and montane riparian shrublands, and aspen forests with shrubby understories, and sometimes in Gambel oak in moist ravines. In migration, riparian forests and shrublands, and wooded urban areas.

Record: Early winter*: 17 Dec 1979, Hotchkiss, Delta County.

Common Yellowthroat

Geothlypis trichas

Summary resident and migrant, mostly at low elevations.

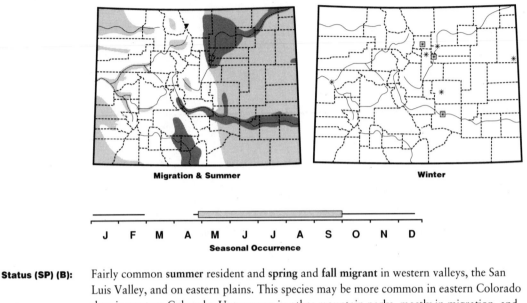

Migration & Summer   **Winter**

J F M A M J J A S O N D

Seasonal Occurrence

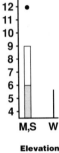

Elevation

Status (SP) (B):   Fairly common **summer** resident and **spring** and **fall migrant** in western valleys, the San Luis Valley, and on eastern plains. This species may be more common in eastern Colorado than in western Colorado. Uncommon in other mountain parks, mostly in migration, and rare in lower mountains and mountain parks (mostly in migration). Accidental in high mountains (one record). Casual **winter** resident on eastern plains, mostly near foothills and mostly in early winter (nine records); accidental in western valleys (one record).

Habitat: Cattail marshes and riparian shrublands.

Records: High mountains: 13 Sep 1939, at 12,000 ft. near Continental Divide in Rocky Mountain National Park (Packard 1946). **Early winter in western valleys:** 2 Dec 1989, Clifton, Mesa County.

Hooded Warbler
Wilsonia citrina

Occasional migrant in eastern Colorado.

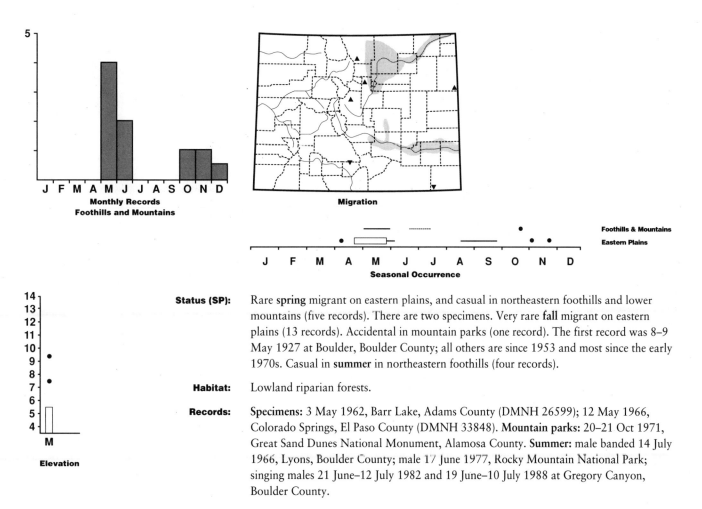

Monthly Records
Foothills and Mountains

Migration

Foothills & Mountains
Eastern Plains

Seasonal Occurrence

Elevation

Status (SP): Rare **spring** migrant on eastern plains, and casual in northeastern foothills and lower mountains (five records). There are two specimens. Very rare **fall** migrant on eastern plains (13 records). Accidental in mountain parks (one record). The first record was 8–9 May 1927 at Boulder, Boulder County; all others are since 1953 and most since the early 1970s. Casual in **summer** in northeastern foothills (four records).

Habitat: Lowland riparian forests.

Records: Specimens: 3 May 1962, Barr Lake, Adams County (DMNH 26599); 12 May 1966, Colorado Springs, El Paso County (DMNH 33848). **Mountain parks:** 20–21 Oct 1971, Great Sand Dunes National Monument, Alamosa County. **Summer:** male banded 14 July 1966, Lyons, Boulder County; male 17 June 1977, Rocky Mountain National Park; singing males 21 June–12 July 1982 and 19 June–10 July 1988 at Gregory Canyon, Boulder County.

Wilson's Warbler
Wilsonia pusilla

Summer resident in high mountains and migrant at lower elevations.

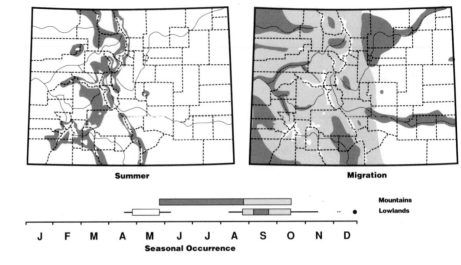

Summer   Migration

Mountains
Lowlands

J F M A M J J A S O N D
Seasonal Occurrence

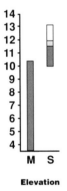

M S

Elevation

Status (SP) (B): Fairly common to common **summer** resident in higher mountains; locally in mountain parks. Common to abundant **fall** migrant and uncommon **spring** migrant in western valleys, foothills, mountains, mountain parks, and on eastern plains. In some areas, may be absent in spring.

Habitat: Breeds in willow thickets of lakeshores, streambanks, and wet meadows, and at or just above timberline. It is the most common breeding passerine in montane and subalpine willow shrublands in Boulder County (Hallock 1984) and probably elsewhere. In migration, riparian forests and shrublands and wooded urban areas and rarely in coniferous forests.

Canada Warbler
Wilsonia canadensis

Occasional migrant in eastern Colorado.

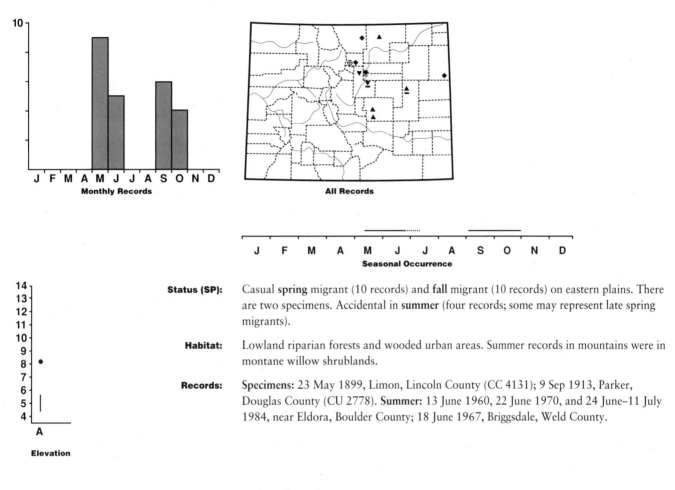

Monthly Records

All Records

Seasonal Occurrence

Elevation

Status (SP): Casual **spring** migrant (10 records) and **fall** migrant (10 records) on eastern plains. There are two specimens. Accidental in **summer** (four records; some may represent late spring migrants).

Habitat: Lowland riparian forests and wooded urban areas. Summer records in mountains were in montane willow shrublands.

Records: Specimens: 23 May 1899, Limon, Lincoln County (CC 4131); 9 Sep 1913, Parker, Douglas County (CU 2778). **Summer:** 13 June 1960, 22 June 1970, and 24 June–11 July 1984, near Eldora, Boulder County; 18 June 1967, Briggsdale, Weld County.

Painted Redstart
Myioborus pictus

Status (PH): Accidental **fall** migrant (three records*) on eastern plains, and accidental **spring** migrant (one record*) in western valleys.

Records: Fall*: 25 Oct–8 Nov 1958, Fountain Valley School, El Paso County; 16–22 Nov 1974, near Loveland, Larimer County (photos in RC files); 7–9 Sep 1987, Lake Hasty, Bent County. **Spring**: 26–31 May 1967, Hotchkiss, Delta County.

Habitat: Lowland riparian forests or wooded urban areas.

Yellow-breasted Chat
Icteria virens

Summer resident in foothills and locally on plains; migrant at lower elevations.

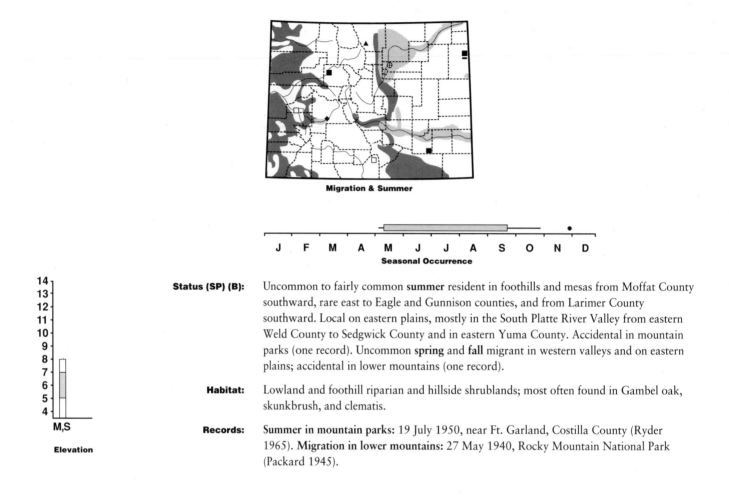

Migration & Summer

Seasonal Occurrence

J F M A M J J A S O N D

Elevation

M,S

14
13
12
11
10
9
8
7
6
5
4

Status (SP) (B): Uncommon to fairly common **summer** resident in foothills and mesas from Moffat County southward, rare east to Eagle and Gunnison counties, and from Larimer County southward. Local on eastern plains, mostly in the South Platte River Valley from eastern Weld County to Sedgwick County and in eastern Yuma County. Accidental in mountain parks (one record). Uncommon **spring** and **fall** migrant in western valleys and on eastern plains; accidental in lower mountains (one record).

Habitat: Lowland and foothill riparian and hillside shrublands; most often found in Gambel oak, skunkbrush, and clematis.

Records: **Summer in mountain parks:** 19 July 1950, near Ft. Garland, Costilla County (Ryder 1965). **Migration in lower mountains:** 27 May 1940, Rocky Mountain National Park (Packard 1945).

Order Passeriformes
Family Emberizidae

Subfamily Thraupinae

Hepatic Tanager
Piranga flava

Local summer resident in southeastern Colorado.

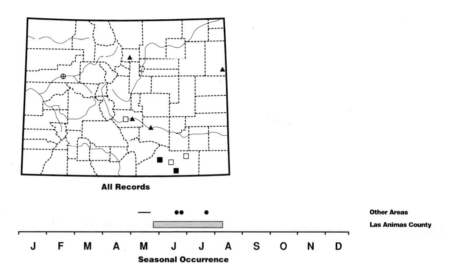

All Records

Other Areas
Las Animas County

J F M A M J J A S O N D
Seasonal Occurrence

Status (SR) (B): Uncommon and very local **summer** resident in central and eastern Las Animas County. It was first found there in 1978 on Mesa de Maya, and was recorded breeding starting in 1980. Breeding was suspected or confirmed in 1989 and 1990 near Kim and at Piñon Canyon (Anonymous 1990, Kingery 1990a). It was seen in 1989 and suspected of breeding in 1990 at Royal Gorge, Fremont County. There are several records of birds in May at Canyon City, Fremont County and at Pueblo, Pueblo County; these were probably birds migrating into their breeding areas. Further field work in southeastern Colorado will undoubtedly reveal additional breeding locations. Accidental in western foothills (one record*).

Accidental in **spring** on northeastern plains (two records*).

Habitat: Breeds in ponderosa pine or ponderosa pine/piñon-juniper forests. Migrants also may occur in lowland riparian forests.

Records: **Western valleys***: pair 21 July 1973, Parachute Creek, Garfield County; no breeding activity was observed, and there have been no subsequent records there; this was the first state record. **Northeastern plains***: 9 May 1977, Boulder, Boulder County; 15 May 1982, Bonny Reservoir, Yuma County.

Elevation

14
13
12
11
10
9
8
7
6
5
4

A

Summer Tanager

Piranga rubra

Migrant at low elevations, mostly in eastern Colorado.

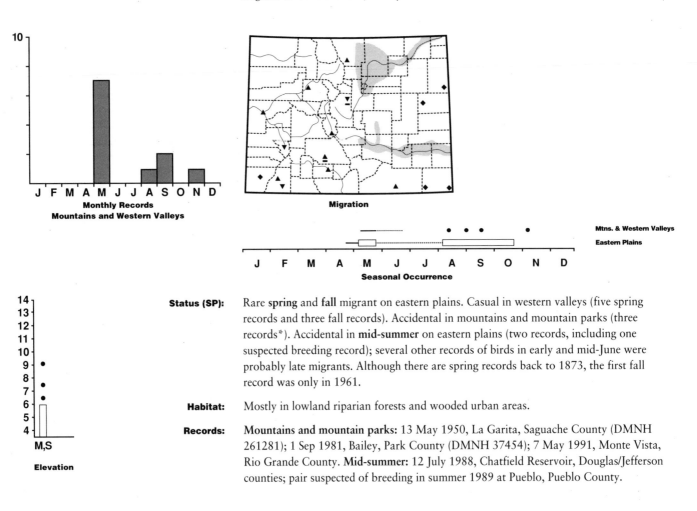

Monthly Records
Mountains and Western Valleys

Migration

Mtns. & Western Valleys

Eastern Plains

Seasonal Occurrence

Elevation

Status (SP): Rare **spring** and **fall** migrant on eastern plains. Casual in western valleys (five spring records and three fall records). Accidental in mountains and mountain parks (three records*). Accidental in **mid-summer** on eastern plains (two records, including one suspected breeding record); several other records of birds in early and mid-June were probably late migrants. Although there are spring records back to 1873, the first fall record was only in 1961.

Habitat: Mostly in lowland riparian forests and wooded urban areas.

Records: **Mountains and mountain parks:** 13 May 1950, La Garita, Saguache County (DMNH 261281); 1 Sep 1981, Bailey, Park County (DMNH 37454); 7 May 1991, Monte Vista, Rio Grande County. **Mid-summer:** 12 July 1988, Chatfield Reservoir, Douglas/Jefferson counties; pair suspected of breeding in summer 1989 at Pueblo, Pueblo County.

Scarlet Tanager
Piranga olivacea

Migrant on eastern plains.

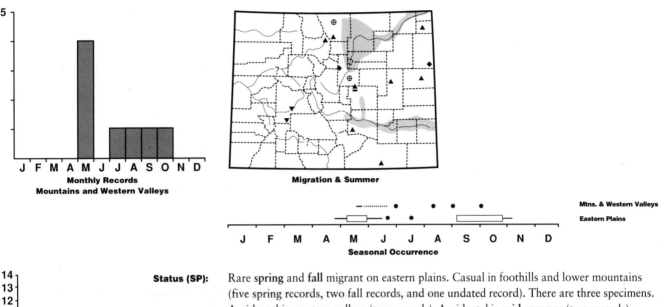

Monthly Records
Mountains and Western Valleys

Migration & Summer

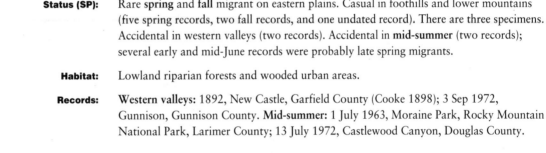

Mtns. & Western Valleys

Eastern Plains

Seasonal Occurrence

Elevation

Status (SP): Rare **spring** and **fall** migrant on eastern plains. Casual in foothills and lower mountains (five spring records, two fall records, and one undated record). There are three specimens. Accidental in western valleys (two records). Accidental in **mid-summer** (two records); several early and mid-June records were probably late spring migrants.

Habitat: Lowland riparian forests and wooded urban areas.

Records: **Western valleys:** 1892, New Castle, Garfield County (Cooke 1898); 3 Sep 1972, Gunnison, Gunnison County. **Mid-summer:** 1 July 1963, Moraine Park, Rocky Mountain National Park, Larimer County; 13 July 1972, Castlewood Canyon, Douglas County.

Western Tanager
Piranga ludoviciana

Summer resident in foothills and mountains and migrant in lowlands.

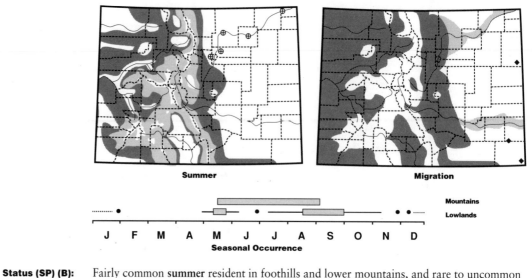

Summer | Migration

Mountains
Lowlands

J F M A M J J A S O N D
Seasonal Occurrence

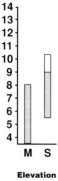

Elevation

Status (SP) (B): Fairly common **summer** resident in foothills and lower mountains, and rare to uncommon locally in higher mountains. Casual on eastern plains, mostly near foothills (seven records). Fairly common **spring** and **fall** migrant in western valleys, foothills, mountain parks, and on eastern plains near foothills. Uncommon on extreme eastern plains in southeastern Colorado and rare in northeastern Colorado. High count: 290+ on 20 May 1979, Chatfield Reservoir, Douglas/Jefferson counties. Accidental in **mid-winter** (two records) and several early winter records in Dec.

Habitat: Breeds most commonly in ponderosa pine and Douglas-fir forests. Also occurs regularly in Gambel oak shrublands, especially those with trees, and in piñon-juniper woodlands and aspen forests. Generally rare in spruce-fir forests, but locally may occur regularly. In migration, lowland riparian forests and wooded urban areas.

Records: Mid-winter: 16 Dec 1960–18 Jan 1961, Boulder, Boulder County; 30 Jan 1983, Monument, El Paso County.

Order Passeriformes
Family Emberizidae

Subfamily Cardinalinae

Northern Cardinal
Cardinalis cardinalis

Occasional year round, mostly in migration and winter, in eastern Colorado.

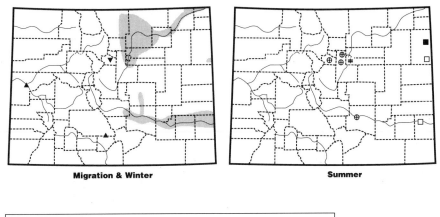

Migration & Winter   Summer

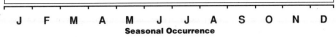

J F M A M J J A S O N D
Seasonal Occurrence

Elevation

Status (SP) (B): Rare on eastern plains, with records in all months but mostly in fall, winter, and spring. High count: 12 on 12 Mar 1983, Orchard, Morgan County. Accidental in mountains and mountain parks (three records) and in western valleys (one record). There are two specimens. There are four confirmed and two probable **breeding** records.

Habitat: Lowland riparian forests and wooded urban areas.

Records: **Specimens:** 5 Dec 1883, Denver County (DMNH 2581); 23 May 1953, Dry Willow Creek, Yuma County (DMNH 26733). **Mountains:** 10 July 1963, Bergen Park, Jefferson County; 5 May 1977, Great Sand Dunes National Monument, Alamosa County; 17 July 1989, Echo Lake, Clear Creek County (Brockner 1989) and probably the same bird 1 Oct–12 Nov 1989, Georgetown, Clear Creek County. **Western valleys:** 27–28 May 1962, Grand Junction, Mesa County; Davis (1969) thought this bird may have been an escape. **Breeding:** pair nested 1924–1926, Littleton, Arapahoe County (Bergtold 1927b); five pairs probably breeding in 1980 at Wray and Laird, Yuma County; pair nested 1982 at Wray; may also nest elsewhere such as at Pueblo, Pueblo County and Holly, Prowers County.

Pyrrhuloxia
Cardinalis sinuatus

Status (PH): Accidental in **early winter** on eastern plains (one record*).

Record: 17–20 Dec 1989, near Holly, Prowers County (Janos 1991); photos are on file with the RC.

Rose-breasted Grosbeak
Pheucticus ludovicianus

Migrant, mostly in eastern Colorado but occasionally elsewhere.

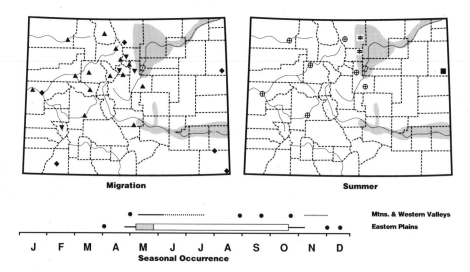

Migration   Summer

Mtns. & Western Valleys

Eastern Plains

J F M A M J J A S O N D

Seasonal Occurrence

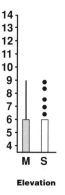

Elevation

M S

Status (SP) (B): Rare to uncommon **spring** migrant on eastern plains and rare in western valleys. Rare in low foothills adjacent to eastern foothills. Very rare in higher foothills and lower mountains (17 records). Rare **fall** migrant on eastern plains and accidental in western valleys (three records) and in lower mountains (two records).

Rare nonbreeding **summer** resident on eastern plains and casual in foothills and lower mountains (five records) and in western valleys (five records). Most summer records are of males, often singing and territorial but usually unmated. There are three confirmed **breeding** records. Accidental in **early winter** (two records*).

This species has become more frequent in Colorado in recent years. In exceptional springs, as many as 135 birds have been reported. The first western Colorado record was 27 May 1962, Grand Junction, Mesa County.

Habitat: Primarily lowland riparian forests and wooded urban areas.

Records: **Fall in western valleys:** 21 Sep 1983, Durango, La Plata County; 9 Nov–2 Dec 1983, Ridgway, Ouray County; 30 Aug 1990, Whitewater, Mesa County. **Fall in mountains:** 22 Oct 1980, Estes Park, Larimer County; 24 Sep 1989, Nederland, Boulder County. **Confirmed breeding:** 1894, Longmont, Boulder County (Cooke 1898); 1924, Loveland, Larimer County (Bailey and Niedrach 1965); pair with recently fledged young 30 July 1974, Bonny Reservoir, Yuma County (Hutchinson 1974). **Early winter*:** 17 Dec 1977, Littleton, Arapahoe County; Dec 1990, Hygiene, Boulder County.

Black-headed Grosbeak

Pheucticus melanocephalus

Summer resident, mostly in foothills, and migrant at low elevations.

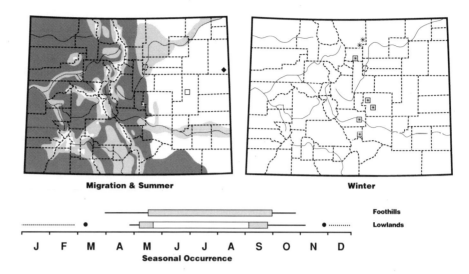

Migration & Summer **Winter**

Foothills
Lowlands

J F M A M J J A S O N D
Seasonal Occurrence

14
13
12
11
10
9
8
7
6
5
4
M,S

Elevation

Status (SP) (B): Fairly common **summer** resident in foothills and lower mountains and rare in higher mountains. Rare in lower western valleys and on eastern plains, mostly near foothills but recorded east to Logan and Lincoln counties. Uncommon **spring** and **fall** migrant in western valleys and on eastern plains near foothills and rare on extreme eastern plains. Rare migrant in mountain parks. Casual in **early winter** in eastern foothill canyons and adjacent plains, Larimer County south to Custer County (seven records); accidental in **mid-winter** (two records).

Habitat: Breeds primarily in ponderosa pine, aspen, and foothill riparian forests, piñon-juniper woodlands, and in Gambel oak shrublands, especially with scattered trees. Much less frequent in lowland riparian forests and spruce-fir forests. In migration, mostly lowland riparian forests and wooded urban areas.

Records: Mid-winter: 1 Dec 1980–28 Feb 1981, Berthoud, Larimer County; 28–30 Jan 1980, Big Thompson Canyon, Larimer County.

Note: There are four sight records of males that appear to be hybrid Rose-breasted X Black-headed Grosbeaks: 2–12 Oct 1975, Four Mile Canyon, Boulder County; 22 May 1976, Boulder, Boulder County; 27 Oct 1979, Durango, La Plata County; hybrid male with female Black-headed Grosbeak at nest 30 May 1983, Tamarack Ranch, Logan County.

Blue Grosbeak

Guiraca caerulea

Summer resident, most common in southeastern Colorado.

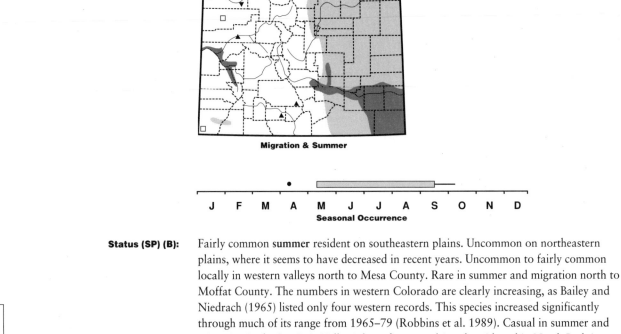

Migration & Summer

J F M A M J J A S O N D

Seasonal Occurrence

Elevation

Status (SP) (B): Fairly common **summer** resident on southeastern plains. Uncommon on northeastern plains, where it seems to have decreased in recent years. Uncommon to fairly common locally in western valleys north to Mesa County. Rare in summer and migration north to Moffat County. The numbers in western Colorado are clearly increasing, as Bailey and Niedrach (1965) listed only four western records. This species increased significantly through much of its range from 1965–79 (Robbins et al. 1989). Casual in summer and migration in the San Luis Valley (about five records) and accidental in North Park in spring and summer (USFWS 1990).

Habitat: Breeds in brushy and weedy edges in agricultural areas and at edges of riparian forests, and in semidesert shrublands. Frequently found in tamarisk, and appears to be one of the main users of that introduced shrub. Rare in grasslands or piñon-juniper woodlands.

Lazuli Bunting

Passerina amoena

Summer resident, mostly in foothills and occasional in lowlands.

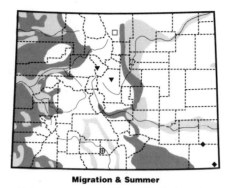

Migration & Summer

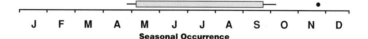

J F M A M J J A S O N D

Seasonal Occurrence

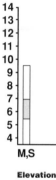

M,S

Elevation

Status (SP) (B): Fairly common **summer** resident in mesas and foothills from Moffat County southward and east to southwestern Grand County, and from Larimer County southward and east to southwestern Baca County. Rare to uncommon in western valleys and on eastern plains near foothills and rare on extreme eastern plains. Rare in lower mountains, mostly in migration. A few occur in summer in the foothills around the San Luis Valley (Ryder 1965, Simmons 1986), but accidental in valley proper (one record). Uncommon to fairly common **spring** and **fall** migrant in western valleys and on eastern plains, mostly near foothills.

Habitat: Breeds most commonly in Gambel oak shrublands, but also in other hillside shrublands (mountain mahogany, serviceberry, etc.), lowland and foothill riparian forests and shrublands, brushy meadows, sage shrublands, and in piñon-juniper woodlands; in all habitats requires low shrubs. In migration, in wooded or brushy areas.

Record: **San Luis Valley:** June 1991, Alamosa National Wildlife Refuge, Alamosa County.

Lazuli X Indigo Bunting hybrids

Passerina amoena X *cyanea*

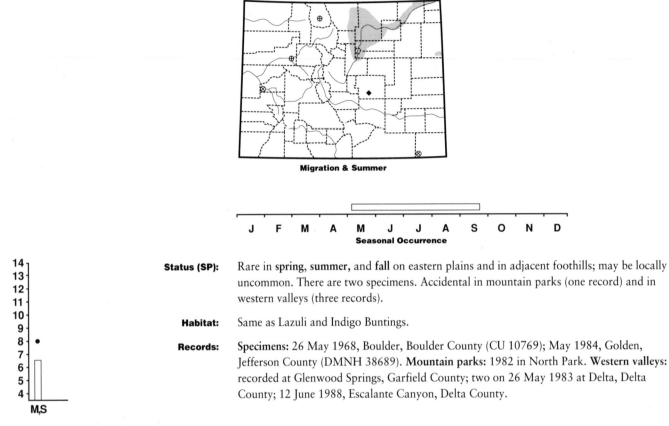

Migration & Summer

J F M A M J J A S O N D

Seasonal Occurrence

Elevation

Status (SP): Rare in **spring, summer,** and **fall** on eastern plains and in adjacent foothills; may be locally uncommon. There are two specimens. Accidental in mountain parks (one record) and in western valleys (three records).

Habitat: Same as Lazuli and Indigo Buntings.

Records: **Specimens:** 26 May 1968, Boulder, Boulder County (CU 10769); May 1984, Golden, Jefferson County (DMNH 38689). **Mountain parks:** 1982 in North Park. **Western valleys:** recorded at Glenwood Springs, Garfield County; two on 26 May 1983 at Delta, Delta County; 12 June 1988, Escalante Canyon, Delta County.

Indigo Bunting
Passerina cyanea

Migrant and summer resident at low elevations, mostly in eastern Colorado.

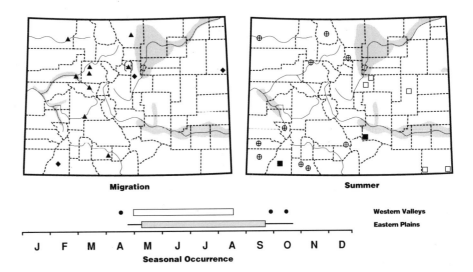

Migration   Summer

Western Valleys

Eastern Plains

J F M A M J J A S O N D

Seasonal Occurrence

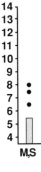

Elevation

Status (SP) (B): Rare to uncommon **spring** and **fall** migrant on eastern plains and rare in western valleys, east to Eagle and Gunnison counties. High count: 12 on 18 May 1985, Colorado Springs State Wildlife Area, El Paso County. Casual in foothills, lower mountains, and mountain parks (five records).

Rare to uncommon local **summer** resident on eastern plains and in western valleys. In western Colorado, it is uncommon locally in Mesa, Delta, and Montrose counties, and rare north to Moffat County, east to Eagle County, and south to Archuleta County. Breeding has been confirmed in western Colorado only at Durango, La Plata County (Durango Bird Club 1988). Accidental in mountains (three records).

This species has been extending its range westward. Although it has been recorded in eastern Colorado since the 1870s, it was not confirmed as a breeder until 1953 (Baily 1954). It was first recorded in the mountains in 1967 and in the western valleys in 1969 (Davis 1970).

Habitat: Riparian forest edges, brushy meadows, thickets, fencerows, and edges of agricultural fields.

Records: **Summer in mountains:** recorded in summer at Great Sand Dunes National Monument, Alamosa County (Simmons 1986); June 1988, Arapaho National Wildlife Refuge, Jackson County; 16 June 1991, Eldora, Boulder County.

Painted Bunting
Passerina ciris

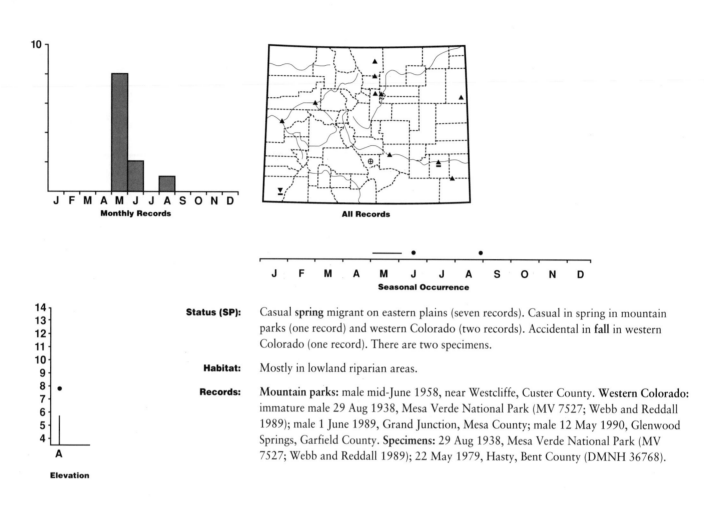

Monthly Records

All Records

Seasonal Occurrence

Elevation

Status (SP): Casual **spring** migrant on eastern plains (seven records). Casual in spring in mountain parks (one record) and western Colorado (two records). Accidental in **fall** in western Colorado (one record). There are two specimens.

Habitat: Mostly in lowland riparian areas.

Records: **Mountain parks:** male mid-June 1958, near Westcliffe, Custer County. **Western Colorado:** immature male 29 Aug 1938, Mesa Verde National Park (MV 7527; Webb and Reddall 1989); male 1 June 1989, Grand Junction, Mesa County; male 12 May 1990, Glenwood Springs, Garfield County. **Specimens:** 29 Aug 1938, Mesa Verde National Park (MV 7527; Webb and Reddall 1989); 22 May 1979, Hasty, Bent County (DMNH 36768).

Dickcissel

Spiza americana

Irregular summer resident, mostly in extreme eastern Colorado.

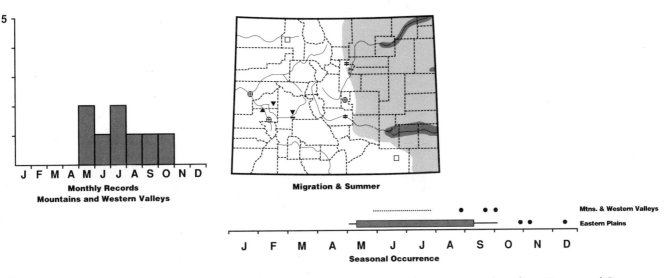

Migration & Summer

Mtns. & Western Valleys
Eastern Plains

Seasonal Occurrence

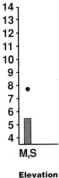

Monthly Records
Mountains and Western Valleys

Elevation

Status (SP) (B): Irregular rare to common **summer** resident on eastern plains from Morgan and Otero counties eastward, and rare and very local west to base of the foothills, primarily in summer but occasionally in migration. Numbers of this species are very irregular; it may be common at a site in one year but rare or absent in other years. There were a number of breeding records on the northeastern plains near the foothills from the 1890s until the 1950s (Alexander 1937, Bailey and Niedrach 1965), but fewer in recent years. Accidental in summer in lower mountains (one record) and western valleys (three records). Breeding has not been confirmed in western Colorado, but the species may breed very locally (Martin et al. 1974); if confirmed in western Colorado, it would be the westernmost breeding location for this species. Casual in migration in western valleys (four records, including one specimen).

Habitat: Breeds most often in alfalfa and clover fields, but also occurs in other types of croplands, meadows, grasslands (especially tall-grass), and in tamarisk.

Records: **Summer in mountains:** 22 June 1981, Manitou Lake, Teller County. **Summer in western valleys:** 10 July 1926, Montrose, Montrose County (McCrimmon 1926); three singing males in an alfalfa field 3 July 1973, Hayden, Routt County (Martin et al. 1974); late May–24 July 1985, Clifton, Mesa County. **Migration in western valleys:** 18 Sep 1956, Gunnison, Gunnison County (DMNH 36718); 4 Oct 1957, Gunnison; 28 Aug 1966, Hotchkiss, Delta County; 27 May 1984, Olathe, Montrose County.

Note: The National Audubon Society considers this species to be of special concern (Tate 1986) due to widespread population declines (Robbins et al. 1986).

Order Passeriformes
Family Emberizidae

Subfamily Emberizinae

Green-tailed Towhee
Pipilo chlorurus

Summer resident in foothills and migrant in lowlands; occasional in winter.

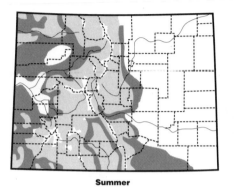

Summer

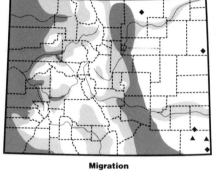

Migration

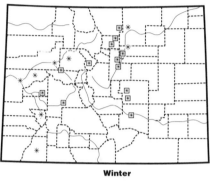

Winter

Foothills

Lowlands

J F M A M J J A S O N D

Seasonal Occurrence

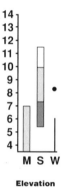

Elevation

Status (SP) (B): Fairly common to common **summer** resident in mesas, foothills, and lower mountains statewide. It is especially numerous on the mesas and foothills of western Colorado. Rare locally in higher mountains to timberline, mostly in late summer.

Fairly common to common **spring** and **fall** migrant in western valleys, foothills, mountain parks, and on eastern plains near foothills; rare on extreme eastern plains. Rare in late summer and early fall in higher mountains to timberline (Packard 1946). In California, juveniles dispersed in late summer to subalpine meadows to complete their molting and to fatten before migrating, especially in dry years (Morton 1991). Such postbreeding dispersal may account for most high elevation records in Colorado for this and many other low elevation species.

Rare **winter** resident in low foothills and adjacent valleys and plains. In western Colorado, it is found from Mesa and Eagle Counties southward, east to Gunnison County, and in eastern Colorado mostly from El Paso County southward, but also north to southern Larimer and western Weld counties.

Habitat: Breeds most commonly in dry, hillside shrublands (Gambel oak, mountain mahogany, serviceberry, sagebrush), and also in riparian shrublands and piñon-juniper woodlands. Migrant in wooded or brushy riparian and urban areas and shrublands.

Rufous-sided Towhee
Pipilo erythrophthalmus

The two field-identifiable forms are treated separately.

Eastern (unspotted) form

Rare resident in extreme eastern Colorado.

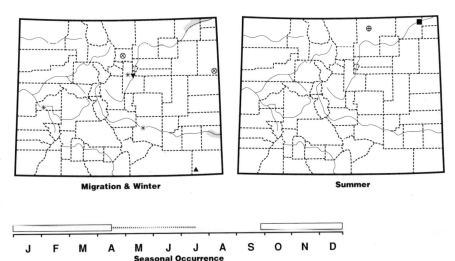

Migration & Winter   Summer

J F M A M J J A S O N D
Seasonal Occurrence

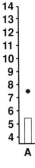

Elevation

Status (SP) (B): Rare to uncommon **resident** on extreme eastern plains, primarily along the South Platte River in Logan and Sedgwick counties and in eastern Yuma County. A few also occur in the Arkansas River Valley from Otero County eastward. Most records are in spring and fall, but this form does breed and there are a few winter records. Intergrades between the spotted and unspotted forms also occur in northeastern Colorado. This species bears study in extreme northeastern Colorado where the two forms overlap as this may help resolve the taxonomic relationship between them (J. V. Remsen, pers. comm.). Very rare west to the base of the foothills, mostly in spring and fall (five records), but also in winter (two records) and summer (one record). There is one specimen. Accidental in mountains (one record) and in western valleys (one record).

Habitat: Lowland riparian forests and shrublands.

Records: Specimen: 24 Sep 1944, Boulder, Boulder County (CU 4282). **Mountains:** 19 Dec 1977–mid May 1978, Conifer, Jefferson County. **Western valleys:** 6 Feb 1983, Delta, Delta County.

Western (spotted) form

Summer resident in foothills and migrant in lowlands; winters mostly in southern half of state.

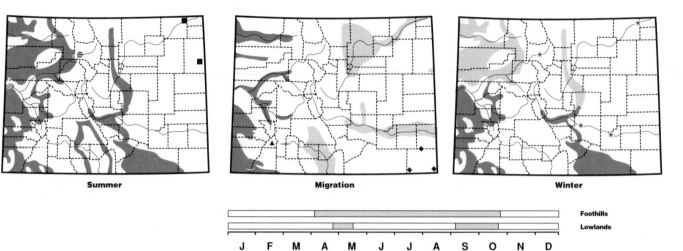

Summer   Migration   Winter

Foothills
Lowlands

J F M A M J J A S O N D
Seasonal Occurrence

Elevation

M S W

Status (SP) (B): Fairly common to common **summer** resident in foothills, and rare in lower mountains. Found in the foothills around the periphery of the San Luis Valley and rarely in southwestern Grand County, but absent from other mountain parks. Also occurs locally in valleys and plains immediately adjacent to foothills. Rare to uncommon locally on eastern plains, mostly along the South Platte River in Logan and Sedgwick counties and in eastern Yuma County.

Winter resident in foothills, fairly common to common in southern Colorado and rare to uncommon in northern Colorado; very rare in lower mountains. Some individuals move into valleys and plains adjacent to lower foothills and very rarely up to 15 mi. from foothills. Accidental on extreme eastern plains (two records) and in mountain parks (one record). Fairly common **spring** and **fall** migrant in western valleys and on eastern plains; rare in lower mountains and mountain parks.

Habitat: Breeds in hillside shrublands (especially Gambel oak) and shrubby pinyon-juniper woodlands. On the eastern plains, breeds in riparian shrublands. In migration, shrublands and wooded riparian and urban areas.

Records: **Winter on extreme eastern plains:** 19 Feb 1979, Rocky Ford, Otero County; 3 Jan 1988, Crook, Logan County. **Winter in mountain parks:** once near Granby, Grand County (D. Jasper, pers. comm.).

Reference: Shier (1967).

Canyon Towhee
Pipilo fuscus

Resident in southeastern foothills.

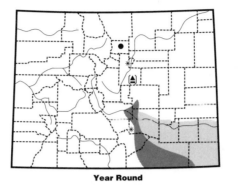

Year Round

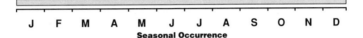

| J | F | M | A | M | J | J | A | S | O | N | D |

Seasonal Occurrence

14
13
12
11
10
9
8
7
6
5
4

A

Elevation

Status (SP) (B): Fairly common **resident** on southeastern mesas and foothills from southern El Paso County southward and east to southwestern Baca County. Rare on southeastern plains along the Arkansas River, mostly in fall and winter. There were numerous reports around Lyons, Boulder County from the 1960s until the mid-1980s, with records in all seasons, perhaps indicating there was a small disjunct breeding population in that area. There seem to have been no records at that site in the last few years. Accidental elsewhere in northeastern foothills (two records).

There have been a number of reports of this species in the foothills of the San Luis Valley and in the western foothills north to Mesa County. None of these records have been documented, and the status of this species in those areas remains unknown. Any observations away from southeastern Colorado should be documented.

Habitat: Piñon-juniper woodlands and shrublands; rarely cholla grasslands.

Records: **Northeastern foothills:** May 1930, Douglas County; 23 Dec 1961, Morrison, Jefferson County.

Note: Formerly known as Brown Towhee.

Cassin's Sparrow
Aimophila cassinii

Summer resident on eastern plains, most common in southeast; numbers irregular.

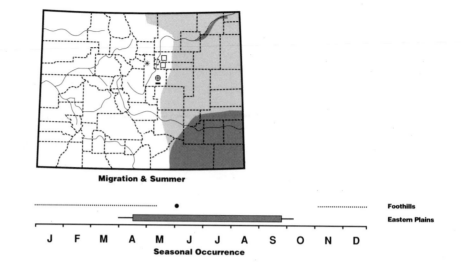

Migration & Summer

Foothills

Eastern Plains

J F M A M J J A S O N D

Seasonal Occurrence

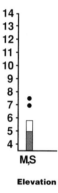

Elevation

Status (SP) (B): Common to abundant **summer** resident on southeastern plains, mostly Otero and central Las Animas counties eastward, and locally west to base of the foothills. High count: 300 on 27 May 1988, Cimarron River area, Baca County. Irregular on the northeastern plains, with abundance varying widely from year to year and site to site. In favorable years, it may be fairly common to common and widespread, while in other years it is much more local, and may be rare or even absent in some areas. The most important area is along the south side of the South Platte River from Morgan to Sedgwick counties. Very locally west to base of the foothills. High count: 50 on 28 May 1977, Pawnee National Grassland, Weld County. Wherever this species occurs, its numbers are irregular, perhaps in relation to rainfall. The species is often absent during years when good rainfall promotes tall grass growth.

Accidental in eastern foothills in summer and **winter** (two records*). There are several undocumented records in the San Luis Valley; observers should be alert for this species in that area, and should document any observations.

Habitat: Breeds primarily in rabbitbrush and sandsage grasslands; avoids both pure grasslands that lack shrubs and shrublands that lack grass (Faanes et al. 1979).

Records: Eastern foothills*: 4 June 1916, 7,000 ft. in Garber Canyon, near Sedalia, Douglas County (CU 2609); 5 Nov 1970–13 May 1971, Evergreen, Jefferson County.

References: Kingery and Julian (1971), Hubbard (1977).

Rufous-crowned Sparrow

Aimophila ruficeps

Resident in mesas of southeastern Colorado.

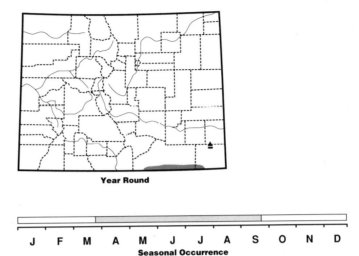

Year Round

J F M A M J J A S O N D

Seasonal Occurrence

Status (SP) (B): Uncommon **resident** in mesas of southern Las Animas and southwestern Baca counties; also recorded at Two Buttes Reservoir, northern Baca County. It may be less common in winter than in summer, but it is less conspicuous in winter, which obscures its true winter status. There are a number of undocumented reports of this species outside its range. This species seems to be quite sedentary, and all out-of-range records need to be carefully documented.

Habitat: Dry, rocky, hillside shrublands.

14
13
12
11
10
9
8
7
6
5
4

A

Elevation

American Tree Sparrow
Spizella arborea

Winter resident, mostly at lower elevations; most common in eastern Colorado.

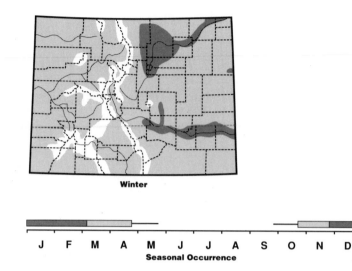

Winter

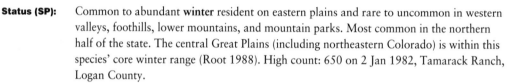

J F M A M J J A S O N D

Seasonal Occurrence

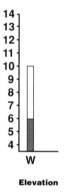

W

Elevation

Status (SP): Common to abundant **winter** resident on eastern plains and rare to uncommon in western valleys, foothills, lower mountains, and mountain parks. Most common in the northern half of the state. The central Great Plains (including northeastern Colorado) is within this species' core winter range (Root 1988). High count: 650 on 2 Jan 1982, Tamarack Ranch, Logan County.

Habitat: Open lowland riparian forests and shrublands, weedy fields, agricultural areas, and windbreaks; rarely in coniferous and aspen forests.

Chipping Sparrow
Spizella passerina

Summer resident in foothills and mountains and migrant throughout Colorado.

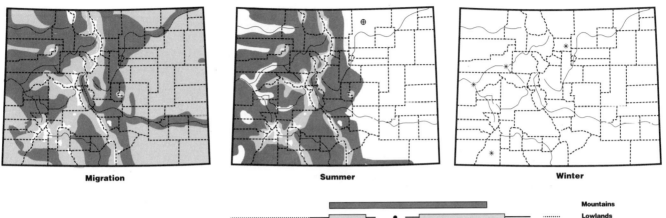

Migration	Summer	Winter

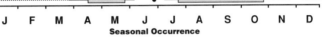

Mountains
Lowlands

J F M A M J J A S O N D

Seasonal Occurrence

Elevation

14
13
12
11
10
9
8
7
6
5
4

M S W

Status (SP) (B): Common **summer** resident in foothills and lower mountains. Rare and local in western valleys, and in higher mountains. Migrating juveniles often appear on the eastern plains in early and mid-July, and this may give the impression that the species nested there. There appear to be no confirmed breeding records on the eastern plains, in spite of statements to the contrary (Bailey and Niedrach 1965). Most records in the higher mountains are in late summer, and are probably due to postbreeding dispersal, but it may breed in small numbers at high elevations. Fairly common to abundant **spring** and **fall** migrant in western valleys, foothills, and on eastern plains, and rare to uncommon in mountains to timberline.

Casual **winter** resident at low elevations (four records*). There are 40+ winter reports of as many as 85 individuals per day. Unfortunately, most of these reports are undocumented, and there are no winter specimens. This species is almost entirely restricted to areas south of 35°N in the interior of the southwestern United States and the southern Great Plains (Root 1988); Colorado's southern border is 37°N. All winter sightings of this species should be made carefully and thoroughly documented. At best, this species is very rare in Colorado in winter.

Habitat: Breeds most commonly in ponderosa pine forests, but also in riparian and piñon-juniper woodlands and shrublands. May also occur occasionally in Douglas-fir, lodgepole pine, aspen, or spruce-fir forests, especially adjacent to meadows. In migration, also in weedy fields, agricultural areas, grasslands, and urban areas.

Records: **Winter***: Feb–Mar 1975, Grand Junction, Mesa County; 1–28 Jan 1982, Durango, La Plata County; 1–6 Jan 1984, Glenwood Springs, Garfield County; 7 Dec 1989–14 Apr 1990, Boulder, Boulder County (photo in RC files).

Clay-colored Sparrow
Spizella pallida

Migrant on eastern plains; most common along eastern border.

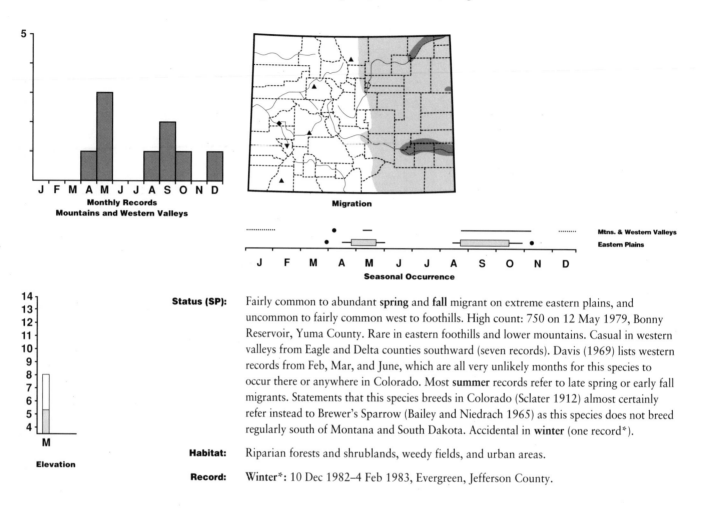

Monthly Records
Mountains and Western Valleys

Migration

Seasonal Occurrence

Mtns. & Western Valleys
Eastern Plains

Elevation

Status (SP): Fairly common to abundant **spring** and **fall** migrant on extreme eastern plains, and uncommon to fairly common west to foothills. High count: 750 on 12 May 1979, Bonny Reservoir, Yuma County. Rare in eastern foothills and lower mountains. Casual in western valleys from Eagle and Delta counties southward (seven records). Davis (1969) lists western records from Feb, Mar, and June, which are all very unlikely months for this species to occur there or anywhere in Colorado. Most **summer** records refer to late spring or early fall migrants. Statements that this species breeds in Colorado (Sclater 1912) almost certainly refer instead to Brewer's Sparrow (Bailey and Niedrach 1965) as this species does not breed regularly south of Montana and South Dakota. Accidental in **winter** (one record*).

Habitat: Riparian forests and shrublands, weedy fields, and urban areas.

Record: Winter*: 10 Dec 1982–4 Feb 1983, Evergreen, Jefferson County.

Brewer's Sparrow

Spizella breweri

Summer resident, most common in western Colorado and in mountain parks, and migrant at low elevations.

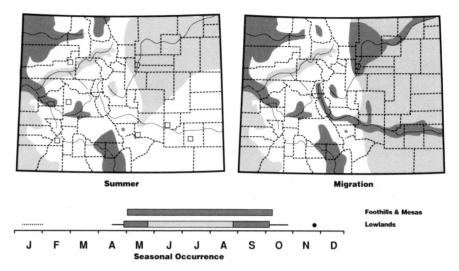

Summer   Migration

Foothills & Mesas

Lowlands

J F M A M J J A S O N D

Seasonal Occurrence

14
13
12
11
10
9
8
7
6
5
4

M,S

Elevation

Status (SP) (B):   Common summer resident on mesas and foothills of western Colorado, and local in lower mountains. Locally uncommon to common on eastern plains (mostly northeastern) and in lower foothills. Fairly common to common in North and Middle Parks and the San Luis Valley; rare in South Park. Local in higher mountains to timberline; primarily in western Colorado. Fairly common to common spring and fall migrant in western valleys, foothills, mountain parks, and on eastern plains near foothills; rare to uncommon on extreme eastern plains and in mountains. Accidental in winter (one record*).

Habitat: Breeds primarily in sagebrush shrublands, but also other shrublands such as mountain mahogany or rabbitbrush. In migration, wooded, brushy and weedy riparian, agricultural, and urban areas.

Record: Winter*: 9 Jan–2 Feb 1985, near Delta, Delta County.

Field Sparrow
Spizella pusilla

Migrant and summer resident along eastern border, and occasionally farther west.

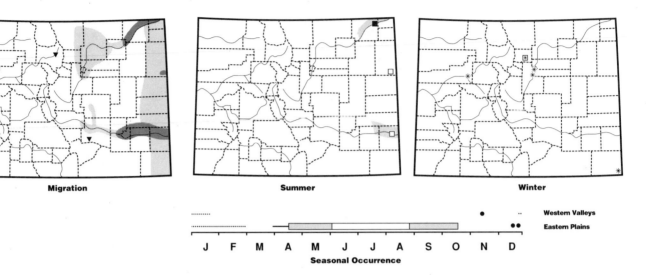

| Migration | Summer | Winter |

Seasonal Occurrence

J F M A M J J A S O N D

Western Valleys
Eastern Plains

Elevation

Status (SP) (B): Uncommon **spring** and **fall** migrant on extreme eastern plains, and rare west to base of foothills. Accidental in mountain parks (one record*) and western valleys (one record*). Uncommon local **summer** resident along eastern border. Most records are at Tamarack Ranch, Logan County, at Julesburg Reservoir, Logan/Sedgwick counties, in the Bonny Reservoir area, Yuma County, and near Holly, Prowers County. There are numerous observations of singing, territorial males and of probable juveniles; the only confirmed breeding was a nest at Tamarack Ranch in 1990.

The **winter** status of this species along the eastern border is unclear. Small numbers have been seen along the Cimarron River, Baca County, indicating that it may be uncommon along the southeastern border. Casual on northeastern plains near foothills (four records*, including one specimen, which is the only state specimen), and accidental in western valleys (one record*). All winter records should be carefully documented.

Habitat: In migration, riparian areas. In summer, fields and pastures with scattered shrubs.

Records: **Fall in mountain parks*:** 7-10 Nov 1989, Shadow Mountain Village, Grand County. **Fall in western valleys*:** 13 Nov 1987, Sweitzer Lake, Delta County. **Winter in western valleys*:** 27 Dec 1986–18 Jan 1987, Glenwood Springs, Garfield County. **Specimen:** 21 Dec 1982, Baseline Reservoir, Boulder County (DMNH 37538).

Note: There are several fall sight reports of the bright, eastern race (*S. p. pusilla*). However, freshly molted individuals of the western race (*S. p. arenacea*) may appear unusually bright, and that may be the explanation for those reports.

Vesper Sparrow
Pooecetes gramineus

Summer resident in foothills and mountain parks and migrant in lowlands.

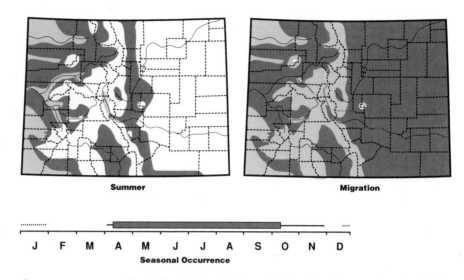

Summer   Migration

J F M A M J J A S O N D

Seasonal Occurrence

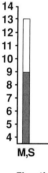

Elevation

Status (SP) (B): Common **summer** resident in foothills (and adjacent lowlands) and mountain parks. Fairly common **spring** migrant and common to abundant **fall** migrant in western valleys, foothills, mountain parks, and on eastern plains. Rare in late summer and fall above timberline. High count: 1,100 on 17 Sep 1988 in northeastern Colorado. There are about 20 **winter** records in the western valleys, mostly in Mesa County, and on the eastern plains near foothills from Larimer County southward, but none are documented. There is one winter specimen. It appears that this species occasionally occurs in winter. All winter reports should be documented.

Habitat: Breeds in grasslands, open shrublands mixed with grasslands, and open piñon-juniper woodlands. In migration, also in open riparian and agricultural areas.

Record: Winter specimen: 28 Jan 1942, Deora, Baca County (DMNH 23835).

Lark Sparrow

Chondestes grammacus

Summer resident and migrant at low elevations and locally in mountains.

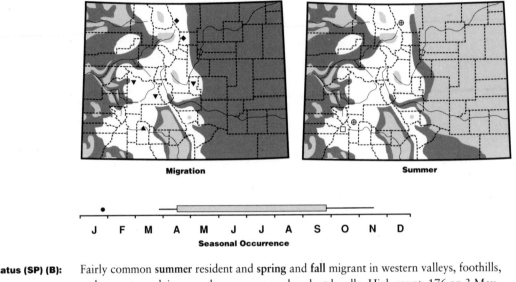

Migration   Summer

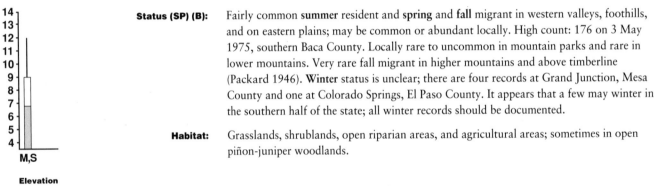

Seasonal Occurrence

Status (SP) (B):   Fairly common **summer** resident and **spring** and **fall** migrant in western valleys, foothills, and on eastern plains; may be common or abundant locally. High count: 176 on 3 May 1975, southern Baca County. Locally rare to uncommon in mountain parks and rare in lower mountains. Very rare fall migrant in higher mountains and above timberline (Packard 1946). **Winter** status is unclear; there are four records at Grand Junction, Mesa County and one at Colorado Springs, El Paso County. It appears that a few may winter in the southern half of the state; all winter records should be documented.

Habitat: Grasslands, shrublands, open riparian areas, and agricultural areas; sometimes in open piñon-juniper woodlands.

Elevation

Black-throated Sparrow

Amphispiza bilineata

Local summer resident in western and southeastern Colorado.

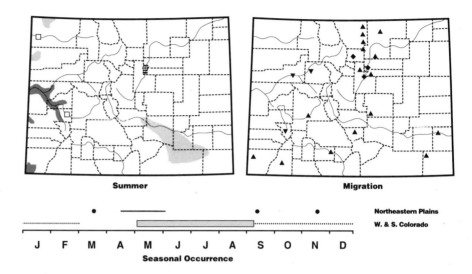

Summer   Migration

Northeastern Plains

W. & S. Colorado

J   F   M   A   M   J   J   A   S   O   N   D

Seasonal Occurrence

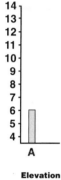

Elevation

Status (SP) (B): Uncommon local **summer** resident on mesas and valleys along western border from Mesa County southward; rare north to western Moffat County. Most records are from Mesa and Delta counties. Rare and local on southeastern plains from eastern Fremont County southeast to northwestern Baca County. Accidental on northeastern plains (one record*). Rare **spring** and **fall** migrant in western valleys and low foothills, east to Eagle and Gunnison counties. Very rare migrant (19+ spring records and two fall records) along eastern plains near foothills north to Larimer County, west to Custer County, and east to western Weld and Prowers counties. Accidental in San Luis Valley (two records). Accidental in **winter** (three records).

Habitat: Breeds in semidesert shrublands and open piñon-juniper woodlands in western Colorado and in cholla grasslands and shortgrass semidesert in southeastern Colorado. Migrants also occur in riparian, urban, and agricultural areas.

Records: **Summer on northeastern plains:** 25 June 1924, Denver County (DMNH 12286). **San Luis Valley:** 1 May 1971, Monte Vista National Wildlife Refuge, Rio Grande County; 18 Apr–1 May 1990, Monte Vista. **Winter:** 10 Feb 1974, Pueblo, Pueblo County; 17 Dec 1978, Grand Junction, Mesa County; Dec 1981–Feb 1982, Pueblo.

Sage Sparrow
Amphispiza belli

Local summer resident in western Colorado; occasional elsewhere in summer and migration.

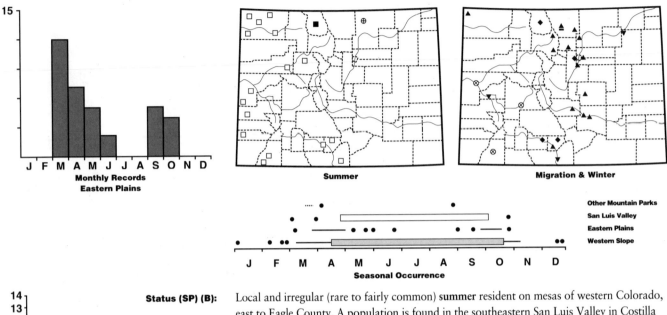

Summer

Migration & Winter

Other Mountain Parks
San Luis Valley
Eastern Plains
Western Slope

Seasonal Occurrence

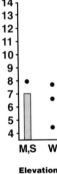

Monthly Records
Eastern Plains

Elevation

Status (SP) (B): Local and irregular (rare to fairly common) **summer** resident on mesas of western Colorado, east to Eagle County. A population is found in the southeastern San Luis Valley in Costilla County. May be most common in northwestern Colorado, especially Moffat County. Rare in North Park. Accidental on northeastern plains (one record). Rare and local **spring** and **fall** migrant in valleys and low foothills of western Colorado; may be fairly common locally, especially in fall. High count: 31 on 4–11 Nov 1979, Delta, Delta County. Rare migrant in San Luis Valley. Very rare spring (25+ records) and casual fall (eight records) migrant on eastern plains along foothills, east to northwestern Washington County. Casual in mountains and mountain parks (four records). Casual in **winter** (five records).

Habitat: Breeds in sagebrush shrublands. This species is very local, which is surprising given the abundance of sagebrush in western Colorado and in some mountain parks. A study of the specific habitat requirements of this species and the factors involved in its localized distribution could prove to be interesting. In migration, also grasslands and other types of shrublands.

Records: **Summer on northeastern plains:** 20 June 1964, Nunn, Weld County. **Mountains and mountain parks:** 24 Mar 1939, Estes Park, Larimer County (DMNH 20070); 16–23 Mar 1972, Estes Park; 20 Mar 1980, Fraser, Grand County; 6 Apr 1980, Grand Lake, Grand County; 23 Aug 1989, Endovalley in Rocky Mountain National Park, Larimer County. **Winter:** 26 Dec 1965, winter of 1982–83, and 3 Jan 1991, in Grand Junction area, Mesa County; 21 Feb 1971, Durango, La Plata County; 19 Dec 1982, Gunnison, Gunnison County.

Lark Bunting
Calamospiza melanocorys

Summer resident on eastern plains; occasionally in mountain parks and in western Colorado, especially in late summer.

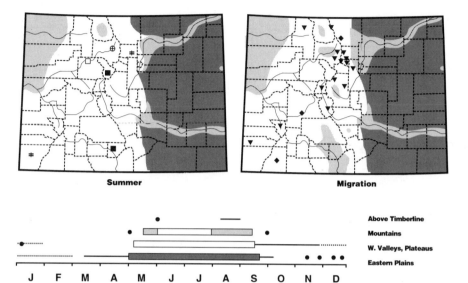

Summer   Migration

Above Timberline

Mountains

W. Valleys, Plateaus

Eastern Plains

J F M A M J J A S O N D

Seasonal Ooourrence

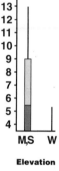

Elevation

Status (SP) (B): Common to abundant **summer** resident on eastern plains. It is somewhat local, being scarce or absent from agricultural areas and river valleys, and it is generally absent near the foothills. Rare to uncommon on the mesas of northwestern Colorado, mostly in Moffat County, but south to Mesa County. Rare to uncommon in mountain parks; most frequent in North Park. Like most grassland birds, local distribution and abundance varies widely from year to year.

Fairly common to abundant **spring** and **fall** migrant on eastern plains. Rare to uncommon in western valleys, foothills, mountains, and (especially) mountain parks; generally most frequent in late summer and fall. Rare late summer and fall migrant above timberline.

This bird's **winter** status is unclear. Flocks have been seen in southeastern Baca County in Jan and Feb (Seltman 1990), and it probably winters in that area regularly. Casual on northeastern plains (four records) and accidental in western valleys (one record).

The distribution of this species has contracted during this century due to conversion of grasslands to agriculture and urbanization. Early in the century it was one of the most abundant breeding species in grasslands between Denver and the foothills (Keyser 1902) and in the Barr Lake area (Hersey and Rockwell 1909); it now is very local in those areas during summer.

Habitat: Breeds primarily in shortgrass grasslands, and also occurs in sagebrush shrublands in mountain parks and in western Colorado. In migration also in agricultural areas. Occurs in late summer and fall on alpine tundra.

Records: **Winter on northeastern plains:** 25 Dec 1901, Denver County (DMNH 27658); Feb 1976, near Platteville, Weld County; 13 Jan 1979 and 7 Jan 1980, near Ft. Morgan, Morgan County. **Winter in western valleys:** 4–6 Jan 1981, Grand Junction, Mesa County.

Note: This is Colorado's state bird.

Savannah Sparrow
Passerculus sandwichensis

Summer resident in mountains and locally in lowlands; widespread migrant.

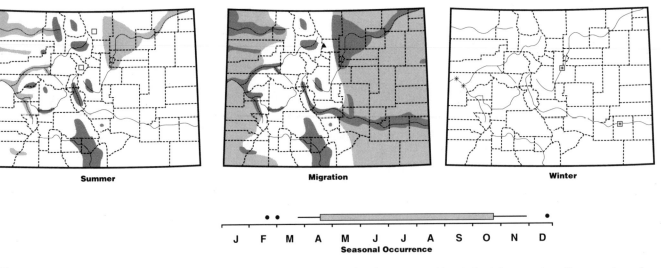

Summer   Migration   Winter

J F M A M J J A S O N D
Seasonal Occurrence

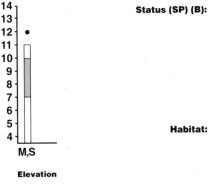

Elevation

Status (SP) (B): Fairly common to common local **summer** resident in both large and small mountain parks and valleys in lower and higher mountains. Rare to uncommon locally in western valleys and on northeastern plains; very local on southeastern plains. Uncommon to fairly common **spring** and **fall** migrant in western valleys, mountain parks, and on eastern plains. Rare in mountains to above timberline. Casual **winter** resident in western valleys and eastern plains from Mesa and Jefferson counties southward (five records). All winter observations should be documented.

Habitat: Breeds in damp meadows, irrigated hayfields, and marsh edges. In migration, also in grasslands, weedy fields, and riparian areas. The loss of moist mountain meadows (the most important breeding habitat in Colorado) to agriculture has caused a decline in breeding populations, and it is a Colorado Species of Special Concern (Webb 1985b).

Baird's Sparrow
Ammodramus bairdii

Migrant on eastern plains; status uncertain.

Status (SP): Casual **fall** migrant (four records*) and accidental **spring** migrant (two records*) on eastern plains. This species probably occurs as a regular migrant, but its true status is obscured by the large number of undocumented or poorly documented observations (67 reports). All observations of this species should be very carefully documented; Zimmer (1985) provided information on the identification of this species.

Habitat: Grasslands; most likely to be found in native grasslands. There are reports from weedy or grassy edges of ditches and roads or in plowed or stubble fields, but this species rarely occurs in such habitats (Zimmer 1985).

Records: Fall*: 22 Aug 1897, Colorado Springs, El Paso County (DMNH 25986–87); 14 Oct 1910, Weld County (CSU 6010); dozen seen and two collected 16 Sep 1939, Neenoshe Reservoir, Kiowa County (DMNH 20425–26); 14 Oct 1989, near Julesburg, Sedgwick County. **Spring***: 8 May 1976, Red Lion State Widlife Area, Logan County; 14 May 1988, Walsenburg, Huerfano County.

Grasshopper Sparrow
Ammodramus savannarum

Summer resident on eastern plains.

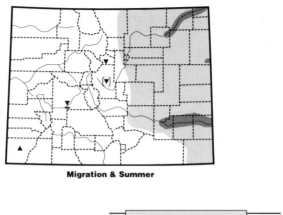

Migration & Summer

J F M A M J J A S O N D

Seasonal Occurrence

14
13
12
11
10
9
8
7
6
5
4

M,S

Elevation

Status (SP) (B): Uncommon to fairly common **summer** resident on eastern plains; may be locally common or abundant. Mostly from Morgan and Otero counties eastward, and very local west to base of foothills and adjacent lower foothills. Local, and numbers fluctuate widely from year to year. Rare **spring** and **fall** migrant on eastern plains. Accidental in western valleys (two records*, including one specimen).

Habitat: Breeds in grasslands, mostly mid and tall grass prairies and sandsage and rabbitbrush grasslands; rarely in agricultural areas (such as wheat) or planted wheatgrass.

Records: **Western valleys***: 15 Oct 1953, Gunnison, Gunnison County (DMNH 36723); 1 Apr 1990, Cortez, Montezuma County.

Note: Due to widespread population declines, this species is listed on the National Audubon Society Blue List (Tate 1986).

References: Strauch and Thompson (1986), Thompson and Strauch (1986).

Henslow's Sparrow
Ammodramus henslowii

Status (SR): Accidental **spring** and **fall** migrant (two records*).

Records: 10 Sep 1985, Jackson Reservoir, Morgan County (Leitner and Halsey 1986); 8 May 1989, Red Lion State Wildlife Area, Logan County.

Habitat: Riparian weedy and brushy areas.

Le Conte's Sparrow
Ammodramus leconteii

Status (SP): Casual in **spring, fall,** and **winter** (three eastern plains records* and one western valley record*). This species occurs regularly in late Oct and early Nov in alfalfa, wheat stubble, and corn stubble fields in western Kansas, and should be looked for in eastern Colorado in appropriate habitats (Bridges and Leatherman 1991).

Records: 6 May 1962, Gunnison, Gunnison County (DMNH 36720); 7 May 1977, near Wellington, Larimer County (photos in RC files); several birds 2 Dec 1990–3 Mar 1991 and 9 Nov 1991, west end of John Martin Reservoir, Bent County (photos in AB).

Habitat: Cattail, sedge, and grassy marshes.

Sharp-tailed Sparrow
Ammodramus caudacutus

Status (SP): Accidental **fall** migrant (two eastern plains records* and one western valley record*). Colorado birds have been of the inland race, *A. c. nelsoni*. This species occurs in late Oct and early Nov in alfalfa, wheat stubble, and corn stubble fields in western Kansas (but in much smaller numbers than Le Conte's Sparrow), and should be looked for in eastern Colorado (Bridges and Leatherman 1991).

Records: 24 Oct 1952, Gunnison, Gunnison County (DMNH 36719); 22 Dec 1973, near Pueblo, Pueblo County; 31 Oct 1982, Cherry Creek Reservoir, Arapahoe County.

Habitat: Marsh edges.

Fox Sparrow

Passerella iliaca

The two field-identifiable forms are treated separately.

Rusty form

P. i. zaboria or P. i. iliaca

Migrant and winter resident on eastern plains.

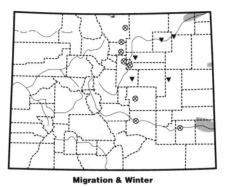

Migration & Winter

J F M A M J J A S O N D

Seasonal Occurrence

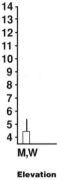

M,W

Elevation

Status (SP): Rare **spring** and **fall** migrant and **winter** resident on eastern plains, mostly on extreme eastern plains. There is one specimen.

Habitat: Lowland riparian shrublands.

Record: Specimen: 1 Nov 1916, Clear Creek, Jefferson County (DMNH 6026).

Rocky Mountain form
P. i. schistacea

Summer resident in mountains.

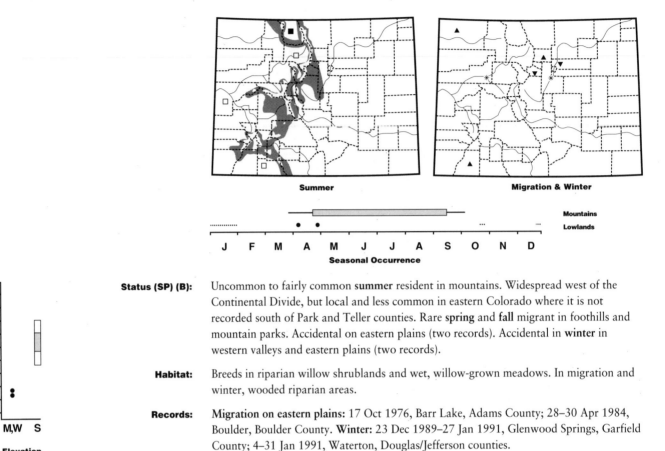

Summer

Migration & Winter

Mountains

Lowlands

J F M A M J J A S O N D

Seasonal Occurrence

Elevation

M,W   S

Status (SP) (B): Uncommon to fairly common **summer** resident in mountains. Widespread west of the Continental Divide, but local and less common in eastern Colorado where it is not recorded south of Park and Teller counties. Rare **spring** and **fall** migrant in foothills and mountain parks. Accidental on eastern plains (two records). Accidental in **winter** in western valleys and eastern plains (two records).

Habitat: Breeds in riparian willow shrublands and wet, willow-grown meadows. In migration and winter, wooded riparian areas.

Records: **Migration on eastern plains:** 17 Oct 1976, Barr Lake, Adams County; 28–30 Apr 1984, Boulder, Boulder County. **Winter:** 23 Dec 1989–27 Jan 1991, Glenwood Springs, Garfield County; 4–31 Jan 1991, Waterton, Douglas/Jefferson counties.

Note: There have been several migration sight records of birds believed to be of one of the northwestern subspecies.

Song Sparrow
Melospiza melodia

Resident, mostly in lowlands and mountain parks.

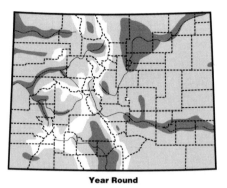

Year Round

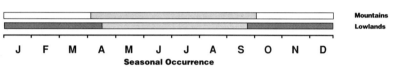

Mountains
Lowlands

J F M A M J J A S O N D

Seasonal Occurrence

Status (SP) (B): Fairly common **resident**. Occurs mostly in western valleys, mountain parks, and on eastern plains. Local and uncommon in summer in foothills and mountains outside main parks, and rare in winter in lower mountains and mountain parks. In the lowlands, it is generally more numerous in winter and migration than in summer, and may be common to abundant.

Habitat: Riparian shrublands (mostly willow) and cattail marshes. This is one of the most common breeding species in montane willow shrublands in Boulder County, but is absent from subalpine and alpine shrublands (Hallock 1984).

14
13
12
11
10
9
8
7
6
5
4

M,W   S

Elevation

Lincoln's Sparrow
Melospiza lincolnii

Summer resident in mountains and widespread migrant.

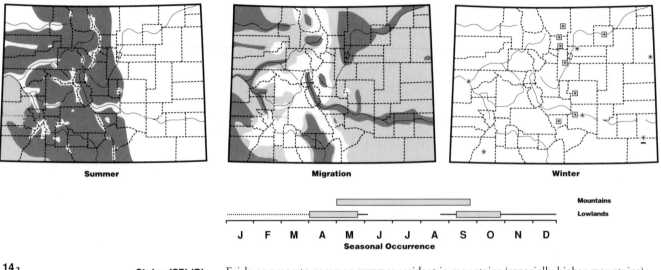

Summer   Migration   Winter

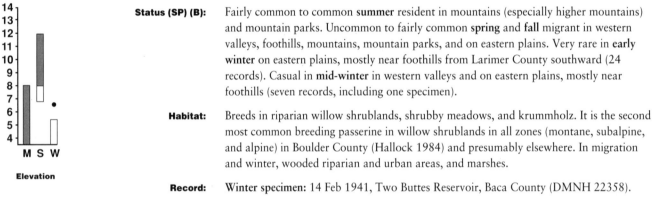

Mountains
Lowlands

J F M A M J J A S O N D
Seasonal Occurrence

Status (SP) (B): Fairly common to common **summer** resident in mountains (especially higher mountains) and mountain parks. Uncommon to fairly common **spring** and **fall** migrant in western valleys, foothills, mountains, mountain parks, and on eastern plains. Very rare in **early winter** on eastern plains, mostly near foothills from Larimer County southward (24 records). Casual in **mid-winter** in western valleys and on eastern plains, mostly near foothills (seven records, including one specimen).

Habitat: Breeds in riparian willow shrublands, shrubby meadows, and krummholz. It is the second most common breeding passerine in willow shrublands in all zones (montane, subalpine, and alpine) in Boulder County (Hallock 1984) and presumably elsewhere. In migration and winter, wooded riparian and urban areas, and marshes.

Record: Winter specimen: 14 Feb 1941, Two Buttes Reservoir, Baca County (DMNH 22358).

14
13
12
11
10
9
8
7
6
5
4

M S W

Elevation

Swamp Sparrow

Melospiza georgiana

Migrant and winter resident on eastern plains.

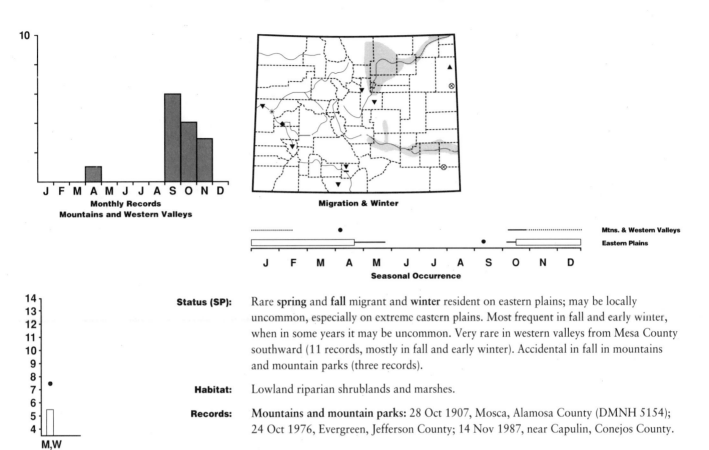

Migration & Winter

Monthly Records
Mountains and Western Valleys

Mtns. & Western Valleys
Eastern Plains

Seasonal Occurrence

Elevation

Status (SP): Rare **spring** and **fall** migrant and **winter** resident on eastern plains; may be locally uncommon, especially on extreme eastern plains. Most frequent in fall and early winter, when in some years it may be uncommon. Very rare in western valleys from Mesa County southward (11 records, mostly in fall and early winter). Accidental in fall in mountains and mountain parks (three records).

Habitat: Lowland riparian shrublands and marshes.

Records: **Mountains and mountain parks:** 28 Oct 1907, Mosca, Alamosa County (DMNH 5154); 24 Oct 1976, Evergreen, Jefferson County; 14 Nov 1987, near Capulin, Conejos County.

White-throated Sparrow
Zonotrichia albicollis

Migrant and winter resident in lowlands, especially in eastern Colorado.

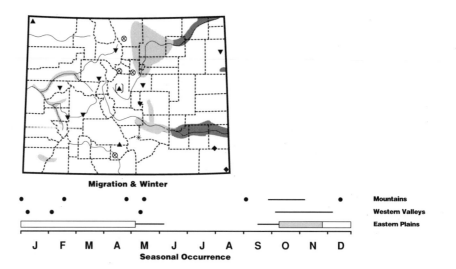

Migration & Winter

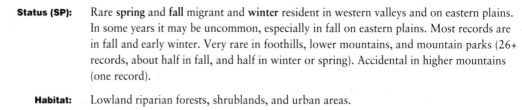

Mountains

Western Valleys

Eastern Plains

Seasonal Occurrence

J F M A M J J A S O N D

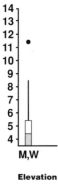

M,W

Elevation

Status (SP): Rare **spring** and **fall** migrant and **winter** resident in western valleys and on eastern plains. In some years it may be uncommon, especially in fall on eastern plains. Most records are in fall and early winter. Very rare in foothills, lower mountains, and mountain parks (26+ records, about half in fall, and half in winter or spring). Accidental in higher mountains (one record).

Habitat: Lowland riparian forests, shrublands, and urban areas.

Record: **High mountains:** 6 Sep 1971, at timberline on Pikes Peak, El Paso County.

Golden-crowned Sparrow
Zonotrichia atricapilla

Migrant and winter resident, mostly in or near northeastern foothills.

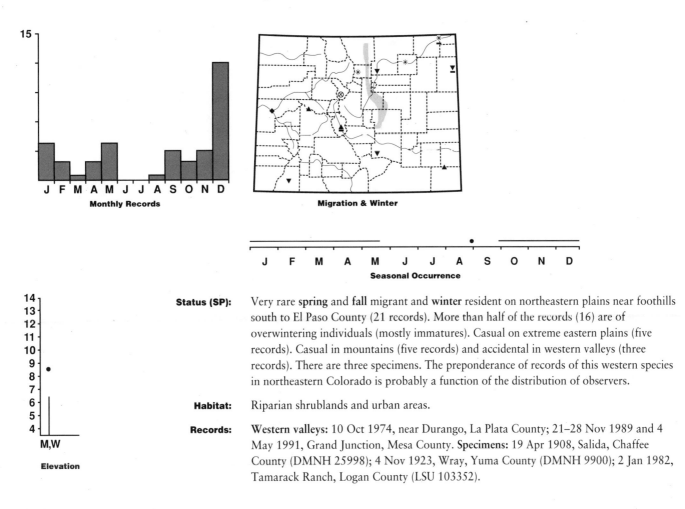

Monthly Records

Migration & Winter

Seasonal Occurrence

Elevation

Status (SP): Very rare **spring** and **fall** migrant and **winter** resident on northeastern plains near foothills south to El Paso County (21 records). More than half of the records (16) are of overwintering individuals (mostly immatures). Casual on extreme eastern plains (five records). Casual in mountains (five records) and accidental in western valleys (three records). There are three specimens. The preponderance of records of this western species in northeastern Colorado is probably a function of the distribution of observers.

Habitat: Riparian shrublands and urban areas.

Records: **Western valleys:** 10 Oct 1974, near Durango, La Plata County; 21–28 Nov 1989 and 4 May 1991, Grand Junction, Mesa County. **Specimens:** 19 Apr 1908, Salida, Chaffee County (DMNH 25998); 4 Nov 1923, Wray, Yuma County (DMNH 9900); 2 Jan 1982, Tamarack Ranch, Logan County (LSU 103352).

White-crowned Sparrow
Zonotrichia leucophrys

Summer resident in mountains, and migrant and winter resident at low elevations.

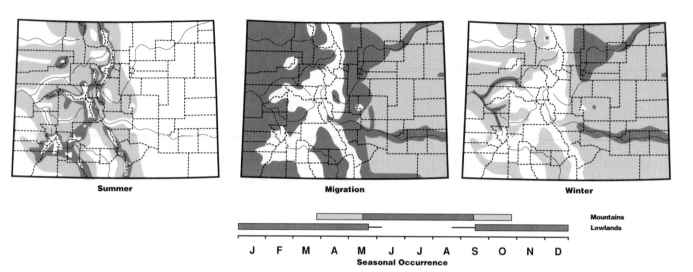

Summer   Migration   Winter

Mountains
Lowlands

J F M A M J J A S O N D
Seasonal Occurrence

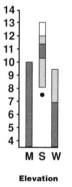

M S W

Elevation

Status (SP) (B): Common **summer** resident in higher mountains, and uncommon to fairly common locally in mountain parks and lower mountains. Common to abundant **spring** and **fall** migrant in western valleys, foothills, mountains, mountain parks, and on eastern plains. Common to abundant **winter** resident in western valleys and on eastern plains near foothills, especially Mesa and El Paso counties southward. Locally uncommon to fairly common in foothills, lower mountains, on extreme eastern plains, and in San Luis Valley; rare in other mountain parks.

Habitat: Breeds in riparian willow shrublands, brushy meadows, and krummholz; rare in dense spruce-fir forest and in willow thickets above timberline (Braun 1980). This is one of the most common breeding passerines in subalpine and alpine willow shrublands in Boulder County; rare in montane zone (Hallock 1984). In migration and winter, most wooded and brushy habitats; often partial to greasewood in western Colorado.

Note: There are two subspecies, which are field-identifiable but seldom reported. *Z. l. oriantha* breeds in the mountains and is a migrant at lower elevations. *Z. l. gambelii* is a migrant and winter resident, mostly at lower elevations.

Harris' Sparrow
Zonotrichia querula

Migrant and winter resident, most common along eastern border and occasional elsewhere.

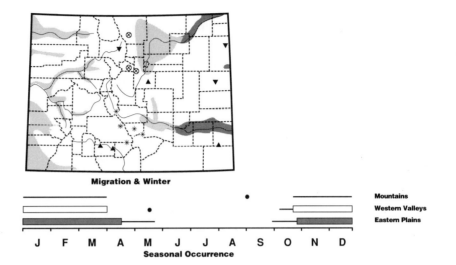

Migration & Winter

Mountains
Western Valleys
Eastern Plains

J F M A M J J A S O N D
Seasonal Occurrence

Elevation

M,W

Status (SP): Fairly common to common **spring** and **fall** migrant and **winter** resident on extreme eastern plains; uncommon west to base of foothills. High count: 195 on 1 Jan 1977, Bonny Reservoir, Yuma County. Very rare in foothills, lower mountains, and mountain parks (22+ records). Rare in western valleys. High count: 10 on 27 Nov 1972, Durango, La Plata County.

Habitat: Wooded or brushy riparian, agricultural, and urban areas.

Dark-eyed Junco
Junco hyemalis

The four field-identifiable forms are treated separately.

White-winged form

Winter resident, mostly in eastern foothills and mountains.

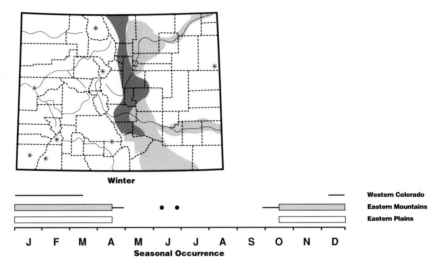

Winter

Western Colorado
Eastern Mountains
Eastern Plains

J F M A M J J A S O N D

Seasonal Occurrence

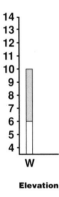

W

Elevation

Status (SP) (FB): Uncommon to fairly common **winter** resident in eastern foothills and lower mountains south to Custer and Pueblo counties. Rare on eastern plains south to Las Animas County, mostly adjacent to foothills. Rare in mountain parks, and in western foothills and mesas, mountains, and lower valleys. Accidental in **summer** (two records, including one breeding record).

Habitat: Coniferous and riparian forests and thickets, shrublands, and wooded urban areas.

Records: Summer: nest with young 11 June 1905, Boulder County (Cary 1909); 26 June 1907, at 10,000 ft. in Clear Creek County (DMNH 9982).

Slate-colored form

Winter resident, most common in eastern Colorado.

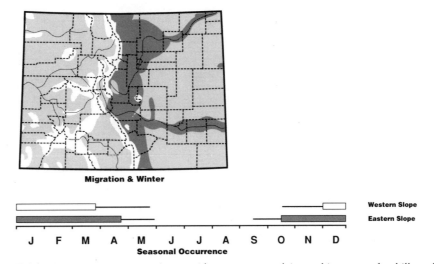

Migration & Winter

Western Slope

Eastern Slope

J F M A M J J A S O N D

Seasonal Occurrence

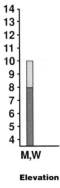

M,W

Elevation

Status (SP): Fairly common to common **winter** resident on eastern plains and in eastern foothills and lower mountains. Rare to uncommon in mountain parks and in western valleys, foothills, and lower mountains.

Habitat: Coniferous and riparian forests and thickets, shrublands, and wooded urban areas.

Oregon and Pink-sided forms

Widespread winter resident.

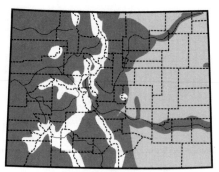

Migration & Winter

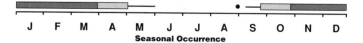

J F M A M J J A S O N D

Seasonal Occurrence

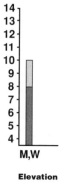

M,W

Elevation

Status (SP): Common to abundant **winter** resident in western valleys, foothills, lower mountains, mountain parks, and on eastern plains. Several late summer records refer to early fall arrivals. The Pink-sided form is more common than the darker-headed Oregon form, but both are numerous and widespread, and have similar distributions.

Habitat: Coniferous and riparian forests and thickets, shrublands, and wooded urban areas.

Gray-headed form

Resident in mountains, moving upward in summer and downward in winter.

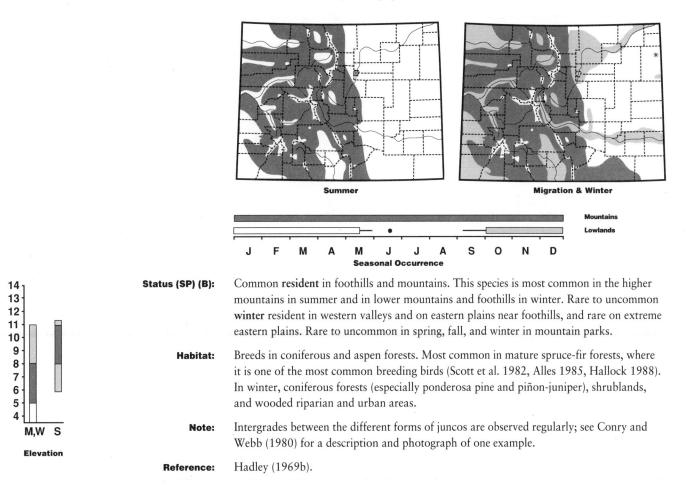

Summer   Migration & Winter

Mountains
Lowlands

J F M A M J J A S O N D
Seasonal Occurrence

Status (SP) (B): Common **resident** in foothills and mountains. This species is most common in the higher mountains in summer and in lower mountains and foothills in winter. Rare to uncommon **winter** resident in western valleys and on eastern plains near foothills, and rare on extreme eastern plains. Rare to uncommon in spring, fall, and winter in mountain parks.

Habitat: Breeds in coniferous and aspen forests. Most common in mature spruce-fir forests, where it is one of the most common breeding birds (Scott et al. 1982, Alles 1985, Hallock 1988). In winter, coniferous forests (especially ponderosa pine and piñon-juniper), shrublands, and wooded riparian and urban areas.

Note: Intergrades between the different forms of juncos are observed regularly; see Conry and Webb (1980) for a description and photograph of one example.

Reference: Hadley (1969b).

M,W S

Elevation

McCown's Longspur

Calcarius mccownii

Summer resident on extreme northeastern plains and migrant elsewhere on eastern plains.

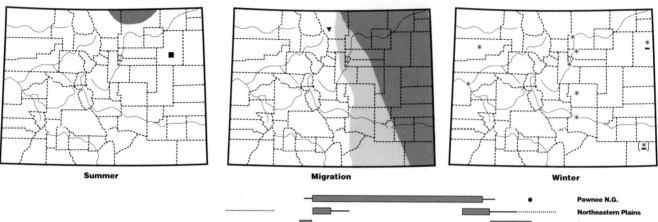

| Summer | Migration | Winter |

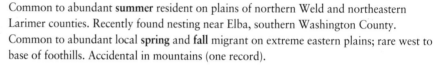

Pawnee N.G.
Northeastern Plains
Southeastern Plains

J F M A M J J A S O N D
Seasonal Occurrence

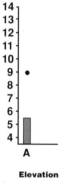

Elevation

Status (SP) (B): Common to abundant **summer** resident on plains of northern Weld and northeastern Larimer counties. Recently found nesting near Elba, southern Washington County. Common to abundant local **spring** and **fall** migrant on extreme eastern plains; rare west to base of foothills. Accidental in mountains (one record).

Casual **winter** resident on eastern plains, mostly near foothills, north to Weld and Yuma counties (eight records); some observations (in mid-Dec and late Feb to early Mar) may represent early or late migrants. There are three late winter specimens but none in mid-winter. It is most likely to occur in winter in Baca County, and should be looked for in that area. All winter records, and all records at any season away from the eastern plains should be documented.

Habitat: Breeds in shortgrass grassland, especially very short, overgrazed areas. In migration, grasslands and agricultural areas.

Records: Mountains: 11 Aug 1984, Pingree Park, Larimer County. Winter specimens: 26–28 Feb 1910, Wray, Yuma County (DMNH 650); 7 Mar 1924, Baca County (DMNH 10606, 10608).

Note: This species is a Colorado Species of Special Concern because it is an excellent indicator species for short-grass prairie (Webb 1985b).

Lapland Longspur
Calcarius lapponicus

Irregular winter resident, most common on northeastern plains.

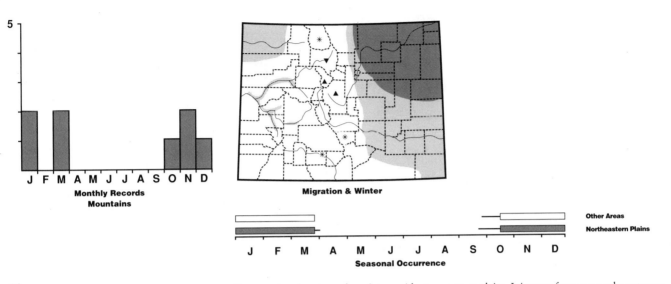

Monthly Records
Mountains

Migration & Winter

Other Areas
Northeastern Plains

Seasonal Occurrence

Elevation

Status (SP): Rare to abundant irregular **winter** resident on eastern plains. It is most frequent on the extreme northeastern plains, west to western Weld and western Adams counties. Numbers fluctuate widely from year to year. Rare to uncommon on northeastern plains adjacent to foothills, on southeastern plains, in mountain parks, and in western valleys south to Delta and Gunnison counties. Often seen mixed with Horned Larks, but pure flocks are sometimes observed.

Habitat: Grasslands and croplands; most often seen in bare or stubble fields.

Chestnut-collared Longspur
Calcarius ornatus

Summer resident on extreme northeastern plains and migrant elsewhere on eastern plains.

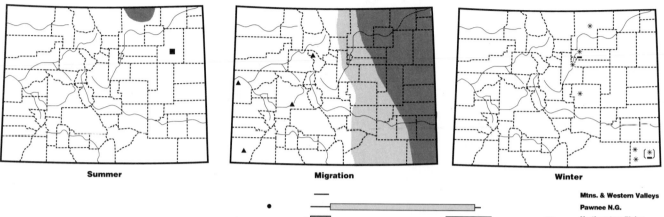

Summer   Migration   Winter

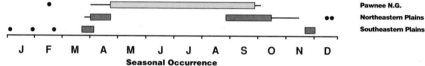

Mtns. & Western Valleys
Pawnee N.G.
Northeastern Plains
Southeastern Plains

J   F   M   A   M   J   J   A   S   O   N   D

Seasonal Occurrence

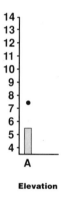

Elevation

Status (SP) (B): Fairly common local **summer** resident on plains of northern Weld County. In the last several years, a small breeding population has been found near Elba, southern Washington County. Fairly common to abundant local **spring** and **fall** migrant on extreme eastern plains; rare west to base of foothills. Casual spring migrant in western valleys and mesas (four records) and accidental in mountains (one record).

Casual **winter** resident on eastern plains from Baca County north to Jefferson and central Weld counties (nine records). There are four winter specimens. Most winter records are in Dec, some of which could represent late migrants. This species is most likely in winter in Baca County, and should be looked for there. All winter records, and all records at any season away from the eastern plains should be documented.

Habitat: Breeds in local patches of slightly tall shortgrass prairie and introduced grasses. In migration and winter, grasslands and croplands.

Records: Western valleys: 4 Apr 1906, Montezuma County (Gilman 1907); 5 Apr 1964 and 24 Apr 1971, Gunnison, Gunnison County; 15 Apr 1972, Glade Park, Mesa County. **Mountains:** 10 Apr 1971, Green Mountain Reservoir, Summit County. **Winter specimens:** 27–28 Dec 1909, Barr Lake, Adams County (DMNH 1752, 1754, 1755); 27 Jan 1949, Baca County (DMNH 24983).

Snow Bunting
Plectrophenax nivalis

Irregular winter resident at low elevations, mostly in northern Colorado.

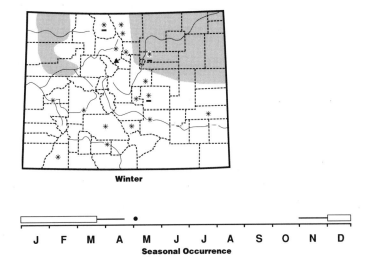

Winter

Seasonal Occurrence

J F M A M J J A S O N D

Elevation

14
13
12
11
10
9
8
7
6
5
4

W

Status (SP): Irregular **winter** resident on northwestern plateau, in western valleys, mountain parks, and on eastern plains. Most records are from northeastern Colorado. Casual in northern mountains outside parks (five records). Occurs mostly in the northern half of the state, but recorded south to La Plata, Rio Grande, Pueblo, and Kiowa counties. Generally rare, and absent in many years; in exceptional years may be more common. In several winters, notable invasions of large flocks have occurred. A flock of 500 was seen 5 Jan–22 Feb 1930, Walden, Jackson County. There were up to 2,500 in Moffat County and up to 10,000 on Pawnee National Grassland, Weld County in Jan and Feb 1978 (Gent 1978). There are four specimens.

Habitat: Grasslands and croplands; sometimes in sagebrush shrublands.

Records: Specimens: 1874, Colorado Springs, El Paso County (CC 1788, 1789); 18 Feb 1978, Walden, Jackson County (DMNH 38941); 30 Dec 1983, western Adams County (LSU 113201).

Order Passeriformes
Family Emberizidae

Subfamily Icterinae

Bobolink
Dolichonyx oryzivorus

Local summer resident and migrant, mostly in northern Colorado.

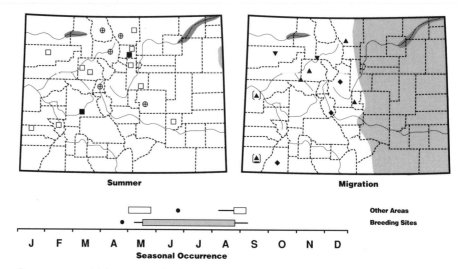

Summer   Migration

Other Areas

Breeding Sites

J F M A M J J A S O N D

Seasonal Occurrence

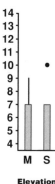

Elevation

Status (SP) (B): Uncommon to fairly common local **summer** resident in western valleys and eastern plains in northern half of state. It is most common and widespread along the South Platte River from Morgan to Sedgwick counties. It occurs more locally on the extreme eastern plains south to Yuma and Crowley counties and near the foothills from Larimer County south to Douglas County. It also occurs in the western valleys south to San Miguel County, but mostly in the Gunnison Basin, Gunnison County, Rio Blanco County, and in the Yampa River Valley in Moffat and Routt counties (Martin et al. 1974). Rare in North Park. There are old records from Middle Park (Bailey and Niedrach 1965) but no recent records (Jasper and Collins 1987); there are also old records from the San Luis Valley (Ryder 1965). Accidental elsewhere in mountains and mountain parks (two records). Rare **spring** and **fall** migrant on eastern plains and in western valleys; casual in northern mountains and mountain parks (about nine records). Most records of migrants are in the northern half of the state, and there are more in spring than in fall.

Habitat: Breeds in moist tallgrass meadows and hayfields. In migration, grasslands and croplands.

Records: **Summer in mountains and mountain parks:** 17 July 1907, Leadville, Lake County (Hersey 1911); 15 June 1910, Estes Park, Larimer County (Widmann 1911).

Reference: Thompson and Strauch (1986).

Red-winged Blackbird

Agelaius phoeniceus

Abundant resident at low elevations, and summer resident in mountains.

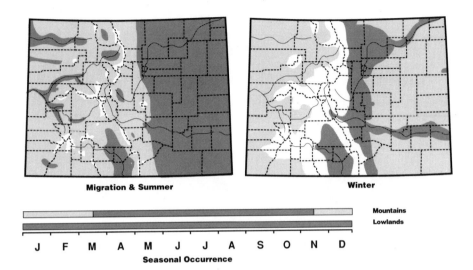

Migration & Summer   **Winter**

Mountains
Lowlands

J F M A M J J A S O N D

Seasonal Occurrence

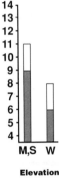

Elevation

Status (SP) (B): Abundant **resident** in western valleys and on eastern plains. Uncommon to fairly common in summer in lower mountains outside main parks; rare in higher mountains. Abundant in summer in mountain parks and rare to uncommon in winter. Rare in lower mountains in winter. Many of the blackbirds seen in eastern Colorado in winter are residents, while many others are individuals that breed north of Colorado from Wyoming to Alberta and Saskatchewan (Royall et al. 1972, 1980). Birds banded in Grand and Summit counties in summer have been recovered in winter from the eastern plains (Cummings 1985). This species is an important host of the Brown-headed Cowbird (Ortega and Cruz 1988, 1991).

Habitat: Cattail marshes, moist meadows, agricultural areas, and wooded riparian areas.

Eastern Meadowlark

Sturnella magna

Local summer resident in extreme northeast corner.

Status (SR): Uncommon **summer** resident at Red Lion State Wildlife Area, Logan/Sedgwick counties. This small population was first discovered in 1975, and birds were observed there annually until 1985, when the fields were burned and the habitat altered (Kingery 1988). This species was observed again in the area in 1990. The birds are present from mid-Apr to late Sep, but breeding has never been confirmed. Accidental elsewhere on eastern plains (two records*). Observers should be very cautious about identifying this species. Because Western Meadowlarks imitate the Eastern song, identifications should not be based only on the song. All reports from localities other than Red Lion should be carefully and thoroughly documented.

Habitat: Tallgrass meadows.

Records: **Eastern plains***: 14 May 1981, Two Buttes Reservoir, Baca County; 12 June-10 July 1988, near Platteville, Weld County.

Western Meadowlark
Sturnella neglecta

Resident at low elevations, and summer resident in mountain parks.

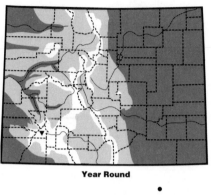

Year Round

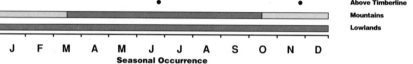

Above Timberline
Mountains
Lowlands

J F M A M J J A S O N D
Seasonal Occurrence

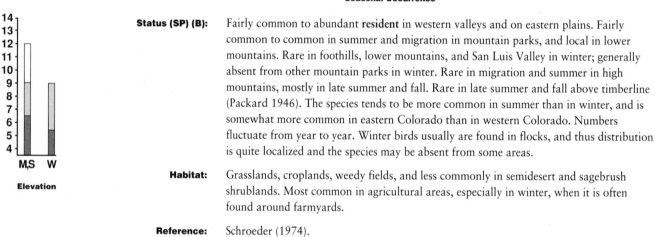

Elevation

Status (SP) (B): Fairly common to abundant **resident** in western valleys and on eastern plains. Fairly common to common in summer and migration in mountain parks, and local in lower mountains. Rare in foothills, lower mountains, and San Luis Valley in winter; generally absent from other mountain parks in winter. Rare in migration and summer in high mountains, mostly in late summer and fall. Rare in late summer and fall above timberline (Packard 1946). The species tends to be more common in summer than in winter, and is somewhat more common in eastern Colorado than in western Colorado. Numbers fluctuate from year to year. Winter birds usually are found in flocks, and thus distribution is quite localized and the species may be absent from some areas.

Habitat: Grasslands, croplands, weedy fields, and less commonly in semidesert and sagebrush shrublands. Most common in agricultural areas, especially in winter, when it is often found around farmyards.

Reference: Schroeder (1974).

Yellow-headed Blackbird

Xanthocephalus xanthocephalus

Summer resident at low elevations and in mountain parks.

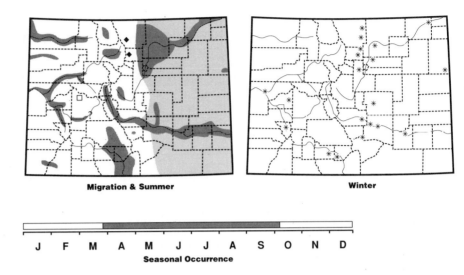

Migration & Summer   **Winter**

J F M A M J J A S O N D

Seasonal Occurrence

Elevation

Status (SP) (B): Abundant **summer** resident in western valleys, mountain parks, and on eastern plains. High count: 2,000 on 15 May 1971, Loveland, Larimer County. Rare and very local in summer and migration in foothills and lower mountains outside parks. In late summer, some individuals wander as high as 7,500 ft. (Packard 1946). Rare **winter** resident in western valleys from Mesa County southward and on eastern plains. Accidental in San Luis Valley (two records).

Habitat: Breeds in large cattail marshes, and forages in adjacent agricultural and riparian areas. In winter, marshes, agricultural, and riparian areas, mostly in association with other icterines; often around farmyards where livestock are kept.

Records: **Winter in San Luis Valley:** 21 Dec 1977, Monte Vista, Rio Grande County; 4 Jan 1981, Alamosa, Alamosa County.

Note: This species is a Colorado Species of Special Concern due to population declines and its specialized habitat requirements (Webb 1985b).

Reference: Ortega and Cruz (1988, 1991).

Rusty Blackbird
Euphagus carolinus

Rare in migration and winter on eastern plains.

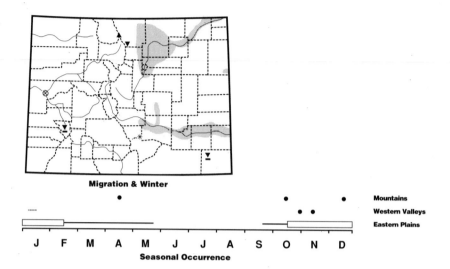

Migration & Winter

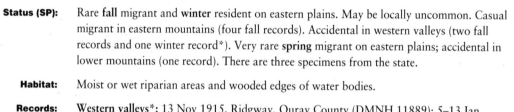

Mountains
Western Valleys
Eastern Plains

J F M A M J J A S O N D

Seasonal Occurrence

Elevation

M,W

Status (SP): Rare **fall** migrant and **winter** resident on eastern plains. May be locally uncommon. Casual migrant in eastern mountains (four fall records). Accidental in western valleys (two fall records and one winter record*). Very rare **spring** migrant on eastern plains; accidental in lower mountains (one record). There are three specimens from the state.

Habitat: Moist or wet riparian areas and wooded edges of water bodies.

Records: **Western valleys*:** 13 Nov 1915, Ridgway, Ouray County (DMNH 11889); 5–13 Jan 1988 and 31 Oct 1991, Clifton, Mesa County. **Spring in mountains:** 16 Apr 1984, Cameron Pass, Larimer County. **Specimens:** Ridgway (see above); 25 Nov 1937, Deora, Baca County (DMNH 22330–22331).

Brewer's Blackbird
Euphagus cyanocephalus

Summer resident at low elevations and in mountain parks; local in winter at low elevations.

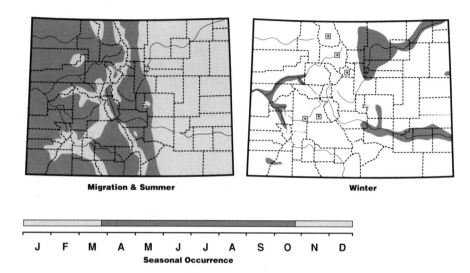

Migration & Summer   Winter

Seasonal Occurrence

J F M A M J J A S O N D

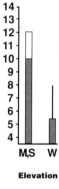

Elevation

Status (SP) (B): Common **summer** resident in western valleys, foothills, and lower mountain valleys and parks. On the eastern plains, it used to be common, but has decreased dramatically in about the last 25 years. It may have been displaced from many areas (especially agricultural and urban areas) by the rapidly increasing Common Grackle. The blackbird is now quite local in the summer, although more widespread in migration. As the Common Grackle spreads into the mountains and western valleys, observers should note if the same replacement occurs. Despite the decrease in eastern Colorado, this species showed an increase on Breeding Bird Survey routes statewide (Robbins et al. 1986). High count: 7,000 on 10 Sep 1986, Lower Latham Reservoir, Weld County. Rare, mostly in late summer and fall, in higher mountains and above timberline (Keyser 1902).

Uncommon to fairly common local **winter** resident in western valleys and on eastern plains; rare in lower mountains and mountain parks. This species has increased in numbers in winter, especially on the eastern plains adjacent to the foothills (Stepney 1975a).

Habitat: Meadows and grasslands, riparian, agricultural, and urban areas; sometimes sagebrush or other shrublands. In winter, most often found near open water (streams and irrigation canals) and farmyards with livestock.

Great-tailed Grackle
Quiscalus mexicanus

Local in summer and winter, mostly in southern Colorado; spreading rapidly.

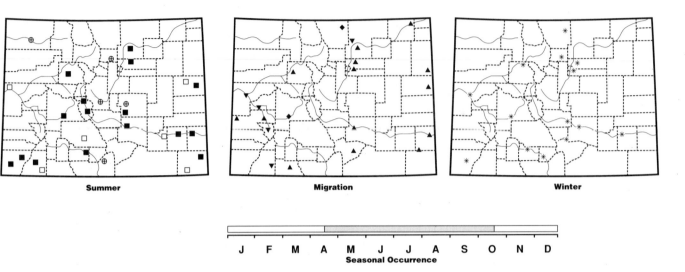

Summer	**Migration**	**Winter**

J F M A M J J A S O N D

Seasonal Occurrence

Elevation

Status (PH) (B): Uncommon to fairly common local **spring** and **fall** migrant and **summer** resident in western valleys, mountain parks, and on eastern plains; may be common or abundant at some sites. Rare to uncommon very local **winter** resident in western valleys, mountain parks, and eastern plains.

The first record in Colorado was a male from 16 May to mid-Aug 1970 at Gunnison, Gunnison County, and the first eastern plains record was 17 Sep 1974 at Pueblo, Pueblo County. Since then, the species has been spreading rapidly, and there are now 150+ records in all seasons. Most records have been in the southern half of the state; recorded north in the western valleys to Moffat and Eagle counties, in the mountains to Park County, and on the eastern plains to Larimer and Logan counties.

The earliest nesting record was in 1973 at Monte Vista, Rio Grande County (Stepney 1975b). Nesting was first recorded in the western valleys in 1981 and on the eastern plains in 1982. Breeding has been recorded at 16 sites in the western valleys north to Eagle County, the San Luis Valley, the upper Arkansas River in Chaffee County, and on eastern plains north to Weld and Kit Carson counties. There are several other sites where breeding has probably occurred but has not been observed. Breeding is confirmed at new sites every year.

This species first wintered in Colorado in 1973–74 at Gunnison, Gunnison County. Wintering has been recorded in the western valleys north to McCoy, Eagle County, in the San Luis Valley, and on the eastern plains north to Ft. Collins, Larimer County. High count: 117 on 6 Jan 1991, Las Animas, Bent County.

Habitat: Nests in trees (especially conifers) or shrubs near water, in marshes, or in windbreaks. Great-tailed Grackles near the edge of their range often favor marshes for nesting (Faanes and Norling 1981). Forages in fields, meadows, and marshes.

Note: There are photos on file with the RC, and there is one published in *American Birds* 38:426 (1984).

Reference: Lambeth (1985).

Common Grackle
Quiscalus quiscula

Summer resident at low elevations, mostly in eastern Colorado; spreading into mountains and western Colorado.

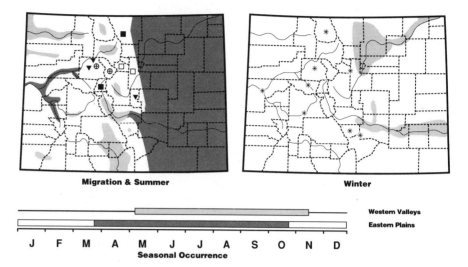

Migration & Summer **Winter**

Western Valleys
Eastern Plains

J F M A M J J A S O N D
Seasonal Occurrence

14
13
12
11
10
9
8
7
6
5
4

S W

Elevation

Status (SP) (B): Abundant **summer** resident on eastern plains. Very local in lower mountains, mountain parks, and in western valleys, mostly rare to uncommon but may be fairly common at some sites. High west slope count: 300–500 during Aug–Sep 1983 at Kremmling, Grand County. Rare **winter** resident on eastern plains. Casual in lower mountains (10 records) and accidental in western valleys (two records).

The numbers and geographic distribution of this species has increased in Colorado. Sclater (1912) noted that this species was "not very common except locally." Since then, it has been steadily increasing in numbers and spreading westward. By the 1970s, it seemed to have displaced Brewer's Blackbird from most urban and agricultural areas on the eastern plains, and was thought to be doing the same in the mountains at Evergreen, Jefferson County. The first mountain records were at Ft. Garland, Costilla County (Sclater 1912) and 2 May–July 1934, Georgetown, Clear Creek County. The first record from the western valleys was 14 June 1969, Steamboat Springs, Routt County. The first breeding record in the western valleys was in 1972 at Gunnison, Gunnison County and in the mountains in 1973 at Estes Park, Larimer County. Breeding is confirmed or strongly suspected at 11 sites in the western valleys and six in the mountains and mountain parks.

Habitat: Lowland riparian forests, agricultural areas, and urban areas.

Records: **Winter in western valleys:** winter of 1976 at Grand Junction, Mesa County; winter 1983 at Gunnison, Gunnison County.

Reference: Mott et al. (1972).

Bronzed Cowbird
Molothrus aeneus

Status (PH): Accidental in **summer** (two records*). This species has been expanding its range due to increased agriculture and urbanization (Robbins and Easterla 1981), and additional records are to be expected.

Records: One 17 May–1 Aug 1990 and 10 May 1991 through rest of month, Lakewood, Jefferson County (photos in RC files).

Brown-headed Cowbird
Molothrus ater

Summer resident at low elevations and in mountain parks.

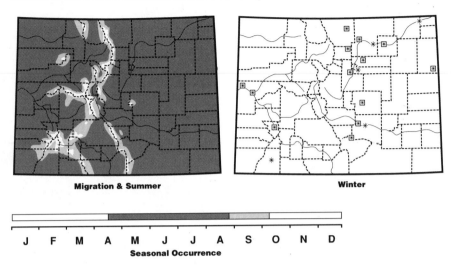

Migration & Summer   Winter

J F M A M J J A S O N D

Seasonal Occurrence

14
13
12
11
10
9
8
7
6
5
4

M,S   W

Elevation

Status (SP) (B): Fairly common to common **summer** resident in western valleys, mountain parks, and on eastern plains. Local in mountains, mostly in lower mountains, but recorded to timberline; most frequent at high elevations in late summer and fall. The original range of this species was at lower elevations; it has spread into the mountains in recent decades (Hanka 1985). It increased in numbers statewide on Breeding Bird Survey routes from 1965–79 (Robbins et al. 1986). Rare fall migrant above timberline. Rare **winter** resident in western valleys from Mesa County southward and on eastern plains.

The eggs of this parasitic species have been found in the nests of 38 species of passerines in Colorado. Only a few studies have examined the rates of cowbird parasitism on particular species in Colorado (see Table 1). The Brown-headed Cowbird is a Colorado Species of Special Concern due to its parasitic nesting behavior (Webb 1985b).

Habitat: Breeds mostly in open areas such as grasslands, shrublands, agricultural areas, mountain meadows, and in adjacent open forests; may be seen flying overhead in virtually any habitat. In winter, most often found around feedlots or farmyards, usually with other icterines.

Table 1 Rates of Brown-headed Cowbird parasitism on host species in Colorado.

Species	Area	%[1]	n[2]	Source
Willow Flycatcher	Jackson County	41	27	Sedgwick and Knopf (1988)
Solitary Vireo	Boulder County	48.7	78	Marvil and Cruz (1989)
Red-winged Blackbird	Colorado & Wyoming[3]	17.5	154	Hanka (1979)
	Boulder County	11-41	650	Ortega and Cruz (1988, 1991)
Yellow-headed Blackbird	Colorado & Wyoming	0.5	381	Hanka (1979)
	Boulder County	0	351	Ortega and Cruz (1988)
Brewer's Blackbird	Colorado & Wyoming	19.4	217	Hanka (1979)
	Jackson County	40	45	Hanka (1985)
Common Grackle	Colorado & Wyoming	0	18	Hanka (1979)

[1] Percentage of nests found with cowbird eggs, including both abandoned nests with cowbird eggs and nests in which cowbird eggs hatched; rate may vary in an area in different habitats or sites, and from year to year.
[2] Number of nests of host species examined.
[3] North-central Colorado and south-central Wyoming.

Additional species (isolated reports of parasitism): Olive-sided Flycatcher, Dusky Flycatcher, Mountain Chickadee (Brockner 1984), Ruby-crowned Kinglet (Spencer 1985), Blue-gray Gnatcatcher, American Robin, Gray Catbird, Gray Vireo, Warbling Vireo (Hanka 1979), Red-eyed Vireo, Virginia's Warbler, Yellow Warbler (Keeler-Wolf et al. 1973), "Audubon's" Warbler, Black-throated Gray Warbler, Grace's Warbler, Common Yellowthroat, Wilson's Warbler, Western Tanager, Lazuli Bunting, Green-tailed Towhee, Cassin's Sparrow (Kingery and Julian 1971), Brewer's Sparrow, Lark Bunting (Porter 1973), Savannah Sparrow, Fox Sparrow, Song Sparrow, Lincoln's Sparrow (Hanka 1979), "Gray-headed" Junco, Orchard Oriole, Northern Oriole (Hanka 1984), House Finch, Lesser Goldfinch.

Orchard Oriole

Icterus spurius

Summary resident in extreme eastern Colorado.

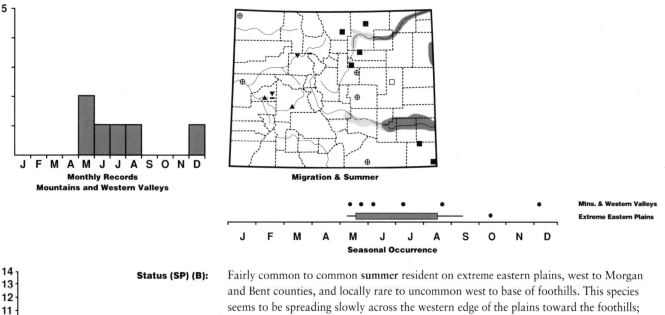

Monthly Records
Mountains and Western Valleys

Migration & Summer

Mtns. & Western Valleys
Extreme Eastern Plains

Seasonal Occurrence

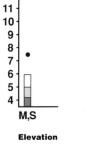

Elevation

Status (SP) (B): Fairly common to common **summer** resident on extreme eastern plains, west to Morgan and Bent counties, and locally rare to uncommon west to base of foothills. This species seems to be spreading slowly across the western edge of the plains toward the foothills; Bailey and Niedrach (1965) listed nesting sites only from the eastern border. There are now breeding records from at least five sites near the foothills, starting in the early and mid-1970s. High count: 200 on 18 May 1983, Bonny Reservoir, Yuma County. Accidental in western valleys (two records). Rare **spring** and **fall** migrant on eastern plains near foothills. Casual in western valleys (four records).

Habitat: Lowland riparian forests.

Records: **Summer in western valleys:** 7 June 1977, Browns Park National Wildlife Refuge, Moffat County; 10 July 1978, Fruita, Mesa County. **Migration in western valleys:** 6 Dec 1906, Paonia, Delta County (DMNH 13008); pair 11 May 1958, Hotchkiss, Delta County (Davis 1969); 21–23 May 1980, Gunnison, Gunnison County; 20 Aug 1989, McCoy, Eagle County. There are also two doubtful records: four specimens collected by E. Carter at Breckenridge, Summit County (DMNH 1598, 1602, 1603, 1604)—it is highly unlikely that so many specimens would have been collected at such an unusual site; one found dead in 1967 at Gunnison and attributed to S. Hyde (Davis 1969), but not listed by Hyde (1979).

Northern Oriole

Icterus galbula

The two field-identifiable forms are treated separately.

Baltimore form

Summer resident along northeastern border.

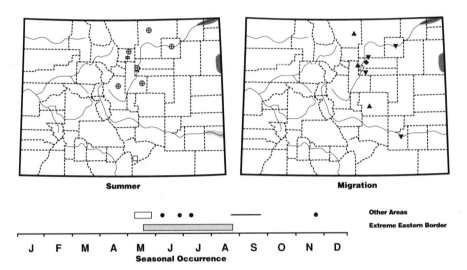

Status (SP) (B): Fairly common **summer** resident along eastern border from Logan and Sedgwick counties south to Yuma County, and rarely to Prowers County. Casual on eastern plains near foothills (five records, including one breeding record). Accidental in mountains (one record). Rare **spring** migrant and casual **fall** migrant (five records) on eastern plains near foothills. Accidental in western valleys (one record).

Habitat: Lowland riparian forests.

Records: **Breeding near foothills:** nest 25 June 1884, Boulder County (Bailey and Niedrach 1965). **Mountains:** 15 June 1982, near Jefferson, Park County. **Western valleys:** 10 May 1982, Gunnison, Gunnison County (based upon the details, this bird could have been either a Baltimore or a Baltimore—Bullock's intergrade).

Bullock's form

Summer resident at low elevations.

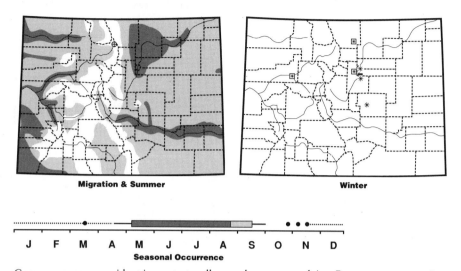

Migration & Summer   **Winter**

J F M A M J J A S O N D

Seasonal Occurrence

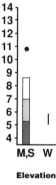

Elevation

Status (SP) (B): Common **summer** resident in western valleys and on eastern plains. Rare to uncommon in migration (mostly spring) and summer in foothills, lower mountains, and mountain parks; accidental in higher mountains (one record). Casual in **winter** on eastern plains near foothills (five records*) and in western valleys (one record*).

The two forms of the Northern Oriole interbreed in the central Great Plains, including extreme northeastern Colorado in Logan and Sedgwick counties (Corbin and Sibley 1977, Rising 1983a, b). At Crook, Logan County between the 1950s and the 1970s, the percentage of intergrades and Bullock's type individuals decreased while Baltimore type individuals increased (Corbin et al. 1979).

Habitat: Lowland riparian forests and urban areas with tall trees; often forages in willow and tamarisk shrublands.

Records: **High mountains:** 9 June 1940, at 10,800 ft. on Milner Pass in Rocky Mountain National Park, Grand/Larimer counties. **Winter*:** 17 Nov–16 Dec 1973, Glenwood Springs, Garfield County; 1 Jan 1976, Denver County (DMNH 36165); male Dec 1977–28 Apr 1978, Littleton, Arapahoe County (Grant 1978); 1 Jan 1980, Colorado Springs, El Paso County; 18 Dec 1982, Denver CBC circle; 16–18 Dec 1990, Loveland, Larimer County.

Scott's Oriole
Icterus parisorum

Local summer resident along western border.

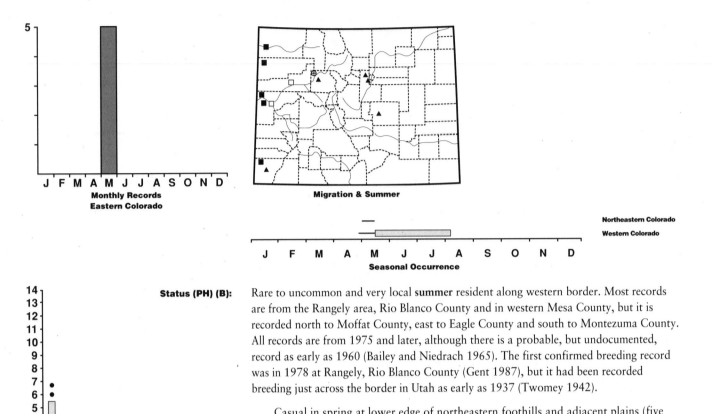

**Monthly Records
Eastern Colorado**

Migration & Summer

Northeastern Colorado

Western Colorado

Seasonal Occurrence

Elevation

Status (PH) (B): Rare to uncommon and very local **summer** resident along western border. Most records are from the Rangely area, Rio Blanco County and in western Mesa County, but it is recorded north to Moffat County, east to Eagle County and south to Montezuma County. All records are from 1975 and later, although there is a probable, but undocumented, record as early as 1960 (Bailey and Niedrach 1965). The first confirmed breeding record was in 1978 at Rangely, Rio Blanco County (Gent 1987), but it had been recorded breeding just across the border in Utah as early as 1937 (Twomey 1942).

Casual in spring at lower edge of northeastern foothills and adjacent plains (five records). The first documented record for the state was an immature male 1–3 May 1975 at Red Rocks Park, Jefferson County (Cooper 1975, Remsen and Cooper 1977; photos in RC files).

Habitat: Breeds in isolated piñon-juniper or juniper groves in semidesert shrublands. Vagrants also occur in foothill and lowland riparian forests.

Note: There are photo records on file with the RC.

Order Passeriformes
Family Fringillidae

Brambling
Fringilla montifringilla

Status (PH): Accidental in **fall** and **winter** (three records*).

Records: 30 Oct–4 Nov 1983, Colorado Springs, El Paso County (Curry and Curry 1984); 16-19 Dec 1983, Pueblo Reservoir, Pueblo County; 17 Dec 1983–3 Mar 1984, Boulder, Boulder County (photos published in Jickling 1984 and Gent 1987).

Habitat: Two of the birds were in suburban areas, coming to feeders.

Rosy Finch
Leucosticte arctoa

Three field-identifiable forms are treated separately.

Gray-crowned form
L. a. tephrocotis

Irregular and local winter resident, mostly in mountains.

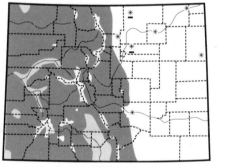

Winter

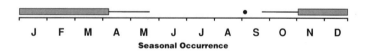

J F M A M J J A S O N D

Seasonal Occurrence

Elevation

Status (SP): Irregular and locally fairly common to abundant **winter** resident, mostly in lower mountains and mountain parks; but also recorded locally to lower edge of foothills and in higher mountains. Local distribution is often influenced by snow depth; deep snow at higher elevations forces the finches to lower elevations. The birds also are seen often around feeders, especially in years when snow depths are greater. Uncommon in lower western valleys. Rare (sometimes common) and very local on eastern plains near foothills; the majority of eastern plains records are from the western Pawnee National Grassland, Weld County. There are two plains specimens. Casual on extreme northeastern plains in Morgan, Logan, and Yuma counties (six records).

Habitat: Most often seen in mountain meadows, shrublands, along roadsides, and in towns. They occur wherever there is bare ground and food supplies; when natural food supplies are scarce or inaccessible due to deep snow, they often concentrate at feeders.

Records: Eastern plains specimens: 25 Jan 1969, Pawnee National Grassland, Weld County (DMNH 38927); 26 Dec 1983, near Barr Lake, Adams County (LSU 113204).

Reference: Shreeve (1980).

Black form

L. a. atrata

Irregular and local winter resident in mountains.

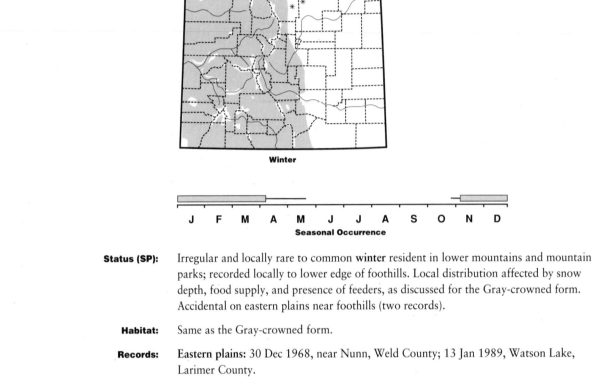

Winter

J F M A M J J A S O N D

Seasonal Occurrence

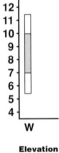

Elevation

Status (SP): Irregular and locally rare to common **winter** resident in lower mountains and mountain parks; recorded locally to lower edge of foothills. Local distribution affected by snow depth, food supply, and presence of feeders, as discussed for the Gray-crowned form. Accidental on eastern plains near foothills (two records).

Habitat: Same as the Gray-crowned form.

Records: **Eastern plains:** 30 Dec 1968, near Nunn, Weld County; 13 Jan 1989, Watson Lake, Larimer County.

Brown-capped form

L. a. australis

Irregular and local winter resident in mountains; summer resident above timberline.

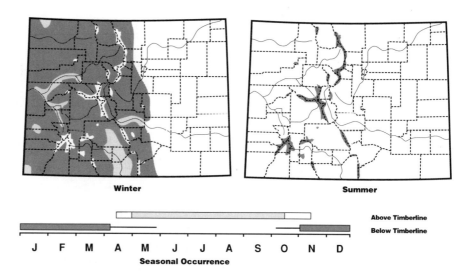

Winter · Summer

Above Timberline
Below Timberline

J F M A M J J A S O N D
Seasonal Occurrence

14
13
12
11
10
9
8
7
6
5
4

S W

Elevation

Status (SP) (B): Irregular and locally rare to common **winter** resident in lower mountains, and mountain parks; recorded locally to lower edge of foothills. Local distribution affected by snow depth, food supply, and presence of feeders, as discussed for the Gray-crowned form. Uncommon to fairly common local **summer** resident above timberline. Widespread above timberline in early and late summer before and after nesting, but while nesting it is very localized around nesting cliffs (Braun 1980).

Habitat: In winter, same as "Gray-crowned" and "Black" forms. In summer, nests around cliffs and often forages on or near alpine tundra snowbanks.

References: Hendricks (1978), Shreeve (1980).

Pine Grosbeak
Pinicola enucleator

Resident in high mountains; occasional at lower elevations in fall and winter.

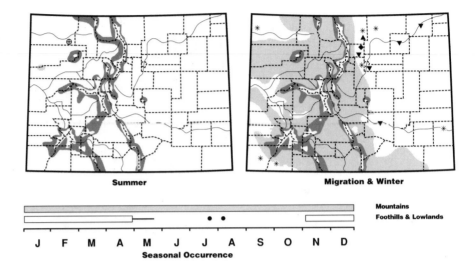

Summer

Migration & Winter

Mountains

Foothills & Lowlands

J F M A M J J A S O N D

Seasonal Occurrence

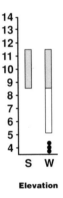

Elevation

Status (SP) (B): Uncommon to fairly common **resident** in higher mountains. Rare in fall and winter in lower mountains and foothills, especially in years of poor spruce and fir cone crops. Casual in spring and summer in lower mountains and foothills. Most frequent at lower elevations in the piñon-juniper zone in western and southern Colorado. High count: 55 on 18 Feb 1989, Loveland Pass, Summit/Clear Creek counties. Casual, mostly in fall and winter on eastern plains near foothills (seven+ records in fall and winter and two in spring) and on extreme eastern plains (four records) east to Logan and Prowers counties.

Habitat: Breeds in spruce-fir forest; also found in other types of coniferous forests in other seasons, primarily in fall, winter, and spring. Often attracted to piñon-juniper woodlands during fall and winter when seed crops in those areas are excellent.

Purple Finch

Carpodacus purpureus

Occasional in fall, winter, and spring in eastern foothills and nearby plains.

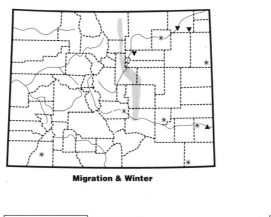

Migration & Winter

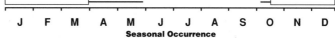

J   F   M   A   M   J   J   A   S   O   N   D

Seasonal Occurrence

Elevation

Status (SP): Rare in **fall, winter, and spring** in lower foothills and adjacent plains from Larimer County south to Pueblo County. There are four specimens. Very rare on eastern plains east to Logan, Yuma, Prowers, and Baca counties (12 records). Accidental in western valleys (one record*). Almost all Colorado records are of females or immatures. Observers should be cautious when identifying this species as it can be easily confused with the much more common Cassin's Finch; see Remsen (1976) and Kaufman (1990) for information on identification.

Habitat: Riparian and urban areas; often at feeders.

Records: Specimens: 15 Nov 1885, Denver County (DMNH 2580); 11 Dec 1976 and 7 Mar 1977, Ft. Collins, Larimer County (DMNH 37694–96). **Western valleys*:** 5 Dec 1974–20 Mar 1974, Durango, La Plata County.

Cassin's Finch

Carpodacus cassinii

Resident in mountains; irregular in fall and winter in foothills and adjacent lowlands.

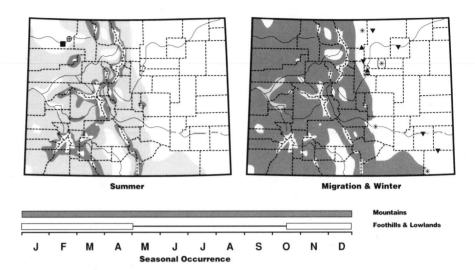

Summer   Migration & Winter

Mountains
Foothills & Lowlands

J F M A M J J A S O N D

Seasonal Occurrence

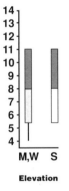

Elevation

Status (SP) (B): Fairly common to common **resident** in mountains. In summer, occurs mostly in higher mountains. In fall and winter, it often withdraws from high elevations and moves down into the lower mountains and foothills, especially to areas where piñon pine cone crops are excellent. Rare to uncommon in summer in foothills, mostly in the piñon-juniper zone. Local abundance and distribution, as in other montane finches, is often quite localized and irregular from year to year due to the influence of food supplies. High count: 3,000 on 14 May 1972, Estes Park, Larimer County. Irregular in fall and winter in western valleys and eastern plains adjacent to mesas and foothills; usually rare, but at times may be common, especially in western Colorado. Casual in fall on extreme eastern plains east to Morgan and Baca counties (seven records).

Habitat: Breeds mostly in high elevation coniferous forests (especially spruce-fir). Breeds in small numbers in piñon-juniper woodlands. There is one nesting record in foothill cottonwood/oak/aspen/sagebrush mixture (Ward 1990). Occurs regularly in fall, winter, and spring in riparian areas, shrublands, and ponderosa pine and Douglas-fir forests, and piñon-juniper woodlands.

House Finch

Carpodacus mexicanus

Resident, mostly in lowlands.

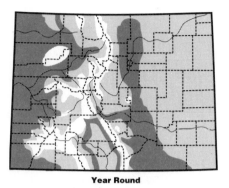

Year Round

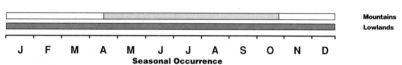

Mountains
Lowlands

J F M A M J J A S O N D

Seasonal Occurrence

Elevation

Status (SP) (B): Abundant **resident** in western valleys, the San Luis Valley, and on eastern plains near foothills. Uncommon in foothills, lower mountains, and mountain parks; rare in higher mountains. In the foothills and mountains, it occurs primarily in spring, summer, and fall (rare in winter). Rare to uncommon on extreme eastern plains.

Habitat: Most common in urban areas and lower piñon-juniper woodlands, but also occurs in agricultural areas, riparian forests, shrublands (sagebrush and rabbitbrush), and cholla grasslands.

Red Crossbill
Loxia curvirostra

Irregular year round in mountains, and occasionally to lowlands.

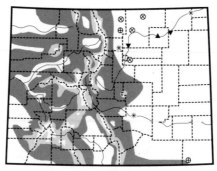

Year Round

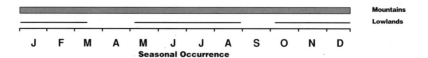

Mountains
Lowlands

J F M A M J J A S O N D

Seasonal Occurrence

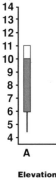

Elevation

Status (SP) (B): Irregular **resident** in foothills and mountains, mostly in foothills and lower mountains, but recorded almost to timberline. In some areas, it may be as common or more common in the higher mountains than at lower elevations. In favorable years, it is common to abundant, but is often completely absent in poor years. Local distribution and year-to-year abundance is controlled by conifer cone crops. Irregular, very rare visitor in western valleys and eastern plains; mostly near foothills, but recorded east to Logan and Baca counties. These vagrant records may be of single birds, but many are of flocks (up to 200). The 40+ records from the eastern plains are distributed throughout the year.

Unlike many montane birds, which wander to lower elevations primarily in fall and winter, season seems to have little or no influence on the wanderings of this species—they may appear at any place in any season. This even holds true for nesting; this species may breed wherever and whenever food supplies are abundant, and there are at least eight records of mid-winter nesting in Colorado. Although there are many summer records at low elevations on the eastern plains, there are no breeding records from that part of the state, and there are also apparently no breeding records from the higher mountains.

Habitat: Coniferous forests. It is especially common in ponderosa pine forests, but in some areas and times may be common also in other forest types such as lodgepole pine and spruce-fir. Vagrants also occur in riparian areas (and flying over most other habitats).

White-winged Crossbill
Loxia leucoptera

Irregular year round in mountains.

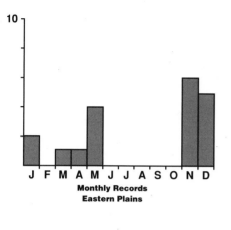

**Monthly Records
Eastern Plains**

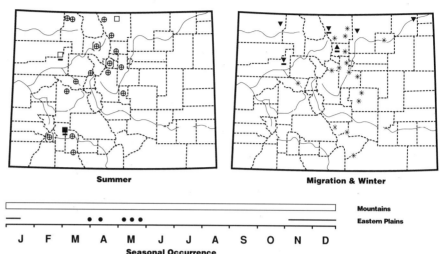

Summer

Migration & Winter

Mountains
Eastern Plains

Seasonal Occurrence

Elevation

Status (SP) (B): Irregular **year round** in mountains; mostly in higher mountains, but also recorded in lower mountains and foothills. At low elevations, it occurs primarily in winter. It is usually rare, but may be locally uncommon, fairly common, or even common. Individuals, pairs, or small flocks are recorded in all seasons, with no discernible seasonal pattern. **Breeding** was confirmed 6–7 June 1987, when adults in breeding condition and a flightless juvenile were collected at Spring Creek Pass, Hinsdale County (Groth 1992). Breeding was suspected in the summer of 1985 on the White River Plateau (Groth 1992) and in 1988 on Cameron Pass, Larimer County. There are six specimens. Very rare in fall and winter (11 records) and casual in spring (four records) on eastern plains adjacent to foothills. Accidental on extreme eastern plains (two records).

Habitat: Primarily spruce-fir forest, but recorded in all other types of coniferous forests, and at low elevations in riparian and urban areas.

Records: **Extreme eastern plains:** 11 Nov 1954, Crook, Logan County; 21 Nov 1984–30 Mar 1985, Ft. Morgan, Morgan County. **Specimens:** 14 Aug 1908, Chambers Lake, Larimer County (CSU 5764); 17 May 1917, Sunset, Boulder County (DMNH 6585); 6 Aug 1985, White River Plateau, Garfield County (MVZ 171137; Groth 1992); 6–7 June 1987, Spring Creek Pass, Hinsdale County (MVZ 171432–34; Groth 1992).

Common Redpoll

Carduelis flammea

Irregular in winter, mostly on northeastern plains.

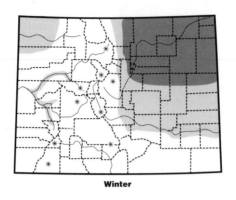

Winter

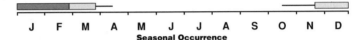

J F M A M J J A S O N D

Seasonal Occurrence

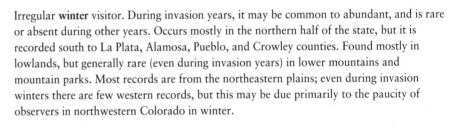

Elevation

Status (SP): Irregular **winter** visitor. During invasion years, it may be common to abundant, and is rare or absent during other years. Occurs mostly in the northern half of the state, but it is recorded south to La Plata, Alamosa, Pueblo, and Crowley counties. Found mostly in lowlands, but generally rare (even during invasion years) in lower mountains and mountain parks. Most records are from the northeastern plains; even during invasion winters there are few western records, but this may be due primarily to the paucity of observers in northwestern Colorado in winter.

Habitat: Open riparian areas, agricultural areas, grasslands, shrublands, and urban areas.

Pine Siskin

Carduelis pinus

Irregular resident in mountains, and winter visitor and migrant in lowlands.

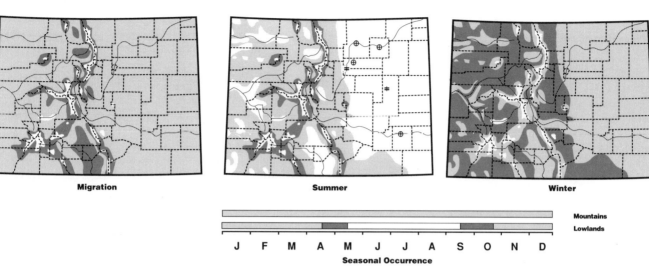

Status (SP) (B): Irregular, uncommon to abundant, **resident** in foothills and mountains. Most common in summer in higher mountains and in winter in lower mountains and foothills. Irregular, rare to common, **spring** and **fall** migrant and **winter** visitor in western valleys and on eastern plains. Rare in summer at low elevations; breeding recorded in Denver County in 1899 (Dille 1900) and at Limon, Lincoln County (Sclater 1912).

Habitat: Breeds primarily in coniferous forests (especially spruce-fir), and rarely in riparian areas, aspen forests, and shrublands. In winter and migration, coniferous forests, riparian areas, shrublands, agricultural, and urban areas, and in flight over grasslands.

Reference: Ryder (1985).

Lesser Goldfinch

Carduelis psaltria

Summer resident in foothills, mostly in southern half of Colorado.

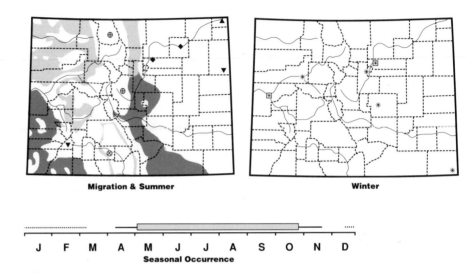

Migration & Summer   **Winter**

J F M A M J J A S O N D

Seasonal Occurrence

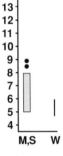

Elevation

Status (SP) (B): Fairly common **summer** resident in mesas, foothills, and adjacent valleys and plains; most common and widespread in the southern half of the state, but it is recorded north to Moffat and Larimer counties. Rare in lower mountains and mountain parks. Very rare on northeastern plains east to Morgan County (six records, mostly in late summer and fall). Most Colorado records of males are of green-backed individuals, but black-backed males are seen regularly as well, with most records along the eastern foothills.

Casual in **winter** in lower foothills and adjacent lowlands north to Mesa and Adams counties (seven records*). There are 70+ winter reports, with as many as 45 individuals/day. The North American winter distribution of this species is almost entirely restricted to the west coast and central and southern Texas (Root 1988). In all parts of Colorado in winter, the American Goldfinch is always far more common than the Lesser Goldfinch. All winter sightings of this species should be thoroughly documented.

Habitat: Breeds in riparian forests, shrublands (mostly Gambel oak), and ponderosa pine forests. Also occurs in agricultural and urban areas, and cholla grasslands in migration.

American Goldfinch
Carduelis tristis

Resident at low elevations.

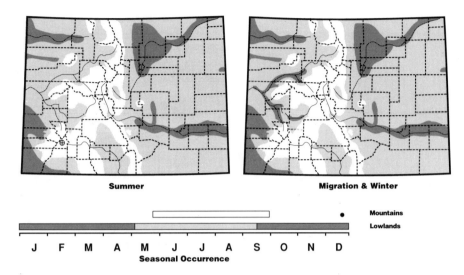

Summer **Migration & Winter**

Mountains
Lowlands

J F M A M J J A S O N D
Seasonal Occurrence

Status (SP) (B): **Resident** in western valleys and eastern plains; uncommon in summer and fairly common to common in migration and winter. Rare in lower mountains and mountain parks, mostly in summer and migration; breeds locally.

Habitat: Occurs mostly in open riparian forests and adjacent fields; also in agricultural and urban areas, and recorded flying over other habitats.

14
13
12
11
10
9
8
7
6
5
4

W   M,S

Elevation

Evening Grosbeak
Coccothraustes vespertinus

Irregular and local year round in mountains and adjacent lowlands.

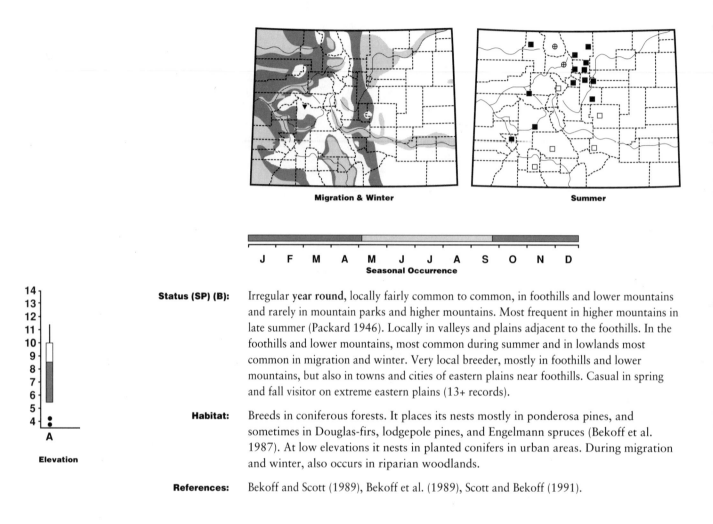

Migration & Winter   Summer

J F M A M J J A S O N D
Seasonal Occurrence

Elevation

Status (SP) (B): Irregular **year round**, locally fairly common to common, in foothills and lower mountains and rarely in mountain parks and higher mountains. Most frequent in higher mountains in late summer (Packard 1946). Locally in valleys and plains adjacent to the foothills. In the foothills and lower mountains, most common during summer and in lowlands most common in migration and winter. Very local breeder, mostly in foothills and lower mountains, but also in towns and cities of eastern plains near foothills. Casual in spring and fall visitor on extreme eastern plains (13+ records).

Habitat: Breeds in coniferous forests. It places its nests mostly in ponderosa pines, and sometimes in Douglas-firs, lodgepole pines, and Engelmann spruces (Bekoff et al. 1987). At low elevations it nests in planted conifers in urban areas. During migration and winter, also occurs in riparian woodlands.

References: Bekoff and Scott (1989), Bekoff et al. (1989), Scott and Bekoff (1991).

Order Passeriformes
Family Passeridae

House Sparrow
Passer domesticus

Widespread resident.

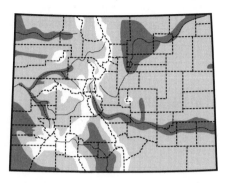

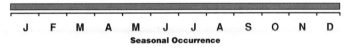

J F M A M J J A S O N D

Seasonal Occurrence

Status (SP) (B): Abundant **resident** in western valleys, foothills, lower mountains, mountain parks, and on eastern plains. This introduced species was first recorded in Colorado on 20 Feb 1895 at Pueblo, Pueblo County (Lowe 1895).

Habitat: Urban and agricultural areas.

14
13
12
11
10
9
8
7
6
5
4

A

Elevation

There are other species that have been reported from the state other than those included in the main section of the book. These additional species fall into four categories. First, some species have been reported by only a single observer. The CFO Records Committee believes that species should not be added to the state list on the basis of a single-observer sight record, even if that report is well-documented. Most such species will be added to the state list when a second documented record is available. Second, some reports most likely refer to escaped individuals rather than wild birds. Third, some species have in the past been included on the state list but were later dropped. Fourth, some difficult records are still under consideration by the Records Committee.

Fulvous Whistling-Duck   *Dendrocygna bicolor*

There was a report of a bird 15 Oct 1990 at Kersey, Weld County. Although wild individuals of this species can be expected to reach Colorado, we believe that it is best to treat observations as possible escapes until a clear pattern is established. Both species of whistling-ducks are popular with collectors, and often escape (R. Ryder, pers. comm.).

Black-bellied Whistling-Duck   *Dendrocygna autumnalis*

Single birds were observed on 21 Sep 1980 at Chatfield Reservoir, Douglas/Jefferson counties and 10–11 July 1991 at Pawnee National Grassland, Weld County. These birds were most likely escapes. This was species was added to the state list, but later deleted (Nelson 1991).

Mottled Duck   *Anas fulvigula*

Several specimens identified as this species (Bailey and Niedrach 1965) were examined and found to be probable hybrids, and this species was dropped from the state list (Andrews 1978, Gent 1986).

Black Vulture   *Coragyps atratus*

There have been about 10 reports of this species from Colorado. Two of these reports have been quite suggestive, but were not sufficiently detailed to warrant adding this species to the list (Chase 1981a). It is likely that this species does wander into Colorado occasionally, especially in southeastern Colorado. Observers are urged to look for this species, and to very thoroughly document any observations.

Common Black-Hawk   *Buteogallus anthracinus*

One adult was seen 20–21 June 1980 along Plum Creek near Chatfield Reservoir, Douglas County. Although this species was added to the state list, there is reason to be uncertain about the origin of this individual, and it was later deleted (Nelson 1991). All other long-distance extralimital records of this species in North America have been discounted as probable escapes (Daniels et al. 1989). However, this species has nested as far north as Bernalillo County in north-central New Mexico (Hundertmark 1974). A clearer pattern of long-distance vagrancy needs to be established before this report can be properly evaluated.

Red-backed Hawk   *Buteo polyosoma*

One individual of this South American species first appeared in Aug 1987 at Gunnison, Gunnison County, and it has returned each year since. In 1988 it mated with a Swainson's Hawk. Although some have argued that this is a wild bird (Wheeler 1988), it is more plausible that it is an escape (Allen 1988) and this species has not been added to the state list (Nelson 1991).

Iceland Gull
Larus glaucoides

Bailey and Niedrach (1965) reported a specimen collected 20 Apr 1938, Barr Lake, Adams County (DMNH 18886). That specimen was also listed in the same reference as a Thayer's Gull. Notations on the label of the specimen confirmed its identity as Thayer's. A well-documented bird was reported 22 Jan–4 Feb 1986, Cherry Creek Reservoir, Arapahoe County. The documentation was examined by J. V. Remsen, Jr., who concluded that the report was suggestive of Iceland, but that key details were not observed, and that any Colorado records of this species would have to be substantiated by specimens or excellent color photographs (RC files).

Common Ground-Dove
Columbina passerina

There is an excellent single-observer record 17 Dec 1981, Tamarack Ranch, Logan County (Chase 1983). There is also a second record that is suggestive but less detailed (Gent 1986). Observers should be on the lookout for this species.

Barred Owl
Strix varia

An adult and two eggs were collected in Mar 1897 at Holyoke, Phillips County (Bailey and Niedrach 1965). However, the specimen is not extant, and so we believe that this species should not be included on the state list. Sight observations are undocumented.

Vaux's Swift
Chaetura vauxi

There have been several sight reports of this species; see Chimney Swift account.

Ruby-throated Hummingbird
Archilochus colubris

A record of a male 13–14 July 1991 at Rye, Pueblo County is being evaluated by the Records Committee.

Acorn Woodpecker
Melanerpes formicivorus

There is a single-observer record 5 Sep 1980, Billy Creek State Wildlife Area, Ouray County (Chase 1982). Observers should look for this species in southwestern Colorado.

Buff-breasted Flycatcher
Empidonax fulvifrons

The Records Committee is currently evaluating a sight report from 19 May 1991 at Colorado Springs State Wildlife Area, El Paso County (Prather 1992).

Cactus Wren
Campylorhynchus brunneicapillus

There were two suggestive reports from southeastern Colorado (Reddall 1973c, 1974a). This species should be looked for in cholla grasslands in southeastern Colorado.

Black-tailed Gnatcatcher
Polioptila melanura

Several birds (including fledged young) and a nest were seen from 7 July 1991 and later, Coal Canyon, near Cameo, Mesa County (Dexter 1991, which includes a photograph). This is notable because the nearest locality for this sedentary species is in southwestern Utah. This record is currently under review by the Records Committee, which also has reviewed records from southwestern Colorado (Chase 1981a, Gent 1984b). Observers are urged to be cautious about identifying this species as Blue-gray Gnatcatchers often show extensive black on the underside of the tail (Dunn and Garrett 1987) and also can be dark in the head (Chase 1981a). There are almost no extralimital records of this highly sedentary species (Dunn and Garrett 1987).

Smith's Longspur
Calcarius pictus

There were several reports of flocks in eastern Colorado in early and mid-Sep 1973 and 1974 which were accepted for the state list. This species was later withdrawn from the state list because the sight records were based on erroneous field marks and because this species is not likely to occur until late fall (Chase 1981a). This species may occur in small numbers in Colorado, and is most likely to be found after mid-Oct on the extreme eastern plains. Observers should be very cautious when identifying this species, and any records would need to be thoroughly documented.

The following are scientific names for plants mentioned in the text; the terminology follows Weber (1987, 1990).

Alder (*Alnus incana*)

Big bluestem (*Andropogon gerardii*)

Big sagebrush
(*Seriphidium tridentatum*)

Bitterbrush (*Purshia tridentata*)

Blueberry (*Vaccinium* spp.)

Blue grama (*Bouteloua gracilis*)

Bog birch (*Betula glandulosa*)

Box-elder (*Negundo aceroides*)

Bristlecone pine (*Pinus aristata*)

Buckbrush (*Ceanothus* spp.)

Buffalo-grass (*Buchloe dactyloides*)

Candelabra cactus
(*Cylindropuntia imbricata*)

Cattail
(*Typha latifolia* and *angustifolia*)

Colorado blue spruce (*Picea pungens*)

Currant (*Ribes* spp.)

Douglas-fir (*Pseudotsuga menziesii*)

Elm (*Ulmus* spp.)

Englemann spruce (*Picea engelmannii*)

Four-winged saltbush
(*Atriplex canescens*)

Gambel oak (*Quercus gambelii*)

Greasewood (*Sarcobatus vermiculatus*)

Green ash (*Fraxinus pennsylvanica*)

Hawthorn (*Crataegus* spp.)

Limber pine (*Pinus flexilis*)

Little bluestem
(*Schizachyrium scoparium*)

Lodgepole pine (*Pinus contorta*)

Mountain mahogany
(*Cercocarpus montanus*)

Mountain maple (*Acer glabrum*)

Mountain sagebrush
(*Seriphidium vaseyanum*)

Narrowleaf cottonwood
(*Populus angustifolia*)

Needle-and-thread (*Stipa comata*)

Ninebark (*Physocarpus monogynus*)

Oneseed juniper (*Sabina monosperma*)

Peach-leaved willow
(*Salix amygdaloides*)

Plains cottonwood (*Populus deltoides*)

Piñon pine (*Pinus edulis*)

Ponderosa pine (*Pinus ponderosa*)

Prickly-pear cactus (*Opuntia* spp.)

Quaking aspen (*Populus tremuloides*)

Rabbitbrush (*Chrysothamnus* spp.)

Red-osier dogwood (*Swida sericea*)

River birch (*Betula fontinalis*)

Rocky Mountain juniper
(*Juniperus scopulorum*)

Rose (*Rosa woodsii*)

Russian-olive (*Elaeagnus angustifolia*)

Sand bluestem (*Andropogon hallii*)

Sand dropseed
(*Sporobolus cryptandrus*)

Sand sagebrush (*Oligosporus filifolia*)

Sandbar willow (*Salix exigua*)

Serviceberry (*Amelanchier* spp.)

Shadscale (*Atriplex* spp.)

Sideoats grama
(*Bouteloua curtipendula*)

Skunkbrush (*Rhus aromatica*)

Smartweed (*Persicaria* spp.)

Snowberry (*Symphoricarpos* spp.)

Subalpine fir (*Abies lasiocarpa*)

Tamarisk (*Tamarix ramosissima*)

Utah juniper (*Juniperus osteosperma*)

Western wheatgrass
(*Pascopyrum smithii*)

Willow (*Salix* spp.)

Winterfat (*Krascheninnikovia lanata*)

White fir (*Abies concolor*)

Whortleberry (*Vaccinium* spp.)

Yucca or Spanish Bayonet
(*Yucca glauca*)

Literature Cited

Aiken, C. E. H. and E. R. Warren. 1914. The birds of El Paso County, Colorado. Colorado College Science Series 12:455–603.

Alexander, G. 1937. The birds of Boulder County, Colorado. University of Colorado Studies 24:79–105.

Allen, J. A. 1872. Notes of an ornithological reconnaissance of portions of Kansas, Colorado, Wyoming, and Utah. Bulletin of the Museum of Comparative Zoology 3:113–183.

Allen, S. 1988. Some thoughts on the identification of Gunnison's Red-backed Hawk (*Buteo polyosoma*) and why it's not a natural vagrant. C.F.O. Journal 22:9–14.

Alles, D. L. 1985. A breeding bird census in the subalpine zone of Colorado's Front Range. Unpublished paper. University of Colorado, Boulder. 15pp.

American Ornithologists' Union. 1983. Check-list of North American birds. 6th ed. Allen Press, Lawrence, Kansas. 877pp.

American Ornithologists' Union. 1985. Thirty-fifth supplement to the American Ornithologists' Union *Check-list of North American Birds*. Auk 102:680–686.

American Ornithologists' Union. 1987. Thirty-sixth supplement to the American Ornithologists' Union *Check-list of North American Birds*. Auk 104:591–596.

American Ornithologists' Union. 1989. Thirty-seventh supplement to the American Ornithologists' Union *Check-list of North American Birds*. Auk 106:532–538.

American Ornithologists' Union. 1991. Thirty-eighth supplement to the American Ornithologists' Union *Check-list of North American Birds*. Auk 108:750–754.

Andrews, R. 1978. Colorado Field Ornithologists Official Records Committee Report 1976 and 1977. C.F.O. Journal 12:4–21.

Andrews, R. 1979. Colorado Field Ornithologists Official Records Committee report 1976–1977. Western Birds 10:57–70.

Andrews, R. and M. Carter. 1992. Birds of the Barr Lake area. In preparation.

Andrews, R., B. Righter, and M. Carter. 1992. A proposed format for local bird checklists. C. F. O. Journal 26:12–18.

Ankney, C. D., D. G. Dennis, and R. C. Bailey. 1987. Increasing Mallards, decreasing American Black Ducks: coincidence or cause and effect? Journal of Wildlife Management 51:523–529.

Anonymous. 1983. Immature Ross' Gull in Colorado. C.F.O. Journal 17:16–17.

Anonymous. 1988. 1988 field season completed now. Colorado Bird Atlas Newsletter No. 5:1.

Anonymous. 1990. Field report—1990 season. Colorado Bird Atlas Newsletter No. 12: 1.

Appleby, R. H., S. C. Madge, and K. Mullarney. 1986. Identification of divers in immature and winter plumages. British Birds 79:365–391.

Armstrong, D. 1972. Distribution of mammals in Colorado. Monograph of the Museum of Natural History, University of Kansas, Lawrence. 415pp.

Aulenbach, S. and M. O'Shea–Stone. 1983. Bird utilization of a ponderosa pine forest after a fire. C.F.O. Journal 17:14–19.

Bailey, A. M. 1926. The ivory gull in Colorado. Condor 28:182–183.

Bailey, A. M. 1945. Rivoli's hummingbird (*Eugenes fulgens*) in Colorado. Auk 62:630–631.

Bailey, A. M. 1957. Hudsonian Godwit in Colorado. Wilson Bulletin 69:112.

Bailey, A. M. 1972. Gyrfalcon specimen from Colorado. Colorado Field Ornithologist No. 12:12.

Bailey, A. M. and F. G. Brandenburg. 1941. Colorado nesting records. Condor 43: 73–74.

Bailey, A. M. and R. J. Niedrach. 1926. Franklin's gull in Colorado. Condor 28: 44–45.

Bailey, A. M. and R. J. Niedrach. 1937. Notes on Colorado birds. Auk 54:524–527.

Bailey, A. M. and R. J. Niedrach. 1938. Brewster's Egret nesting in Colorado. Condor 40:44–45.

Bailey, A. M. and R. J. Niedrach. 1939. Notes on jaegers and gulls of Colorado. Auk 56:79–81.

Bailey, A. M. and R. J. Niedrach. 1965. Birds of Colorado. Denver Museum of Natural History. 2 vols. 895pp.

Bailey, A. M. and R. J. Niedrach. 1967. Pictorial checklist of Colorado birds. Denver Museum of Natural History. 168pp.

Bailey, S. F. 1991. Bill characters separating Trumpeter and Tundra Swans: a cautionary note. Birding 23:89–91.

Baily, A. L. 1954. Indigo bunting nesting in Colorado. Auk 71:330.

Baker, W. L. 1984. A preliminary classification of the natural vegetation of Colorado. Great Basin Naturalist 44:647–671.

Balda, R. P., B. C. McKnight, and C. D. Johnson. 1975. Flammulated Owl migration in the southwestern United States. Wilson Bulletin 87:520–533.

Balch, L. G. 1979. Separation of Northern and Loggerhead Shrikes in the field. Birding 11:9–12.

Baldwin, P. H. and J. R. Koplin. 1966. The Boreal Owl as a Pleistocene relict in Colorado. Condor 68:299–300.

Barrows, C. W. 1981. Roost selection by Spotted Owls: an adaptation to heat stress. Condor 83:302–309.

Bartol, D. A. 1973. 1972 records of the Blue-throated Hummingbird in Colorado. Colorado Field Ornithologist No. 15:20–21.

Bass, K.H. 1977. Cape May Warbler at Rocky Mountain National Park. C.F.O. Journal 31:14–15.

Beaver, D. L. and P. H. Baldwin. 1975. Ecological overlap and the problems of competition and sympatry in the Western and Hammond's Flycatchers. Condor 77:1–13.

Bechard, M. J. and C. S. Houston. 1984. Probable identity of purported Rough-legged Hawk nests in the western U. S. and Canada. Condor 86:348–352.

Behle, W. H. 1981. The birds of northeastern Utah. Utah Museum of Natural History Occasional Publication No. 2, University of Utah, Salt Lake City. 136pp.

Behle, W. H. 1985. Utah birds: geographic distribution and systematics. Utah Museum of Natural History Occasional Publication No. 5, University of Utah, Salt Lake City. 147pp.

Behle, W. H. and M. L. Perry. 1975. Utah birds: check-list, seasonal and ecological occurrence charts and guides to bird finding. Utah Museum of Natural History, Salt Lake City. 144pp.

Behle, W. H., E. D. Sorensen, and C. M. White. 1985. Utah birds: a revised checklist. Utah Museum of Natural History Occasional Publication No. 4, University of Utah, Salt Lake City. 108pp.

Beidleman, R. G. undated. Birds of Rocky Mountain National Park: a check list.

Bekoff, M. and A. C. Scott. 1989. Aggression, dominance, and social organization in Evening Grosbeaks. Ethology 83:177–194.

Bekoff, M., A. C. Scott, and D. A. Conner. 1987. Nonrandom nest-site selection in Evening Grosbeaks. Condor 89:819–829.

Bekoff, M., A. C. Scott, and D. A. Conner. 1989. Ecological analyses of nesting success in evening grosbeaks. Oecologia 81:67–74.

Benedict, A. and O. Williams. 1981. Winter territoriality and diet of Colorado solitaires. Journal of the Colorado—Wyoming Academy of Science 13:61–62.

Bergtold, W. H. 1921. The season. Bird-Lore 23:38, 96, 147, 207, 312.

Bergtold, W. H. 1924. A summer occurrence of the Bohemian Waxwing in Colorado. Auk 41:614.

Bergtold, W. H. 1927a. The season. Bird-Lore 29:60-62.

Bergtold, W. H. 1927b. The Cardinal in Colorado. Auk 44:108.

Bergtold, W. H. 1928. A guide to Colorado birds. Smith-Brooks Printing Co., Denver. 207pp.

Bergtold, W. H. 1931. The season. Bird-Lore 33:19, 134, 201, 273, 338, 413.

Bergtold, W. H. 1932. The season. Bird-Lore 34:18, 147, 213, 278, 346, 405.

Betts, N. D. 1913. Birds of Boulder County, Colorado. University of Colorado Studies 10: 177–232.

Binford, L. C. and J. V. Remsen, Jr. 1974. Identification of the Yellow-billed Loon (*Gavia adamsii*). Western Birds 5:111–126.

Bock, C. E. 1971. Pairing in hybrid flicker populations in eastern Colorado. Auk 88:921–924.

Bock, C. E. 1982. Factors influencing winter distribution and abundance of Townsend's Solitaire. Wilson Bulletin 94:297–302.

Bock, C. E., H. H. Hadow, and P. Somers. 1971. Relations between Lewis' and Red-headed Woodpeckers in southeastern Colorado. Wilson Bulletin 83: 237–248.

Bock, C. E. and L. W. Lepthien. 1975. Distribution and abundance of the Black-billed Magpie (*Pica pica*) in North America. Great Basin Naturalist 35: 269–272.

Bock, C. E. and L. W. Lepthien. 1976a. Geographical ecology of the common species of *Buteo* and *Parabuteo* wintering in North America. Condor 78: 554–557.

Bock, C. E. and L. W. Lepthien. 1976b. Changing winter distribution and abundance of the Blue Jay. American Midland Naturalist 96:232–236.

Bosley, B. 1975. Chestnut-sided Warbler—second Colorado nest. C.F.0. Journal No. 24:10.

Bottorff, R. L. 1974. Cottonwood habitat for birds in Colorado. American Birds 28:975–979.

Bouricius, S. M. 1992. A Scissor-tailed Flycatcher in a montane meadow. C.F.O. Journal 26:76–78.

Braun, C. E. 1973. Distribution and habitats of Band-tailed Pigeons in Colorado. Proceedings of the Western Association of State Game and Fish Commissions 53:336–344.

Braun, C. E. 1979. Migration routes of Mourning doves west of the Continental Divide in the Central Management Unit. Wildlife Society Bulletin 7:94–97.

Braun, C. E. 1980. Alpine bird communities of western North America: implications for management and research. Pages 280–291 *in* R. M. DeGraff and N. G. Tilghman, compilers. Workshop Proceedings Management of western forests and grasslands for nongame birds. USDA Forest Service General Technical Report INT–86.

Braun, C. E., M. F. Baker, R. L. Eng, J. S. Gashwiler, and M. H. Schroeder. 1976. Conservation committee report on effects of alteration of sagebrush communities on the associated avifauna. Wilson Bulletin 88:165–171.

Braun, C. E., R. B. Davies, J. R. Dennis, K. A. Green, and J. L. Sheppard. 1992. Plains Sharp-tailed Grouse Recovery Plan. Colorado Division of Wildlife, Denver. 31pp.

Braun, C. E., K. M. Giesen, R. W. Hoffman, T. E. Remington, and W. D. Snyder. 1991. Upland bird management analysis guide: draft. Colorado Division of Wildlife, Denver. 90pp.

Braun, C. E., V. H. Reid, T. D. Ray, and R. L. Boyd. 1979. Additional records of White-winged Doves in Colorado. Condor 81:96.

Braun, C. E. and G. E. Rogers. 1971. The White-tailed Ptarmigan in Colorado. Colorado Division of Game, Fish and Parks Technical Publication No. 27, Denver. 80pp.

Breiding, G. H. 1943. Starling nesting in Colorado. Wilson Bulletin 55:247.

Brewer, T. M. 1879. The Rocky Mountain goldeneye (*Bucephala islandica*). Bulletin of the Nuttall Ornithological Club 4:148–152.

Bridges, D. 1985. White Ibis—first Colorado record. C.F.O. Journal 19:75–76.

Bridges, D. 1992a. Black Rail saga. C.F.O. Journal 26:57–60.

Bridges, D. 1992b. Relative abundance of owls in Colorado: a preliminary estimate. C.F.O. Journal 26:27–28.

Bridges, D. 1992c. Northern Saw-whet Owls vs. Boreal Owls above 10,000 feet in the Wet, Sangre de Cristo, and Culebra mountains of south-central Colorado: a preliminary report. C.F.O. Journal 26:29–31.

Bridges, D. and D. A. Leatherman. 1991. Sprague's Pipits and some associated bird species in extreme northeastern Colorado. C.F.O. Journal 25:115-118.

Brockner, W. W. 1984. Brown-headed Cowbird parasitizing Mountain Chickadee nest. C.F.O. Journal 18:109–110.

Brockner, W. W. 1989. A Northern Cardinal (*Cardinalis cardinalis*) at 10,710 feet elevation in Colorado. C.F.O. Journal 23:132–133.

Browning, M. R. 1974. Comments on the winter distribution of the Swainson's Hawk (*Buteo swainsoni*) in North America. American Birds 28:865–867.

Buechert, C. 1980. Summer occurrence of a Yellow-throated Vireo in Colorado. C.F.O. Journal 14:27–28.

Bunn, R. L. 1986. Breeding records for Clark's Grebe in Colorado and Nevada. Great Basin Naturalist 46:581–582.

Bunn, R. L. 1988. Colorado Field Ornithologists Records Committee report for reports submitted in 1986. C.F.O. Journal 22:85–90.

Bunn, R. L. 1989a. Colorado Field Ornithologists Records Committee report for reports submitted in 1987 (Part I). C.F.O. Journal 23: 13–18.

Bunn, R. L. 1989b. Colorado Field Ornithologists Records Committee report for reports submitted in 1987 (Part II). C.F.O. Journal 23: 114–120.

Burget, M. L. 1957. The wild turkey in Colorado. Colorado Department of Game and Fish P.–R. Project W–30–R, Denver. 68pp.

Burnell, K. L. and D. F. Tomback. 1985. Steller's Jays steal Gray Jay caches: field and laboratory observations. Auk 102:417–419.

Burnett, L. E. 1904. Whip-poor-will (*Antrostomus vociferus*), a new bird for Colorado. Auk 21:278–279.

Buttery, R. F. 1971. Bendire's Thrasher nesting in Colorado. Colorado Field Ornithologist No. 9:29.

Cade, B. S. and R. W. Hoffman. 1990. Winter use of Douglas-fir forests by Blue Grouse in Colorado. Journal of Wildlife Management 54:471–479.

Cairo, J. 1985. King Rail—second Colorado record. C.F.O. Journal 19:38.

Calder, W. A. III. 1987. Southbound through Colorado: migration of Rufous Hummingbirds. National Geographic Research 3:40–51.

Calder, W. A. III. 1991. Territorial hummingbirds. National Geographic Research and Exploration 7:56–69.

Calder, W. A. III., N. M. Waser, S. M. Hiebert, D. W. Inouye, and S. Miller. 1983. Site-fidelity, longevity, and population dynamics of Broad-tailed Hummingbirds: a ten year study. Oecologia 56:359–364.

Campbell, C. L. 1978. Migrating swallows and nutcrackers in Mosquito Range. C.F.O. Journal No. 32:25.

Carter, M. 1990. Status of Least Terns and Piping Plovers in Colorado. C.F.O. Journal 24:115–116 (abstract only).

Carter, M. and J. Reddall. 1991. First successful nesting of the Piping Plover in Colorado. Unpublished report, Colorado Bird Observatory, Brighton, Colo.

Cary, M. 1909. New records and important range extensions of Colorado birds. Auk 26:180–185, 312.

Cary, M. 1911. A biological survey of Colorado. North American Fauna No. 33. USDA—Bureau of Biological Survey. 256pp.

Catlett, R. H., R. G. Beidleman, and G. W. Esch. 1958. An analysis of Long-eared Owl pellets from northern Colorado. Journal of the Colorado—Wyoming Academy of Science 4:48 (abstract only).

Chase, C. A. III. 1979. Breeding shorebirds in the Arkansas Valley. C.F.O. Journal 13:3–6.

Chase, C. A. III. 1980. Summer report, June 1-August 31, 1979. C.F.O. Journal 14: 38–51.

Chase, C. A. III. 1981a. Colorado Field Ornithologists Records Committee Report—1977-1980-Part 1. C.F.O. Journal 15:24–30.

Chase, C. A. III. 1981b. Colorado Field Ornithologists Records Committee Report—1977-1980-Part 2. C.F.O. Journal 15:54–59.

Chase, C. A. III. 1982. Colorado Field Ornithologists Records Committee Report—1980-1981. C.F.O. Journal 16:46–52.

Chase, C. A. III. 1983. Colorado Field Ornithologists Records Committee Report—1981. C.F.O. Journal 17:75–82.

Chase, C. A. III. 1984. Gull hybridization: California X Herring. C.F.O. Journal 18:62 (abstract only).

Chase, C. A. III. 1985. Identification of Laughing and Franklin's Gulls. C.F.O. Journal 19:102–106.

Chronic, H. 1980. Roadside geology of Colorado. Mountain Press Publishing Co., Missoula, Mont. 322pp.

Chronic, J. and H. Chronic. 1972. Prairie, peak and plateau: a guide to the geology of Colorado. Colorado Geological Survey Bulletin 32, Colorado Geological Survey, Denver. 126pp.

Clark, W. S. 1987. A field guide to hawks. Houghton Mifflin Co., Boston. 198 pp.

Cohen, R. R. 1976. Nest-site selection by the Tree Swallow [*Iridoprocne bicolor*] and its avian competition in the Colorado mountains: initial findings. Journal of the Colorado—Wyoming Academy of Science 8:73 (abstract only).

Cohen, R. R. 1977. On the breeding biology of the Tree Swallow, *Iridoprocne bicolor*, in the Colorado Rocky Mountains. Journal of the Colorado—Wyoming Academy of Science 9:47 (abstract only).

Cohen, R. R. 1978. Behavioral adaptations for cavity-nesting in the Tree Swallow, *Iridoprocne bicolor*. Journal of the Colorado—Wyoming Academy of Science 10:41 (abstract only).

Cohen, R. R. 1982. A comparison of Violet-green Swallow and Tree Swallow breeding biology at high altitudes in Colorado. Journal of the Colorado—Wyoming Academy of Science 14:60 (abstract only).

Cohen, R. R. 1984. Weather and early spring activity patterns of Tree Swallows at a mountain breeding area in Colorado. American Zoologist 4:61A (abstract only).

Colborn, T. E. and O. Reames. 1971. Anna's Hummingbird in Colorado. Colorado Field Ornithologist No. 9:26.

Collister, A. 1970. Annotated checklist of birds of Rocky Mountain National Park and Shadow Mountain Recreation Area. Denver Museum of Natural History Pictorial No. 18. 64pp.

Colorado Division of Wildlife. 1989. Colorado Statewide Waterfowl Management Plan 1989–2003. Colorado Division of Wildlife, Fort Collins. 98pp.

Conover, M. R. 1983. Recent changes in Ring-billed and California Gull populations in the western United States. Wilson Bulletin 95:362–383.

Conry, J. A. and B. E. Webb. 1980. Intergrade Juncos (*Junco hyemalis mearnsi* X *J. caniceps caniceps*) in eastern Colorado. Western Birds 11:205–206.

Conry, J. A. and B. E. Webb. 1982. An extant specimen of Arctic Tern from Colorado. Western Birds 13:37–38.

Cook, A. G. 1984. Birds of the desert region of Uintah County, Utah. Great Basin Naturalist 44:584–620.

Cooke, F., D. T. Parkin, and R. F. Rockwell. 1988. Evidence of former allopatry of the two color phases of Lesser Snow Geese (*Chen caerulescens caerulescens*). Auk 105:467–479.

Cooke, W. W. 1897. The birds of Colorado. State Agricultural College (Colorado State University), Bulletin 37 (Technical Series 2). Smith-Brooks Printing Co., Denver.

Cooke, W. W. 1898. Further notes on the birds of Colorado: an appendix to Bulletin 37. State Agricultural College (Colorado State University), Agricultural Experimental Station, Fort Collins, Bulletin 44 (Technical Series 4), pp. 147–176. Smith-Brooks Printing Co., Denver.

Cooke, W. W. 1900. The birds of Colorado: a second appendix to Bulletin 37, Agricultural College of Colorado (Colorado State University), Bulletin 56 (Technical Series 5), published by Agricultural Experimental Station, Fort Collins, pp. 179–239.

Cooke, W. W. 1909. The birds of Colorado—third supplement. Auk 26:400–422.

Cooper, J. R. 1975. Scott's Oriole—first Colorado record. C.F.O. Journal No. 24:22–23.

Corbin, K. W. and C. G. Sibley. 1977. Rapid evolution in orioles of the genus *Icterus*. Condor 79:335–342.

Corbin, K. W., C. G. Sibley, and A. Ferguson. 1979. Genic changes associated with the establishment of sympatry in orioles of the genus *Icterus*. Evolution 33: 624–633.

Costello, D. F. 1964. Vegetation zones in Colorado. Pages iii-x *in* Harrington, H. D. Manual of the plants of Colorado. Sage Books, Denver.

Coues, E. 1874. Avifauna of Colorado and Wyoming. American Naturalist 8:240.

Cox, G. W. 1973. Hybridization between Mourning and MacGillivray's Warblers. Auk 90:190–191.

Craig, G. R. 1971. Gyrfalcon trapped in Colorado. Colorado Field Ornithologist No. 9:20.

Craig, G. R. 1981. Raptor investigations. Job Progress Report, Colorado Division Wildlife Research Report, pp.130–139, Denver.

Craig, G. R. 1991a. Bald Eagle nest site protection and enhancement program. Job Progress Report, Colorado Division Wildlife Research Report, pp. 1–6, Denver.

Craig, G. R. 1991b. Peregrine Falcon restoration program. Job Progress Report, Colorado Division Wildlife Research Report, pp. 1–9, Denver.

Cranson, B. F. 1972. Mississippi Kite nesting in Colorado. Colorado Field Ornithologist No. 11:5–11.

Crockett, A. B. and H. H. Hadow. 1975. Nest site selection by Williamson and Red-naped Sapsuckers. Condor 77:365–368.

Crockett, A. B. and P. L. Hansley. 1977. Coition, nesting, and postfledging behavior of Williamson's Sapsucker in Colorado. Living Bird 16:7–19.

Crockett, A. B. and P. L. Hansley. 1978. Apparent response of *Picoides* woodpeckers to outbreaks of the pine bark beetle. Western Birds 9:67–70.

Cruz, A. 1975. Ecological analysis of the breeding birds of a ponderosa pine forest. Journal of the Colorado—Wyoming Academy of Science 7 (6):37-38 (abstract only).

Cummings, J. L. 1985. Movements of adult male red-winged blackbirds color-tagged in Colorado. North American Bird Bander 10:73–75.

Curry, E. and M. Curry. 1984. A Brambling in Colorado. C.F.O. Journal 18:3.

Daniel, J. C. 1953. A note on the common loon in southern Colorado. Great Basin Naturalist 13:74.

Daniels, B. E., L. Hays, D. Hays, J. Morlan, and D. Roberson. 1989. First record of the Common Black-Hawk for California. Western Birds 20:11–18.

Darling, J. L. 1970. New breeding records of *Toxostoma curvirostre* and *T. bendirei* in New Mexico. Condor 72:366–367.

Davis, D. 1976. Comments on the distribution of Turkey Vultures in Colorado. Journal of the Colorado—Wyoming Academy of Science 8:74 (abstract only).

Davis, W. A. 1969. Birds in Western Colorado. Colorado Field Ornithologists. 61pp.

Davis, W. A. 1970. Additions and corrections to "Birds in Western Colorado." Colorado Field Ornithologist No. 8:30–32.

DeHaven, R. W. and J.L. Guarino 1970. Breeding of Starlings using nest-boxes at Denver, Colorado. Colorado Field Ornithologist No. 8:1-10.

Dennis, J. R. 1985. Whooping Cranes in eastern Colorado. C.F.O. Journal 19:77–79.

Dexter, C. 1991. Breeding Black-tailed Gnatcatchers? In Colorado? C.F.O. Journal 25:103.

Dille, F. M. 1887. A week's trip after hawk's eggs in Colorado. Ornithologist and Oologist 12:97–100.

Dille, F. M. 1900. Nesting of the pine siskin at Denver, Colorado. Condor 2:73.

Dille, F. M. 1903. Nesting dates for birds in the Denver district, Colorado. Condor 5:73–74.

Doerr, P. D. and J. H. Enderson. 1965. An index of abundance of the Goshawk in Colorado in winter. Auk 82:284–285.

Dorn, J. L. and R. D. Dorn. 1990. Wyoming birds. Mountain West Publishing, Cheyenne, Wyo. 139pp.

Douglass, J. R. and M. M. Douglass. 1958. First Ancient Murrelet collected in Colorado. Auk 75:216.

Downing, H. 1981. The first nesting of Vermilion Flycatchers in Colorado. C.F.O. Journal 15:75–76.

Drew, F. M. 1881. Field notes on the birds of San Juan County, Colorado. Bulletin of the Nuttall Ornithological Club 6:85–91, 138–143.

Drewien, R. C. and E. G. Bizeau. 1974. Status and distribution of Greater Sandhill Cranes in the Rocky Mountains. Journal of Wildlife Management 38:720–742.

Droger, H. K. 1979. Female Least Bittern with young. C.F.O. Journal 13:62–63.

Ducey, J. E. 1988. Nebraska birds: breeding status and distribution. Simmons-Boardman Books, Omaha. 148pp.

Dunn, J. L. and K. L. Garrett. 1983a. The identification of wood-pewees. Western Tanager 50, No. 4:1–3.

Dunn, J. and K. Garrett. 1983b. The identification of thrushes of the genus *Catharus*. Western Tanager 49, No. 6:1–2, No. 7:4, 9, No. 8:7–9, No. 9:1–3.

Dunn, J. L. and K. L. Garrett. 1987. The identification of North American gnatcatchers. Birding 19:17–29.

Dunn, P. O. and R. A. Ryder. 1986. Notes on the birds of Cold Spring Mountain, northwestern Colorado. Great Basin Naturalist 46:651–655.

Durango Bird Club. 1988. A checklist of the birds of Southwestern Colorado (west of the Continental Divide and south of the San Miguel County line—since 1950).

Eckhardt, R. C. 1976. Polygyny in the Western Wood Pewee. Condor 78:561–562.

Eckhardt, R. C. 1977. Effects of late spring storm on a local Dusky Flycatcher population. Auk 94:362.

Eckhardt, R. C. 1979. The adaptive syndromes of two guilds of insectivorous birds in the Colorado Rocky Mountains. Ecological Monographs 49:129–149.

Ellis, K. L. and J. Haskins. 1985. Unusual nest site for Greater Sandhill Cranes in Colorado. Western Birds 16:185–186.

Ely, C. A. 1970. Migration of Least and Traill's Flycatchers in west-central Kansas. Bird-Banding 41:198–204.

Enderson, J. H. 1964. A study of the prairie falcon in the central Rocky Mountain region. Auk 81:332–352.

Enderson, J. H. 1965. A breeding and migration survey of the Peregrine Falcon. Wilson Bulletin 77:327–339.

Enderson, J. H., F. A. Colley, and J. Stevenson. 1970. Aerial eagle count in Colorado. Condor 72:112.

Erickson, K. A. and A. W. Smith. 1985. Atlas of Colorado. Colorado Associated University Press, Boulder. 73pp.

Evans, K. 1966. Observations on a hybrid between the Sharp-tailed Grouse and the Greater Prairie Chicken. Auk 83:128–129.

Evans, K. and D. L. Gilbert. 1969. A method for evaluating the Greater Prairie Chickens habitat in Colorado. Journal of Wildlife Management 33:643–649.

Faanes, C. A., B. A. Hanson, and H. A. Kantrud. 1979. Cassin's Sparrow—first record for Wyoming and recent range extensions. Western Birds 10: 163–164.

Faanes, C. A. and W. Norling. 1981. Nesting of the Great-tailed Grackle in Nebraska. American Birds 35:148–149.

Felger, A. H. 1909. Colorado notes. Auk 26:85–86.

Felger, A. H. 1910. Birds and mammals of northwestern Colorado. University of Colorado Studies 7:132–146.

Felger, A. H. 1917. Blue Jay in Jefferson Co., Colorado. Auk 34:209–210.

Figgins, J. D. 1913. The status of the Gambel quail in Colorado. Condor 15:158.

Findholt, S. L. 1986. The Ring-billed Gull: a rediscovered nesting species in Wyoming. Western Birds 17:189–190.

Fitton, S. D. and O. K. Scott. 1984. Wyoming's juniper birds. Western Birds 15: 85–90.

Flack, J. A. D. 1976. Bird populations of aspen forests in western North America. Ornithological Monographs No. 19. American Ornithologists' Union, Allen Press, Lawrence, Kan. 97pp.

Fox, E. 1978. Black Phoebe at Durango. C.F.O. Journal 12:43.

Franks, E. C., E. C. Franks, and R. C. Beason. 1971. Blackburnian Warbler in Rocky Mountain National Park, Colorado. Colorado Field Ornithologist No. 9:33.

Frederick, R. B. and R. R. Johnson. 1983. Ross' Geese increasing in central North America. Condor 85:257–258.

Friedmann, H. and C. F. Kiff. 1985. The parasitic cowbirds and their hosts. Proceedings of the Western Foundation of Vertebrate Zoology 2:226–303.

Gadd, S. 1942. Spotted owl nesting in Colorado. Condor 44:35.

Gadd, S. 1969. Chestnut-sided Warbler breeds in Colorado. Auk 86:552–553.

Gatz, T. A. and P. L. Hegdal. 1986. Local winter movements of four raptor species in central Colorado. Western Birds 17:107–114.

Gent, P. 1978. Snow Bunting blizzard. C.F.O. Journal No. 33:9–11.

Gent, P. 1984a. The CFO Records Committee Report for 1982. C.F.O. Journal 18: 51–57.

Gent, P. 1984b. A Pygmy Owl on Mount Shavano. C.F.O. Journal 18:80.

Gent, P. 1985a. The CFO Records Committee Report for 1983. C.F.O. Journal 19: 28–33.

Gent, P. 1985b. The CFO Records Committee Report for 1984. C.F.O. Journal 19: 82–87.

Gent, P. 1986. The CFO Records Committee Report for 1985. C.F.O. Journal 20: 44–50.

Gent, P. 1987. Colorado Field Ornithologists' Records Committee report for 1978–1985. Western Birds 18:97–108.

Giesen, K. M. 1988. Status of Lesser Prairie-Chickens in Colorado. C.F.O. Journal 22:57–58 (abstract only).

Giesen, K. M., C. E. Braun, and T. A. May. 1980. Reproduction and nest-site selection by White-tailed Ptarmigan in Colorado. Wilson Bulletin 92: 188–199.

Giezentanner, J. B. 1970. Avian distribution and population fluctuations on the shortgrass prairie of north-central Colorado. U. S. International Biological Program, Grassland Biome Technical Report 62. 112pp.

Gilman, M. F. 1907. Some birds of southwest Colorado. Condor 9:152–158, 194–195.

Glahn, J. F. 1974. Study of breeding rails with recorded calls in north-central Colorado. Wilson Bulletin 86:206–214.

Gorenzel, W. P. 1977. Eared Grebes' and Forster's Terns' nesting attempts at Lake John. C.F.O. Journal No. 31:13–14.

Gorenzel, W. P., R. A. Ryder, and C. E. Braun. 1981a. American Coot distribution and migration in Colorado. Wilson Bulletin 93:115–118.

Gorenzel, W. P., R. A. Ryder, and C. E. Braun. 1981b. American Coot response to habitat change on a Colorado marsh. Southwestern Naturalist 26:59–65.

Gorenzel, W. P., R. A. Ryder, and C. E. Braun. 1982. Reproduction and nest site characteristics of American Coots at different altitudes in Colorado. Condor 84:59–65.

Grant, A. L. 1978. Bullock's Oriole winters in Littleton. C.F.O. Journal No. 33:12.

Graul, W. D. 1971. Observations at a Long-billed Curlew nest. Auk 88:182–84.

Graul, W. D. 1973. Adaptive aspects of the Mountain Plover social system. Living Bird 12:69–94.

Graul, W. D. 1975. Breeding biology of the Mountain Plover. Wilson Bulletin 87:6–31.

Graul, W. D. 1976a. The Mountain Plover's mating system. C.F.O. Journal No. 26: 17–18.

Graul, W. D. 1976b. Food fluctuations and multiple clutches in the Mountain Plover. Auk 93:166–167.

Graul, W. D. and L. E. Webster. 1976. Breeding status of the Mountain Plover. Condor 78:265–267.

Gray, M. T. 1990. The Piping Plover: a rare bird comes to Colorado. Colorado Outdoors March/April 1990:20–21.

Gregg, H. R. 1938. Birds of Rocky Mountain National Park. Publication 4, Rocky Mountain Nature Association Estes Park, Colo. 80pp.

Gregg, R. E. 1963. The ants of Colorado. University of Colorado Press, Boulder. 792pp.

Griese, H. J., R. A. Ryder, and C. E. Braun. 1980. Spatial and temporal distribution of rails in Colorado. Wilson Bulletin 92:96–102.

Griffiths, D. A. 1976. King Rail—first Colorado record. C.F.O. Journal No. 28:17.

Griffiths, D. A., C. Griffiths, and D. Silverman. 1980. Grace's Warbler nesting on Colorado's eastern slope. C.F.O. Journal 14:37.

Groth, J. G. 1992. White-winged Crossbill breeding in southern Colorado, with notes on juvenile calls. Western Birds 23:35–37.

Grudzien, T. A., W. S. Moore, J. R. Cook, and D. Tagle. 1987. Genic population structure and gene flow in the Northern Flicker (*Colaptes auratus*) hybrid zone. Auk 104:654–664.

Gutiérrez, R. 1970. Birds of the upper Sand Creek drainage, Sangre de Cristo Mountains, Colorado. Colorado Field Ornithologist No. 8:11–16.

Gutiérrez, R. 1971. Observations on the breeding biology and behavior of Mourning Doves in Fort Collins, Colorado. Colorado Field Ornithologist No. 10:10–16.

Gutiérrez, R., C. E. Braun, and T. P. Zapatka. 1975. Reproductive biology of the Band-tailed Pigeon in Colorado and New Mexico. Auk 92:665–677.

Ha, J. C. and P. N. Lehner. 1990. Notes on Gray Jay demographics in Colorado. Wilson Bulletin 102:698–702.

Hadley, N. 1969a. Microenvironmental factors influencing the nesting sites of some subalpine fringillid birds in Colorado. Arctic and Alpine Research 1: 121–126.

Hadley, N. 1969b. Breeding biology of the Gray-headed Junco, *Junco caniceps* (Woodhouse) in the Colorado Front Range. Colorado Field Ornithologist No. 5:15–21.

Hadow, H. H. 1973. Winter ecology of migrant and resident Lewis' Woodpeckers in southeastern Colorado. Condor 75:210–224.

Hall, G. A. 1979. Hybridization between Mourning and MacGillivray's Warblers. Bird–Banding 50:101–107.

Hallock, D. 1984. Status and avifauna of willow carrs in Boulder County. C.F.O. Journal 18:100–105.

Hallock, D. 1988. Breeding birds of an old-growth spruce-fir forest. C.F.O. Journal 22:44–55.

Hallock, D. 1990. A study of breeding and winter birds in different age-classed lodgepole pine forests. C.F.O. Journal 24:2–16.

Hansen, H. A. and U. C. Nelson. 1957. Brant of the Bering Sea—migration and mortality. Pages 237-256 *in* Transactions of the Twenty-second North American Wildlife Conference, March 4, 5, and 6, 1957. Wildlife Management Institute, Washington D.C.

Hanka, L. R. 1979. Choice of host nest by the Brown-headed Cowbird in Colorado and Wyoming. Condor 81:436–437.

Hanka, L. R. 1984. A Brown-headed Cowbird parasitizes Northern Orioles. Western Birds 15:33–34.

Hanka, L. R. 1985. Recent altitudinal range expansion by the Brown-headed Cowbird in Colorado. Western Birds 16:183–184.

Harmata, A. R. 1981. Recoveries of Ferruginous Hawks banded in Colorado. North American Bird Bander 6:144–147.

Harrington, H. D. 1964. Manual of the plants of Colorado. Sage Books, Denver. 666pp.

Hayworth, A. M. and W. W. Weathers. 1984. Temperature regulation and climatic adaptation in Black-billed and Yellow-billed Magpies. Condor 86: 19–26.

Hendee, R. W. 1929. Notes on birds observed in Moffat County, Colorado. Condor 31:24–32.

Henderson, J. 1905. A Blue Jay at Yuma, Colorado. Auk 22:82.

Henderson, J. 1909. An annotated list of the birds of Boulder County, Colorado. University of Colorado Studies 6:219–242.

Hendricks, P. 1978. Notes on the courtship behavior of Brown-capped Rosy Finches. Wilson Bulletin 90:285–287.

Henshaw, H. W. 1875. Report upon ornithological collections made in portions of Nevada, Utah, California, Colorado, New Mexico, and Arizona, during the years 1871, 1872, 1873, and 1874, in report upon geographical and geological explorations and surveys west of the one hundreth meridian. (First Lieut. George M. Wheeler, Corps of Engineers, in charge; 6 vols., GPO, Washington D. C.). Vol. 5 Zoology, Chap. 3, pp.133-507.

Hersey, L. J. 1911. Some new birds for Colorado. Auk 28:490.

Hersey, L. J. and R. B. Rockwell. 1909. An annotated list of the birds of the Barr Lake district, Adams County, Colorado. Condor 11:109–122.

Hoag, A. W. and C. E. Braun. 1990. Status and distribution of Plains Sharp-tailed Grouse in Colorado. Prairie Naturalist 22:97–102.

Hoffman, R.W. 1963. The Lesser Prairie Chicken in Colorado. Journal of Wildlife Management 27:726–732.

Hoffman, R.W. 1965. The Scaled Quail in Colorado: range, population status, and harvest. Technical Publication No. 18, Colorado Game, Fish and Parks Department. 47pp.

Hoffman, R.W. 1968. Roosting sites and habits of Merriam's Turkeys in Colorado. Journal of Wildlife Management 32:859–866.

Hoffman, R.W. and B. S. Cade. 1982. Occurrence of Sage Grouse above treeline. C.F.O. Journal 16:22–23.

Hoffman, R.W. and C. E. Braun. 1975. Migration of a wintering population of White-tailed Ptarmigan. Journal of Wildlife Management 39:485–490.

Hoffman, R.W. and C. E. Braun. 1977. Characteristics of a wintering population of White-tailed Ptarmigan in Colorado. Wilson Bulletin 89:107–115.

Hoffman, R.W. and C. E. Braun. 1978. Characteristics and status of Ruffed Grouse and Blue Grouse in Colorado. Western Birds 9:121–126.

Hoffman, R.W. and K. M. Giesen. 1983. Demography of an introduced population of white-tailed ptarmigan. Canadian Journal of Zoology 61: 1758–1764.

Hoffman, S., W. Potts, and S. Vander Wall. 1978. Communication. C.F.O. Journal No. 32:4

Holmgren, M. 1981. Wood Duck and Vermilion Flycatcher in far western Oklahoma. Bulletin of the Oklahoma Ornithological Society 14:13–14.

Holt, H. R. 1970. Colorado type bird localities. Colorado Field Ornithologist No. 7:18–22.

Holt, H. R. 1989. Migration calendar of birds of the plains of Colorado—Denver area—north and east. Lark Bunting 24:98–106.

Holt, H. R. and J. A. Lane. 1987. A birder's guide to Colorado. L & P Press, Denver. 163pp.

Howe, W. H. and D. A. Leatherman. 1991. Swainson's Warbler in Fort Collins, Colorado. C.F.O. Journal 25:125–129.

Hubbard, J. D., A. B. Crockett, and P. L. Hansley. 1975. Second record for the Phainopepla in Colorado. Western Birds 6:28.

Hubbard, J. P. 1977. The status of Cassin's Sparrow in New Mexico and adjacent states. American Birds 31:933–941.

Hubbard, J. P. 1978. Revised check-list of the birds of New Mexico. New Mexico Ornithological Society Publication No. 6, Albuquerque. 110pp.

Hudler, G. W., N. Oshima, and F. G. Hawksworth. 1979. Bird dissemination of dwarf mistletoe on ponderosa pine in Colorado. American Midland Naturalist 102:273–280.

Hundertmark, C. A. 1974. Breeding range extensions of certain birds in New Mexico. Wilson Bulletin 86:298–300.

Hutchinson, D. (ed.). 1974. Rose-breasted Grosbeak observed at Bonny Reservoir. Lark Bunting 9, No. 11.

Hyde, A. S. 1979. Birds of Colorado's Gunnison country. Western State College Foundation, Gunnison, Colorado. 140pp.

Inkley, D.B., R.W. Andrews, and S.H. Anderson. 1981. Patterns of bird distribution in Colorado. C.F.O. Journal 15:91–94.

Jacobs, B. 1986. Birding on the Navajo and Hopi Reservations. Jacobs Publishing, Sycamore, Mo. 131pp.

Janos, M. 1985a. Status of Ross' Goose in western Colorado. C.F.O. Journal 19:69–72.

Janos, M. 1985b. An observation of a Least Tern in western Colorado. C.F.O. Journal 19:73–74.

Janos, M. 1985c. Second record of Black Phoebe in western Colorado. C.F.O. Journal 19:25–26.

Janos, M. 1989. Identification guide—Gray Vireo. Colorado Bird Atlas Newsletter, No. 8: p. 4.

Janos, M. 1991. First record of Pyrrhuloxia (*Cardinalis sinuatus*) from Colorado. C.F.O. Journal 25:41–42.

Janos, M. and I. Prather. 1989. A second specimen record of Lesser Nighthawk (*Chordeiles acutipennis*) from Colorado, with notes on its occurrence and identification. C.F.O. Journal 23:134–138.

Jasper, D. A. and W. S. Collins. 1987. The Birds of Grand County, Colorado, including Rocky Mountain Nat'l Park west of the Continental Divide and Arapaho National Recreation Area. 3rd. ed.

Jehl, J. R., Jr. 1979. The autumnal migration of Baird's Sandpiper. Studies in Avian Biology No. 2:55–68.

Jeske, C. W. 1989. A specimen of Surf Scoter (*Melanitta perspicillata*) from western Colorado. C.F.O. Journal 23:75.

Jickling, B. 1984. The Boulder Brambling. C.F.O. Journal 18:3–4.

Johnsgard, P. A. 1979. Birds of the Great Plains: breeding species and their distribution. University of Nebraska Press, Lincoln. 539pp.

Johnsgard, P. A. 1990. Hawks, eagles, and falcons of North America. Smithsonian Institution Press, Washington. 403pp.

Johnsgard, P. A. and R. E. Wood. 1968. Distributional changes and interactions between prairie chickens and Sharp-tailed Grouse in the Midwest. Wilson Bulletin 80:173–188.

Johnson, B. R. and R. A. Ryder. 1977. Breeding densities and migration periods of Common Snipe in Colorado. Wilson Bulletin 89:116–121.

Johnson, C. G., L. A. Nickerson, and M. J. Bechard. 1987. Grasshopper consumption and summer flocks of nonbreeding Swainson's Hawks. Condor 89:676–678.

Jones, S. 1987. Breeding status of small owls in Boulder County, Colorado. C.F.O. Journal 21:35 (abstract only).

Jones, S. 1988. Owling tips for atlasers. Colorado Bird Atlas Newsletter, No. 3, p. 4–5.

Jones, S. 1991. Distribution of small forest owls in Boulder County, Colorado. C.F.O. Journal 25:55–70.

Jordan, M. 1988. Distinguishing Tundra and Trumpeter Swans. Birding 20: 223–226.

Kaufman, K. 1990. Advanced birding. Peterson Field Guide Series. Houghton Mifflin, Boston. 299pp.

Kaufman, K. 1991. The practiced eye. American Birds 45:330–333.

Keeler-Wolf, T., V. Keeler-Wolf, and W. A. Calder, Jr. 1973. Bird fauna of the vicinity of the Rocky Mountain Biological Laboratory. Colorado Field Ornithologist No. 15:22–26.

Keyser, L. S. 1902. Birds of the Rockies. A. C. McClurg and Co., Chicago. 355pp.

Killpack, M. L. 1970. Notes on Sage Thrasher nestlings in Colorado. Condor 72: 486–488.

Kingery, H. E. 1971. Great Basin-Central Rocky Mountain Region. American Birds 25:882–888.

Kingery, H. E. 1972. Great Basin-Central Rocky Mountain Region. American Birds 26:882-887.

Kingery, H. 1973a. Mountain West region. American Birds 27:897–902.

Kingery, H. 1973b. The Curve-billed Thrasher (*Toxostoma curvirostre*)—its status in Colorado and the first recorded nest for the state. Colorado Field Ornithologist No. 17:16–18.

Kingery, H. 1975. Prairie Warbler—first state record. C.F.O. Journal No. 24:24.

Kingery, H. (ed.). 1988. Colorado Bird Distribution Latilong Study. Colorado Division of Wildlife, Denver. 81pp.

Kingery, H. 1990a. Breeding bird atlas update. C.F.O. Journal 24:119.

Kingery, H. 1990b. Mountain West region. American Birds 44:298–301.

Kingery, H. 1990c. Mountain West region. American Birds 44:468–472.

Kingery, H. 1991a. Mountain West Region. American Birds 45:296–299.

Kingery, H. 1991b. Spotted Owl records in Colorado. C.F.O. Journal 25:15–18.

Kingery, H. 1991c. Breeding Bird Atlas update. C.F.O. Journal 25:104–105.

Kingery, H. E. 1992. First Colorado nest for Carolina Wren. C.F.O. Journal 26:67–70.

Kingery, H. E. and P. R. Julian. 1971. Cassin's Sparrow parasitized by cowbird. Wilson Bulletin 83:439.

Kingery, H. and U. Kingery. 1989. Barrow's Goldeneyes summer in Flat Tops Wilderness. C.F.O. Journal 23:86–90.

Kladder, N. 1971. Common Scoter in western Colorado. Colorado Field Ornithologist No. 9:18.

Knopf, F. L. 1985. Significance of riparian vegetation to breeding birds across an altitudinal cline. Pages 105–111 *in* R. R. Johnson et al., technical coordinators, Riparian ecosystems and their management: reconciling conflicting uses. USDA Forest Service General Technical Report RM-120, Fort Collins, Colo. 523pp.

Knopf, F. L. 1986. Changing landscapes and the cosmopolitism of the eastern Colorado avifauna. Wildlife Society Bulletin 14:132–142.

Knopf, F. L. 1988. Conservation of steppe birds in North America. ICBP Technical Publication No. 7:27–41.

Knopf, F. L. 1991. Status and conservation of Mountain Plovers: the evolving regional effort. Report of research activities, USFWS National Ecology Research Center, Fort Collins. 9pp.

Knopf, F. L., R. R. Johnson, T. Rich, F. B. Samson, and R. C. Szaro. 1988. Conservation of riparian ecosystems in the United States. Wilson Bulletin 100: 272–284.

Knopf, F. L. and T. E. Olson. 1984. Naturalization of Russian-olive: implications to Rocky Mountain wildlife. Wildlife Society Bulletin 12:289–298.

Knopf, F. L. and J. A. Sedgwick. 1987. Latent population responses of summer birds to a catastrophic, climatological event. Condor 89:869–873.

Knopf, F. L., J. A. Sedgwick, and R. W. Cannon. 1988. Guild structure of a riparian avifauna relative to seasonal cattle grazing. Journal of Wildlife Management 52:280–290.

Knopf, F. L., J. A. Sedgwick, and D. B. Inkley. 1990. Regional correspondence among shrubsteppe bird habitats. Condor 92:45–53.

Knorr, O. A. 1961. The geographical and ecological distribution of the black swift in Colorado. Wilson Bulletin 73:155–170.

Knorr, O. A. and A. L. Baily. 1950. First breeding record of the black swift, *Nephoecetes n. borealis*, in Colorado. Auk 67:516.

Knowles, C. J., C. J. Stoner, and S. P. Gieb. 1982. Selective use of black-tailed prairie dog towns by mountain plovers. Condor 84:71–74.

Koplin, J. R. 1969. The numerical response of woodpeckers to insect prey in a subalpine forest in Colorado. Condor 71:436–438.

Kowalski, M. P. 1978. Golden-winged Warbler—discovery of a specimen from Colorado. C.F.O. Journal No. 32:25.

Lamb, R. E. 1950. The birds of Logan County, Colorado and the Prewitt Reservoir region of Washington County, Colorado. MS desposited in the Denver Museum of Natural History. 22pp.

Lambeth, R. 1985. The Mesquite Grackle in Mesa County. C.F.O. Journal 19:97–99.

Lambeth, R. and T. Armstrong. 1985. Checklist of the birds of Mesa County. Audubon Society of Western Colorado.

Lanner, R. M. 1981. The piñon pine: a natural and cultural history. University of Nevada Press, Reno. 208pp.

Laymon, S. A. and M. D. Halterman. 1987. Can the western subspecies of the Yellow-billed Cuckoo be saved from extinction? Western Birds 18:19–25.

Leachman, B. and B. Osmundson. 1990. Status of the Mountain Plover: a literature review. USFWS, Fish and Wildlife Enhancement, Golden, Colo. 83pp.

Lehman, P. 1980. The identification of Thayer's Gull in the field. Birding 12:198–210.

Leitner, W. and L. R. Halsey. 1986. First recorded sighting of Henslow's Sparrow in Colorado. C.F.O. Journal 20:18–19.

Levad, R. 1989. Western Screech-Owls in the Grand Valley. C.F.O. Journal 23:107–109.

Ligon, J. C. and D. A. Griffiths. 1972. Black Phoebe nesting in Colorado. Colorado Field Ornithologist No. 13:3–4.

Lincoln, F. C. 1919. Additional notes and records from Colorado. Condor 21:237–238.

Lincoln, F. C. 1920. Birds of the Clear Creek district, Colorado. Auk 37:60–77.

Lindauer, I. E. 1983. A comparison of the plant communities of the South Platte and Arkansas River drainages in eastern Colorado. Southwestern Naturalist 28:249–259.

Linkhart, B. D. and R. T. Reynolds. 1987. Brood division and postnesting behavior of Flammulated Owls. Wilson Bulletin 99:240–243.

Lockhart, J. M. and G. R. Craig. 1985. Ferruginous Hawk status in Colorado. Proceedings of the Raptor Research Foundation Symposium, Management of Birds of Prey, Nov. 3-6, Sacramento (abstract only).

Loeffler, C. 1977. California Gulls—new nesting site. C.F.O. Journal No. 31:13.

Lowe, W. P. 1894. A list of the birds of the Wet Mountains, Huerfano County, Colorado. Auk 11:266–270.

Lowe, W. P. 1895. The arrival of the English sparrow at Pueblo, Colo. Nidologist 2:99.

Marr, J. W. 1967. Ecosystems of the east slope of the Front Range in Colorado. University of Colorado Studies in Biology, No. 8. 134pp.

Marsh, T. G. 1968. A history of the first records of all the birds reported to have been seen within the present boundaries of the state of Colorado prior to settlement. Colorado Field Ornithologist No. 3:12–21.

Marti, C. D. 1968. Double broods of the Barn Owl in Colorado. Colorado Field Ornithologist No. 3:7–8.

Marti, C. D. 1973a. Ten years of Barn Owl prey data from a Colorado nest site. Wilson Bulletin 85:85–86.

Marti, C. D. 1973b. Food consumption and pellet formation rates in four owl species. Wilson Bulletin 85:178–181.

Marti, C. D. 1974. Feeding ecology of four sympatric owls. Condor 76:45–61.

Marti, C. D. and C. E. Braun. 1975. Use of tundra habitats by Prairie Falcons in Colorado. Condor 77:213–214.

Martin, S. G., P. H. Baldwin, and E. B. Reed. 1974. Recent records of birds from the Yampa Valley, northwestern Colorado. Condor 76:113–116.

Marvil, R. E. and A. Cruz. 1989. Impact of Brown-headed Cowbird parasitism on the reproductive success of the Solitary Vireo. Auk 106: 476–480.

McCaffery, B. J., T. A. Sordahl, and P. Zahler. 1984. Behavioral ecology of the mountain plover in northeastern Colorado. Wader Study Group Bulletin 40:18–21.

McCallum, D. A., W. D. Graul, and R. Zaccagnini. 1977. The breeding status of the Long-billed Curlew in Colorado. Auk 94:599–601.

McCrimmon, A. R. 1926. Dickcissel in western Colorado. Auk 43:550.

McDonald, R. 1991. Black jewel of the marsh. Birder's World 5:21–23.

McEllin, S. M. 1979. Nest sites and population demographies of White-breasted and Pigmy Nuthatches in Colorado. Condor 81:348–352.

McGovern, M. and J. M. McNurney. 1986. Densities of Red-tailed Hawks in aspen stands in the Piceance Basin, Colorado. Raptor Research 20:43–45.

McKinley, D. 1964. History of the Carolina Parakeet in its southwestern range. Wilson Bulletin 76:68–93.

Mesa Verde Museum Association. 1986. Checklist of the birds: Mesa Verde.

Miller, G. C. 1978. Riverside Reservoir, Colorado 1977 nesting season report. C.F.O. Journal No. 33:19–20.

Miller, G. C. and W. D. Graul. 1987. Inventories of Colorado's Great Blue Herons. C.F.O. Journal 21:59–66.

Miller, G. C. and R. A. Ryder. 1979. Cattle Egret in Colorado. Western Birds 10: 37–41.

Millsap, B. A. and P. A. Millsap. 1987. Burrow nesting by Common Barn-Owls in north central Colorado. Condor 89:668–670.

Morgan, C. A. 1975. Great Egret nesting. Colorado Field Ornithologist No. 24: 24–25.

Monson, G. and A. R. Phillips. 1981. Annotated checklist of the birds of Arizona. 2nd ed. University of Arizona, Tucson. 240pp.

Morton, M. L. 1991. Postfledging dispersal of Green-tailed Towhees to a subalpine meadow. Condor 93:466–468.

Morrison, C. F. 1886. Field notes on some birds of Colorado. Ornithologist and Oologist 11:153–154, 164–165.

Morrison, C. F. 1888. A list of some birds of La Plata County, Colo., with annotations. Ornithologist and Oologist 13:70–75, 107–108, 115–116, 139–140.

Morrison, C. F. 1889. A list of the birds of Colorado. Ornithologist and Oologist 14:6–9, 65–68, 145–150.

Morrison, M. L. and M. P. Yoders-Williams. 1984. Movements of Steller's Jays in western North America. North American Bird Bander 9(No. 2):12-15.

Mott, D. F., J. L. Guarino, P. P. Woronecki, and W. C. Royall, Jr. 1972. Long-distance recoveries of Common Grackles banded in north-central Colorado. Colorado Field Ornithologist No. 12:16–17.

Moulton, P., M. Moulton, and J. Sundine. 1976. Observations of nesting Long-eared Owls. C.F.O. Journal No. 28:4–7.

Mutel, C. F. and J. C. Emerick. 1984. From grassland to glacier: the natural history of Colorado. Johnson Books, Boulder. 238pp.

National Park Service. 1988. Dinosaur National Monument, Colorado/Utah: Bird Checklist.

Neff, J. A. and J. C. Culbreath. 1946. The status of Colorado band-tailed pigeon in Colorado: season of 1946. Management Division, Federal Aid Section, Colorado Game and Fish Department, Denver. 24pp.

Nelson, D. 1990. Raptor migration along the Dakota hogback in Jefferson County, Colorado, spring 1990. Unpublished report to HawkWatch International. 25 pp.

Nelson, D. 1991. The C.F.O. Records Committee report for 1989. C.F.O. Journal 25:119–125.

Nelson, D. 1992. Ruffed Grouse in Moffat County, Colorado: some thoughts about their status in the state. C.F.O. Journal 26:1–3.

Nelson, D. 1990 and M. F. Carter. 1990a. Birds of selected wetlands of the San Luis Valley. Unpublished report to Colorado Division Wildlife, Denver. 38pp.

Nelson, D. 1990 and M. F. Carter. 1990b. Nesting of Least Tern and Piping Plover, Southeast Colorado, 1990. Unpublished report to Colorado Division Wildlife, Denver.

Nicholls, T. H. and L. M. Egeland. 1989. Birds of the Fraser Experimental Forest, Colorado and their role in dispersing lodgepole pine dwarf mistletoe. C.F.O. Journal 23:3–12.

Niedrach, R. J. and R. B. Rockwell. 1939. Birds of Denver and mountain parks. Denver Museum of Natural History Popular Series No. 5. 203pp.

Oakleaf, B., H. Downing, B. Raynes, and O. K. Scott. 1982. Wyoming avian atlas. Wyoming Game and Fish Department, Cheyenne. 87pp.

Olsen, K. M. 1989. Field identification of the smaller skuas. British Birds 82: 143–176.

O'Meara, T. E., J. B. Haufler, L. H. Stelter, and J. G. Nagy. 1981. Nongame wildlife responses to chaining of pinyon-juniper woodlands. Journal of Wildlife Management 45:381–389.

Ortega, C. P. and A. Cruz. 1988. Mechanisms of egg acceptance by marsh-dwelling blackbirds. Condor 90:349–358.

Ortega, C. P. and A. Cruz. 1991. A comparative study of cowbird parasitism in Yellow-headed Blackbirds and Red-winged Blackbirds. Auk 108:6–16.

Packard, F. M. 1945. The birds of Rocky Mountain National Park, Colorado. Auk 62:371–94.

Packard, F. M. 1946. Midsummer wandering of certain Rocky Mountain birds. Auk 63:152–158.

Pakulak, A. J., C. D. Littlefield, and R. A. Ryder. 1969. Black brant observed in Larimer County, Colorado. Colorado Field Ornithologist No. 5:5–7.

Palmer, D. A. 1983. Northern Saw-whet Owl nesting at Chatfield State Recreation Area. C.F.O. Journal 17:83–86.

Palmer, D. A. 1984. Current status of the Boreal Owl in Colorado. C.F.O. Journal 18:62 (abstract only).

Palmer, D. A. 1987. Annual, seasonal, and nightly variation in calling activity of Boreal and Northern Saw-whet Owls. 1987. Pages 162-168 *in* Nero, R. W. et al., eds. Biology and conservation of northern forest owls: symposium proceedings. General Technical Report RM—142. U.S. Department of Agriculture, Forest Service, Rocky Mountain Forest and Range Experimental Station. Fort Collins. 309pp.

Palmer, D. A. and R. A. Ryder. 1984. The first documented breeding of the Boreal Owl in Colorado. Condor 86:215–217.

Parker, J. W. and J. C. Ogden. 1979. The recent history and status of the Mississippi Kite. American Birds 33:119–129.

Parkes, K. C. and C. H. Nelson. 1976. A definite Colorado breeding record for the Harlequin Duck. Auk 93: 846–847.

Patti, S. T. and M. L. Myers. 1976. A probable Mourning X MacGillivray's Warbler hybrid. Wilson Bulletin 88:490–491.

Peet, R. K. 1981. Forest vegetation of the Colorado Front Range. Vegetatio 45: 3–75.

Phillips, A. R. 1990. Identification and southward limits, in America, of *Gavia adamsii*, the Yellow-billed Loon. Western Birds 21:17–24.

Phillips, A. R., C. Chase III, B. Webb, and D. Casey. 1984. Fourth annual CFO/DMNH taxonomy clinic. C.F.O. Journal 18:19–26.

Phillips, A. R. and M. Holmgren. 1979. The second DMNH/CFO taxonomy clinic. C.F.O. Journal 13:92–100.

Phillips, A. R. and M. Holmgren. 1980. The second DMNH/CFO taxonomy clinic. C.F.O. Journal 14:4–10.

Phillips, A., J. Marshall, and G. Monson. 1964. The birds of Arizona. University of Arizona Press, Tucson. 212pp.

Porter, D. K. 1973. First observation of cowbird parasitism on Lark Buntings in Colorado. Colorado Field Ornithologist No. 16:18.

Porter, D. K., M. A. Strong, J. B. Giezentanner, and R. A. Ryder. 1975. Nest ecology, productivity, and growth of the Loggerhead Shrike on the shortgrass prairie. Southwestern Naturalist 19:429–436.

Prather, B. 1988. Least Flycatcher nesting in Colorado. C.F.O. Journal 22:134–136.

Prather, J. 1992. First record of the Buff-breasted Flycatcher (*Empidonax fulvifrons*) for Colorado. C.F.O. Journal 26:37–38.

Pratt, H. D. 1976. Field identification of White-faced and Glossy Ibises. Birding 8:1–5.

Prevett, J. P. and C. D. MacInnes. 1972. The number of Ross' Geese in central North America. Condor 74:431–438.

Price, F. E. 1979. Nest site factors affecting reproductive success of dippers at different population sizes. American Zoologist 19:1003 (abstract only).

Price, F. E. and C. E. Bock. 1973. Polygyny in the Dipper. Condor 75:457–459.

Price, F. E. and C. E. Bock. 1983. Population ecology of the Dipper (*Cinclus mexicanus*) in the Front Range of Colorado. Studies in Avian Biology No. 7. 84pp.

Pyle, P. and P. Henderson. 1990. On separating female and immature *Oporornis* warblers in fall. Birding 22:222–229.

Rawinski, J. J. and R. A. Ryder. 1991. Western Screech-Owl at Sand Dunes is first record for San Luis Valley. C.F.O. Journal 25:89–90.

Rea, A. M. 1975. The Scaled Quail (*Callipepla squamata*) of the southwest: systematic and historical consideration. Condor 75:322–329.

Reddall, J. 1973a. Reports from the CFO Official Records Committee. Colorado Field Ornithologist No. 15:9–15.

Reddall, J. 1973b. Reports from the CFO Official Records Committee. Colorado Field Ornithologist No. 16:19–26.

Reddall, J. 1973c. Reports from the CFO Official Records Committee. Colorado Field Ornithologist No. 18:9–20.

Reddall, J. 1974a. Reports from the CFO Official Records Committee. C.F.O. Journal No. 19:11-37.

Reddall, J. 1974b. Reports from the CFO Official Records Committee. Colorado Field Ornithologist No. 21/22:28–34.

Reddall, J. 1975. Reports from the CFO Official Records Committee. C.F.O. Journal No. 23:17–34.

Reddall, J. 1976a. CFO Official Records Committee 1975 report. C.F.O. Journal No. 27:5–19.

Reddall, J. 1976b. Colorado Field Ornithologists Official Records Committee report 1972 through 1975. Western Birds 7:81–97.

Rees, J.R. 1977. Pygmy Owl observations from Gunnison County, Colorado. C.F.O. Journal No. 29:4–5.

Reeser, W. 1979. Rare warblers in Rocky Mountain National Park. C.F.O. Journal 13:20.

Remsen, J. V. Jr. 1976. Identification of Purple and Cassin's Finch. C.F.O Journal, No. 25:4–7.

Remsen, J. V. Jr. and L. C. Binford. 1975. Status of the Yellow-billed Loon (*Gavia adamsii*) in the western United States and Mexico. Western Birds 6:7–20.

Remsen, J. V. Jr. and J. R. Cooper. 1977. First record of Scott's Oriole from Colorado. Western Birds 8:157–158.

Renner, L., P. Gray, and V. Graham. 1990. Greater Sandhill Crane nesting success and recruitment in northwest Colorado. Colorado Division of Wildlife, Terrestrial Wildlife Section, Grand Junction. 56pp.

Renner, L., P. Gray, and V. Graham. 1991. Greater Sandhill Crane nesting success and recruitment in northwest Colorado. Colorado Division of Wildlife, Terrestrial Wildlife Section, Grand Junction. 56pp.

Rennicke, J. 1986. Colorado mountain ranges. Colorado Geographic Series No. 2. Falcon Press Publishing Co., Helena and Billings, Mont. 128pp.

Reynolds, R. T. 1990. Distribution and habitat of Mexican Spotted Owls in Colorado: preliminary results. Unpublished report, Rocky Mountain Forest and Range Experiment Station, Laramie, Wyo.

Reynolds, R. T. and B. D. Linkhart. 1987a. The nesting biology of Flammulated Owls in Colorado. Pages 239-248 *in* Nero, R. W. et al., eds. Biology and conservation of northern forest owls: symposium proceedings. General Technical Report RM—142. U.S. Department of Agriculture, Forest Service, Rocky Mountain Forest and Range Experimental Station. Fort Collins. 309pp.

Reynolds, R. T. and B. D. Linkhart. 1987b. Fidelity to territory and mate in Flammulated Owls. Pages 234-238 *in* Nero, R. W. et al., eds. Biology and conservation of northern forest owls: symposium proceedings. General Technical Report RM—142. U.S. Department of Agriculture, Forest Service, Rocky Mountain Forest and Range Experimental Station. Fort Collins. 309pp.

Reynolds, R. T., D. P. Kane, and D. M. Finch. 1991. Tree-nesting habitat of Purple Martins in Colorado. Unpublished report. 9pp.

Reynolds, R. T., S. Joy, and T. B. Mears. 1990. Predation and observation records of Boreal Owls in western Colorado. C.F.O. Journal 24:99–101.

Richmond, M. L., L.R. DeWeese, and R. E. Pillmore. 1980. Brief observations on the breeding biology of the Flammulated Owl in Colorado. Western Birds 11:35–46.

Ridgway, R. and H. Friedman. 1946. The birds of North and Middle America. U. S. National Museum Bulletin 50, Part X. U. S. Government Printing Office, Washington, D. C. 463pp.

Righter, B. 1988. Some new information on the identification of juvenile and winter plumaged loon with reference to the National Geographic Field Guide to the Birds of North America, second edition. C.F.O. Journal 22:91–95.

Righter, B., H. Kingery, and R. Wilson. 1989. A House Wren singing at 11,800 feet. C.F.O. Journal 23:106.

Ringelman, J. K. 1990. Buffleheads. Colorado Outdoors 39:8–9.

Ringelman, J. K. and K. J. Kehmeier. 1990. Buffleheads breeding in Colorado. C.F.O. Journal 24:46–48.

Rising, J. D. 1974. The status and faunal affinities of the summer birds of western Kansas. University of Kansas Science Bulletin 50:347–388.

Rising, J. D. 1983a. The Great Plains hybrid zone. Pages 131-157 *in* F. Johnston, ed. Current Ornithology, Vol. 1. Plenum Press, New York.

Rising, J. D. 1983b. The progress of oriole hybridization in Kansas. Auk 100: 885–897.

Rising, J. D. and F. W. Schueler. 1980. Identification and status of wood pewees (*Contopus*) from the Great Plains: what are sibling species? Condor 82: 301–308.

Robbins, C. S., J. R. Sauer, R. S. Greenberg, and S. Droege. 1989. Population declines in North American birds that migrate to the neotropics. Proceedings of the National Academy of Science 86:7658–7662.

Robbins, M. B. and D. A. Easterla. 1981. Range expansion of the Bronzed Cowbird with the first Missouri record. Condor 83:270–272.

Rockwell, R. B. 1908. An annotated list of the birds of Mesa Cty, Colorado. Condor 10:152–180.

Rockwell, R. B. 1911. Notes on the nesting of the Forster and black terns in Colorado. Condor 13:57–63.

Rockwell, R. B. 1912. Notes on the wading birds of the Barr Lake region, Colorado. Condor 14:117–131.

Rockwell, R. B. and A. Wetmore. 1914. A list of birds from the vicinity of Golden, Colorado. Auk 31:309–333.

Rogers, G. E. 1964. Sage Grouse Investigations in Colorado. Colorado Game, Fish and Parks Department Technical Publication No. 16, Denver. 132pp.

Rogers, G. E. 1968. The Blue Grouse in Colorado. Colorado Game, Fish and Parks Department Technical Publication No. 21, Denver. 64pp.

Rogers, G. E. 1969. The Sharp-tailed Grouse in Colorado. Colorado Game, Fish and Parks Department Technical Publication No. 23, Denver. 94pp.

Root, T. 1988. Atlas of wintering North American birds—an analysis of Christmas Bird Count data. University of Chicago Press. 312pp.

Roppe, J. A. and D. Hein. 1978. Effects of fire on wildlife in a lodgepole pine forest. Southwestern Naturalist 23:279–287.

Rosenberg, G. H. and S. B. Terrill. 1986. The avifauna of Apache County, Arizona. Western Birds 17:171–187.

Royall, W. C., Jr. and J. L. Guarino. 1976. Movements of Starlings banded in north-central Colorado, 1960–74. North American Bird Bander 1:58–62.

Royall, W. C., Jr., J. L. Guarino, and J. F. Besser. 1972. Movements of Redwings color-marked in north-central Colorado in 1971. Colorado Field Ornithologist No. 14:20–23.

Royall, W. C., Jr., J. L. Guarino, and A. W. Spencer. 1980. Seasonal dispersal of Red-winged Blackbirds banded in four western states. North American Bird Bander 5:91–96.

Ryder, R. A. 1952. Bird notes from southern Colorado. Condor 54:317–318.

Ryder, R. A. 1964. California Gulls nesting in Colorado. Condor 66:440.

Ryder, R. A. 1965. A checklist of the birds of the Rio Grande Drainage of southern Colorado. Unpublished report. 41pp.

Ryder, R. A. 1967a. Distribution, migration and mortality of the White-faced Ibis (*Plegadis chihi*) in North America. Bird-Banding 38:257–277.

Ryder, R. A. 1967b. Migration and movements of some gulls from Colorado. Colorado Field Ornithologist No. 2:16–20.

Ryder, R. A. 1971a. Banding studies of White Pelicans nesting in Colorado. Colorado Field Ornithologist No. 9:14–15 (absract only).

Ryder, R. A. 1971b. Snowy Egret, Black-crowned Night Heron and White-faced Ibis banding in Colorado. Colorado Field Ornithologist No. 9:15 (abstract only).

Ryder, R. A. 1975. Possible hibernation of the Poor-will in Colorado. Journal of the Colorado—Wyoming Academy of Science 7 (6):42–43.

Ryder, R. A. 1978. Gulls in Colorado: their distribution, status and movements. Proceedings of the 1977 Conference of the Colonial Waterbird Group, De Kalb, Ill., pp. 3–9.

Ryder, R. A. 1981. Movements and mortality of White Pelicans fledged in Colorado. Colonial Waterbirds 4:72–76.

Ryder, R. A. 1985. The Pine Siskin in northern Colorado: some results from censuses and bandings. C.F.O. Journal 19:6 (abstract only).

Ryder, R. A. 1986. The North American Breeding Bird Survey: the first eighteen years in Colorado. C.F.O. Journal 20:21.

Ryder, R. A. 1991a. Distribution, status, migration and harvest of Colorado Redheads. C.F.O. Journal 25:102 (abstract only).

Ryder, R. A. 1991b. Distribution and status of the Boreal Owl in western North America: an update. Journal of the Colorado–Wyoming Academy of Science 23:26.

Ryder, R. A., D. A. Palmer, and J. J. Rawinski. 1987. Distribution and status of the Boreal Owl in Colorado. Pages 169-174 *in* Nero, R. W. et al., eds. Biology and conservation of northern forest owls: symposium proceedings. General Technical Report RM–142. U.S. Department of Agriculture, Forest Service, Rocky Mountain Forest and Range Experimental Station. Fort Collins. 309pp.

Ryder, R. A. and L. A. Roper. 1961. Recent waterfowl records for Colorado. Condor 63:418.

Ryder, R. A., W. D. Graul, and G. C. Miller. 1979. Status, distribution, and movements of ciconiiforms in Colorado. Proceedings of the Colonial Waterbird Group 3:49–58.

Ryder, R. A. , R. W. Schnaderbeck, and C. W. Jeske. 1989. The Little Blue Heron, a new breeding bird for Colorado. C.F.O. Journal 23:102 (abstract only).

Schmutz, J. A. 1988. Wild Turkey reproductive performance and nest habitat use. Journal of the Colorado–Wyoming Academy of Science 20: 8 (abstract only).

Schmutz, J. K., R. W. Fyfe, U. Banasch, and H. Armbruster. 1991. Routes and timing of migration of falcons nesting in Canada. Wilson Bulletin 103:44–58.

Schroeder, R. L. II. 1974. A study of the nesting behavior of Western Meadowlarks near Fort Collins, Colorado. Colorado Field Ornithologist No. 21/22:6–10.

Schultz, M. P. 1971. Second state record for the Louisiana Heron. Colorado Field Ornithologist No. 9:16.

Sclater, W. H. 1912. A history of the birds of Colorado. Witherby and Co., London. 576pp.

Scott, A. C. and M. Bekoff. 1991. Breeding behavior of Evening Grosbeaks. Condor 93:71–81.

Scott, V. E., G. L. Crouch, and J. A. Whelan. 1982. Responses of birds and small mammals to clearcutting in a subalpine forest in central Colorado. Research Notes RM-422. Fort Collins, Colo. 6pp.

Sealy, S. G. 1979. Extralimital nesting of Bay-breasted Warblers: response to forest tent caterpillars? Auk 96:600–603.

Sealy, S. G., H. R. Carter, and D. Alison. 1982. Occurrences of the Asiatic Marbled Murrelet (*Brachyramphus marmoratus perdix*) in North America. Auk 99: 778–781.

Sedgwick, J. A. 1987. Avian habitat relationships in pinyon-juniper woodland. Wilson Bulletin 99:413–431.

Sedgwick, J. A. and F. L. Knopf. 1986. Cavity-nesting birds and the cavity-tree resource in plains cottonwood bottomland. Journal of Wildlife Management 50:247–252.

Sedgwick, J. A. and F. L. Knopf. 1987. Breeding bird response to cattle grazing of a cottonwood bottomland. Journal of Wildlife Management 51:230–237.

Sedgwick, J. A. and F. L. Knopf. 1988. A high incidence of Brown-headed Cowbird parasitism of Willow Flycatchers. Condor 90:253–256.

Sedgwick, J. A. and F. L. Knopf. 1989. Regionwide polygyny in Willow Flycatchers. Condor 91:473–475.

Sedgwick, J. A. and F. L. Knopf. 1990. Habitat relationships and nest site characteristics of cavity-nesting birds in cottonwood floodplains. Journal of Wildlife Management 54:112–124.

Seltman, S. 1990. Winter bird summary. Horned Lark 17:3–6.

Senner, S. E. and E. F. Martinez. 1982. A review of Western Sandpiper migration in interior North America. Southwestern Naturalist 27:149–159.

Shenk, T. M. 1988. Roost site selection of Whooping Cranes in Colorado. Journal of the Colorado–Wyoming Academy of Science 20: 9 (abstract only).

Shier, G. R. 1967. Rufous-sided Towhee range in Colorado. Colorado Field Ornithologist No. 1:7–9.

Short, L. L. Jr. 1965. Hybridization in the flickers (*Colaptes*) of North America. Bulletin of the American Museum of Natural History 129:307-428.

Shreeve, D. F. 1980. Behaviour of the Aleutian Grey-crowned and Brown-capped Rosy Finches *Leucosticte tephrocotis*. Ibis 122:145–165.

Shuster, W. C. 1974. An analysis of Great Horned Owl pellets and prey species from Spring Canyon, Larimer County, Colorado. Colorado Field Ornithologist No. 19:4–8.

Shuster, W. C. 1976. Northern Goshawk nesting densities in montane Colorado. Western Birds 7:108–110.

Shuster, W. C. 1980. Northern Goshawk nest site requirements in the Colorado Rockies. Western Birds 11:89–96.

Silverman, D., D. Griffiths, and C. Griffiths. 1978. Suspected nesting of Grace's Warbler on eastern slope. C.F.O. Journal 12:41–42.

Simmons, V. 1986. A checklist of the birds of Great Sand Dunes National Monument, Colorado. Rabbitbrush Enterprises, Alamosa, Colo.

Smith, H. G. 1896. Some birds new to Colorado—with notes on others of little known distribution in the state. Nidologist 3:65, 76.

Smith, H. G. 1905. The blue jay and other eastern birds at Wray, Yuma County, Colorado. Auk 22:81–82.

Smith, H. G. 1908. Random notes on the distribution of some Colorado birds, with additions to the state avifauna. Auk 25:184–191.

Smith, K. G. 1978. Range extension of the Blue Jay into western North America. Bird-Banding 49:208–214.

Smith, K. G. 1979. Migrational movements of Blue Jays west of the 100th meridian. North American Bird Bander 4:49–52.

Snow, C. 1973. Habitat management series for unique or endangered species: Golden Eagle. U. S. Department of Interior, Bureau of Land Management Technical Note 239, Washington D.C. 52pp.

Snyder, W. D. 1978. The bobwhite in eastern Colorado: a study. Colorado Division of Wildlife Technical Publication No. 32, Denver. 88pp.

Snyder, W. D. 1984a. Ring-necked Pheasant nesting ecology and wheat farming on the High Plains. Journal of Wildlife Management 48:878-888.

Snyder, W. D. 1984b. Management procedures for Northern Bobwhites in eastern Colorado. Colorado Division of Wildlife Special Report, Denver. 22pp.

Spear, L. B., M. J. Lewis, M. T. Myres, and R. L. Pyle. 1988. The recent occurrence of Garganey in North America and the Hawaiian Islands. American Birds 42:385–392.

Spencer, R. A. 1985. Brown-headed Cowbird fledgling feeding incidents. C.F.O. Journal 19:39.

Stahlecker, D. W. and T. E. Behlke. 1974. Winter diurnal raptor populations of three habitat types in northeastern Colorado. Colorado Field Ornithologist No. 20:6-17.

Stahlecker, D. W. and H. J. Griese. 1977. Evidence of double brooding by American Kestrels in the Colorado high plains. Wilson Bulletin 89:618–619.

Stahlecker, D. W.and J. J. Rawinski. 1990. First records for the Boreal Owl in New Mexico. Condor 92:517–519.

Stamper, M. N., R. Ryder, and M. M. Lett. 1972. New nesting site for White-faced Glossy Ibis, *Plegadis chihi*, in Colorado. Journal of the Colorado–Wyoming Academy of Science 7(No.2-3):113 (abstract only).

Stelter, L. S. 1979. Riparian birds of Piceance Creek basin, Colorado and a new method of express-ing bird census data. C.F.O. Journal 13:64–70.

Stelter, L. S. and J. G. Nagy. 1979. Raptor food habits in the oil shale region of northwestern Colorado. C.F.O. Journal 13:7–12.

Stepney, P. H. R. 1975a. Wintering distribution of Brewer's Blackbird: historical aspect, recent changes, and fluctuations. Bird—Banding 46: 106–125.

Stepney, P.H.R. 1975b. First recorded breeding of the Great-tailed Grackle in Colorado. Condor 77:208–210.

Stevens, L. 1991. Sandhill Crane (*Grus canadensis*) recovery plan. C.F.O. Journal 25:49–51.

Stone, D. D. 1884. Colorado notes; extracts from my note-book. Ornithologist and Oologist, part 1, 9:9–10; part 2, 9:20–21.

Strauch, J. G., Jr. and R. W. Thompson. 1986. The status of the Grasshopper Sparrow in Boulder County. C.F.O. Journal 20:63–69.

Strong, T. R. 1983. Winter territorial behavior of the Townsend's Solitaire (*Myadestes townsendi*) near Morrison, Colorado. C.F.O. Journal 17:42–51.

Sutton, G. M. 1967. Oklahoma birds. Univ. Oklahoma Press, Norman. 674pp.

Sutton, G. M. 1974. A check-list of Oklahoma birds. Stovall Museum of Science and History. Univ. Oklahoma Press, Norman. 48pp.

Svoboda, P. L., K. E. Young, and V. E. Scott. 1980. Recent nesting records of Purple Martins in western Colorado. Western Birds 11:195–198.

Swanson, G. A. 1971. An unusual Townsend's Solitaire nest. Colorado Field Ornithologist No. 9:30.

Szymczak, M. R. 1975. Canada goose restoration along the foothills of Colorado. Colorado Division of Wildlife Technical Publication No.31, Denver. 63pp.

Tate, J., Jr. 1986. The Blue List for 1986. American Birds 40:227–236.

Thompson, C. F. 1971. Two 19th century Cerulean Warbler specimens from Colorado. Colorado Field Ornithologist No. 9:32–33.

Thompson, M. C. and C. Ely. 1989. Birds in Kansas. Vol. 1. University of Kansas Museum Natural History, Public Education Series No. 11. Lawrence, Kan. 404pp.

Thompson, R. W. and J. G. Strauch, Jr. 1986. Habitat use by breeding birds on city of Boulder Open Space, 1985. Report for city of Boulder, Western Ecosystems, Inc. Lafayette, Colo. 167pp.

Thorne, T. W. 1889. The olivaceous flycatcher and phoebe in Colorado. Auk 6: 276–277.

Trautman, M. B., M. A. Trautman, and H. G. Deignan. 1950. A sight record of the knot in Colorado. Condor 52:135.

Tully, R. J. 1974. Spring status of the Greater Prairie Chicken and other observations in the northern sandhills of Yuma County, Colorado. Colorado Field Ornithologist No. 20:18–26.

Twomey, A. C. 1942. The birds of the Uinta Basin, Utah. Annals of Carnegie Museum 28:341–490.

Unitt, P. 1987. *Empidonax traillii extimus*: an endangered subspecies. Western Birds 18:137–162.

US Fish and Wildlife Service. 1989. Birds of the Alamosa—Monte Vista National Wildlife Refuge Complex.

US Fish and Wildlife Service. 1990. Wildlife of Arapaho National Wildlife Refuge.

Vander Wall, S. B., S. W. Hoffman, and W. K. Potts. 1981. Emigration behavior of Clark's Nutcracker. Condor 83:162–170.

Van Sant, B. F. and C. E. Braun. 1990. Distribution and status of Greater Prairie-Chickens in Colorado. Prairie Naturalist 22:225–230.

Van Sickle, A. and H. B. Thurlow. 1971. First nesting of the Chestnut-sided Warbler in Colorado. Colorado Field Ornithologist No. 9:34–35.

Vaughan, S. 1985. Distribution and identification of eagles in Colorado. C.F.O. Journal 19:6 (abstract only).

Vos, D. K., R. A. Ryder, and W. D. Graul. 1985. Response of breeding Great Blue Herons to human disturbance in north-central Colorado. Colonial Waterbirds 8:13–22.

Wagner, J. L. 1984. Post–breeding avifauna and mixed insectivorous flocks in a Colorado spruce–fir forest. Western Birds 15:81–84.

Walters, R. E. 1983. Utah bird distribution: latilong study. Nongame section, Utah Division of Wildlife Resources, Salt Lake City. 97pp.

Ward, J. 1990. Cassin's Finch nesting in atypical habitat. C.F.O. Journal 24: 102–104.

Warkentin, I. G. and P. C. James. 1988. Trends in winter distribution and abundance of Ferruginous Hawks. Journal of Field Ornithology 59:209–214.

Warren, E. R. 1904. A sandhill crane's nest. Condor 6:39–40.

Warren, E. R. 1906. A collecting trip to southeastern Colorado. Condor 8:18–24.

Warren, E. R. 1907. An interesting occurrence of the canyon wren. Condor 9 111.

Warren, E. R. 1908. Northwestern Colorado bird notes. Condor 10:18–26.

Warren, E. R. 1910. Some central Colorado bird notes. Condor 12:23–39.

Warren, E. R. 1912. Some north-central Colorado bird notes. Condor 14:81–104.

Waser, N. M. 1976. Food supply and nest timing of Broad-tailed Hummingbirds in the Rocky Mountains. Condor 78:133–135.

Waser, N. M. 1978. Competition for hummingbird pollination and sequential flowering in two Colorado wildflowers. Ecology 59:934–944.

Waser, N. M. and D. W. Inouye. 1977. Implications of recaptures of Broad-tailed Hummingbirds banded in Colorado. Auk 94:393-394.

Webb, Betsy. 1985a. Against all odds: first record of a Magnificent Frigatebird in Colorado. C.F.O. Journal 19:94–96.

Webb, Betsy. 1985b. Birds subgroup report. Pages 33–39 *in* B. L. Winternitz and D. W. Crumpacker, eds. Colorado wildlife workshop-species of special concern. Colorado Division of Wildlife, Denver.

Webb, Betsy and J. Reddall. 1989. Recent state record specimens of birds at the Denver Museum of Natural History. C.F.O. Journal 23:121–127.

Webb, Betsy A. and A. R. Phillips. 1992. A new state record specimen of Sprague's Pipit at the Denver Museum of Natural History. C.F.O. Journal 26:61-62.

Webb, Bruce. 1975. Little Gull—first Colorado record. Colorado Field Ornithologist No. 23:16.

Webb, Bruce. 1976. A Groove-billed Ani in northeastern Colorado. Western Birds 7:153–154.

Webb, Bruce. 1978. The occurrences of the Red-shouldered Hawk in Colorado. C.F.O. Journal No. 32:19–21.

Webb, Bruce. 1981. An instance of long distance movement by a Steller's Jay in Colorado. C.F.O. Journal 15:102.

Webb, Bruce. 1982a. Distribution and nesting requirements of montane forest owls in Colorado. Part III: Flammulated Owl (*Otus flammeolus*). C.F.O. Journal 16:76–82.

Webb, Bruce. 1982b. Distribution and nesting requirements of montane forest owls in Colorado. Part II: Northern Pygmy Owl (*Glaucidium gnoma*) and Boreal Owl (*Aegolius funereus*). C.F.O. Journal 16:58–65.

Webb, Bruce. 1982c. Distribution and nesting requirements of montane forest owls in Colorado. Part I: Saw-whet Owl *Aegolius acadicus*. C.F.O. Journal 16: 26–32.

Webb, Bruce. 1983. Distribution and nesting requirements of montane forest owls in Colorado. Part IV: Spotted Owl (*Strix occidentalis*). C.F.O. Journal 17: 2–7.

Webb, Bruce and J. A. Conry. 1978. First record of a Lesser Black-backed Gull in Colorado. Western Birds 9:171–173.

Webb, Bruce and J. A. Conry. 1979. A Sharp-tailed Sandpiper in Colorado, with notes on plumage and behavior. Western Birds 10:86–91.

Weber, W. A. 1987. Colorado flora: western slope. Colorado Associated University Press, Boulder. 530pp.

Weber, W. A. 1990. Colorado flora: eastern slope. University Press of Colorado, Niwot. 396pp.

Webster, H. Jr. 1944. A survey of the prairie falcon in Colorado. Auk 61:609–616.

Wheat, P. 1980. Hybridization of the Blue and Steller's Jays. C.F.O. Journal 15: 9–23.

Wheeler, B. 1988. A Red-backed Hawk in Colorado. C.F.O. Journal 22:5–8.

White, C. M., G. D. Lloyd, and G. L. Richards. 1965. Goshawk nesting in the Upper Sonoran in Colorado and Utah. Condor 67:269.

Whitney, B. 1983. Bay-breasted, Blackpoll, and Pine Warblers in fall plumage. Birding 15:219–222.

Whitney, B. and K. Kaufman. 1985a. The *Empidonax* challenge. Part I. Birding 17:151–158.

Whitney, B. and K. Kaufman. 1985b. The *Empidonax* challenge. Part II. Birding 17:277–287.

Whitney, B. and K. Kaufman. 1986a. The *Empidonax* challenge. Part III: "Traill's" Flycatcher: The Alder/Willow problem. Birding 18:153–159.

Whitney, B. and K. Kaufman. 1986b. The *Empidonax* challenge. Part IV. Birding 18:315–327.

Whitney, B. and K. Kaufman. 1987. The *Empidonax* challenge. Part V. Birding 19:7–15.

Widmann, O. 1911. List of birds observed in Estes Park, Colorado, from June 10 to July 18, 1910. Auk 28:304–319.

Wilds, C. 1984. ID Points: Snowy Egret/Little Blue Heron/Reddish Egret (white phase). Birding 16:15.

Wilds, C. 1990. The dowitchers. Pages 68–75 *in* Kaufman, K. Advanced birding. Peterson Field Guide Series. Houghton Mifflin, Boston. 299pp.

Wilds, C. and M. Newlon. 1983. The identification of dowitchers. Birding 15: 151–166.

Williams, O. and P. Wheat. 1971. Hybrid jays in Colorado. Wilson Bulletin 83: 343–346.

Winn, R. 1970. Status of breeding Flammulated Owls in Colorado. Audubon Warbler, December: 2–4. Denver, Colo.

Winn, R. 1979. Bay-breasted Warblers summer in Colorado. C.F.O. Journal 13: 21–23.

Winn, R. 1981. The Williamson's Sapsucker—a timetable for bird watching. C.F.O. Journal 15:42–43.

Winternitz, B.L. 1976. Temporal change and habitat preference of some montane breeding birds. Condor 78:383–393.

Woffinden, N. D. 1986. Notes on the Swainson's Hawk in central Utah: insectivory, premigratory aggregations, and kleptoparasitism. Great Basin Naturalist 46:302–304.

Wood, D. S. and G. D. Schnell. 1984. Distributions of Oklahoma birds. University of Oklahoma Press, Norman. 209pp.

Yaeger, M. 1987. Second Colorado nesting site for Black Phoebe. Colorado Bird Atlas Newsletter, No. 2, p. 2.

Zerbi, V. 1985. Purple Martins nesting on McClure Pass. C.F.O. Journal 19:53–54.

Zimmer, K. 1985. The western bird watcher. Phalarope Books, Prentice-Hall. Englewood Cliffs, N. J. 278pp.

Zwinger, A. H. and B. E. Willard. 1972. Land above the trees: a guide to American alpine tundra. Harper and Row, New York. 489pp.

INDEX